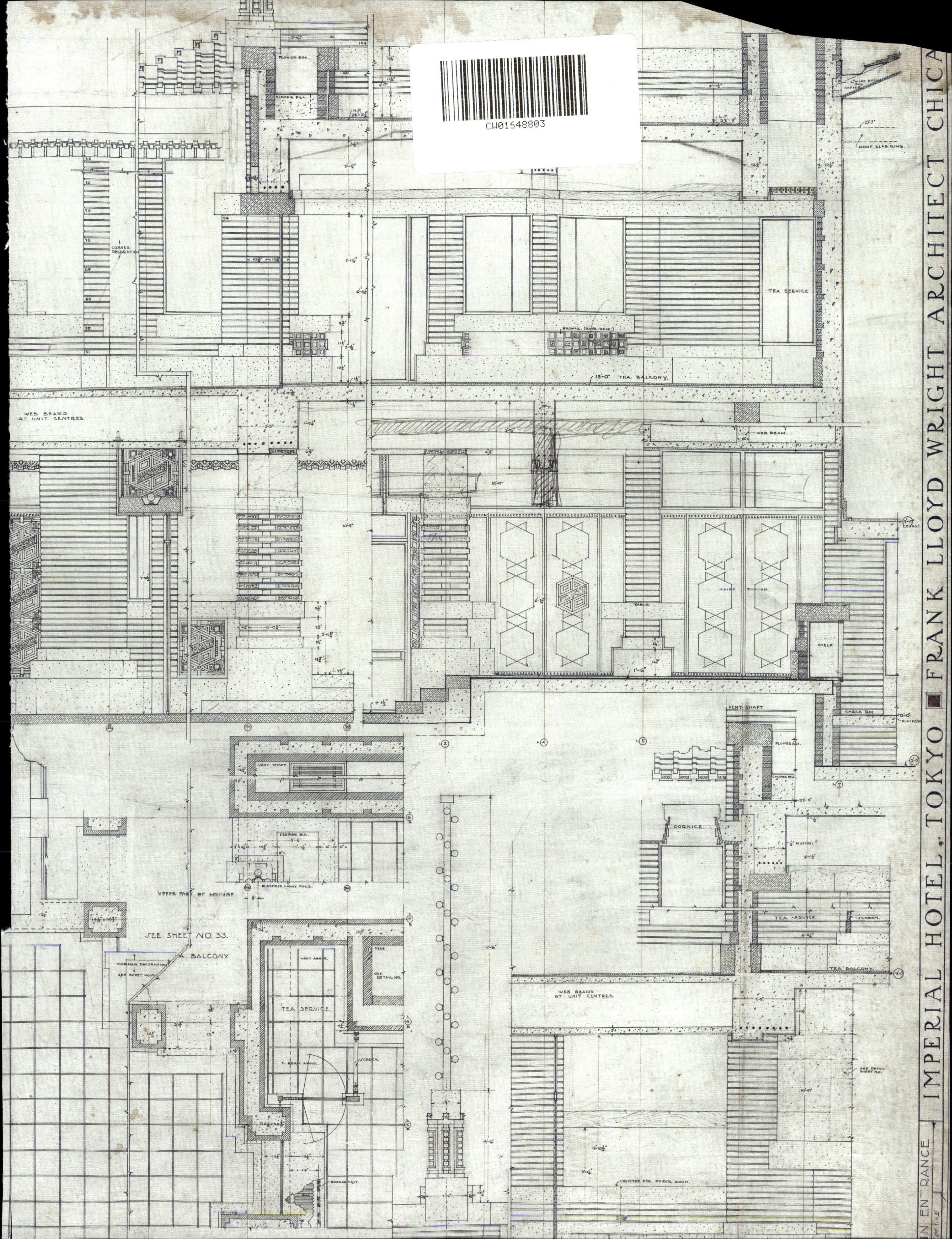
FLOWER BOX
TEA SERVICE
13'-0" TEA BALCONY
WEB BEAMS AT UNIT CENTRES
WEB BEAM
TABLE
SHELF
CHECK RM
VENT SHAFT
FLOWER BOX
CORNICE
TEA SERVICE
SCREEN
TEA BALCONY
WEB BEAMS AT UNIT CENTRES
UPPER PART OF LOUNGE
ELECTRIC LIGHT POLE
SEE SHEET NO. 33.
BALCONY
CORNICE DECORATION
TEA SERVICE
COUNTER FOR CHECK ROOM
N EN TRANCE
IMPERIAL HOTEL, TOKYO ■ FRANK LLOYD WRIGHT ARCHITECT CHICA

1

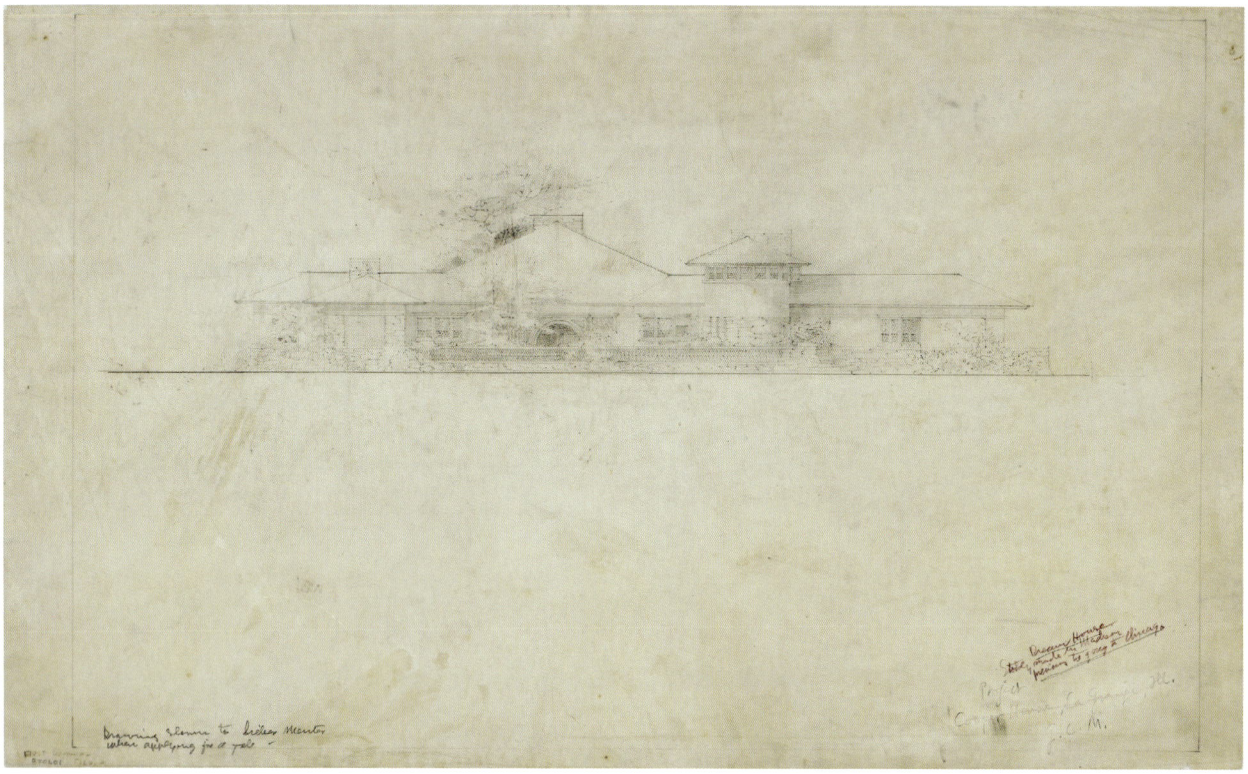

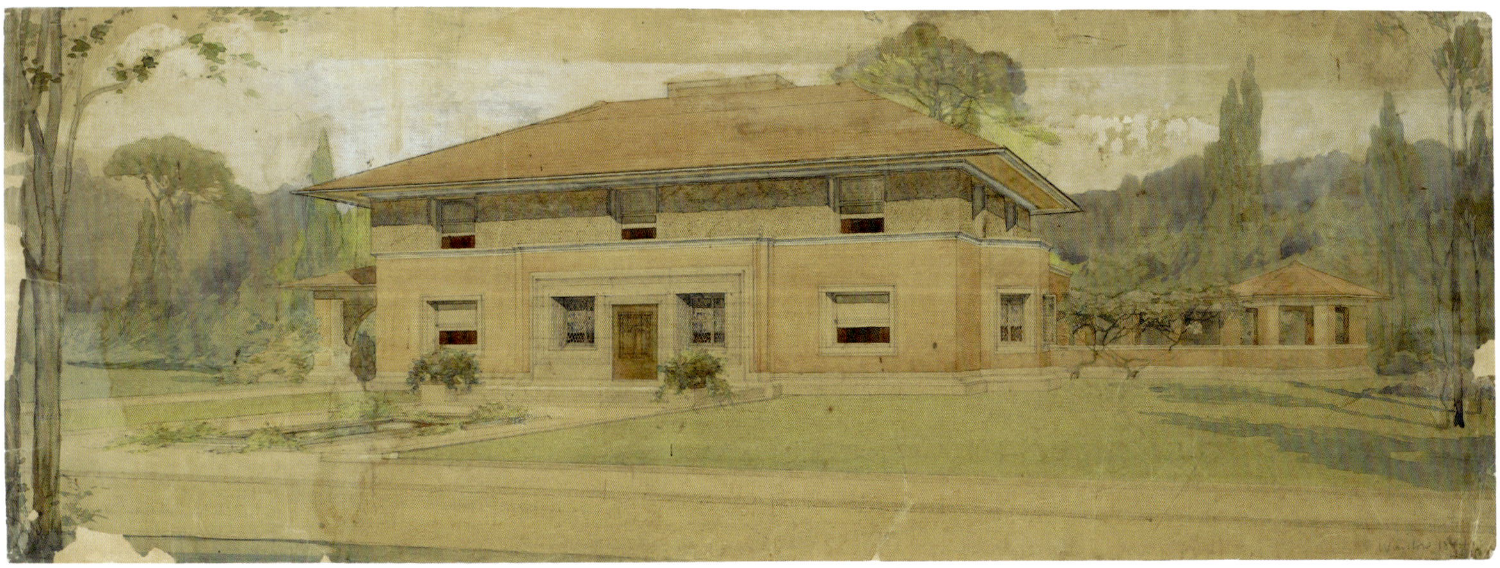

3

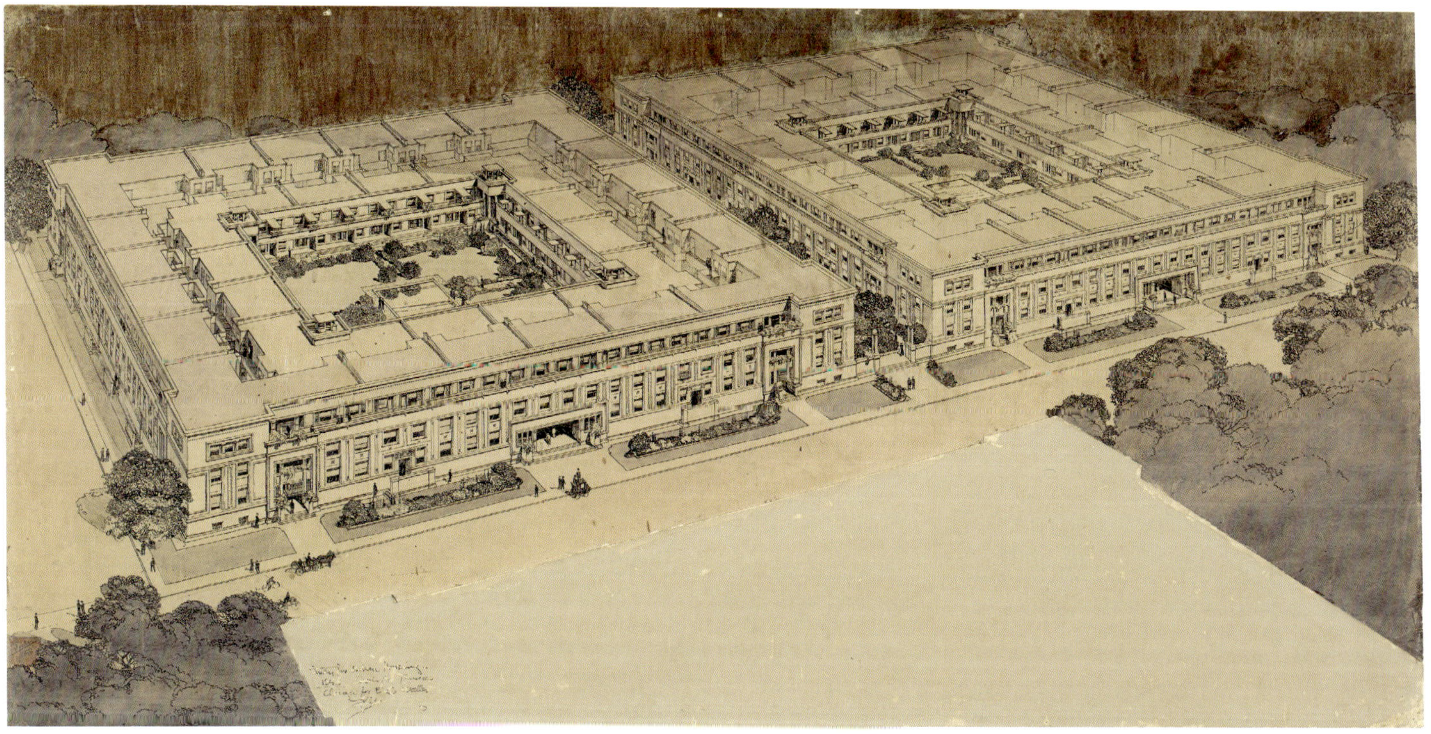

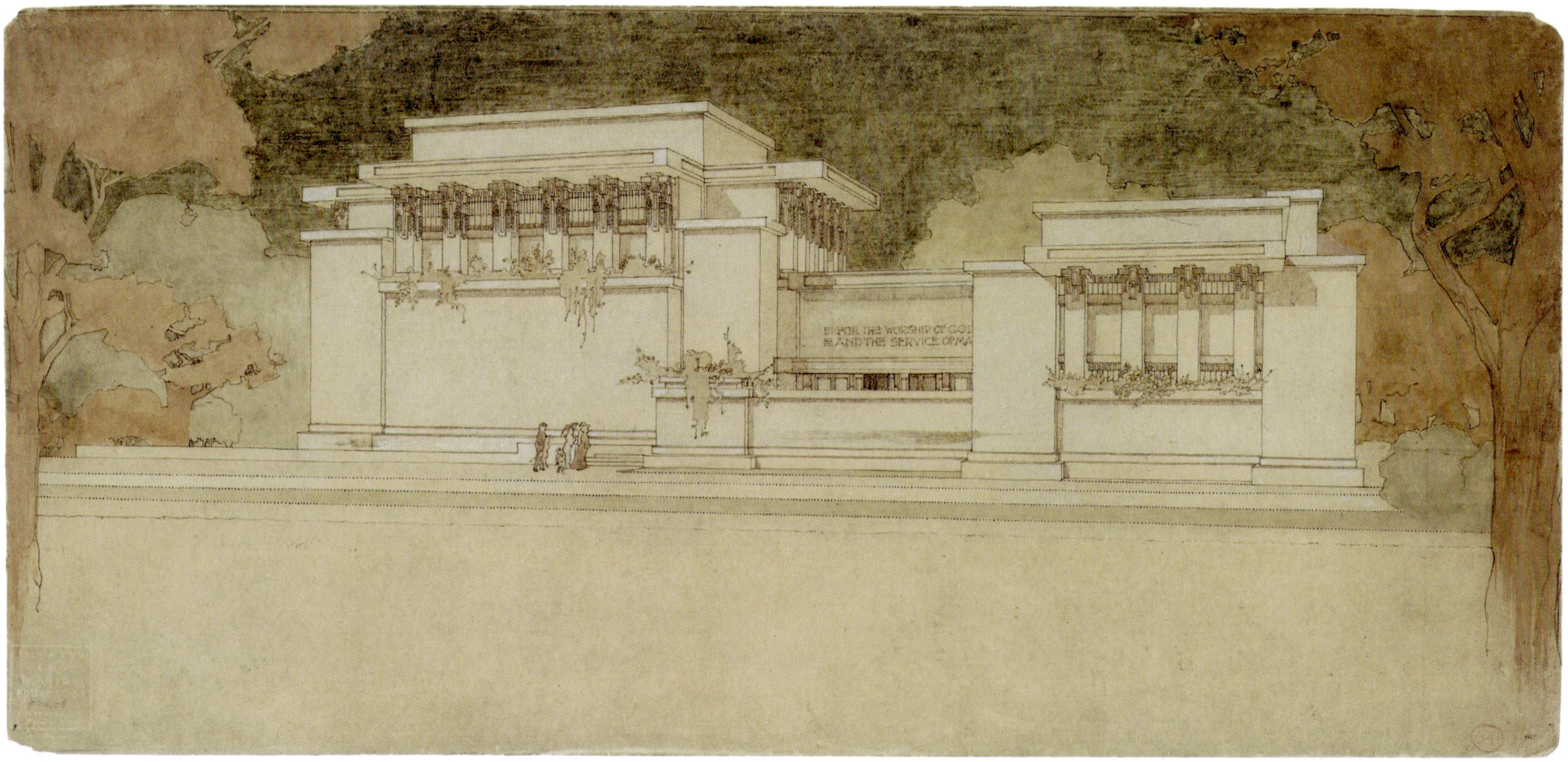
FOR THE WORSHIP OF GO
AND THE SERVICE OF MA

BARRY BERGDOLL
JENNIFER GRAY

FRANK LLOYD WRIGHT

UNPACKING THE ARCHIVE

with essays by
Michael Desmond
Carole Ann Fabian
Elizabeth S. Hawley
Juliet Kinchin
Neil Levine
Ellen Moody
Therese O'Malley
Ken Tadashi Oshima
Michael Osman
Spyros Papapetros
Janet Parks
Matthew Skjonsberg
David Smiley
Mabel O. Wilson

THE MUSEUM OF MODERN ART NEW YORK

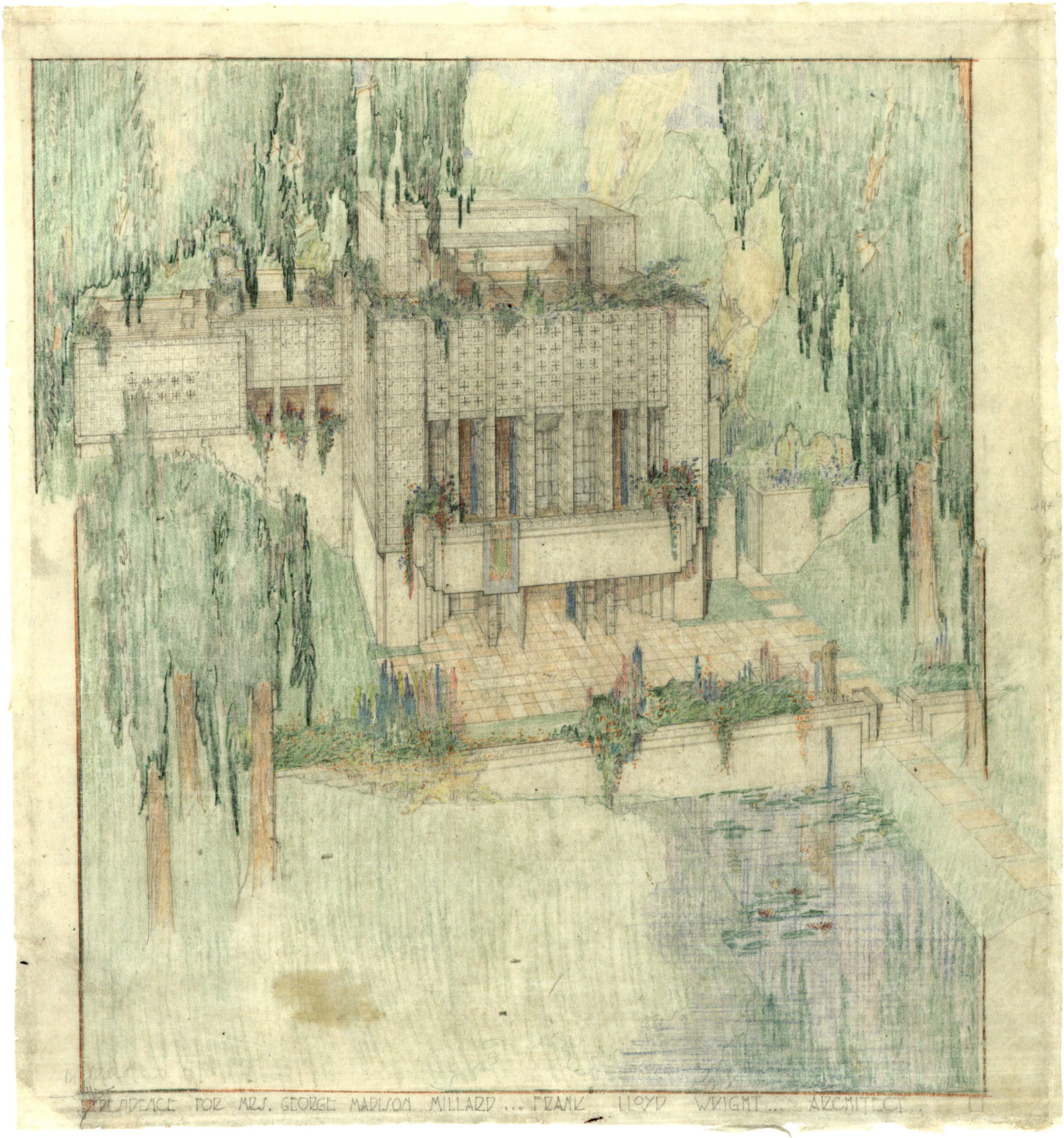
RESIDENCE FOR MRS. GEORGE MADISON MILLARD ... FRANK LLOYD WRIGHT ... ARCHITECT ..

CONTENTS

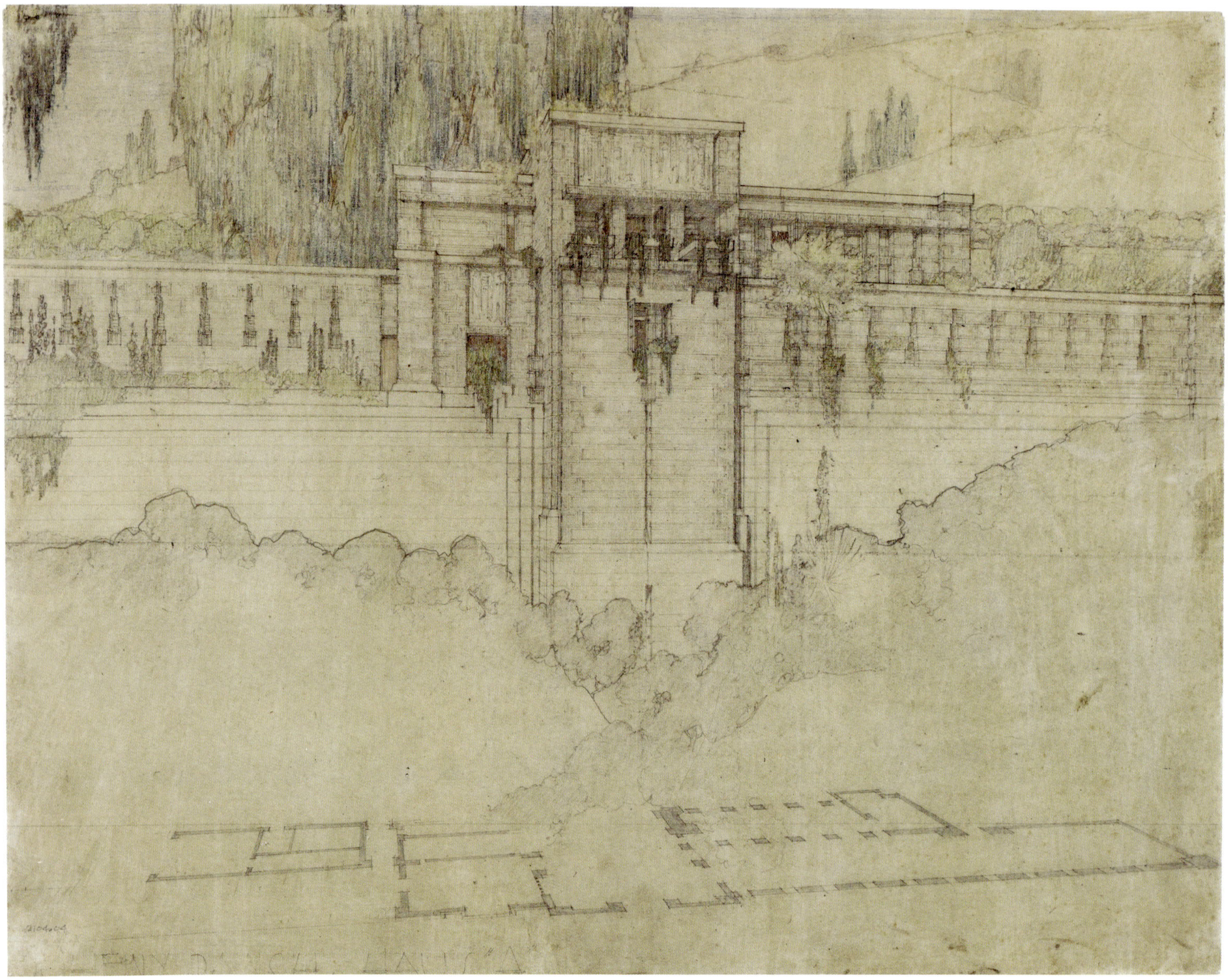

FOREWORD

In September 2012 The Museum of Modern Art and Avery Architectural & Fine Arts Library at Columbia University, along with the Frank Lloyd Wright Foundation, announced an agreement for the transfer of ownership and stewardship of the archives documenting the work and career of Frank Lloyd Wright. These vast holdings, including drawings, correspondence, building models and fragments, photographs, and films, would be transferred from Wright's two studio-residences—the campuses of the two Taliesins, in Wisconsin and Arizona—to the Museum and University. At Taliesin West the materials had been organized and catalogued over decades under the leadership of Bruce Brooks Pfeiffer and had often been lent to major exhibitions, including a comprehensive retrospective organized at MoMA in 1994 by Terence Riley and Peter Reed. Since that exhibition the Frank Lloyd Wright Foundation Archives have begun a new life, with greater access to them made possible by archival management, gallery displays, and regular teaching.

Even in his seeming contradictions, Wright provides a valuable lens for interpreting modern architecture and twentieth-century American culture. Wright's projects, both built and hypothetical, continue to engage us, and the questions addressed in his work resonate with contemporary debates in land use and planning. The exhibition accompanying this volume, *Frank Lloyd Wright at 150: Unpacking the Archive*—the opening of which coincides with Wright's birthday—evidences the joint conviction of MoMA and Avery Library that even an artist as protean and thoroughly studied as Wright remains of interest for current generations. No other architect has been exhibited as frequently and consistently in the eighty-five years since Wright was included in MoMA's inaugural architectural exhibition, in 1932. The first architectural exhibition in the Fifty-third Street building, in 1940, was devoted to Wright, and Avery Library's online catalogue contains nearly 1,400 publications related to him. Rather than offer a comprehensive interpretation of Wright's career, however, this book and exhibition propose that now, as the monumental task of unpacking the thousands of drawings, letters, manuscripts, and photographs is nearing completion, the task of interpretation—of scholarly unpacking—remains open-ended. This undertaking, then, is both a catalyst for research and an approach to displaying the very nature of an archival collection.

I am grateful to Barry Bergdoll, assisted by Jennifer Gray, for orchestrating this curatorial and scholarly experiment. In its ambitious constellation of research, planning, and preparation, this project is indebted to Avery Architectural & Fine Arts Library. We extend our sincerest thanks to its Director, Carole Ann Fabian, and to Janet Parks, Curator of Drawings & Archives, for their unstinting devotion to and stewardship of the Archives. On behalf of the Trustees and staff of the Museum, I would especially like to thank Hyundai Card for its major support of this exhibition. Additional generous support is provided by Sue and Edgar Wachenheim III, the Graham Foundation for Advanced Studies in the Fine Arts, and the Annual Exhibition Fund.

For their major support for this publication I thank The Dale S. and Norman Mills Leff Publication Fund and The Museum of Modern Art's Research and Scholarly Publications endowment established through the generosity of The Andrew W. Mellon Foundation, the Edward John Noble Foundation, Mr. and Mrs. Perry R. Bass, and the National Endowment for the Humanities' Challenge Grant Program.

Glenn D. Lowry
Director, The Museum of Modern Art

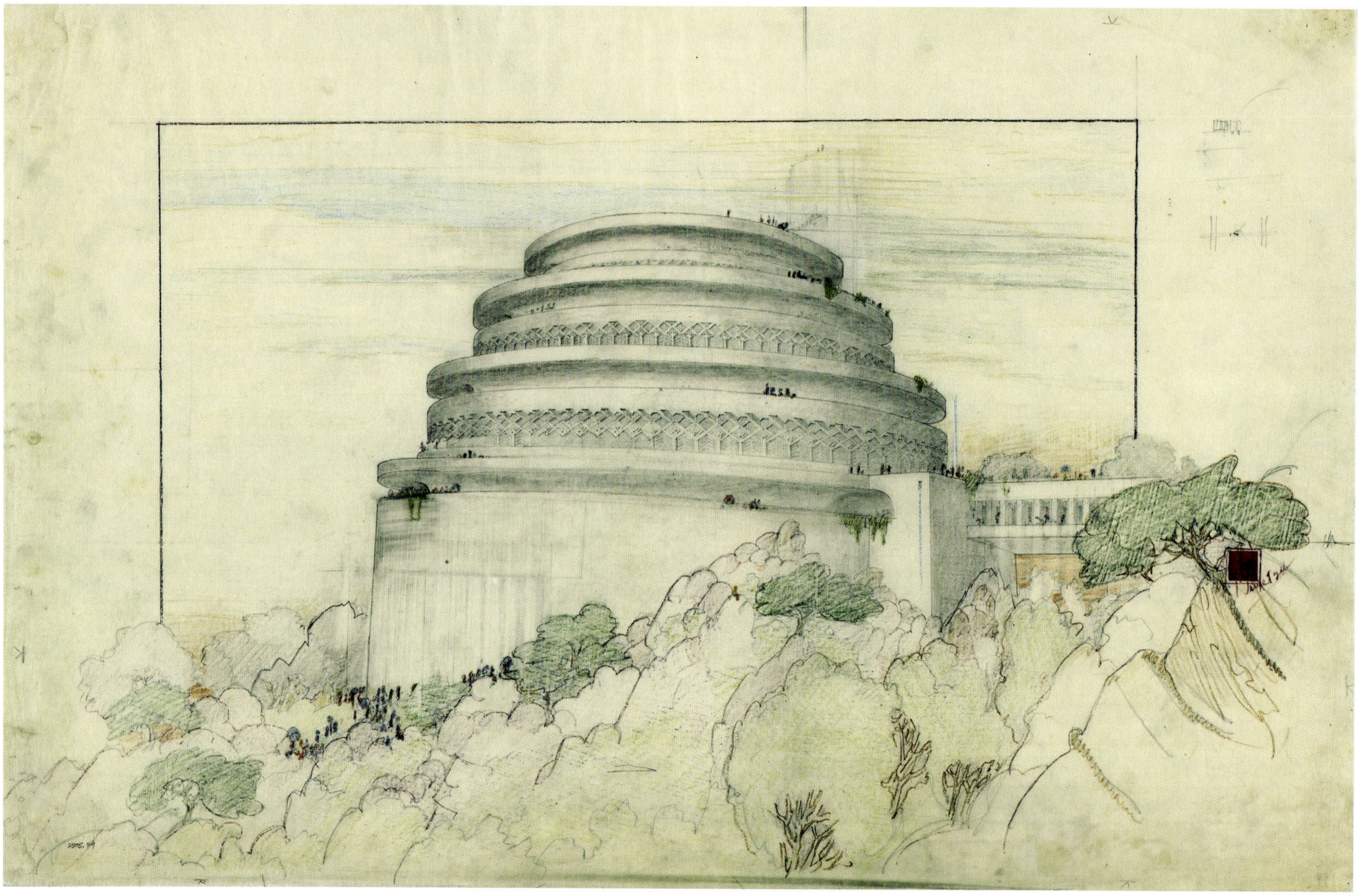

Hyundai Card

Hyundai Card is proud to sponsor the exhibition *Frank Lloyd Wright at 150: Unpacking the Archive* at The Museum of Modern Art. There is no better way to commemorate the 150th birthday of this radically intellectual architect than to explore the historic archive that bears his name.

Frank Lloyd Wright at 150 will reveal new sides to Wright as it interprets his greatest works in contexts that include events from his own life as well as from outside his field. In this anthological presentation, we will see Wright as not only a master architect but also as a social activist, a savvy mass communicator, and a surprisingly international figure.

Hyundai Card celebrates figures like Wright, who drew inspiration broadly from many fields in order to create paradigm-shifting work. As Korea's foremost issuer of credit cards, Hyundai Card is committed to challenging convention with disruptive ideas. Whether we're hosting tomorrow's cultural pioneers at our stages and art spaces, building libraries for our members on design, travel, and music, or designing credit cards and digital services as beautiful as they are functional, Hyundai Card's most inventive endeavors all draw from the creative well that the arts provide.

An eight-year sponsor of The Museum of Modern Art, Hyundai Card is delighted to make *Frank Lloyd Wright at 150* possible.

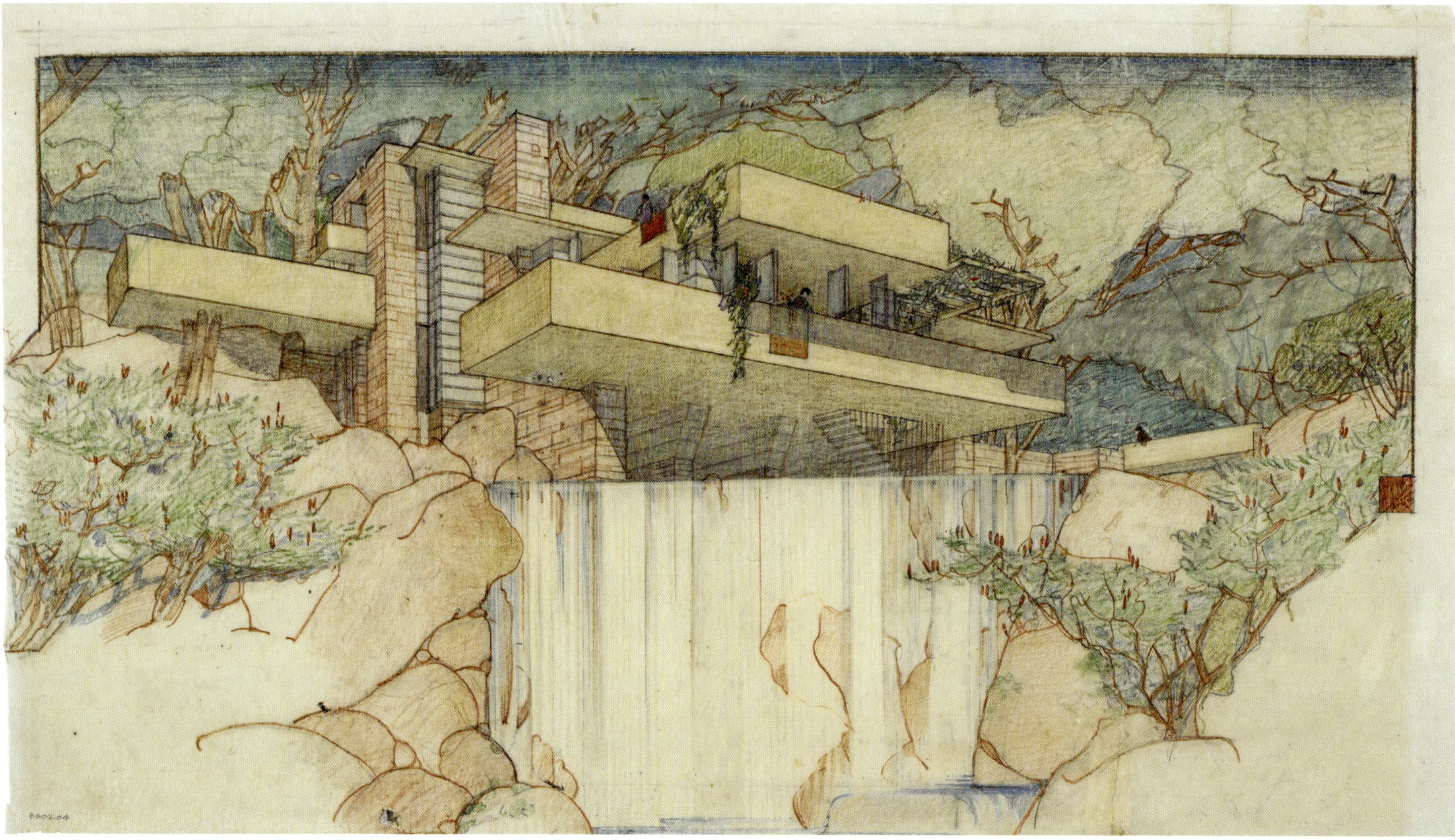

INTRODUCTION

When The Museum of Modern Art and Avery Architectural & Fine Arts Library of Columbia University jointly acquired the Frank Lloyd Wright Foundation Archives—an endeavor years in the making—it brought the work of America's most famous, and arguably most influential, architect together with the research forces of the country's leading architectural library and the exhibition programs of the country's oldest museum department of architecture and design. A steering committee of representatives from all three entities thus helped Wright's archival legacy make the trip east from the two bases, in rural Wisconsin and the Arizona desert, that had been the loci of so much of his creative outpouring in design, writing about architecture, and training of future architects in his precepts and design approaches. In New York, Wright's drawings and papers have found not only brilliant, and sometimes familiar, company (notably Ludwig Mies van der Rohe in the architecture collections of MoMA and Louis Sullivan at Avery), but also an institutional infrastructure to support the scholarly and public engagement that Wright's work continues to command.

The sheer scale of the Archives is remarkable: some 55,000 drawings, 125,000 photographs and other photographic items, 285 films, 300,000 sheets of correspondence, 2,700 manuscripts, and counting, since the numbers have gradually been adjusted upward as the elements have been processed by staff at Avery Library. These materials, housed at Columbia, have been made available to researchers with a swiftness never imagined when the daunting task of moving and unpacking such a vast collection began. In addition, there are dozens of models—including the monumental model of Broadacre City (1929–35)—and fragments of buildings along with material studies now stored with MoMA's collection of architectural models and used regularly for exhibition purposes. While materials up until 1959, the year of Wright's death, were moved first, as of 2016 the final shipment of materials of Taliesin Associated Architects (TAA) has been transferred, fulfilling the commitment to keep the collections formerly housed at the two Taliesins integral. The result is one of the most complete and important archives of an American architect in an institutional setting, and it rivals in scale and complexity other major resources for studying the figures who have often been called the "form givers" of modern architecture: the Mies van der Rohe Archive at MoMA and at the Library of Congress, the Walter Gropius Archive at Harvard University, the Le Corbusier archive at the Fondation Le Corbusier in Paris, and the Alvar Aalto archive in Finland. Like those archives, the Wright Foundation Archives offer insights into the larger culture of architecture of an extended period, in this case from the 1890s into the 1960s, and record not only the built and unbuilt work of a master architect but the creation and functioning of a significant—and ongoing—educational experiment, namely the Taliesin Fellowship.

This exhibition and catalogue celebrate the unpacking of Wright's archives in both the literal and metaphorical senses of the word: the physical unpacking and collection management, and the intellectual work of opening up the contents to new interpretations. Far from sequential, these activities have been intertwined from the first months of the mammoth transfer of materials from Arizona and Wisconsin. In both library and museum, the decision was made to integrate Wright both physically and intellectually into the existing holdings, ending the preference during the architect's lifetime—and for decades after under Olgivanna Wright—of showing Wright's work primarily monographically. Both Columbia and MoMA are leaders in collection conservation, with complementary strengths. Conservation of works on paper began almost immediately at the Columbia University Libraries, where the conservation lab has recognized expertise in the treatment of paper documents. At MoMA work also rapidly began on conservation assessment of the building fragments and architectural models in the Archives. For two years, with the aid of a grant from the Andrew W. Mellon Foundation, a dedicated conservator studied Wright's models and not only stabilized their condition but made possible many novel lines of thinking about Wright's designs and his use of models, most of which were made for exhibition and promotion purposes rather than for design development. The first results of that conservation work are featured here in a report by Ellen Moody on work done on two models for Wright's most prominent New York projects: the residential St. Mark's Tower (1927–29) and the Solomon R. Guggenheim Museum (1943–59). Together with students from Columbia University's program in historic preservation, an inquiry was begun into various fragments and building studies and Wright's experiments with materials. At both Avery and MoMA, new standards of digital imaging are transforming use of the collection in ways large and small.

Avery Library is leading the inter-institutional data development project for the Archives in consultation with the registrars and technical teams at MoMA. Informational control of the materials is being achieved first by item-level inventorying and accessioning, and second by cataloging using a hierarchy of several core record types: collection-level records by format type, item level records for individual works, transactional records to track the location and use of materials, and archival finding aids to establish an organized structure and overview of the holdings. Cataloging the Archives requires recording physical characteristics of the works (format, materials, dimensions, extent, etc.); identifying less apparent elements that often require extensive research to derive definitive data (authoritative and vernacular title, date and date range, provenance, and status of built/unbuilt works), and mapping relationships between items across formats (drawings, correspondence, photography). These efforts to document in detail all items in the Archives—while crossing the boundaries of professional practices from curator to librarian to archivist to registrar to technologist—contribute valuable descriptive and technical information. This information must flow easily across multiple platforms at Avery and MoMA, and the integration of complex data systems between both institutions is essential to the co-stewardship of such a vast array of materials. The cataloging data also provides the basis for revealing the contents of the Archives to the public through easily understood points of discovery. Carole Ann Fabian's essay on data visualization in this volume demonstrates the potential of such new modes of representation that derive from the digital management of the collection.

Use of the collection for research, teaching, and exhibition has not awaited this first large-scale exhibition. In addition to semester-long seminars on Wright at both the undergraduate and graduate levels, numerous individual classes have been held and research projects developed. One of these, taught by Barry Bergdoll, led directly to the 2014 exhibition at MoMA *Frank Lloyd Wright and the City: Density vs. Dispersal.* That presentation—much more modest than the present one—welcomed Wright's archives to New York by asking new questions about his complex views on the proliferation of cities in twentieth-century America, notably juxtaposing his fascination with decentralized urbanization of the countryside in Broadacre City with his lifelong pursuit of unprecedented height for the skyscraper, culminating in The Mile-High Illinois project of 1956. In addition, a lecture series honoring Bruce Brooks Pfeiffer, a Wright apprentice and original curator and director of the Archives at Taliesin, has been inaugurated, and periodic lectures are organized jointly or separately by Avery and MoMA. And in 2013 the Temple Hoyne Buell Center for the Study of American Architecture held a Wright dissertation colloquium, marking the hope that the presence of the Archives, at the heart of a major research university, will catalyze younger scholars to take up their own approaches to Wright's work—its historical importance as well as its ongoing relevance. The Buell Center's continued engagement with the Archives is reflected in a concurrent exhibition presented in the Miriam and Ira D. Wallach Art Gallery at the Lenfest Center for the Arts on Columbia's new Manhattanville campus. This exhibition, in fall 2017, offers another context for understanding Wright's Broadacre model and is represented in this catalogue by an essay penned by David Smiley.

This book and exhibition do not propose a comprehensive view or overarching interpretation of Wright's long and protean career. Rather they celebrate the discoveries that the institutional settings of the Archives make possible. If previously these holdings were largely exploited by established Wright scholars, their presence at Avery and MoMA makes them regularly available to new voices, new contexts, and new questions. Because most of the contributors to this volume—historians, archivists, librarians, and art conservators—have not previously focused on Wright, their inquiries present original perspectives and avenues of research. Internally we have referred to them as the second-generation "unpackers." If the first set of unpackers was the team organized by Janet Parks—Curator of Drawings & Archives at Avery, whose essay here draws on her deep knowledge to highlight the contributions of the many designers whose hands can be detected in the Wright drawings—the second generation consists of scholars who have established expertise in many of the questions that are central to thinking about Frank Lloyd Wright. Only a few—Neil Levine and Michael Desmond—have devoted years to studying Wright. Each has chosen an object in the Archives that intrigued them, sometimes resonating with themes they have addressed in other scholarship and writing. This object is a point of entry into the Archives—something that illuminates many spheres, as in the famous micro-histories of Carlo Ginzburg or Robert Darnton, for instance—and the exhibition and the catalogue record both the process of historical inquiry and interpretation and the resulting reflections. Little-known aspects of Wright's work are explored. For example, landscape historian Therese O'Malley takes up the unusual planting plan for the Darwin D. Martin House in Buffalo (1903–06), called the "Floricycle," to explore Wright's relationship to debates about native versus imported plants; and Mabel O. Wilson examines a prototype design of a school for African-American children commissioned by the Julius Rosenwald Fund. Well-known projects are looked at as well, utilizing documents that have previously been overlooked, as Ken Tadashi Oshima considers the famed Imperial Hotel (1913–23) in Tokyo—Wright's most important commission during the lean years of the late teens and early 1920s and one of the largest of his career—by examining an extremely rare photographic volume found in the Archives.

This exhibition is an invitation to this rich repository, a first set of reports following the thought processes of some of the country's leading historians of architecture and landscape, and of the professionals who have taken up the stewardship of the records of this towering figure in the history of architecture.

Barry Bergdoll
Curator, Department of Architecture and Design
The Museum of Modern Art

Carole Ann Fabian
Director, Avery Architectural & Fine Arts Library
Columbia University

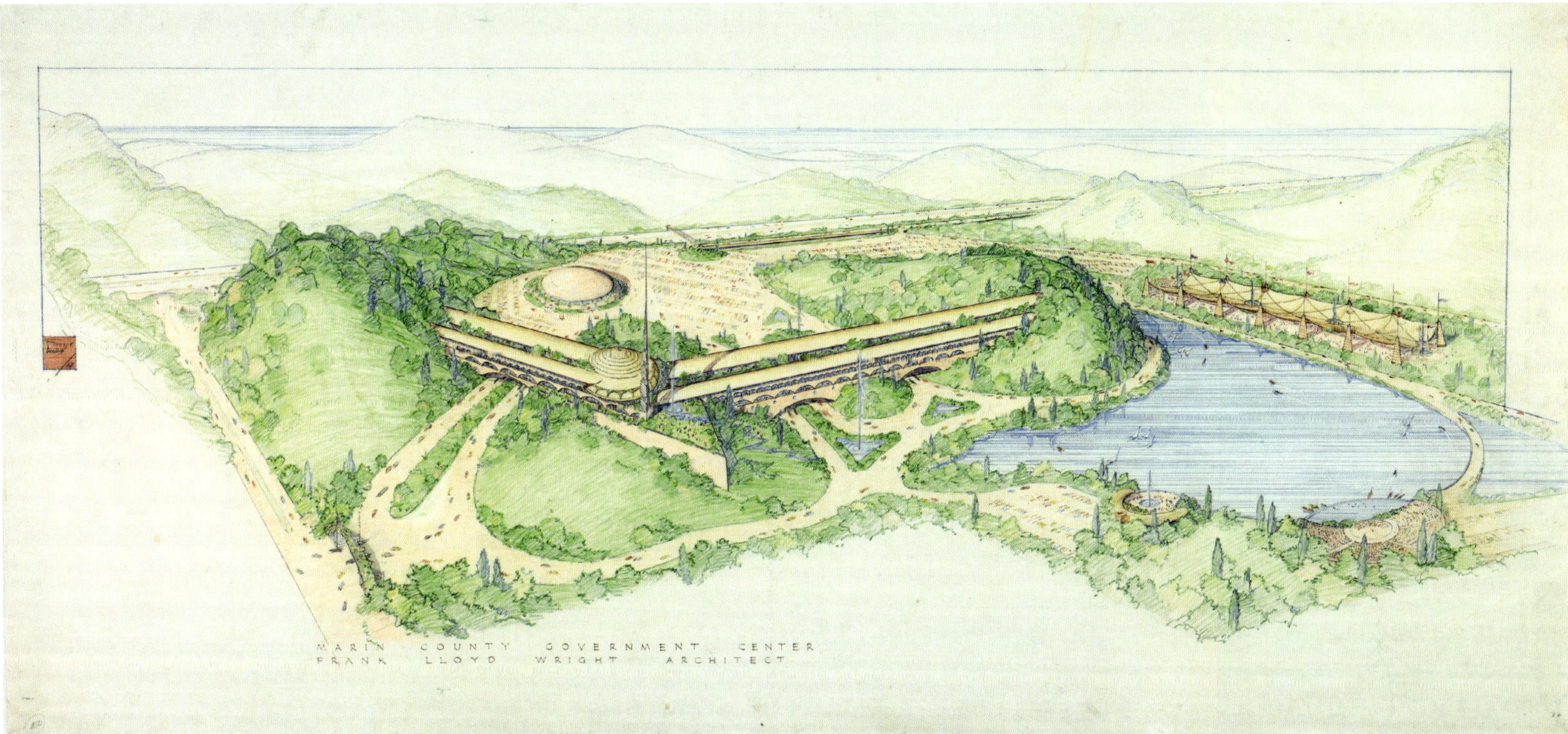
MARIN COUNTY GOVERNMENT CENTER
FRANK LLOYD WRIGHT ARCHITECT

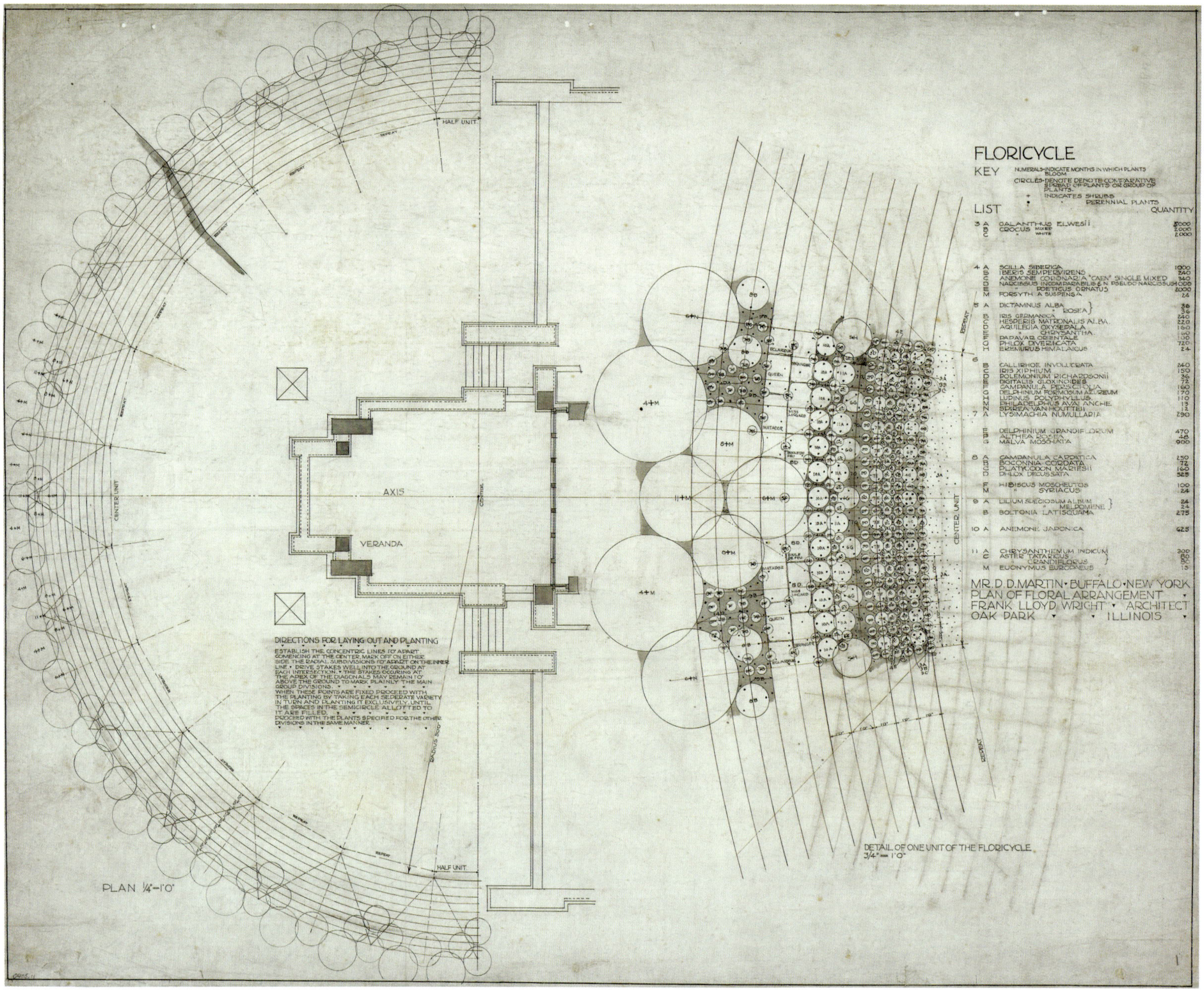

THERESE O'MALLEY

THE FLORICYCLE

DESIGNING WITH NATIVE AND EXOTIC PLANTS

Darwin D. Martin House, Buffalo, New York. 1903–06. "Floricycle." Ink on drafting cloth, 32 1/8 x 39 3/4 in. (81.6 x 100.1 cm)

Frank Lloyd Wright's drawing titled "Floricycle" (opposite), an unusual planting plan made for the Darwin D. Martin House, invites a close reading of the use of plants in the architect's garden designs and the function of landscape in creating a unified work of art. It raises the issue of the status of native and exotic plants at a moment when the profession of landscape design was emerging and the value of indigeneity and naturalization was under debate.[1] The Martin House was built from 1903–06 in Parkside, a Buffalo, New York, neighborhood laid out in the 1880s according to the designs of Frederick Law Olmsted, Sr. The Floricycle indicates plant species and quantities in great detail, proposing thousands of native and non-native bulbs, perennials, biennials, and flowering shrubs and trees to be planted in a half circle around the east porch of the main house. Drawings such as this one, covered in plant names, are rarely published or exhibited, yet they offer a level of specify about Wright's approach to garden design that has remained rarely studied.

While some have claimed that Wright knew little about or had limited interest in garden design, several facts point in the opposite direction: in many projects, he emphasized garden spaces and their plantings early in the design process, when buildings were still under development; he gave a lecture, in 1900, titled "Concerning Landscape Architecture" that illustrated his awareness of current trends; and he had ties to the most important landscape architects during a critical period of the profession's formation, including the Olmsteds, Walter Burley Griffin, Frank Lloyd Wright, Jr. (the architect's own son), Jens Jensen, and J. Elliot Wilkinson, all of whom interacted with Wright directly or indirectly through their projects. To understand his garden designs, we must shift from a focus on Wright alone to his collaborations with clients and other designers.

The undated and unattributed Floricycle plan represents the replanting of a preexisting bed in the shape of a hemicycle. The drawing is schematic in execution and exists in three versions—pen and ink on drafting cloth and two blueprints. Its highly diagrammatic character calls to mind Ebenezer Howard's influential 1898 garden city drawings, specifically Diagram No. 3, in which a wedge is pulled out and enlarged to explicate the detail. It has been noted that Walter Burley Griffin, who had joined Wright's studio in 1901 and oversaw both the architecture and gardens for the Martin project, was particularly interested in Howard's publications.[2] In the Floricycle, the wedge represents the unit that is to be replicated around the hemicycle eleven times with half units at either end.

The half-circle garden feature appeared in earlier stages of the Martin House project, including a freehand block plan by Wright from 1904 (plate 1). A sketch by Griffin from 1905, covered with hand-written plant names, also indicates a dense planting of both native and exotic species (fig. 1). According to correspondence among Darwin Martin, Wright, and Griffin, the Floricycle planting was carried out gradually between 1906 and 1913 (plate 2), replacing an original unsuccessful planting campaign. Wright included the Martin House plan and perspective in the Wasmuth portfolio, the 1910 German publication of a selection of his work. The Floricycle, called the Blumen Halbkreis (flower semicircle), was rendered with less exuberance than that conveyed by the original planting schemes.

The function of the large hemicycle seems to have been to create a privacy screen for the verandah against the open corner of the property. Unlike the pinwheel or circular shapes that appear in other Wright designs, in which either panoramic or sequentially changing distant views are created, here the density and height of the planting created a living wall that enclosed private space from public. Griffin returned to the project in 1910 to design a buffer shrubbery to provide even more protection from increasing traffic and development.[3]

Planting schemes for other projects by Wright's studio from this period similarly illustrate complex proposals for the domestic garden. For the Willits House, in Highland Park, Illinois (1902–03), Griffin planned a hemicycle landscape feature with a profusion of interlocking flowering plants, and two circular driveways (plate 3). The planting scheme for the Little House, in Peoria, Illinois (1902), also by Griffin, includes rectilinear borders, in which native and exotic plants are labeled in irregular drifts. When landscape designer and plantsman Jens Jensen laid out the grounds for Wright's Booth House, in Glencoe, Illinois (1911–12), he detailed the planting scheme with names of species on overlapping irregular swaths arranged in color bands with full seasonal blooming times.[4] The Frank Lloyd Wright Foundation Archives also contain a handwritten list of native and exotic plants for the Avery and Queene Coonley House in Riverside, Illinois, another Olmsted-planned community, which includes Japanese quince (*Chaemomeles speciosa*) and Oriental poppies (*Papaver orientalis*). For the Coonley garden, Jensen followed the hardscape designs of Wright, which included a walled garden at its center (plate 4). A grove of native birch trees and ferns, sited in the front of the house, was echoed on the interior in a mural by George Niedecken (fig. 2). This repetition of plant motifs, whether living or ornamental, outside or inside buildings, was characteristic of Wright's synthesizing approach, or creation of a *Gesamtkunstwerk*.

These planting plans are clues to the landscape and garden milieu in which Griffin, Jensen, and Wright worked. Wright's projects from the early twentieth century are often associated with the Prairie School of landscape design, as defined by Wilhelm Miller, whose treatise emphasized

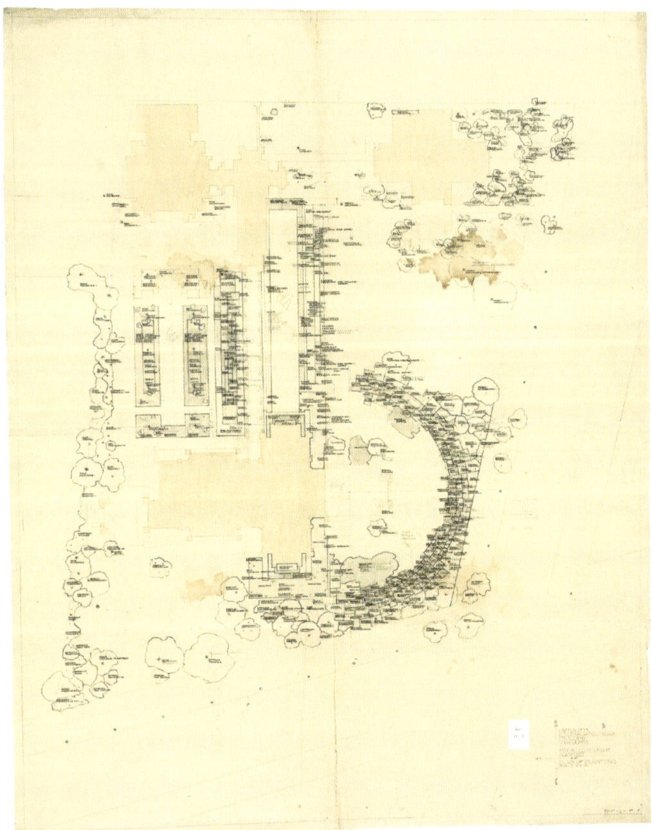

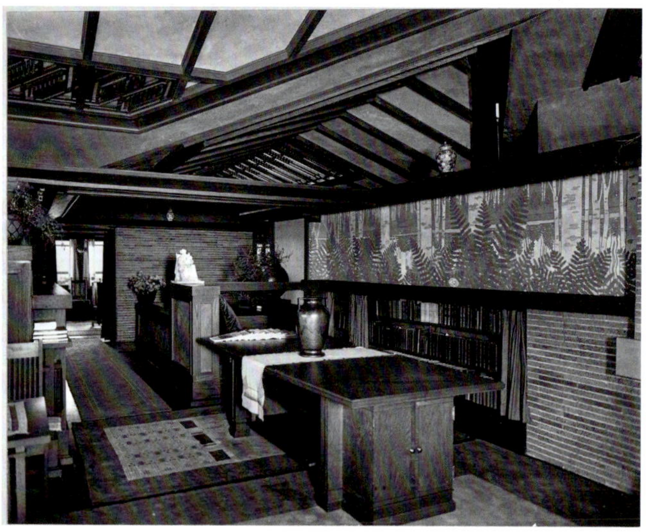

Fig. 1. Darwin D. Martin House, Buffalo, New York. 1903–06. Planting plan by Walter Burley Griffin. Ink and pencil on linen-backed tracing paper, 39 ¾ x 31 ⅜ in. (101 x 79.7 cm). University Archives, State University of New York at Buffalo

Fig. 2. Coonley House, Riverside, Illinois. 1906–09. Interior view with birch trees and fern mural

the use of indigenous plants.[5] Miller lauded Griffin and Jensen as leading practitioners. Indeed, planting plans featured hawthorn (*Craetageous*), staghorn sumac (*Rhus typhina*), false Aster (*Boltonia latisquama*), and many other natives. However, the schemes also include Japanese iris (*Iris kaempferi*), hollyhock (*Althea rosea*), Rose of Sharon (*Hibiscus syriacus*), snowball or mock orange (*Philadelphus avalanche*), tiger lily (*Lilium auratum*), and Boston Ivy (*Parthenocissus tricuspidata*), all originating in East Asia, as well as many plants from Europe and Africa. These non-native species were integral to the designs and suggest a less orthodox approach than that which we associate with Jensen and his followers, given their nativist rhetoric. This more inclusive practice represents what Philip Pauly has called an "ecological cosmopolitanism," an influential movement that encouraged increasing diversity in the American domesticated landscape and promoted the naturalization of foreign plants.[6]

There may be another explanation for the presence of so many Asian plants in Wright's designs in the first decades of the twentieth century. These are the same species that appear often in Japanese woodblock prints: hollyhock, peony, iris, magnolia, viburnum, and honeysuckle. Much has been written about the impact of Japanese prints on the Oak Park studio's architectural design, decorative arts, and style of graphic presentation drawing.[7] The hallmark style of Marion Mahony Griffin, an architect and graphic artist in Wright's studio, was inspired in palette and composition by Japanese prints (plate 5). Could it also be that this passion carried through to the level of living plant material used in the gardens?

Although the taste for Japanese gardens and plants was well primed by the Arts and Crafts movement, it was only in the 1890s that both American and Japanese nurseries were sufficiently established in the import-export business to ensure a stable supply of plants.[8] The inspiration of World's Fairs featuring Japanese pavilions and their gardens stimulated this taste in a broader audience.[9] Correspondence between Martin and the Wright studio in October 1904 suggests that Griffin was working out the final details for the Martins' planting plan while traveling to St. Louis to attend the Louisiana Purchase Exposition.[10] Wright also visited what was the first fully realized Japanese stroll garden in America (fig. 3), replete with vast quantities of plants shipped directly from Asia. Although the Ho-o-den, a Japanese pavilion set in Olmsted's naturalistic landscape at the 1893 World's Fair in Chicago, is often credited with influencing Wright's architecture, the Japanese gardens at the St. Louis Exposition eleven years later exemplified the interpenetration of garden and house in a far more complete display with imported flora. It is also important to note that the grounds of the Japanese pavilion were rimmed with American trees and shrubs, many from local woodlands, modeling a blend of native and exotic plants that was found in the projects of Wright's studio.

In the development of Wright's designs, clients certainly played a critical role in the selection of plant materials. The Willitses traveled to Japan with Wright in 1905. The Littles and the Martins became avid collectors of Japanese prints, usually provided by Wright, who was a major collector and dealer during these years.[11] In the Martin House, Japanese prints were the only decoration in the hall, receiving room, and living room. Prints by Utagawa Hiroshige hung in the Little House on special stands designed by Wright, on which a "weed vase" and flower arrangement could also sit.[12] In a period when avant-garde architecture featured a harmonious integration of decorative and architectural design and dynamic interaction of interior and exterior spaces the garden contributed to the total work of art and its unified character down to its most basic element: the living plant.

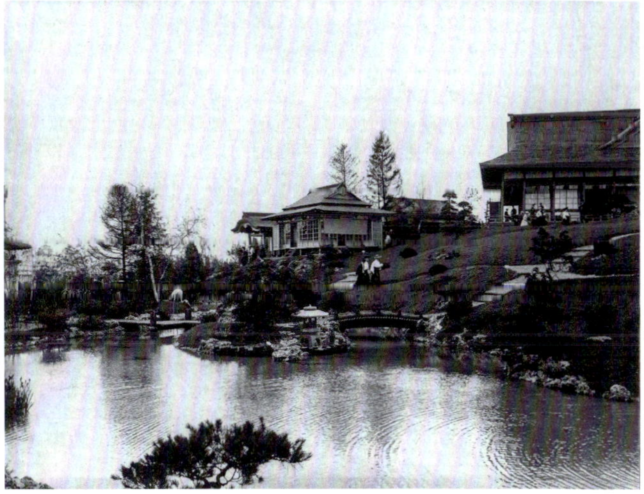

Fig. 3. Japanese pavilion and garden at the Louisiana Purchase Exposition, St. Louis. 1904. Missouri History Museum, St. Louis

Many of Wright's clients were interested in horticulture and the art of garden design. The Martins, for example, were eager gardeners, and Queene Ferry Coonley was the daughter of D. W. Ferry, founder of a Detroit seed company that would become the largest seed company in the world. They were also caught up in a nature conservation crusade that swept the progressive reformist circles to which they belonged.[13] In terms of garden aesthetics, this clientele shared the preferences of the international Arts and Crafts movement, which was active in America, especially in the Chicago area. Wright himself was a charter member of the Chicago Arts and Crafts Society, established in 1897.[14] In landscape design, this movement opposed the artificiality of bedding out hothouse plants, and championed both local and imported plants, treated in such a way that allowed a natural growth pattern rather than one that was clipped and shaped.

Within this movement, the influential garden writer, designer, and plantswoman Gertrude Jekyll promulgated the naturalistic treatment of native and exotic plants.[15] Among her many innovative methods were the emphasis on color and texture in plants, and, in practice, the use of photography and the graphic convention of drifts of plants in clusters of hot and cool tones.[16] In his 1900 lecture on landscape architecture, Wright recommended Jekyll's latest book, *Home and Garden*, because it "shows very well this attitude toward our subject, and it should be in every library." The subject to which Wright refers is the symbiosis of gardens and buildings as part of a modern approach to design: "Landscape architecture has a decidedly architectural basis—that is an architectural plan in arrangement and division, which provides for massing and grouping of foliage according to its true nature—that is, as it naturally grows best to show its full beauty as a lilac, a syringa, an elm, an oak, or a maple."[17] Wright called the Victorian mode, in which yews and boxwood are trimmed into animal shapes, tortured and forced, a "degeneracy." He argued for an integrated composition of building and grounds, as a way to "harmonize these growing things with man's surrounding. . . . It is no longer permitted to reach into and mar the natural grace of foliage."[18] Walls, steps, pools, pergolas, and terraces were elements both Wright and Jekyll employed to connect houses and their gardens.

In the same year Wright gave this lecture, Jekyll's book was reviewed in *Architectural Review*.[19] The account emphasizes two issues that seem relevant to Wright: the extension of the house into the garden and reconciling architectural and organic forms. Would Wright have seen the review? It seems likely since the rest of the issue was the first comprehensive publication of Wright's work. Robert Closson Spencer, Jr., an architect and friend with whom Wright shared offices, wrote the essay, "The Work of Frank Lloyd Wright," allegedly with text and images supplied by Wright.[20] The article employs the ecological metaphor of the indigenous versus the alien in the opening sentences: "The last year of the century finds the majority of our prominent and successful architects still busily engaged in the transplanting of exotics. From every favorable foreign source, the outward forms of the various styles and periods are being 'adapted,' plagiarized or caricatured."[21] In contrast, Spencer praises Wright: "A younger man . . . swinging easily along amid the beauties of the forests and flower-sown prairies of his own country." The author claims Wright's work as an "original native effort," arguing that in order to attain "a great national architecture," our buildings must be the "natural bloom of a hardy native growth with its roots deep in the soil."[22] The trope of the native and exotic was played out in texts and designs during these years in which the gardens of Wright's studio were born from a rich and varied theoretical and aesthetic milieu.[23]

In spite of the inclusiveness shown in the planting plans, the rhetoric that surrounded Wright's designs was more often in favor of native species. Wright published photos of local "weeds" and decorated homes with wildflowers. For the Dana House in Springfield, Illinois, he commissioned murals featuring the prairie staghorn sumac and asters by George Niedecken (plate 6). The sumac, as Wilhelm Miller wrote, was a "red badge of courage which is often considered a symbol of the indomitable western spirit." Formerly a weed "despised by farmers, [it] is now much planted about middle-western homes because of its gorgeous autumnal colors."[24] Jensen is credited with planting a whole hillside at Taliesin with sumac, whose "leafy crowns," according to Jensen, "autumn's frosty breath turned . . . into a flaming red"[25] The sumac's feathery leaves also generated decorative elements that unified interior and exterior spaces. Abstractions of plants ornamented objects such as Wright's studio's distinctive art glass and light screens that marked the threshold across which space flowed in and out. Even in winter, which is long and hard in this region, the abstracted plant motifs created garden views.

Wright favored another flower, the hollyhock, which was commonly used in prairie gardens but also in New England colonial revival and British cottage gardens. The fact that it was not truly native, but Asian, did not stop anyone from claiming it as authentic. Even Jensen could not resist this stalwart flower and provides poetic justification for its use: "Hollyhocks, although not a true product of native soil, has [*sic*] truly become a part of our rural countryside as the immigrant, for the pioneer so loved the hollyhock that he brought it with him and planted it at his cabin and dugout door. Traveling throughout our western plains, a clump of hollyhocks, or lilac bush, and a few apple trees, are all that remains to tell of the struggle of some early settler, who later, for some reason or another, had to give up the struggle and move onwards."[26] Evocative of both the pioneer's prairie and Japanese aesthetics, the hollyhock served multiple symbolic and design purposes for Wright, as a garden specimen and source for decorative motifs.

In 1917 Wright moved to Los Angeles, joining his son Lloyd, a landscape architect. Wright and studio were faced with a new environment, economically, socially, and ecologically: the Pacific Rim. Wright was developing a "form language" of circles, triangles, and squares, yet his or his assistants' close studies of plants continued to yield motifs that inspired fundamental structure and harmonious works, internally and externally.[27] Botanical imagery, as always, fueled Wright's oratory. In his autobiography Wright recalls that the 1923–24 Millard House, also known as La Miniatura, happened, "as the cactus grows."[28] He is comparing the evolution of his design to the growth of the saguaro cactus: a strong central spine with arms branching out. The house was built in a wooded eucalyptus ravine that formed a sunken garden into which balconies and terraces projected out from the house's core.[29] Wright describes the building "as a kind of tree standing at home among other trees in its own native land."[30] Once again, the native trope emerges as the fundamental principle, however inaccurate. The highly combustible eucalyptus, introduced from Australia and planted by the millions in California in the late nineteenth and early twentieth centuries, was by this time considered a blight on the landscape.[31] The saguaro cactus (*Carnegiea gigantean*), which Wright references as if it is indigenous and uses as a metaphorical source for his design, would probably not have originated in this coastal area either, but further south in Arizona and Mexico.

The Barnsdall House, in Los Angeles (1918–21), was named Hollyhock House because its owner, Aline Barnsdall, true to Jensen's thesis, favored this "prairie" flower from back home in the Midwest. The iconic plant inspired the building's ornament and interior decoration (plate 7). The living gardens included a hemicycle and woods planted with imported species, such as Italian stone pine (*Pinus pinea*), blue gum eucalyptus (*Eucalyptus globulus*), and olive trees, planted in orderly rows.[32] Californians at this moment were in the process of transforming the native landscape with Mediterranean, South African, and South American plants that suited the climate of the Pacific coast. To fill the increasing demand for cacti and succulents, landscapers raided the nearby Sonoran and Anza Borega deserts. If, as has been said, Wright was exploring a romantic primitivism in the architecture of this project, he was also creating a romantic environment of exotic sources in the landscape.[33]

In 1927 Wright and his apprentices encountered another new (for them) ecology, the Sonoran Desert, which would become their winter home over the next thirty years. George Kastner, draftsman and photographer for Wright in the late 1920s, produced a series of photographs documenting the transplanted studio camp of wood and canvas tents, Ocatilla, named after the common desert plant ocotillo (*Fouquieria splendens*).[34] A photograph indicates the location of key landscape elements, the commanding saguaro, around which the camp was laid out, and the model for the vertically serrated concrete blocks for the proposed San Marcos-in-the-Desert Hotel (fig. 4).[35]

Eugene Masselink, who joined the Fellowship in 1933, captured in both words and images the sensory revolution the group experienced each autumn when leaving Wisconsin for Taliesin West. He described arriving in the Arizona desert for the first time: "Tall ancient saguaro and graceful waving ocotillo and the vivid green on the floor of the desert and the purple mountains beyond. A garden like none I had ever seen. A desert like something I had never dreamed."[36] Masselink's studies of staghorn cholla, lichen, and rocks attests to the continuing inspiration by natural forms (plates 8–11). In terms of graphic representation, the three-dimensional quality of these studies contrasts with the flatness of earlier depictions of plants and landscapes and those made, for example, for the mural (see p. 58) and curtain for the Taliesin Fellowship Complex and the *Liberty* magazine covers. Marc Treib has written that modernist garden practice would move away from an ecological interaction of plants in the designed environment to using plants more as sculptural entities. This is certainly how the large-scale cacti were treated in Wright's desert work, as individual monumental specimen.[37]

From his earliest house designs, Wright displayed a passionate interest in the living elements of design. Collaborating with associates and clients, he generated new vocabularies of plant texture, color, and behavior inspired by a complex marriage of form and meaning. Whether on Lake Erie or in the Arizona desert, plants and plant imagery proved a vital way to bridge the architectural interior, the garden, and the wider landscape. What seems constant in his work is best summarized by Wright himself: "We have no . . . longer an outside and an inside as two separate things. Now the outside may come inside, and the inside may and does, go outside. They are of each other. Form and function become one in design and execution of the nature of materials and method and purpose are all in unison."[38]

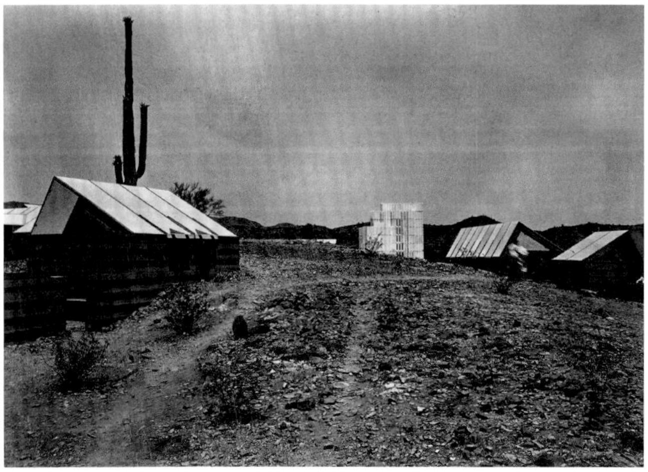

Fig. 4. Ocatilla (Wright camp), Phoenix South (formerly Salt River) Mountains, Phoenix, Arizona. 1929. Central court with concrete-block model for San Marcos-in-the-Desert Hotel (1928–29) in the background

Notes

1. For in-depth study of this project, see Charles E. Aguar and Berdeana Aguar, *Wrightscapes: Frank Lloyd Wright's Landscape Designs* (New York: McGraw-Hill, 2002), pp. 87–96; and Mark H. Bayer and Zakery D. Steele, Bayer Landscape Architecture, PLLC, *Darwin D. Martin House, Cultural Landscape Report* (Buffalo, N.Y.: Martin House Restoration Corporation, 2014), http://martinhouse.z-paper.com/mh_cultural_rep/.

2. Sir Ebenezer Howard, *Garden Cities of Tomorrow* (London: Swan, Sonnenschein, 1902). Christopher Vernon, " 'Expressing Natural Conditions with Maximum Possibility': The American Landscape Art of Walter Burley Griffin," *Journal of Garden History* 15 (1995): 26–28; Lance Necker, "Fast-tracking Culture and Landscape: Horace William Shaler Cleveland and the Garden in the Midwest," in *Regional Garden Design in the United States*, ed. Therese O'Malley and Marc Treib (Washington, D.C.: Dumbarton Oaks, 1995), p. 69n3; and David Van Zanten, "The Ambition and Reach of Chicago's Progressive Architects," in *Drawing the Future: Chicago Architecture on the International Stage* (Evanston, Ill.: Northwestern University Press, 2013), pp. 45, 47.

3. Bayer and Steele, *Darwin D. Martin House, Cultural Landscape Report*, p. 75.

4. Aguar and Aguar, *Wrightscapes*, pp. 143–49.

5. Wilhelm Miller, *The Prairie Spirit in Landscape Gardening*, repr. in O'Malley and Treib, *Regional Garden Design*, Appendix, pp. 271–310.

6. Philip J. Pauly, *Biologist and the Promise of American Life* (Princeton, N.J.: Princeton University Press, 2000), pp. 72–74.

7. See Christopher Vernon, "The Silence of the Mountains and the Music of the Sea: The Landscape Artistry of Marion Mahony Griffin," in *Marion Mahony Griffin: Drawing the Form in Nature*, ed. Debora Wood (Evanston, Ill.: Museum of Northwestern University, 2005), p. 9; and Margo Stipe, "Wright and Japan," in *Frank Lloyd Wright: Europe and Beyond*, ed. Anthony Alofsin (Berkeley: University of California Press, 1999), p. 24.

8. Judith M. Taylor, *The Global Migrations of Ornamental Plants* (St. Louis: Missouri Botanical Garden Press, 2009), pp. 154–58.

9. Cathy Jean Maloney, *World's Fair Gardens: Shaping American Landscapes* (Charlottesville: University of Virginia Press, 2011), p. 22. See also Seiko Goto, "The First Japanese Garden in the Western World: The Garden in the Louisiana Purchase Exposition," *Studies in the History of Gardens and Designed Landscapes* 27, no. 3 (July–September 2007): 244–53.

10. Aguar and Aguar, *Wrightscapes*, p. 93.

11. Edgar Kaufmann, Jr., "Frank Lloyd Wright Exhibited," in "Frank Lloyd Wright at the Metropolitan Museum of Art," *Met Bulletin* 40, no. 2 (Fall 1982): 32.

12. Julia Meech-Pekarik, "Frank Lloyd Wright and Japanese Prints," in Kaufmann, Jr., *Met Bulletin* 40, no. 2 (Fall 1982): 52. The Littles had three hundred prints from Wright's collection.

13. Alice T. Friedman, "Girl Talk: Feminism and Domestic Architecture at Frank Lloyd Wright's Oak Park Studio," in *Marion Mahony Reconsidered*, ed. David Van Zanten (Chicago: University of Chicago Press, 2011), pp. 23–50.

14. Andrew Saint, "Wright and Great Britain," in *Frank Lloyd Wright: Europe and Beyond*, ed. Alofsin, p. 123.

15. Judith B. Tankard, "An American Perspective on Gertrude Jekyll's Legacy," reprinted from the *Journal of the New England Garden History Society* 6 (Fall 1998), https://www.masshort.org/Garden-History-Articles.

16. Judith B. Tankard and Michael R. Van Valkenburgh, *Gertrude Jekyll: A Vision of Garden and Wood* (New York: Harry N. Abrams, 1988).

17. Frank Lloyd Wright, "Concerning Landscape Architecture," *Frank Lloyd Wright: Collected Writings*, Bruce Brooks Pfeiffer, ed. (New York: Rizzoli, 1992), pp. 54–57.

18. Ibid., p. 56.

19. "Home and Garden, by Gertrude Jekyll," *Architectural Review* 7, no. 6 (June 1900): 76.

20. Robert C. Spencer, Jr., "The Work of Frank Lloyd Wright," *Architectural Review* 7, no. 6 (June 1900): 59–72. Joseph Connors, "Wright on Nature and the Machine," in *The Nature of Frank Lloyd Wright*, ed. Carol R. Bolon, Robert S. Nelson, and Linda Seidel (Chicago: University of Chicago Press, 1988), p. 3.

21. Spencer, "The Work of Frank Lloyd Wright," p. 59.

22. Ibid., pp. 59, 61–62.

23. Wilhelm Miller, *The Prairie Spirit in Landscape Gardening*, repr. in *The Native Landscape Reader*, ed. Robert E. Grese (Amherst: University of Massachusetts Press, 2011), p. 117.

24. Ibid.

25. Cited in Derek Fell, *The Gardens of Frank Lloyd Wright* (London: Frances Lincoln Limited, 2009), p. 113.

26. Jensen, quoted in Grese, ed., *The Native Landscape Reader*, p. 7.

27. Anthony Alofsin, "Frank Lloyd Wright and Modernism," in *Frank Lloyd Wright, Architect*, ed. Terence Riley with Peter Reed (New York: The Museum of Modern Art, 1994), p. 37.

28. Frank Lloyd Wright, *Frank Lloyd Wright: Writings and Buildings*, ed. Edgar Kaufmann and Ben Raeburn (Cleveland: Meridian Books, 1960), p. 211.

29. David G. DeLong, *Frank Lloyd Wright: Designs for an American Landscape* (New York: Harry N. Abrams, 1996), p. 41.

30. Wright, *Frank Lloyd Wright: Writings and Buildings*, ed. Kaufmann and Raeburn, p. 216. Aguar and Aguar, *Wrightscapes*, pp. 192, 211–19. Quoted in Catherine Howett, "Modernism and American Landscape Architecture," in *Modern Landscape Architecture: A Critical Review*, ed. Marc Treib (London: MIT Press, 1993), p. 23.

31. Jared Farmer, *Trees in Paradise: A California History* (New York: W. W. Norton, 2013), p. 130.

32. Aguar and Aguar, *Wrightscapes*, p. 182.

33. Delong, *Frank Lloyd Wright: Designs for an American Landscape*, p. 36.

34. Frank Lloyd Wright, *An Autobiography* (New York: Horison, 1977), p. 312; and Penny Fowler, *Frank Lloyd Wright: Graphic Artist* (San Francisco: Pomegranate, 2002).

35. Fell, *The Gardens of Frank Lloyd Wright*, p. 74.

36. Randolph C. Henning, ed., *"At Taliesin": Newspaper Columns by Frank Lloyd Wright and the Taliesin Fellowship, 1934–1937* (Carbondale: Southern Illinois University Press, 1992), pp. 109–10; quoted in Anne Whiston Spirn, "Frank Lloyd Wright, Architect of Landscape," in DeLong, *Frank Lloyd Wright: Designs for an American Landscape*, p. 149.

37. Marc Treib, "Aspects of Regionality and the Modern(ist) Garden in California," in O'Malley and Treib, *Regional Garden Design*, p. 6. Modernist cactus gardens are documented in Sao Paolo in 1925–28. In 1931 Wright went to Brazil and visited them. Annette Condello, "Cacti Transformation from the Primitive to the Avant-Garde: Modern Landscape Architecture in Brazil and Mexico," *Studies in the History of Gardens and Landscapes* 34, no. 4 (October–December 2014): 339–51.

38. Wright, *An Autobiography*, p. 363.

JENNIFER GRAY

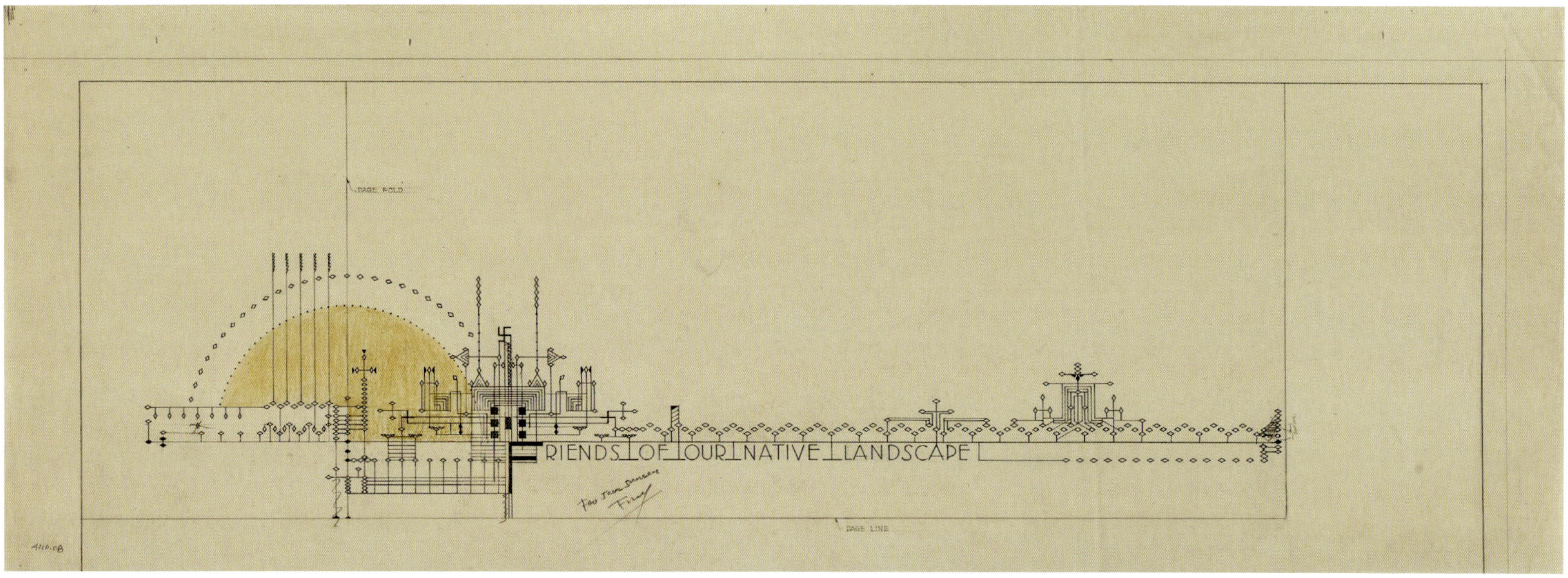

PATTERN BEHIND THE REALISM THE JENSEN GRAPHIC

Graphic design for Jens Jensen. n.d. Ink, pencil, and colored pencil on tracing paper, 11 7/8 x 33 in. (30.2 x 83.8 cm)

Sometime between 1913 and 1927 Frank Lloyd Wright designed a graphic for the landscape architect Jens Jensen that encodes—both in its geometric design and in the copious, handwritten notations explaining its symbolism—the substance of Wright's views on nature, and especially its political significance. The design abstracts the prairie topography into a logo for the Friends of Our Native Landscape, an advocacy group founded by Jensen in 1913 to advance conservation causes and whose membership would come to include many influential and well-connected figures, including several of Wright's clients.[1] The prairie is represented as a horizontal line, together with the moon, a flowering tree, and a group of dried weeds with their seedpods (opposite). In the preliminary sketch, Wright includes lengthy notations to Jensen explaining the composition's symbolism (fig. 1). The prairie is fundamental, Wright explains, "because Jensen and I love it!" The moon signals "elemental conditions" incomprehensible to man. The flowering tree "decorates the prairie sympathetically," while the dried weeds and seedpods are "nature's most effective readymade decoration." Atop the weeds is a swastika, an "Indian symbol" that Wright equates with fecundity and productivity, a "good Earth symbol, antedating Confucius," and also relates to the displacement of Native Americans, because, as he explains, "we are taking over the landscape and trust from the Indians." The prairie thus conjured is existential and terrestrial, universal and historically specific, and reveals nature to be a contested territory where competing political interests play themselves out.

Little is known about the origin of this design, which would have adorned newsletters or other literature published by the Friends of Our Native Landscape (FONL). Changes to the composition, as well as the varying conditions and types of papers used in its multiple iterations, suggest that the graphic may have been reworked several times, possibly over years. The design appears never to have been implemented and has never been the object of analytical study, and in fact Wright never joined the FONL, though he was elected an honorary member.[2] Why is this seemingly minor and unexecuted logo significant? The literature on Wright and nature is practically endless, with much of it centered on existential readings of the natural world, heroic interpretations of the Midwest prairie, and Wright's extraordinary sensitivity to both. However true, the FONL graphic complicates these received narratives, especially in the way it reveals the ideological nature of nature. It raises questions about the politics of regional ecologies and indigenous plants—usually, and uncritically, assumed to be positive—as well as debates over colonization, immigration, and displacement that pervaded political and architectural discourse in the early twentieth century. It also sheds light on Wright's lifelong relationship with Jensen, widely acknowledged but little explored.[3] Ultimately this design raises questions about the relationships between nature and Wright's larger social project, the revivification of democracy.

Given that the datum of the graphic is an abstracted prairie, it seems reasonable to begin our inquiry by asking: what was the meaning of the prairie at this time? For Wright and Jensen, as well as many other architects, activists, and thinkers in Chicago during these years, the expansive and purportedly native prairie landscape not only represented the openness, freedom, and uniqueness of American democracy—famously theorized by Frederick Jackson Turner in 1893—but it also actively cultivated similar political beliefs among the public.[4] Such ideas circulated among a group of progressive designers who shared offices in Chicago, including Wright, Jensen, Dwight Perkins, Irving and Allen Pond, Robert Spencer, and Walter Burley Griffin, prompting historians to dub them the Prairie School of architecture, identifiable by shared tropes such as horizontal lines and ribbon windows, though in practice no such coherent school existed. These ideas also manifested themselves in publications celebrating the virtues of the prairie landscape and native plants, such as Wilhelm Miller's seminal text *The Prairie Spirit in Landscape Gardening* (1915), as well as in countless philanthropic agencies, vacation schools, and walking clubs that organized prairie excursions in order to reunite the people of Chicago, especially immigrants and children, with this genius loci of democracy.[5]

The prairie, however, was a myth. Industrialization had eradicated or fundamentally altered most of the Midwest prairie by the early twentieth century.[6] The Friends of Our Native Landscape was a political vehicle for advancing awareness and conservation of remaining endangered native landscapes. Since the 1890s Jensen had been a vocal supporter of natural gardens and indigenous plant species, for both economic and environmental reasons. Together with Henry C. Cowles, a botanist at the University of Chicago, Jensen pioneered the emerging field of ecology, called "plant sociology" at the time, which studied plants as "living communities" in which flora coexisted in ecological association rather than as autonomous organisms.[7] This was an irresistible metaphor for the kinds of democratic communities that many activists hoped to forge from the largely foreign-born and sometimes volatile mix of races, ethnicities, and ideologies that comprised Chicago in 1900. Jensen and the FONL conducted environmental surveys; hosted prairie walks; published preservation recommendations; and lobbied public officials on conservation matters—activities that, paradoxically, interested middle-class reformers more than their intended audience of working-class immigrants. With chapters in Illinois, Wisconsin, and Michigan, the FONL was highly successful, conserving dozens of prominent sites around the Midwest, such as the Indiana Dunes southwest of Chicago, developing rural planning and highway beautification plans, and advancing environmental legislation for forty years.

That the central graphic device of the FONL design is an abstracted prairie landscape encapsulates critical dif-

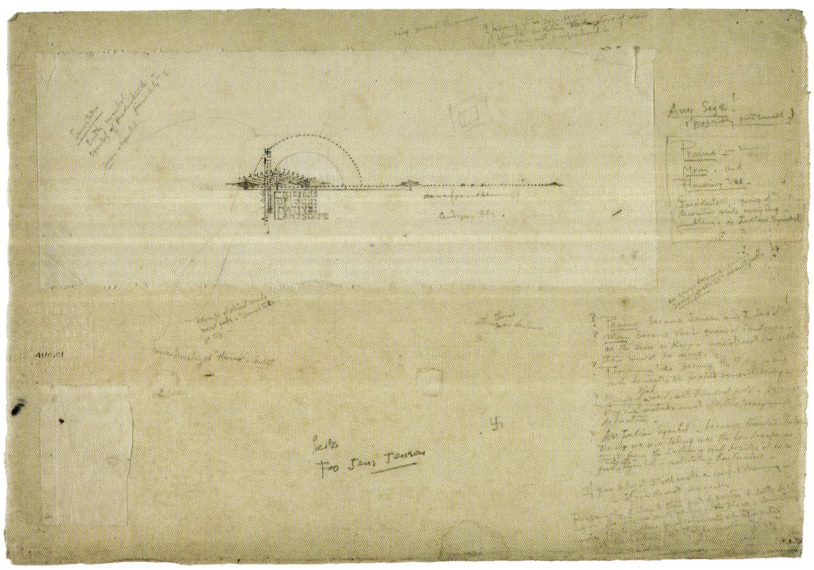

Fig. 1. Graphic design for Jens Jensen. n.d. Pencil on tracing paper, 9 7/8 × 14 5/8 in. (25.1 × 37.1 cm)

ferences in how Wright and Jensen approached nature. Wright saw in nature ordering geometries and underlying structure—a kind of architecture—not particular plants. Schooled in the tradition of Ralph Waldo Emerson, Wright understood natural forms, a beautiful leaf or bloom, to be outward manifestations of an underlying, divine order that was Nature, a philosophy substantiated by his exposure to the pedagogy of Friedrich Froebel, who insisted that students master formal geometric exercises before drawing directly from real objects, from nature.[8] He distinguished ideas of nature and natural from Nature in his autobiography, where he describes nature as "some sentimental feeling about animals, grass and trees, and the out-of-doors."[9] Believing that the artist approximated Nature through a process of "conventionalization,"[10] Wright criticized Jensen for being a "realistic landscapist," whereas he was "an abstractionist seeking pattern behind the realism—the interior structure instead of the comparatively superficial exterior effects [*sic*] you delight in."[11]

As such, Wright often engaged plants and landscapes at a critical remove. In 1896 he prefaced his reprint of *The House Beautiful* with a series of photogravures illustrating abstract arrangements of weeds and seedpods—the very "readymade decorations" he refers to in the FONL graphic (fig. 2).[12] That Wright used the term readymade is particularly poignant in the context of avant-garde artistic experiments in the early twentieth century, suggesting that weeds and native plants were found objects and that their artistic qualities resided in their creative arrangement or unexpected setting. However much Wright criticized formal gardens—calling them perverted, decadent, and abusive in what, tellingly, would be his only text to address landscape architecture[13]—the weeds he illustrated in *The House Beautiful* are removed from their natural habitats and arranged into abstract designs, genuine readymades, their dislocation furthered by the vertical cropping and negative space that are distinctly Japanese in composition. Four years later, in 1900, Wright made a series of collotypes depicting the landscape of Jones Valley, Wisconsin, to accompany promotional materials for Hillside Home School, a progressive educational center founded by his aunts that engaged farming, gardening, and nature study in its curriculum. Many of the images—presumably intended to advertise the fertile environs of the school—depicted the valley during the winter (fig. 3), when very little agriculture could be seen let alone practiced, because he preferred the simplicity of the denuded prairie. Wright noted in the FONL graphic that the abstracted prairie depicted was covered in snow—which "simplifies it beautifully"—and indeed, the linearity of the design calls to mind the collotypes, in which dark angular branches of bare trees and shrubs punctuate otherwise white fields.[14] Compared to Jensen's taxonomic nature photography—close-up shots documenting specific species, always in situ—Wright's abstractions were formal and conceptual exercises.

Despite being critical of Jensen's realism, Wright collaborated with him on numerous occasions, including residential designs for Sherman Booth, Abby Beecher Roberts, and Avery Coonley. The Booth estate was a particularly ambitious collaboration—at one point encompassing public parks accessible by two railroad stations—and reveals the extent to which seemingly natural or realistic landscapes can be artificial, manufactured environments. In addition to being a founding member and secretary of the

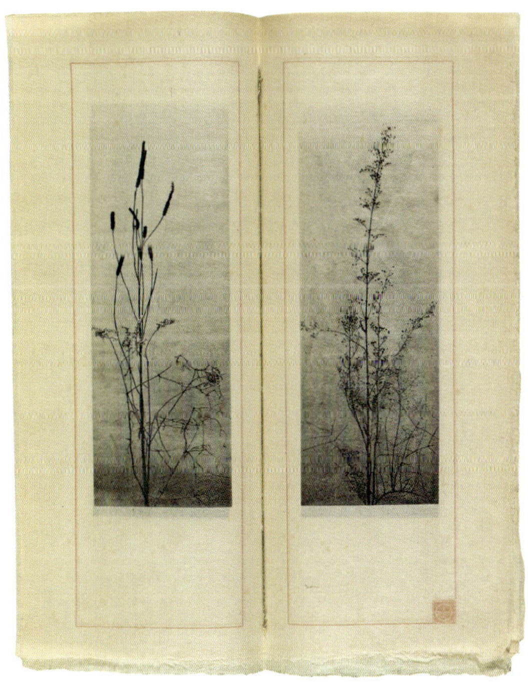

Fig. 2. Weeds and seedpods. n.d. Photogravures on Japanese paper, page 7 1/2 x 2 3/4 in. (19.1 x 7 cm). Inset in William C. Gannett. *The House Beautiful* (River Forest, Ill.: Auvergne Press, 1896–98). Avery Architectural & Fine Arts Library, Columbia University, New York

FONL, Booth was a member of the Glencoe Park District and chairman of its Board of Trustees. The fifteen-acre (six-hectare) site he selected for his estate in Glencoe, Illinois, was a dramatic environment sliced through with glacial ravines and a tributary stream that emptied into nearby Lake Michigan.[15] The estate was located adjacent to a surviving prairie forest that Jensen was lobbying to preserve during these years—a project that re-created as much natural scenery as it conserved and that likewise proposed to modernize nature by incorporating sewers, parkways, and railroads.[16] If fully realized, Booth's estate would have been part of the very same network of nature preserves and parks that Jensen and the FONL envisioned transforming social relations.

The landscape design for the estate is a veritable inventory of Jensen's signature landscape concepts (plate 12). Dense groupings of native plants nearly obscure the escarpments, bluffs, and ravines, especially on the northeastern portion of the site, interrupted only by the curving drive and various trails that provide access through what almost could be described as a botanical garden. An open meadow, called The Clearing—endowed by Jensen with metaphysical associations as a clearing in the woods, as well as a clearing in the mind—punctuates the densely planted site.[17] To the south of the central vegetable garden is an irregularly shaped, spring-fed swimming pool. Jensen was renowned for his water features: meandering "prairie rivers" and swimming holes lined with stratified rocks that recalled the long-evaporated riverbeds of the preindustrial prairie, a tradition of natural artifice stemming back to Frederick Law Olmsted and beyond.[18] Two campfires, or "council rings" as Jensen called them, one adjacent to the house, the other among the trees, provide places for outdoor gatherings. Council rings were, for Jensen, symbols of American identity, deriving from Native American and pioneer rituals (fig. 4). In his estimation they encouraged democratic social relations: "In this friendly circle, around the fire . . . there is no social caste. All are on the same level, looking each other in the face."[19] Like many wilderness advocates, Jensen romanticized direct contact with native landscapes for their associations with frontier life and the origins of American democracy,[20] going so far as to describe them as fragments of land "as the white man found it—a different world from the manmade one"[21]—a mythology that Wright enacted in his annual pilgrimages to Arizona and the camp-like accommodations of Ocatilla and Taliesin West.

Wright's renderings for the Booth estate (plates 13, 14) are particularly compelling, and it is difficult to resist the temptation to read an organic wholeness or transcendental unity in the interpolation of landscape, infrastructure, and architecture depicted in them. The sheer beauty of the representations—their persuasive "naturalness"—is the stuff of Wright lore. Indeed, Wright captioned the perspective drawing as an illustration of what he called "Simplicity," a state of equilibrium whereby all parts coexist in harmonious unity: "Nothing at all as simple in itself . . . but must achieve simplicity—as an artist should use the term—as a perfectly realized part of some organic whole."[22] Beneath the intoxicating surface, however, the paradisiacal garden in which the Booth House is situated was an entirely constructed environment, one inhospitable for building mansions precariously perched over rocky ravines and also inaccessible without modern infrastructure. The challenging topography of the property necessitated extensive land surveys and infrastructure to site and grade roadways and bridges, as well as an ambitious reforestation project to re-create the native landscape destroyed by clearing and farming.[23] The presence of hollyhocks in the foreground of the perspective, clearly identifiable at the entrance to the bridge, reveals a second fiction, one centered on the authenticity and even ethical attributes of indigenous plants and native landscapes. Hollyhocks are not native to the Midwest. Most advocates of natural gardens used a mixture of natives and exotics to achieve various effects

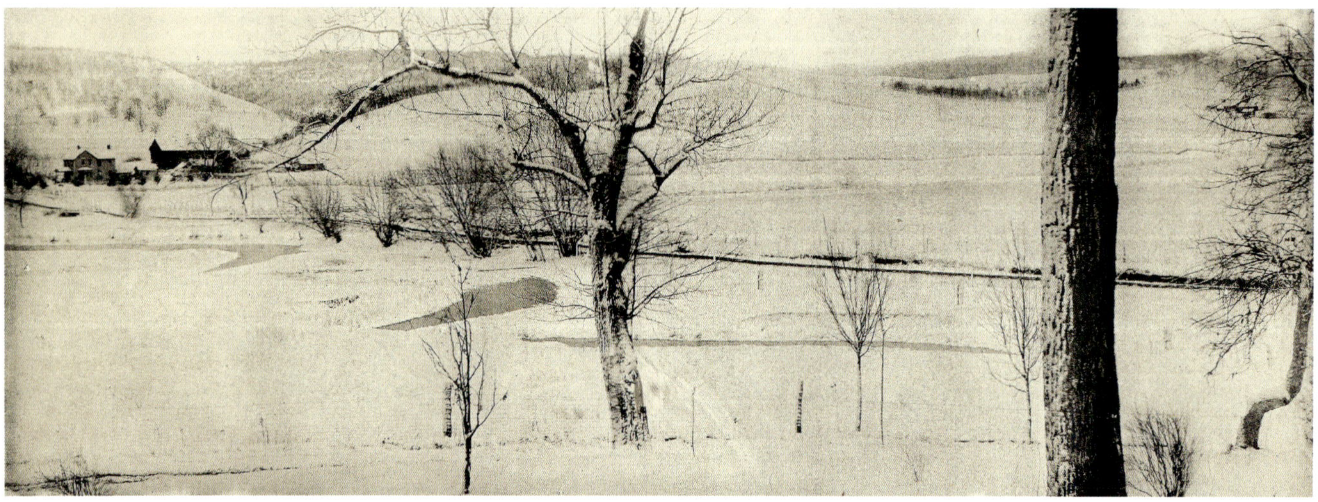

Fig. 3. Jones Valley, Wisconsin, c. 1900. Photograph by Frank Lloyd Wright. Collotype on Japanese paper, 3 1/2 x 9 3/8 in. (8.9 x 23.8 cm). Wisconsin Historical Society, Madison

throughout changing seasons. Jensen readily acknowledged as much, categorizing hollyhocks along with lilacs, geraniums, and the verbena as examples of non-native plants well adapted to the Midwest prairies—assimilated, one could say, to the local environment.[24]

That nature is constructed is not a new idea, of course.[25] Wright himself frequently engaged in large-scale environmental planning projects, such as dams, dredging, canals, and other kinds of hard infrastructures, that reshaped the landscape in ways that today are widely understood to damage, if not destroy, local ecologies. His first such project came in 1895, when Edward Waller commissioned Wright to create an amusement park out of the swampy wetlands along the beaches of Wolf Lake, just inland from Lake Michigan. Wright imagined the ambitious program—concessions, gaming, boating, a garden, and bandstand for musical concerts—housed in a megastructure designed according to Beaux-Arts principles of symmetry and axial relations (plate 15). He makes almost no attempt to respond to the natural wetland environment, instead proposing to dredge the lake; to construct an expansive circular causeway into nearby Hyde Lake, thus forging a connection to existing commuter railroads; and to dig a canal linking Wolf Lake and Lake Michigan to accommodate large excursion boats. The project was one of land reclamation as much as architecture, whereby Wright molded and restructured the existing prairie landscape into pavilions, infrastructure, and beaches.[26] Following on the heels of Chicago's 1893 World's Fair—itself a miracle of engineering and infrastructure that transformed a swampy wasteland into a cosmopolitan vision, even incorporating into its center a domesticated wilderness called the wooded isle—the Wolf Lake project demonstrates the degree to which Wright was still digesting the lessons of the Fair. Indeed the legendary impact on Wright made by the Ho-o-den, a Japanese temple located on the wooded isle, was surely equaled by his encounter with such a metamorphic example of environmental planning.

Wright's project for San Marcos-in-the-Desert Hotel, a luxury resort near Chandler, Arizona, is arguably one of the architect's most ambitious environmental planning projects, its tract consisting of several thousand acres of "pure mountain desert" that would have to be made accessible, habitable, and comfortable.[27] Wright earlier had experimented with creating cooling microclimates amid the arid landscape in his project for a desert compound for A. M. Johnson in Death Valley, California. For this undertaking he envisioned an extensive system of corbeled concrete walls that integrated the surrounding topography, the roadways, and even an irrigation system, the latter enabling the cultivation of alfalfa and other crops in an environment otherwise unsuited to agricultural production (fig. 5).[28] But the client for San Marcos, Dr. Alexander Chandler, envisioned building an "undefiled-by-irrigation desert resort," a considerable challenge given the high water demands of most elite tourist destinations.[29] Wright's design proposed a massive complex of terraced rooms interwoven with cooling gardens, plunge pools, and fountains, all of which straddled an existing arroyo that he transformed into a driveway leading directly into the building underneath a tower (plate 16).[30] These water features, together with the fact that Wright intended to build the hotel almost entirely of patterned concrete blocks—not only walls but interior and exterior finishes, structural floors, and ceilings, all made from the very desert soil surrounding the hotel—invites additional interpretation of its program: San Marcos would have operated as a veritable dam. Its concrete structure was intended to capture and redirect large amounts of water—the same water lost during flash floods generated by the region's occasional but torrential winter rainstorms that carved the arroyo—in order to create pools for recreation behind the hotel. These waters were to be chaneled underneath the hotel, presumably feeding the smaller plunge pools and fountains, and then emptied outside the front to form a waterfall (plates 17, 18).[31] Wright had long been fascinated with

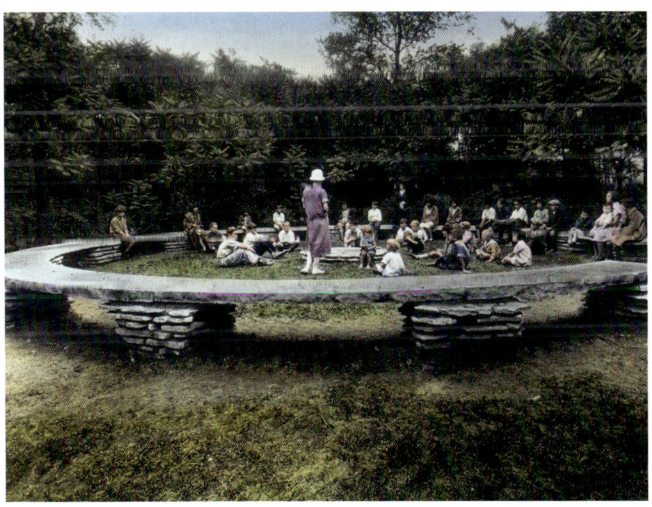

Fig. 4. Jens Jensen (American, born Denmark, 1860–1951). Columbus Park, Chicago. 1916. Council ring in the children's playground. Photograph by Frank A. Waugh. Department of Special Collections and University Archives, W. E. B. Du Bois Library, University of Massachusetts Amherst Libraries

dams, evidenced by his well-known experiments with hydroelectricity at Taliesin, but also with Henry Ford's unrealized project for Muscle Shoals, Alabama, and ultimately with the Tennessee Valley Authority—both projects that integrated infrastructure and nature into new, modern landscapes and endeavored to advance social democracy by reimagining industrial relations.[32] Though critics doubt the feasibility of the San Marcos scheme, the idea is remarkable for how it attempts to productively harness and recycle runoff water, advancing a more sustainable kind of ecotourism in the process.[33]

However interventionist his designs for Johnson and San Marcos, Wright was enamored with the stratified geological environment of the Arizona desert—calling it a "vast battleground of titanic natural forces"—because its very terrain appeared architectural.[34] The tectonics of the desert extended to its plant forms, especially the saguaro, cholla, and staghorn cactuses, because their cellular structure offered lessons in economical construction, such as "the perfect lattice . . . and welded tubular construction in the stalk of the cholla or staghorn." Indeed, Wright argued that the saguaro cactus—the "perfect example of reinforced building construction"—was the architectural progenitor of San Marcos. The patterned concrete block used throughout the hotel created a fretted line in its refraction of the desert sun that was inspired by this desert species: "Every horizontal line in San Marcos in the Desert is a dotted line . . . grosgrained patterned like the Sahuaro itself . . . the entire building is in pattern an abstraction of mountain region and cactus life." The generative relationship between desert ecologies and architecture is nowhere more persuasive than in the pattern studies conducted by Wright's apprentice, Eugene Masselink, in which various cactuses, rock formations, and even lichen are distilled to their essential organizing patterns (plates 8–11). The design process behind these extraordinary abstractions, however, did not originate in the desert, but rather was imported from the Midwest, where Wright first conventionalized nature. Wright's description of Arizona—an environment that "seems to cry out for a space-loving architecture of its own . . . the straight line and flat plane must come here—of all places"—suggests that the straight line and flat plane already existed elsewhere, perhaps even among the lush and gently rolling prairies where Wright established his reputation designing geometrically abstract houses. Indeed Wright's persistent and various misspellings of "saguaro" make one wonder as to the depth of his allegiance to this desert plant or its ecological setting.

All of which brings us back to the graphic. With the physical metrics of the prairie—native plants, natural landscapes, straight lines, or flat planes—revealed to be stagecraft, one must ask again, what was the meaning of the prairie for Wright, Jensen, and their progressive milieu? The invocation of indigenous plants and native lands was as much the reaction of a bourgeois, Anglo-Saxon majority culture threatened by an urbanized, primarily immigrant working class as it was an environmental movement—the politicization of the prairie. Recent scholarship has raised questions about the racist and fascist motivations driving native-plant advocates, including Jensen as well as German landscape architects working under Adolf Hitler, whereby natural gardens would be purged of their foreign species in concert with the Reich's social policies.[35]

In spite of rebuttals, argument continues over this issue,[36] and the broad politics of nativism, conservation, and land reform advanced by Wright and by organizations such

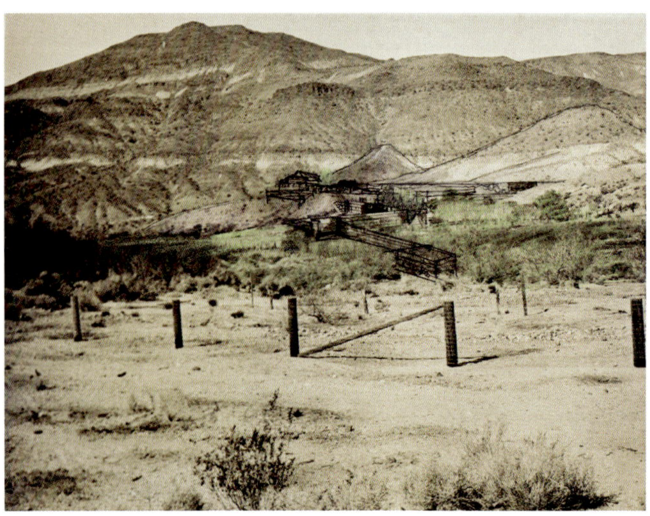

Fig. 5. A. M. Johnson Desert Compound and Shrine, Death Valley, California. Project, 1924–25. Preliminary sketch over a photograph

as the Friends of Our Native Landscape provoke troubling questions with regard to their purportedly democratic goals. The most compelling evidence of this in the FONL graphic is the swastika that Wright included as an ancient earth symbol, consistent with his views on a universal, metaphysical nature, but which he also connected to the displacement of Native Americans and to the author Hamlin Garland, two associations with specific historical and geographic resonances. Garland was a founding member of the FONL and an advocate for Native American rights, spending years on Western reservations documenting the experiences of those who had been displaced. He also spearheaded a federal project to rename all Native Americans according to state-recognized standards—a necessity due to the expansion of land ownership and its attendant deeds, titles, and taxes that accompanied Anglo-Saxon colonization—because he believed this was a prerequisite for native people's assimilation and advancement, even at the risk of losing their cultural heritage.[37] That Wright could simultaneously critique the displacement of Native Americans and endorse the activism of Garland speaks to the paradoxes underlying progressive reform at this time. Such contradictions were embodied in a ceremonial masque performed at meetings of the FONL. The play—which reenacted the expulsion of Native Americans from their lands, the myth of the enterprising pioneer, and the advancement of industrialization—is striking for how it recapitulates American imperialism.[38] The setting rotated to various endangered landscapes that the FONL hoped to conserve, thus naturalizing the genocide, xenophobia, and violence that accompanied manifest destiny. Native landscapes, in these contexts, did not embody existential nature, nor were they simply untouched remnants of a pristine, primitive nature; they were instruments for advancing the political ambitions of the ruling class, thus reproducing rather than overcoming the structural inequalities of society.

What do the shortcomings of nature to advance democracy mean for Wright and his dedication to those very ideas? One answer lies toward the end of his singular text on landscape architecture, which he concluded not with commentary about plants or garden design, but with a discussion of social relations—the communal nature of nature—namely, that despite private property rights, individuals have a social responsibility to cultivate their landscapes for the well-being of their neighbors.[39] Wright framed landscape in terms of citizenship. Perhaps understanding that all nature was already constructed, he shifted the conversation from one about ecosystems to one about social systems. Indeed, when the Booth project fell through, Wright developed an alternative plan for the site—a subdivision of houses in which "strict building restrictions will run with the land to protect" the neighborhood as a whole—thus negotiating between private and public, individual and social priorities, the very crux of democratic exchange.[40] In this context, the mythologies surrounding native plants and prairie landscapes are less important than understanding that access to nature of any kind is unequal. It is in understanding that landscape and nature are mutually imbedded with, and indeed created by, sociopolitical systems that Wright is closest to realizing his democratic ambitions.

Notes

1. Sherman Booth, Avery and Queene Coonley, and Augusta Rosenwald, wife of philanthropist Julius Rosenwald, were all members of FONL and clients of Wright. See *Friends of Our Native Landscape, Yearbook* (1913); Jens Jensen Archive, Morton Arboretum, Chicago, and Bentley Historical Library, University of Michigan; and William H. Tishler and Erik M. Ghenoiu, "Conservation Pioneers: Jens Jensen and the Friends of Our Native Landscape," *Wisconsin Magazine of History* 86, no. 4 (Summer 2003): 2–15.

2. On October 8, 1927, Franz Aust, a professor of landscape at the University of Wisconsin and founder in 1920 of the Wisconsin chapter of Friends of Our Native Landscape, wrote to Wright asking to use the graphic design for a FONL publication, which indicates that the graphic already existed in 1927. Though some of the working drawings are labeled for the Wisconsin chapter, others refer only generally to the FONL, no chapter specified, and are clearly addressed to Jensen. This suggests the possibility that Wright designed the graphic sometime between 1913, when Jensen founded the FONL, and 1920, when the organization expanded into state chapters.

3. Virginia L. Russell, "You Dear Old Prima Donna: The Letters of Frank Lloyd Wright and Jens Jensen," *Landscape Journal* 20, no. 2 (January 2001): 141–55.

4. Frederick Jackson Turner, "The Significance of the Frontier in American History" (1893), repr. in *Rereading Frederick Jackson Turner: The Significance of the Frontier in American History and Other Essays*, with commentary by John Mack Faragher (New York: Henry Holt, 1994), pp. 31–32.

5. Wilhelm Miller, *The Prairie Spirit in Gardening* (Urbana: University of Illinois, 1915; repr. Amherst: University of Massachusetts Press in association with Library of American Landscape History, 2002).

6. See William Cronon, *Nature's Metropolis: Chicago and the Great West* (New York: W. W. Norton, 1991).

7. Robert Grese, *Jens Jensen: Maker of Natural Parks and Gardens* (Baltimore: Johns Hopkins University Press, 1998), p. 52.

8. William Cronon, "Inconstant Unity: The Passion of Frank Lloyd Wright," in *Frank Lloyd Wright: Architect*, ed. Terence Riley (New York: The Museum of Modern Art, 1994): 13–16.

9. Frank Lloyd Wright, *An Autobiography* (New York: Duell, Sloan and Pearce, 1943), p. 89.

10. Frank Lloyd Wright, "A Philosophy of Fine Art," speech delivered to the Architectural League of the Art Institute of Chicago in 1909; repr. in *Frank Lloyd Wright: Collected Writings*, vol. 1, ed. Bruce Brooks Pfeiffer (New York: Rizzoli, 1992), p. 42.

11. Wright, letter to Jens Jensen, March 1, 1943, in *Frank Lloyd Wright: Letters to Architects*, ed. Bruce Brooks Pfeiffer (Fresno: The Press at California State University, 1984), p. 104

12. William C. Gannett, *The House Beautiful*, redesigned and reprinted by Frank Lloyd Wright and William Winslow (River Forest, Ill.: Auvergne Press, 1896–98).

13. Frank Lloyd Wright, "Concerning Landscape Architecture" (1900), unpublished address read to the Fellowship Club, Oak Park, Illinois; repr. in Pfeiffer, ed., *Frank Lloyd Wright: Collected Writings*, pp. 54–57.

14. Wright also opens his *Autobiography* with a description of the snow-covered prairie.

15. Charles E. Aguar and Berdeana Aguar, *Wrightscapes: Frank Lloyd Wright's Landscape Designs* (New York: McGraw-Hill, 2002), pp. 143–45.

16. See Dwight Heald Perkins, *Report of the Special Park Commission to the City Council of Chicago on the subject of a Metropolitan Park System* (Chicago: W. J. Hartman Company, 1905), esp. Jens Jensen, "Report of the Landscape Architect"; and Jennifer Gray, "An Everyday Wilderness: Dwight Perkins and the Cook County Forest Preserve," *Future Anterior* (Summer 2013).

17. Grese, *Jens Jensen: Maker of Natural Parks and Gardens*, pp. 136–37; The Clearing was also the name Jensen gave to his "school of the soil" in Ellison Bay, Wisconsin.

18. Ibid., pp. 172–73.

19. Lester Pottenger, "The Council Ring as Jensen Sees It," typescript copied from *Vistas*, a student paper published by the Landscape Council Ring at the University of Wisconsin, Morton Arboretum, Chicago; Jensen, "The Camp Fire or Council Fire," *Outdoors with the Prairie Club* (1941), repr. in William H. Tischler, ed., *Jens Jensen: Writings Inspired by Nature* (Madison: Wisconsin Historical Society Press, 2012), pp. 121–22.

20. Jens Jensen, "Thoughts" (November 3 and December 3, 1940), typescript, pp. 1, 3, 5, Morton Arboretum, Chicago.

21. Jens Jensen, *A Greater West Park System* (Chicago: West Chicago Park Commissioners, 1920), p. 15.

22. Wright, *An Autobiography*, p. 144.

23. Aguar and Aguar, *Wrightscapes*, p. 146.

24. Jens Jensen, unpublished excerpt from Ragna Eskil, n.d., Morton Arboretum, Chicago.

25. See William Cronon, ed., *Uncommon Ground: Toward Reinventing Nature* (New York: W. W. Norton & Company, 1995).

26. Aguar and Aguar, *Wrightscapes*, pp. 41–43.

27. Wright, *An Autobiography*, p. 306.

28. David De Long, "Frank Lloyd Wright: Designs for an American Landscape, 1922–1932," in De Long, ed., *Frank Lloyd Wright: Designs for an American Landscape, 1922–1932* (New York: Harry N. Abrams, 1996), p. 74.

29. Wright, *An Autobiography*, p. 306.

30. Aguar and Aguar, *Wrightscapes*, p. 210.

31. Ibid., p. 210.

32. Alvin Rosenbaum, *Usonia: Frank Lloyd Wright's Design for America* (Washington, D.C.: The Preservation Press, National Trust for Historic Preservation, 1993), esp. pp. 45–62, 83–94.

33. Aguar and Aguar, *Wrightscapes*, p. 210.

34. Wright, *An Autobiography*, p. 315. All remaining quotes in this paragraph are from this same book, pp. 308–09, 309, 314, 309.

35. Michael Pollan, "Against Nativism," *New York Times Magazine*, May 15, 1994; Gert Gröening and Joachim Wolschke-Bulmahn, "Politics, Planning, and the Protection of Nature: Political Abuse of Early Ecological Ideas in Germany, 1933–1945," *Planning Perspectives* 2 (1987): 127–48; Gröening and Wolschke-Bulmahn, "Some Notes on the Mania for Native Plants in Germany," *Landscape Journal* 11, no. 2 (Fall 1992): 116–26; Gröening and Wolschke-Bulmahn, "Response: If the Shoe Fits, Wear It!" *Landscape Journal* 13, no. 1 (Spring 1994): 62–63.

36. See Kim Sorvig, "Natives and Nazis: An Imaginary Conspiracy in Ecological Design," *Landscape Journal* 13, no. 1 (Spring 1994): 58–61; and Dave Egan and William H. Tishler, "Jens Jensen, Native Plants, and the Concept of Nordic Superiority," *Landscape Journal* 18, no. 1 (Spring 1999): 11–29.

37. Lonnie E. Underhill, "Hamlin Garland and the Indian," *American Indian Quarterly* 1, no. 2 (Summer 1974): 103–13.

38. Jensen originally asked Garland to write the masque, but the author declined. Ultimately written by Kenneth Sawyer Goodman, the masque was first published in the first *FONL Yearbook* (1913) and subsequently republished in numerous of the organization's annual yearbooks, pamphlets, and brochures; see also Regina B. Eskil, "Notes on the Masque," typescript, n.d.; and Carol L. Doty, "The Story of the Masque," typescript, n.d., all at Morton Arboretum, Chicago.

39. Wright, "Concerning Landscape Architecture," p. 57.

40. 1516.015, Frank Lloyd Wright Foundation Archives (The Museum of Modern Art | Avery Architectural & Fine Arts Library, Columbia University, New York).

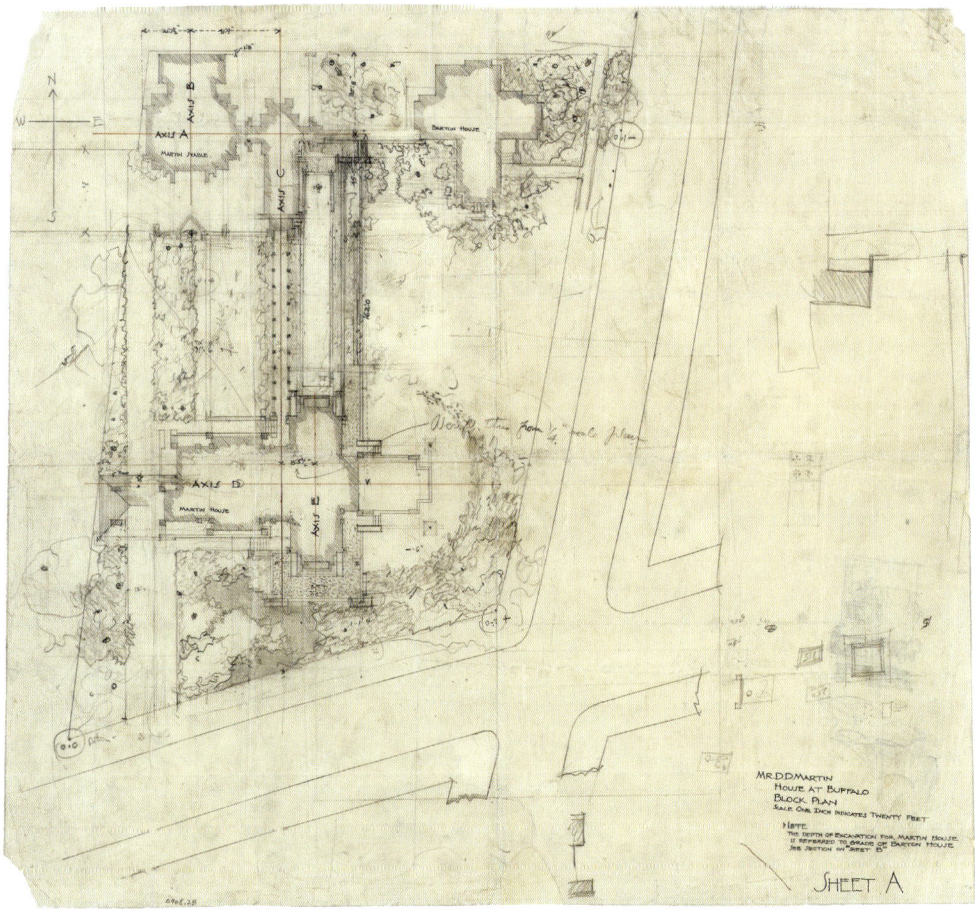

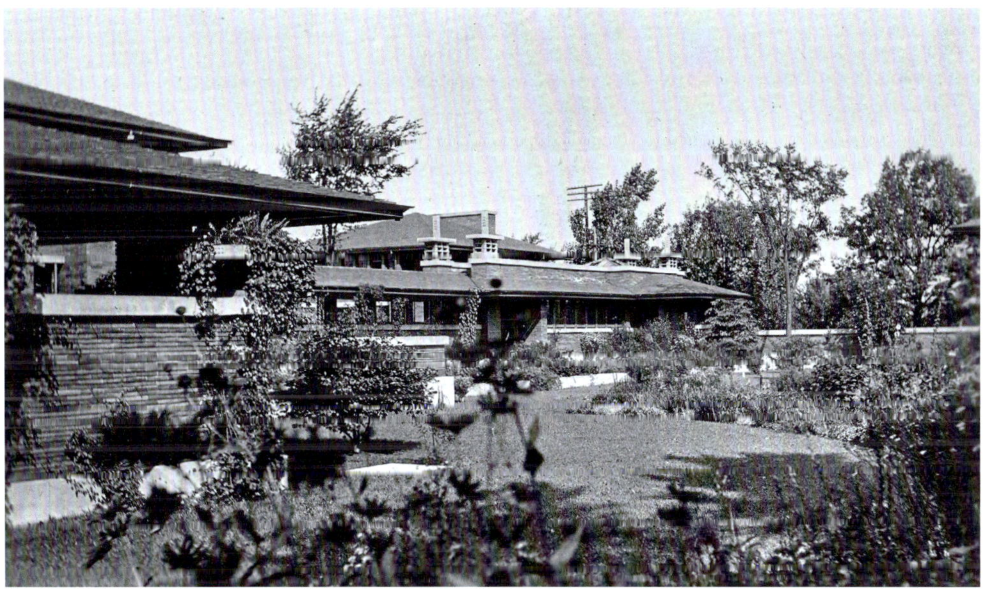

1. Darwin D. Martin House, Buffalo, New York. 1903–06. Block plan.
Ink and pencil on paper, 20 ½ x 22 ⅜ in. (52.1 × 56.8 cm)

2. Darwin D. Martin House, Buffalo, New York. 1903–06.
View of the Floricycle from the southeast

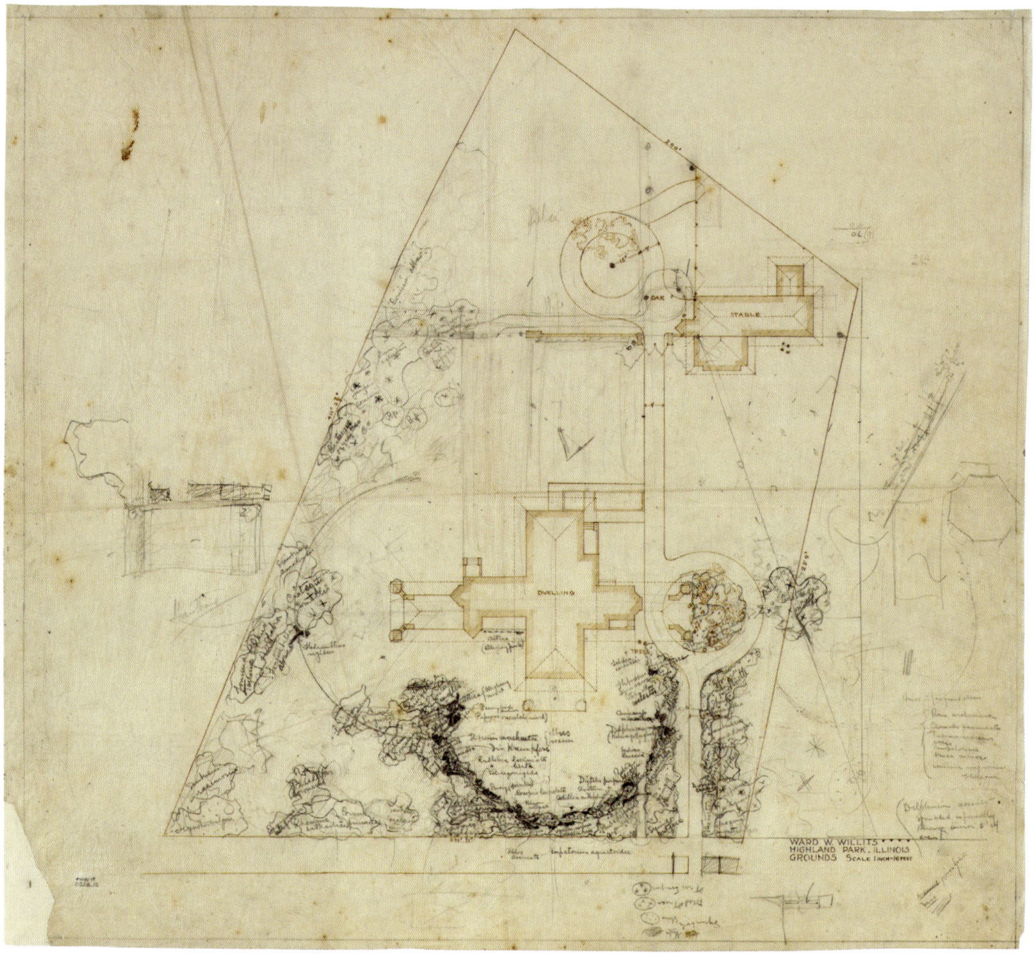

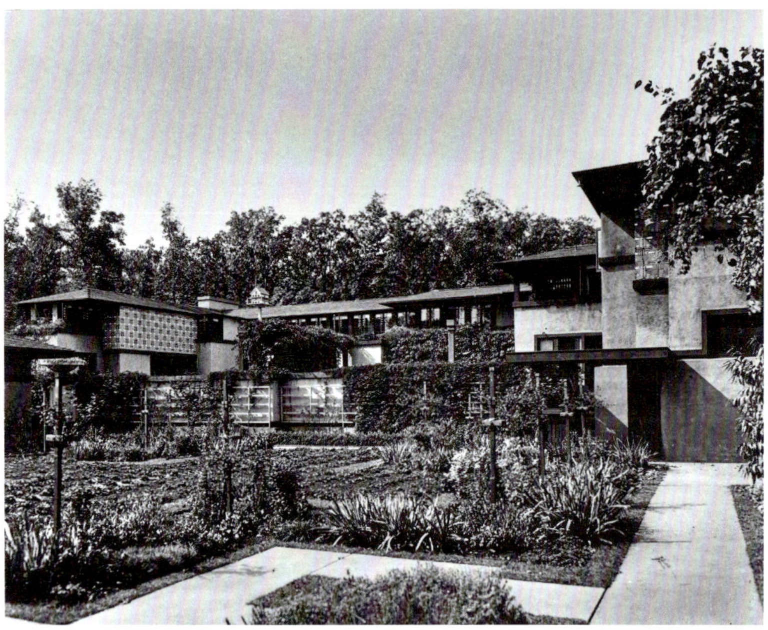

3. Willits House, Highland Park, Illinois. 1902–03. Planting plan by Walter Burley Griffin. Ink and pencil on tracing paper, 27 1/8 x 29 5/8 in. (68.9 x 75.2 cm)

4. Coonley House, Riverside, Illinois. 1906–09. View of the garden

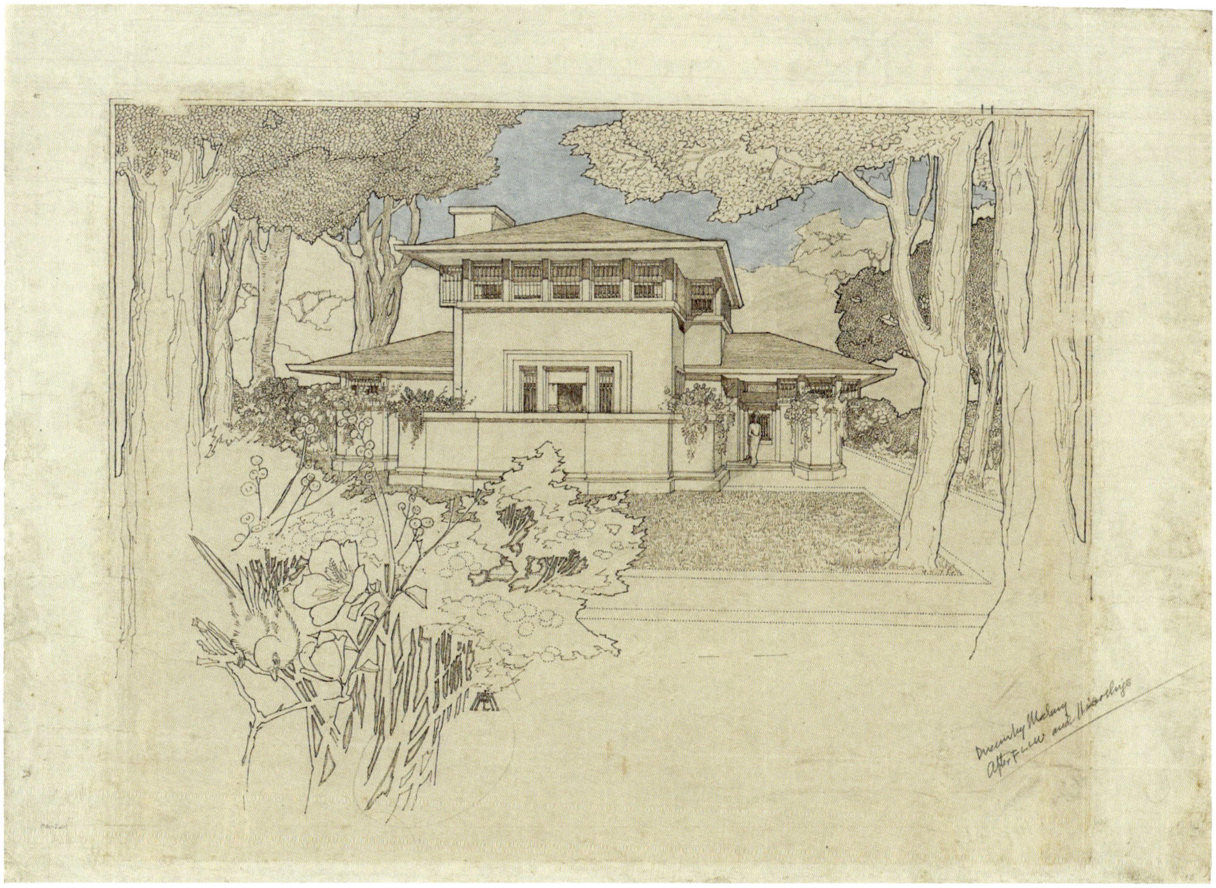

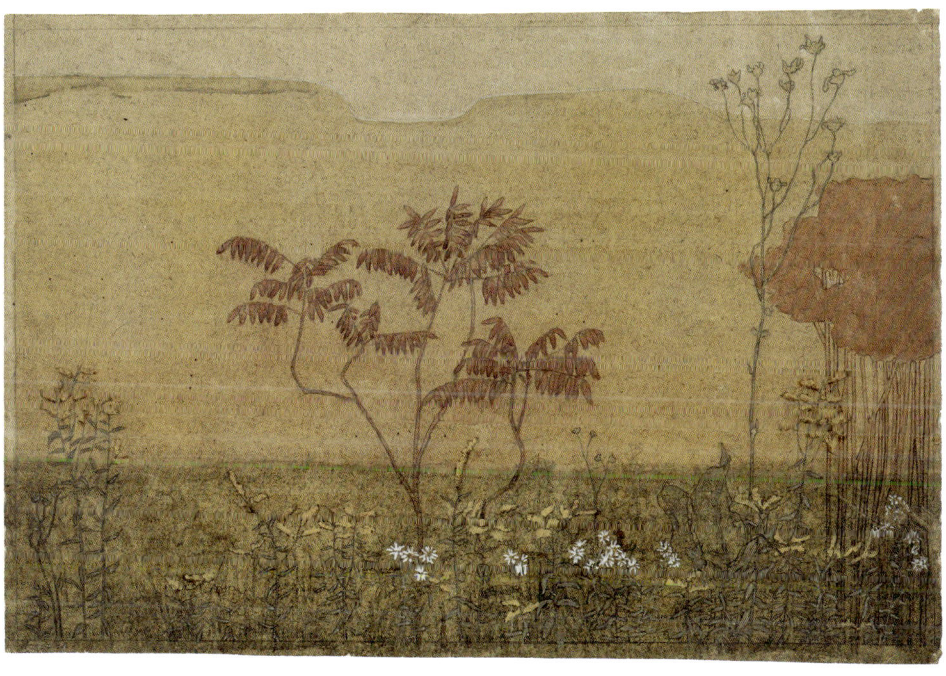

5. DeRhodes House, South Bend, Indiana. 1906. Perspective rendered by Marion Mahony Griffin.
Ink, pencil, and colored pencil on paper, 18 ½ x 25 ¾ in. (47 × 65.4 cm)

6. Dana House, Springfield, Illinois. 1902–04. Mural design by George Niedecken.
Ink, watercolor, and tempera on paper, 11 x 16 ½ in. (27.9 × 41.3 cm)

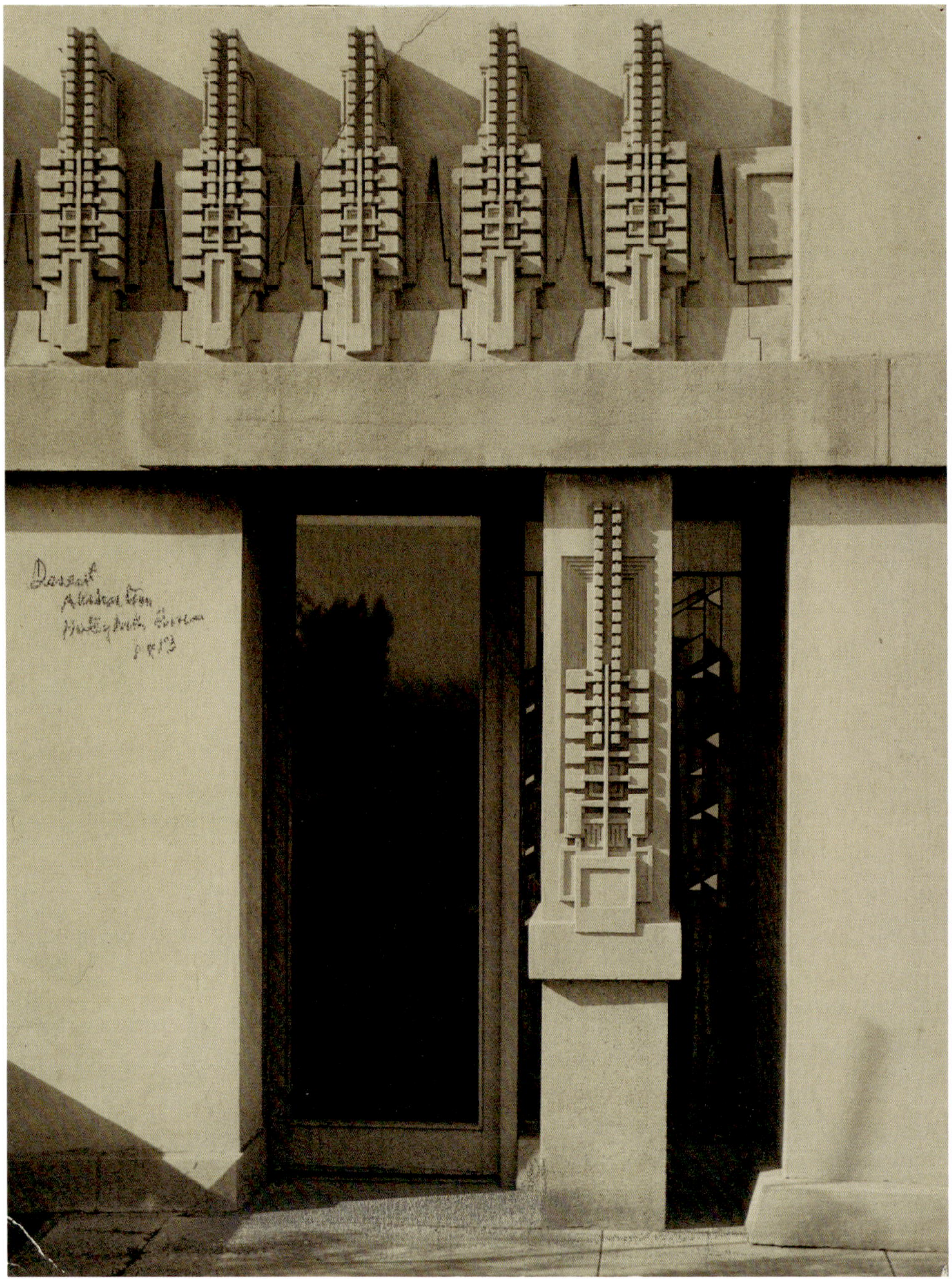

7. Hollyhock (Barnsdall) House, Los Angeles. 1918–21. Detail of the southwest terrace

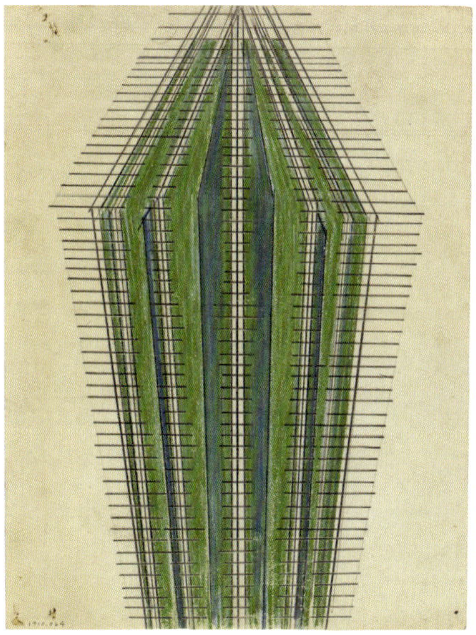

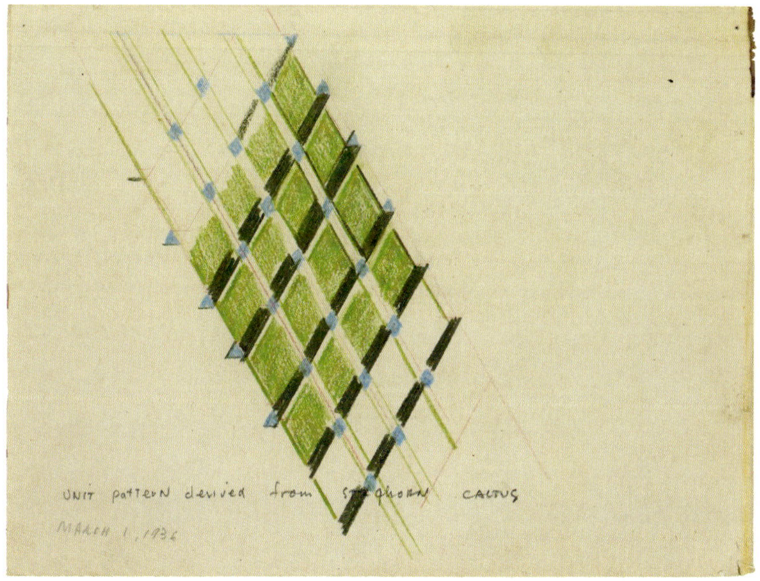

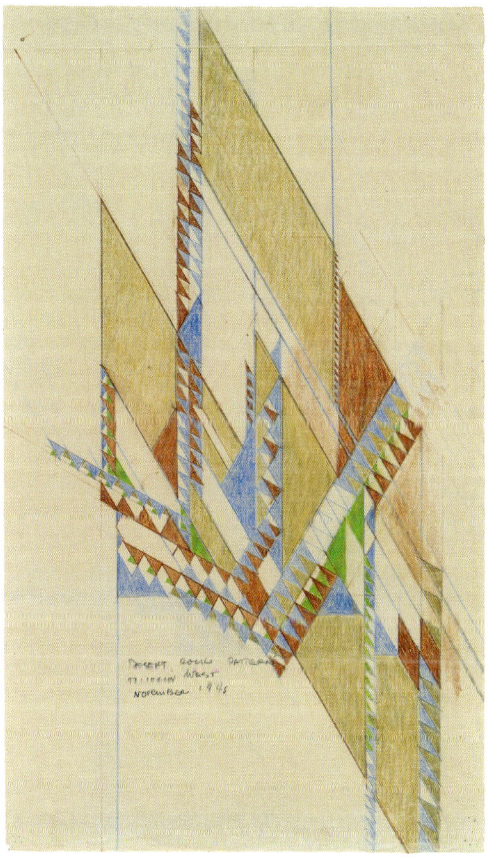

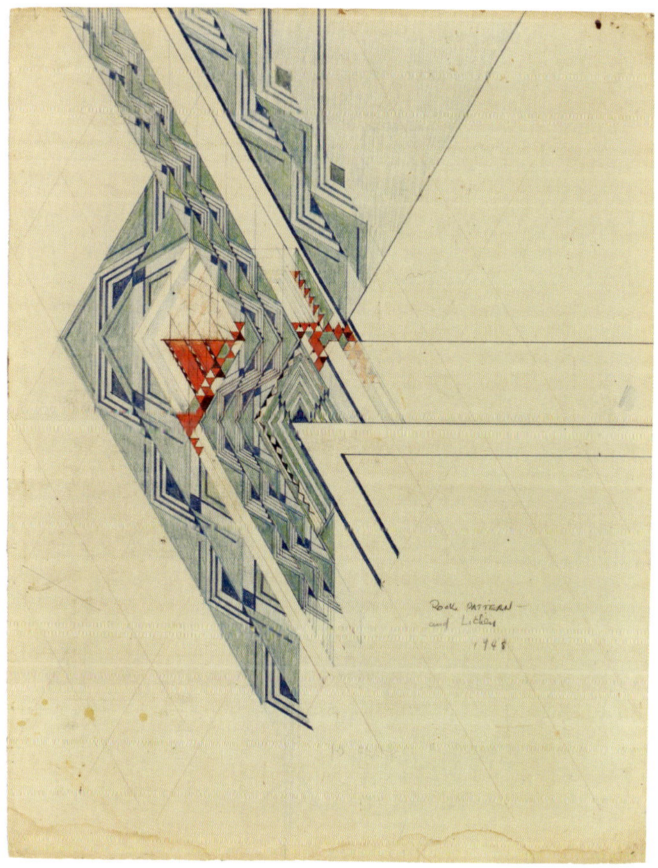

8. Eugene Masselink (American, born South Africa. 1910–1962). Pattern study of a barrel cactus. n.d.
Pencil and colored pencil on paper, 12 x 9 in. (30.5 x 22.9 cm)

9. Eugene Masselink. Pattern study of a desert rock, Taliesin West, Scottsdale, Arizona. 1948. Pencil and colored pencil on paper mounted to paper, 25 x 18 7/8 in. (63.5 x 47.9 cm)

10. Eugene Masselink. Pattern study of a staghorn cactus. 1936. Pencil and colored pencil on paper mounted to paper, 14 7/8 x 24 3/4 in. (37.8 x 62.9 cm)

11. Eugene Masselink. Pattern study of rock and lichen. 1948. Pencil and colored pencil on paper, 26 x 20 in. (66 x 50.8 cm)

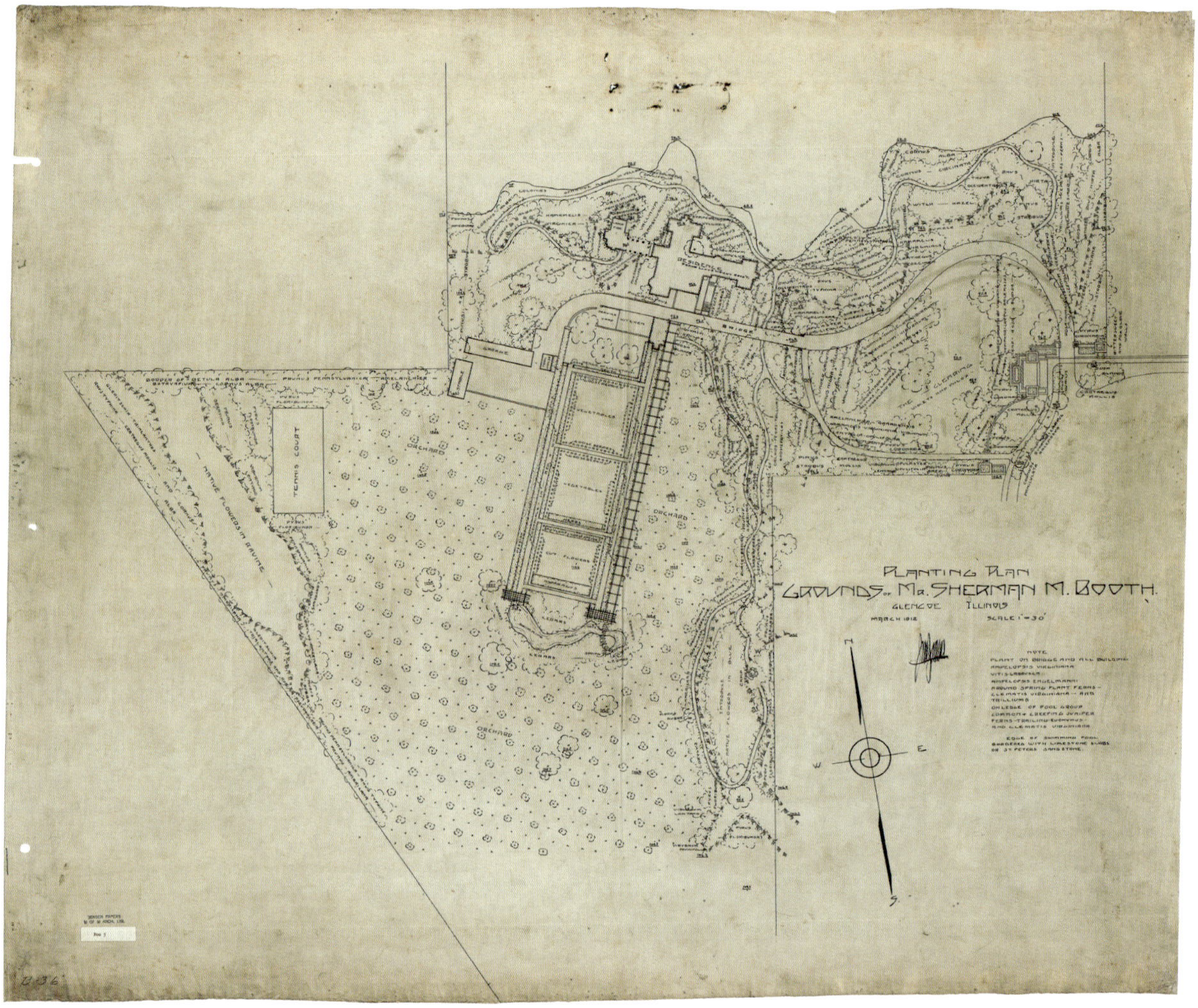

12. Booth House, Glencoe, Illinois. Project, 1911–12. Planting plan by Jens Jensen for the first scheme.
Ink on linen, 37 ⅜ x 31 ½ in. (95 x 80 cm).
Jens Jensen Drawings and Papers, Bentley Historical Library, University of Michigan, Ann Arbor

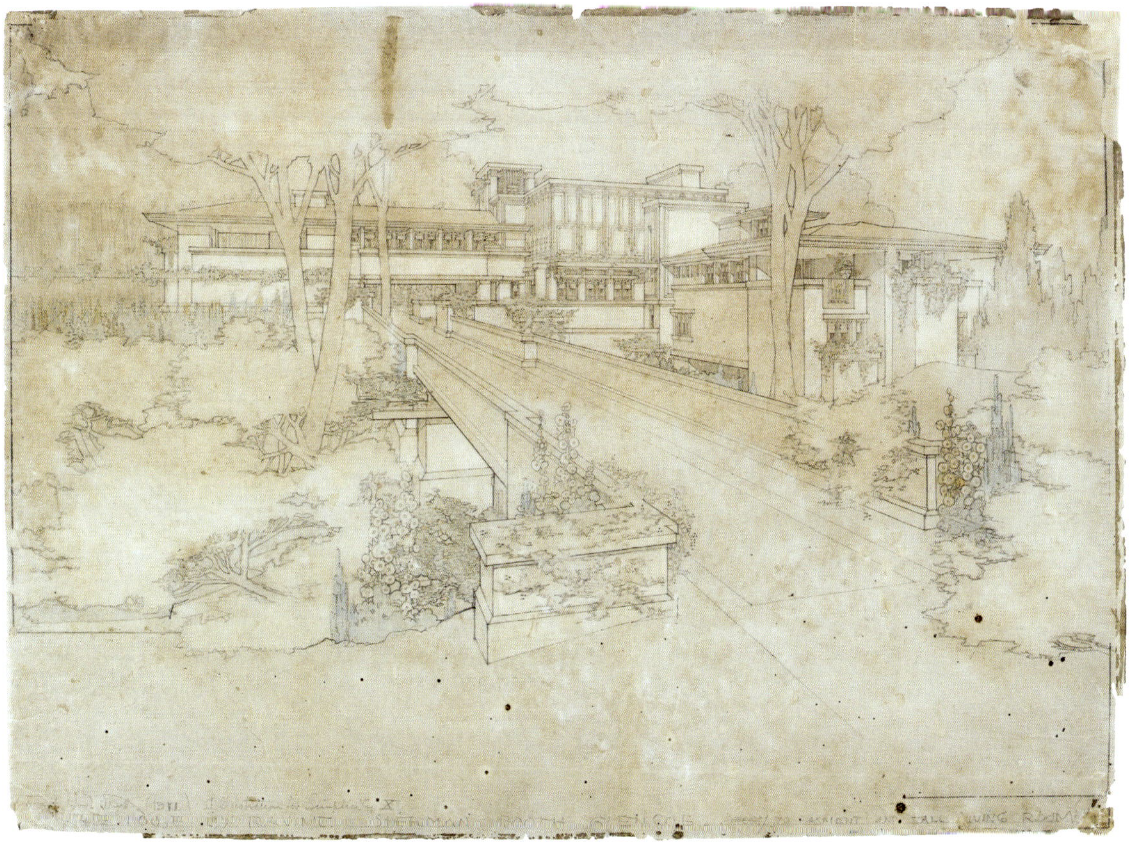

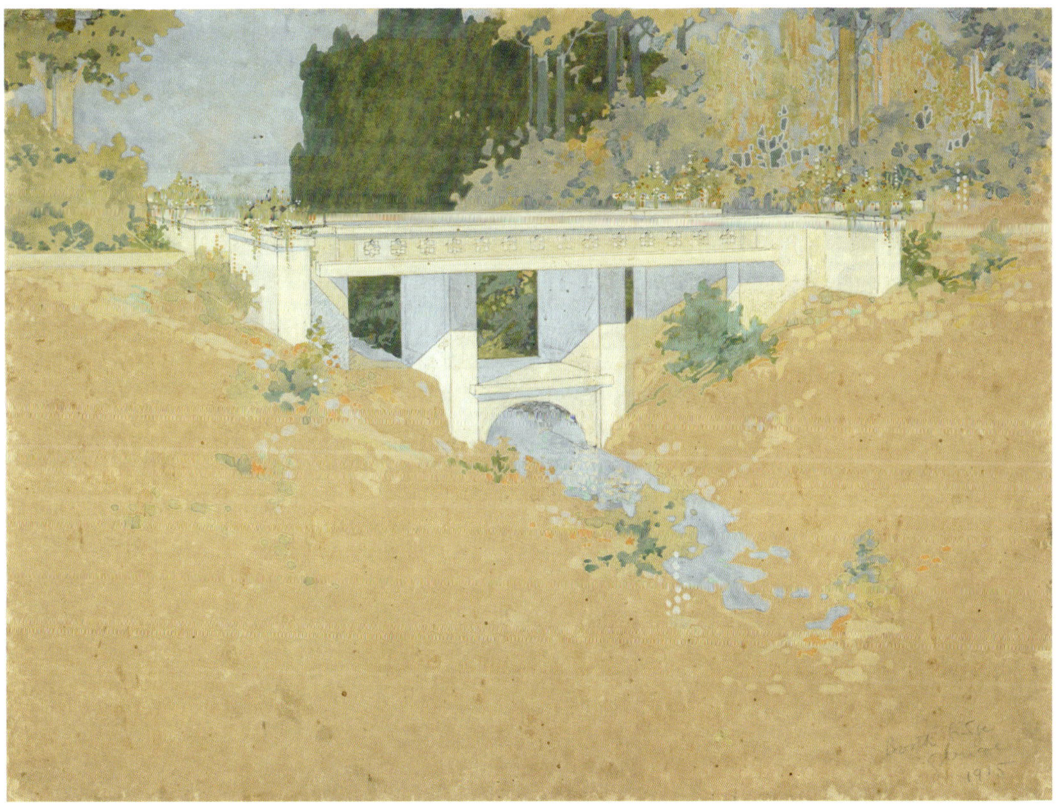

13. Booth House, Glencoe, Illinois. Project, 1911–12. Perspective of the first scheme, 1911.
Pencil and colored pencil on tracing paper, 20 x 27 3/8 in. (50.8 x 69.5 cm)

14. Ravine Bluffs Development for Sherman Booth, Glencoe, Illinois. 1915.
Perspective of the bridge for Sylvan Road.
Gouache and pencil on paper, 17 3/8 x 23 1/4 in. (44.1 x 59.4 cm)

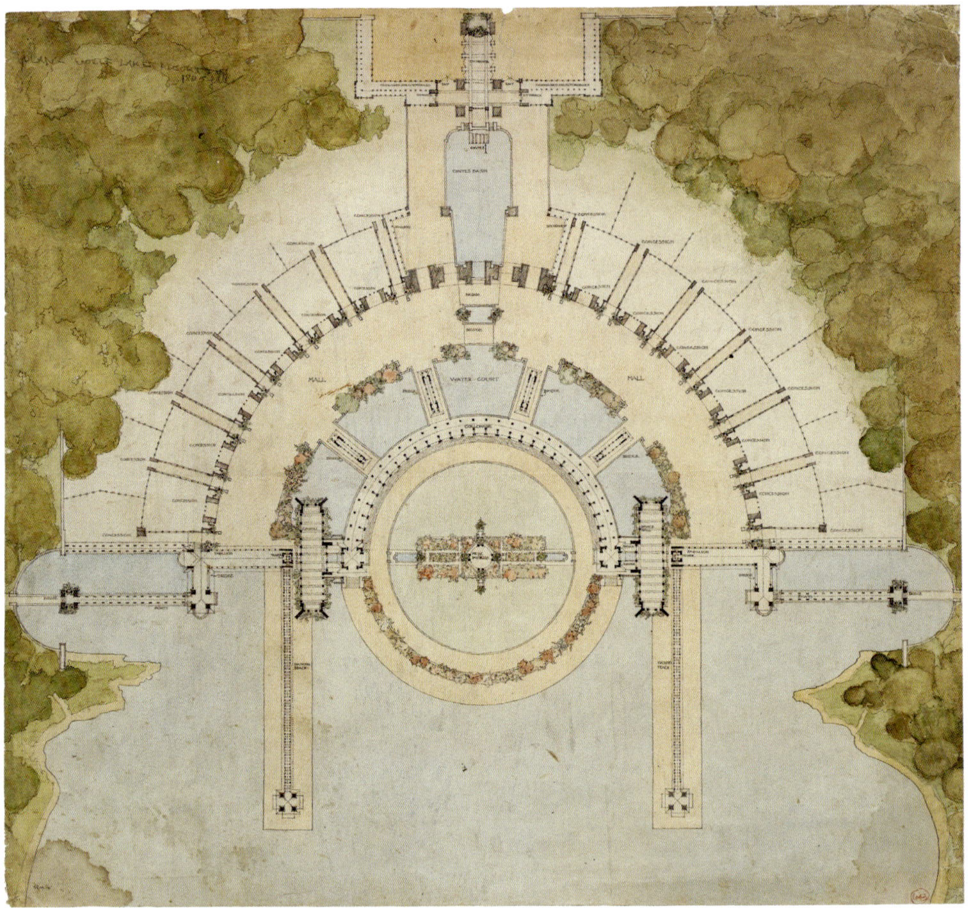

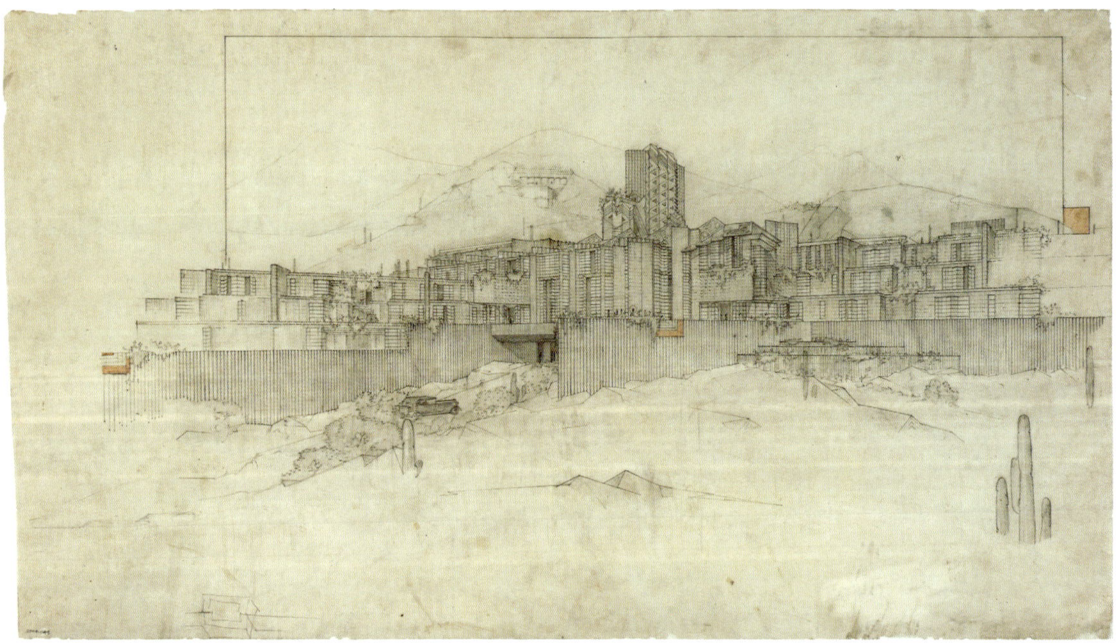

15. Wolf Lake Amusement Park, Chicago. Project, 1895. Plan.
Watercolor, ink, and pencil on paper, 27 x 29 ⅜ in. (68.6 x 74.6 cm)

16. San Marcos-in-the-Desert Hotel, Phoenix South (formerly Salt River) Mountains, Phoenix, Arizona. Project, 1928–29. Perspective of the entrance.
Ink, pencil, and colored pencil on paper, 19 ¾ x 35 in. (50.2 x 88.9 cm)

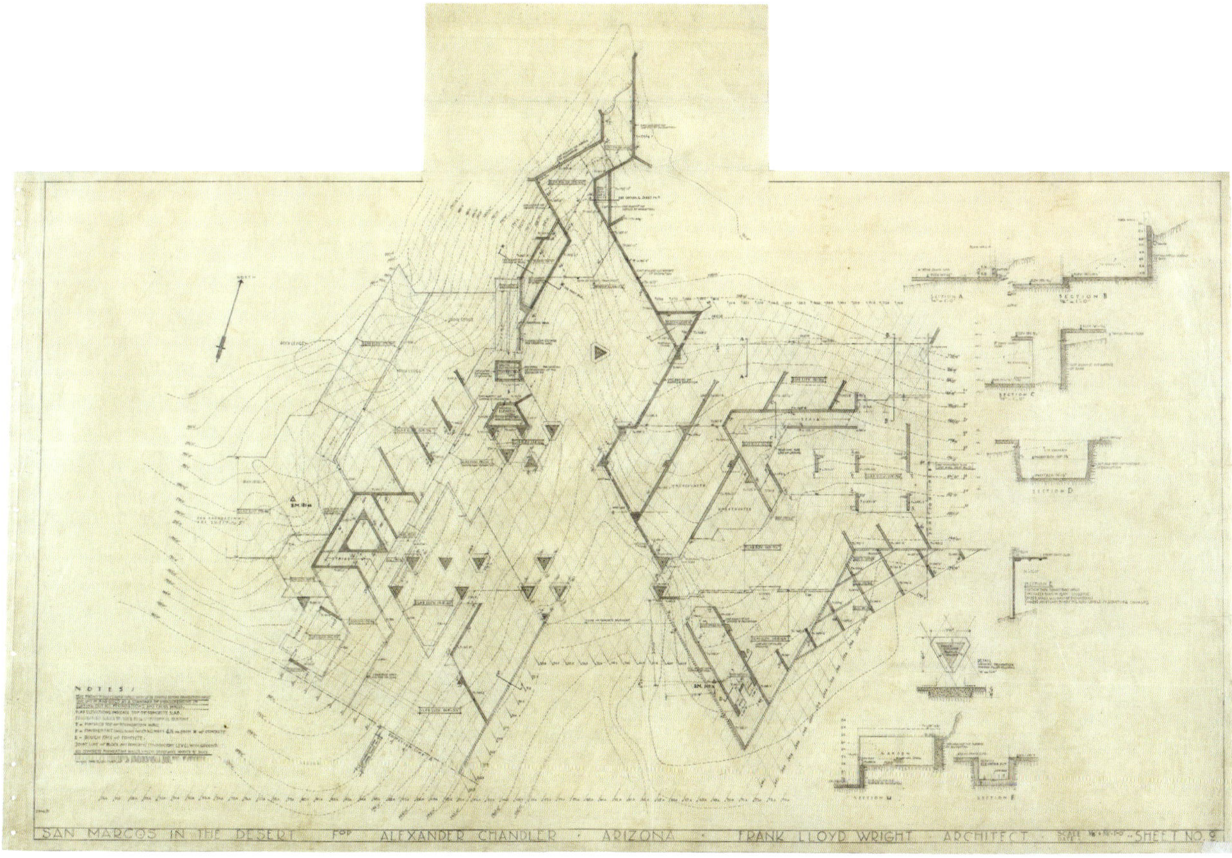

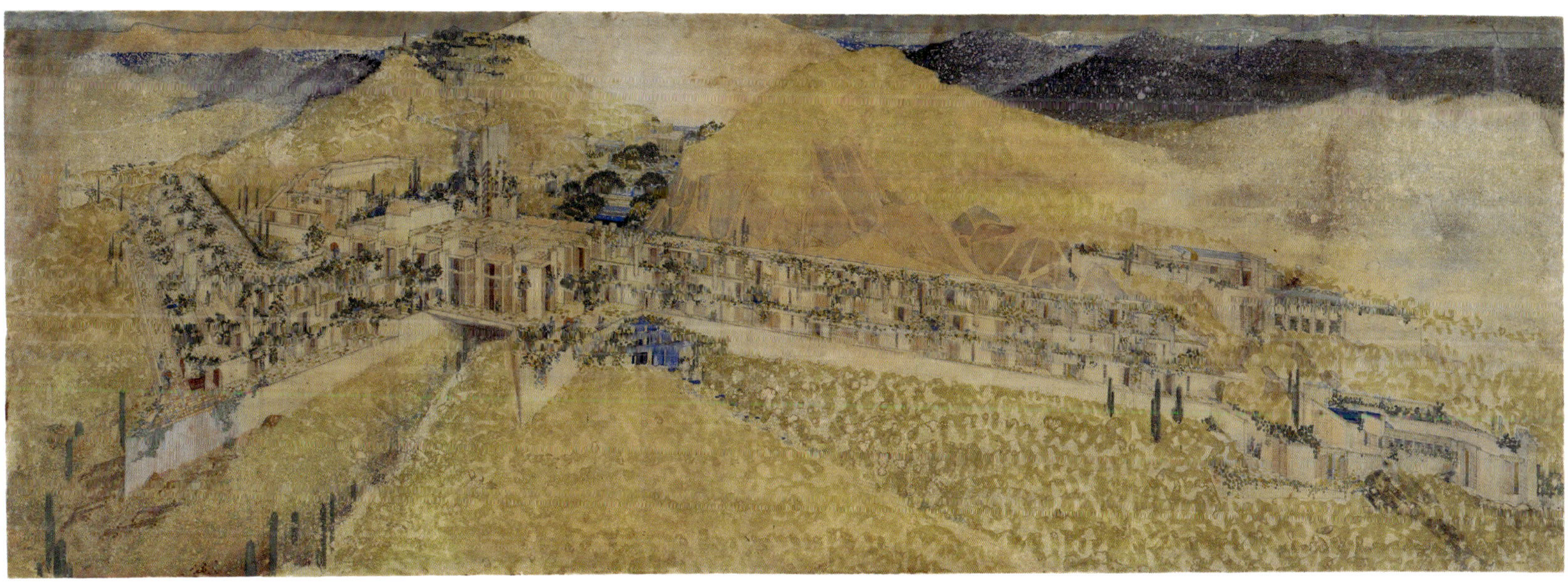

17. San Marcos-in-the-Desert Hotel, Phoenix South (formerly Salt River) Mountains, Phoenix, Arizona. Project, 1928–29. Topographic plan with section details. Pencil on tracing paper, 37 1/8 x 54 1/2 in. (94.2 x 137.5 cm)

18. San Marcos-in-the-Desert Hotel, Phoenix South (formerly Salt River) Mountains, Phoenix, Arizona. Project, 1928–29. Perspective. Watercolor on board, 22 5/8 x 64 1/4 in. (57.5 x 163.2 cm)

JULIET KINCHIN

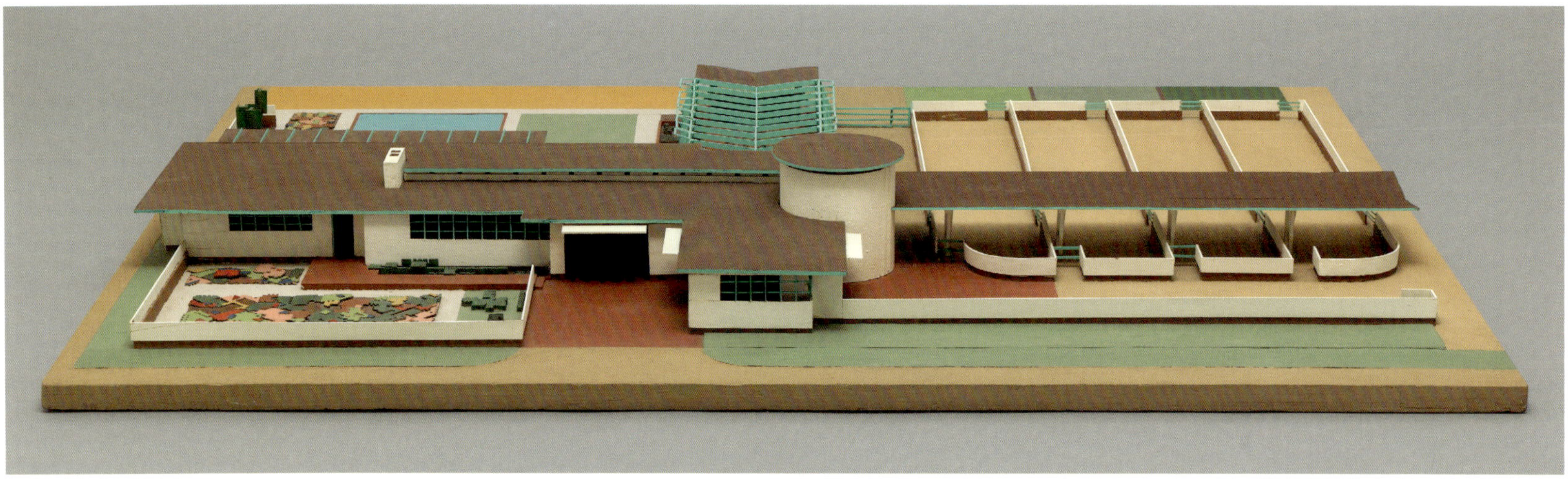

LITTLE FARMS UNIT

NATURE, ECOLOGY, AND COMMUNITY

Davidson Little Farms Unit. Project, 1932–33. Model.
Painted wood and particle board, 7 3/4 x 70 x 54 3/4 in. (19.7 x 177.8 x 139.1 cm)

During the Great Depression, the United States was in the grip of a crisis that struck at the core of the nation's mythologized identity as a land of pioneers crafting a civilization from the earth, and the thoughts of many were trained upon the farm as both the root of complex problems and a harbinger of better times to come. Economists, politicians, environmentalists, planners, entrepreneurs, and social activists wrestled with strategies to get food on plates, to alleviate rural poverty and urban unemployment, to stem foreclosures, and to reverse the depletion and pollution of natural resources. Wright staked out his own position on such issues in *The Disappearing City*, first published in September 1932, through a narrative that leads from an aerial view of New York's waterfront belching out smoke to a farmland vista bathed in sunlight "beyond the vortex," in which a woman walks across a field of stubble toward a laden hay cart (fig. 1). "The door of the urban cage is about to open," predicts Wright, ushering in an era of good citizenship and new physical and mental freedoms.[1] The modern farm was key to his vision of urban and environmental renewal, in which people could lead independent, productive lives while benefiting from restorative contact with nature (opposite).

The spur to these ideas and their materialization in architectural form was a commission earlier in 1932 from Walter V. Davidson, a friend and client from Wright's early days in Buffalo.[2] "I have been steadily developing the Little Farms–Davidson Market idea," Davidson wrote excitedly. "This will be a long letter, because I want to get you 'thinking out' your indispensable contributions to the plan. Some stormy day at Taliesin sit down with this letter and mull over the possibilities."[3] In four densely typed pages, accompanied by his own annotated layouts of a typical little farm unit and a roadside market (plates 1, 2), Davidson outlined the financial basis and integrated operation of the scheme. He already had his eye on 640 acres (259 hectares) in central Long Island for a first tract of two hundred farms of 1 to 5 acres (0.4 to 2 hectares) each, connected by daily truck deliveries to a central market facility. Instead of trying to compete with colossal grain and beef-rearing operations of the Midwest, these Little Farms would grow food for their own consumption with some land set aside for cash crops under a local cooperative arrangement. "You see, Frank, there are no middlemen, no cost to the farmer of finding a market, no cost to him of delivery, no cost of railroad transportation, no waste, and no losses from payment collections. . . . The market volume will be vast, because produce and flowers on the day gathered will be beyond all competition."[4]

Each compact farm unit was to combine five elements: living quarters, garage, packing station, stable and pens, and greenhouse with mushroom cellar. To illustrate the brief, Davidson had also written a fictitious journal titled "The Diary of Mary, a Little Farmer's Wife" ("Mary" became the project's nickname).[5] A week after Davidson's letter, New York Governor Franklin D. Roosevelt spoke about his administration's attempts to foster a practical regionalism in the state that would bring producers and consumers together on their own acres of farmland. He noted in conclusion, "This country will remain progressive just as long as we are willing to make experiments, just as long as we are able to say: 'Here is a suggestion that sounds good. We can't guarantee it, but let's try it out somewhere and see if it works.'"[6] Wright immediately scribbled a note to Davidson: "Get to Franklin Roosevelt with your plan—tell him I am with you."[7]

Over the next three years Davidson and Wright elaborated their conception of radical farm relief in tandem with Roosevelt's developing New Deal initiatives as President (fig. 2). It was a collaborative venture in which both men were deeply invested—personally, economically, and philosophically—at a make-or-break moment in their respective careers following the economic meltdown of 1929. Davidson was struggling to sustain a management consultancy in food distribution and warehousing, while Wright, hunkered down on his family's Wisconsin farmlands, with no architectural commissions in sight, was teetering on insolvency. An ideological rift opened between them as Davidson's efforts to secure financial backing became more desperate, and ultimately "Mary" came to nothing. This relatively minor project received scant attention either at the time or in subsequent scholarship, yet it was clearly an important catalyst for Wright's Broadacre City, the Taliesin Fellowship, and his Usonian houses, as well as a platform for his polemical stance against functionalist modernism. Davidson's role in all this is ripe for evaluation, not least because his ideas were recycled by Wright, without acknowledgment, from the 1932 publication of *The Disappearing City* up to *The Living City* in 1958.

WAYSIDE MARKETS

Client and architect brought complementary skills and experiences to the "Mary" project. Davidson, a successful engineer turned accountant and entrepreneur, was a management consultant in the food industry specializing in inventory control and the physical planning of retail and warehouse operations.[8] He had smoothed the flow of raw materials, goods, and services in huge concerns, starting with the Larkin Company in Buffalo, where he first encountered Wright. Like his good friend Christine Frederick—renowned the world over for her application of Frederick Taylor's time and motion studies to kitchen design—Davidson was one of a new breed of "efficiency experts" and "packaging engineers."[9] One of his clients in 1927 was First National Stores, reputedly the largest food-packaging and warehouse complex in the world, that had just built its headquarters next to the Ford Motor Company assembly plant in Somerville, Massachusetts. Motorized transport was transforming the food industry, and there was growing interest in roadside markets as a

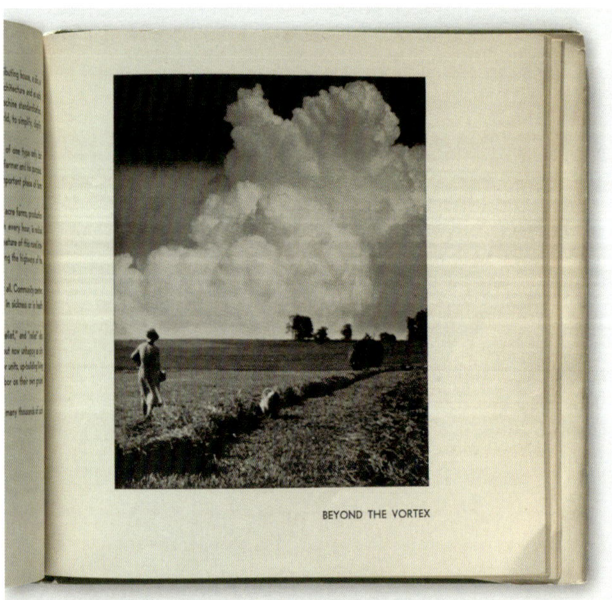

Fig. 1. "Beyond the Vortex." From Frank Lloyd Wright, *The Disappearing City* (New York: W. F. Payson, 1932)

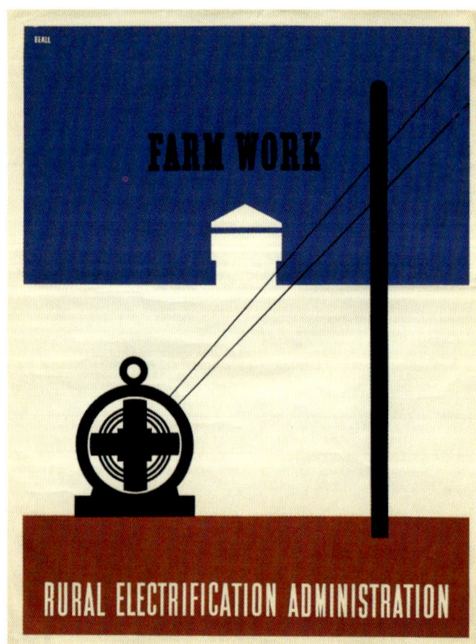

Fig. 2. Lester Beall (American, 1903–1969). "Farm Work—Rural Electrification Administration." 1937. Silkscreen, 40 1/4 x 30 in. (102 x 76.2 cm). Printer: U.S. Government Printing Office, Washington, D.C. The Museum of Modern Art, New York. Gift of the designer

means of connecting newly mobile consumers with fresh, locally sourced food.

Set on launching his own packaging brand and a chain of fifteen food markets, Davidson initially approached Wright in 1927 for designs to help him raise $1.5 million in capital.[10] Davidson wanted easily memorable designs for trademarks named Blazing Sun, Shining Star, and Silver Moon, which were to be "repeated over and over again in the store decoration, in the store advertising and on the store front" (plate 3).[11] He also specified that each can or package label was to carry a stripe at a uniform distance from the bottom that could continue right down the shelves in self-service aisles. Wright took eighteen months to produce the drawings, at which point the 1929 stock-market crash stalled the project. Undeterred, Davidson revived the market idea three years later, on an even more ambitious scale embracing food production as well as distribution.

As governor of New York from 1929 to 1932, Roosevelt commissioned a report on decentralized markets and made strenuous efforts to improve dirt roads, the crucial arteries for produce, as part of a proposed statewide farm-to-market system.[12] Henry Ford had also been working along similar lines by envisioning Muscle Shoals, Alabama, as a networked city of small farms and factories stretching 75 miles (120 kilometers) along the Tennessee River. Wright declared this "one of the best things that I have heard of."[13] Clara Ford's contribution to her husband's vision was to champion roadside markets that would allow rural women to sell produce directly to city folk rather than through wholesalers and commission merchants. Mrs. Ford exhibited full-scale models of her open-source design that farmers could build themselves from white-painted boards.[14] By comparison the Davidson-Wright wayside markets were larger and more architecturally ambitious. Davidson was keen to develop an "outdoor effect inside."[15] Wright understood the importance of spectacle, and developed his earlier design into the form of a terraced ziggurat filled with greenery—a veritable temple of consumerism constructed of copper, glass, and reinforced concrete (plate 4). The interior was arranged around a fountain below a large suspended goldfish bowl. The ziggurat form, one of the classic building types associated with indigenous societies of the pre-Columbian Americas, appears to grow organically from the land, and the Mayan influence continues in the interlocking patterns of the floor plans (plate 5). Davidson may have lacked Wright's farming experience and aesthetic sense, but he knew about retailing food and flowers, and he developed extremely detailed floor plans for Wright to adapt (see plate 2). The interior was a sequence of courts devoted to flowers and produce, a delicatessen and bakery, machinery for popcorn, candy, doughnuts, peanut butter, etc., three grades of eateries, a section for housewares and a model kitchen, a beauty parlor, crèche, and women's lounge, plus offices for telephone orders and accounting. A traffic-flow system around the exterior accommodated deliveries from nearby Little Farms (plate 6) and connected shoppers with valet parking and a gas station. This concentration of farm produce, leisure facilities, and variegated merchandise was designed to make the market a destination and community center rather than a pit stop for motorists looking to buy a few vegetables.

LIVING THE FARM

Wright was himself part of the Depression-era back-to-the-land movement.[16] In 1928, after battling the banks to retain possession of Taliesin, he and his new wife, Olgivanna Milanoff, settled back in the valley farmed by Wright's maternal family since the early nineteenth century. There he felt himself as much a part of the landscape as the trees, birds, red barns, or the animals. The seasonal rhythms of farm life punctuate the autobiography that he wrote over the next four years while planning the resuscitation of Taliesin as a productive landscape: "I saw the hill crown at the back of the house as one mass of apple trees in bloom . . . abundant asparagus in rows and a stretch of great sumptuous rhubarb. . . . And the herd I would have! The gentle Holsteins . . . . Those grunting sows to turn all waste into solid gold" (plates 7, 8).[17] Wright's attempts to sustain a diversified pattern of cultivation, the balanced ecology of the valley, and respect the natural contours of the land, posited an alternative to the ravages of chemical exhaustion and wind and water erosion that were threatening large portions of the Midwest.[18] As an autonomous unit, however, Taliesin was not economically viable, even with the free labor of fee-paying students starting in 1932.[19]

Wright's practical ideas about self-sufficiency were rooted in childhood experience of lean times on the family farm. His autobiography reflected on practical and spiritual lessons learned from laboring as a boy on his Uncle James's farm, reliving the dust, mud, and flies, the backbreaking, monotonous chores, and the sweat and heat of the harvest field (fig. 3). At the same time, he communicated the sense of farming as a kinetic and multisensory experience structured around musical rhythms and geometric patterns: "The entire field is becoming a linear pattern of Work. . . . Rhythm is regular and patterned order is everywhere established in this work of the harvest" (plate 9).[20] In this cosmic drama the farmer became the hero, bound into the landscape in an intimate, creative way rather than standing apart from nature. Wright's phraseology and the frequent analogies between architectural thought and patterns of cultivation were redolent of "The Gospel of the Farm" preached by his Uncle Jenkin Lloyd Jones, a Unitarian minister in early-twentieth-century Chicago.[21] Whether eulogizing cows, farm machinery, and prairie pioneers or describing aspects of plowing, sowing, weeding, reaping, and barn-building, uncle and nephew emphasized the unity of processes governing material and spiritual realities.

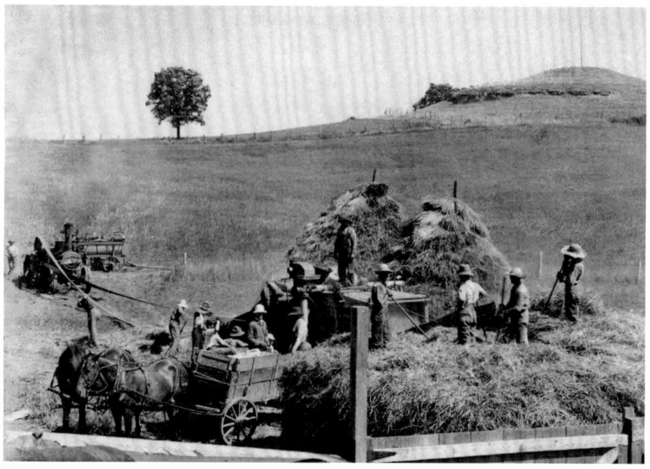

The farm as a model of organic architecture, community values, and simple yet civilized living also referred back to precepts of the international Arts and Crafts movement. "Back to the land!" was how British architect-designer C. R. Ashbee, a close friend of Wright's since 1898, had described the move in 1902 of his Arts and Crafts Guild of Handicraft from the overcrowded East End of London to rural Chipping Camden. Ashbee's whole venture, which placed value on working the land and growing the food they ate, was soon in financial difficulties. But in 1908, with help from a Philadelphia philanthropist, Ashbee purchased a 70-acre (28.3-hectare) farm to secure his little community's future.[22] Wright also saw himself as extending the legacy of the Hillside Home School run by his aunts Ellen and Jane Lloyd Jones. Since the 1890s their progressive curriculum had embraced farming as conducive to "physical development, mental discipline, and moral growth."[23] A premium was placed on cooperation in work and play, with farm life providing real situations to which all could contribute.

Fig. 3. Harvesting on the farm of James Lloyd Jones, Spring Green, Wisconsin. n.d. Wisconsin Historical Society, Madison, Wisconsin

Botany, geology, geography, physics, and zoology were taught by direct observation, in conjunction with the study of authors such as Herbert Spencer and Edward Clodd on evolution and ecology. In the spirit of learning by doing, students spent one hour each day on manual work in the barn, henhouse, garden, or kitchen. Leading educators "are beginning to realize that the farm is a great laboratory which will make clear and interesting the study of the sciences," declared the aunts' 1907 prospectus.[24] This farm-laboratory idea resurfaced in Wright's Broadacre City plans (1929–35) for an agricultural research complex—replete with experimental tracts, engineering labs and a library—that would serve as an educational resource for local small farmers (plate 10).

While working on the Davidson Little Farms, Wright and the first intakes of fee-paying apprentices at Taliesin were living the experience of sustainable, small-scale agriculture. As part of the Fellowship scheme devised with Olgivanna in 1932, manual labor on the land was combined with the apprentices' architectural and environmental studies. Wright took his part alongside them—whether on the potato planter, hand-racking hay, or in the drawing studio—and took pleasure in personally trading the Taliesin milk, cows, and horses (figs. 4, 5). "The whole farm thing was nourishment for Mr. Wright," recalled John de Koven Hill, a former apprentice, "and a little bit of every day somehow went toward it, whether it was just planning or actually going and doing something."[25] City dwellers like Betty Bauer—who would subsequently become head of MoMA's Architecture Department—having married fellow apprentice Rudolf Mock, were brought into direct contact with materials and nature's processes. "Betty is in the trenches in blue overalls—and all outdoors sweating like a colt," wrote Wright to a friend. "Much of the 'New Yorker' has been shed with the perspiration."[26] Edgar Kaufmann, Jr., another MoMA curator in the making, joined the Fellowship in 1934. There is a strong likelihood that both he and Bauer were involved in the two models of the Little Farms Unit (see p. 42) that were made by apprentices at Taliesin during this time. Wright was keen to proceed with a full-scale pilot farm unit at Taliesin, a move that could have put Taliesin on a secure financial footing as the experimental engine of Davidson's scheme, recasting Ralph Waldo Emerson's vision of sustainable farming for the 1930s. The poet's 1858 essay on "The Man with a Hoe" was studied in the Hillside Home School and remained a touchstone for Wright throughout his life, appearing as an appendix to his last book, *The Living City*: "The glory of the farmer is that, in the division of labors, it is his part to create. All trade rests at last on his primitive activity. The food which was not, he causes to be."[27]

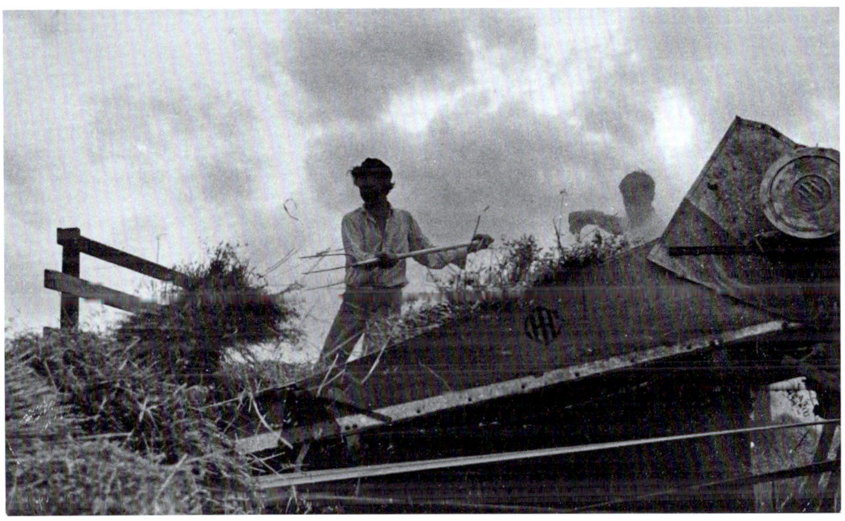

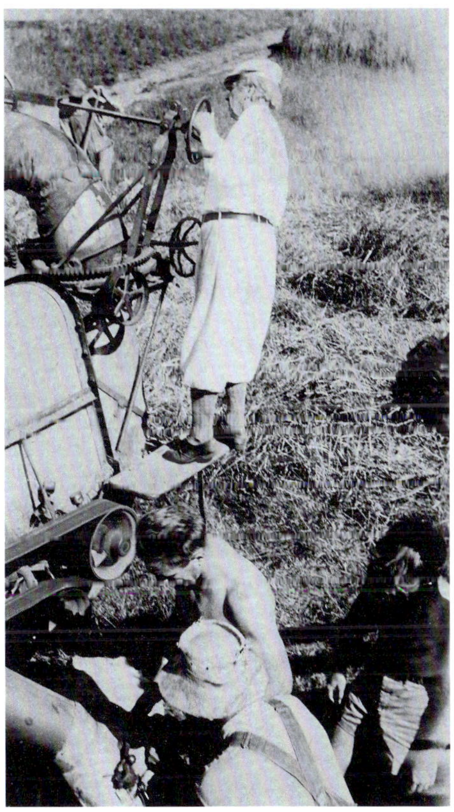

Fig. 4. Apprentices racking hay at the Taliesin Fellowship Complex. n.d. Edgar Tafel Architectural Records and Papers, Avery Architectural & Fine Arts Library, Columbia University, New York

Fig. 5. Wright harvesting. n.d. Edgar Tafel Architectural Records and Papers, 1919–2005. Avery Architectural & Fine Arts Library, Columbia University, New York

TOWARD AN ORGANIC, BIOTECHNIC ARCHITECTURE

The Little Farms were not to be a cookie-cutter, quick-fix solution to the problems that beset the Depression-era farm, but rather an architectural suggestion for what Wright considered a better way of living, working, and building communities. The standardized parts and built-in features of the compact plan were designed to be cost effective and built around the balanced and healthy coexistence of people, livestock, crops, and machinery. Wright estimated that, built separately, the facilities specified by Davidson would have cost around $10,850 for a "heap of rubbish all requiring perpetual upkeep and soon 'cut.'"[28] For the same money, or less, Wright felt he could enlarge the farmer's facilities for work and comfort, and at the same time cut down maintenance costs and unnecessary expenditure of time and labor by means of rationalizing and unifying the farm's layout. Such a farm would become one of the most desirable and beautiful units in any community. This innovative design offered a sophisticated yet functional alternative to singly built farmhouses, soulless industrial-scale units, and the kind of pinched "emergency" farms being erected by government Home Relief agencies.

The open, cruciform design was centered on a cylindrical silo and deployed harmonious combinations of the square, circle, and rectangle. Such geometric forms reflected Wright's conviction that "nature-pattern and nature-texture in materials themselves often approach conventionalization, or the abstract."[29] As in his Prairie-style houses, an earth-hugging layout fused farm with landscape to create an effect both intimate and expansive. Schematic renderings of varied livestock in the pens illustrate how Wright was attuned to the color and shape of the animals and birds as a form of mobile decoration, creating shifting patterns in the landscape that were composed of his favored breeds. Textures and hues added by the crops were also inflected by seasonal change, the composition crafted like a carpet from the rhythms of the regulated planting, as in his mural design for Taliesin (see plate 9).

Wright's belief that daily contact with variegated crops would refine the farmer's aesthetic sensibilities was most apparent in the vegetable and flower gardens (the "soul" of the farm) adjacent to the house. Floor-to-ceiling glazed walls opened onto the garden and terrace offering a cinematic screen of seasonal change from the interior. The whole unit was like a living organism in which fresh produce from field and garden was either processed for dispatch via the packing area, or brought directly into the farmhouse for consumption. Wright conceived the composite plan as a flexible combination of elements that could be modified to suit various terrains and combinations of crops and livestock. His ultimate concern, as at Taliesin, was to encourage biodiversity and the ecological management of nature's life force. From the outset Davidson had seen the farm tract as having its own sewer system and electric power plant that would channel hot water, central heating, and air conditioning to each Little Farm. State-of-the-art humidifiers in the mushroom cellar and sunlamps in the greenhouses would aid natural processes through electrical technology rather than polluting chemicals. There was provision for a truck and car on each unit, but tractors and other farm equipment were to be used cooperatively.

In 1932 the American Institute of Steel Construction was aggressively promoting the factory production and sale of small homes.[30] Prefabrication had been a preoccupation of Wright's since his experimentation with American System-Built Houses in 1915–17, and his initial drawing for the Little Farms is fittingly marked "Standardized sheet steel construction" (see plate 6). Davidson too had relevant

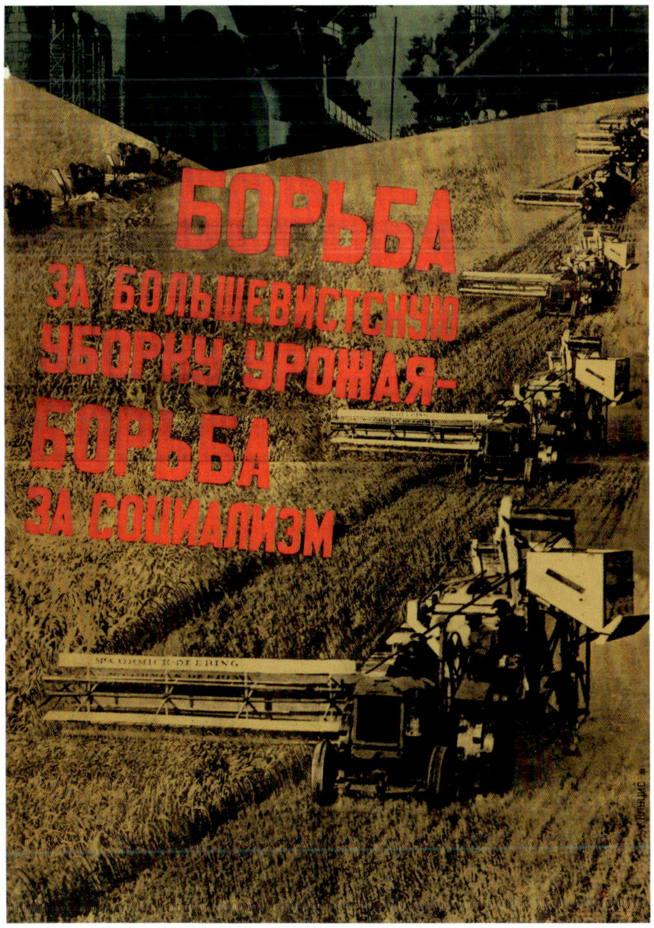

experience in this area. During World War I he had worked briefly for an airplane construction company and at Philadelphia's Hog Island, one of the largest shipbuilding concerns in the world, helping to manage the experimental design of prefabricated ships for the U.S. war effort. He was keen to link up the Little Farms with steel companies, but not so Wright: "The factory is to come to the house on this job as it is laid out and not the house go to the factory."[31] Wright believed in the automobile as an agent of potential diffusion and cohesion, but did not dream of fully formed farms rolling off the factory assembly lines like Ford's Model T. His preference was the assembly of prefabricated elements on site—a process that the *architect* could control.[32] Farm-as-factory and factory-built farms were ideas linked in Wright's mind with either the controlling interest of commercial corporations or the collectivist ethos of Soviet-style architecture and agriculture (fig. 6), both unacceptable as the way forward.[33]

In the *New York Times Magazine* from March 20, 1932, published a month after Davidson sent Wright his initial proposals, Wright imagines a "network of fine roads . . . passing roadside markets, integrated with groups of three, five, ten acre intensive farm units."[34] What better focus for a polemical stance against the cold functionalism and high-rise urbanism of architects such as Le Corbusier and Ludwig Mies van der Rohe than a radical rethink of the farm as technologically progressive and at the heart of a redefined cityscape? Wright was feeling marginalized by the efforts of Philip Johnson and Henry-Russell Hitchcock to promote a severe European modernism in the United States and found an influential ally in architectural critic and cultural theorist Lewis Mumford, with whom he was in regular correspondence. From Germany in June 1932, Mumford wrote reassuringly to Wright that he had found "much formula, much dogma, much paper," and that only about a tenth of the modern work was genuinely good. He did note, however, a farm by Hugo Häring, near Lübeck, "which would have delighted you" (fig. 7).[35] Häring's organic design of 1922–26 and the way he wrote about architecture as an expression of materials, place, and human activities had much in common with the direction Wright was developing. In summer 1933 Davidson tracked down Mumford, who was immersed in writing *Technics and Civilization*, and presented him with a copy

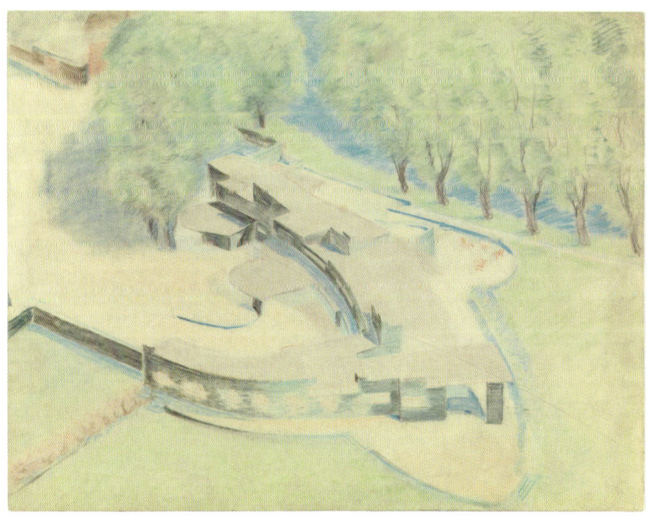

Fig. 6. Gustav Klutsis (Latvian, 1895–1938) and Sergei Senkin (Russian, 1894–1963). "The Bolshevik Struggle for the Harvest Is the Struggle for Socialism." 1931. Lithograph, 56 3/8 x 39 5/8 in. (143.2 x 100.7 cm). The Museum of Modern Art, New York. Gift of Karl Gerstner

Fig. 7. Hugo Häring (German, 1882–1958). Farmhouse at Gut Garkau, near Lübeck, Germany. Project, 1922–26. Perspective. Pastel on paper, 19 3/4 x 25 5/8 in. (50.2 x 65.1 cm). The Museum of Modern Art, New York. Gift of the Architecture and Design Committee in honor of Kenneth Frampton

of "The Diary of Mary, a Little Farmer's Wife," illustrated with Wright's drawings.[36] Mumford was fascinated, presumably because he could see the relevance of the system of farms and markets to his broad-ranging survey of the human dimensions and ethical dilemmas of technological change. *Technics and Civilization* was heavily influenced by Mumford's mentor Patrick Geddes, the Scottish biologist and polymath, in its concepts of ecology, the relationship between place, people, and work, and Geddes's synthetic characterization of cultural evolution from Neolithic to Paleolithic and Biotechnic eras.[37] Mumford saw around him the negative fallout of exploitative capitalists who "threw their money in the rivers, let it escape in smoke in the air, handicapped themselves with their own litter and filth, prematurely exhausted the agricultural lands upon which they depended for food and fabrics."[38] Yet, in Wright's work, Mumford saw the first signs of "a return to nature, a new confidence in the organism as a harmonious, self-equilibrating unit."[39] On May 21, 1934, he inscribed a copy of *Technics and Civilization*: "To Frank Lloyd Wright who made the difference between the mechanical and the organic visible in architecture—and so helped to initiate the *biotechnic* phase."[40]

Two years after his initial proposal, his own finances steadily dwindling, Davidson was still frantically trying to align his farm-market project with larger commercial and government agendas. After months of hunting down Julius Rosenwald, who had funded a program for schoolhouses in the rural south, including a design by Wright, the final interview was "somewhat disappointing, as he gave me the feeling that he did not know very much about life, nothing about farming and less about flowers."[41] Initially promising approaches to Thomas Dewey, the Russell Sage Foundation, the Brookings Institute, and members of Roosevelt's so-called "brain trust," including Stuart Chase, Wroe Anderson, and Bruce Melvin, all petered into nothing. Meanwhile, an irreparable rift was developing between architect and client, with Wright sensing that Davidson was selling out to corporate interests and bureaucratic number crunchers. Their falling out enacted what Mumford saw on a meta level as a clash between a high-tech, resource-hungry civilization and a holistic, deep-rooted, and organic culture. Mumford felt agriculture was not for turning a quick profit and that nurturing it into a biotechnic age required small measures and incremental changes. Wright ranted at Davidson:

Organic design isn't an affair of a budget mind or a case of budget in any way. . . . Mary is in danger of landing in a tin Lizzie [a reference to Henry Ford's Model T car] *instead of something organic and higher up in the human scale of values. . . . If you are forming another corporation to make money quick by lip service to Mary as an ideal for a "come-on"—you will be just a little bit worse than the others because you will prostitute an intelligence to become just another of those things we are cursed by. No Dave—I believe that old corp stuff is just as dead as the old type of building and the old way of building it, and the old corp type of business man is dead or dying.*[42]

The last bit was true in that Davidson died penurious in 1941. His obituary made no reference to the farms and markets or their inclusion in Wright's retrospective exhibition at MoMA, *Frank Lloyd Wright: American Architect*, which opened in November 1940, that helped propel the architect back into the limelight. Yet his beloved "Mary" lived on, albeit namelessly subsumed into Wright's ongoing projects—Broadacre City, his Usonian houses, and the Taliesin Fellowship. Multiple images of both a Unified Farm and Roadside Market were featured in Wright's last publication and exhibition, *The Living City*, as his sole creation, and as the epitome of "forces tearing the vortex down."[43]

Notes

1. Frank Lloyd Wright, *The Disappearing City* (New York: W. F. Payson, 1932), p. 81.

2. In 1908 Wright designed a house for Davidson in Buffalo. The fullest account of their relationship appears in Jack Quinan, *Frank Lloyd Wright's Buffalo Venture: From the Larkin Building to Broadacre City: A Catalogue of Buildings and Projects* (San Francisco: Pomegranate, 2012).

3. Davidson, letter to Wright, January 18, 1932, D010A06, Frank Lloyd Wright Foundation Archives (The Museum of Modern Art | Avery Architectural & Fine Arts Library, Columbia University, New York).

4. Ibid. Emphasis in original.

5. Davidson went on to privately publish five hundred copies of the "diary," none of which have yet been traced.

6. Roosevelt, speech marking the completion of the New York Regional Plan, as reported in "Growing Up by Plan," *Survey Graphic*, February 1932.

7. Wright, letter to Davidson, January 25, 1932, D008B02, Wright Foundation Archives (MoMA | Avery).

8. D016C09, Wright Foundation Archives (MoMA | Avery). Obituary, "W. V. Davidson, 65, Engineer, Is Dead," *New York Times*, March 9, 1941.

9. Davidson tried to interest Wright in designing a house for Frederick in a letter to Wright, January 25, 1930, C009A06, Wright Foundation Archives (MoMA | Avery).

10. Davidson, letter to Wright, March 11, 1927, D003B02, Wright Foundation Archives (MoMA | Avery).

11. Davidson, letter to Wright, April 4, 1927, D003B05, Wright Foundation Archives (MoMA | Avery). Wright's drawings for the trademarks and market interior are lost.

12. See Gertrude Almy Slichter, "Franklin D. Roosevelt's Farm Policy as Governor of New York State, 1928–1932," *Agricultural History* 33, no. 4 (Oct. 1959): 167–76.

13. Frank Lloyd Wright, *On Architecture: Selected Writings, 1894–1940* (New York: Grosset and Dunlap, 1941), p. 144. Ben Bassham, "FLLW, Henry Ford and the Road Back to the Farm," *Journal of the Taliesin Fellows*, no. 8 (Fall 1992): 8–15; and Alvin Rosenbaum, "2. Muscle Shoals," in *Usonia: Frank Lloyd Wright's Design for America* (Washington, D.C.: The Preservation Press, 1993), pp. 45–62.

14. In 1927 Clara Ford became president of the Women's National Farm and Garden Association. "Mrs. Ford Exhibits Model Farm Store," *New York Times*, November 5, 1929.

15. Wright, letter to Davidson, April 17, 1928, D003C01, Wright Foundation Archives (MoMA | Avery).

16. Newspapers were full of discussion about the creation of small farm communities to rehabilitate the unemployed and colonize idle farms, with one prominent spokesperson being Ralph Borsodi, author of *Flight From the City: The Story of a New Way to Family Security* (New York: Harper and Brothers, 1933).

17. Frank Lloyd Wright, *An Autobiography* (New York: Duell, Sloan and Pearce, 1943), p. 169.

18. Ibid., p. 168.

19. Wright wrote in a letter to Davidson about anxiously looking for a shipment of grocery stuff to supplement what he could grow, July 19, 1933, D016A10, Wright Foundation Archives (MoMA | Avery).

20. Wright, *An Autobiography*, p. 121.

21. See Jenkin Lloyd Jones and Thomas Graham, *The Agricultural Social Gospel in America: the Gospel of the Farm* (Lewiston, N.Y.: Edwin Mellen Press, 1986); and Thomas Graham, "Jenkin Lloyd Jones and 'The Gospel of the Farm,' " *Wisconsin Magazine of History* 67, no. 2 (Winter 1983–84): 121–48.

22. The millionaire Joseph Fels was an advocate of Henry George's single tax system and of land nationalization. See Alan Crawford, *C. R. Ashbee: Architect, Designer and Romantic Socialist* (New Haven, Conn.: Yale University Press, 1985), p. 148.

23. "Hillside Home School" prospectus (1891–92), p. 4, Lloyd Jones Papers, Wisconsin Historical Society.

24. "Hillside Home School" prospectus (1907), p. 3, Lloyd Jones Papers, Wisconsin Historical Society.

25. John de Koven Hill, audio interview by Diana Balmori, January 28, 1994, transcript, Wright Foundation Archives (MoMA | Avery).

26. Wright, letter to Lewis Mumford, January 1, 1933, in *Frank Lloyd Wright and Lewis Mumford: Thirty Years of Correspondence*, ed. Bruce Brooks Pfeiffer (New York: Princeton Architectural Press, 2001), p. 153.

27. Ralph Waldo Emerson, "On Farming," appendix to Frank Lloyd Wright, *The Living City* (New York: Horizon, 1958).

28. Wright, letter to Davidson, February 2, 1934, D018C08, Wright Foundation Archives (MoMA | Avery).

29. Wright, *An Autobiography*, p. 157.

30. See report of the Small House Forum organized by the Institute in "Everyman's House," *New York Times*, May 29, 1932.

31. Wright, letter to Davidson, February 15, 1934, D018C03, Wright Foundation Archives (MoMA | Avery).

32. Ibid.

33. The rapid industrialization of Soviet agriculture on a massive scale was widely publicized in the United States. Wright visited several collective farms during a visit to the Soviet Union in June 1937 to attend the First All-Union Congress of Soviet Architects held in Moscow. See Donald Leslie Johnson, "Frank Lloyd Wright in Moscow: June 1937," *Journal of the Society of Architectural Historians* 46, no. 1 (March 1987): 65–79; and Jean-Louis Cohen, "Useful Hostage: Constructing Wright in Soviet Russia and France," in *Frank Lloyd Wright: Europe and Beyond*, ed. Anthony Alofsin (Berkeley: University of California Press, 1999), pp. 100–20.

34. Frank Lloyd Wright, "Broadacre City: An Architect's Vision," *New York Times Magazine*, March 20, 1932, p. 9. This was Wright's first published reference to little farms and wayside markets. Le Corbusier had been afforded prominent coverage in the same magazine on January 3, 1932, and it is clear from correspondence with Lewis Mumford at the time that Wright felt his position at the forefront of architectural debates in the United States was being eroded.

35. Mumford, letter to Wright, in *Frank Lloyd Wright and Lewis Mumford: Thirty Years of Correspondence*, p. 148.

36. Davidson, letter to Wright, July 22, 1933, D016B01, Wright Foundation Archives (MoMA | Avery).

37. Wright was certainly familiar with Geddes's work and possibly even heard him lecture at Hull House to the Chicago Arts and Crafts Society, in 1899, on the importance of electricity and environmental controls as factors in human progress.

38. Lewis Mumford, *Technics and Civilization* (New York: Harcourt, Brace, 1934), p. 255.

39. Ibid., p. 247.

40. *Frank Lloyd Wright and Lewis Mumford: Thirty Years of Correspondence*, p. 161.

41. Davidson, letter to Wright, July 20, 1932, D010D09, Wright Foundation Archives (MoMA | Avery).

42. Wright, letter to Davidson, February 2, 1934, D018C08, Wright Foundation Archives (MoMA | Avery).

43. Wright, *The Living City*, pp. 57–61, 99–101.

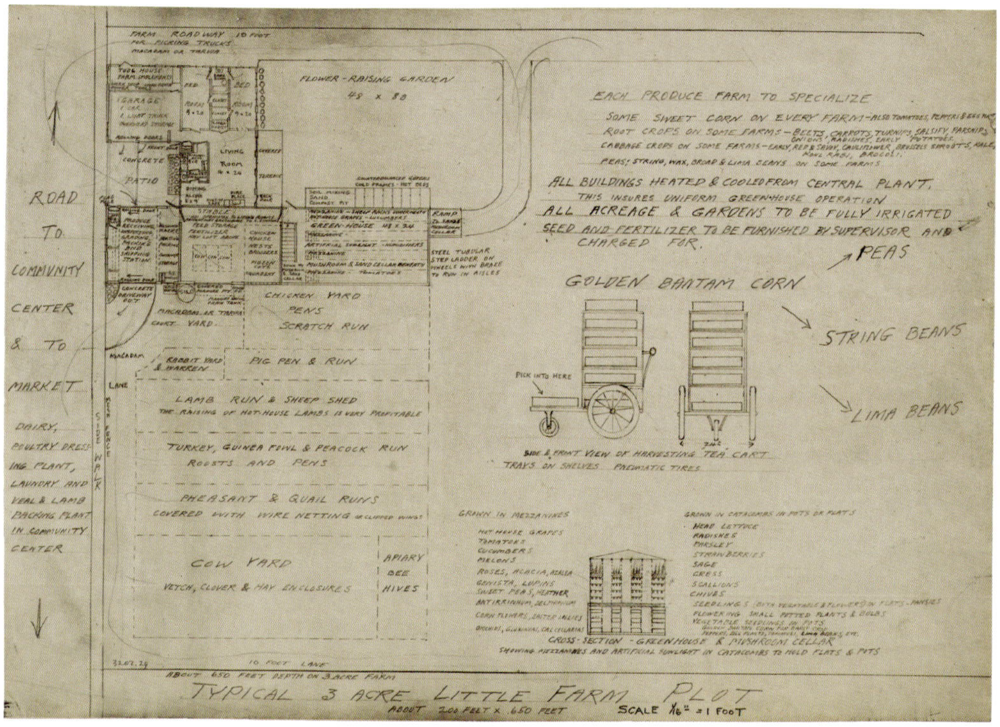

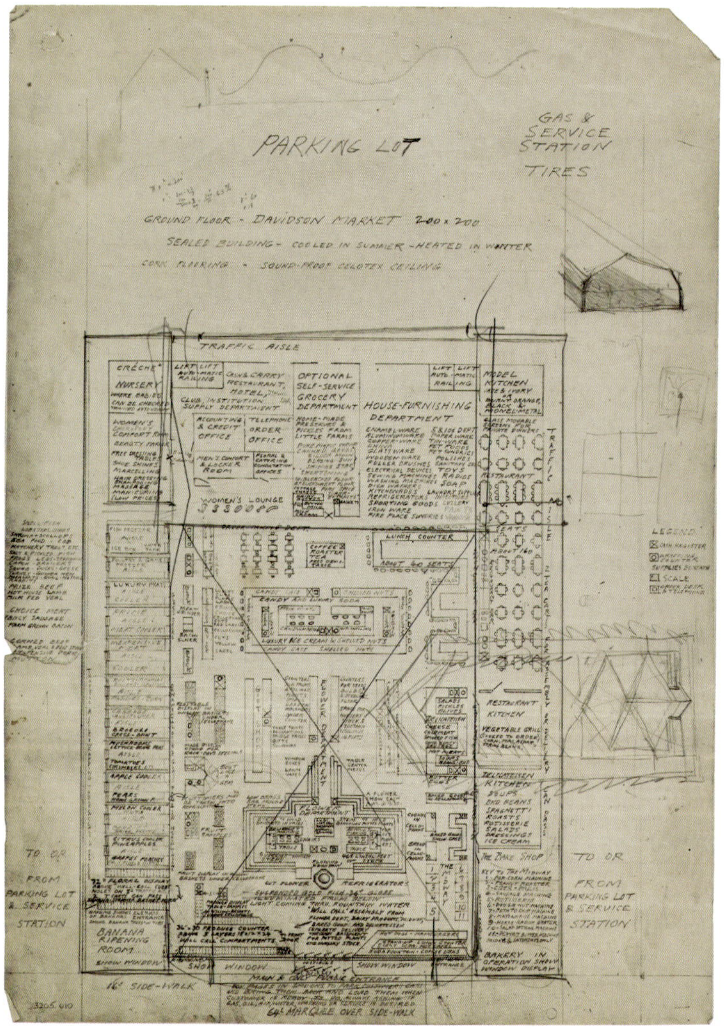

1. Davidson Little Farms Unit. Project, 1932–33.
Plan and details for a typical three-acre plot drawn by Walter V. Davidson.
Pencil on positive Photostat, 14 1/8 x 20 in. (35.9 x 50.8 cm)

2. Davidson Wayside Markets. Project, 1932–33.
Ground-floor plan drawn by Walter V. Davidson.
Pencil on positive Photostat, 20 x 14 1/4 in. (50.8 x 36.2 cm)

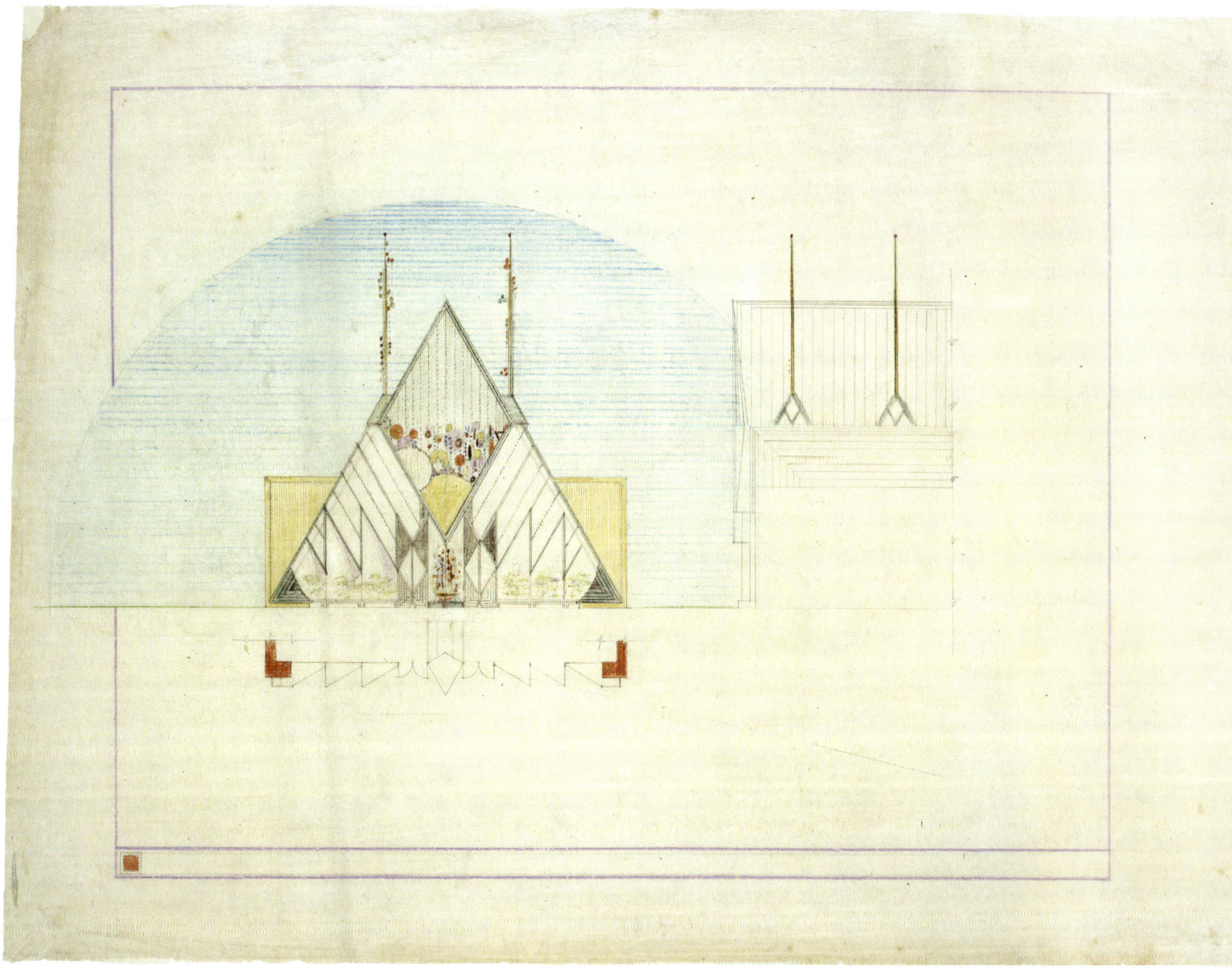

3. Preliminary proposal for Davidson Wayside Markets. Project, 1927.
Elevation and partial plan. Colored pencil and pencil on paper, 27 15/16 x 40 3/16 in. (71 x 102 cm).
Prints and Photographs Division, Library of Congress, Washington, D.C.

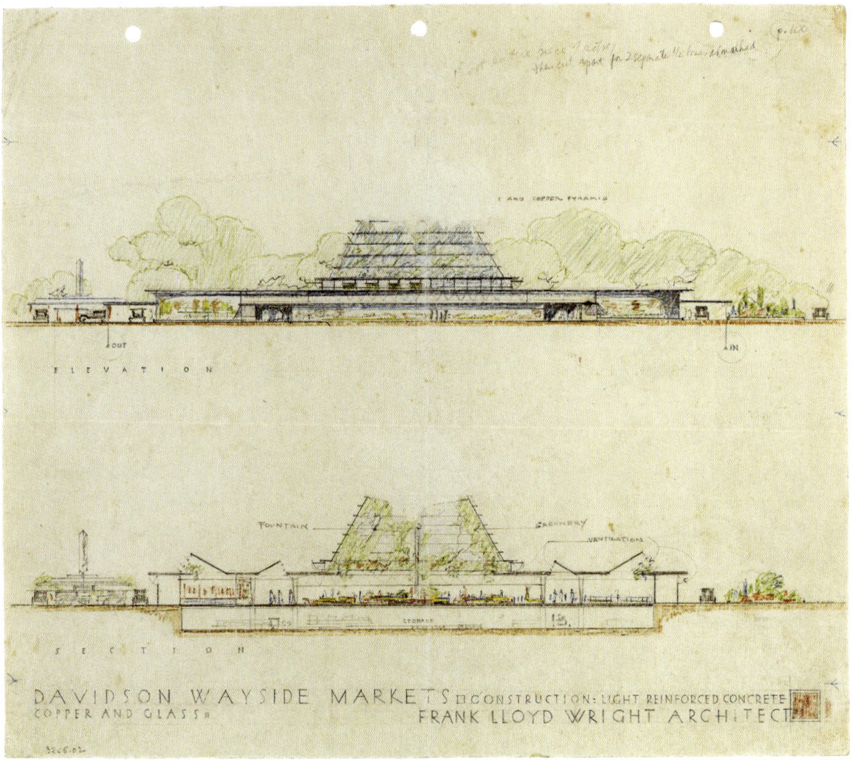

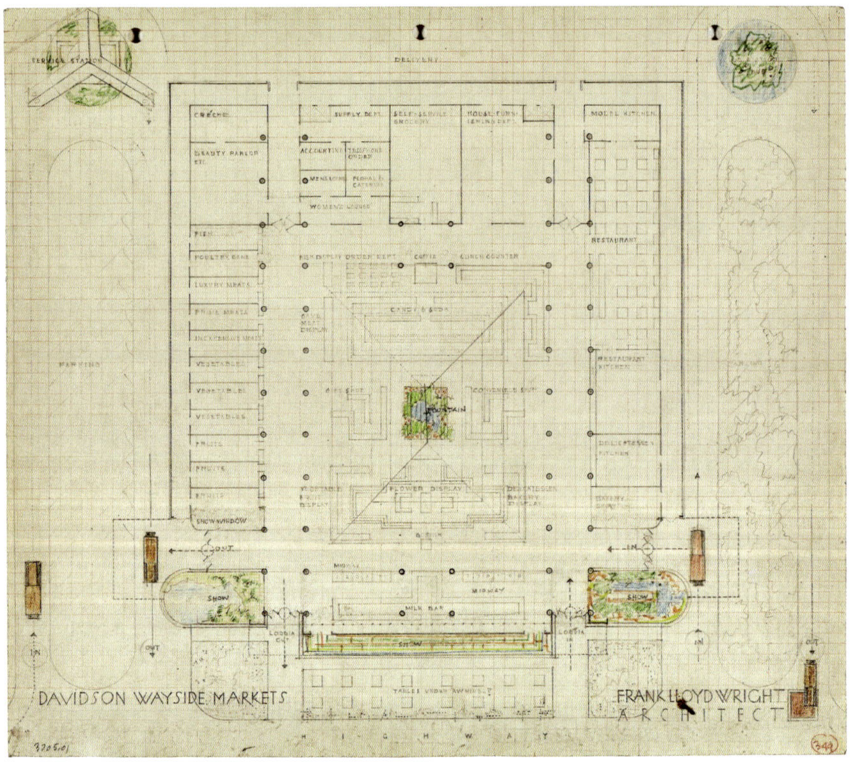

4. Davidson Wayside Markets. Project, 1932–33. Elevation and section.
Pencil and colored pencil on paper, 11 1/8 x 14 in. (28.3 x 35.6 cm)

5. Davidson Wayside Markets. Project, 1932–33. Ground-floor plan.
Pencil, colored pencil, and ink on paper, 11 1/8 x 14 in. (28.3 x 35.6 cm)

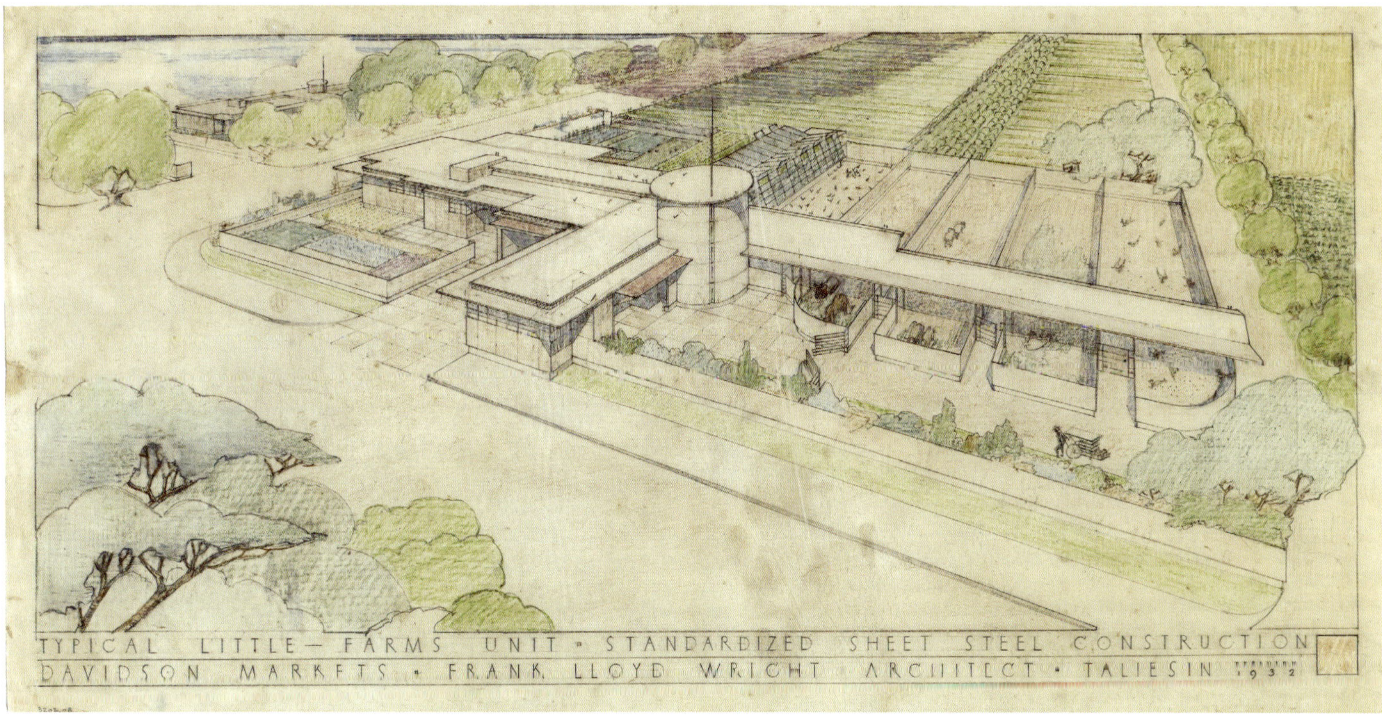

6. Davidson Little Farms Unit and Markets. Project, 1932–33. Aerial perspective.
Pencil and colored pencil on tracing paper. 11 5/8 x 22 7/8 in. (29.5 x 58.1 cm)

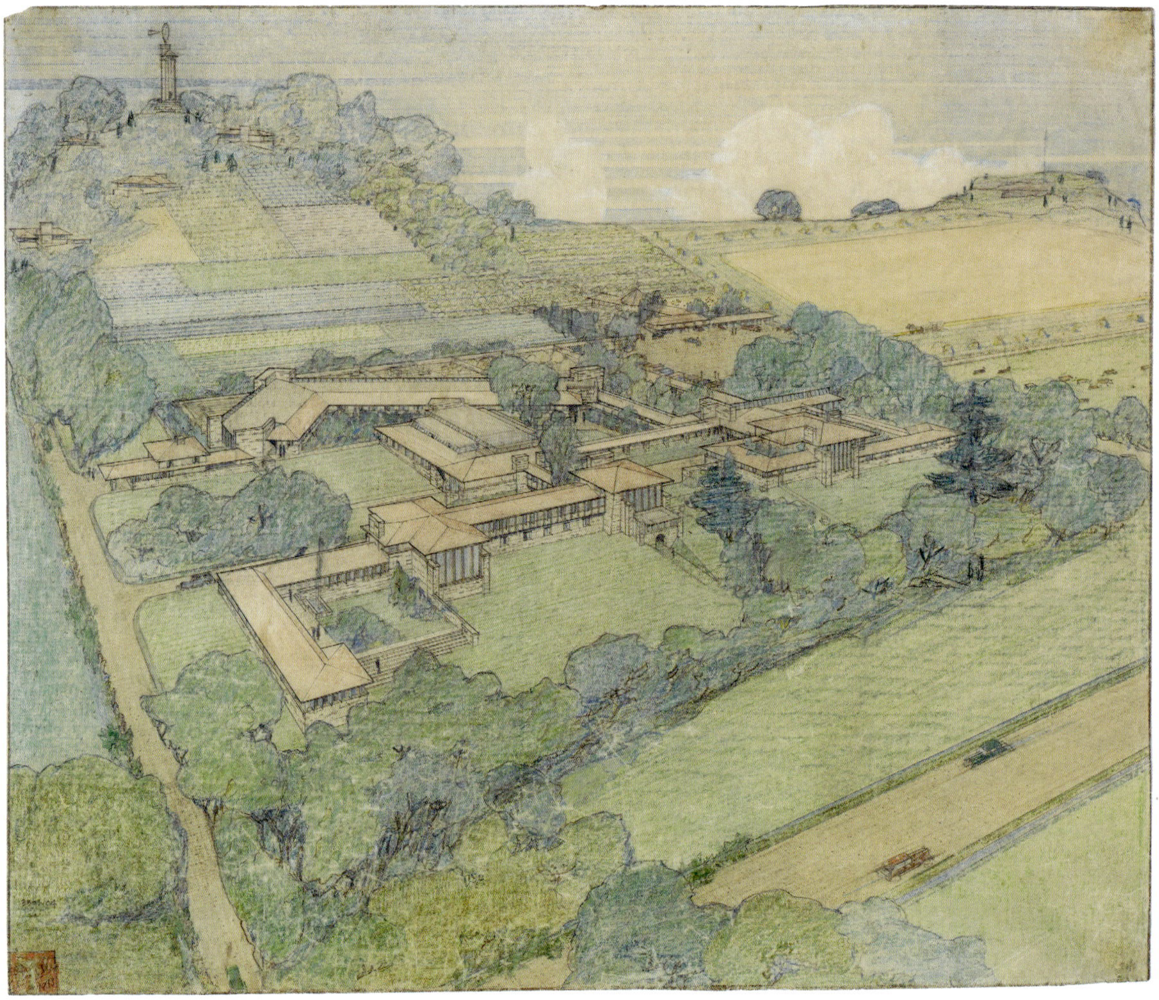

7. Taliesin Fellowship Complex, Spring Green, Wisconsin. Begun 1932–33. Aerial perspective.
Pencil and colored pencil on tracing paper, 17 ⅛ x 20 ⅛ in. (43.5 x 51.1 cm)

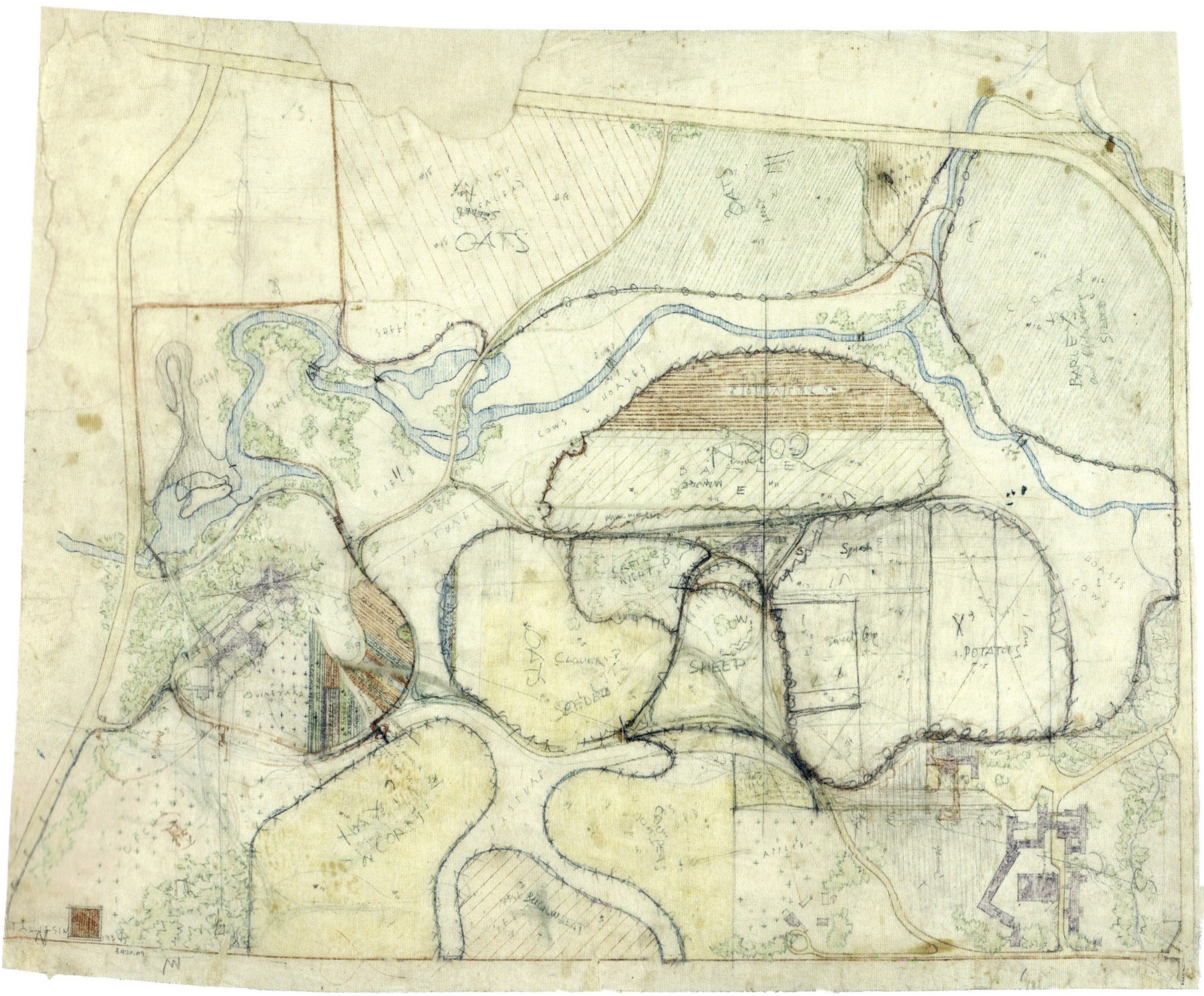

8. Taliesin Fellowship Complex, Spring Green, Wisconsin. Begun 1932–33. Crop plan. Pencil and colored pencil on tracing paper, 28 x 35 ¼ in. (73 x 89.5 cm)

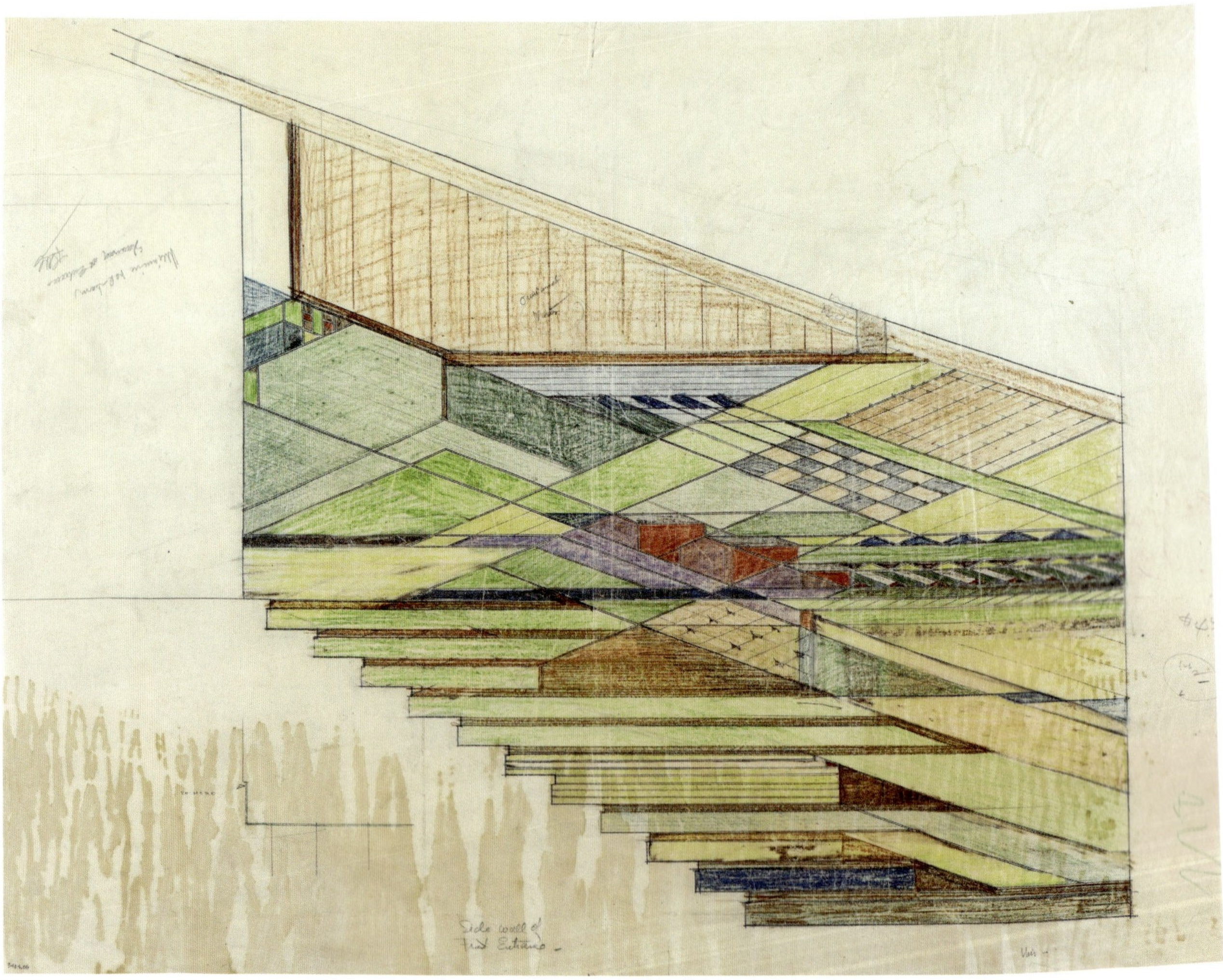

9. Taliesin Fellowship Complex, Spring Green, Wisconsin. Begun 1932–33. Mural design for the front entrance. Pencil and colored pencil on tracing paper, 26 3/8 x 33 1/4 in. (67 x 84.5 cm)

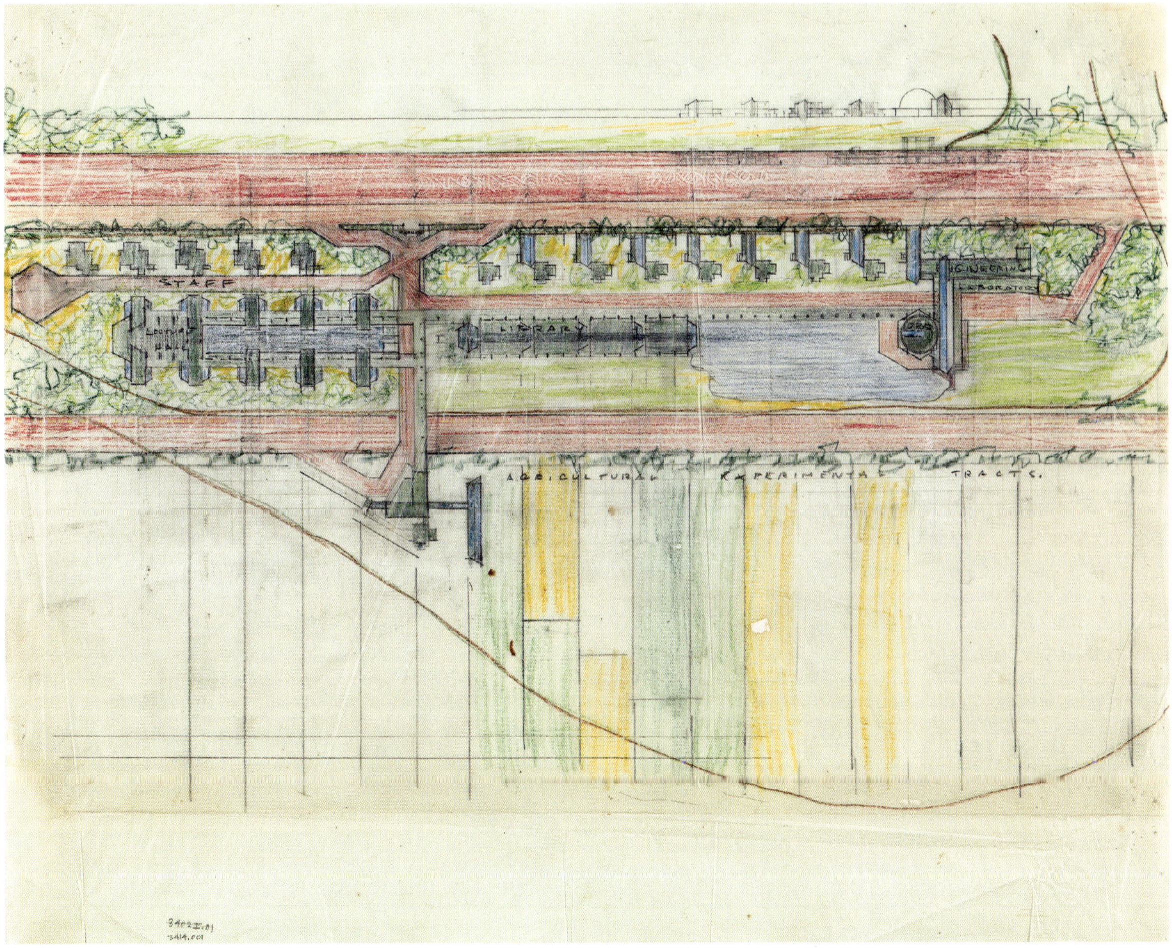

10. Broadacre City. Project, 1929–35. Plan of the agricultural research center.
Pencil and colored pencil on tracing paper, 16 3/4 x 20 7/8 in. (42.5 x 53 cm)

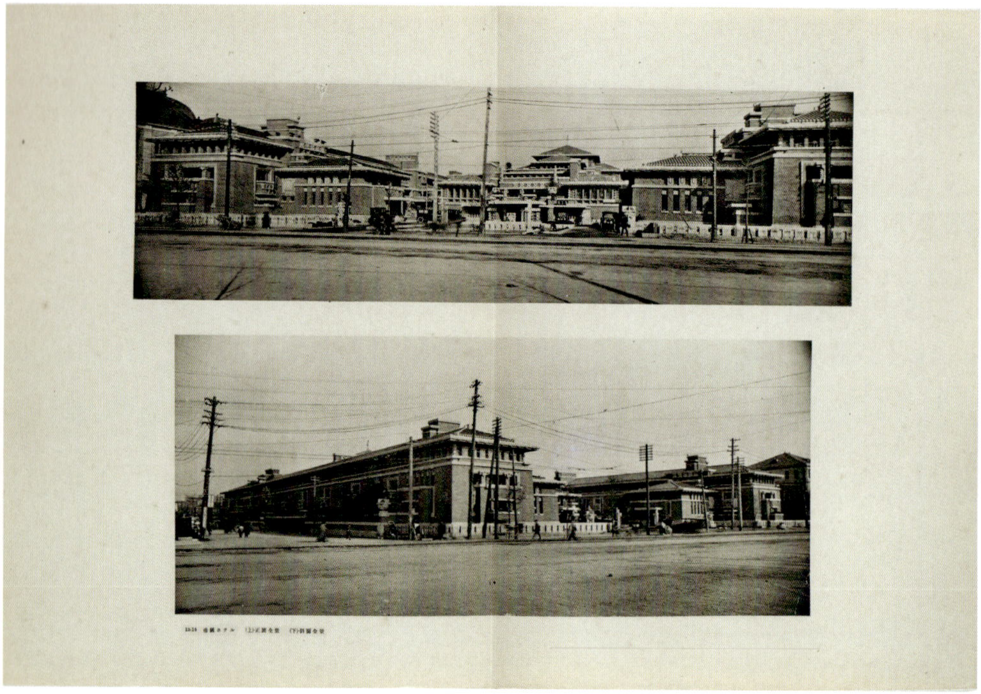

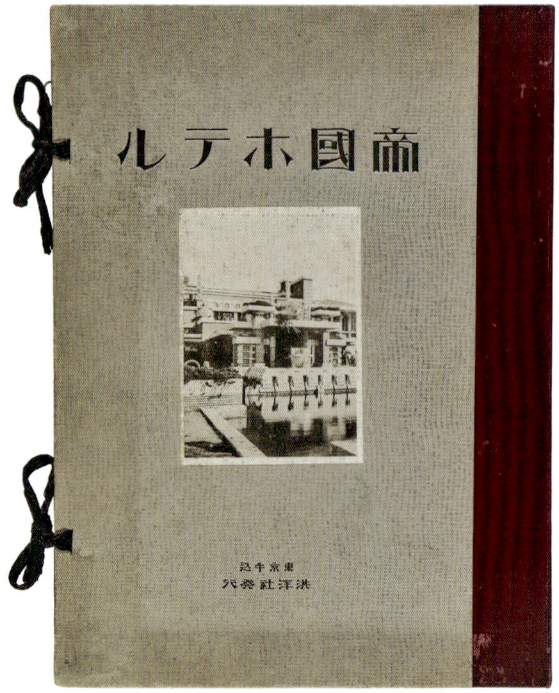

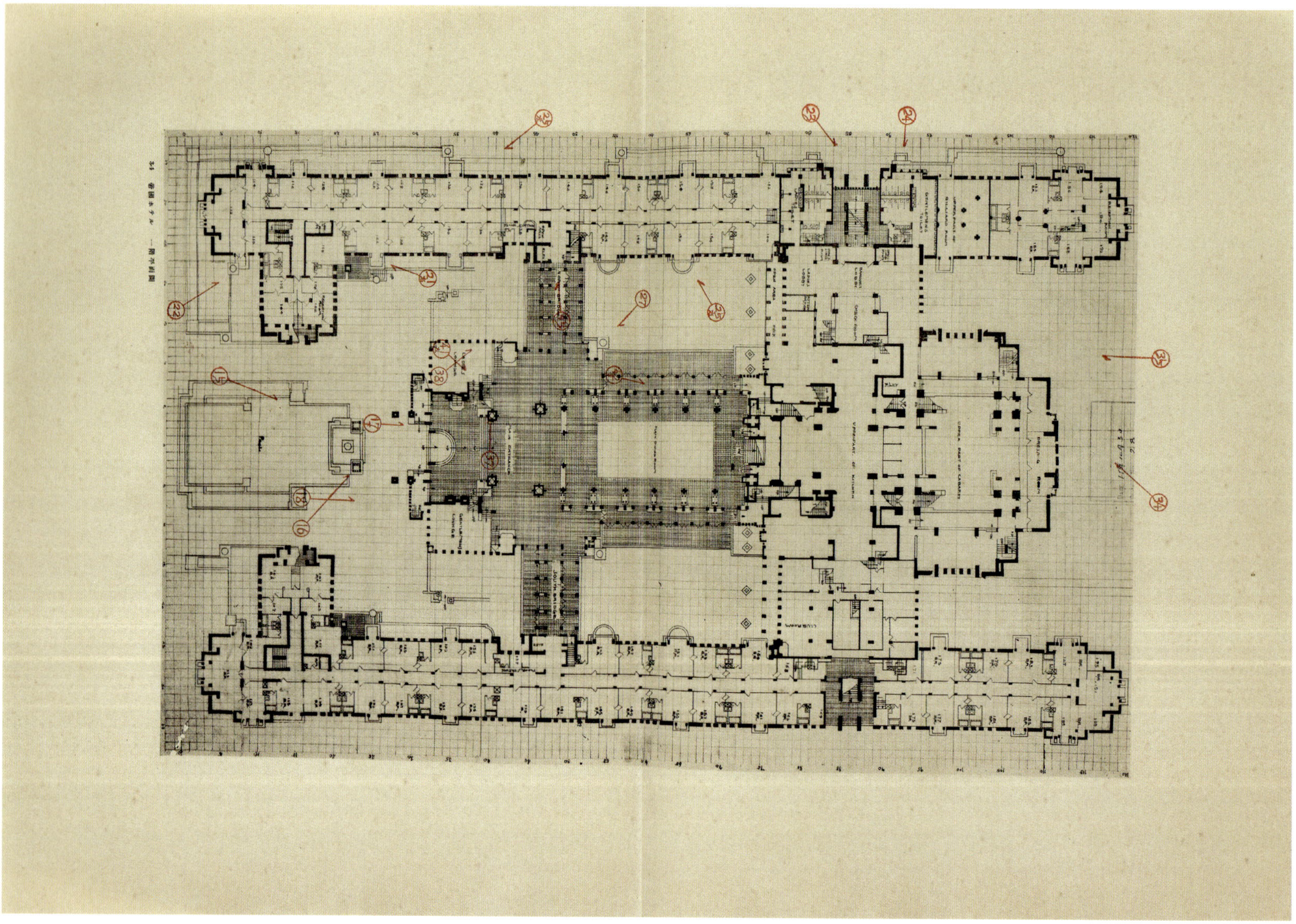

Cover and interior spreads of *Teikoku Hoteru*, ed.Takanashi Yūtarō (Tokyo: Kōyōsha, 1923)

KEN TADASHI OSHIMA

REFRAMING THE IMPERIAL HOTEL BETWEEN EAST AND WEST

Cultural definitions and interpretations of Frank Lloyd Wright's epic masterwork of the Imperial Hotel (1913–23) have been fluid in the century since its inception. This pioneering hotel has been seen as both a symbolic expression of Japan, underscored by its proximity to the Imperial Palace and by direct investment from the Imperial Household, and a site of direct social encounter within the modernizing, Westernizing nation. Parallel to the transformation of Wright's design, from its inception to built form and subsequent evolution before and after World War II, the hotel's surrounding urban context and the nation itself underwent rapid, ongoing changes. Wright himself described the Imperial Hotel commission as a "relief" from the tragedies of fire and murders in 1914 at Taliesin, his estate in Wisconsin, and as a bridge linking his early and later career.[1] The reception of Wright's design has ebbed and flowed, and its destruction in 1968 has prevented subsequent generations from experiencing the hotel's grandeur in its original context.

The fully illustrated book, *Teikoku Hoteru* (Imperial Hotel), displays Wright's realized vision in its pristine glory. It follows the eleven hundred drawings through their progression from Taliesin to Tokyo over a decade. It was published in August 1923, a year after Wright's final departure from Japan, on July 27, 1922, and right before the Great Kanto Earthquake struck on September 1, 1923.[2] Wright viewed the completed hotel through his personal copy of this rare publication (opposite). The photographic narrative, with the architect's own sketches and visual enhancements, provides a more vivid understanding of both the hotel's architecture and how guests experienced it than do later accounts, which emphasize its survival of the earthquake over any other attributes.[3] In departing Japan in 1922, Wright did not see the completion of the hotel's south wing and full growth of the landscaping. He subsequently drew on the photographs in his copy of the volume, highlighting his vision for more extensive foliage, as well as sketched in various details he must have been trying to further work out. Though published in the age of black-and-white photography, a few colorized photographs

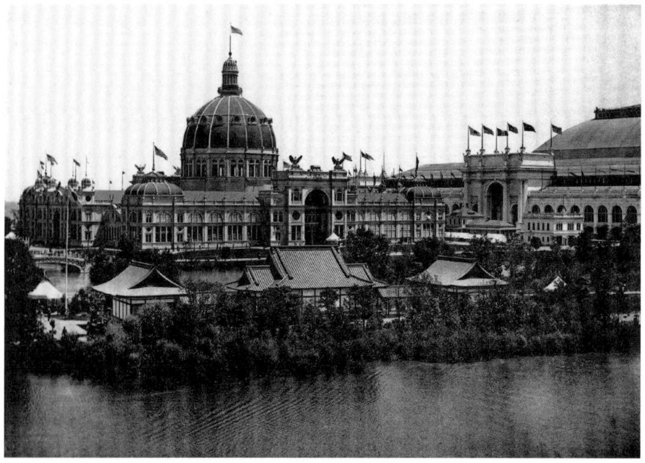

highlight the material character of the building elements. In counterpoint to books in English that read from left to right, this book follows Japanese custom by reading from right to left, and mistakenly credits its architect as "FRANK LLOYD WRGHIT." Such errors and miscommunication must have challenged Wright throughout his extended stays in Japan for a cumulative period of four years.

The plans featured in the volume include red markings that precisely indicate the position where each photograph was taken (see p. 60). Each image presents a framed scene, like the Japanese prints Wright had long collected and acknowledged were his source of inspiration for the design. While the hotel's symmetrical massing and serial placement of columns physically frame a one-point perspectival experience, many of the book's photographs highlight its dynamic compositional details from an angle as a two-point perspective. The Frank Lloyd Wright Foundation Archives also contain photographs that the architect cropped to emphasize either the horizontal or vertical elements of the hotel's composition (plates 1, 2). These include the dichotomous symbolic icons of samurai versus viking sculptural sprites, affirming Wright's conscious framing of the Imperial Hotel as the dialogue between East and West. The broader context of this cultural dialogue is also seen in the duality of the cycle rickshaws and automobiles pictured in front of the hotel. The appearance of electric power lines on the hotel's exterior serve as another prominent expression of modernization. Most notably, these lines contributed to the Imperial's legendary survival after the 1923 earthquake: the hotel credits its complete electrification as the reason for escaping fire in the aftermath of that natural disaster.[4]

Wright's own encounter with Japanese design on American soil, at the 1893 Chicago World's Fair, was followed by a lifelong dialogue with the country's art and architecture. The presentation at the fair of the Ho-o-den pavilion (fig. 1), a reconstruction of the eleventh-century Byōdō-in Phoenix Hall, noted for its symmetrical design and extended composition of corridors, would resonate in Wright's own Imperial Hotel design.[5] Wright had also been exposed to a circle of Asian art enthusiasts, including

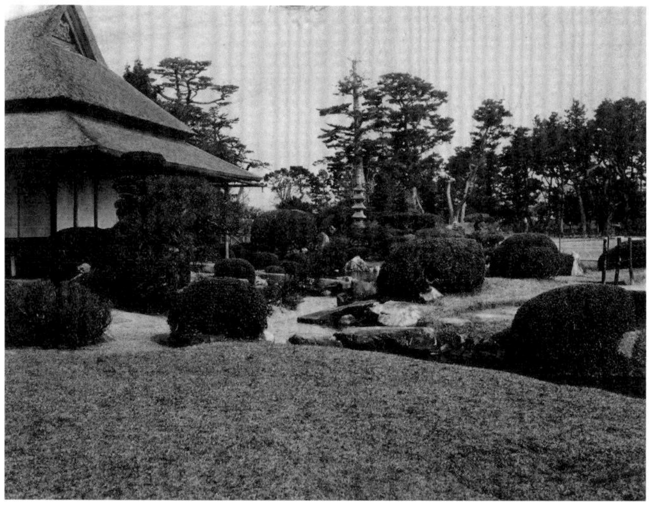

Fig. 1. Ho-o-den pavilion (foreground) at the 1893 Chicago World's Fair. From C. D. Arnold and H. D. Higinbotham, *Official Views of the World's Columbian Exposition* (Chicago: Chicago Photo-gravure, Co., 1893)

Fig. 2. Korakuen Garden, Okayama, Japan. 1687–1700. Photograph from Wright's 1905 trip

his mentors Joseph Silsbee and Louis Sullivan, in the age of *Japonisme* and the imagining of Japan by those outside the country.[6] Wright expressed his own interpretation of Japanese prints with his photographs of weeds and wildflowers in his 1896 book *The House Beautiful*—collotype prints on Japanese paper that recall Utagawa Hiroshige's *Nadeshiko (Pink) Butterfly and Poem* (c. 1840), from his own collection (see p. 27, fig. 2).[7] He further took photographs, around 1900, of snow-covered landscapes around Spring Green, Wisconsin, that recall the minimal composition of Japanese ink paintings on hand scrolls, underscoring his passion for this artistic view (see p. 28, fig. 3).

Wright's interest in Japanese landscapes and traditional structures deepened during his seven weeks spent traveling throughout Japan in 1905 (fig. 2).[8] This journey provided a dynamic spatial understanding of buildings in the context of surrounding mountains and forests, which he noted was "a great educational experience."[9] As Japanese art historian Julia Meech has suggested, the principles of the large garden estates that he saw in Japan—which combined "small hills, rivers, ponds, and bridges, with carefully constructed 'views'"—may have inspired Wright in the landscape design of Taliesin.[10] They clearly also influenced his approach to the Imperial's gardens and greenery. The hotel was, in Wright's words, "designed as a system of gardens and sunken gardens and terraced gardens—of balconies that are gardens and loggias that are also gardens and roofs that are gardens—until the whole arrangement becomes an interpenetration of gardens. Japan is Garden-land."[11]

Wright also brought his self-described "obsession" with Japanese art—as a collector, teacher, and dealer—from Japan back to America.[12] He returned to Chicago with several hundred Hiroshige prints, which he exhibited in March 1906 at the Art Institute of Chicago, also publishing his first essay on prints.[13] Wright's intense interest led him to meet avid Japanese print collector Frederick William Gookin, who is thought to have suggested Wright for the Imperial Hotel commission.[14] He also encouraged his clients to hang Japanese prints on the walls of their homes.[15] For a second, even larger exhibition of ukiyo-e prints at the Art Institute, in March 1908, Wright designed special stands tailored to fit the space—akin to his high-backed dining chairs from his home in Oak Park, Illinois—that vertically framed the works. Gookin organized this later exhibition, and Wright designed the exhibition space, with its system of prints hanging from a rail installed above precisely placed benches. Wright developed further iterations of these ideas in designs such as the Japanese Print Gallery for William Spaulding (fig. 3) and the S. Mori Japanese Print Shop (1914), a remodeled interior in the Fine Arts Building in Chicago. In both instances, he designed the entire space around the precise viewing of the prints. Everything—the cabinets, picture rails, fabrics, carpets, wall treatments, and a remarkably

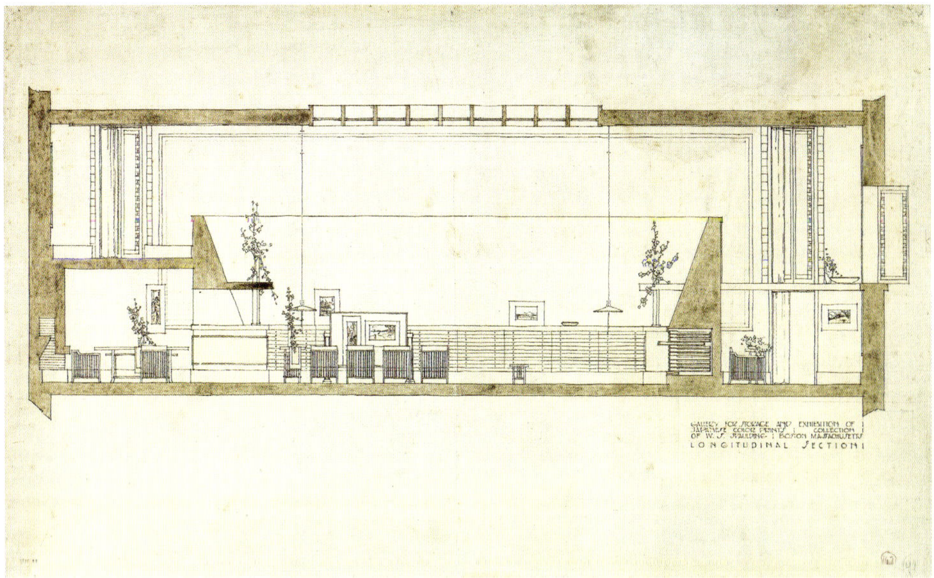

Fig. 3. Japanese Print Gallery for William Spaulding. Boston. Project. 1914. Longitudinal section. Ink, colored pencil, and pencil on paper, 20 1/4 x 32 5/8 in. (51.4 x 82.9 cm)

minimal square chair design—focused attention on the artwork. Wright's total environments, with their framed artistic views of natural subjects, akin to the windows of his residential designs, thus provide a counterpoint in Chicago to his concurrent design for the Imperial Hotel in Tokyo.

From the Japanese perspective, Wright's Imperial Hotel followed in the more than forty-year history of providing accommodations in a consciously Western architectural idiom for foreign visitors. In contrast to traditional Japanese inns with tatami-based rooms, the Western hotel provided guests beds and chairs. The Rokumeikan (1883), a two-story French Renaissance-style party palace in Tokyo's central Hibiya district, designed by British architect Josiah Conder, was the most prominent symbolic setting for accommodating governmental guests and hosting social events where Japanese officials embraced Western manners for the first time.[16] This area just outside the Imperial Palace, which was formerly the site of samurai mansions and the Tokyo National Museum (1837–81), became the site for a sequence of Imperial Hotels.[17] Prussian firm Ende and Böckmann, architects of many of the nearby neoclassical governmental offices and the civic plan for the rising Meiji Government (1868–1912)—which embraced both Western culture and political systems to create a modern nation—designed the first Imperial Hotel (1890), which then was completed by Japanese architect Yuzuru Watanabe (fig. 4).[18] The three-story hotel with mansard roofs featured sixty rooms and social spaces such as a newspaper reading room, dance hall, billiard room, parlor, and music hall. While the hotel initially struggled to attract guests, it flourished in the period following the Russo-Japanese War (1904–05), engendering the need for a new, larger hotel in the following decade, and the commissioning of Wright.[19]

Wright's journeys between East and West, experienced through various linguistic, visual, and cultural modes of translation, shaped his decade-long design phase for the Imperial Hotel. Wright returned to Tokyo in early 1913 for four months to study the proposed site, consider appropriate building materials, and work on a preliminary scheme for the new hotel, to be located just east of the first Imperial Hotel, which faced Hibiya Park, and north of the Rokumeikan.[20] Wright was now designing for an increasingly internationalized Japan in the Taisohō period that had begun on July 30, 1912, upon the death of the Meiji Emperor. During this time he examined the unstable soil conditions for the site, which was originally part of the Hibiya inlet of Tokyo Bay before being filled in as part of the construction of the feudal capital of Edo. Both the first and second Imperial Hotel sites had faced the outer moats of Edo Castle before they were filled in, around 1903, with the completion of Hibiya Park. Although the residence of the Minister of Home Affairs was located on the site, its planned demolition would provide an open stage for the wide range of fantastic, varied visions beyond the realized form depicted in the 1923 book.

Wright's preliminary scheme, from 1913–14, depicted in a bird's-eye perspective a complex defined by symmetrical

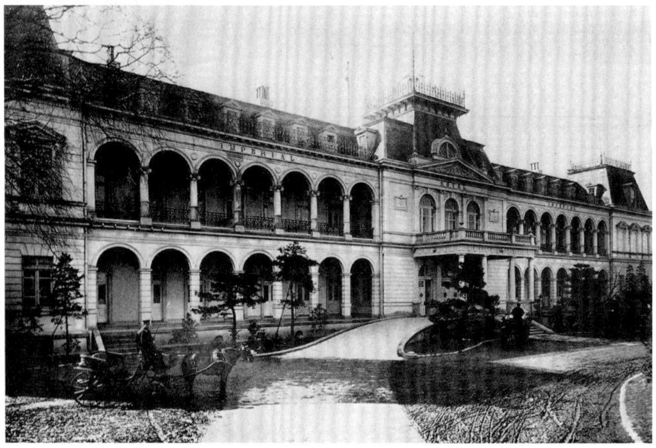

Fig. 4. Yuzuru Watanabe (Japanese, 1855–1930). Imperial Hotel, Hibiya, Tokyo. 1890

wings, forming public courtyard space (plate 3).[21] On the one hand, this symmetrically composed building parti resonated with Japanese temple schemes, such as the Higashi-Honganji Temple in Nagoya that Wright had seen on his 1905 trip.[22] On the other hand, Wright scholar Neil Levine also highlights it as a Beaux-Arts palatial type, as seen in Julien Guadet's Grand Prix project of 1864 for a Hospice in the Alps.[23] In any case, the strict symmetry is depicted from the side, emphasizing an asymmetrical perspective that would have been seen from the direction of the Imperial Palace.

This preliminary design could be seen to bring symbolic imagery of East and West together through its central stepped pyramidal roof. The precise proportions and details of the abstracted geometric scheme of the Imperial's central roof would undergo many different iterations, underscoring its symbolic importance and multiplicity of interpretations. Wright's own photographic collection included diverse precedents of stepped pyramidal forms, from Mesoamerica (El Castillo, Chichen Itza, Mexico) and Indonesia, as well as Japanese pyramidal roof forms such as the Sutra Library at Higashi-Honganji Temple (Nagoya-Betsuin), featured in his 1905 photo album,[24] though the Imperial's lower courtyard composition, with its lobby and dining room, certainly differed from these precedents.

Wright's initial presentation of the Imperial Hotel design, at the 1914 annual Chicago Architectural Club exhibition, highlighted his interpretation of Japanese aesthetics expressed in his curation of prints and flower arrangements (fig. 5).[25] The renderings of the hotel's surrounding greenery corresponded with the landscape prints of Hiroshige and ikebana flower arrangements displayed on the print stands that Wright had designed for the 1908 Art Institute showing. The exhibition for the Architectural Club also presented the model for the concurrent design of Midway Gardens that would officially open in the month after the exhibition, on June 27, 1914. Wright developed both the Imperial Hotel and Midway Gardens following his return to Chicago in 1913, elaborating on the initial Imperial scheme, and they shared similar basic symmetrical plan and section strategies. Moreover, both designs could be seen to be equally hybrid, with Wright traveling back and forth between Chicago and Tokyo, himself recalling of Midway Gardens: "To many it was all Egyptian, Mayan to some, very Japanese to others. But strange to all, it awakened a sense of mystery and romance in the beholder."[26] By this point, Wright's travels and direct work experiences had dissolved a strict Oriental/Occidental divide, enabling him to freely draw from multiple sources, with new meanings found in his translations from Chicago to Tokyo and back.

In contrast to the Imperial Hotel's stated purpose to establish a proper Western hotel that symbolized Japan's rise as a modern nation, Wright consciously took "off his hat to Japanese traditions"; he asserted "the West has much to learn from the East—and Japan was the gateway to that great East of which I had been dreaming since I had seen my first Japanese prints—and read my first Laotze."[27] The development of Wright's Imperial Hotel design between 1914 and 1916 (plate 4) expresses clear affinities with the roofs and spatial composition of traditional Japanese temples and pagodas that he had photographed during his 1905 trip. The siting of the central auditorium and Peacock Room and the symmetrical room wings, for example, is analogous to Japanese temple compositions, such as the main hall of Chion-in Temple in Kyoto and its roofed wings from Wright's 1905 album. Moreover, the distinctly flared corners of Wright's Imperial Hotel roofs express his translation of Japanese traditions, especially in the roofs and finials atop the hotel's elevator towers. Such attempts by foreign architects to consciously inflect prominent buildings with

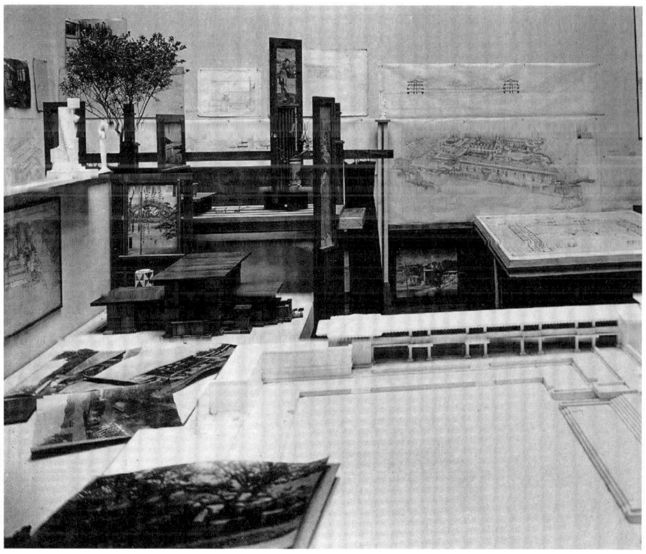

Fig. 5. Imperial Hotel drawings (upper right) at the annual Chicago Architectural Club exhibition, Art Institute of Chicago, 1914

Japanese traditions, in contrast to Japanese attempts to design "Western" buildings, were common, as seen notably in Ralph Adams Cram's "proposal for the Parliament Houses in Tokyo" from 1908 that similarly crowned the composition with temple and pagoda roofs.[28]

Upon closer inspection, Wright's fantastic scheme could be seen as a site for direct interaction between international guests and "the Japanese social life of the Capital." Grand corridors such as the "Promenade" provided space for socializing and cross-cultural interactions. Wright himself noted that the two hundred eighty-five hotel rooms consisted of "less than one-half the substance of the whole, or its function, or its cost."[29] His design called for a one-thousand-person theater with a revolving stage, top-floor ballroom/banquet hall, a terraced cabaret with table seating for three hundred and room for dancing, extensive dining rooms, and a grand cross-axial 300-foot-long (91.4-meter-long), 24-foot-wide (7.3-meter-wide) promenade with ample seating to connect to the relatively minimal rooms. The Imperial Hotel, rising seven stories on a 4-acre (1.6-hectare) site—Wright's largest commission to date—could thus be seen as a mini-city, an urban microcosm at the center of the Japanese capital.

The hotel's design further evolved upon Wright's arrival back in Tokyo, in December 1917, for a five-month stay, highlighting the ongoing tensions and ambiguity between East and West. The drawing set of "Preliminary Prints" (plate 5) feature the title block IMPERIAL HOTEL FRANK LLOYD WRIGHT ARCHITECT CHICAGO next to the 4'20'17 TOKYO dating with a graphic logo and signature square reminiscent of woodblock print signatures. While the gable roofs of the front elevation are less overtly "Japanese" than the previous schemes, certain drawings can be seen to emphasize supposedly Japanese elements—such as the portals recalling a Japanese *mon* (gate) with flanking pagoda-like towers—while other drawings lack such specific domestic references. The crowning banquet hall, which would become known as the Peacock Room (plates 6–8), similarly expresses an ambiguity of a Western cruciform plan and possible domed roof, versus the realized pyramidal roof that Neil Levine argued would be the symbolic expression of Mount Fuji.[30]

The translation of Wright's Imperial Hotel drawings into built form proved to be a daunting task (plates 9, 10). The construction period was projected to be a year and a half, but the hotel ended up taking five years to build, with both time and budget almost three times initial projections.[31] The original drawings remained schematic, without precise material specifications for the Japanese carpenters, and drawn in feet and inches rather than the customary system of *shaku* and *sun*. Wright noted, "Most all of the plans I had prepared at Taliesin were thrown away and my presence on the work [site] enabled me to make such changes in the work itself as were required or I desired."[32] For Wright, the realization of this total environment (figs. 6, 7) demanded close collaboration with craftsmen, whom he praised for their skill and patience. This close contact was afforded by Wright taking residence in a penthouse apartment in the adjacent Imperial Hotel Annex, also designed by him, and working from a site office located across the street, in Hibiya Park. He noted, "I modified many original intentions to make the most of [a building process] I now saw was naturally theirs."[33] This transformative design process included the extensive development of the hotel's seismic structure to employ a floating pier system, which Wright

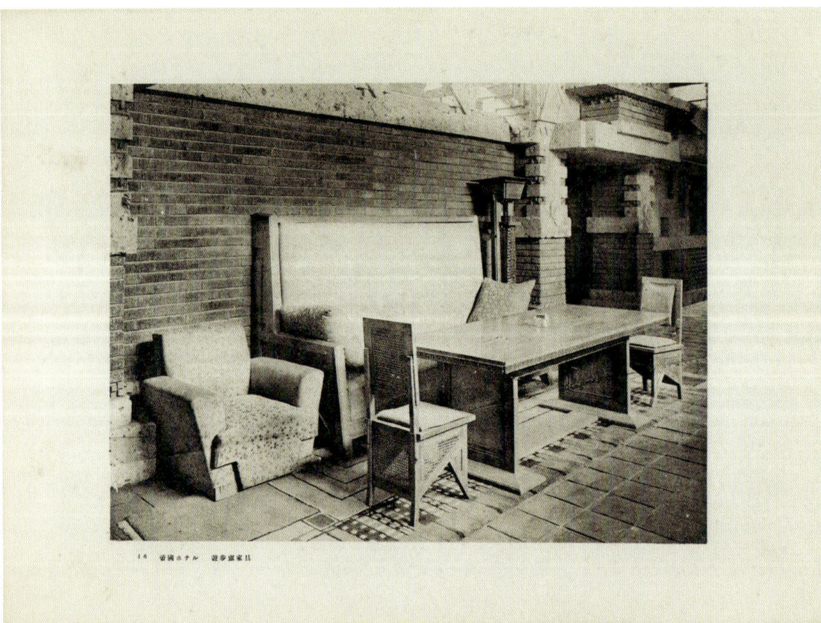

Fig. 6. Imperial Hotel, Tokyo. 1913–23. Interior view. From *Teikoku Hoteru*, ed., Takanashi Yūtarō (Tokyo: Kōyōsha, 1923)

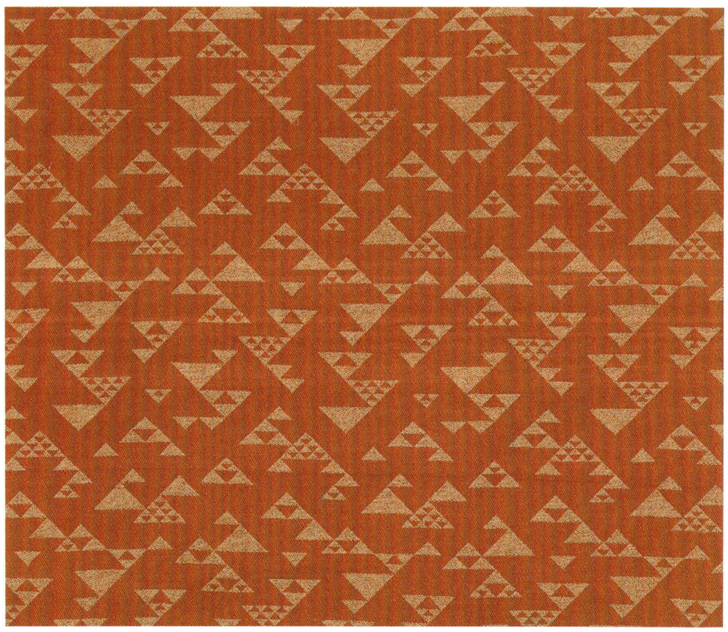

Fig. 7. Imperial Hotel, Tokyo. 1913–23. Upholstery fabric. Silk and viscose, 19 x 35 in. (48.3 x 88.9 cm)

likened to the way "a waiter carries his tray on raised fingers at the center—balancing the load."[34]

To express the material character of this earthquake-prone nation, Wright looked to new possibilities in place of brick and stone. Rather than using unreinforced brick that had failed in Meiji-period buildings, Wright developed, along with a local producer, "scratch tiles": hollow tiles textured to appear like brick that would face reinforced concrete.[35] He then sought to complement these tiles with Oya tuff (volcanic stone) that added porous texture to his composition of ornamented columns, capstones, and bases (plate 11). While Oya stone was used for everyday needs, such as sidewalk paving and common building faces, Wright advocated the prominent use of some 60,000 cubic feet (1,700 cubic meters) of this material for the Imperial Hotel.[36] He further developed terra cotta textile blocks, whose square frame composition evoked the overall form of the hotel.

Beyond the Imperial, Wright worked in Japan on multiple scales and typologies. For the Jiyu Gakuen School (1921; plate 12), in Tokyo, he employed the Imperial's symmetrical courtyard organization, but on a smaller scale appropriate to young children and constructed using a wood frame. Houses, including those for the Imperial Hotel's manager, Aisaku Hayashi (1917), would be completed by the circle of architects around Wright in Japan, including Arata Endo and others. While Wright's ambitious Odawara Hotel (1917; plate 13)—which would have bridged a waterfall with cantilevered trays—would not be completed, the design's fundamental concepts would take form later in projects, such as his masterwork Fallingwater (1934–37) in Mill Run, Pennsylvania.

Within Japan, Wright's design for the Imperial Hotel resonated in prominent buildings that followed, such as the stepped pyramid form of the National Diet Building (1936) just across Hibiya Park, and in so-called Imperial Crown Style designs of the 1930s that embraced traditional Japanese roofs on top of neoclassical structures with bands of clerestory windows.

The Imperial, however, would remain Wright's most heroic work embodying his intense interest in Japan. Sadly, the completed hotel was compromised almost instantly through damage sustained in the Great Kanto Earthquake, and then again during fire bombings in World War II that would destroy the Peacock Room and much of the south wing. The hotel would be taken over by the Allied Occupation administration, with transformations unsympathetic to Wright's original vision, such as painting the Oya stone white. A move to tear down the hotel, in order to further modernize and add floors, began as early as the 1930s in preparation for the unrealized 1940 Tokyo Olympics, to be repeated by a push to build higher for the 1964 Olympics. While efforts to save the hotel initially curtailed demolition, the wrecking ball struck in 1967 to make way for a new high-rise Imperial Hotel in anticipation of additional visitors from the Osaka Expo 1970. By this time, the hotel had fallen into decay, with the unsightly addition of air conditioners and other compromises to Wright's original design. Preservation efforts resulted in the reconstruction of the hotel at the Meiji Mura architectural park, though within a very different, rural setting. Taken together, the book, drawings, and remaining artifacts related to this now iconic structure illuminate the evolution of Wright's dynamic vision that fused East and West, past and future.

Notes

1. Frank Lloyd Wright, *An Autobiography* (New York: Horizon, 1977), p. 193.
2. Takanashi Yūtarō, ed., *Teikoku Hoteru* (Tokyo: Kōyōsha, 1923).
3. See *The Imperial: The First 100 Years* (Tokyo: Imperial Hotel, 1990), pp. 130–36.
4. Ibid., p. 133.
5. For a further discussion of Wright's encounter with the 1893 World's Fair, see Julia Meech, *Frank Lloyd Wright and the Art of Japan: The Architect's Other Passion* (New York: Japan Society/Harry N. Abrams, 2001), pp. 30–33.
6. See ibid., pp. 28–47; and Kevin Nute, *Frank Lloyd Wright and Japan* (New York: Van Nostrand, 1993), pp. 9–34.
7. See Meech, *Frank Lloyd Wright and the Art of Japan*, pp. 35–37; and W. C. Gannett et al., *The House Beautiful* (River Forest, Ill.: Auvergne Press, 1896–98).
8. See Meech, *Frank Lloyd Wright and the Art of Japan*, pp. 37–40; and Melanie Birk, ed., *Frank Lloyd Wright's Fifty Views of Japan: The 1905 Photo Album* (San Francisco: Pomegranate, 1996).
9. Transcript of a Sunday morning print party talk, Taliesin West, Scottsdale, Arizona, February 5, 1956. Quoted in Meech, *Frank Lloyd Wright and the Art of Japan*, pp. 38, 273n29.
10. Meech, *Frank Lloyd Wright and the Art of Japan*, p. 40.
11. Frank Lloyd Wright, "In the Cause of Architecture: The New Imperial Hotel," *Western Architect* 32 (April 1923): 42.
12. See Meech, *Frank Lloyd Wright and the Art of Japan*.
13. Frank Lloyd Wright, *Hiroshige: An Exhibition of Colour Prints from the Collection of Frank Lloyd Wright* (Chicago: Art Institute of Chicago, 1906).
14. Gookin had heard by the first half of 1911 about the proposal to build a new Imperial Hotel. Kathryn Smith, "Frank Lloyd Wright and the Imperial Hotel: A Postscript," *Art Bulletin* (June 1, 1985): 297.
15. Meech, *Frank Lloyd Wright and the Art of Japan*, p. 55.
16. Toshio Watanabe, "Josiah Conder's Rokumeikan: Architecture and National Representation in Meiji Japan," in "Japan, 1868–1945: Art, Architecture, and National Identity," special issue, *Art Journal* 55, no. 3 (Autumn 1996): 21–27.
17. For a full chronology of the Imperial Hotel design history, see *The Imperial: The First 100 Years*; and Kathryn Smith, "Frank Lloyd Wright and the Imperial Hotel: A Postscript," *Art Bulletin* 67, no. 2 (June 1, 1985): 296–310.
18. David Stewart, *The Making of a Modern Japanese Architecture: 1868 to the Present* (Tokyo: Kodansha, 1987), pp. 43–47.
19. The precise dating of Wright's Imperial Hotel commission is complex. See Shindō Akashi and Osamu Murai, *Furanku Roido Raito no Teikoku Hoteru=Frank Lloyd Wright: Imperial Hotel* (Tokyo: Kensetsu Shiryō Kenkyūsha, 2004), p. 35.
20. Smith, "Frank Lloyd Wright and the Imperial Hotel: A Postscript," p. 298.
21. For a further discussion of Wright's "Courtyard Public Space" typology, see Robert McCarter, *Frank Lloyd Wright*, *Critical Lives* (London: Reaktion, 2006), pp. 136–59.
22. Birk, *Frank Lloyd Wright's Fifty Views of Japan*, pp. 22–28.
23. Neil Levine, *The Architecture of Frank Lloyd Wright* (Princeton, N.J.: Princeton University Press, 1996), p. 115.
24. Birk, *Frank Lloyd Wright's Fifty Views of Japan*, p. 36.
25. See Meech, *Frank Lloyd Wright and the Art of Japan*, pp. 106–10; and Ron McCrea, *Building Taliesin: Frank Lloyd Wright's Home of Love and Loss* (Madison: Wisconsin Historical Society Press, 2012), pp. 142–45, 194.
26. Wright, *An Autobiography*, p. 214.
27. Ibid., p. 237.
28. For a further discussion of the National Diet Building (which Cram refers to as the Parliament Houses) competition designs, see Jonathon Reynolds, "Japan's Imperial Diet Building," *Art Journal* 55, no. 3 (1996): 38–47.
29. Wright, "In the Cause of Architecture," p. 40.
30. Levine, *The Architecture of Frank Lloyd Wright*, pp. 122–23.
31. Akashi and Murai, *Furanku Roido Raito no Teikoku Hoteru*, p. 34.
32. Wright, *An Autobiography*, p. 247.
33. Ibid., p. 241.
34. For a comprehensive discussion of the hotel's seismic structure, see Joseph Siry, "The Architecture of Earthquake Resistance: Julius Kahn's Truscon Company and Frank Lloyd Wright's Imperial Hotel," *Journal of the Society of Architectural Historians* 67, no. 1 (March 2008): 78–105.
35. *The Imperial: The First 100 Years*, p. 98.
36. Ibid., p. 99.

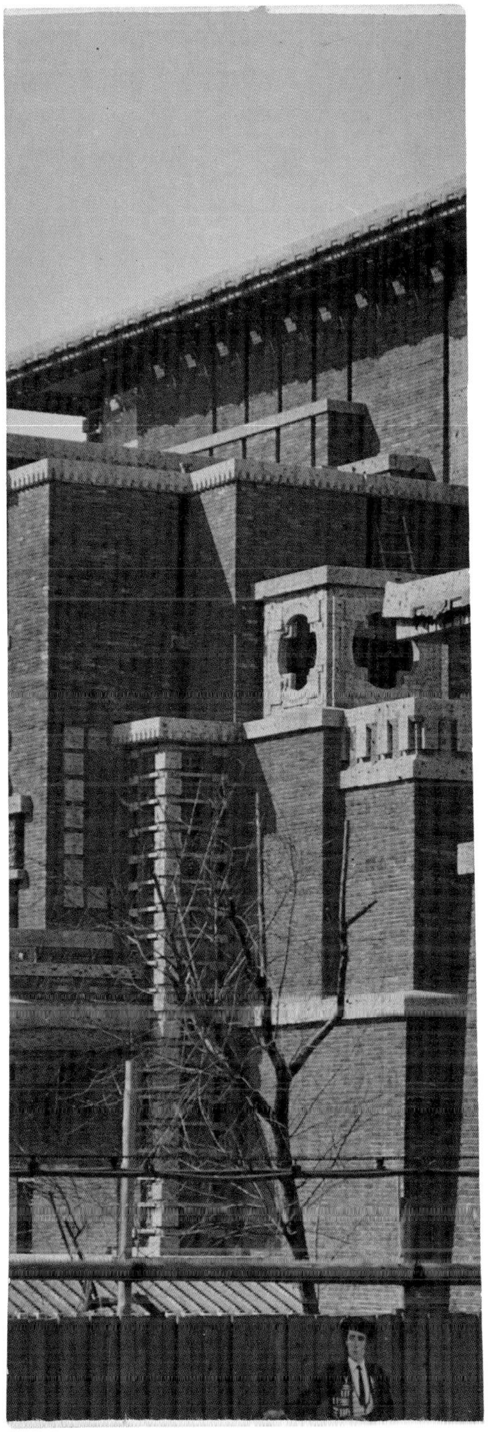

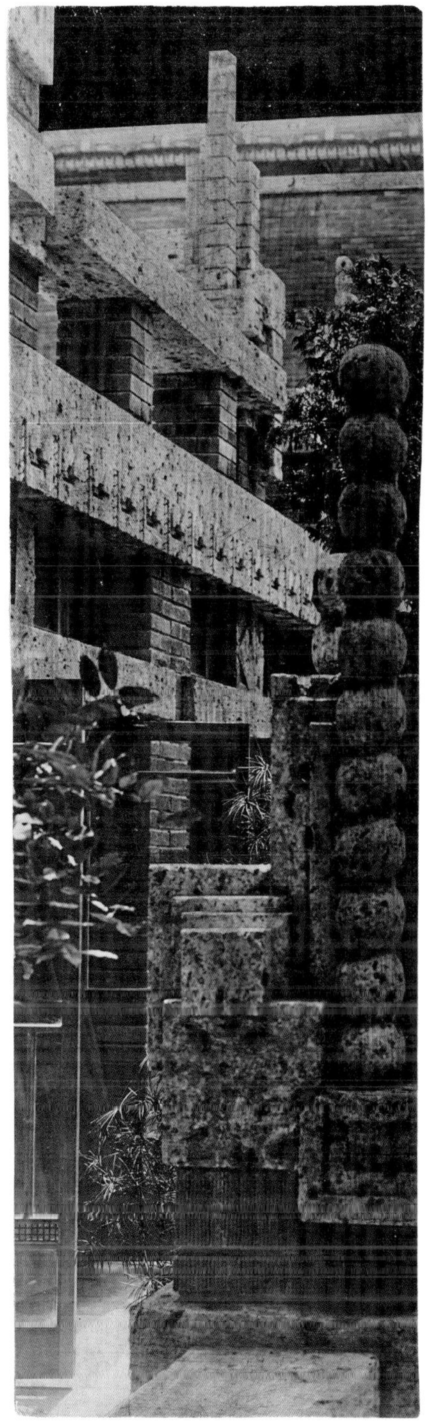

1. and 2. Imperial Hotel, Tokyo. 1913–23. Cropped views of the exterior

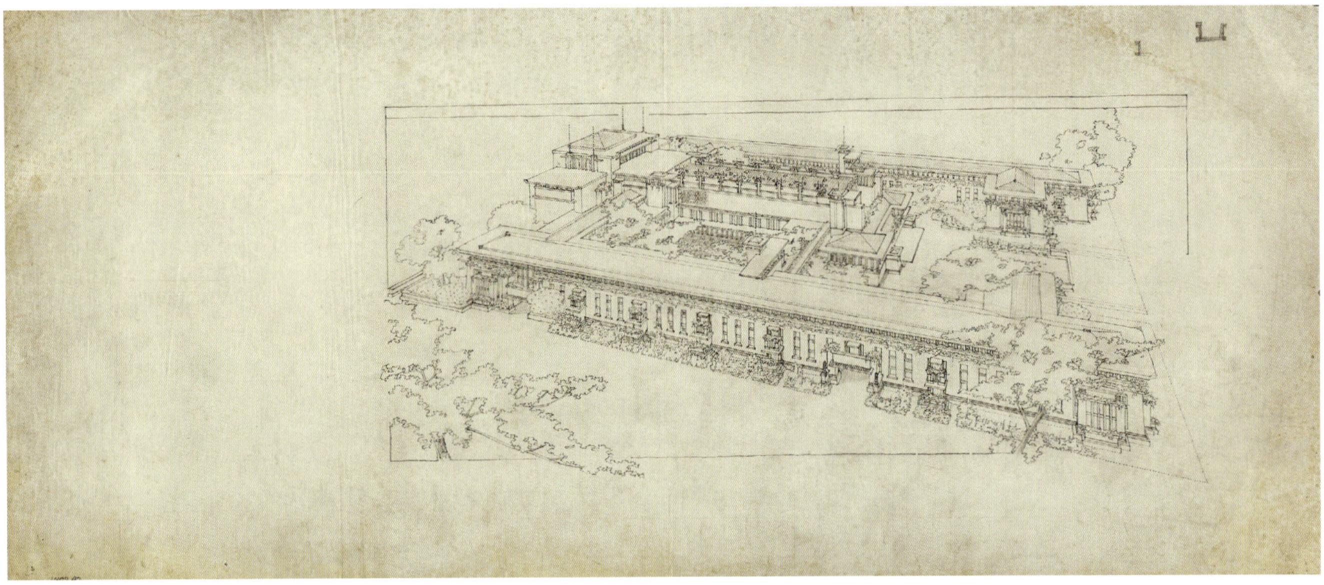

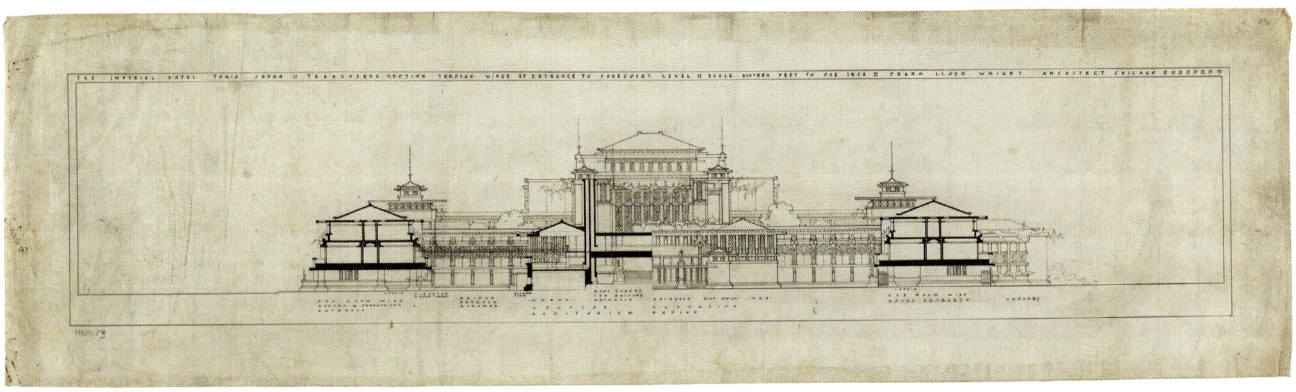

3. Imperial Hotel, Tokyo. 1913–23. Perspective of the preliminary scheme, 1913–14. Ink, colored pencil, and pencil on drafting cloth, 15 ¼ x 35 in. (38.7 x 88.9 cm)

4. Imperial Hotel, Tokyo. 1913–23. Cross-section looking east of the preliminary scheme, 1914–16. Ink and pencil on drafting cloth, 10 ¼ x 32 ⅞ in. (26 x 83.5 cm)

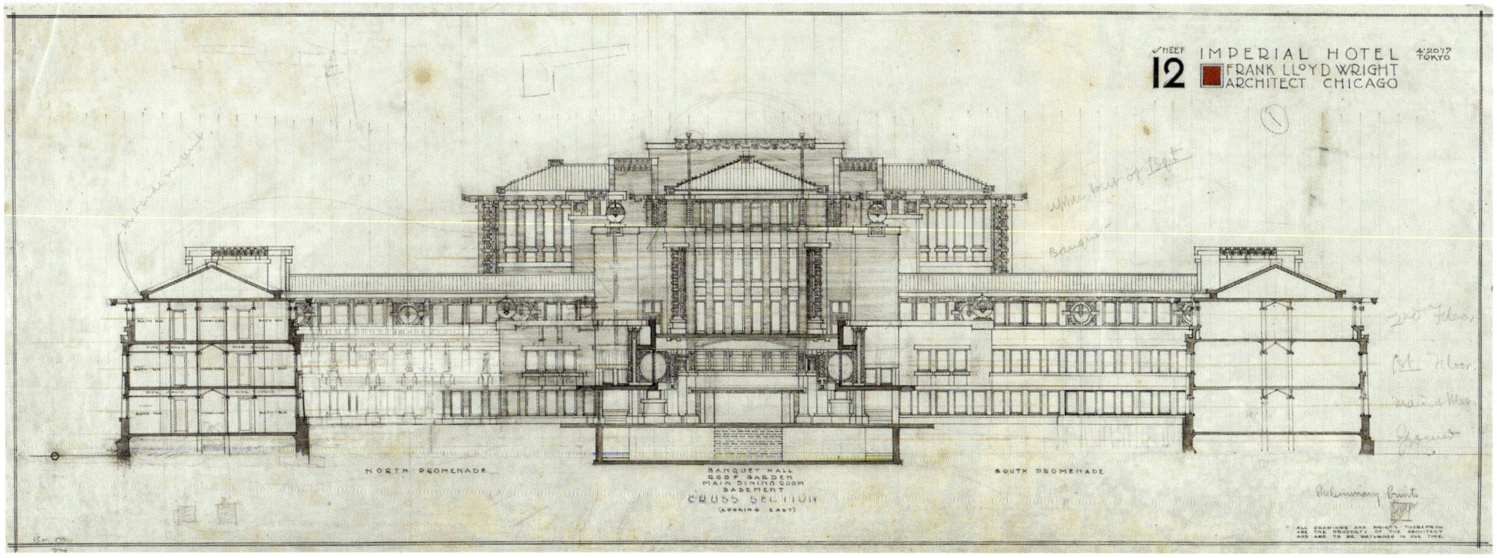

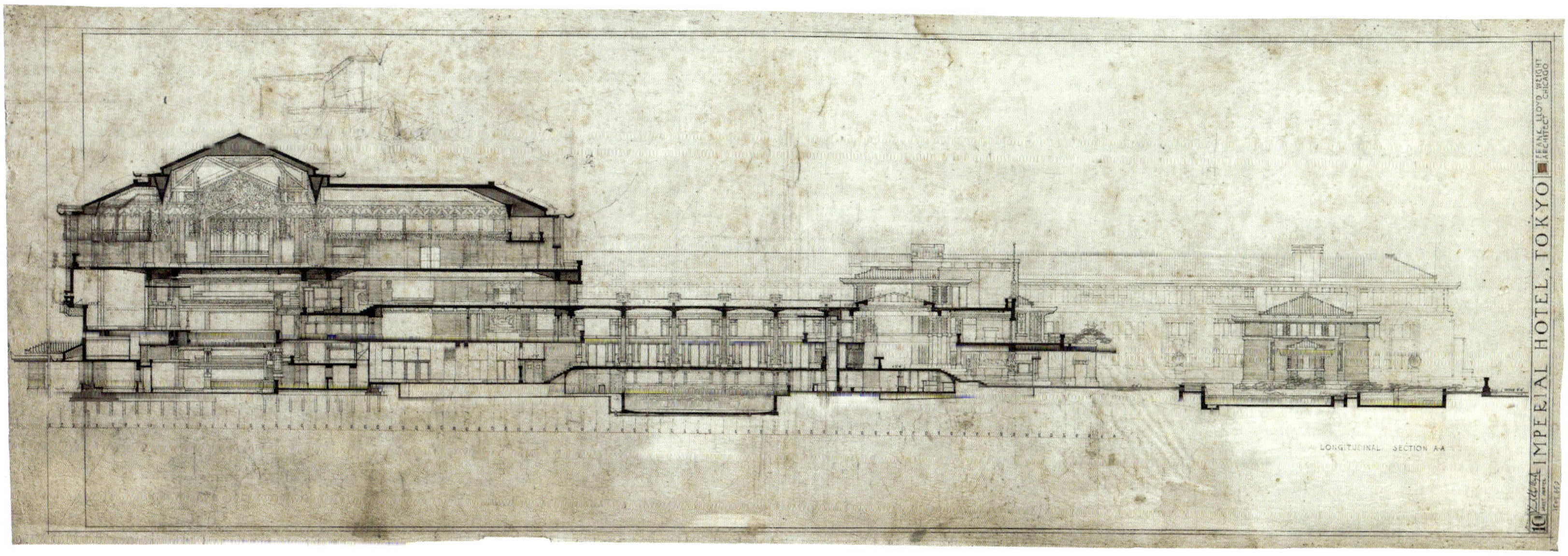

5. Imperial Hotel, Tokyo. 1913–23. Cross section looking east.
Ink, pencil, and colored pencil on drafting cloth, 15 x 40 in. (38.1 x 101.6 cm)

6. Imperial Hotel, Tokyo. 1913–23. Longitudinal section showing Peacock Room at top left.
Ink and pencil on drafting cloth, 20 3/8 x 60 5/8 in. (51.8 x 154 cm)

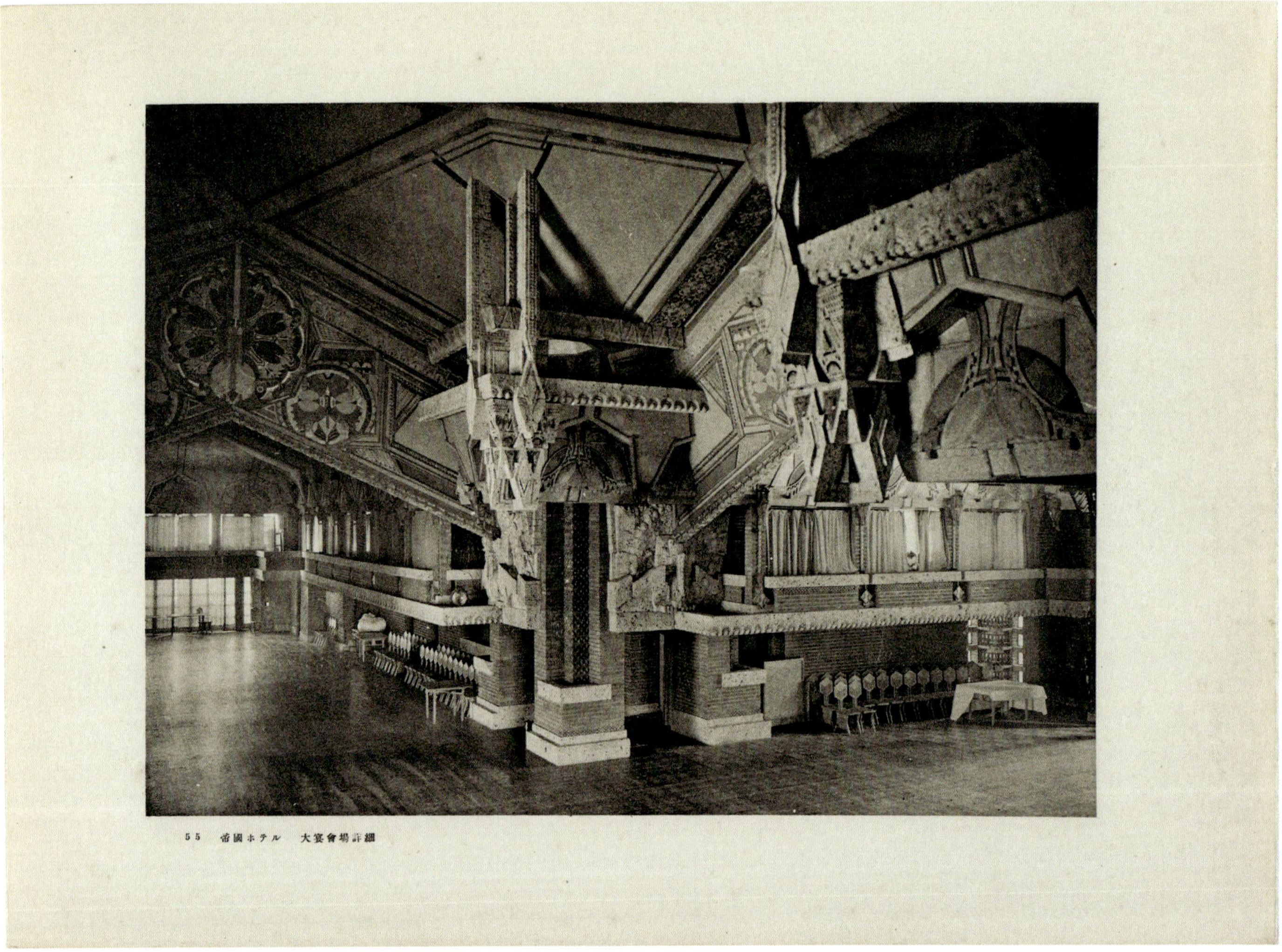

7. Imperial Hotel, Tokyo. 1913–23. Peacock Room.
From *Teikoku Hoteru*, ed. Takanashi Yūtarō (Tokyo: Kōyōsha, 1923)

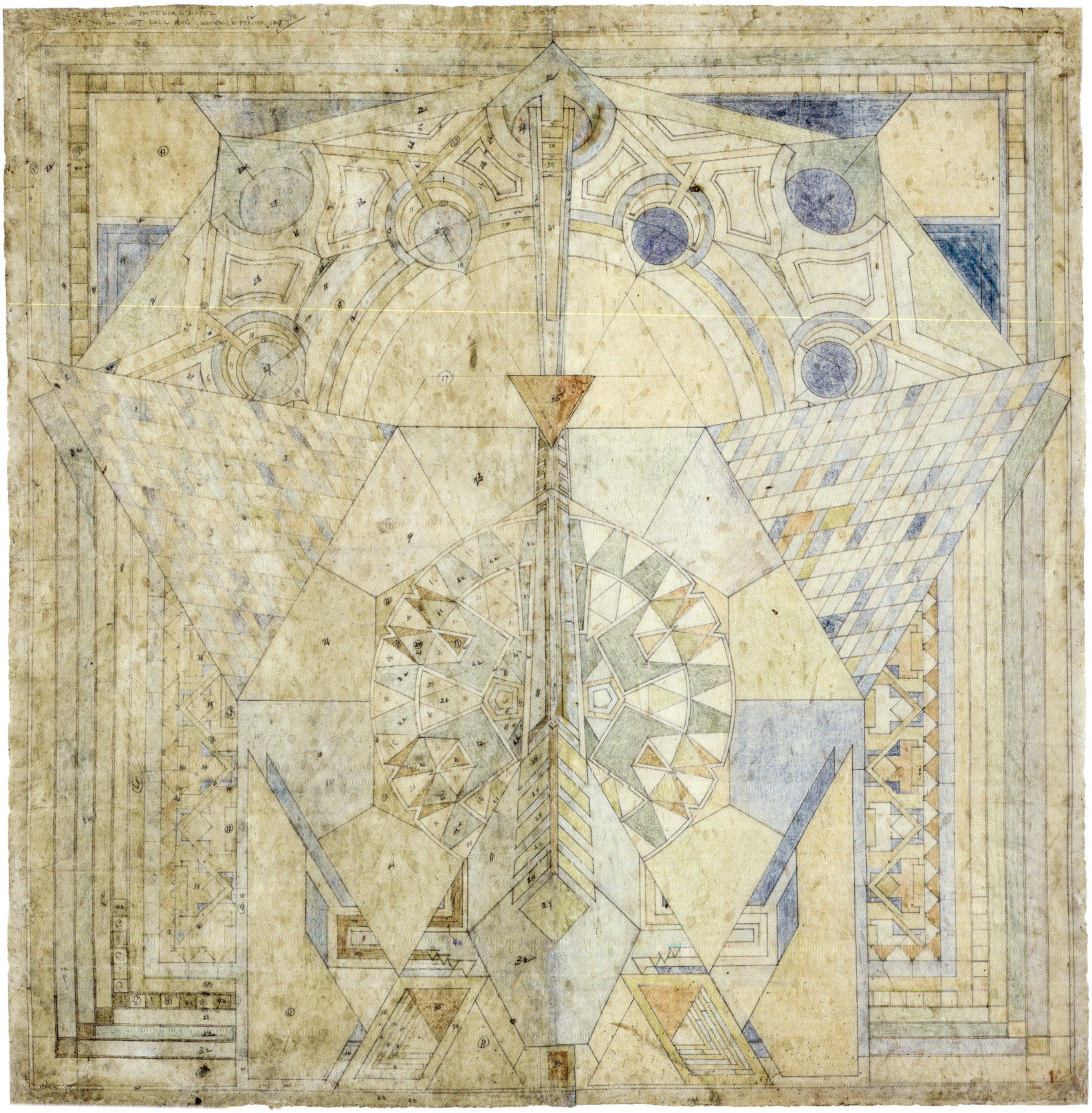

8. Imperial Hotel, Tokyo. 1913–23. Rug design for Peacock Room.
Pencil and colored pencil on tracing paper, 45 1/2 x 45 1/2 in. (115.6 x 115.6 cm)

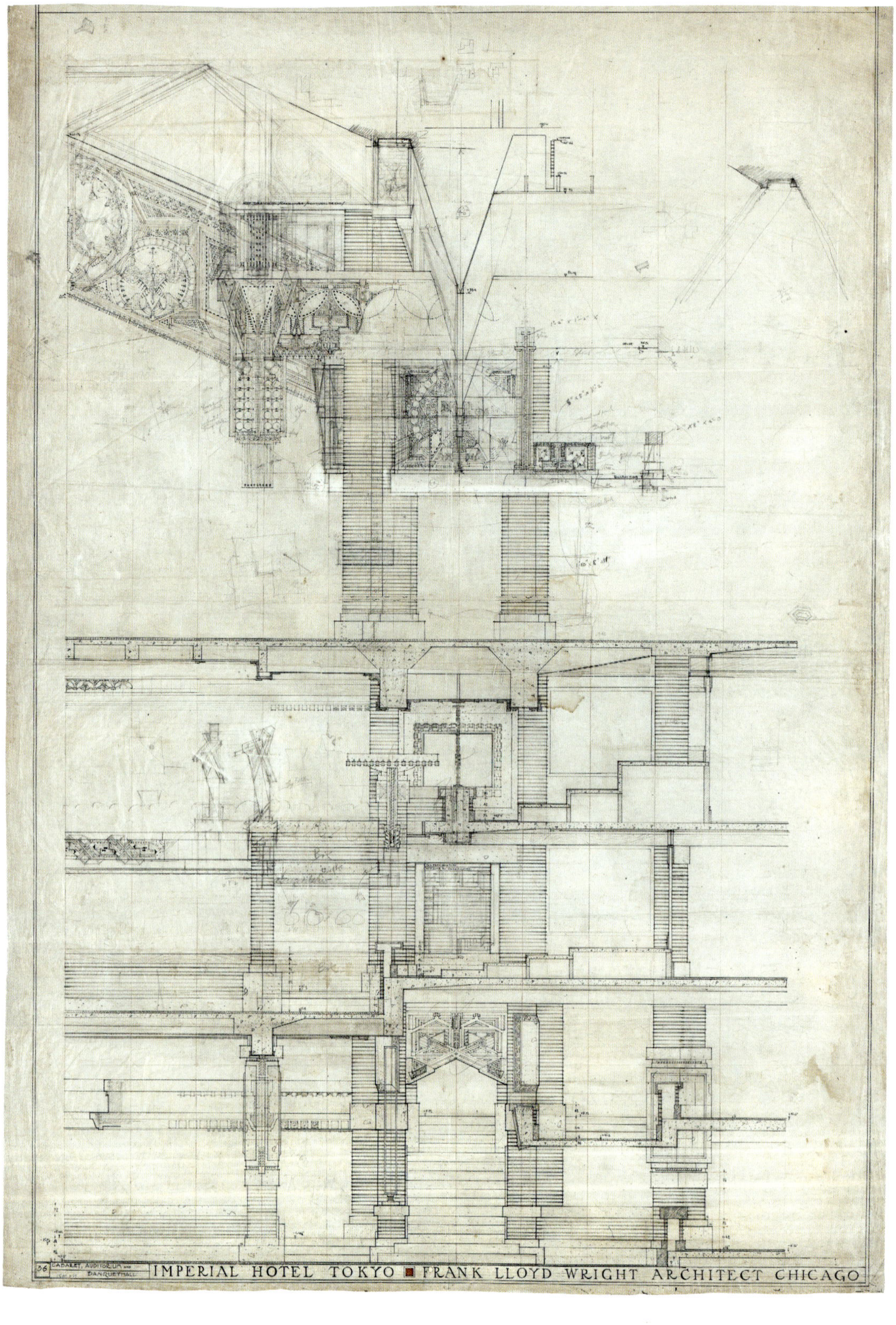

9. Imperial Hotel, Tokyo. 1913–23. Section through the cabaret, auditorium, and banquet hall.
Ink, pencil, and colored pencil on drafting cloth, 58 x 40 ³⁄₄ in. (147.3 x 103.5 cm)

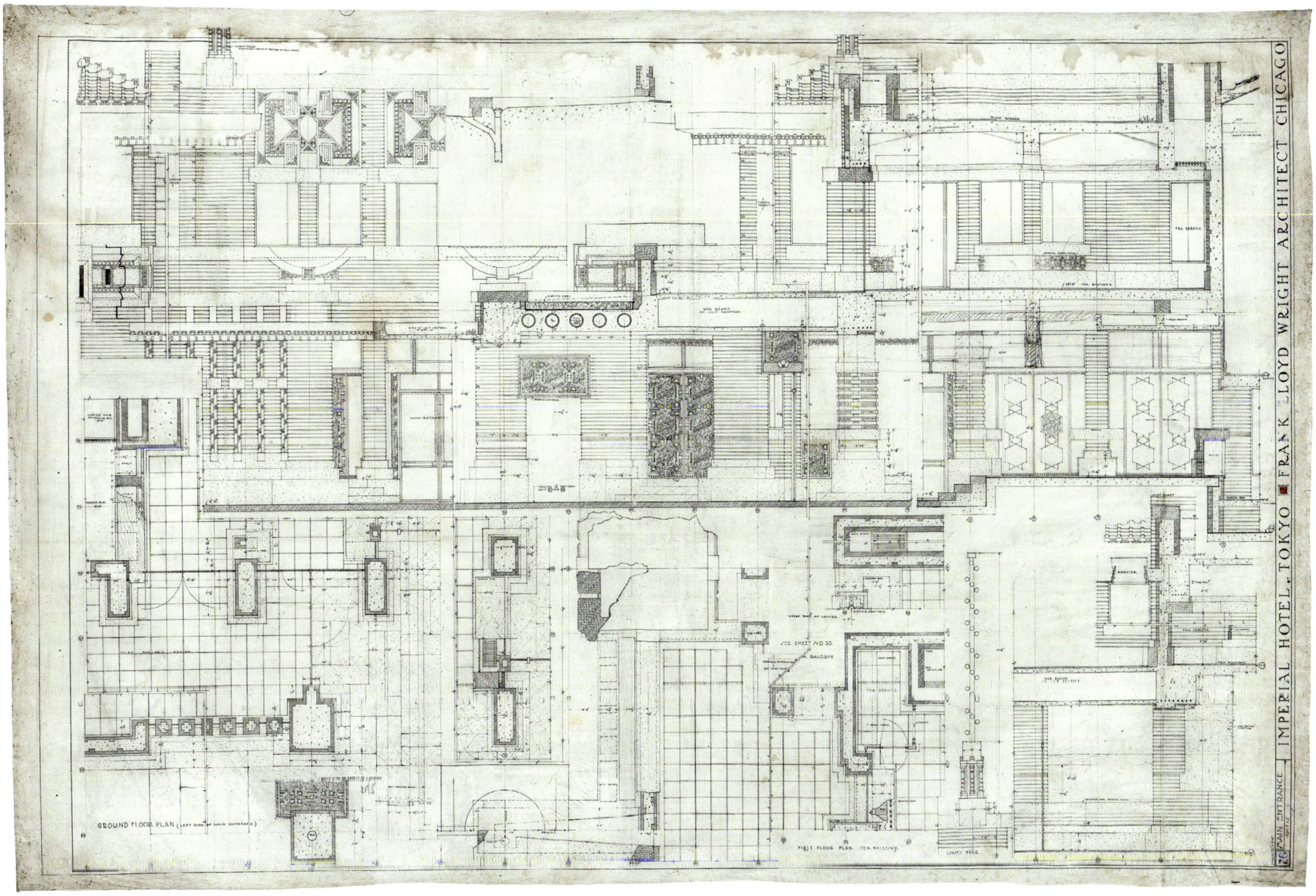

10. Imperial Hotel, Tokyo. 1913–23. Plan and section details of the main entrance.
Ink with pencil on drafting cloth, 40 5/8 x 60 5/8 in. (103.2 x 154 cm)

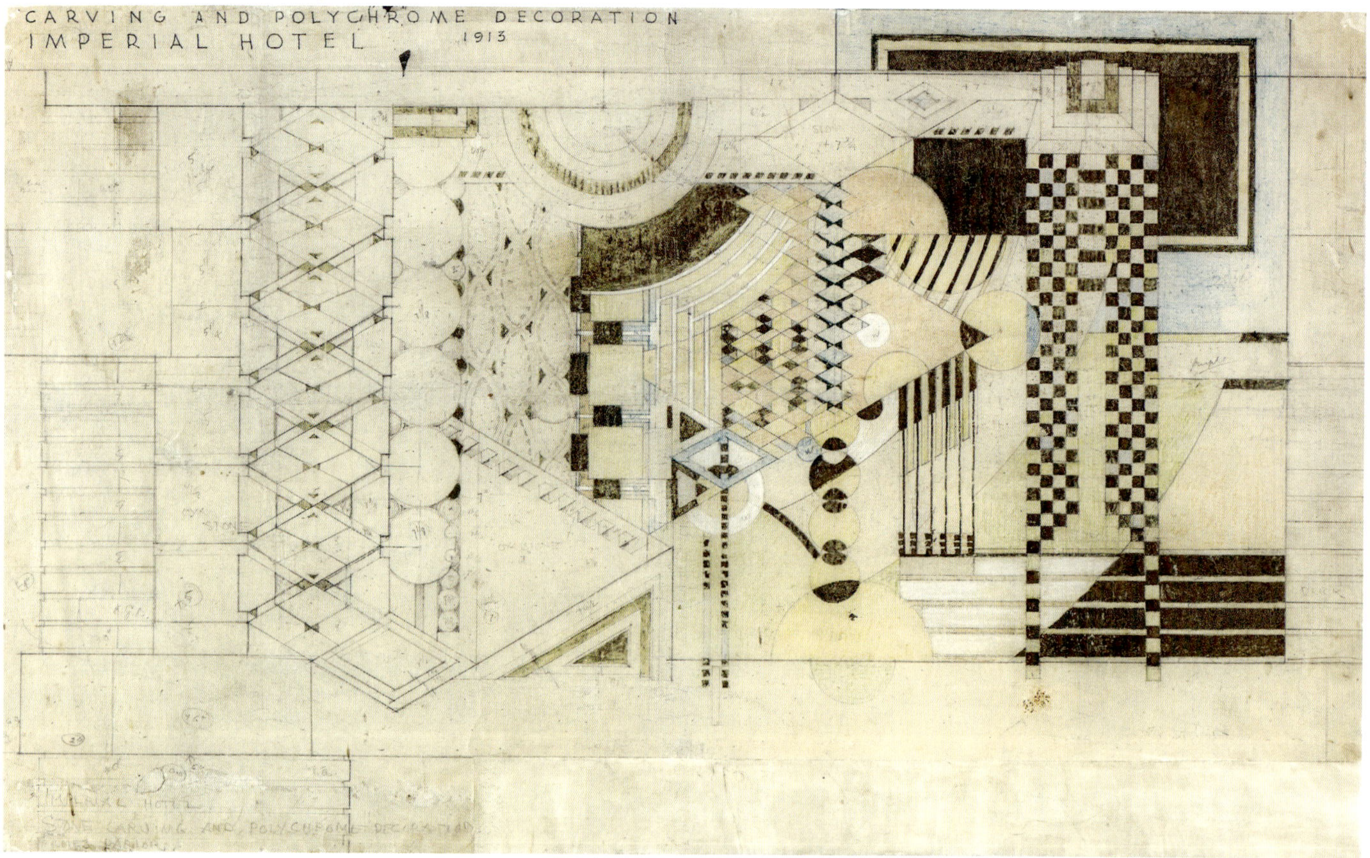

11. Imperial Hotel, Tokyo. 1913–23. Stone carving and polychrome decorations for the north parlor. Gold paint, pencil, and colored pencil on tracing paper, 21 ⅞ x 35 ⅞ in. (55.6 x 91.1 cm)

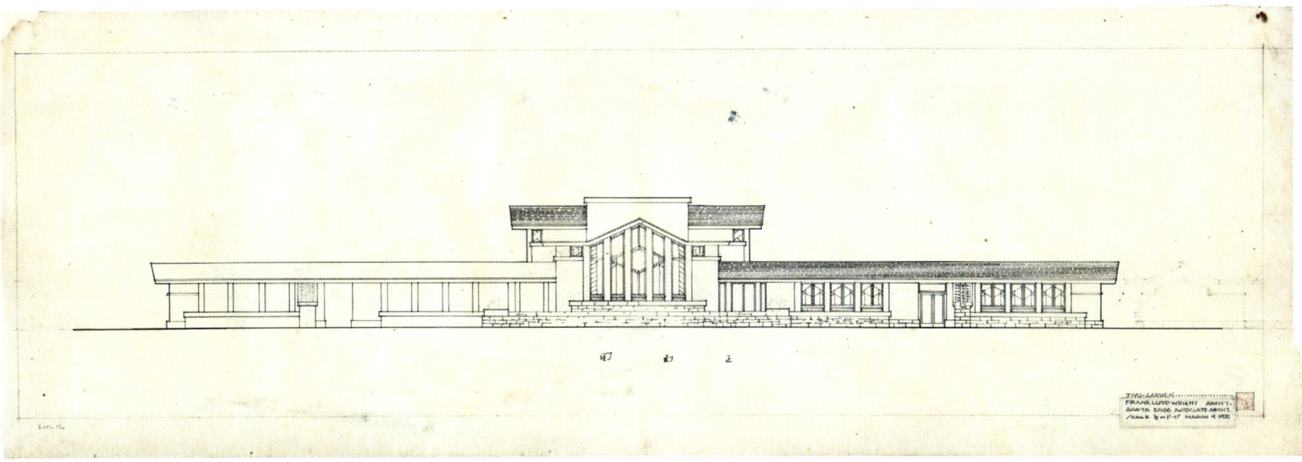

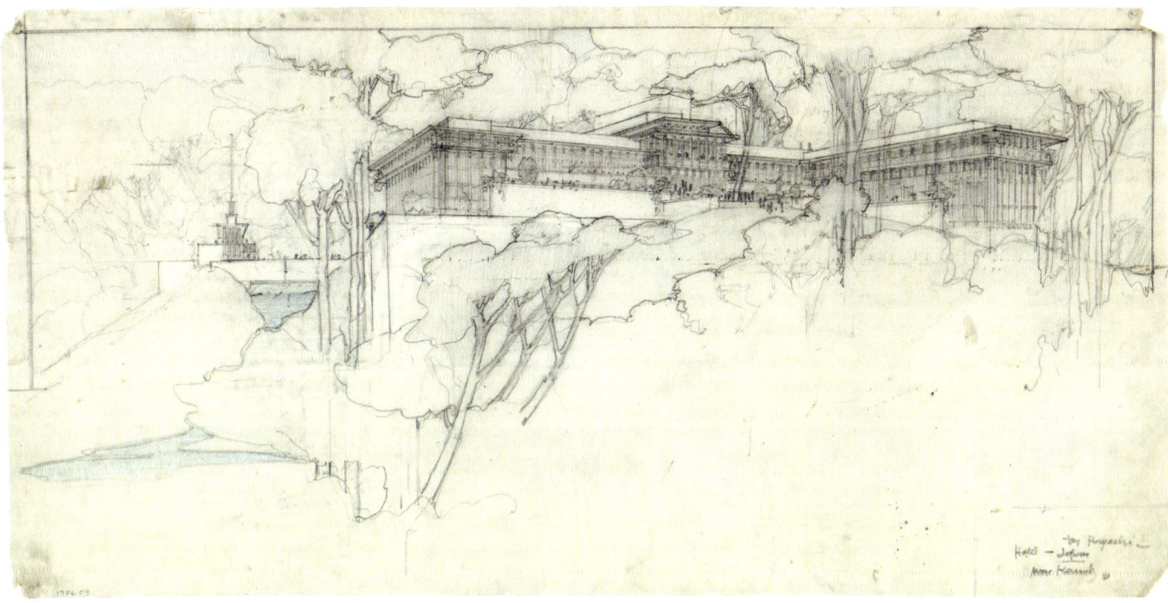

12. Jiyu Gakuen School, Tokyo. 1921. Elevation.
Ink on tracing paper, 10 7/8 x 32 in. (27.6 x 81.3 cm)

13. Odawara Hotel, Japan. Project, 1917. Perspective.
Pencil and colored pencil on tracing paper, 12 1/8 x 24 3/8 in. (30.8 x 61.9 cm)

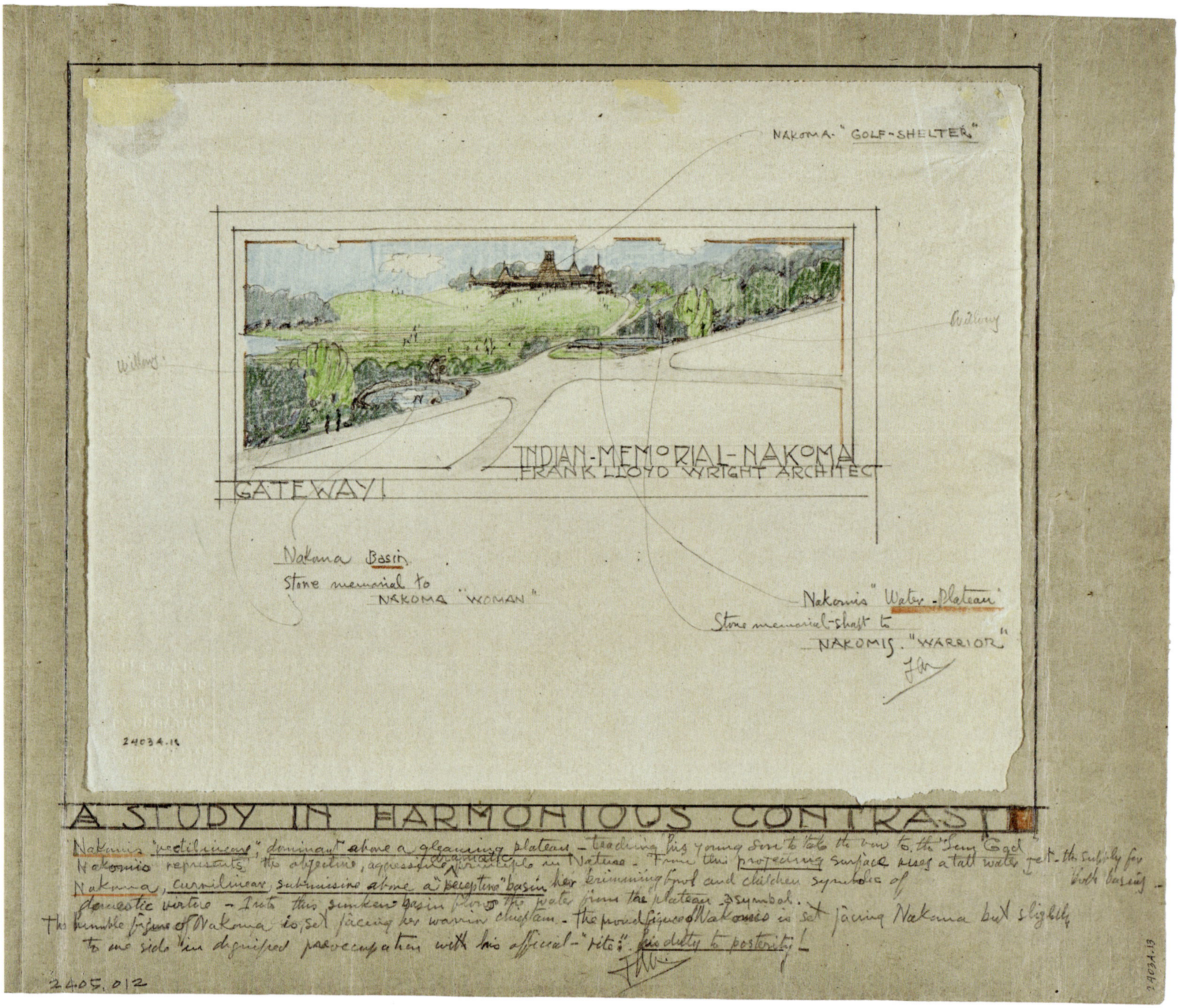

Nakoma Memorial Gateway, Madison, Wisconsin. Project, 1924. Perspective. Pencil and colored pencil on tracing paper mounted on cloth, 11 3/8 x 13 3/8 in. (28.9 x 34 cm)

ELIZABETH S. HAWLEY

"PLAYING INDIAN" AT THE NAKOMA COUNTRY CLUB

In 1923 the Nakoma Country Club, a golf resort in Madison, Wisconsin, commissioned Frank Lloyd Wright to design its clubhouse. Soon afterward, the real estate developers for the surrounding suburb offered to pay for the drive up to the clubhouse, and asked Wright to design a set of sculptures for the gateway. At first glance, Wright's preparatory drawings for these projects are surprisingly clichéd in their reference to American Indians.[1] An early sketch reveals a cluster of tipi-shaped buildings labeled "Nakoma 'Golf-Shelter'" on a hill in the distance, with two sculptures denoted as "Nakoma 'Woman'" and "Nakomis 'Warrior'" positioned by pools on either side of the approaching roadway (opposite). The drawing is small and sketchy, yet it gives a sense of the approach that club members would have taken to reach their clubhouse quarters: turning off the main road onto the club drive, passing the looming figures of Nakoma and Nakomis, winding up the willow-lined path, and finally arriving at the resort. A larger perspective drawing of the clubhouse shows the series of conical tent-like structures more clearly, and scribbled text substantiates Wright's intentional use of American Indian motifs (plate 1). "High tipi," for example, is scrawled in reference to the large assembly room in the center of the complex, whereas the umbrella-covered picnic tables to the lower right—which echo the pointed, tent-like look of the resort buildings—are accompanied by the terms "wigwams" and "tepee." Using these terms interchangeably, Wright imbues the project with a generic sense of "Indianness" rather than referencing any specific form of American Indian architecture.[2]

A 1924 *Wisconsin State Journal* article on Wright's plans continues this conflation of indigenous architectural types, describing the designs as carrying out "the idea of wigwams in an Indian village . . . each surmounted by a tepee-like structure."[3] Yet tipis are conical, portable, and used by Native peoples of the Great Plains area of North America, whereas wigwams are domed, more permanent, and used by Native peoples of the Northeast and Great Lakes region.[4] The article goes on to describe Wright's "wigwams in an Indian Village" as "distinctly American in design." Portraying the Indian aspect of the work as particularly American speaks to a long history of non-Native peoples in the United States crafting a national identity through the performance of Indian-ness. Historian Philip Deloria characterizes this phenomenon as "playing Indian," noting that American Indians—or the rhetorical trope thereof—first gave the otherwise young United States a history and the possibility of a non-European identity, and later offered an experience of American authenticity that quelled anxieties about industrialization and modernization.[5] During the late nineteenth and early twentieth centuries, wealthy Anglo-Americans joined Indian-themed societies, decorated their homes with American Indian wares, and sent their children to summer camps suffused in "Indian" play.

Wright referenced American Indian imagery and designs throughout his career, in keeping with his early rejection of the ornate, classicizing Beaux-Arts approach as well as his subsequent disavowal of the stripped-down, austere International Style. He bemoaned the American turn to the Beaux-Arts during the late nineteenth century, criticizing the resuscitation of classical forms that were neither American nor modern. He called instead for a homegrown American architecture that would reflect the spirit of the times.[6] When the International Style gained traction decades later, Wright declared it another betrayal of American architecture, arguing: "Whatever is really modern in architecture should . . . intensify the individualities of all nations, not strip them of the charms of their innate distinctions."[7] Periodically incorporating American Indian imagery into his works, Wright distanced himself from European architectural traditions by calling upon the long-standing association between Indian-ness and American-ness.[8] Wright rarely took into account the specificities of particular Native peoples' histories and traditions; instead, he turned to his own *perception* of American Indian designs and architectural forms. The "innate distinctions" he drew between nations collapsed in his generalized conception of American Indians.

Wright intended to decorate the interior space of the Nakoma clubhouse tipi (plate 2) with animal symbols of the twelve clans of the Winnebago Tribe, a design feature that would have added a degree of specificity to his American Indian references, since Winnebago peoples had once inhabited the land around Madison.[9] Tipis, however, are more associated with Plains Indians than with the Winnebago, although this discrepancy would have hardly registered for the larger Nakoma community, which had long participated in the broad application of Indian themes to non-Native programs and institutions.[10] By the time Wright presented his plans to the Nakoma members, they had already termed the club property the Reservation, dubbed the area awaiting the clubhouse Wigwam Hill, and given names like Many Scalps, Big Smoke, and Eaglefeather to the various golf greens.[11]

Recognizing that the golf club would raise the value of properties in Nakoma, the Madison Realty Company, which had developed the 225-acre (91-hectare) residential suburb, offered to pay for the approaching roadway and commissioned Wright to produce the large sculptures to be placed at the base of the drive: the 18-foot-tall (5.5-meter-tall) male Nakomis and 16-foot-tall (4.9-meter-tall) female Nakoma (plates 3–5).[12] On the sketch with which this essay begins, Wright labeled the sculptures "A Study in Harmonious Contrast," and the figures reveal gender as well as racial stereotypes. Wright described Nakomis as "rectilinear," "dominant," and representative of "the aggressive, dramatic principle in nature," while he referred to Nakoma as "curvilinear," "submissive," with "brimming bowl and children symbolic of domestic virtue." Nakomis appears to be teaching his son to shoot an arrow at the sun, a rite of manhood that captured the imagination of many non-Native artists.

Two children accompany Nakoma: a daughter at her side, and a small child on her back. Wright's dichotomous language is representative of the way Anglo ideals of masculinity and femininity were foisted upon American Indians. While gender roles among American Indian peoples vary, Wright projects the Western doctrine of separate spheres onto his figures. In this nineteenth-century ideology, men belong in the competitive public sphere encompassing work and politics, whereas women belong in the domestic sphere of home and family.

Wright referred to this sculptural project as "Indian Memorial for Winnebago Camping Grounds."[13] The sculptures themselves, however, reveal his generalizing attitude: Nakomis's headwear resembles a Plains headdress, while the pottery accompanying Nakoma is associated with Pueblo peoples. This imagery further divides the figures along Wright's projection of gender difference: in the early twentieth century, American Indians of the Plains region were characterized as aggressive, warlike, and thus masculine, while Pueblo peoples of the Southwest were viewed as peaceable, domestic, and thus feminine.[14]

Wright rarely acknowledged the influence of American Indians on his work, but living in Chicago at the turn of the century certainly exposed him to popular conceptions of Indian-ness. A number of American Indians, dubbed "show Indians," performed at the 1893 World's Fair in Chicago, which Wright visited. Under the leadership of American anthropologist Frederic Ward Putnam, the Fair's Department of Ethnology put several American Indian peoples on display in an "Indian Village," instructing them to remove all signs of modernity from their self-presentation. Buffalo Bill's Wild West Show, set up just outside the fairgrounds, demanded a similar anachronistic positioning, albeit toward sensationalist entertainment rather than ostensible anthropological education.[15] Wright was also a charter member of the Cliff Dwellers, an Indian-themed Chicago club for "men of artistic and literary tastes."[16] Founded by American author Hamlin Garland in 1907, the Cliff Dwellers' club name "was intended to point a finger toward the ancient cliff-dwelling Indians of the Southwest."[17] The club quarters were called the "khiva," in reference to Pueblo ceremonial spaces, and the interior was decorated with various American Indian motifs. The inauguration of the club included a fire-lighting ceremony and a song penned by Garland that pays homage to "grave warriors" with their "peace pipe."[18] Garland authored works of fiction and nonfiction addressing the struggles of contemporary American Indians. Like other writers and intellectuals of the time, he viewed Indian peoples as a "vanishing race," whose disappearance through annihilation or assimilation seemed imminent. Garland and Wright became close friends; Wright's first wife, Catherine, even declared Garland one of the few friends "able to understand him."[19]

Garland may have introduced Wright to sculptor Hermon Atkins MacNeil, whose pieces adorned some of Wright's early houses. Captivated by the American Indian peoples he came across at the 1893 World's Fair, MacNeil began producing sculptures depicting Indians, which became quite popular. Wright was an early collector of these works. In his autobiography, Wright notes that he decorated "The Garrick," his early offices in the Schiller Building, with MacNeil's sculptures.[20] We also see MacNeil's *A Primitive Chant to the Great Spirit* in an oft-published photograph showing the interior of Wright's Winslow House (1893–94; plate 6), as well as in Wright's drawing of the library for his Dana House (1902–04; plate 7). MacNeil's model for this work was Black Pipe, a Sioux man who had been a performer in Buffalo Bill's Wild West Show during the World's Fair. In need of work after the fair closed, Black Pipe agreed to pose for MacNeil, and he continued working in the sculptor's studio for a year and a half.[21] It was not uncommon for American Indians—often due to a lack of other employment options—to stage themselves to fit stereotypical non-Native conceptions of Indian identity.

In the summer of 1895, MacNeil and Garland traveled throughout New Mexico and Arizona. They observed Pueblo and Zuni ceremonies and dances, and were particularly fascinated by the Snake Dance they saw at Walpi Pueblo. Upon their return to Chicago, MacNeil sculpted *The Moqui Runner*, based on his recollection of the Snake Dance. A cast of this work can be seen in at least one photograph of Wright's home in Oak Park, Illinois.[22]

Photographs of Wright's home also reveal two murals depicting American Indians in the master bedroom, which Wright commissioned from Orlando Giannini.[23] Wright's son John Lloyd Wright recalled: "'Skinny' Giannini from Italy painted American Indians in brilliant colors on the walls of Papa's bedroom. On one wall was a full-length Indian chief peering out over the plains, one hand shading his eyes. On the opposite wall, his squaw stood holding a water jug."[24] Between MacNeil's sculptures and the imagery of Giannini, it is not hard to imagine where Wright sought inspiration when designing Nakoma and Nakomis years later.

Wright was also influenced by the Chicago Arts and Crafts Society, a group he helped inaugurate at Hull House in 1897. Several American Arts and Crafts societies formed during these years, but the Chicago group paid particular attention to American Indian arts and crafts, admiring the way these designs were often abstracted, geometricized forms derived from nature.[25] This imagery dovetailed with the theories of John Ruskin and Owen Jones, important British predecessors to the American Arts and Crafts Movement, whose works had a profound effect on Wright. Ruskin declared that artists and architects must abstract from nature in order to convey the deepest truths, while Jones argued that all ornament must be based on geometric construction, with every form a multiple of a simple base unit.[26] As William Cronon has argued, to these influences on Wright we must add Ralph Waldo Emerson's call for artists to transform the raw material of nature into something more perfect and universally harmonious, as well as Eugène Viollet-le-Duc's insistence that architects develop their style by closely observing preexisting universal principles in nature. Cronon also cites the early influence of German educational philosopher Friedrich Froebel's "gifts," which Wright's mother purchased for him as a young boy. These included geometric blocks used by children to create modular patterns and constructions, teaching that Euclidian geometries undergird all natural forms.[27]

Such theories of nature-inspired geometric forms resonated with the language and imagery found in the articles promoting American Indian works that pepper Arts and Crafts journals with which Wright would have been familiar. Wright's son Lloyd recalled finding copies of *House Beautiful* and *The Craftsman* in his father's office and drafting studio at Oak Park, and Wright himself had published in *Brush and Pencil*.[28] In that same journal, E. A. Burbank praised Indian craftspeople for their works' truth to nature: "Be the patterns what they may, the Indian finds the prototype of all his curves and colors in the natural objects with which he is familiar."[29] This point is illustrated with a photograph of a Chippewa medicine bag, which features a geometricized floral design (fig. 1).

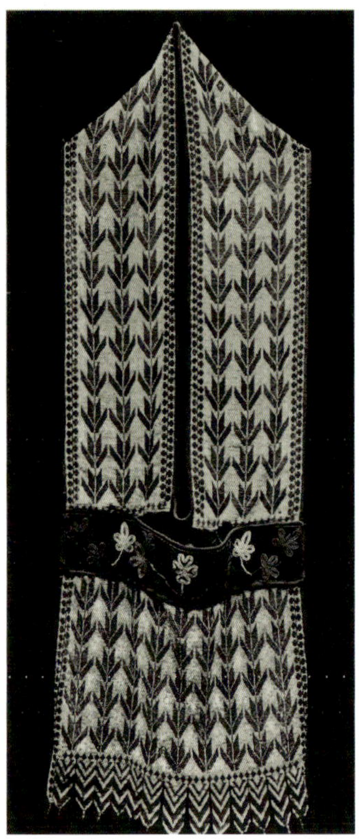

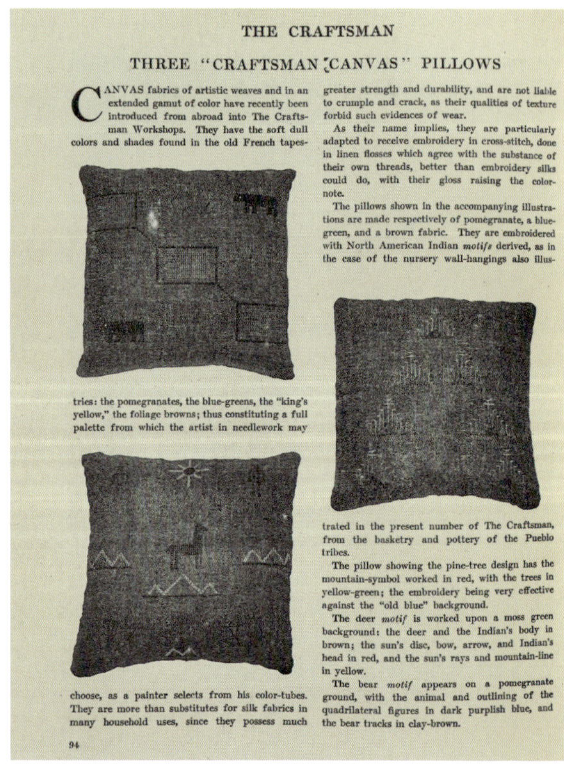

THE CRAFTSMAN

THREE "CRAFTSMAN CANVAS" PILLOWS

CANVAS fabrics of artistic weaves and in an extended gamut of color have recently been introduced from abroad into The Craftsman Workshops. They have the soft dull colors and shades found in the old French tapestries: the pomegranates, the blue-greens, the "king's yellow," the foliage browns; thus constituting a full palette from which the artist in needlework may choose, as a painter selects from his color-tubes. They are more than substitutes for silk fabrics in many household uses, since they possess much greater strength and durability, and are not liable to crumple and crack, as their qualities of texture forbid such evidences of wear.

As their name implies, they are particularly adapted to receive embroidery in cross-stitch, done in linen flosses which agree with the substance of their own threads, better than embroidery silks could do, with their gloss raising the color-note.

The pillows shown in the accompanying illustrations are made respectively of pomegranate, a blue-green, and a brown fabric. They are embroidered with North American Indian *motifs* derived, as in the case of the nursery wall-hangings also illustrated in the present number of The Craftsman, from the basketry and pottery of the Pueblo tribes.

The pillow showing the pine-tree design has the mountain-symbol worked in red, with the trees in yellow-green; the embroidery being very effective against the "old blue" background.

The deer *motif* is worked upon a moss green background: the deer and the Indian's body in brown; the sun's disc, bow, arrow, and Indian's head in red, and the sun's rays and mountain-line in yellow.

The bear *motif* appears on a pomegranate ground, with the animal and outlining of the quadrilateral figures in dark purplish blue, and the bear tracks in clay-brown.

94

Fig. 1. "Chippewa Medicine-Bag." From E. A. Burbank, "Studies of Art in American Life—III: In Indian Tepees," *Brush and Pencil* 7, no. 2 (November 1900)

Fig. 2. "Three 'Craftsman Canvas' Pillows." From *The Craftsman* 5, no. 1 (October 1903). Avery Architectural & Fine Arts Library, Columbia University, New York

The design is comparable to Wright's light screens for Dana House, which include abstracted, geometric representations of sumac (plate 8). Arts and Crafts journals also frequently featured items inspired by American Indian designs, but produced by non-Native craftsmen, as in *The Craftsman* article "Three 'Craftsman Canvas' Pillows" (fig. 2). The "pillow showing the pine-tree design" bears some resemblance to one of Wright's 1906 rug designs (plate 9).

Advertisements for American Indian wares often featured in these Arts and Crafts publications. *House Beautiful* circulated ads such as "The Coffeen Indian Collection," which displays a room teeming with American Indian products (fig. 3). Traders like Coffeen ran brisk catalog businesses, although department stores in larger cities such as Chicago also sold these items. Navajo rugs—noticeably given pride of place in Coffeen's advertisement—were particularly popular.[30] Historical photographs reveal that Wright decorated his personal spaces, such as his Oak Park studio and his desert shelter at Ocatilla, with Navajo rugs (plate 10 and fig. 4).

In 1915 Wright traveled to San Diego to visit the Panama-California Exposition, where he was introduced to a theory of a pan-American indigenous culture encompassing American Indians as well as Mesoamerican peoples. We know that Wright saw the Maya exhibit there, and given his interest in American Indians, he likely also visited the Painted Desert exhibit. Like the Indian Village at the 1893 World's Fair, this exhibit put living American Indian peoples—primarily of the Southwest—on display. Anthropologist Edgar Hewett was tasked with illustrating "the progress of man"; but unlike most anthropologists in 1893, Hewett viewed American Indians not as inferior peoples, but as present-day examples of America's grand ancient past, who should be seen as akin to the peoples of European classical antiquity. In conceptualizing this American classical world, he sought to connect ancient Mesoamerican civilizations with contemporary North American Indians, arguing that "all native American remains, whether of plains tribes, mound-builders, cliff-dwellers, Pueblo, Navaho, Toltec, Aztec, Maya, Inca, are just the works of the Indian."[31]

While this was an oversimplification, it accounts for the imagery found in some of Wright's subsequent projects, such as the sculptural frieze at the Bogk House (1916–17) in Milwaukee. A glittering partial rendering of the frieze in watercolor, gouache, and metallic paint shows two winged figures hovering over a ledge (plate 11). Their blocky, geometric forms are frequently compared to those of Maya as well as Aztec motifs.[32] However, the wings of the figures also resemble the eagle imagery prominent in the Pueblo Eagle Dance—which involves two men, costumed as eagles, replicating the movements of the birds—one of the most popular ceremonial dances performed at the 1915 Exposition (fig. 5). The straight rows of feathers adorning their arms resemble the winged appearance of the Bogk House figures.

Nakoma and Nakomis, which Wright designed less than ten years later, reveal no discernible Mayan sources, as he was likely trying to keep to the more narrowly defined American Indian themes of the Nakoma Country Club. While the clubhouse and sculptures were never built in Nakoma, Wright's Indian figures continue to appear in various ways in his work.[33] His designs for the Taliesin Fellowship Complex (begun 1932–33) in Spring Green, Wisconsin, include several renderings of the fellows' dormitories, and small Nakoma figurines can be found in most of them, perched on shelves and nightstands (plate 12). Their placement resembles the position of MacNeil's Indian sculptures in Wright's early interiors. And the appropriation went

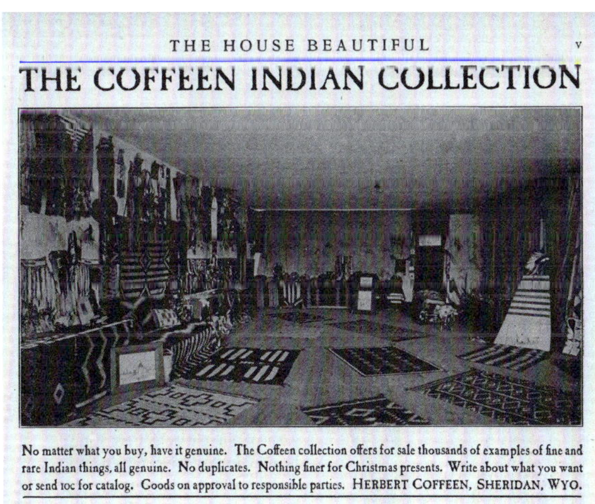

Fig. 3. "The Coffeen Indian Collection." Advertisement in *House Beautiful* 15, no. 6 (May 1904)

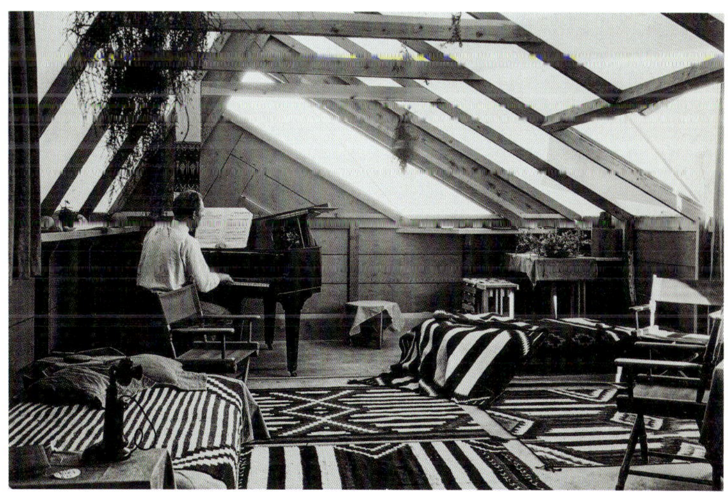

Fig. 4. Ocatilla (Wright camp), Phoenix South (formerly Salt River) Mountains, Phoenix, Arizona. 1929. Interior of Wright's living quarters

beyond décor: When German architect Erich Mendelsohn visited Wright at Taliesin in 1924, he was asked to don "a fantastic garment with something Indian about it," which included bark shoes, a staff, gloves, and a tomahawk. Wright wore something similar, and they went for a walk in the surrounding hills—land Mendelsohn described as "abandoned by the redskins."[34]

But of all Wright's projects, Taliesin West, the western outpost of the Fellowship in Scottsdale, Arizona, is the one that scholars most often associate with his interest in American Indians.[35] Built on lands once inhabited by the ancient Hohokam peoples, Wright took traces of this prehistoric culture into consideration when devising site plans. Upon finding a number of boulders incised with petroglyphs, Wright incorporated them into the complex. The Hohokam symbols on these stones included a double-square spiral, which Wright famously reproduced in a deep red hue as the logo of the Taliesin Fellowship.

A sketch shows that Wright also designed a "totem pole for private garden court at Taliesin West" (plate 13).[36] There is no extant totem pole at Taliesin West, but archival photographs show that Wright's design indeed came to fruition, and for a time a wooden totem structure existed on the grounds (plate 14). This indigenous reference is less geographically specific than that of the Hohokam: while totem poles have become an enduring stereotype of Indian-ness, they are produced by American Indians of the Pacific Northwest, far from the Arizona desert. The poles are a way of marking ancestral histories and material wealth, and they cannot be read without extensive knowledge of the families they are meant to represent.

Totem poles, along with tipis and Plains headdresses, could be found in many twentieth-century summer camps, where the Woodcraft Boys, Camp Fire Girls, and other youth groups engaged in "playing Indian" as a way of escaping modern life and embracing the invigorating, primitive existence associated with American Indians.[37] Taliesin West can itself be seen as a camp of sorts, the desert outpost to which Wright's apprentices decamped each winter to escape the harsh Wisconsin temperatures. Fellows in their first year were required to live in canvas tents resembling tipis, after which they were expected to build their own living spaces. Just as younger campers were expected to exhibit the self-reliance and wilderness survival skills associated with American Indians, so too were Wright's fellows. Wright's totem pole fits this rhetoric: he produced it himself in the context of a seasonal residence that served as an escape from civilization, a space he associated with a symbolic, primordial indigenousness.

Wright's lack of concern for cultural specificity in his American Indian references belies his deep deliberation on other aspects of his architecture, such as the location of his buildings and how best to situate them in the landscape. Throughout his career, he retained a concept of universal Indian-ness from which he drew when "playing Indian" in his designs and décor. Wright's appreciation for the American Indian peoples from whom he selected design motifs did not extend to their particularized histories and traditions, and what was no doubt a genuine respect for their imagery and designs was tempered by the indiscriminately broad lens through which he viewed American Indian cultures.

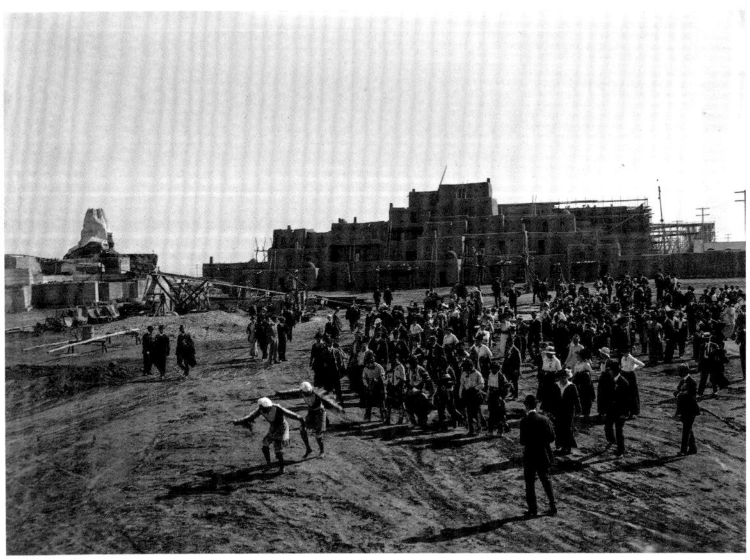

Fig. 5. Eagle Dance at the Painted Desert exhibit, Panama-California Exposition, San Diego. 1915. Jesse Nusbaum Collection, Palace of the Governors Photo Archives (NMHM/DCA), Santa Fe

Notes

1. While it is always preferable to refer to specific Native communities Pueblo, Navajo, etc. such cultural specificity is impossible in this essay, which addresses Frank Lloyd Wright's generalized conception of "Indian-ness" writ large, rather than the actualities of particular peoples. I deliberated over the two most commonly accepted—albeit both flawed—terms, "Native American" and "American Indian." Taking my cue from Choctaw scholar Devon Abbott Mihesuah, I have chosen to use the terms "American Indian" and "Native." Devon Abbott Mihesuah, *So You Want to Write About American Indians? A Guide for Writers, Students, and Scholars* (Lincoln: University of Nebraska Press, 2005), pp. xi–xii.

2. I use the term "Indian-ness"—and occasionally "Indian"—to refer to the Anglo construction of a monolithic, stereotypical American Indian identity. For the classic text on this subject, see Robert F. Berkhofer, *The White Man's Indian: Images of the American Indian from Columbus to the Present* (New York: Knopf, 1978).

3. "Unique Lodge, Plan in Nakoma," *Wisconsin State Journal*, August 4, 1924, p. 2.

4. Bently Spang, "Of Tipis and Stereotypes," in *Tipi: Heritage of the Great Plains* (Seattle: University of Washington Press, 2011), p. 110.

5. Philip J. Deloria, *Playing Indian* (New Haven, Conn.: Yale University Press, 1998).

6. Frank Lloyd Wright, "The Architect," *Brickbuilder* 9 (June 1900): 124–28.

7. Frank Lloyd Wright, "Frank Lloyd Wright Speaks Up," *House Beautiful* (July 1953): 88.

8. See Deloria, *Playing Indian*, pp. 181–91.

9. See "Unique Lodge, Plan in Nakoma"; and Mary Jane Hamilton, "Wright's Nakoma Country Club: An Unrealized Masterpiece," *Journal of Historic Madison* 7 (1981–82): 10.

10. Mary Jane Hamilton, "The Nakoma Country Club," in *Frank Lloyd Wright and Madison: Eight Decades of Artistic and Social Interaction* (Madison, Wis.: Elvehjem Museum of Art, 1990), p. 77.

11. Ibid.

12. Henry Wadsworth Longfellow refers to Nokomis in his poem "The Song of Hiawatha" (1855). Wright was likely aware of this reference, although he describes Nakomis as a warrior, while Longfellow's Nokomis is an old woman.

13. 2405.013, Frank Lloyd Wright Foundation Archives (The Museum of Modern Art | Avery Architectural & Fine Arts Library, Columbia University, New York).

14. Elizabeth Cromley, "Masculine/Indian," *Winterthur Portfolio* 31, no. 4 (Winter 1996): 265.

15. Rosalyn R. LaPier and David R. M. Beck, *City Indian: Native American Activism in Chicago, 1893–1934* (Lincoln: University of Nebraska Press, 2015), pp. 17–33.

16. Wright, letter to the Cliff Dwellers, July 12, 1947, Cliff Dwellers Records, The Newberry Library, Chicago; and Henry Regnery, *The Cliff Dwellers: The History of a Chicago Cultural Institution* (Chicago: Chicago Historical Bookworks, 1990), p. 9.

17. Regnery, *The Cliff Dwellers*, p. 7.

18. Ibid., pp. 13, 16–17.

19. Robert C. Twombly, *Frank Lloyd Wright: His Life and His Architecture* (New York: John Wiley & Sons, 1979), p. 120.

20. Frank Lloyd Wright, *An Autobiography* (New York: Longmans, Green, 1932), p. 147.

21. J. Walker McSpadden, *Famous Sculptors of America* (Freeport, N.Y.: Books for Libraries Press, 1924), p. 312.

22. 8901.029, Wright Foundation Archives (MoMA | Avery).

23. 8901.018 and 8901.033, Wright Foundation Archives (MoMA | Avery).

24. John Lloyd Wright, *My Father Who Is on Earth* (New York: G. P. Putnam's Sons, 1946), p. 34.

25. Judith A. Barter, *Window on the West: Chicago and the Art of the New Frontier, 1890–1940* (New York: Hudson Hills Press, 2003), pp. 53–54.

26. John Ruskin, *The Seven Lamps of Architecture* (2nd ed., 1880; reprint ed., New York: Dover, 1989), p. 105; Owen Jones, *The Grammar of Ornament* (1856; reprint ed., London: B. Quaritch, 1910), p. 5.

27. William Cronon, "Inconsistent Unity: The Passion of Frank Lloyd Wright," in *Frank Lloyd Wright: Architect* (New York: The Museum of Modern Art, 1994), pp. 8–31.

28. David Gebhard and Harriette Von Breton, *Lloyd Wright, Architect: 20th Century Architecture in an Organic Exhibition* (Santa Barbara: University of California, Santa Barbara Art Gallery, 1971), p. 15.

29. E. A. Burbank, "Studies of Art in American Life—III: In Indian Tepees" *Brush and Pencil* 7 no. 2 (November 1900): 76.

30. Erika Marie Bsumek, *Indian-Made: Navajo Culture in the Marketplace, 1868–1940* (Lawrence: University Press of Kansas, 2008).

31. Edgar L. Hewett, "America's Archaeological Heritage" *Art and Archaeology* 4, no. 6 (December 1916): 259.

32. Dimitri Tselos, "Exotic Influences in Frank Lloyd Wright," *Magazine of Art* 47 (April 1953): 167, 184; Anthony Alofsin, *Frank Lloyd Wright: The Lost Years, 1910–1922* (Chicago: The University of Chicago Press, 1993), pp. 251–52.

33. Neither the original clubhouse nor the sculptures were built. However, in 1995 Dariel and Peggy Garner contacted the Taliesin Associated Architects to design a clubhouse for a planned golf resort in Northern California. Upon seeing the original Nakoma plans, they asked the architects to use them as a basis for their designs. The project—which included both the clubhouse and the sculptures—was completed in 2001. See Douglas M. Steiner, *Frank Lloyd Wright's Nakoma Clubhouse and Sculptures: A Historic Perspective* (Edmonds, Wash.: Milbourn, 2013), p. 27.

34. Eric Mendelsohn, "A Visit with Wright (1924)," in *Writings on Wright: Selected Comment on Frank Lloyd Wright*, ed. H. Allen Brooks (Cambridge, Mass.: MIT Press, 1981), p. 7.

35. Neil Levine, *The Architecture of Frank Lloyd Wright* (Princeton, N.J.: Princeton University Press, 1996), pp. 255–97.

36. Wright also referred to the cinema-theater space at Taliesin West as a kiva, echoing the Cliff Dwellers' characterization of their club quarters.

37. Abigail A. Van Slyck, *A Manufactured Wilderness: Summer Camps and the Shaping of American Youth, 1890–1960* (Minneapolis: University of Minnesota, 2006), pp. 169–213.

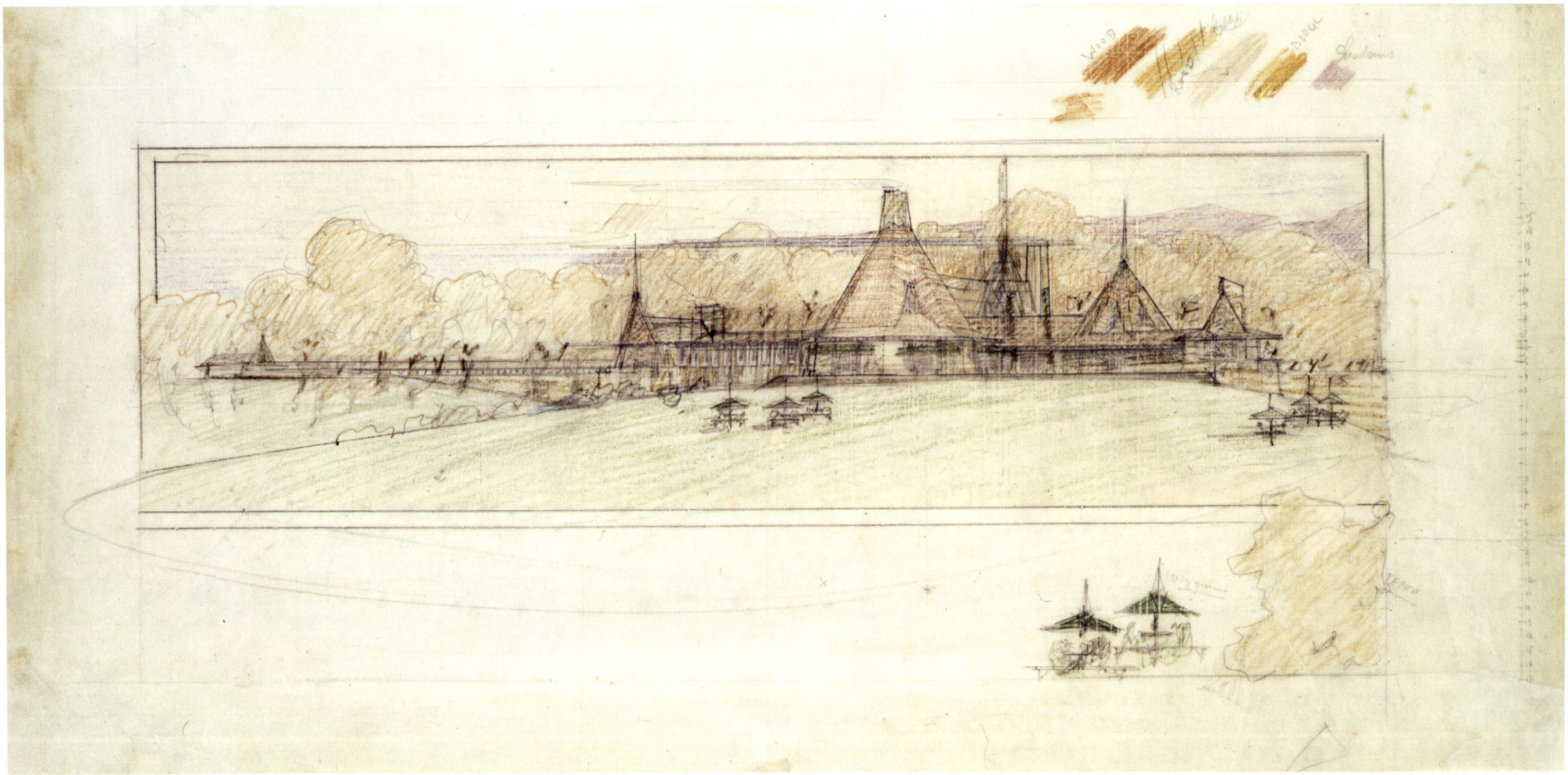

1. Nakoma Country Club, Madison, Wisconsin. Project, 1923–24. Perspective of the clubhouse. Graphite and colored pencil on tracing paper, 13 ¼ x 27 ⅞ in. (33.7 x 70.8 cm). Prints and Photographs Division, Library of Congress, Washington, D.C.

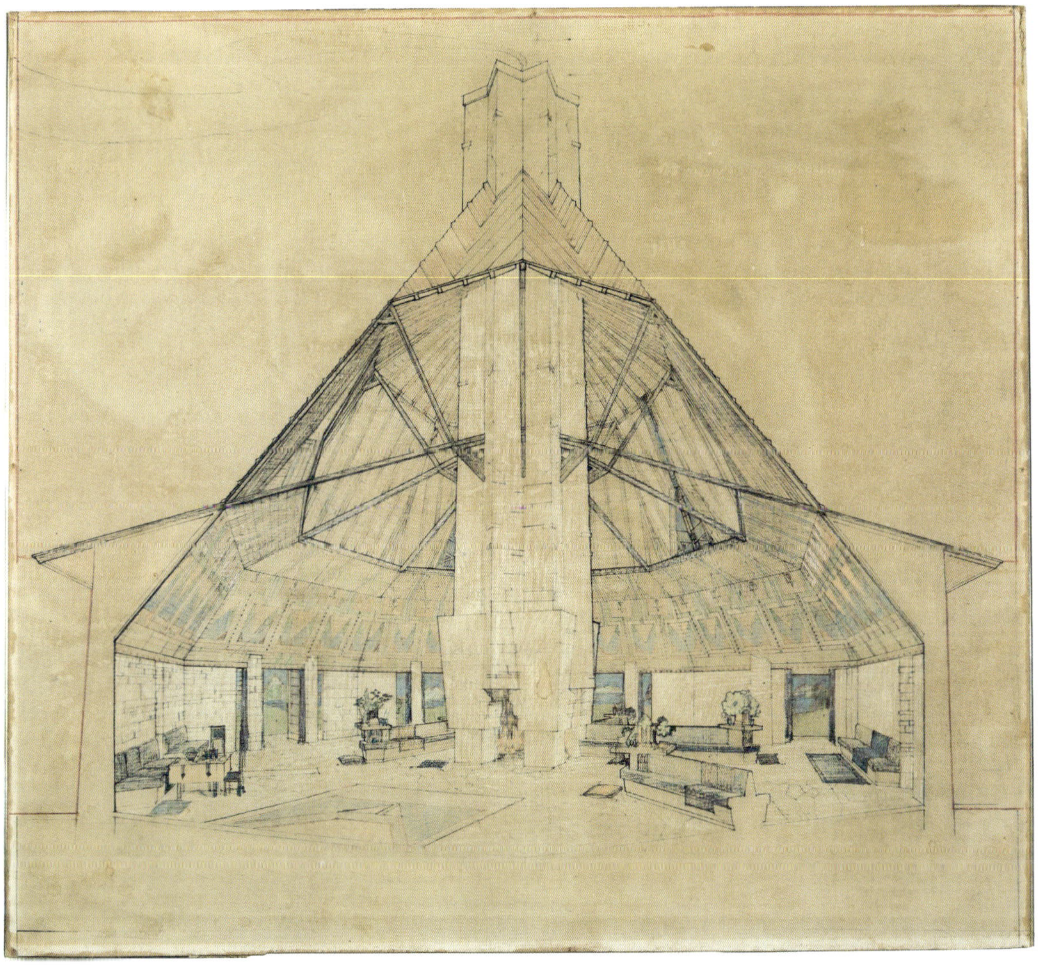

2. Nakoma Country Club, Madison, Wisconsin. Project, 1923–24. Cutaway perspective of the interior. Graphite and colored pencil on transparent paper mounted on board, 18 ⅛ x 20 in (46 x 50.8 cm). The Aust Family Trust

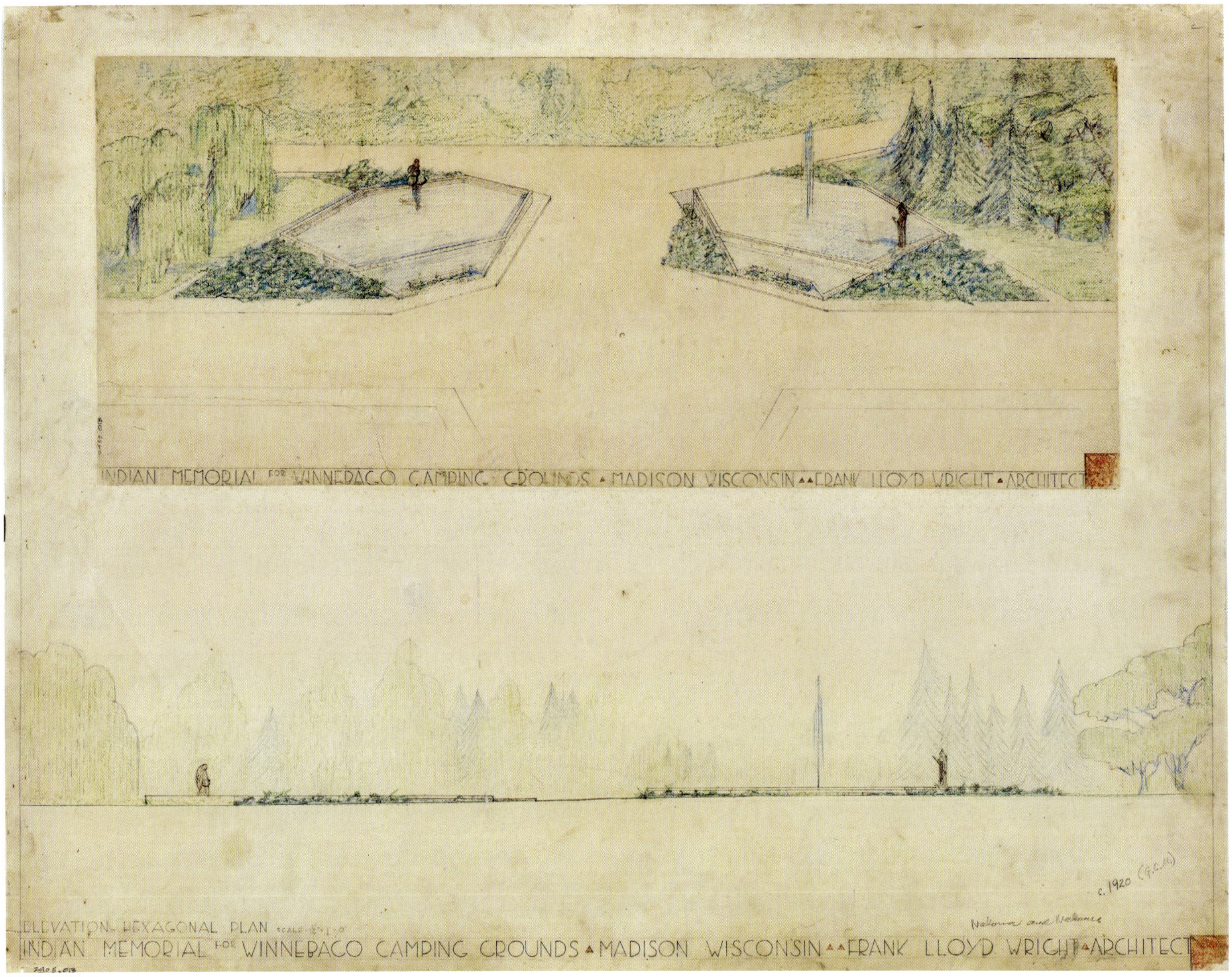

3. Nakoma Memorial Gateway, Madison, Wisconsin. Project, 1924. Perspective and elevation.
Pencil and colored pencil on tracing paper, 23 ½ x 30 ⅛ in. (59.7 x 76.5)

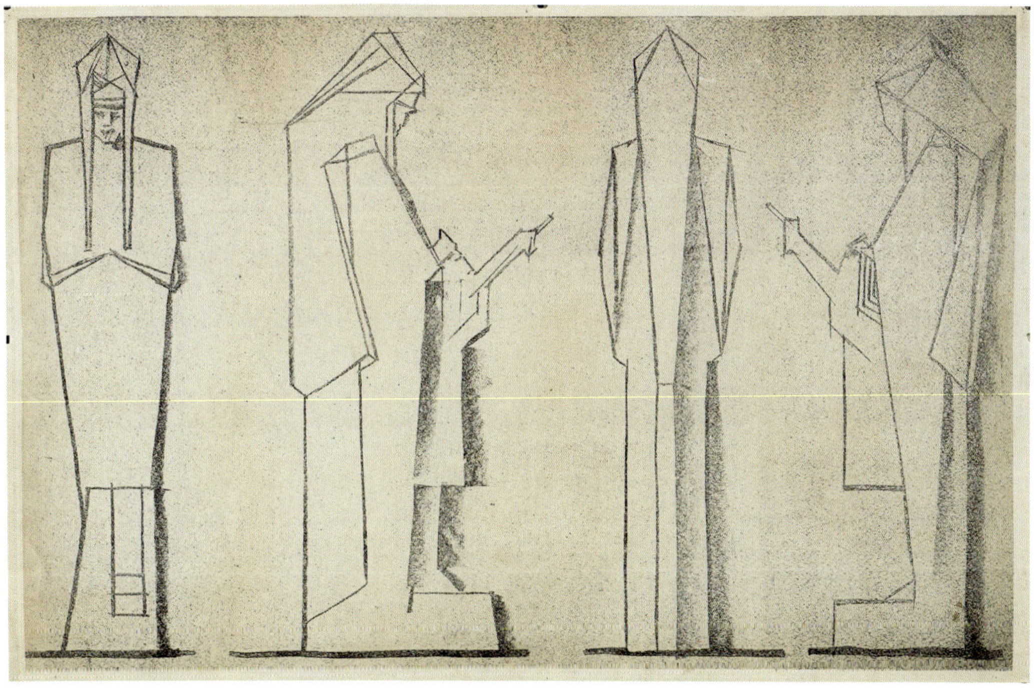

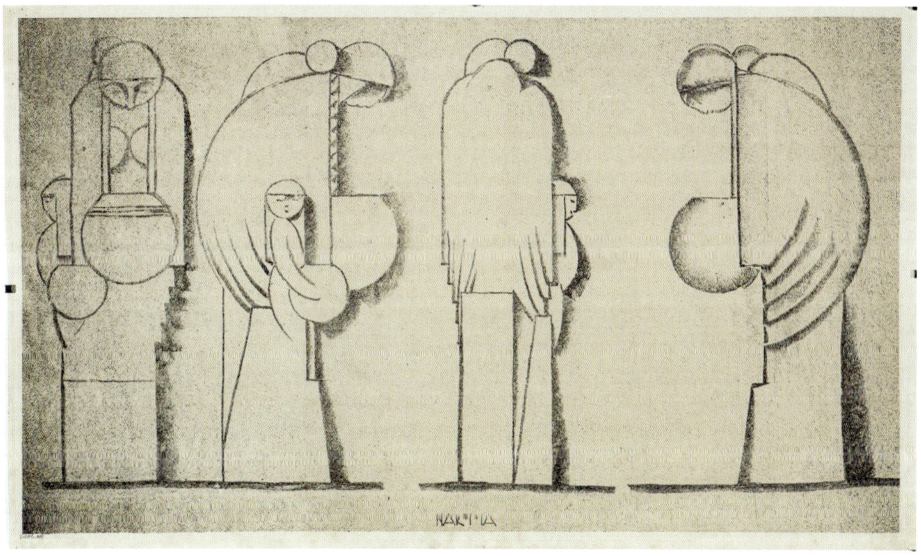

4. Nakoma Memorial Gateway, Madison, Wisconsin. Project, 1924. Elevations of the Nakomis sculpture. Lithograph, 20 7/8 x 31 1/4 in. (53 x 79.4 cm)

5. Nakoma Memorial Gateway, Madison, Wisconsin. Project, 1924. Elevations of the Nakoma sculpture. Lithograph, 17 5/8 x 29 3/8 in. (44.8 x 74.6 cm)

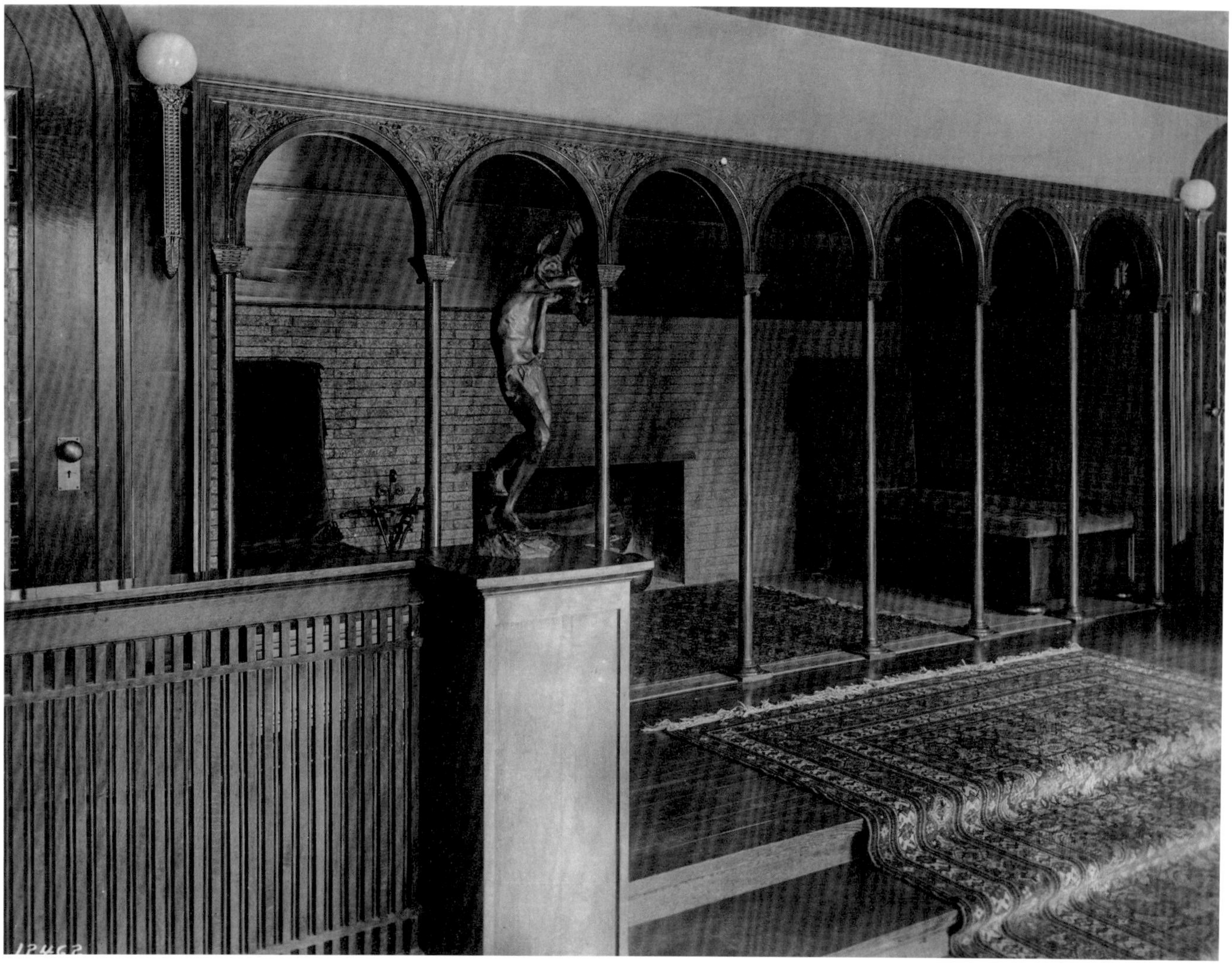

6. Winslow House, River Forest, Illinois. 1893–94. View of the inglenook with Hermon Atkins MacNeil's sculpture *A Primitive Chant to the Great Spirit*. Photograph by Henry Fuermann. Historic Architecture and Landscape Image Collection, Ryerson and Burnham Archives, The Art Institute of Chicago

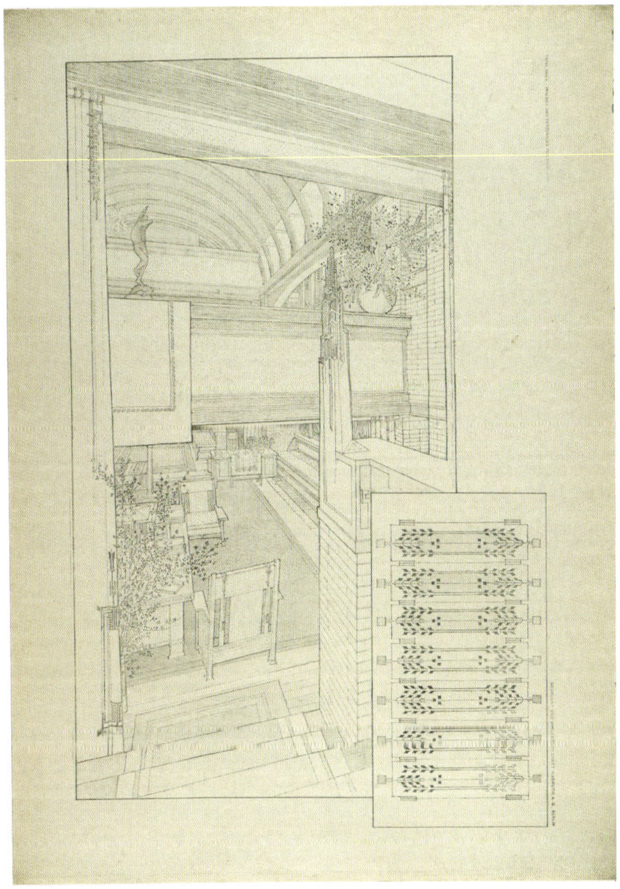

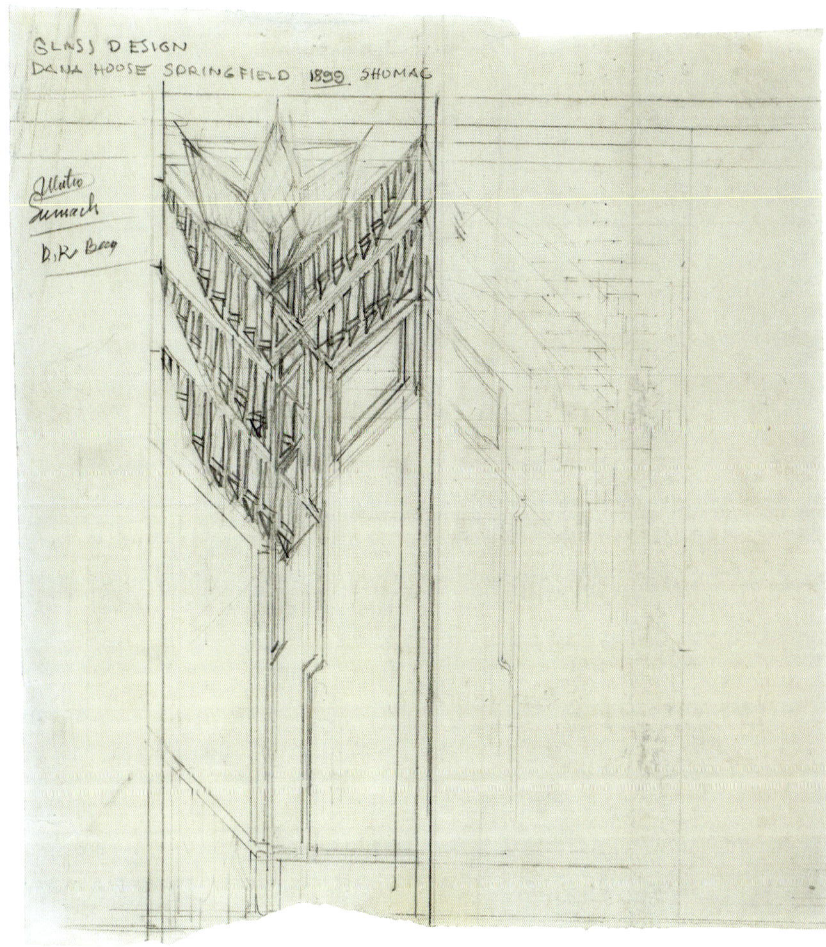

7. Dana House, Springfield, Illinois. 1902–04. Interior perspective. Plate XXXIb from *Ausgeführte Bauten und Entwürfe von Frank Lloyd Wright* (Berlin: Ernst Wasmuth, 1910). Avery Architectural & Fine Arts Library, Columbia University, New York

8. Dana House, Springfield, Illinois. 1902–04. Stained-glass design. Pencil on tracing paper, 12 3/8 x 10 7/8 in. (31.4 x 27.6 cm)

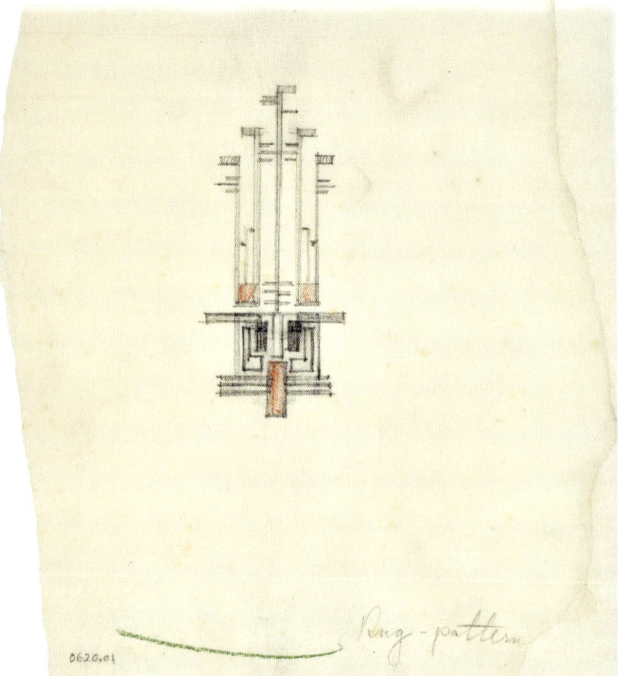

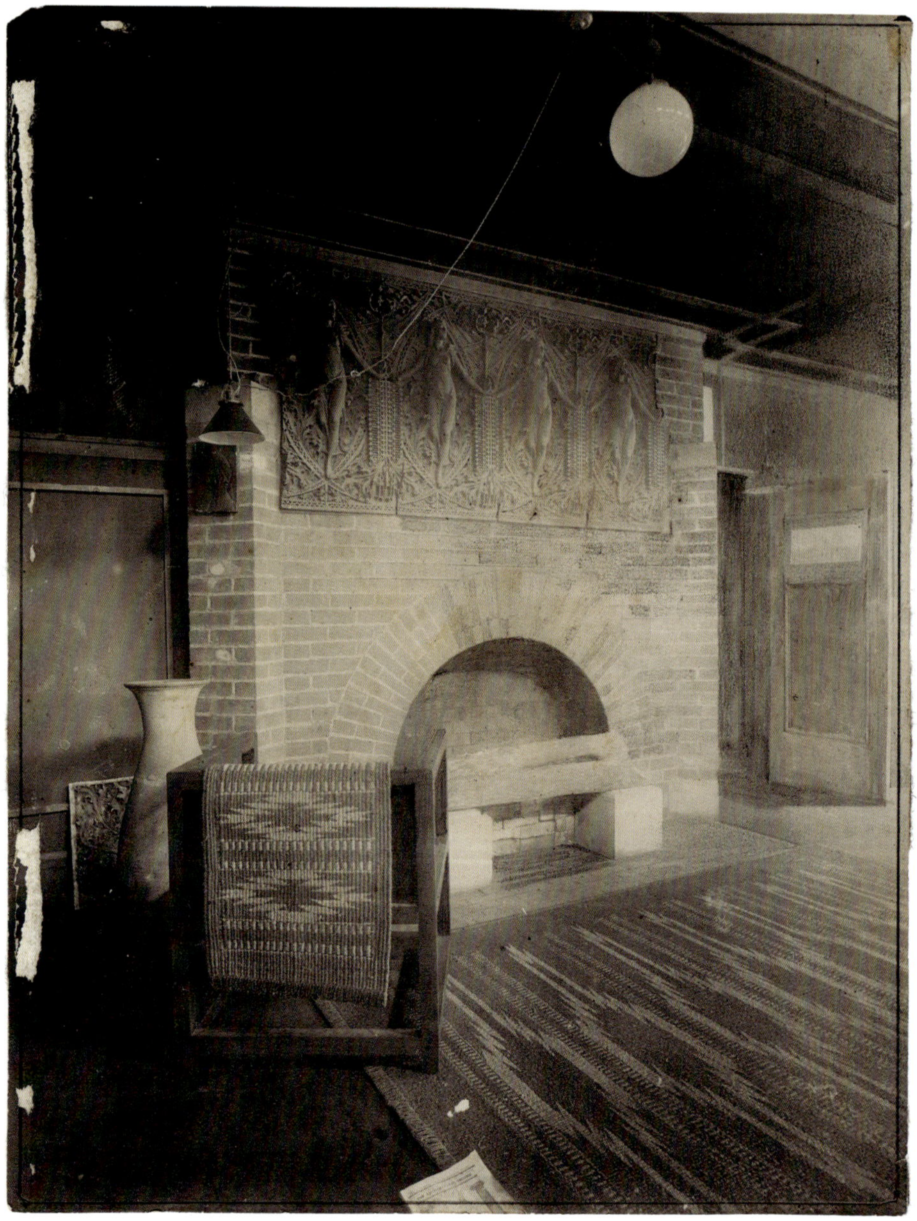

9. Design for a rug. 1906.
Pencil and colored pencil on tracing paper, 10 5/8 x 11 5/8 in. (27 x 29.5 cm)

10. Wright House and Studio, Oak Park, Illinois. 1895–98.
Studio interior with Navajo rug and runner, n.d.

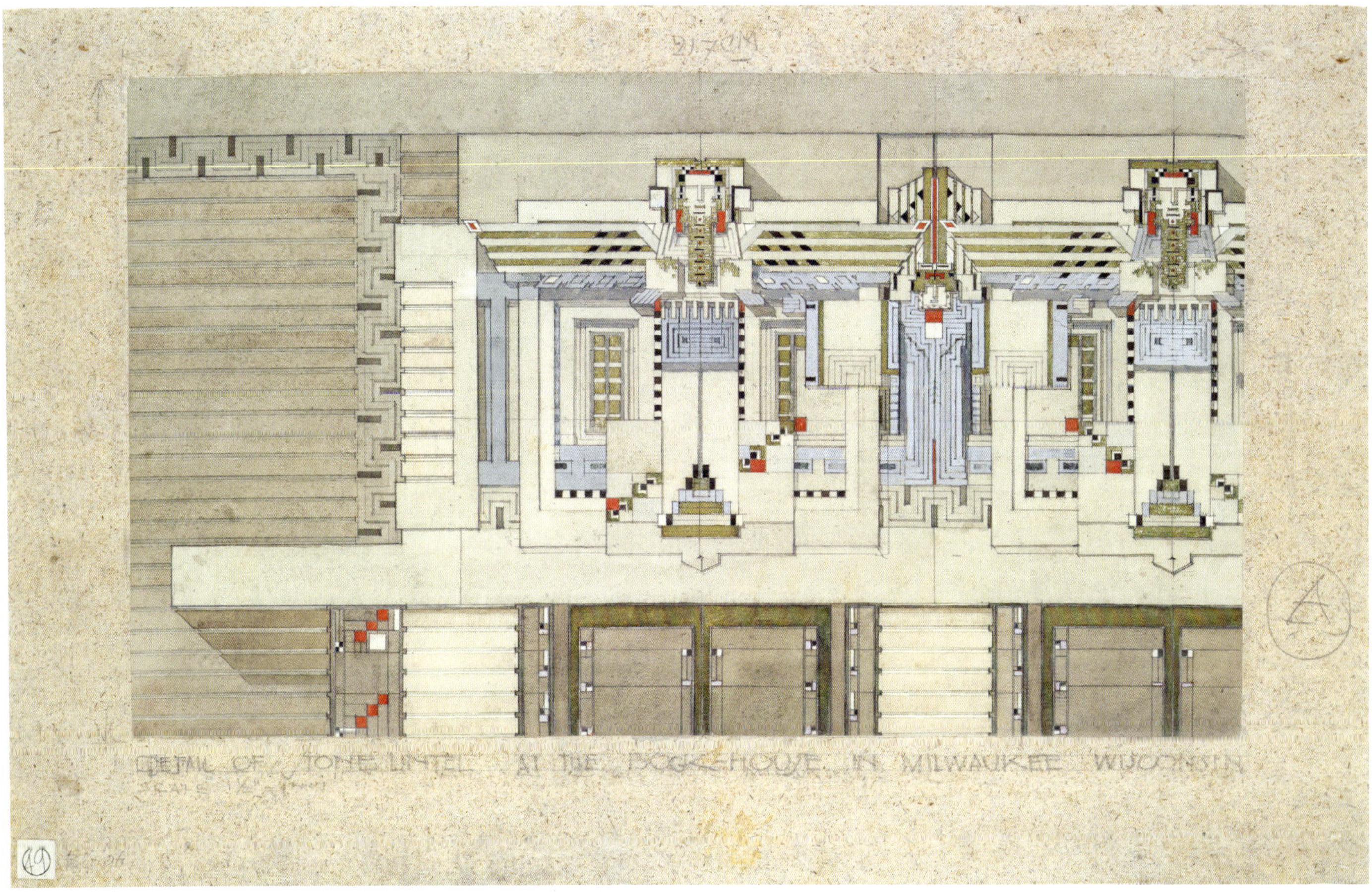

11. Bogk House, Milwaukee, Wisconsin. 1916–17. Detail of the stone lintel.
Watercolor, gouache, gold paint, and graphite on paper
mounted on Japanese paper, 15 1/2 x 24 1/4 in. (39.4 x 61.6 cm).
Prints and Photographs Division, Library of Congress, Washington, D.C.

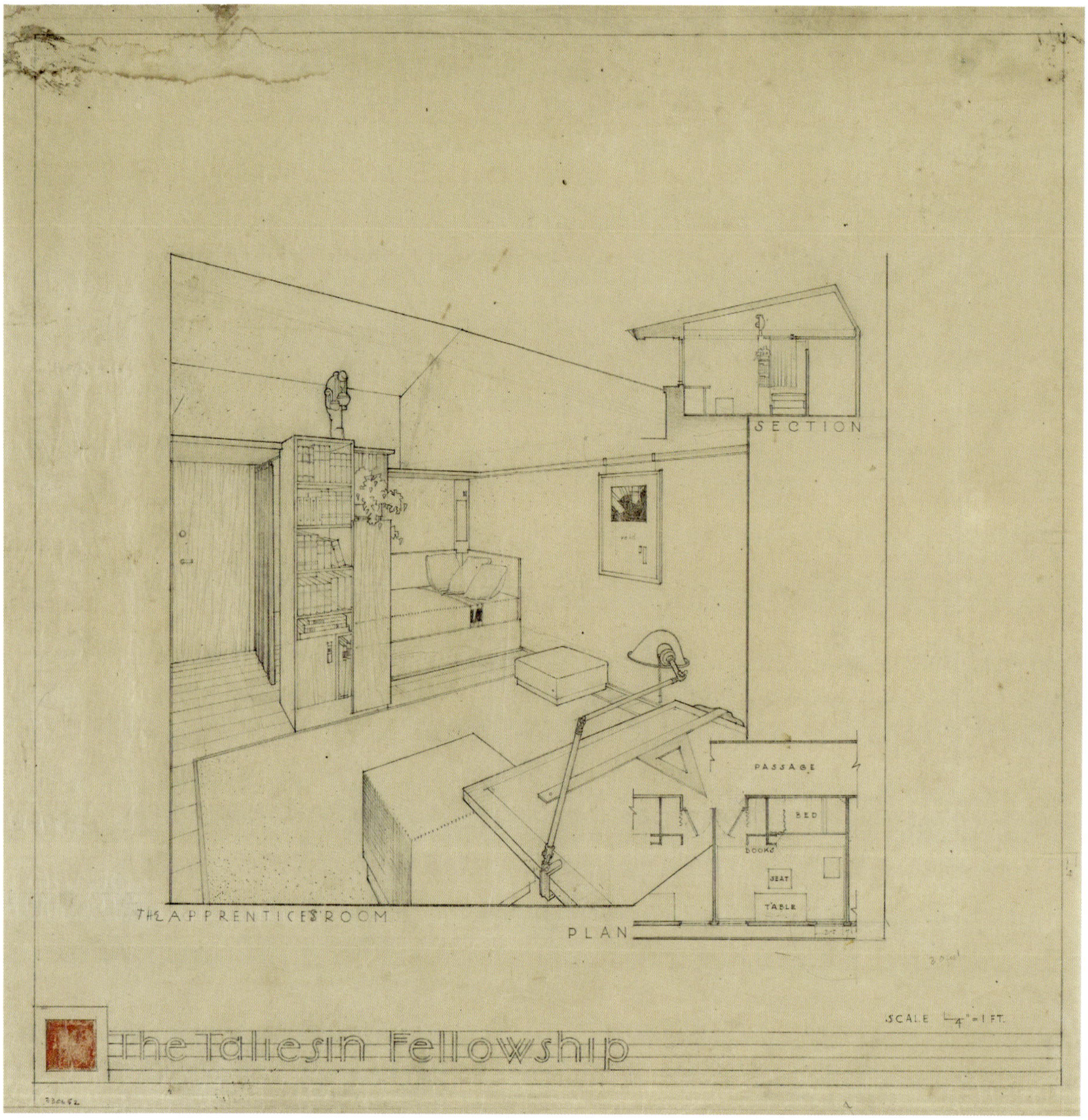

12. Taliesin Fellowship Complex, Spring Green, Wisconsin. Begun 1932–33.
Perspective, plan, and section of an apprentice's room.
Pencil and colored pencil on tracing paper, 22 ½ x 22 ⅜ in. (57.2 x 56.8 cm)

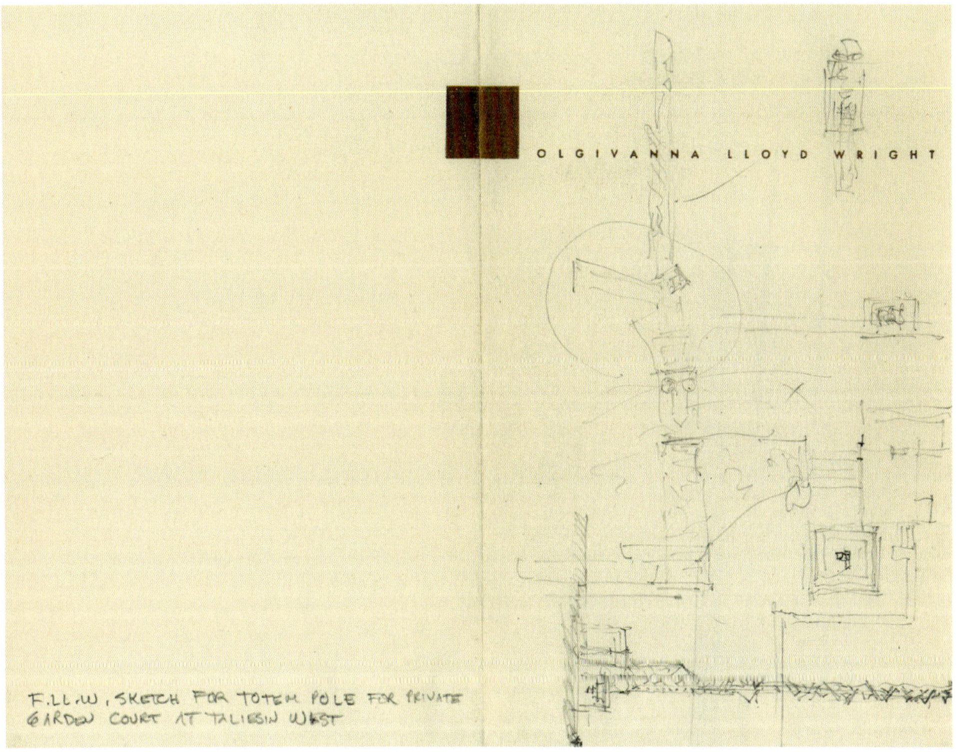

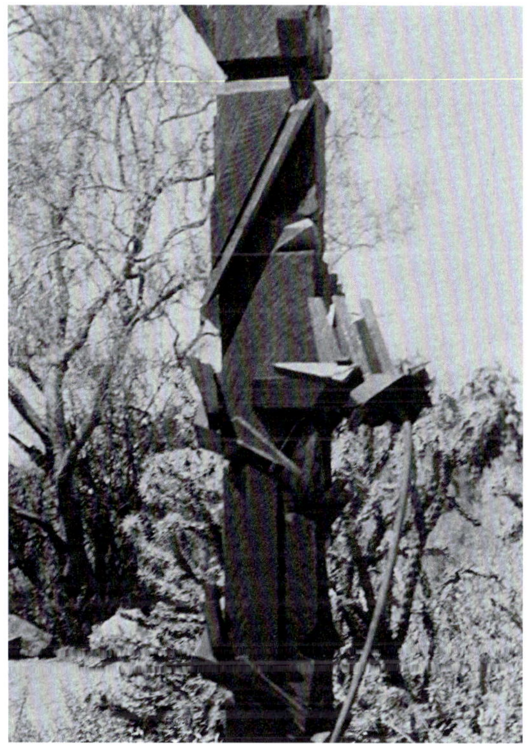

13. Taliesin West, Scottsdale, Arizona. Begun 1938.
Study for a totem pole for a private garden court, n.d.
Pencil on stationary, 11 x 8 ½ in. (27.9 x 21.6 cm).
Wisconsin Historical Society, Madison, Wisconsin

14. Taliesin West, Scottsdale, Arizona. Begun 1938.
Totem pole, n.d.

MABEL O. WILSON

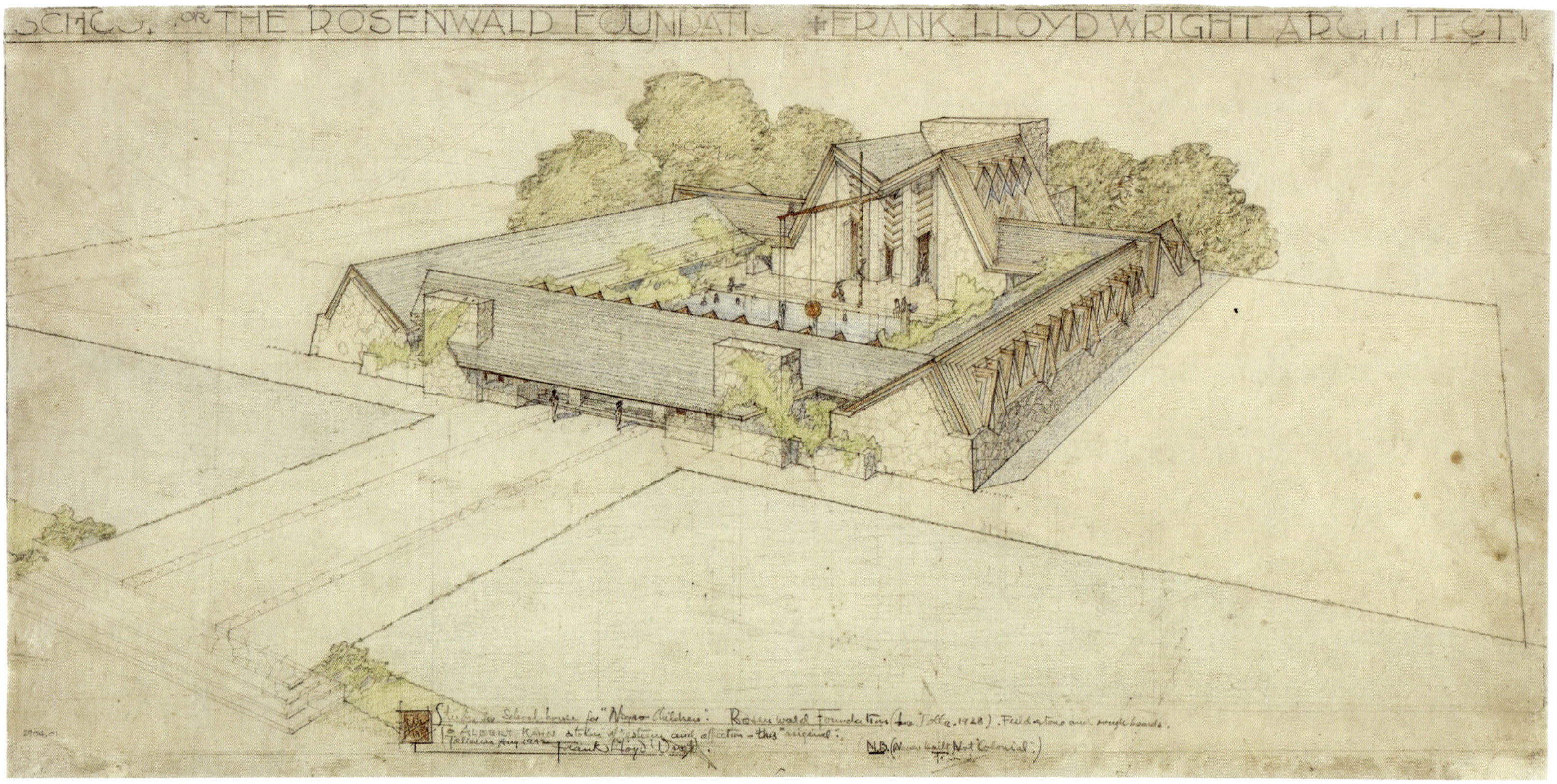

ROSENWALD SCHOOL LESSONS IN PROGRESSIVE EDUCATION

Rosenwald School, Hampton Normal and Agricultural Institute, Virginia. Project, 1928. Perspective. Pencil and colored pencil on tracing paper, 12 ¾ x 25 ⅞ in. (32.4 x 65.7 cm)

"School should be a happy place—even for the negro [*sic*]," wrote Frank Lloyd Wright to his friend and longtime patron Darwin D. Martin in July 1928.[1] Along with the letter, Wright sent Martin presentation drawings for the Rosenwald School, a practice teaching school for African-American students in coastal Virginia. The school was never built, and only a few drawings remain, including the color perspective opposite. Only once does Wright refer to the design in his writings, a 1929 *Architectural Record* essay, and it remains a relatively unknown project.[2] While it lacks a wealth of documentation, the Rosenwald School nonetheless illuminates Wright's vision of education that nurtured individualism and strengthened democratic solidarity, linking him to leading social and educational reformers, while also advancing his experimentation with affordable construction techniques. His exploration of form, ornament, and site for the school (plate 1) also reveals the racial underpinnings of his theories on organic architecture, ideas that advanced Anglo-American culture beyond what Wright described as the "colorful, joyful spirit of the negro [*sic*]."[3]

THE NEGRO RURAL SCHOOL PROGRAM

Wright designed his practice school for the Hampton Normal and Agricultural Institute, which was founded by white abolitionists from the American Missionary Association after the Civil War. Hampton's curriculum offered instruction in teaching and industrial trades through the eleventh grade. An impressive roster of politicians and philanthropists, including Presidents James Garfield and William Taft, George Foster Peabody, and Collis Huntington, supported the school's white administration and faculty in their mission to transform former enslaved blacks into wage earners. The school became famous for the "Hampton Ideal," an educational and disciplinary model that endeavored to lift up black students from illiteracy and poverty. To project an aura of respectability, boys had to wear military uniforms and girls had to observe strict dress codes. By disciplining "the head, heart and hands"—the Hampton mantra—the school graduated farmers, domestics, bricklayers, and teachers.[4] Though Hampton's mission of "racial uplift" posited that social equality was something African Americans must work to achieve, it was a cause that some believed validated black inferiority and Jim Crow segregation.

In 1881, nearly fifty years before Wright's Rosenwald design, Hampton's most distinguished graduate, Booker T. Washington, had become the head of a black-led teacher-training school in rural Alabama—the Tuskegee Normal School for Colored Teachers, which counted Andrew Carnegie and John D. Rockefeller as patrons. Tuskegee lacked facilities, and Washington put students to work building the campus: "To have them erect their own buildings . . . the school would not only get the benefit of their efforts, but the students themselves would be taught to see not only the utility in labour, but beauty and dignity."[5] Hard work and self-help exemplified the Tuskegee creed, which some African-Americans criticized for pandering to white racists who wanted to ensure blacks remained in society's lowest ranks.

In Alabama's Black Belt, named for its dark, fertile soil and for its concentration of poor black sharecroppers, Washington attempted to replicate the success of Tuskegee Institute (as the school was commonly known) by starting a program to help black communities build schools. Jim Crow segregation had separated schools according to race, with many black students attending crowded one-room shacks. Washington approached his trustee, Julius Rosenwald, a Chicago-based Jewish philanthropist, to donate funds, asking that local black communities raise the other half (fig. 1). Rosenwald, who was president of the Sears, Roebuck & Co. mail-order business, enthusiastically agreed and suggested adopting Sears's prefabrication methods used for its catalog houses. Despite the constraints of time and material availability as well as Washington's philosophy of self-help, which prohibited standardization, black communities near Tuskegee erected six one-teacher schools between 1913 and 1914. Impressed with the outcome, Washington expanded the program. Rosenwald's charity would donate one-third of the funds, black communities would raise another third, and white-run education boards would allocate the rest.[6] The fact that black Americans had to pay for even part of their schools was a stark reminder of the unequal distribution of state education monies.

In February 1915, Rosenwald finally witnessed the fruits of his investments. He toured the schools with an entourage of Chicago's social progressives who were committed to improving the lives of that city's growing immigrant and black populations. Among Rosenwald's guests was the social reformer Jane Addams, who had established Hull House, a settlement house aiding Chicago's poor. Also in the group was Unitarian minister Jenkin Lloyd Jones, founder of the All Soul's Unitarian Church on Chicago's Southside.[7]

Lloyd Jones was one of Chicago's first clergymen to welcome black congregants and had supported a young Washington, praising his strategy to improve black education and race relations. He was also Wright's maternal uncle, and the young architect regularly attended lectures at All Soul's when he lived in Chicago. Lloyd Jones had severed ties with Unitarian leadership to form the Abraham Lincoln Center (1898–1905), open to all classes and races. The interdenominational settlement house-cum-office building was one of Wright's first projects.[8] The center, where Rosenwald served on the board, offered a broad range of social services. It would be Wright's vast

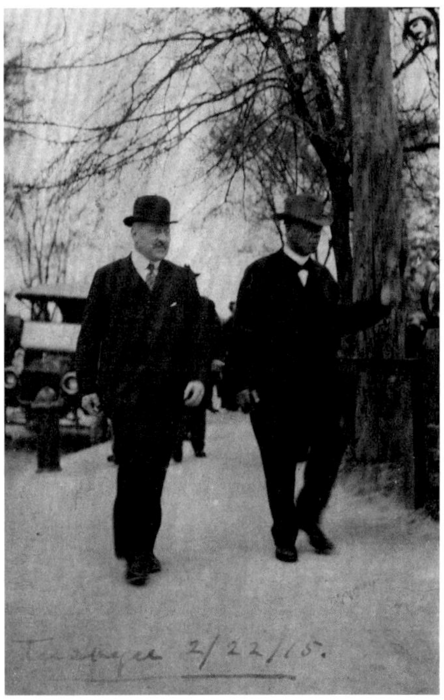

Fig. 1. Julius Rosenwald (left) and Booker T. Washington at the Tuskegee Institute, Alabama. February 22, 1915. Special Collections Research Center, University of Chicago Library

nine-hundred-seat auditorium, with its open-span interior, similar to his Unity Temple (1905–08), that embodied Lloyd Jones's vision of sanctuary for spiritual and intellectual engagement, one that nurtured individual life and strengthened communal bonds.[9] These innovations influenced Wright's Rosenwald School design at Hampton.

THE ROSENWALD SCHOOL DESIGNS

To build momentum for its school-building program, Tuskegee published *The Negro Rural School and Its Relation to the Community* (1915) that featured different designs, for a single-teacher school up to a ten-teacher school. The pattern book showed plans and perspectives for schools in Colonial and Arts and Crafts styles, some drawn by the country's first licensed black architect, Robert R. Taylor.[10] The book illustrated how to landscape around each school, along with how to build privies and teacher residences. The wood-frame construction could be affordably erected using basic carpentry skills.[11] Black communities that had received Rosenwald funds followed these plans and standards when they built their local schools. Though Washington died in November 1915, the program continued at Tuskegee for four more years.

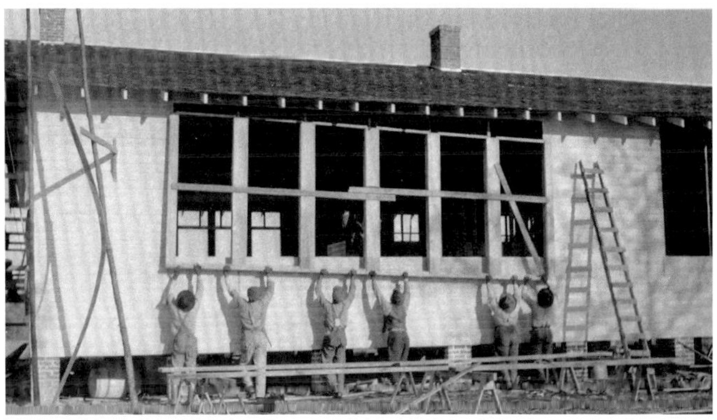

Concerned about the program's administration, in 1919 Rosenwald decided to move it from Tuskegee Institute to the Julius Rosenwald Fund in Nashville, Tennessee, under the stewardship of white staff working with black field agents. Fletcher Dressler, a white educational reformer, revised the original school models to comply with new construction and hygiene standards. One of Dressler's recommendations, for example, was that classrooms have east or west orientations to prevent eye strain from blackboard glare.[12] In 1921 the Rosenwald Fund issued the booklet "Community School Plans," featuring the new model plans developed by Dressler and staff with the same spare Colonial Revival exteriors of the previous Tuskegee prototypes (figs. 2, 3). By 1928 the fund had increased financial allowances and developed a new group of plans to erect more permanent brick-and-concrete schools. To secure Rosenwald Fund support, Hampton Institute proposed its practice school would follow the classroom plans and design standards for a ten-teacher school built from brick, identified as the "10A" plan (plates 3, 4).[13]

In December 1928, Darwin Martin, for whom Wright had built a sprawling Prairie-style house in Buffalo, New York, initiated correspondence with James E. Gregg, the principal of Hampton Institute. Martin inquired about the administration's plans to replace the old wood-frame Whittier School in nearby Phoebus, Virginia, with a new practice-school building, partially financed by the Rosenwald Fund, on the Hampton campus.[14] Martin had professionally supported educational initiatives at Tuskegee Institute and he had personally made donations to Hampton Institute.[15] Keen on finding new projects to restart Wright's office after the architect suffered a series of personal travails and near financial collapse, Martin wrote to Gregg with an offer to donate to the new school if Wright could be its designer.[16] In Wright's favor, Martin was also professionally acquainted with Julius Rosenwald, as both had contributed their expertise

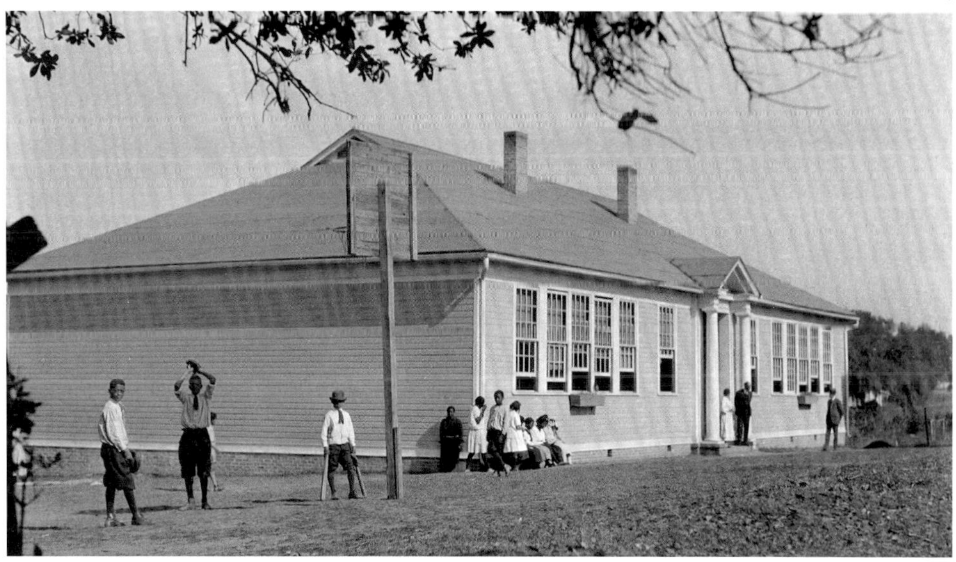

Fig. 2. Installing the window frames at a Rosenwald School in Gregg County, Texas. March 1921. Photograph by Jackson Davis. Albert and Shirley Small Special Collections Library, University of Virginia

Fig. 3. Rosenwald Practice School, Florida Agricultural and Mechanical School, Tallahassee, Florida. April 7, 1923. Photograph by Jackson Davis. Albert and Shirley Small Special Collections Library, University of Virginia

to the procurement effort during World War I.[17] If Rosenwald were making a personal donation, Martin speculated that would further make the case to hire Wright.[18] But Rosenwald would not be directly involved, and the architect's selection would be the purview of Hampton's administration in consultation with the Rosenwald Fund's leadership. Gregg, a New England Congregationalist minister, valued thrift and discipline, both hallmarks of the Hampton Ideal. He would entertain Martin's offer and his architect, but only if this contributed financially to the school's construction and if Wright's design enhanced the original plan of the Rosenwald ten-teacher school.

The Rosenwald Fund's effort to efficiently build affordable schools on a national scale, a strategy that by July 1928 had erected more than 4,300 schools (fig. 4), piqued Wright's own interest in designing for everyday Americans. One goal of building a Rosenwald School at Hampton was to serve as a model for those planning to erect similar low-cost masonry schools.[19] This resonated with Wright: throughout his career, he had experimented with handcraft methods adapted to modern production techniques, such as his ongoing research to produce on-site masonry "textile blocks" that when stacked created tapestry-like wall patterns. Martin seemed to think that Wright might convince Hampton's administration to use textile blocks for the new school.[20] Under this complicated chain of funding and institutional accountability, Hampton asked Wright to submit a design by mid-July.[21]

The only remaining detailed drawing of the plan—a faint pencil sketch on tracing paper (plate 2)—reveals that Wright's schematic design closely followed the plan of the 10A model school (see plate 4). The final design, however, transformed the school from an austere colonial farmhouse to a colorful crystalline outcrop of fieldstone and shingles, while maintaining the essence of its organization (see p. 96 and plate 1). The entire structure sat on a slab-on-grade concrete foundation, a cost-saving method that allowed for other alterations to the plan.[22] Like the model plan, the front of the school hosted the administrative functions of the office and library. Six classrooms and four recitation rooms were divided between two wings. With the entrance on the north or south facade, the two wings would have the recommended east-west daylighting, although Wright incorporated triangular windows in a row of dormers 6 feet (1.8 meters) above the floor, replacing the suggested banks of tall sash windows. This allowed for the sloped roof to be extended, thus lowering the height of the east and west walls and reducing cost. On the interior, the slope of the classroom ceilings reflected daylight upon the desks, which for the architect was "an ideal section for school purposes as well as for working purposes."[23] The school's elevations show how Wright expanded every fourth window into a diamond shape to offer students glimpses of the surrounding campus.

Instead of building with brick, as the Rosenwald 10A plan stipulated, or with textile-block units, Wright's final design for the exterior wall construction proposed fieldstone on concrete. The technique "a la Flagg," as Wright described, was adapted from architect Ernest Flagg, a Beaux-Arts trained New York architect.[24] Like Wright, Flagg was interested in inexpensive, non-labor-intensive methods of construction to build modest cottage houses. Flagg developed a construction technique called "mosaic rubble" that minimized the use of formwork and scaffolding, which Wright found to be efficient and affordable.[25] Beyond the cost savings, Wright's use of stone proved aesthetically compelling because it, along with the low eaves, rooted the school's mass into the flat tidewater landscape.

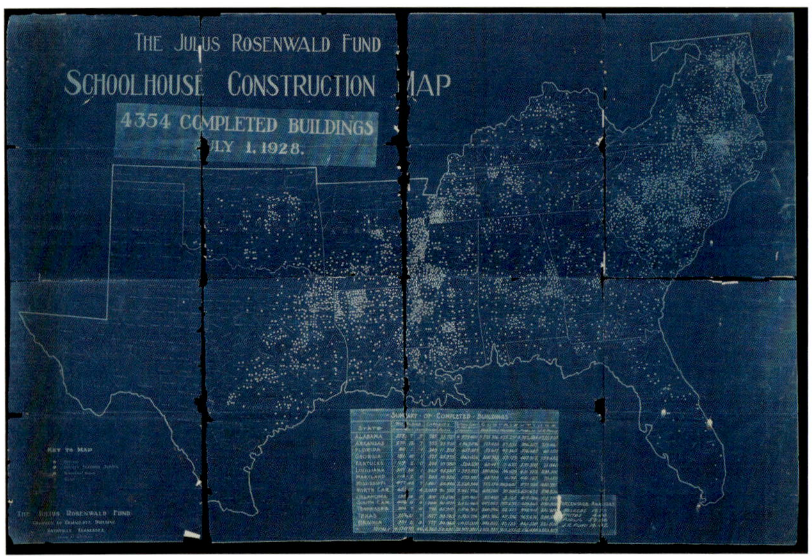

Fig. 4. Construction map of the Julius Rosenwald Fund's 4,354 completed buildings. July 1, 1928. Blueprint, 32 ½ x 49 in. (82.6 x 124.5 cm). State Archives of North Carolina

Wright retained most of the original Rosenwald 10A plan, but in a brilliant move that transformed the character of the entire scheme, he pushed the auditorium, renamed the Little Theater, from the front to the rear of the building (see plate 2). The new location of the auditorium enclosed a courtyard patio with a pool to encourage play and exercise. These new amenities increased the cost, but Wright argued it would "be worth it—Physical Culture should be 3/5 of 'Education.'"[26]

Wright had learned from his upbringing and several earlier projects that a good education depended on the cultivation of the mind and body within a thriving egalitarian milieu. Wright's mother, Anna Lloyd Wright, for example, educated her children at home employing the techniques of German pedagogue Friedrich Froebel, who promoted games and other forms of play. Froebel, the inventor of kindergarten, advocated giving children tools, or "gifts"—objects in elemental colors, forms, and patterns—to aid in learning basic forces and geometries. These exercises formed the foundation for Wright's interpretation of organic architecture that derived line, color, and form from nature.

Throughout the early decades of the twentieth century, progressive educational reformers were establishing experimental schools and popularizing their ideas through public lectures and publications. In *Schools of To-morrow* (1915), the pragmatist philosopher John Dewey and his daughter Evelyn Dewey praised Froebel as a pivotal figure in education reform with "his emphasis upon play, dramatization, songs and storytelling."[27] One model of progressive education featured in the Deweys' study was a photograph of the Cottage School in Riverside, Illinois, with students costumed in Grecian togas posing in front of Wright's Coonley House (1906–09). Wright's client, Queene Coonley, a former social worker in Chicago's settlement houses and a prominent advocate of early childhood education, and her husband, Avery Coonley, also commissioned Wright to build the Coonley Playhouse (1912), with an assembly room and stage for musical performances and dramatizations. Around the main assembly hall's clerestory windows, Wright designed iconic stained-glass windows, that showcased a parade of primary-colored circles and rectangles to stimulate the children's imaginations.

In 1923 Wright designed a community theater, the Little Dipper (plate 5), for Aline Barnsdall's arts compound around the Hollyhock (Barnsdall) House (1918–21), one of Wright's Los Angeles houses. Fascinated by Dalcroze Eurythmics and a form of experimental theater known as the Little Theater Movement, Barnsdall wanted to bring together structured rhythmic movement with theatrical performance in an educational curriculum, and she hired Wright to create the playhouse school for her daughter and friends. The perspective views capture the playhouse's mass of intersecting rhomboids clad in textile blocks rising from the hillside. Wright's design choreographed theatrical and dance performance, study, swimming, and play into one imaginative, educational experience.

Wright also pursued public projects to test his ideas on education. Reformers like Jane Addams pressured municipalities to build playgrounds, pools, sports fields, gymnasiums, and field houses in city parks and schoolyards. In 1926 Wright proposed four field houses, called the Kindersymphonies, for a competition for Oak Park, Illinois (plates 6–9). Although each pavilion shared the same plan for playrooms and wading pools (plate 10), Wright composed different exterior configurations with a palette of gabled roofs, windows, and candy-striped columns. In perspective views, he dotted the pavilions with primary-colored orbs reminiscent of balloons to craft a fantastical playscape.

The educational ideas that Wright explored in these earlier projects influenced his transformation of the Rosenwald School 10A model. He designed the courtyard area for the patio and pool to stimulate a "physical culture" critical for the children's educational advancement. In the new rear wing, he topped the Little Theater with a two-story, double-gabled roof, diamond-shaped dormers, and brightly colored eaves. A three-bay entrance welcomed visitors to the large assembly hall that could be arranged for group exercise, public assembly, or performances. Like the sanctuary of the Abraham Lincoln Center, fellowship in the hall would strengthen communal ties within the school and among Hampton's students and the local townspeople.

Wright disliked the appearance of the "innocuous" Rosenwald School designs, declaring their New England aesthetic "the 'extreme' of timidity and sterility."[28] Built from fieldstone, concrete, shingles, and cypress boards stained bright colors and integrated into Virginia's flat coastal plains, Wright's inventive proposal to merge architecture, landscape, learning, and physical fitness in his new Rosenwald School made architecture "a factor in education!"[29] He based his work on the principles of organic architecture that merged form, material, ornament, and site into an expression of cultural and racial character. As Wright noted on a photocopy of one of the drawings, a perspective given to architect Albert Kahn, it had been "an attempt to make a school building a little warmer in color and form and nearer to the negro [*sic*] heart than the little old New England Schoolhouse."[30] Through its brightly colored ornament, chevron-patterned shingles, and geometric roof massing, Wright believed he had captured the spirit of "the negro [*sic*]." The African American, he wrote to Martin, "ought not to be pared down to our less colorful standards. Let him live, as he does in this building. Why not let the joy that is in him live and educate him in the light of his own colorful capacity for that joy?"[31] Wright's organic sensibilities created an authentic "colorful vivacious thing" so that "the Darkies would have something that belonged to them. Something exterior of their own lively interior color and charm."[32] Wright believed he had captured the spirit of African-American culture in his modern school design, and yet old stereotypes of racial difference persisted.

THE NEW NEGRO SPIRIT

Wright was not alone in his assessment that Hampton's puritanical ways were outmoded. In October 1927, two months before Wright and Martin became involved with the Rosenwald School project, students launched a strike protesting the paternalistic treatment by the white administration and faculty that shut down the school for two weeks and garnered national attention. They asserted that the industrial training curriculum that had made Hampton popular with white donors was no longer relevant to the outspoken culturally aware "New Negro," an emerging black intellectual, creative, and political movement that sought to efface the subservient and deferential ways of the "Old Negro."[33] Sociologist and activist W. E. B. Du Bois wrote a scathing critique in *The Nation*: "Hampton was no longer dealing with docile and half-grown elementary students, regimented to strict military discipline; she had to deal with older college men [and women] who were thinking for themselves."[34] Students wanted curricula like those taught in white liberal arts colleges, but Gregg refused to abandon the Hampton Ideal.[35] Protesters demanded better teachers and courses as well as a more liberal dress code and social policies. Defiant, they no longer wanted to serenade white visitors with plantation songs at Sunday evening service. Wright had been regaled by one such memorable performance: "Went to an evening service to hear the singing of the spirituals which surpassed anything I have ever heard or expect to hear. One thousand or more darky voices rising in that auditorium with a simple [*sic*] touching songs that bring the tears to anyones [*sic*] eyes."[36] Gregg resisted, expelled the troublemakers, and restored calm to reassure trustees and donors.

Characterizing African Americans as "Darkies," a demeaning minstrel stereotype, reveals the paradoxes and tensions in Wright's Rosenwald School design. On one hand, Wright's organic architecture expressed cultural and racial character through style, ornament, and form. His architecture of the "negro spirit" represented, in the same manner as the Hampton Ideal, black culture as primitive. This aligned with whites who viewed black Americans as a docile, childlike people who find happiness in rudimentary artistic creations, which masked the devastating oppression wrought by white racism. On the other hand, however, Wright's inventive Rosenwald School, an architecture that served as a "factor in education," embodied the progressive ethos of a liberal education, one that produced ethical individuals and cultivated better citizens, values that both Washington and Du Bois championed. Wright believed his model of modern architecture created for his well-to-do white clients could be adapted to serve black students. This progressive educational agenda was echoed by Hampton's protesters who also wanted a school that stimulated the imagination and nurtured the intellect, and whose graduates would strive to build a better world and uphold the egalitarian values of a democratic society.

Hampton never built Wright's Rosenwald School. After Wright submitted his scheme, vice principal George Phenix wrote in a report to Gregg: "I do not think the plans for beautifying the Rosenwald building will please any of us. The ground plan of the revised Rosenwald building is in some respects superior, but the exterior is an entire misfit."[37] The typical Rosenwald school was not only austere as disciplinary reinforcement, but its simplicity ensured the schools appeared inferior to ones for white children.

In November 1928, Gregg invited Wright to Hampton to continue discussions.[38] Due to illness, Wright declined. Finally in October 1929, Wright, still interested in the commission, traveled to Hampton with his wife, Olgivanna. By then, however, Gregg had retired and been replaced by Phenix. While plans for a new teaching school had been expanded, thus making Wright's scheme obsolete, Phenix was not as enthused as his predecessor by Wright's scheme, and the project stalled. Wright retrieved his drawings, and his effort to shake off the campus's Yankee solemnity ended.

Notes

1. Wright, letter to Martin, July 11, 1928, Folder Darwin D. Martin, Frank Lloyd Wright Files, Hampton University Archives.
2. Frank Lloyd Wright, "Surface and Mass—Again!" *Architectural Record*, no. 66 (July 1929): 92–94. Jack Quinan, "Frank Lloyd Wright, Darwin D. Martin, and Whittier School for Hampton Institute," *Arris* 21 (2010).
3. Wright, letter to Martin, July 11, 1928.
4. Walton C. John, *Hampton Normal and Agricultural Institute: Its Evolution and Contribution to Education as a Land-Grant College*, Department of the Interior, Bureau of Education, Bulletin no. 27, 1923 (Washington, D.C.: Government Printing Office, 1923), p. 7.
5. Booker T. Washington, *Up from Slavery: An Autobiography* (New York: Doubleday, Page, 1904), p. 143.
6. Mary S. Hoffschwelle, *The Rosenwald Schools of the American South* (Gainesville: University Press of Florida, 2006), pp. 242–43.
7. Ibid., p. 48.
8. The project was designed with architect Dwight Heald Perkins. See Joseph Siry, "The Abraham Lincoln Center in Chicago," *Journal of the Society of Architectural Historians* 50, no. 3 (September 1991): 242.
9. Ibid.
10. Taylor studied at Tuskegee and was the first black graduate of Massachusetts Institute of Technology. See Ellen Weiss, *Robert R. Taylor and Tuskegee: An African American Architect Designs for Booker T. Washington* (Montgomery, Ala.: New South Books, 2012).
11. Ibid., pp. 125–27.
12. Samuel L. Smith, Julius Rosenwald Fund director, letter to Martin, April 21, 1928, Folder Julius Rosenwald Fund, Frank Lloyd Wright Files, Hampton University Archives. Also see Hoffschwelle, *The Rosenwald Schools of the American South*, p. 48.
13. Conference of Trustees and Guests Julius Rosenwald Fund, April 29, 1928, Box 57, Folder 1, Julius Rosenwald Papers, Special Collections Research Center, University of Chicago Library.
14. Gregg, letter to Martin, January 4, 1928, Folder Darwin D. Martin, Frank Lloyd Wright Files, Hampton University Archives.
15. Gregg, letter to Rosenwald, May 24, 1928, Box 208 Projects/Persons Requesting Aid, Folder 15, Julius Rosenwald Fund Archives, 1917–1948, Julius Rosenwald Collection, Special Collections, Fisk University Archive.
16. Martin, letter to Gregg, April 5, 1928, Folder Darwin D. Martin, Frank Lloyd Wright Files, Hampton University Archives.
17. Quinan, "Frank Lloyd Wright, Darwin D. Martin, and Whittier School for Hampton Institute," p. 25.
18. Martin, letter to Gregg, June 12, 1928, Folder Darwin D. Martin, Frank Lloyd Wright Files, Hampton University Archives.
19. Smith, letter to Martin, April 21, 1928.
20. Martin, letter to Wright, June 8, 1928. Folder Frank Lloyd Wright, Frank Lloyd Wright Files, Hampton University Archives.
21. Martin, letter to Gregg, June 12, 1928, Folder Darwin D. Martin, Frank Lloyd Wright Files, Hampton University Archives.
22. Wright, letter to Martin, July 27, 1928, Folder Darwin D. Martin, Frank Lloyd Wright Files, Hampton University Archives.
23. Ibid. Wright also sketched a tiny sectional diagram in his letter to Martin.
24. Darwin Martin, letter to James E. Gregg, July 11, 1928, Folder Darwin D. Martin, Frank Lloyd Wright Files, Hampton University Archives.
25. Ernest Flagg, *Flagg's Small Houses: Their Economic Design and Construction, 1922* (Mineola, N.Y.: Dover, 2006), pp. 18–21. Wright, letter to Martin, July 27, 1928.
26. Ibid.
27. John Dewey and Evelyn Dewey, *Schools of Tomorrow* (New York: E. P. Dutton, 1916), p. 108.
28. Wright, letter to Martin, July 27, 1928.
29. Wright, letter to Martin, July 11, 1928.
30. From a typewritten note on a photocopy, 2904.009, Frank Lloyd Wright Foundation Archives (The Museum of Modern Art | Avery Architectural & Fine Arts Library, Columbia University, New York).
31. Wright, letter to Martin, July 11, 1928.
32. Address at Milwaukee Art Institute, Talk No. II, December 4, 1945, transcript, pp. 24–25, 2401.276A, Wright Foundation Archives (MoMA | Avery).
33. Alaine Locke, "Harlem Mecca of the New Negro," *Survey Graphic* 6, no. 6 (March 1926).
34. W. E. B. Du Bois, "The Hampton Strike," *The Nation*, November 2, 1927, pp. 471–72.
35. "Annual Report of the Principal, April 26, 1928," Folder Trustees Report, Dr. James E. Gregg Files, General Correspondence, Hampton University Archives.
36. Wright, letter to Martin, October 21, 1929, M010A08, Wright Foundation Archives (MoMA | Avery).
37. Phenix, letter to Gregg, August 17, 1928. Frank Lloyd Wright Files, Folder Whittier School, Hampton University Archives.
38. James E. Gregg, letter to Frank Lloyd Wright, November 16, 1928, Folder Frank Lloyd Wright/Darwin D. Martin, Frank Lloyd Wright Files, Hampton University Archives.

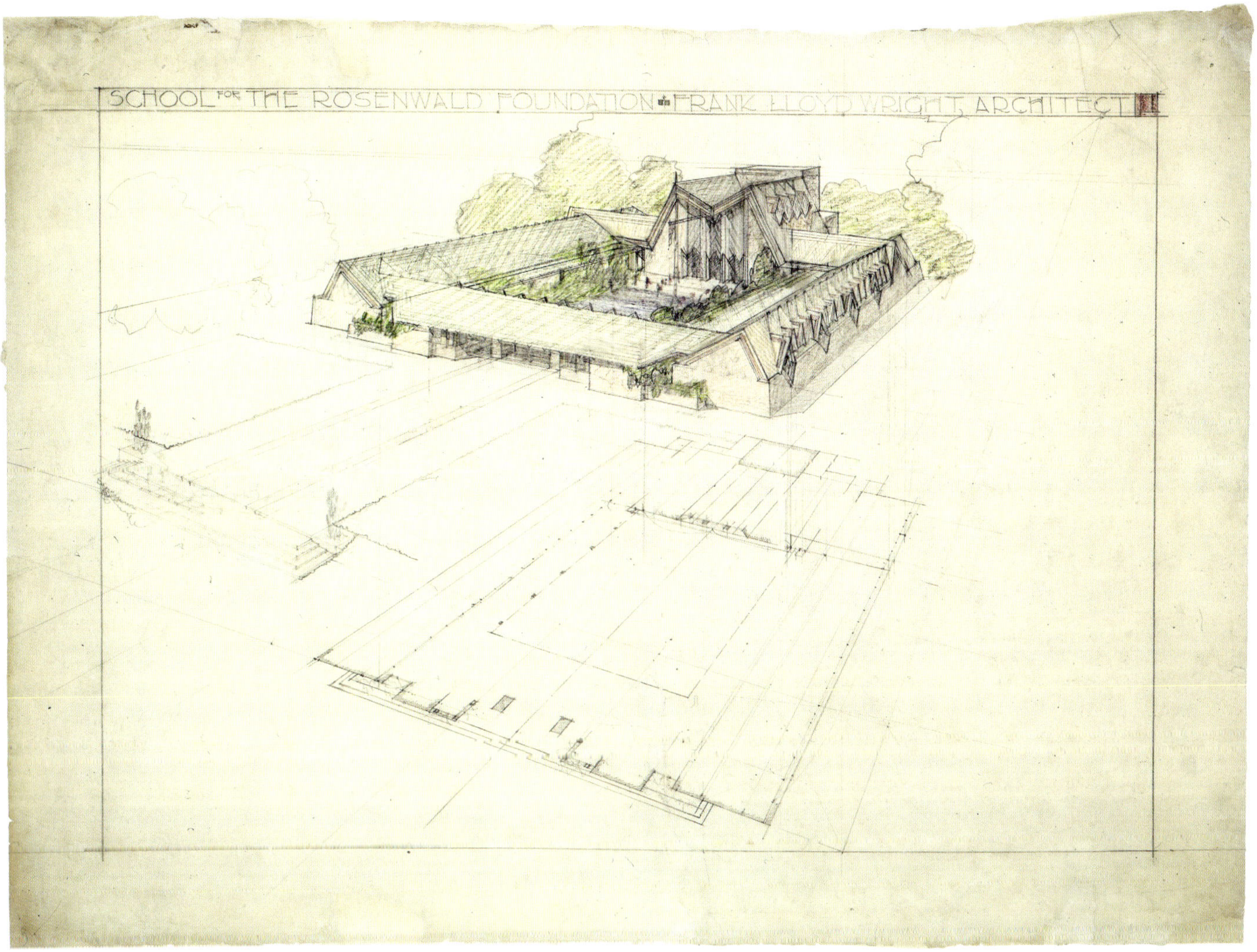

1. Rosenwald School, Hampton Normal and Agricultural Institute, Virginia. Project, 1928. Perspective with plan.
Graphite and colored pencil, 28 x 40 ¼ in. (71 x 102 cm).
Prints and Photographs Division, Library of Congress, Washington, D.C.

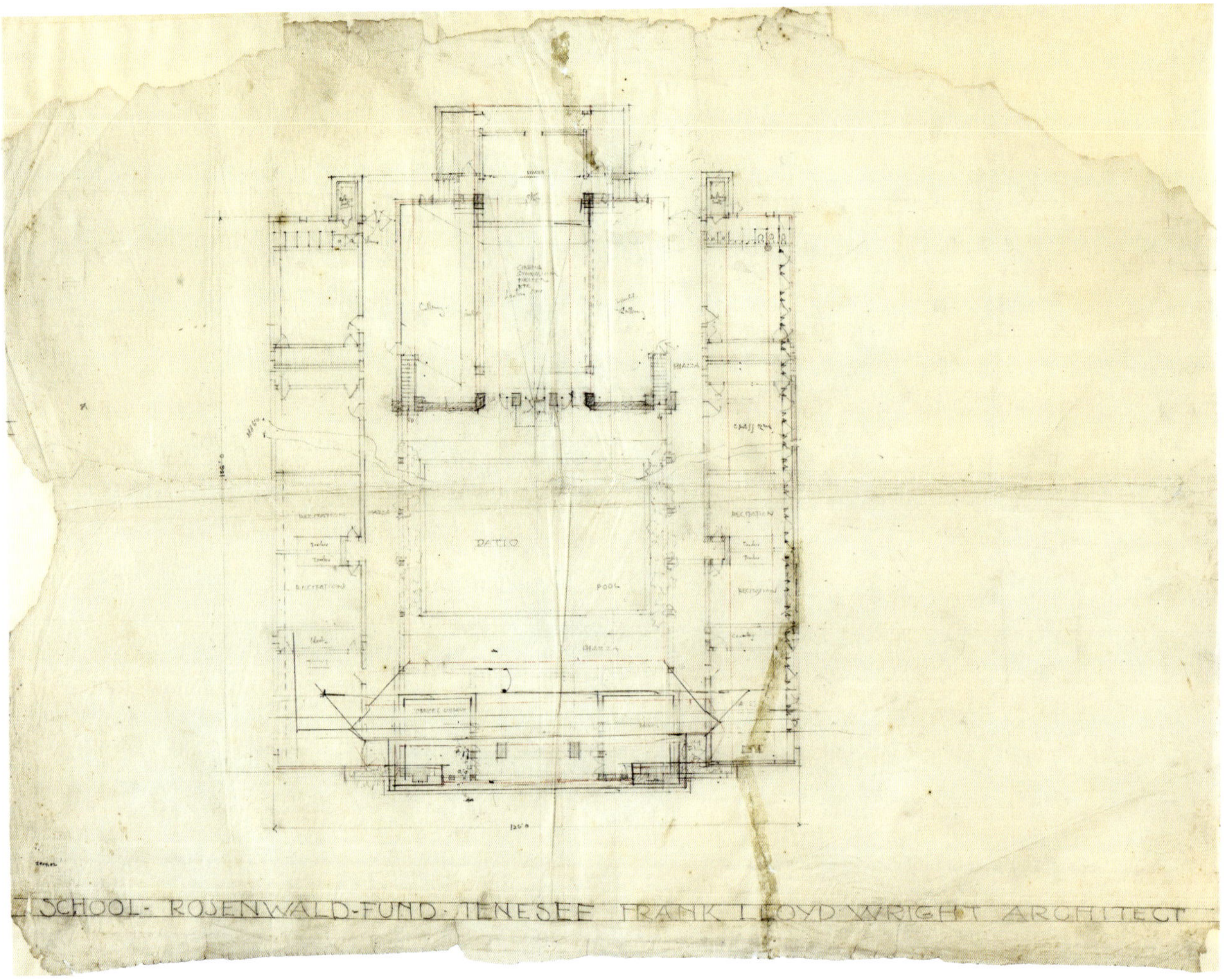

2. Rosenwald School, Hampton Normal and Agricultural Institute, Virginia. Project, 1928. Plan.
Pencil and colored pencil on tracing paper, 27 x 35 ⅞ in. (68.6 x 91.1 cm)

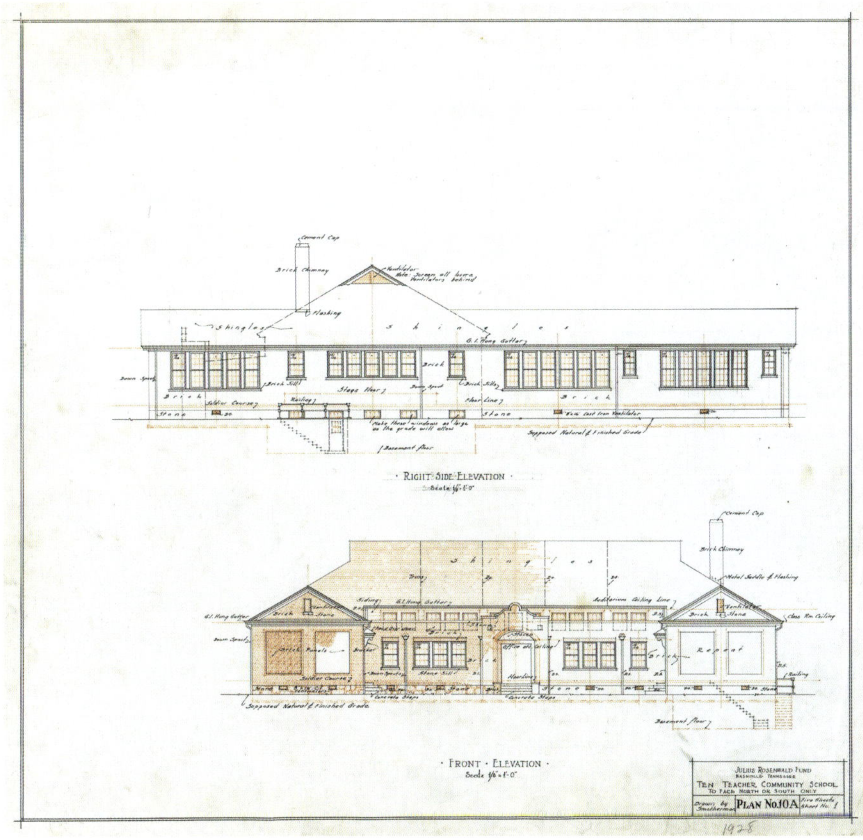

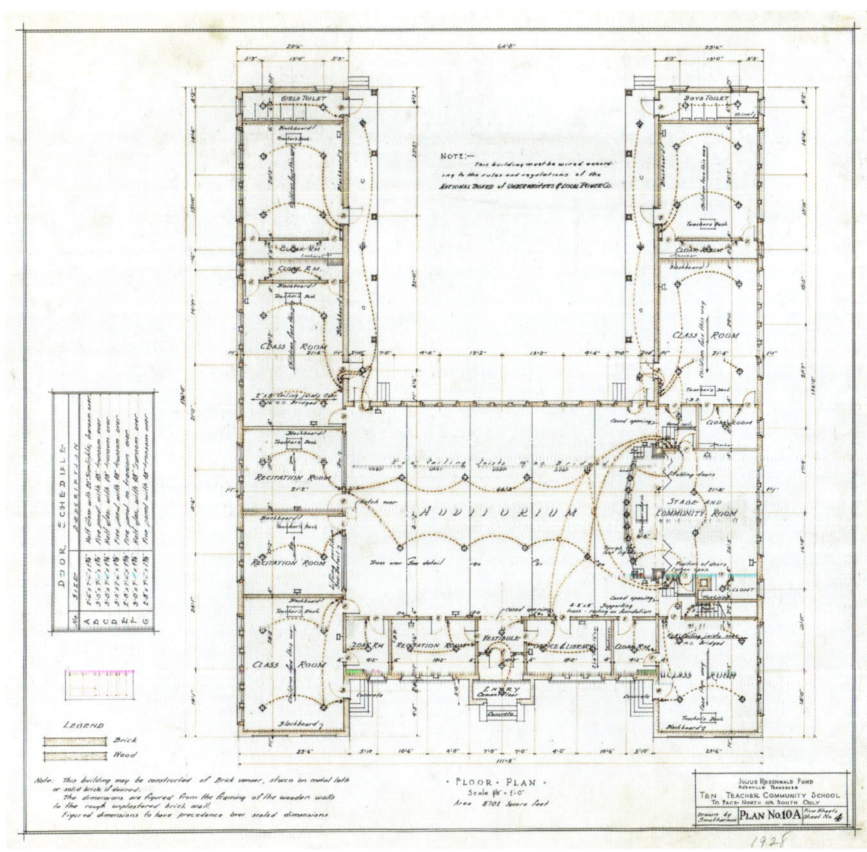

3. and 4. Julius Rosenwald Fund. Plan No. 10A. 1927. Elevations and plan for a ten-teacher school. Ink on linen, 22 x 22 in. (55.9 x 55.9 cm).
Julius Rosenwald Fund Collection, John Hope and Aurelia E. Franklin Library, Special Collections, Fisk University

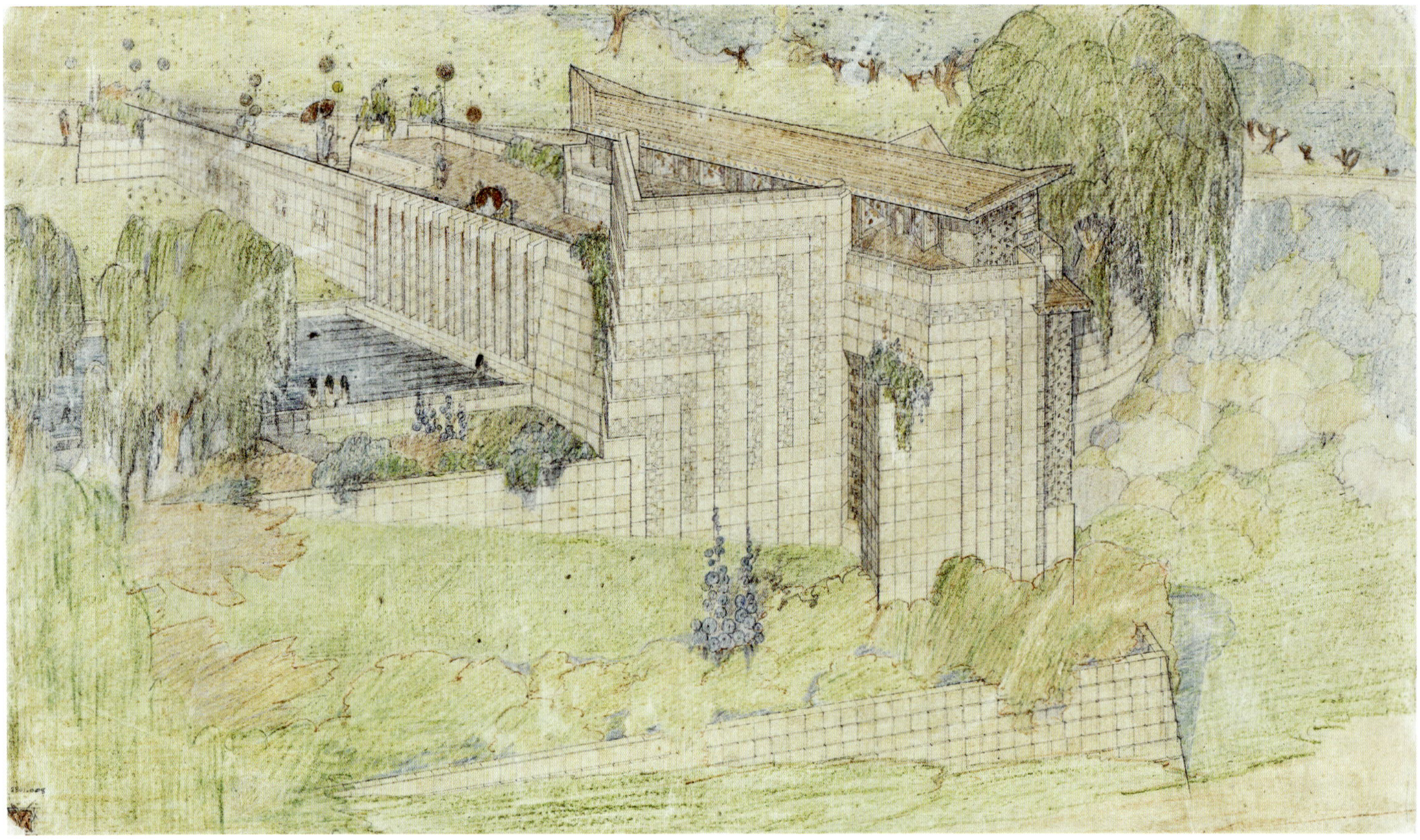

5. Little Dipper School and Community Playhouse, Los Angeles. 1923.
Perspective from the west. Pencil and colored pencil on tracing paper,
15 3/4 x 26 7/8 in.(40 x 68.3 cm)

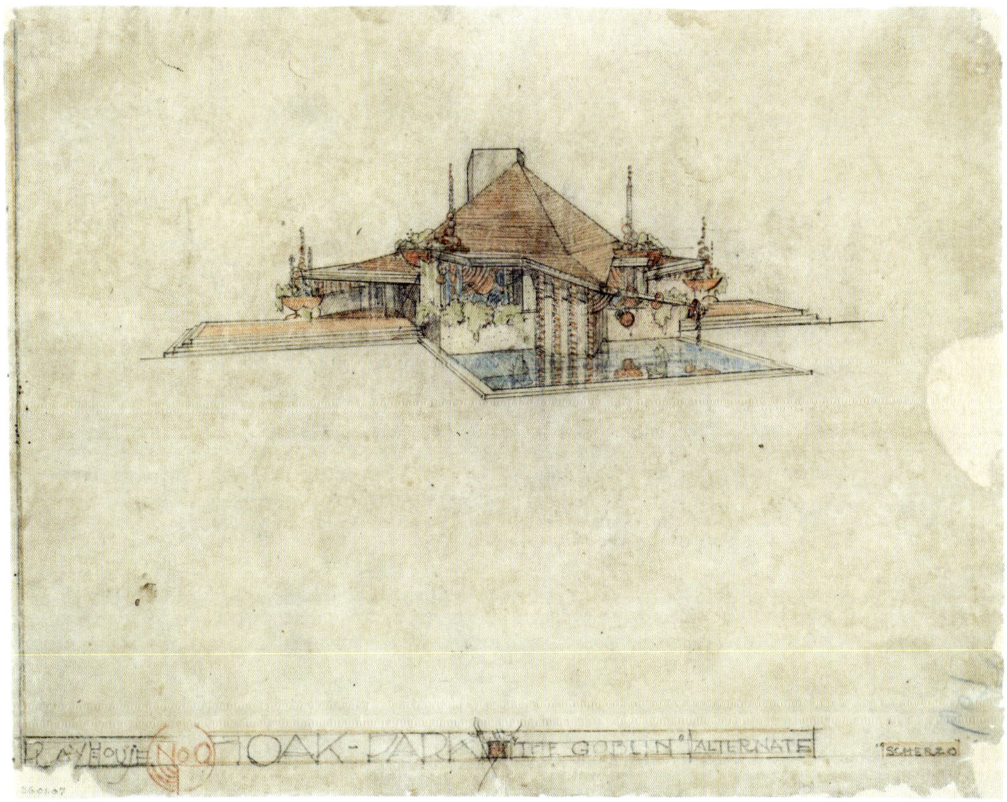

6. Playhouses for the Oak Park Playground Association (Kindersymphonies),
Oak Park, Illinois. Poject, 1926. Perspective of the "Goblin" house.
Pencil and colored pencil on tracing paper, 9 ⅞ x 12 ½ in. (25.1 x 31.8 cm)

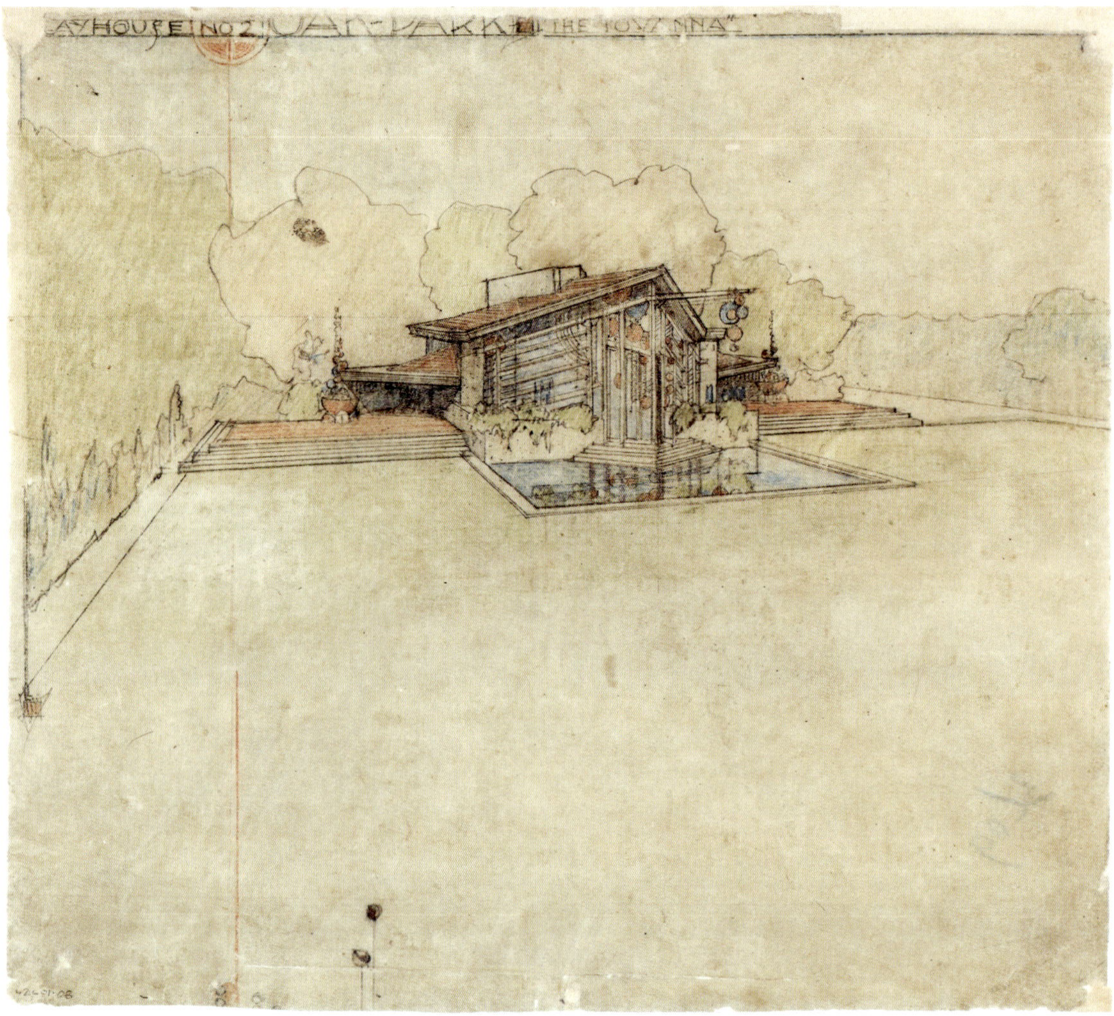

7. Playhouses for the Oak Park Playground Association (Kindersymphonies),
Oak Park, Illinois. Project, 1926. Perspective of the "Iovanna" house.
Pencil and colored pencil on tracing paper, 11 ⅛ x 11 ½ in. (28.3 x 29.2 cm)

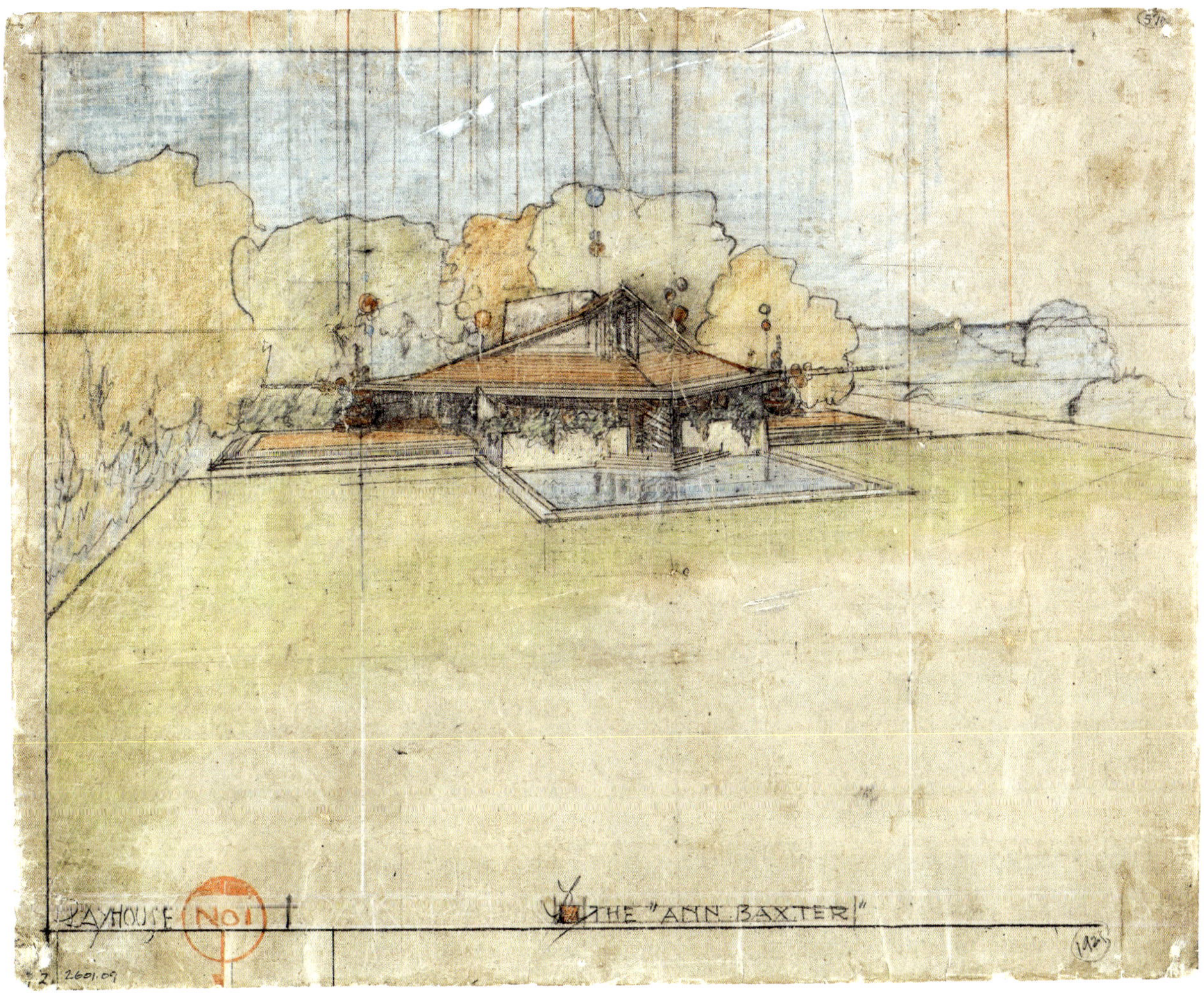

8. Playhouses for the Oak Park Playground Association (Kindersymphonies), Oak Park, Illinois. Project, 1926. Perspective of the "Ann Baxter" house. Pencil and colored pencil on tracing paper, 11 ⅛ x 13 ⅝ in. (28.3 x 34.6 cm)

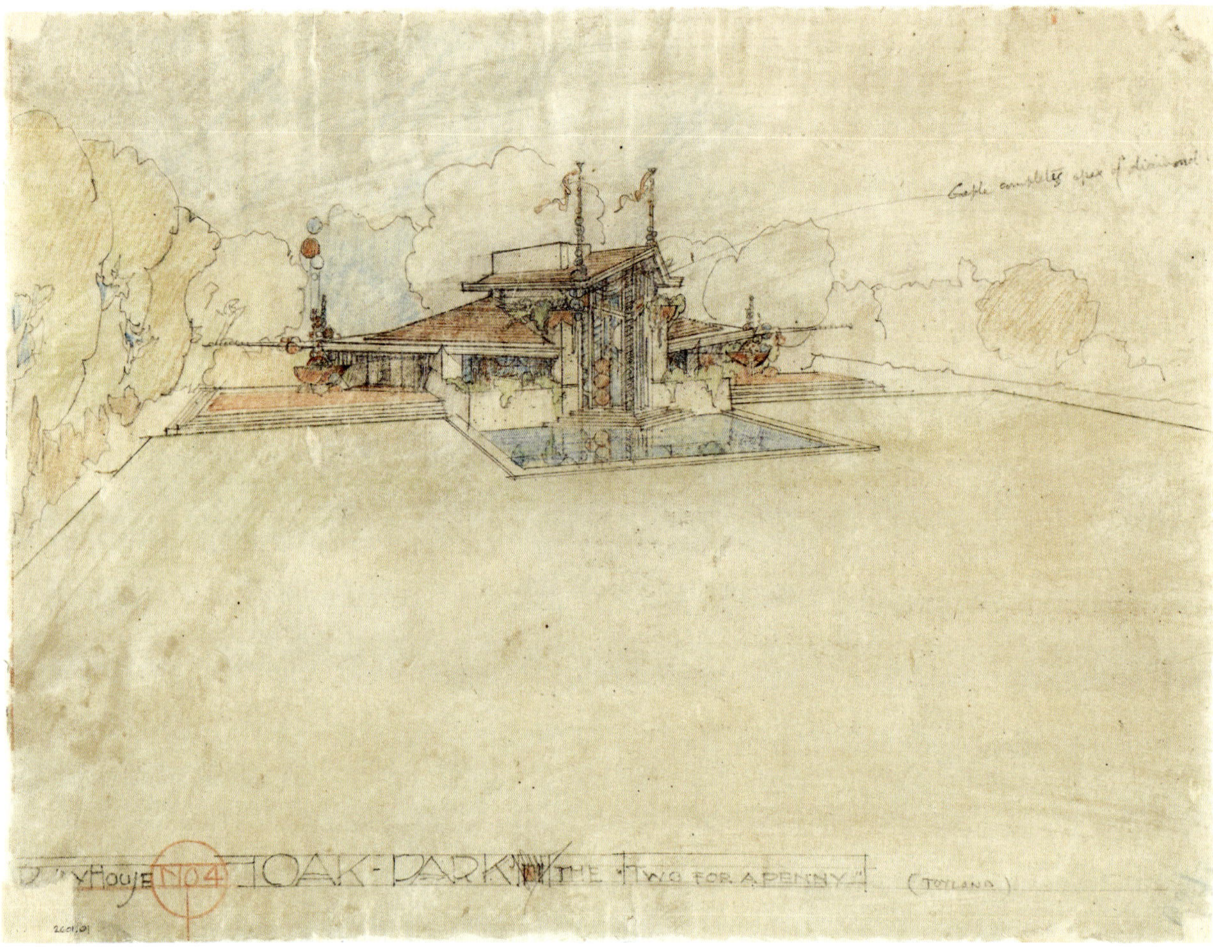

9. Playhouses for the Oak Park Playground Association (Kindersymphonies), Oak Park, Illinois. Project, 1926. Perspective of the "Two for a Penny" house. Pencil and colored pencil on tracing paper, 10 ½ x 13 ⅞ in. (26.7 x 35.2 cm)

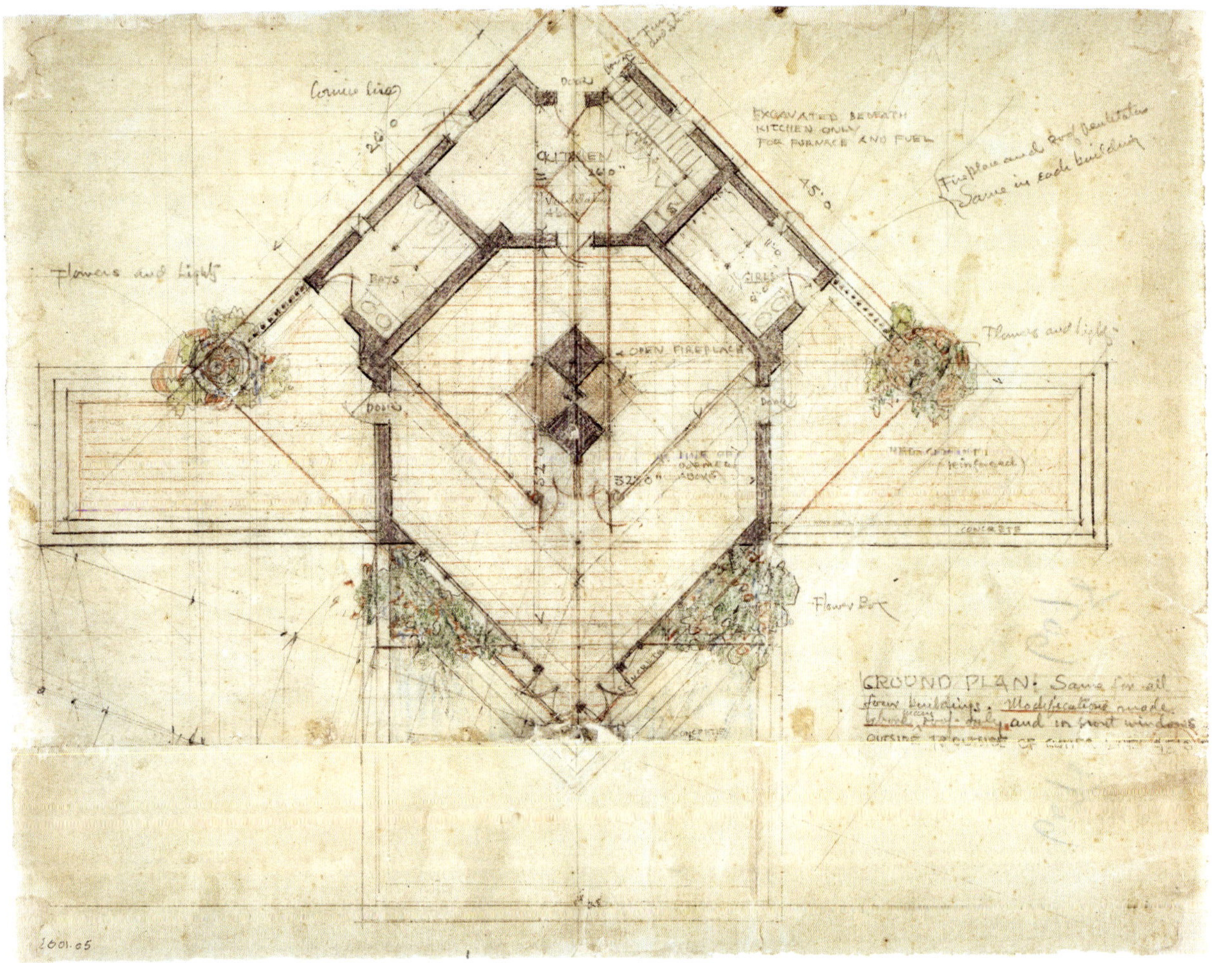

10. Playhouses for the Oak Park Playground Association (Kindersymphonies),
Oak Park, Illinois. Project, 1926. Ground-floor plan.
Pencil and colored pencil on tracing paper, 10 x 12 7/8 in. (25.4 x 32.7 cm)

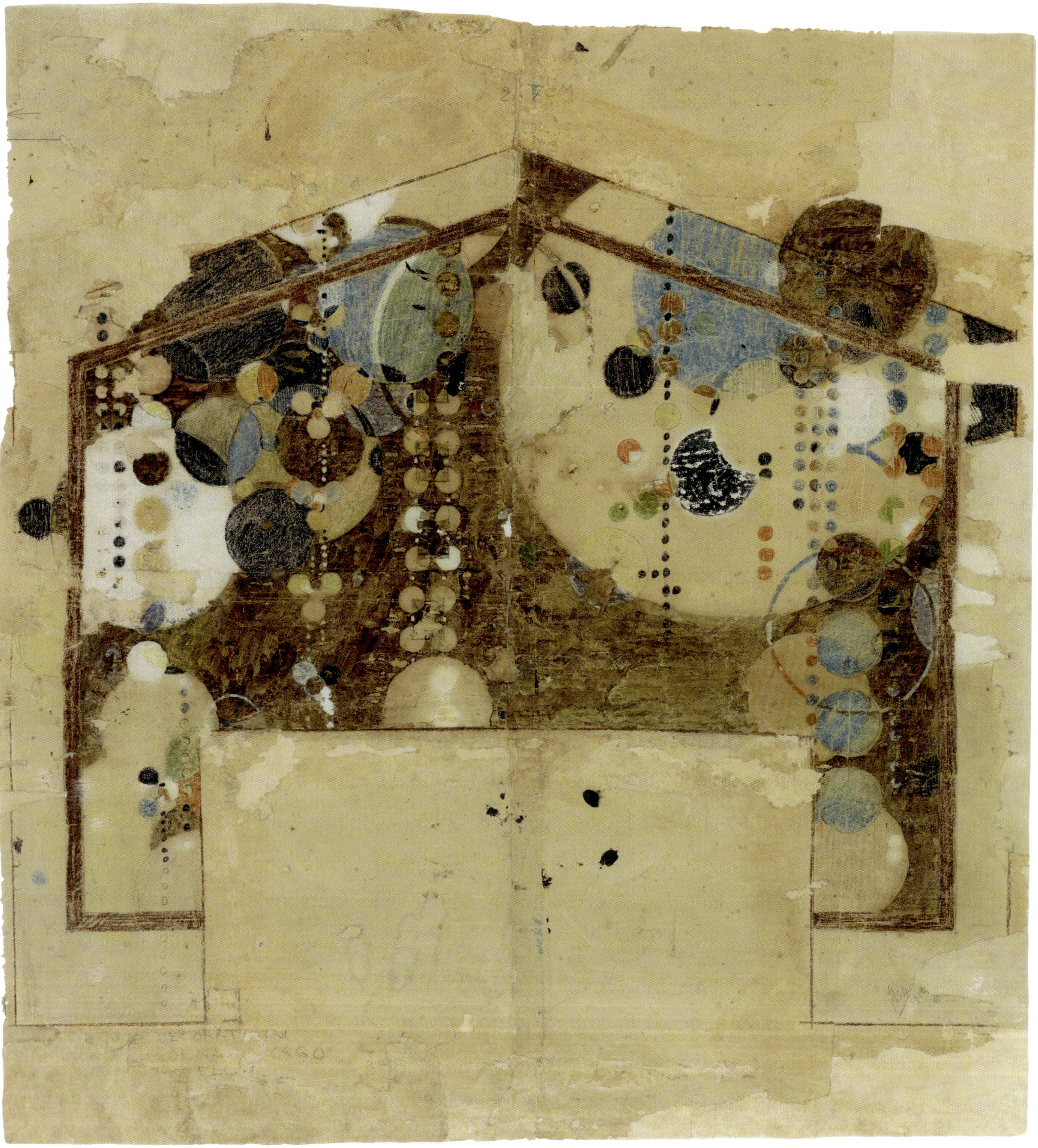

Midway Gardens, Chicago. 1913–14. Mural design for the tavern. Ink, pencil, and colored pencil on tracing paper, 23 5/8 x 21 3/4 in. (60 x 55.2 cm)

SPYROS PAPAPETROS

THE FINIAL AND THE MOUSETRAP ORNAMENT FROM MIDWAY GARDENS TO THE V. C. MORRIS GIFT SHOP

Among the many legends trailing the demolition of Frank Lloyd Wright's Midway Gardens (1913–14) is the story of a finial seen "rising grotesquely from the water" after the entertainment complex in Chicago was bulldozed and thrown into Lake Michigan to support the building of a breakwater.[1] While the rest of the sturdy edifice had long expired, the surviving building crown appeared to keep up the fight against financial speculation by refusing to become functionally repurposed as landfill. Instead, the defiant finial would remain resolutely an ornament signaling the building's location even when its ruins were long buried underwater.

Since Wright designed a variety of vertical markers symmetrically installed on top of Midway's terraces (fig. 1), we may never know exactly what this particular vampire finial looked like. Yet we can imagine that in its original setting it would have been surrounded by Midway's tall electric-light towers, which oriented visitors driving toward the popular establishment at night. An elevation of Midway's towering "stacks" labels the large rectangular frames on top of these central pylons "cement finials" and shows them supporting long "string" pendants, each a cascade of spherical, cubic, and pyramidal ornaments painted in "red, white, orange, blue, and gold."[2] However, just like the white balloons seen rising from the terraces in an aerial perspective of the project (plate 1), these pendants never materialized due to the financial limitations that from the start curtailed Wright's vast ornamental program for the establishment.

While missing from the exterior, the circles of these phantom finials and evanescent balloons would haunt the interior decoration of Midway, as their cascades of annular ornaments would reverberate in the multiple columns of colorful circles on the tavern murals (opposite). It appears prophetically ironic that the murals' effervescent circles, suggesting the "bubbles in sparkling drinks" once consumed on the premises, would eventually fizzle in the marine environment of Lake Michigan.[3]

The very ornamentation that once bolstered Midway's consumerist euphoria transformed into a harbinger of its evaporation into building debris, owing to financial failure fifteen years after its opening. Now the diagonal lines of the "dancing glass" pattern on the decorative concrete blocks once unifying Midway's arcade and belvedere balconies would striate the sand on the bottom of the lake, until they too would be smoothed out by erosion (plate 2).[4]

In their quasi-mythical marine afterlife, Midway's finials, murals, and decorative blocks function as allegorical emblems for Wright's practice of ornamentation as a whole. In an era when ornamental motifs started vanishing from buildings, ornament resiliently survived in Wright's designs, persisting despite periodic financial cataclysms by transforming and, just like the displaced finial, learning how to "float" within an increasingly "liquid" economic environment where no building or artifact could ever be stable. Even if clad in a geometry of harmonious symmetry and order, Wright's ornaments function as prognosticating graphic symbols of pervasive instability and disarray.

Critics and historians, like Wright himself, have portrayed his ornament as "integral," demonstrating an "organic" coherence both within itself and with the rest of the structure of which it is a genuine member rather than a superficially applied layer.[5] Using the story of Midway Gardens as departure point, this essay follows a different pathway to the organic, one less concerned with integration and more reflective of the rupture and disintegration that Wright's rhythmic ornaments often confronted when exposed to the financial hardships and professional discordances of the real world.

Economic concerns play a prominent role not only in Wright's ornamental practice but also in his writing about ornament. In a lecture on the "ethics of ornamentation" given in January 1909 in Oak Park, Wright presents ornament as a primeval "desire" that is "coexistent with the earliest attempts of civilization of every people" but that today "consumes at least two thirds of [the nation's] economic resources."[6] One could perhaps object that in several of Wright's own projects, whether for the private residences of wealthy clients or for grand commercial establishments like Midway, the parts of the design related to the ornamental "dressing" of the building represented a major expense that could cause the project to go over budget. A drawing of furniture for two studio residences for Aline Barnsdall (fig. 2) is remarkable in this respect: next to the dimensions of each piece of furniture, drawn in front and side elevation, Wright noted the price, as one might in the pages of a furniture catalog. The lower half of the same sheet includes two detailed budget lists with the total cost of furniture and all other artifacts that could be called "decoration," including "light stands," "overstuffed ottomans," "rugs," and "shades."[7] Lines and mathematical figures together draw a "projection" of the house, juxtaposing a figurative with a numerical perspective. One might further speculate that the allegedly "organic" or "integral" character of Wright's ornamentation was part of a business strategy that made it very hard to remove any part of the design as "extra." In any case, ornaments left out due to financial shortage, such as the Midway balloons and finial pendants, would accumulate in the architect's treasury of design ideas and return in future projects in even greater quantity and cost.

Steep economic expenditure on ornament reappears in a later text of Wright's, "An Apology for the Decorator," written in 1931 but unpublished during his lifetime. In the opening paragraphs Wright mentions that a "recent drive across the country from Los Angeles to New York convinced me that 97 percent was the decorators' in one form or another."[8] What could Wright have seen in this

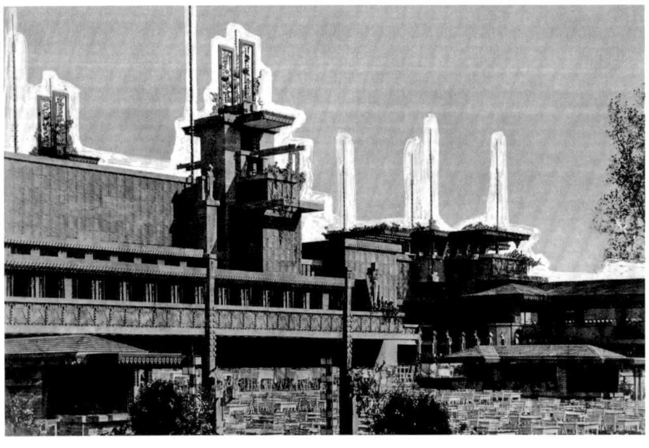

Fig. 1. Midway Gardens, Chicago. 1913–14. View of the finials

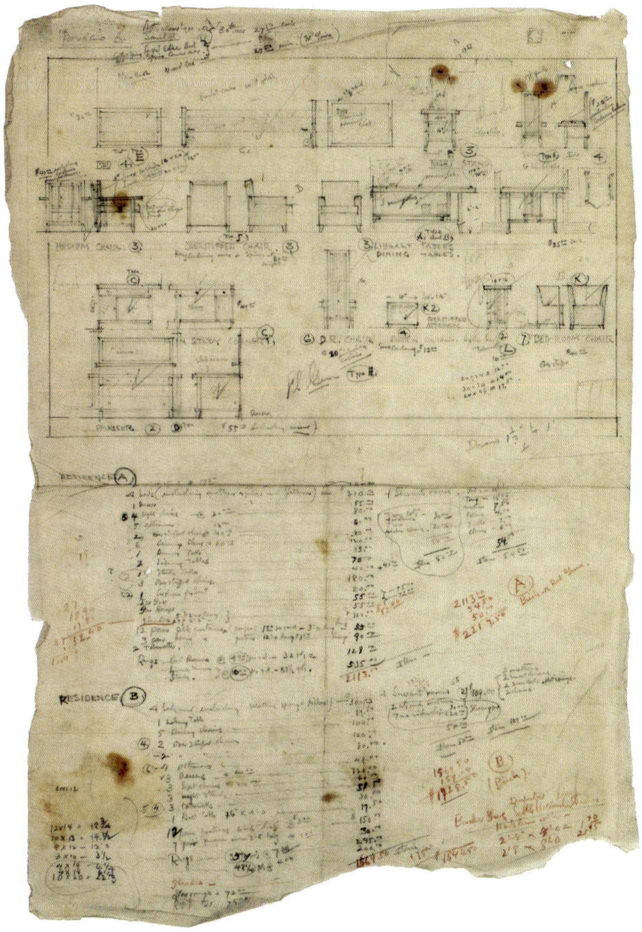

long drive that convinced him of the precipitous increase of the decorator's property (a rise of approximately 30 percent in twenty years, if we compare the 1931 percentage with the "two thirds" of Wright's 1910 lecture)? Here the architect obviously refers to something much vaster than buildings or furniture. Like a host of cultural and social theorists of his period, Wright appears dumbfounded by the increasing "ornamentalization" of both culture and economy. He described the proliferation of "peripheral" artifacts—such as clothing accessories, gadgets, appliances, billboards, and electrical marquees (like the one Wright resisted installing in Midway Gardens)—that would quickly take over the entrances of department stores, hotels, and entertainment centers from New York to Los Angeles.

The titles attached to Wright's 1909 and 1931 texts would seem to mark a gradual transition from "ornament" to "decoration," that is, from an individual surface pattern to an organized system of objects that expands beyond a building environment and is controlled—or even personified, according to Wright—by the professional circle of the "decorator." Wright's often contentious encounters with the "club" of interior decorators (whom in the mid-1930s he would address as "inferior desecrators") suggest that while decorators could exist near the professional territory of the architect they would always be disavowed.[9] "The architect is a decorator," but is the decorator "such an architect?" Wright asks.[10]

As projected by the use of geometry in Wright's early decorative designs, his strongest method of branding his work was his peculiar form of abstraction or "conventionalization" of nature, which distinguished his ornament from that of other architects and "decorators." Patron and architect would "co-own" the building through an ornamental pattern that colonized all interior and exterior surfaces and was designed for that project alone. The vast house for Susan Lawrence Dana (1902–04) in Springfield, Illinois, for example, is unified by the extensive use of stained glass ornamented by variants of a sumac-tree pattern (see p. 91, plate 8), transforming the interior space into a sheltered microcosm that nonetheless remains in intimate dialogue with nature (plate 3). Outside, on the plaster frieze of the upper facade, variations of the same vegetal pattern are

Fig. 2. Hollyhock (Barnsdall) House and Olive Hill Cultural Center, Los Angeles. 1918–21. Furniture and millwork for Studio Residences A and B. 1920–21. Ink, pencil, and colored pencil on tracing paper, 22 1/2 x 15 5/8 in. (57.2 x 39.7 cm)

organized into a geometric network, extending the dialogue initiated by nature's conventionalization to the inorganic world of the machine, electricity, and industrial infrastructure (plates 4, 5).

Despite embracing "the art and craft of the machine," Wright's own ornament and decorative designs had a tentative and somewhat challenging relation with industrial reproduction. His designs for electric lamps, rugs, and furniture were usually produced in limited numbers for a specific project.[11] A rare exception is the copper urn (plate 6), with an embossed ornamental pattern of circles and squares, that figures prominently in the interior of the Dana House. This is one of the architect's few decorative artifacts to be selectively reinstalled in a limited number of his residential and commercial interiors from the early 1890s to the late 1940s.

Wright's designs for glassware and dinner service for the Dutch glass company Leerdam (1929; plate 7) are ostensibly his first explicit attempts to design household artifacts for industrial production and without a specific house design in mind. Since they were originally conceived as "ceramic forms," however, Wright's glassware designs were "not amenable" to mass production and almost none of them were industrially reproduced.[12] The architect's designs test the limits of the application of the same forms and ornamental patterns across different materials—a transference that had proliferated since the second half of the nineteenth century, when workshops and factories started to mechanically reproduce formerly luxurious ornamental artifacts in less precious materials for public consumption.

While turning from the three-dimensionality of artifacts to the flatness of the printed page, Wright's colorful designs for the cover of the magazine *Liberty* (1927–28) offered him the opportunity to extend the possibilities of ornament's transference across materials and scales. *Liberty* rejected the covers, but the architect creatively recycled them for other journals and books, as well as in a variety of artifacts and building designs. The original graphic designs expand Wright's process of conventionalization from the world of plants, such as fruit and cactus flowers, to the domain of human artifacts and architectural structures, such as balloons, flags, jewelry, gift packages, and a shopping window, each representing a particular month or season of the year.

The background of financial transaction underlying Wright's ornament is in full display in his design for a *Liberty* cover, "The Jeweler's Window," that depicts a series of necklaces and pendants suspended inside the vacuum of a shop window (plate 8). The jewels appear suspended in midair with no obvious support, yet a sense of gravity is restored by the thick black horizontal base, which the pendants appear to penetrate as if they were in front of rather than behind the "window" frame. This means that we, the spectators, are also inside the shop window, in empathy with these commercial articles, not outside looking at them from the street. Tellingly, however, some of the colorful objects displayed in the window depict not handcrafted jewels but raw precious stones "conventionalized" into circular, square, and triangular forms and piled on top of the dark horizontal frame as if just unearthed.[13] What we previously perceived as the base of a window frame proves to be a geological section, signaling the original connection of bodily adornment to the earth, and the role of natural ecology in forming the material content of adornment before the laws of human economy and its (archi)tectonic forms transpired.

Unlike the colorful mosaics that the Chicago architect and artist Charles Morgan produced in 1929 in strict imitation of Wright's *Liberty* covers, Wright's own translations of these designs into other forms went beyond the literal. In a drawing of the floor plan and rug design for the house of David Wright (1950–51; plate 9), the pneumatic circles of another *Liberty* cover, "March Balloons," appear not only to have landed on the living room carpet but to have spread around circular columns, curvilinear interior and exterior walls, fireplace, windows, and landscape elements. Such sprawling expansion is possible because the strings that appear to tie all the balloons on the original cover are now almost absent, signaling the transition from the verticality of the balloons (or of the columns of bubbles on the Midway murals) to the horizontal plane of the rug. A 1955 presentation drawing adapted from the same "March Balloons" cover, but based on the rug design for David Wright, converts the textile composition of the rug plan back into a graphic pattern (plate 10). Since Wright signs his name along the long side of the sheet, the drawing implies a stronger ambiguity of orientation, suggesting a possible turn from the original, vertical format of the journal cover to the horizontal layout of the rug.[14] While Wright's conventionalization of plant motifs principally preserved the vertical direction of vegetal growth, the ornamental abstraction of human artifacts facilitated a nonconventionalizing design behavior, breaking away from the laws of gravity and bolstering the liberal circulation inflating human economic growth.

Wright's annular ornaments would perform another "revolution" in transferring from residential and commercial establishments to religious ones. If, in earlier designs, the organizing structure of the building plan was merely suggested in the main decorative pattern for the same project, some of the distinctly ornamental plans in Wright's late building designs display themselves overtly as iconic miniature plan-logos spread across interior and exterior building surfaces. This transformation of ornament to both plan and icon applies, for example, to the symmetrical design of the Annunciation Greek Orthodox Church in Wauwatosa, Wisconsin (1955–61), one of Wright's last religious buildings, whose construction and interior decoration were completed three years after his death (plate 11). The floor plan's circle-and-cross pattern—echoing not only the principal Christian Orthodox liturgical symbols but also the main ornamental motifs of Wright's early designs, including his urn and signature logo from the 1890s—is created by the intersection of four circles of equal diameter, each centered on one of the four corners of a square and each inscribing the main circle of the auditorium and its large spherical dome. The same geometric ornament is quoted in various scales in all the decorative features of the church interior, as well as in the design of the surrounding landscaping.

Of particular interest in the church is the ornamentation of the altar screen, which separates the sanctuary from the elevated chancel and the auditorium and comprises two gold-painted metal panels featuring variations of the circle-and-cross motif in contrasting scales (plate 12). On its front is an "icon screen" with an elevated canopy of large intersecting circles that frame the religious icons and are supported by a series of thin steel pipe columns forming a sequence of arched gates. Behind the icon screen is a more densely "perforated ornamental metal screen," a series of rotating panels whose design is again based on the church's plan, miniaturized in densely intersecting circles of 2 1/2 inches (6.4 centimeters) in radius.

This double screen can be opened and closed, periodically veiling and unveiling the religious ritual to the audience and in doing so underlining the role of decoration as a threshold between the visible and the invisible, between iconic figuration and symbolic abstraction. The intrinsic rhetorical capacity of ornament allows the screen to mediate between the spaces of attendance and of performance, both encircled by the same geometric pattern. The screen is the supreme speaker of the church. The very act of annunciation is performed by the seemingly infinite repetition of the screen's circular patterns as they reverberate not only the divine word but also the architect's emblematic plan and decoration.

Both the religious icons originally installed on the altar screen and the colorful geometric designs intended for the stained-glass bay windows were designed by Eugene Masselink (plate 13). Wright's designer employed a mixed Byzantine and abstract style, diverging from the stylistic precepts of the traditional Byzantine iconography normatively required in Greek Orthodox churches. For that reason, Masselink's icons were later removed from the screen and his window designs never materialized. The graphic artist's designs had centered on a religious figure framed by intricate ornamental patterns, which represented clouds or waves and repeated the geometric motifs of Wright's gate screen and elevated chancel railing. By converting Wright's ornamental plan into both a visual element implying landscape and an organic part of the religious iconography, Masselink's icons and glass designs aspired to be not merely framed by but embedded in the building's geometric decoration. Perhaps the testament encrypted in the last church designs of an architect who portrayed himself as a "natural heretic" was that architectural decoration and ornament have the capacity to convey a more universal message than the typified repertoire of any orthodox religion.[15] It is precisely decoration that allows the architect to become a *superior* "desecrator."

Wright's expanded practice of ornamentation reached its most "integral" postwar expression not in a church but in a more modest chapel of commerce, the V. C. Morris Gift Shop in San Francisco (1948–49), a work that reestablishes ornament's organic link with the world of artifacts and commercial exchange. Here Wright condensed the circular floor plan and ramp of his first design for the Solomon R. Guggenheim Museum (1943–59) inside the much smaller envelope of an existing building set within a dense city block. The ramp is hidden from the street behind a tall brick wall ornamented only by a radial-patterned arch over the vaulted glass gateway that leads to the shop's entrance door (plate 14). The facade is incised by a horizontal row of small "translucent glass squares" with light bulbs for "night lighting," and, on the store's left border, by a tall "vertical railway 30 feet long" with projecting brick tiles and "receptacles for sixteen 40 watt bulbs" to be lit at night—yet another reminder of Midway Gardens' freestanding light towers, here immured on the brick wall like a relief (fig. 3).[16] The flatness of the facade gives it a graphic quality anticipating its conversion by Masselink into stationery design embossed with the semicircular arch and the store owner's name (fig. 4). As with "March Balloons" and the David Wright rug and floor plan, the conversion from graphic ornament to building plan can work both ways. By means of graphic ornament, the building facade becomes a personal emblem, which, even if it prominently bears the name of the client, also unmistakably carries the signature of the architect.

The store's lack of an open storefront or even a single glass vitrine was noted by the contemporary architectural press and used by Wright almost as a banner to advertise the shop as a unique and unorthodox design.[17] Equally noted is Wright's response to Vere Morris's concerns over the absence of any public display of the artifacts for sale in his shop: "We are not going to dump your beautiful merchandise on the street," Wright replied, adding that his intention was to "entice" passersby to look inside through the arched glass tunnel. Then, led to "penetrate further" and see the shop's ramp and tables "set with fine

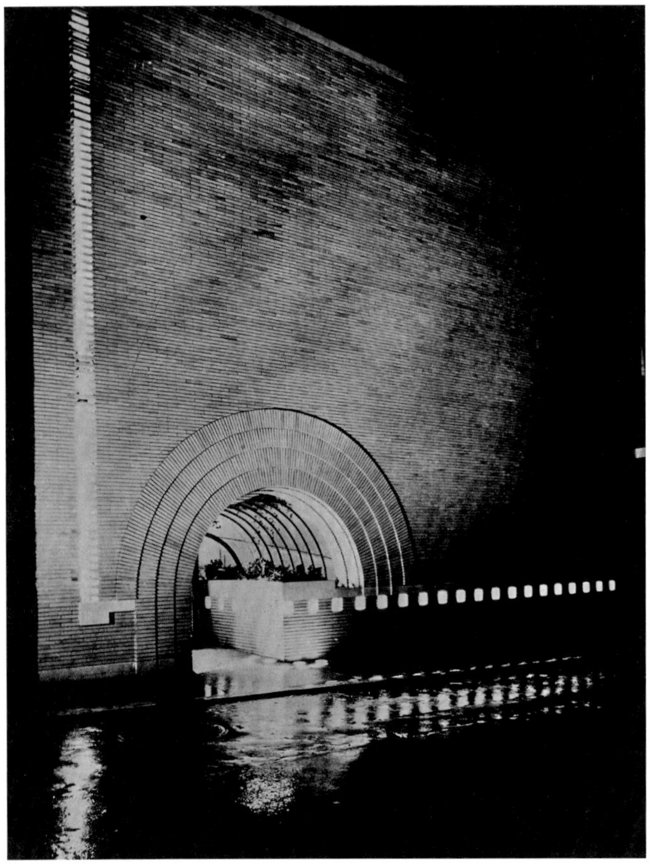

Fig. 3. V. C. Morris Gift Shop, San Francisco. 1948–49. View of the facade at night

china and crystal," prospective customers would "suddenly" be compelled to "push open the door, and . . ." added the architect with a smile, "you've got them. Just like a mousetrap!"[18] It may be that the vaulted tunnel of the glass-and-metal entryway, recalling an antique mousetrap made of metal wire, provided the model for the animal analogy, yet it was the profuse interior decoration behind the store's plain facade that materialized its architectural logic of deception.

Next to the fictively animalized patrons, the most vivid inhabitants of this entrapping enclosure were the artifacts for sale, the "beautiful merchandize" for which Wright appeared to be concerned in designing an envelope that would shield them from exposure to the street. Carefully staged photographs of the Morris shop in its original state capture the luster the glass artifacts added to the dark wood of the cabinetry in which they sat in order, like the displays in an arts-and-crafts museum. Large spherical vases designed by Wright, emulating the copper or stone urns on the exteriors of his early projects, were embedded in the display of the rest of the commercial artifacts. Made of clear plastic, some of them contained fish and aquatic plants, standing in for the aquarium included in the original floor plan for the store. The profuse vegetation in the large planter suspended from the ceiling (the sole remnant of a circular constellation of spherical planters that Wright intended to suspend over the ramp, as shown in the section) and the ambient light descending from the circular "clouds" in the translucent Plexiglas "visor" further embellished the mimicry between nature and commerce, private and public space (plate 15).[19] Protected by the opaque facade, the interior decoration bestowed a domestic ambience on this private commercial establishment, giving the impression of entering someone's home—and Wright was in fact commissioned to design a home for the Morrises, which, however, despite multiple design efforts, never materialized.[20] Contributing to the ornamental recovery of domesticity, the shop's ground-floor plan also features a small sketch of Wright's original copper urn from the 1890s (drawn in plan yet absent from the original photographs of the shop), set next to a large transparent hemispheric bowl, filled with small clear-plastic balls, on a "stone table" directly behind the glass wall of the entry tunnel. Glimpsing the balls inside the large "globe," the passersby would see the anamorphic reflections of their own faces, as if they were already trapped in the store's interior before they even crossed its entrance.

Wright also designed a series of circular niches carved into the circular wall of the ramp, some acting as stands or vitrines for items clustered in vertical sequences (like the hanging pendants in the "Jeweler's Window" *Liberty* cover or the columns of circles on the Midway murals). From flat surface and sunken relief to three-dimensional artifacts and architectural features, the Morris shop diagrams the transition from ornament to object through building. Wright not only designed some of the objects displayed in the store but also chose artifacts from its "gift" collection for other projects of his. This reciprocal exchange of professional services between architect and client provided the organizational core of the gift shop and is reflected in its formal organization. The fulcrum of the shop is the spiral ramp, which mediates between the sky of the ceiling and the earthly tile floor. The skylight's geometric "clouds" would be reflected in the floating islands of built-in displays and mobile furniture on the ground floor, including a large semicircular table (designed by Manuel Sandoval) with two rotating quarters nesting a few smaller circular tables and stools tacked underneath. One of these tables was specifically requested by Morris for the display of jewelry, as documented in a letter to Wright on the back of which the architect drew a sketch of the table set on casters with a rotating glass top, swivel side shelves, and

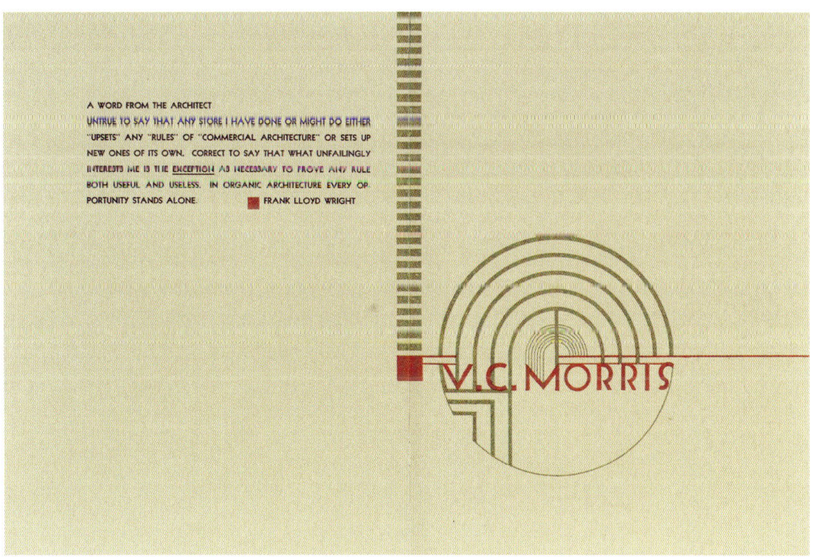

Fig. 4. Eugene Masselink (American, born South Africa, 1910–1962). Graphic design for V. C. Morris. 1948. Stationary, 11 7/16 x 17 1/4 in. (29.1 x 43.8 cm)

removable trays (fig. 5). This circular artifact served as a conceptual model for the entire shop, which operated on a similar rotating schedule recalling the combined rotation and levitation of the "March Balloons," whose circles would touch, overlap, or nest inside one another, granting the graphic design a seemingly infinite possibility of rearrangement.

This circular transformation applies to the afterlife of Wright's project: following the deaths of the original owners, who wanted the shop to be preserved as "a museum for its architect," it was eventually converted to a clothing department store and later a private gallery for "ethnic art" from around the globe.[21] Surveying the transformations, conversions, and "desecrations," as well as the cancellations, financial failures, and building collapses associated with Wright's projects, one might view the resilient presence of ornament in all of the architect's efforts not only as a wholesome symbol of the harmonious cooperation between the geometric circles of architecture and the real world but also as a rudiment of their catastrophic collision. The divided legacy of Wright's ornament lies in its double function as a "seed germ" (to use a term of Louis Sullivan's) of new ideas and simultaneously as a remnant of abandoned or canceled plans—private or collective revolutions that were never completed yet are destined to return in ever-more-elaborate constellations. Wright's own mythic personality and organic ideology share a deep affinity with ornament in that both were essentially rudiments of a nineteenth-century mentality surviving deep into the twentieth century, and even experiencing a vigorous afterlife during the last two decades of the architect's lifetime. From the underwater wreckage of Midway Gardens to the posthumously commodified aquarium of the V. C. Morris Gift Shop, ornament functions as the memorializing sign of Wright's production in its transformative encounters with the overlapping circles of economic and ecological transformation. If the machine-age ornament in Wright's early designs represented a conventionalization *of* nature, then the eroded concrete block blossoming with moss in the underwater Midway Gardens embodies the *re-* or *de*-conventionalization of geometric ornament *by* nature. This is the new "organic" direction signaled by Midway's lost finial, still beckoning from the gutter of the lake.

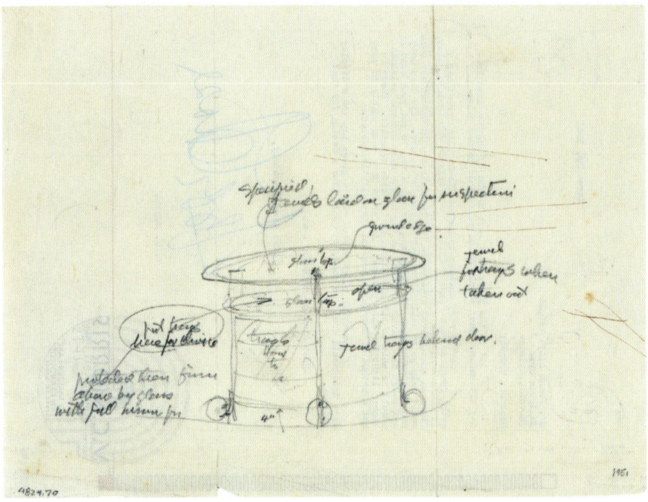

Fig. 5. V. C. Morris Gift Shop, San Francisco. 1948–49. Study for a table. Pencil on paper (verso) with typed letter, signed (recto), 8 x 11 in. (20.3 x 27.9 cm)

Notes

1. See Brendan Gill, *Many Masks: A Life of Frank Lloyd Wright* (New York: Da Capo, 1998), p. 228.
2. 1401.082, Frank Lloyd Wright Foundation Archives (The Museum of Modern Art | Avery Architectural & Fine Arts Library, Columbia University, New York).
3. Anthony Alofsin, *Frank Lloyd Wright: The Lost Years, 1910–1922. A Study of Influence* (1993; repr. Austin: InnerformsLtd.com, 2009), p. 164.
4. Ibid., p. 264.
5. See the section "Integral Ornament at Last!" in Frank Lloyd Wright, *An Autobiography* (1943; repr. New York: Barnes & Noble, 1998), pp. 346–48.
6. Wright, quoted in Jessie Higly, "On Ornamentation: Frank Lloyd Wright pleads for a new culture," *Oak Leaves*, January 16, 1909, p. 20.
7. 2002.012, Wright Foundation Archives (MoMA | Avery).
8. Frank Lloyd Wright, "An Apology for the Decorator," in Wright, *Collected Writings*, ed. Bruce Brooks Pfeiffer (New York: Rizzoli, 1993), 3:32.
9. See Eugene Masselink, letter (on behalf of Wright) to Gwendolen Thorpe (Lecture Committee Chair of New York's Decorators Club), October 6, 1935, D024C01, Wright Foundation Archives (MoMA | Avery).
10. Wright, "An Apology for the Decorator," p. 33.
11. Wright, "The Art and Craft of the Machine" (1901), in Wright, *Collected Writings*, 1:58–72.
12. David Hanks, *The Decorative Designs of Frank Lloyd Wright* (New York: Dutton, 1979), pp. 185–86.
13. For the analogy of Wright's ornamental forms for this *Liberty* cover with precious stones, such as "topaz," "emerald," and "turmaline," see Penny Fowler, *Frank Lloyd Wright, Graphic Artist* (Rohnert Park, Calif.: Pomegranate Press, 2002), p. 84.
14. In a contemporary photograph, however, Wright seems to be working in front of the same drawing in its vertical orientation. See ibid., p. iv.
15. Frank Lloyd Wright, *A Testament* (New York: Bramhall House, 1957), p. 23.
16. See notes in ground-floor plan, 4826.006, Wright Foundation Archives (MoMA | Avery).
17. "Gift Shop by Frank Lloyd Wright," *Architectural Forum* 92, no. 2 (February 1950): 79–85.
18. Wright, quoted in Pfeiffer and Yokio Futagawa, eds., *Frank Lloyd Wright* (Tokyo: A.D.A. Edita, 1984–88), 7:228.
19. V. C. Morris, letter to Wright, November 17, 1948, p. 2, B128D05, Wright Foundation Archives (MoMA | Avery).
20. See Paul V. Turner, *Frank Lloyd Wright and San Francisco* (New Haven, Conn.: Yale University Press, 2016), pp. 58–74.
21. Lilian Morris, letter to Wright, July 16, 1957, M263B05, Wright Foundation Archives (MoMA | Avery). Also quoted in Turner, *Frank Lloyd Wright and San Francisco*, p. 74.

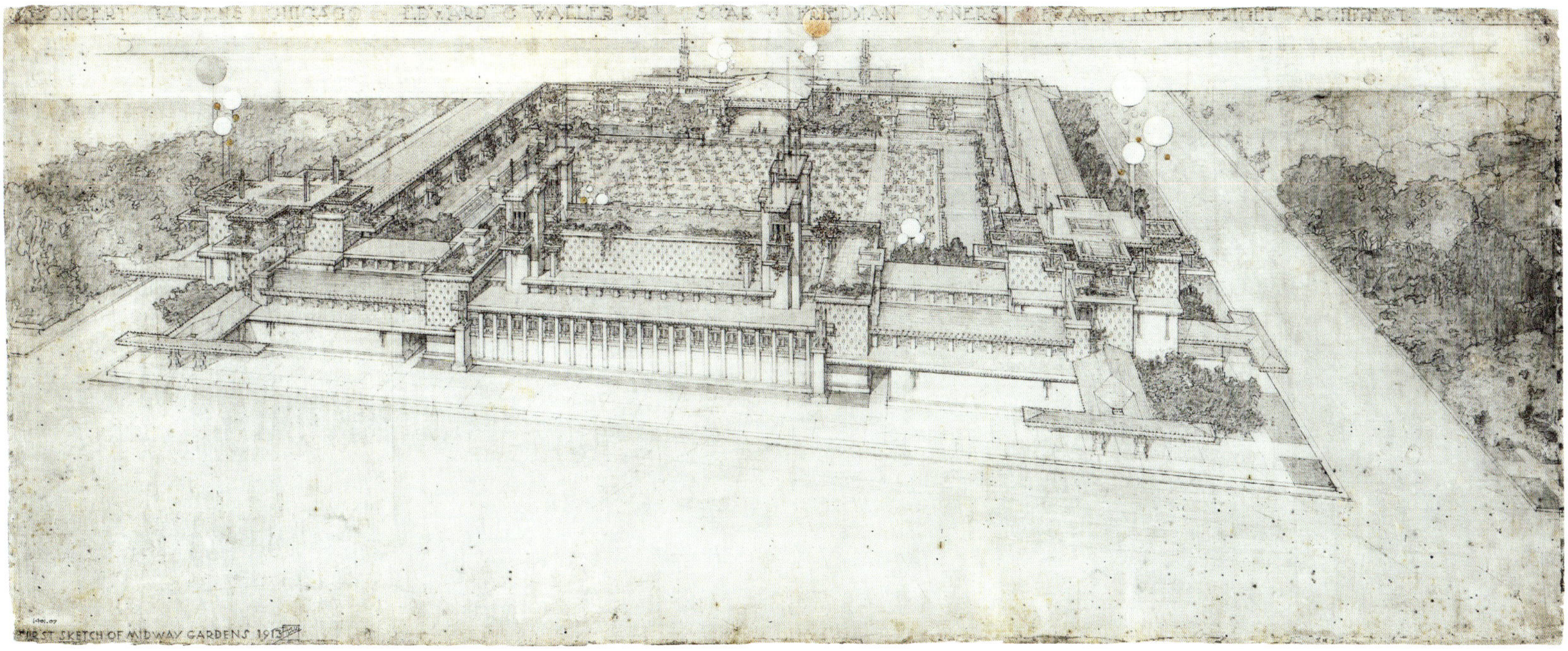

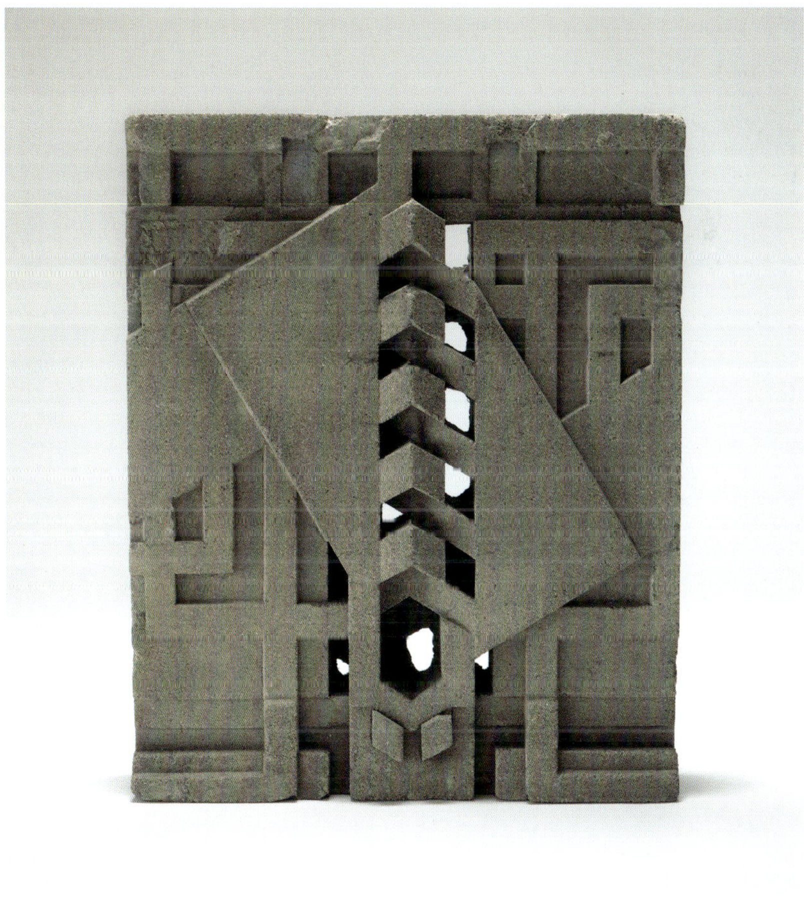

1. Midway Gardens, Chicago. 1913–14. Aerial perspective.
Pencil and colored pencil on drafting cloth, 16 ¼ x 40 in. (41.3 x 101.6 cm)

2. Midway Gardens, Chicago. 1913–14. Sculpted block.
Concrete, 32 ¾ x 27 x 6 ½ in. (83.2 x 68.6 x 16.5 cm)

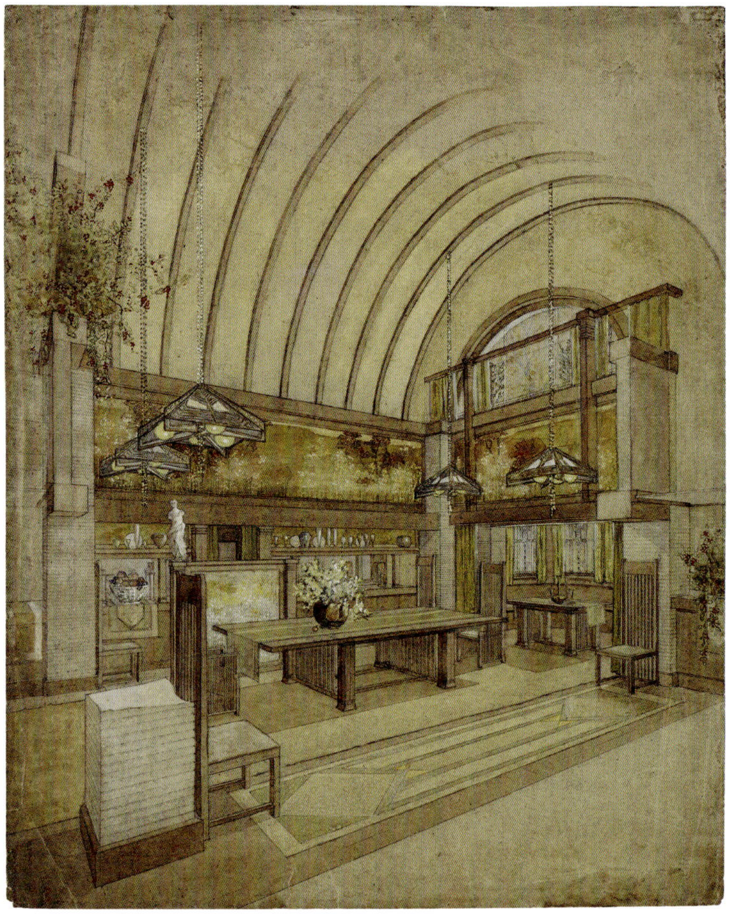

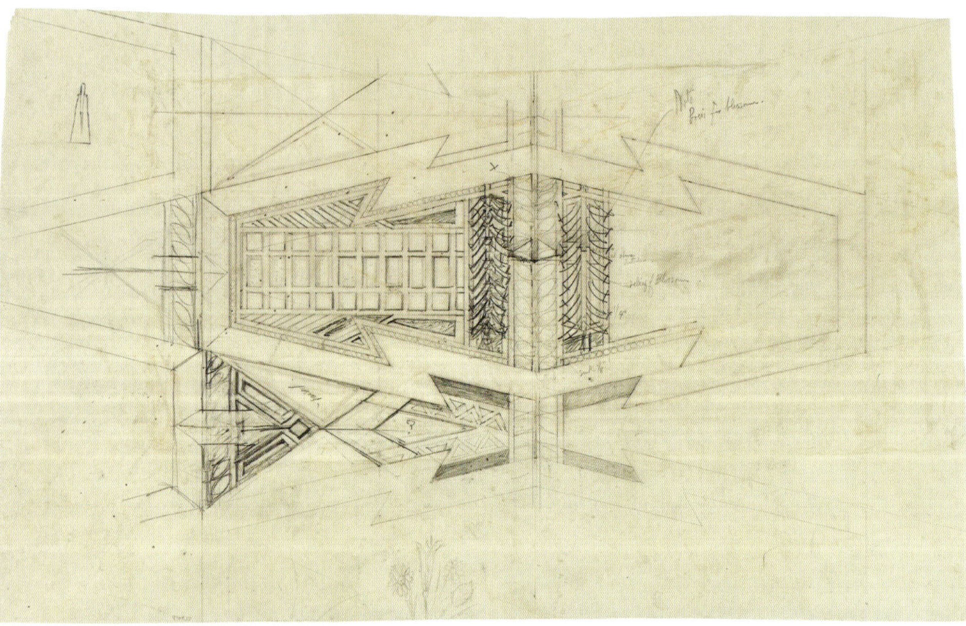

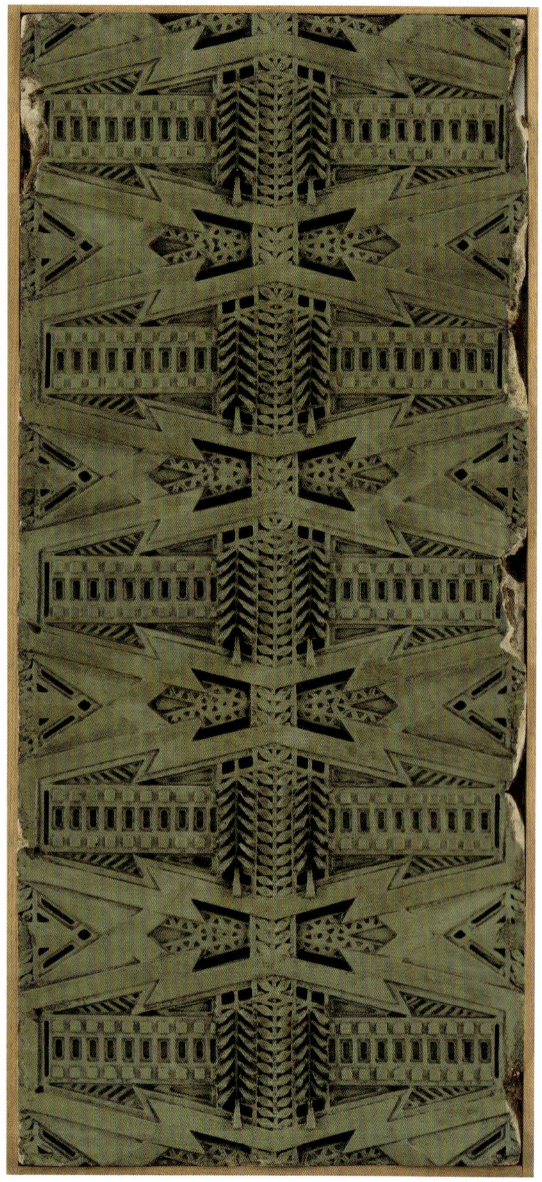

3. Dana House, Springfield, Illinois. 1902–04. Interior perspective of the dining room.
Graphite and watercolor on paper, 25 x 20 3/8 in. (63.5 x 51.6 cm).
Avery Architectural & Fine Arts Library, Columbia University, New York

4. Dana House, Springfield, Illinois. 1902–04. Study for the frieze.
Pencil and colored pencil on tracing paper, 21 5/8 x 34 7/8 in.
(54.9 x 88.6 cm)

5. Dana House, Springfield, Illinois. 1902–04. Exterior frieze.
Plaster and paint, 55 1/4 x 24 5/8 x 1 3/4 in. (140.3 x 62.5 x 4.4 cm).
The Museum of Modern Art, New York. Gift of Don Magner and Edgar Smith

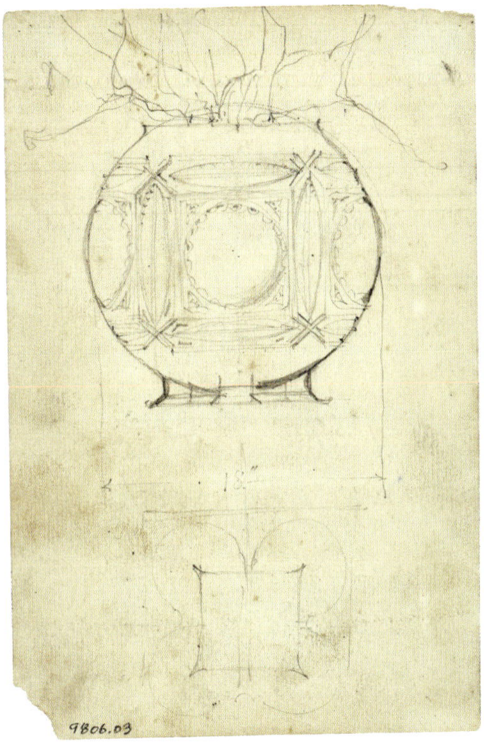

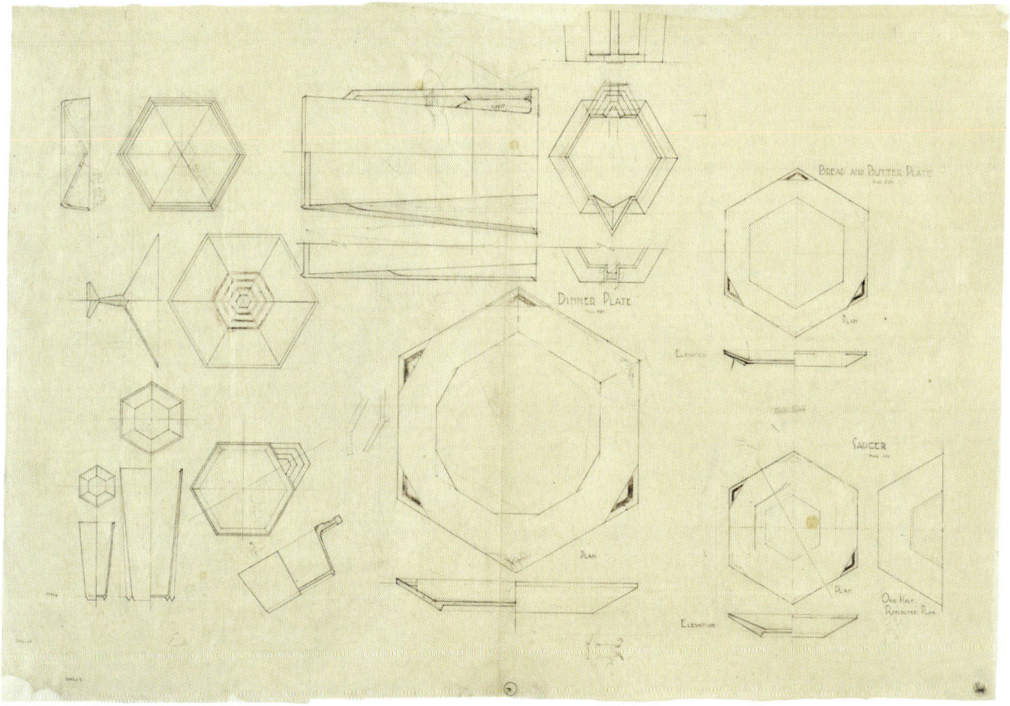

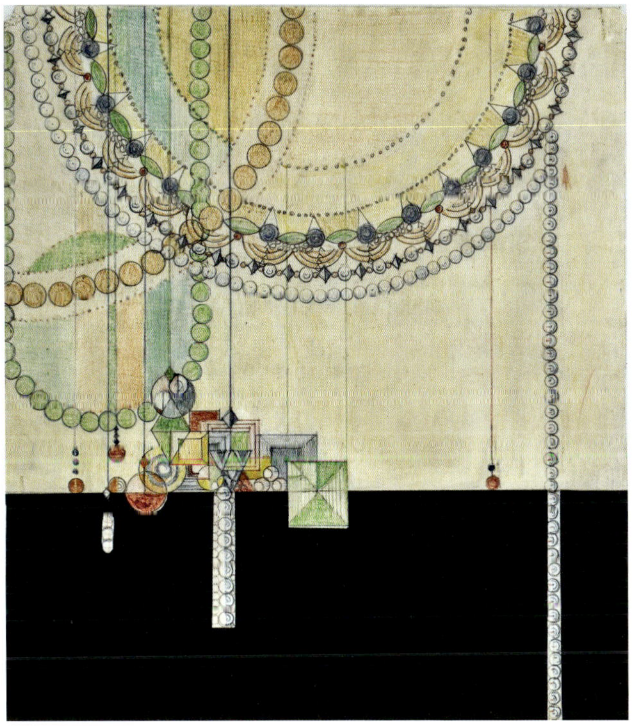

6. Urn design. 1898. Elevation and plan.
Pencil on tracing paper, 17 3/4 x 9 1/2 in. (45.1 x 24.1 cm)

7. Glassware designs for Leerdam Glasfabriek. 1929. Plans, sections, and elevations.
Pencil and colored pencil on tracing paper, 29 x 42 in. (73.7 x 106.7 cm)

8. "The Jeweler's Window." 1927. Cover design for *Liberty* magazine.
Pencil and colored pencil on tracing paper with colored paper, 13 1/4 x 12 in. (33.7 x 30.5 cm)

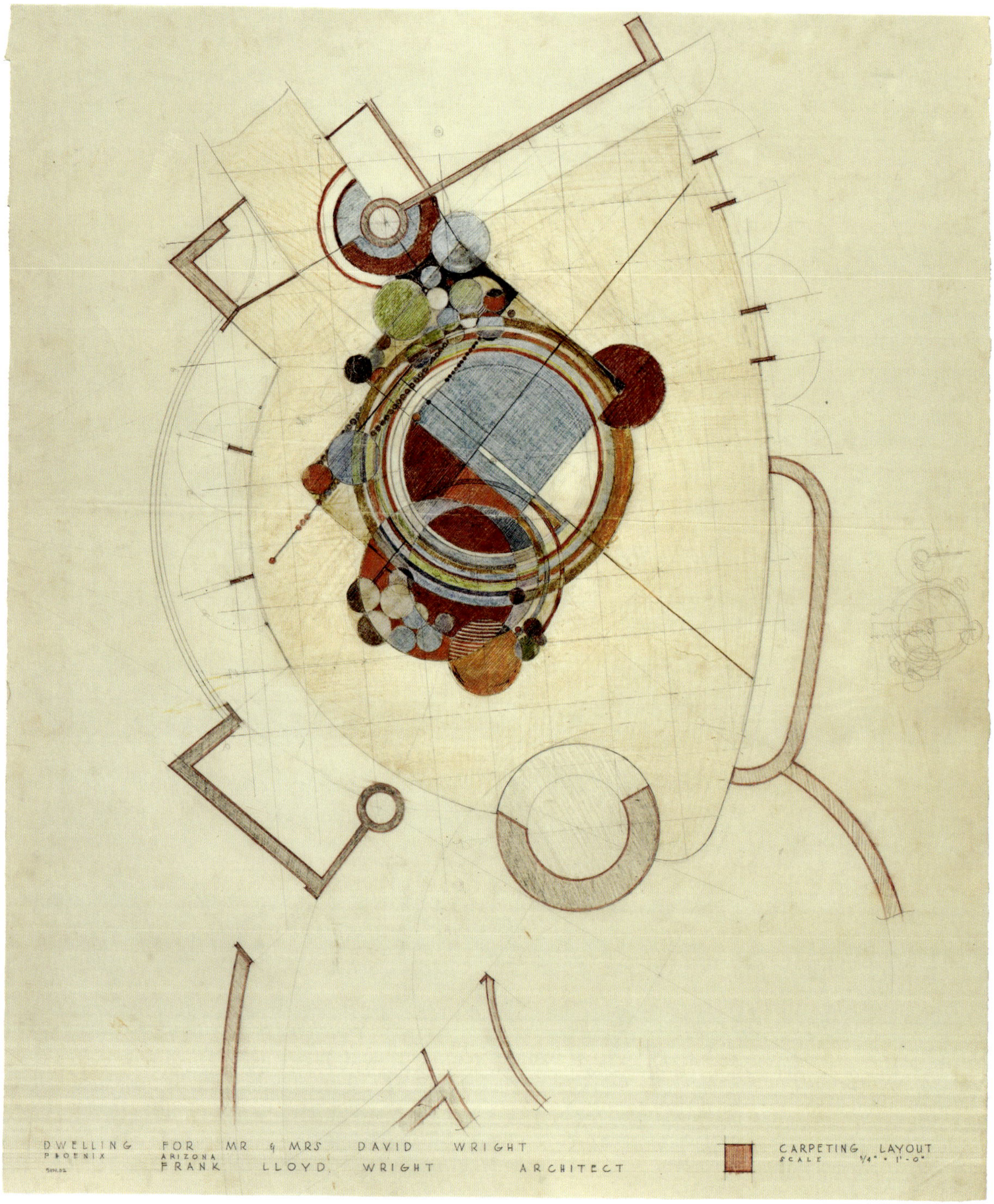

9. David Wright House, Phoenix, Arizona. 1950–51. Living room plan with rug design.
Pencil and colored pencil on tracing paper, 35 x 29 ½ in. (88.9 x 74.9 cm)

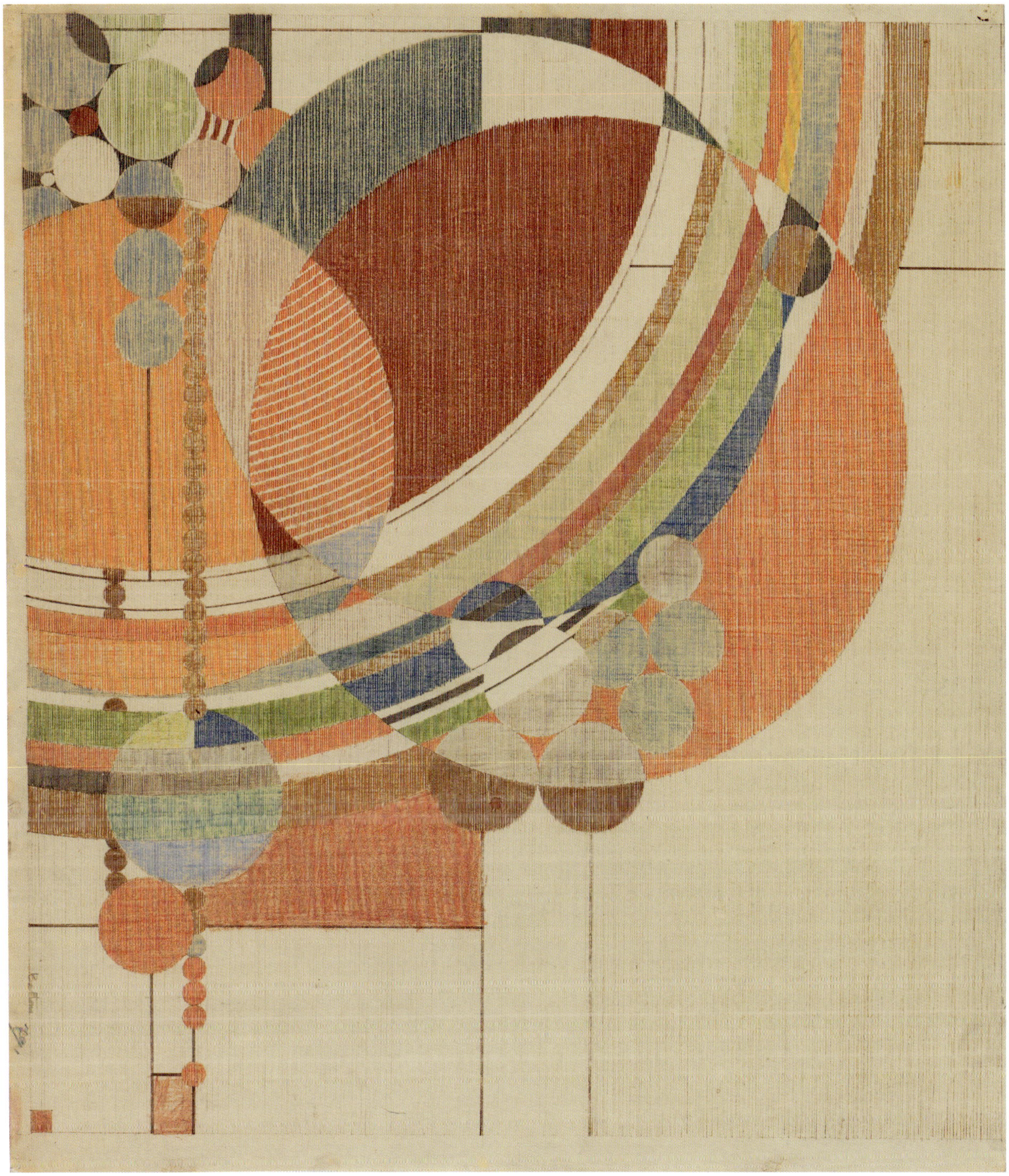

10. "March Balloons." 1955. Drawing based on a c. 1926 design for *Liberty* magazine.
Colored pencil on paper, 28 ¼ x 24 ½ in. (71.8 x 62.2 cm)

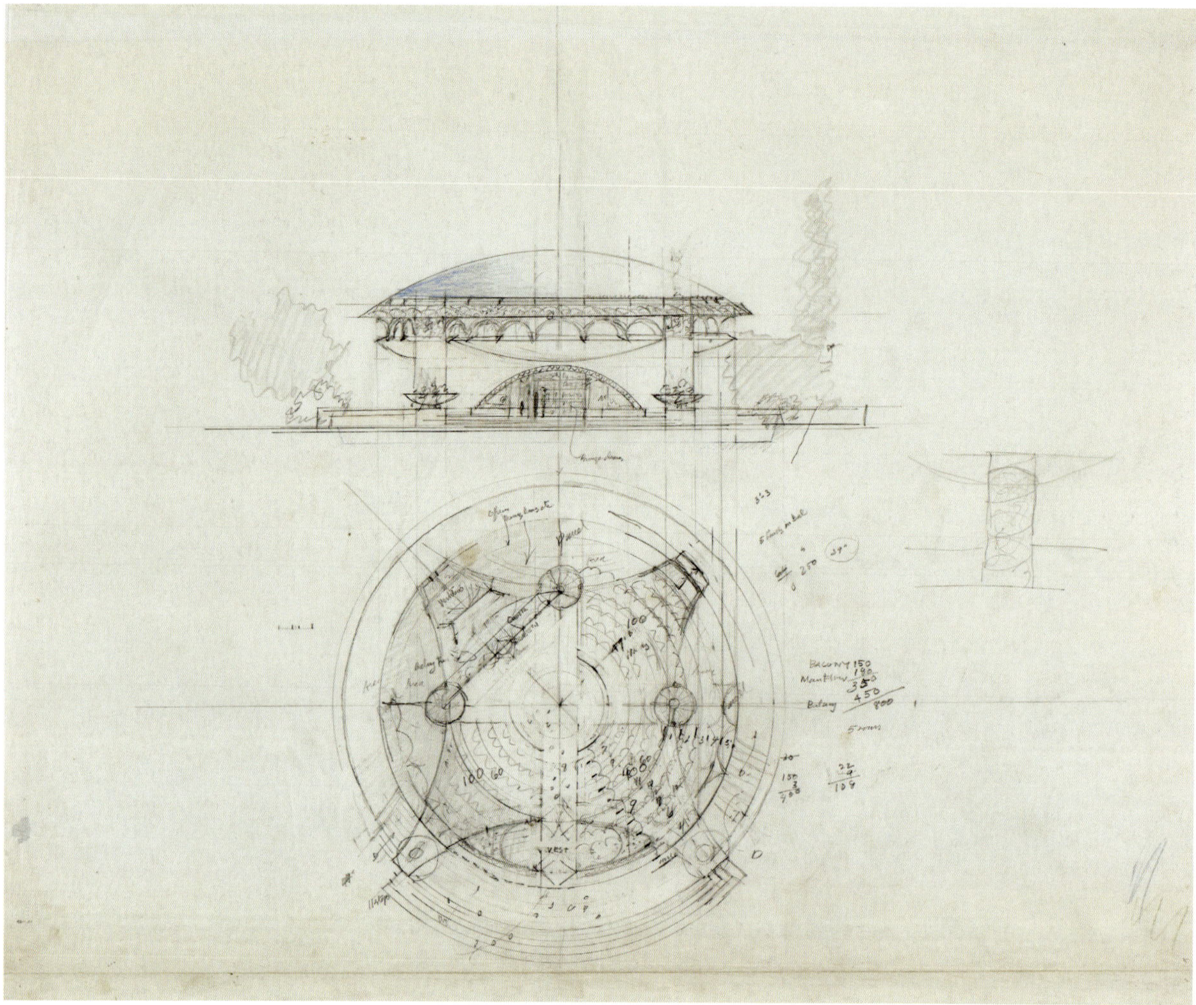

11. Annunciation Greek Orthodox Church, Wauwatosa, Wisconsin. 1955–61. Elevation and plan. Pencil and colored pencil on paper, 29 3/4 x 36 in. (75.6 x 91.4 cm)

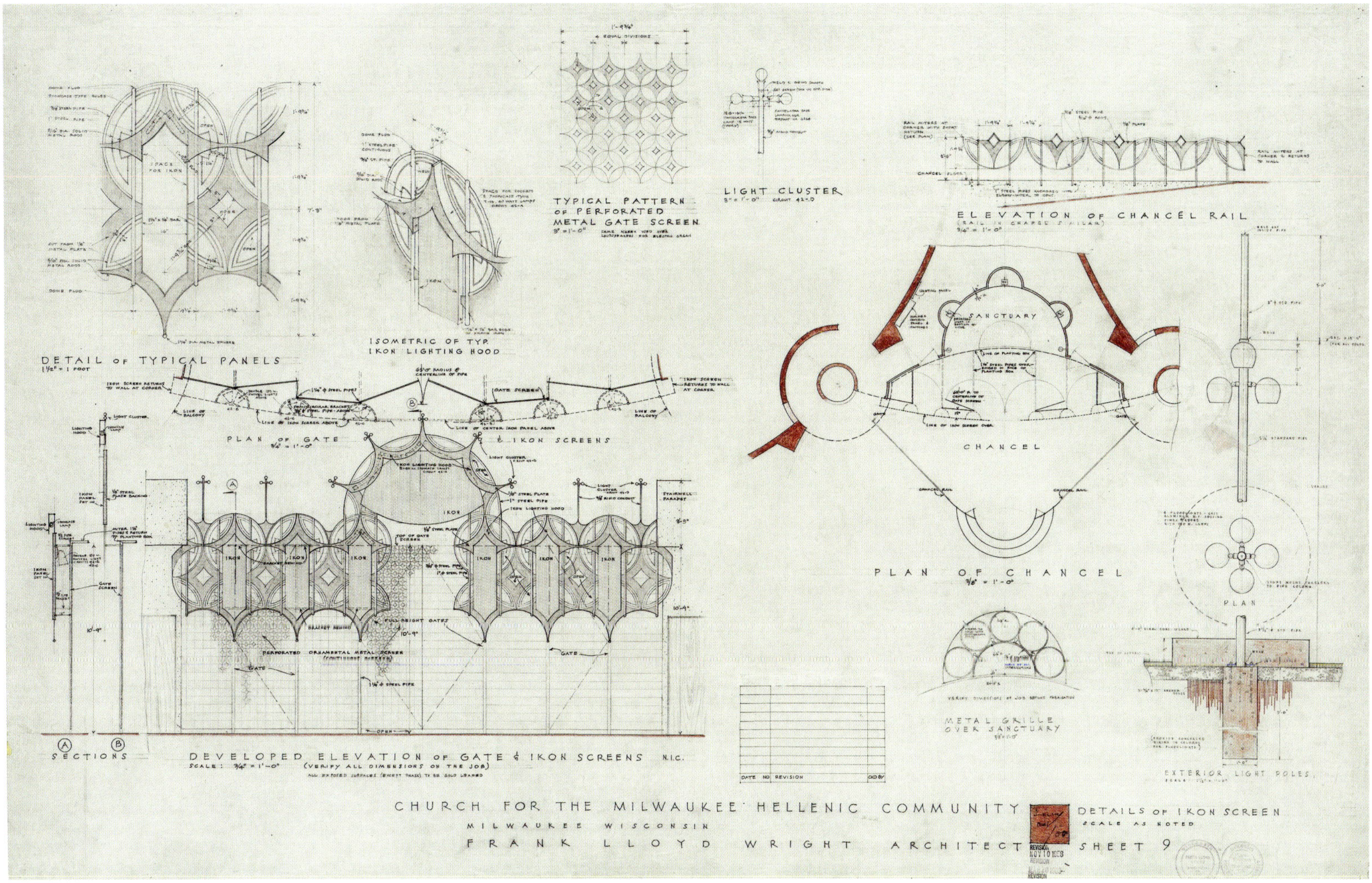

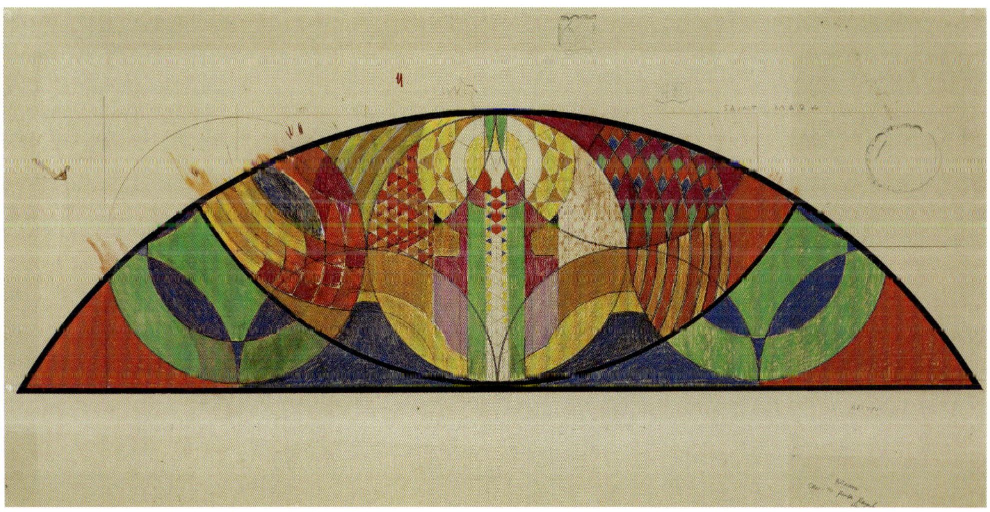

12. Annunciation Greek Orthodox Church, Wauwatosa, Wisconsin. 1955–61.
Plan, section, and elevation details for the gate and icon screens at the chancel.
Ink, pencil, and colored pencil on drafting cloth, 38 x 60 in. (96.5 x 152.4 cm)

13. Annunciation Greek Orthodox Church, Wauwatosa, Wisconsin. 1955–61.
Stained-glass design by Eugene Masselink.
Pastel and pencil on paper, 24 1/4 x 48 1/4 in. (61.6 x 122.6 cm)

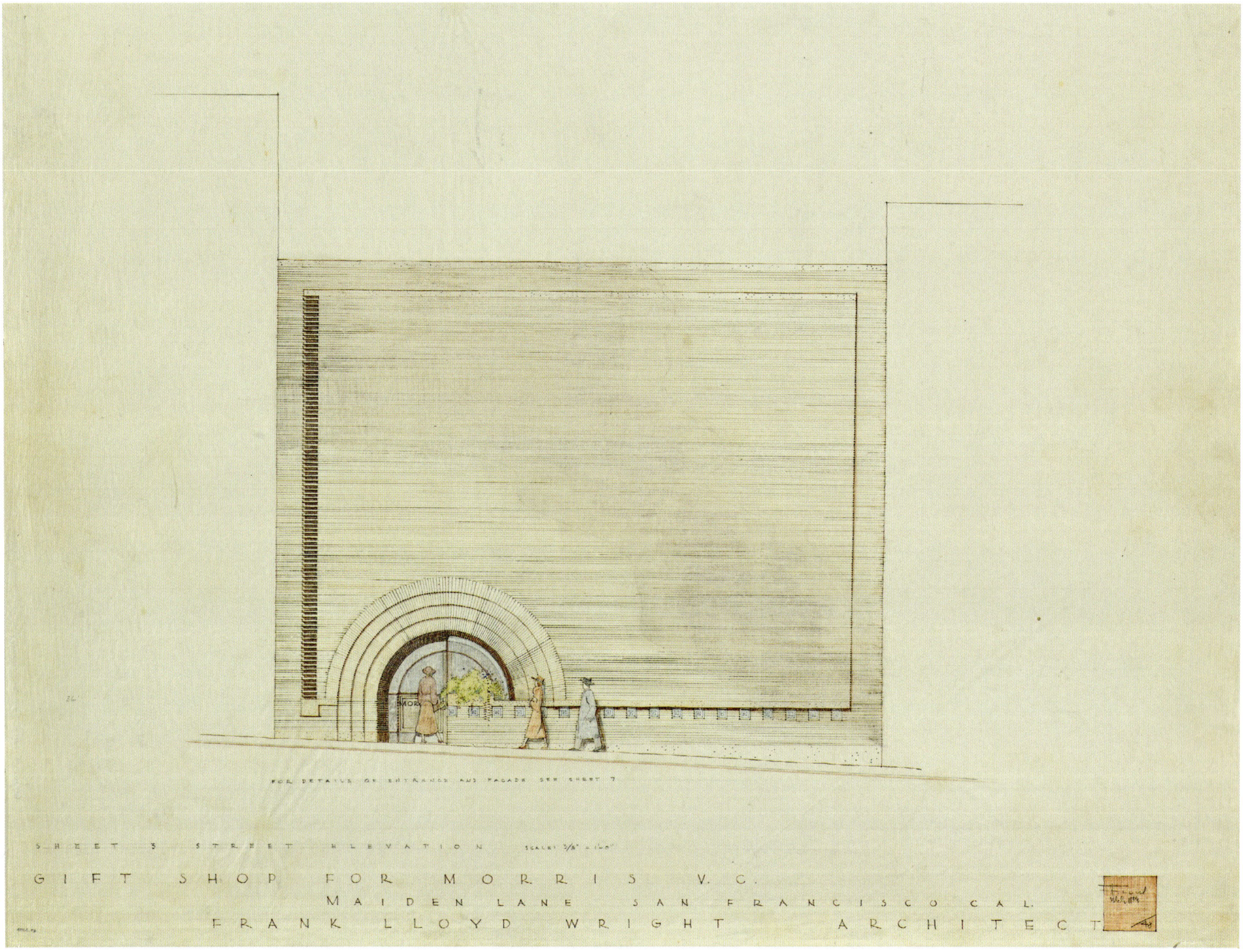

14. V. C. Morris Gift Shop, San Francisco. 1948–49. Street elevation.
Ink, pencil, and colored pencil on tracing paper, 30 x 36 in. (76.2 x 91.4 cm)

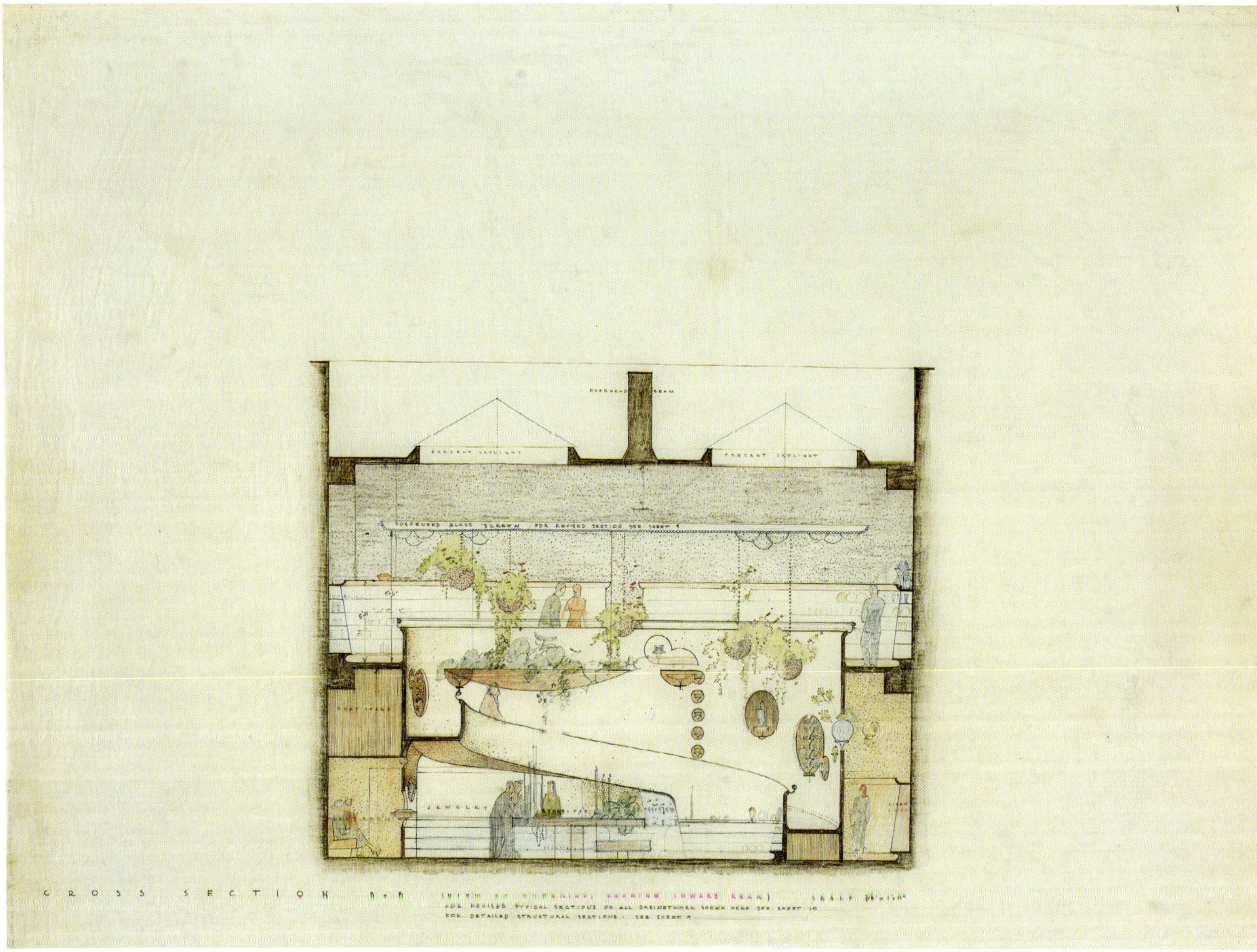

15. V. C. Morris Gift Shop, San Francisco. 1948–49. South-north section.
Ink, pencil, and colored pencil on tracing paper, 29 ½ x 35 in. (74.9 x 88.9 cm)

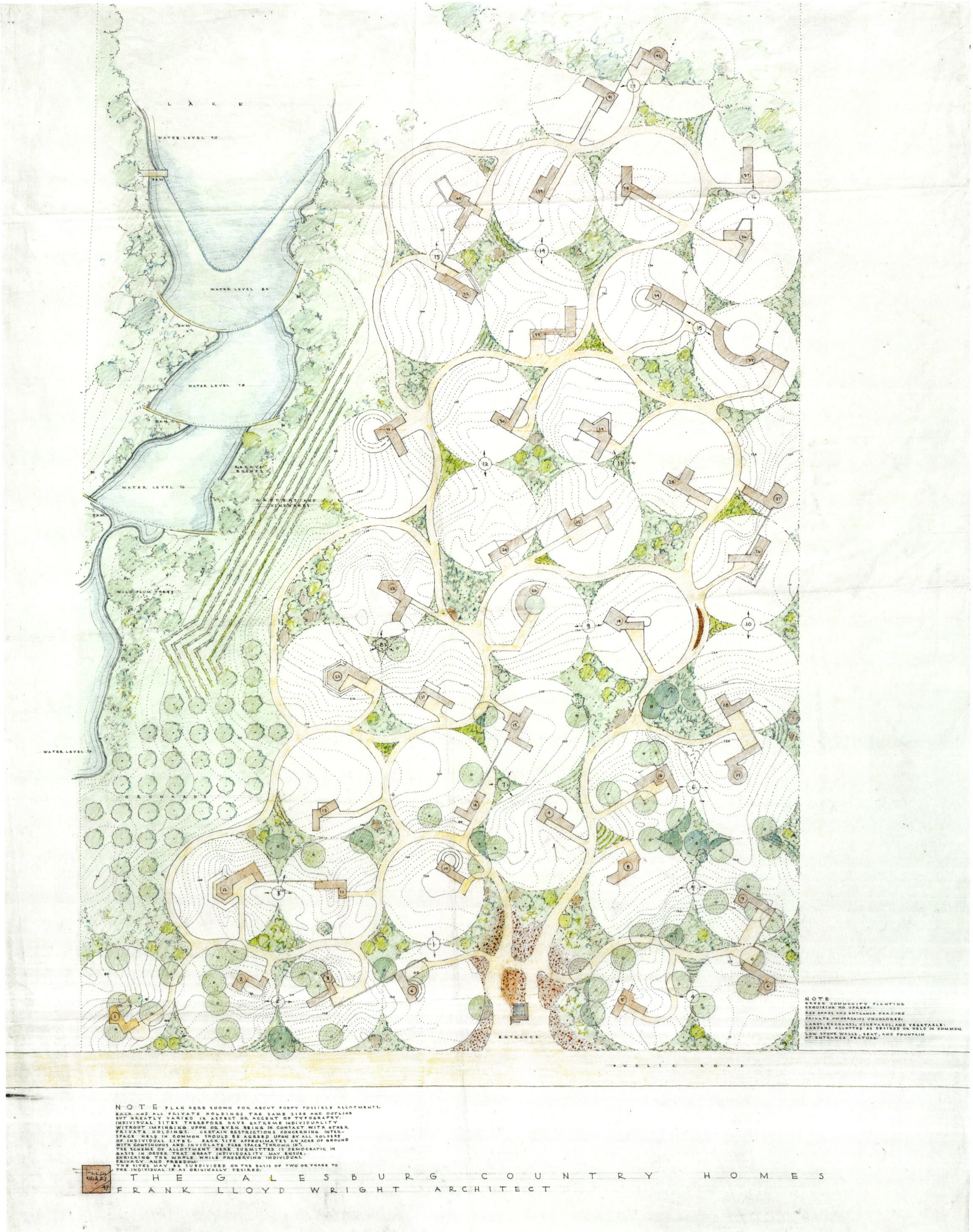

Galesburg Country Homes, Galesburg, Michigan. 1946–49. Site plan, 1947. Ink and colored pencil on tracing paper, 46 5/8 x 37 1/8 in. (118.4 x 94.3 cm)

MICHAEL DESMOND

ABSTRACTING THE LANDSCAPE GALESBURG ABOVE AND BELOW THE SURFACE

Frank Lloyd Wright's design for the Michigan community of Galesburg Country Homes stands out as one of the most enigmatically beautiful conceptions of his entire career. The colored pencil master plan—its multitude of circles tumbling together over the drawing, the large round lots laid over gently rolling hills indicated by swirling topographic lines, the broken angularity of twisting and turning house forms, the many existing green trees, the order of an intended orchard, the rows of garden and grape vines, the cascading pools of water and constantly curving gravel roadway—captures the imagination (opposite). Wright's use of geometric abstraction to encourage identification with landscape, heightening its potential to serve as a basis for community, is seen nowhere more beautifully than in this drawing. The Galesburg members, who commissioned the drawings, responded, "We are overwhelmed with the concept of your proposed development of our land—it is the stuff dreams are made of."[1]

In contrast to the dominance of the urban grid seen in his neighborhood planning projects from the turn of the century, Wright's postwar community-scale designs developed new ways in which to intertwine perceptions of architecture and of self/group associations with the natural environment. The development of this approach can be seen in a series of planning projects he produced in the decade following the revolutionary designs of Fallingwater (1934–37) and the Johnson Wax Administration Building (1936–39), as the obvious presence of his otherwise ubiquitous planning grids gives way to representations of motion and multiplicity that reflect an intensified scale of engagement with landscapes made possible by the automobile. With designs such as the one for Galesburg, the concept of a distinct boundary between the natural and the manmade—or even of a difference between these as categories of definition—begins to fade with the experience of interdependency. Wright expressed this interest in his London lectures of 1939, "We are talking about the countryside itself developing into a type of building in which will lie naturally building becoming part of the countryside, building belonging there naturally with grace. Such buildings will exist.

There are already a few of them. . . . The more of such buildings we have in the country the more beautiful community life will become and the less you will be aware of the fact that buildings are there at all as intrusion."[2]

One beginning of this strategy is found in the large house known as Wingspread (fig. 1), designed for the owner of the Johnson Wax company, Herbert Johnson, at the same time as the Administration Building was being constructed. In this design, Wright replaced any traditional bilateral symmetry with a more complex foursquare rotational expression seen in house plan, site plan, and some of his earliest aerial photography. Similar qualities of form appeared again the next year in the Suntop Homes project for Ardmore, Pennsylvania. In this partially completed project, Wright twisted, rotated, and juxtaposed small floor plans of four-sided apartment buildings—literally incorporating rotational movement into the design process—to create an overall site plan of striking angularity wherein building form, driveways, and layers of planting all work together to form an abstracted landscape (fig. 2). In the unbuilt U.S. defense workers' housing design for Pittsfield, Massachusetts, known as Cloverleaf (1941–42), altered versions of the Suntop structures are surrounded by differently planted individual yards, rounded at their edges to reflect the movement patterns of the automobile (plate 1). The houses are positioned in relation to each other in ways that enliven shifting conceptions of group identity while not privileging any single point of view. In the aerial rendering for Cloverleaf we see these associations of individuality and group identity slide through various scales, continually transformed by the implied motion of the cars weaving in and out and around the buildings. The multiplication of curving forms found throughout the site would replicate the dance of rotating tires, steering wheels, and changing vistas through which the potential of the automobile, as a central aspect of modern life, is brought to the fore.

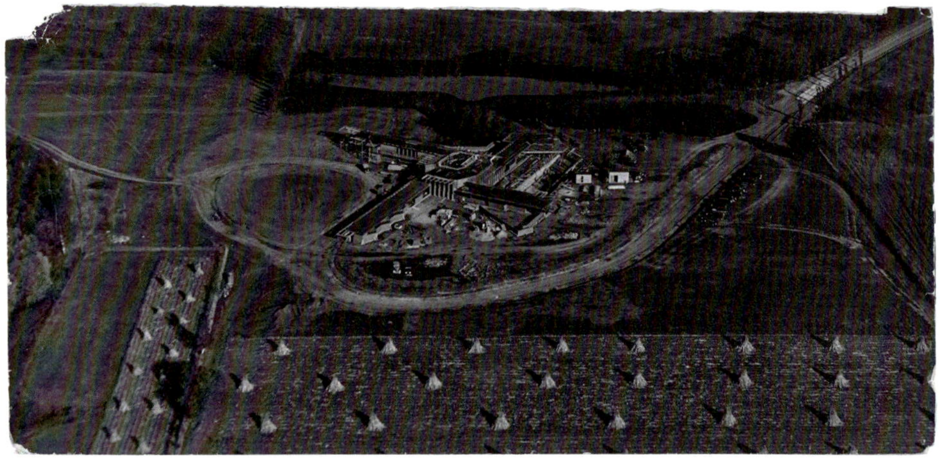

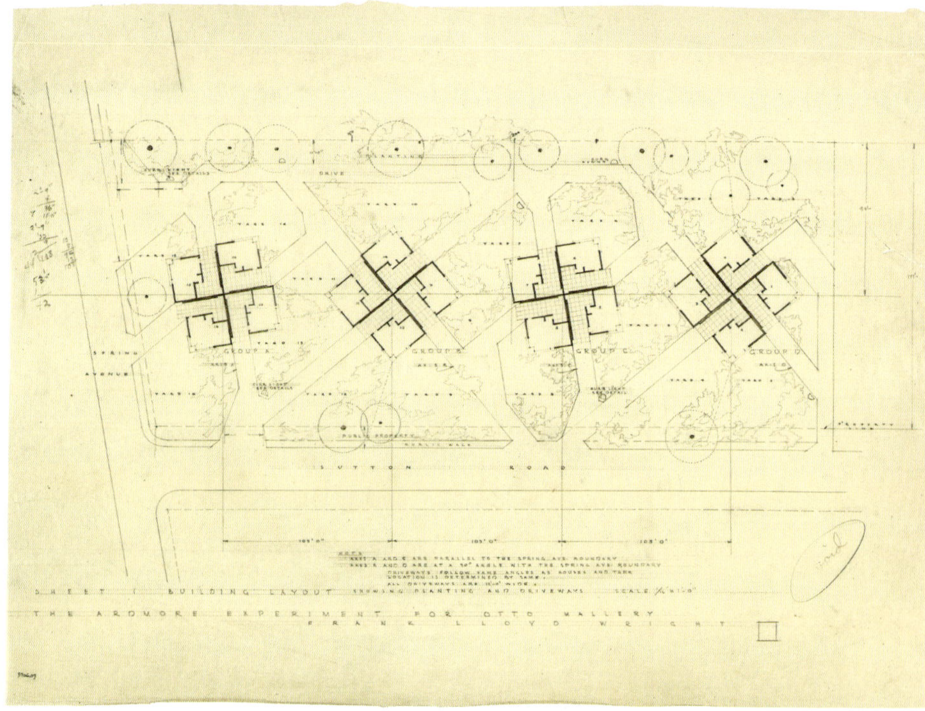

Fig. 1. Wingspread (Johnson House), Wind Point, Wisconsin. 1937. Aerial view

Fig. 2. Suntop Homes, Ardmore, Pennsylvania. 1938–39. Site plan. Pencil and ink on paper, 27 x 41 in. (68.6 x 104.1 cm)

Wright's use of arcs and rotational movement seen in this series of planning projects culminated in the partially executed subdivision designs for Galesburg (March 1947), for Parkwyn Village (April 1947), in nearby Kalamazoo; and for Usonia Homes (May 1947), in Pleasantville, New York. The two Michigan projects were initaited by a group of employees from the growing pharmaceuticals company Upjohn in Kalamazoo to take advantage of economies of scale through the communal purchase of large tracts of land, one near town and the other some 10 miles (16.1 kilometers) out. It is the first, unbuilt plan Wright made for Galesburg that set the character of the designs for all three projects. The Galesburg group had five members and wanted to limit its eventual size to fifteen and their families. The site they purchased consisted of a section along a county highway composed of rolling hills loosely covered with apple trees and other mature hardwoods giving way to open land through a small central valley next to a fully wooded rear area. A small stream, which the members wanted to dam for swimming and fishing, occupied the northern portion of the tract.

Wright responded with a plan of great literal and conceptual beauty, showing forty-two circular lots of 200 feet (61 meters) in diameter sprinkled about the low hills and connected by networks of narrow path-like roadways (see p. 132). The rendered plan includes the topographic description of the land seen beneath the uncolored circular lots, each surrounded by shrubs and background vegetation, the whole interspersed with existing tree canopies. It represents an unprecedented ordering of forms, movement, and landscape. On closer inspection one can see that the individual lots are joined in groups of two or three by small, numbered circular marks indicating choices to be made between them. Wright intended that each member would select one lot from these smaller groups, with unselected lots added to other common lands such as ponds, gardens, fields, and orchards. Each selection required members to choose a relationship to the overall topography and the position of the roadway, and to react to the choices made by other members, creating clusters or remaining more isolated. The plan presents a total of seventeen such selections with countless possible variations.

While there are many exemplars of order in this remarkable drawing, what seems to be missing is the grid. Its influence is there, however, as virtually all of the lots shown are centered on one of the orthogonal surveyor grid lines describing the land that the group sent to Wright. His first layout of this plan was completed directly on the survey print he received, and he utilized this grid extensively. In the presentation plan, the presence of that grid was entirely suppressed. After members chose their lots, the only further development Wright suggested was that additional tree plantings be kept out of the commonly held lands between the selected lots, and that those common areas be planted with a low, naturally occurring shrub, such as barberry or sumac, "throwing a network of color in pattern over the entire tract."[3] Given the character of the softly rolling hills, this would have created an entrancing vision, with the roadway bending as it rose and fell across the land among the disconnected individually landscaped circles. Even more than in the Cloverleaf plan, here perceptions of individuality, landscape, and group would shift as one moved through the environment. The ability to distinguish between manmade and natural would blur as the power of abstraction is highlighted, reminding each individual of a ceaseless intertwining of human purpose and natural environment, of the idea that, according to one person who grew up in the community, home "meant more than a house."[4]

This process of intertwining perceptions of architectural form and landscape developed through the designs of many of the individual houses Wright made over this period as well. It is an approach that negotiates a shift from the use of multiple, overlapping, partially incomplete orthogonal frames of reference in his Prairie-style and Usonian houses, to more active ones of arcs and circles inclusive of motion. This interest was explored in one of Wright's most unexplained residential designs, for the Hollywood film artist Ralph Jester, intended for a site on the coast just south of Los Angeles (1938–39; plate 2). The sketches show the first results of a new spatial exploration of grid and motion coupled with the pleasant year-round climate of southern California. The design for the unbuilt Jester House responded to its dramatic hillside site. Perched between an encircling ring of high hills on one side and spectacular views outward over the Pacific Ocean, it juxtaposes a governing planning grid with a range of circular forms, from stools and other seating, tables, beds, fireplaces, columns, and room enclosures to a flamboyant projecting infinity pool whose surface would have merged with the horizon. Here definitions of "outside" and "inside" begin to blur as Wright positioned architectural elements in relation to one another and to views of the site with a new freedom. Enclosure, envelope, inside and outside, even near and far, take on new dimensions of meaning.

In the early 1940s, at almost the same moment that Wright was designing Cloverleaf—shifting layers of perception through the grid and representations of curving motion—he designed a stunningly original house for Lloyd Burlingham in El Paso, Texas, overlooking the Rio Grande Valley (1940–42; plate 3). This unbuilt design develops a relationship between its controlling grid and the plan's centers of organization that is different from that of the projects just described. In the Jester project's presentation plan, the pattern of stone flooring was composed of randomly shaped pieces organized in such a way that the underlying grid of 4-foot (1.2-meter) squares is clearly present in some areas and wavering in others as the circular rooms, columns, and furnishings float about with a disengaged unity. In contrast, for the earliest studies of the Burlingham design, Wright utilized the orthogonal modules of the survey to anchor the house to the topography before allowing the grid to disappear entirely. This house was composed of arcing lines of enclosure, containment, and circulation organized with respect to two centers selected from grid survey points (plate 4). One of these, nestled against a rocky outcropping on the high side of the site, defines a series of concentric arcs that form the driveway, an enclosed private garden, and the living and bedroom wing of the house. The other, located out in space toward the vista, establishes a complementary series of arcs that define the kitchen and service wing surrounding a luna-shaped court containing a pool. The push-pull of the two centers establishes an operational drama for the design—suspended between the protective rocky mountainside and the distant river valley—as a new enlivening of the prospect-and-refuge dynamic often referred to in Wright's domestic designs.

The emerging structure of form, symbol, and perception used in the Jester and Burlingham designs appears clearly in Wright's domestic architecture in the second home he designed for Herbert Jacobs, known as the Solar Hemicycle (fig. 3), just as his work on the Solomon R. Guggenheim Museum was beginning. The curving shape of this design is governed by a single center divided into two halves. The slightly lowered house looks out over a sunken circular garden as it reciprocates the daily path of the sun. A bank of low planting completes the circle, evoking the prairie horizon that was fully apparent when the house was originally built. The house's interior and exterior spaces are gathered by the continuous arc of a rear-enclosing wall. The obvious redundancy of the circle

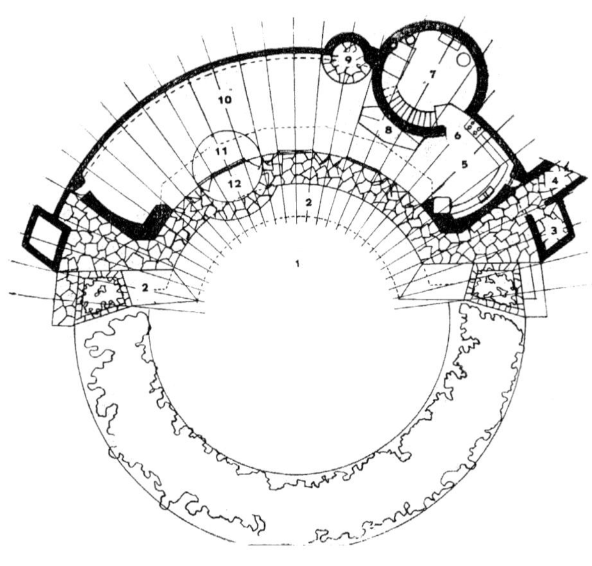

Fig. 3. Jacobs House (Solar Hemicycle), Middleton, Wisconsin. 1943–48. Site plan. From *L'Architecture d'aujourd'hui* 24, no. 50 (December 1953)

is reserved for the hearth, bathroom/utility core, and an inside-outside pool that reinforces the dualism of the whole. A suspended bedroom loft hovers, allowing the large, steadily curving wall of glass and French doors to sweep through the entire experience, uniting inside and out with the sky—a disengaged unity. The use of the circle in this design presents a merging of symbolic reference, cognitive process, and cumulative experience as the two-sided, narrative dimension of the Burlingham design is folded into a unity, a duality of one where reading the symbol is inextricably woven into the architectonics.

The unity of the Jacobs design was loosened as Wright encountered various landscapes over the coming years. Designs for Kenneth Hargrove (fig. 4) and J. J. Vallarino Jr. (1951–57; plates 5, 6) expanded this strategy for sites in Orinda, California, and Panama City. Although Wright designed several modified versions for each of these clients they both remain unbuilt. Both houses share with the Jester and Burlingham plans a relationship to sites with distant outward views backed by rising ground utilized to create a sense of sanctuary. In these designs the steady datum of a constantly curving rear wall is countered by a polyphony of arcs about many centers describing spaces of all kinds, including living rooms, dining areas, outdoor terraces and steps, circular playrooms, and pools held out toward the vista. Moreover, this multiplicity occurs at different levels, as the living rooms rise toward the vista, the dining areas slide off toward the kitchen and playrooms, while an upper bedroom wing hovers privately in the middle of it all. Shifting, sliding, moving definitions of enclosure are all gathered together into one continuous reach outward toward the natural world. In these circular-themed house designs Wright expanded the Usonian geometric framework with the perception of spatial enclosure projected outward to engage features of the landscape, evoking a new architectonic of "continuity." "We have no longer an outside as outside," he wrote. "We have no longer an outside and an inside as two separate things. Now the outside may come inside, and the inside may and does go outside. They are of each other. . . . Open reaches of the ground may enter as the building and the building interior may reach out and associate with these vistas of the ground."[5]

In 1951 Wright offered Liliane Kaufmann one of the most expressive designs of his career, as a complement perhaps to Fallingwater, built for her husband almost two decades earlier. The simple organizing idea of the Boulder House (plate 7) seems almost obvious at first glance, seen in contrast between the three parts making up the body of the house and the expanding circles of court, yard, and boulder-strewn landscape—the former seemingly contingent, the latter totalizing. But the interactions of forms are only part of the story, as these are animated by intended relationships and perceptions of the surrounding landscape not seen in the plan. The renderings of the unbuilt project convey Wright's intentions in this regard. One's experience of the house would have begun with the central forecourt receiving the automobile, abruptly half-lawn and half-gravel, framed by the carport wing as it encircles the dominant rising stone mass of the hearth that anchors the composition. The drawing suggests a grouping of trees rising toward the nearest of several ridges that extend into the canyon along its western edge, establishing an affinity with the ridges as they march off into the deep perspective of greater Palm Canyon toward the Santa Rosa Mountains. The entryway pulls one toward the curving side of the dining pavilion, up across a bridge over the pool surrounding the main body of the house before being swept into the living room, which itself follows a counter motion defining the central luna of the house. It is a process composed of fluid changes of direction and orientation—first this way then

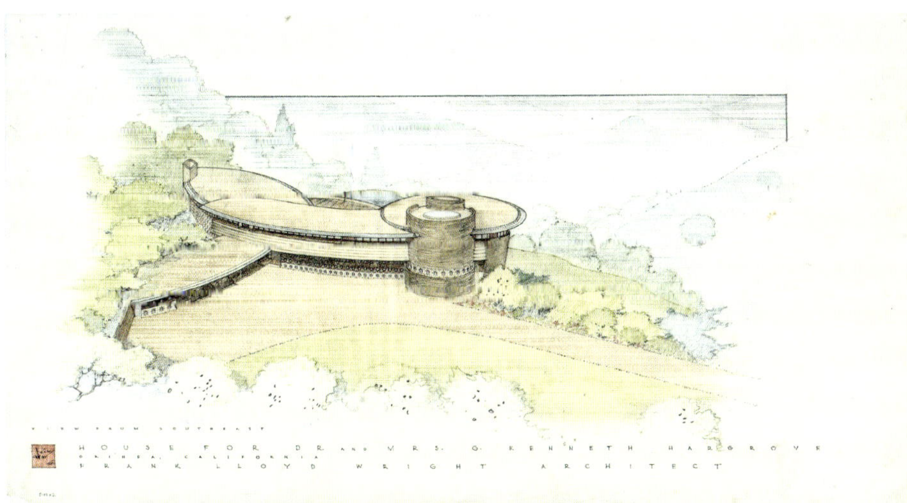

Fig. 4. Hargrove House, Orinda, California. Project, 1950. Aerial perspective from the southeast. Pencil, colored pencil, and ink on tracing paper, 18 7/8 x 35 in. (47.9 x 88.9 cm)

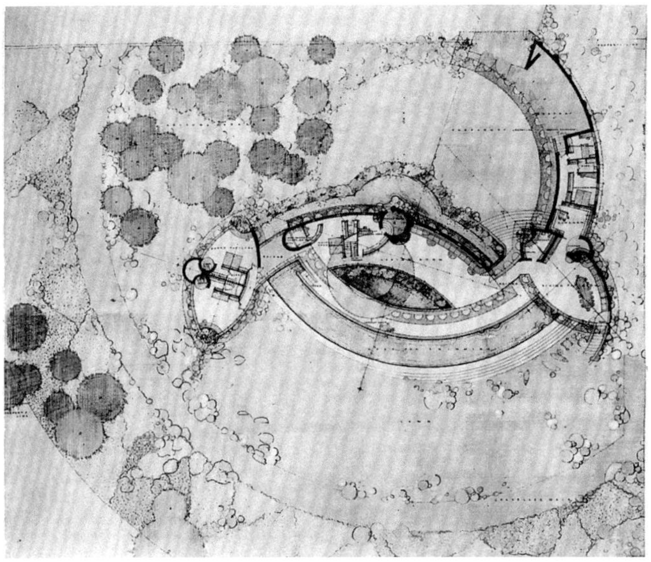

that, through compressive spaces then expansive vistas as the house curves around you—constantly changing your frame of reference to it and to the ever-present visible world outside. The dining and guest bedroom pavilions pull attention outward as they echo and multiply the curving structures of the design. Finally, an upper-level circular terrace held up to the sky and the desert landscape is indicated in the plan (fig. 5) as a lightly shaded circle, surrounded on one side by the mountains, embraced on the other side by the house. The aerial perspective (see plate 7) shows the house's luna-shaped masses strewn across the desert floor in dialogue with the mountainous forms pulling one's eye to the distance. The design resembles an orrery, a dynamic moving model of a solar system showing the orbits of planets and other bodies around a central point, yet without ever clearly stating a totalizing order. There is a constantly moving dialogue between the lines of the building and the lines of the earth, everything is akilter, awry, off axis, dislocated slightly, creating a spatial experience more like those we find in the natural world where we constantly establish frames of reference with our perceptions as we go along. It is a new kind of architecture, the epitome of dozens of such designs from the last decades of his life, very few of which he was able to build, and none at this scale of richness.[6]

The house Wright designed for Mexican businessman Raúl Baillères is the veritable embodiment of his idea that "architecture properly studied in relation to the natural features surrounding it is a great clarifier and developer of the beauty of landscape. . . ."[7] Located on a spectacular site in Acapulco, Wright designed the house around an open-air living patio perched above Acapulco Bay and looking northward through a sweep of cascading boulders, steps, terrace, pool, and ramp to the beach below. One feels a sense of exuberance in the plan and elevation drawings and in the overarching enclosure of the cutaway perspective (plates 8–10). The experience begins at a gatehouse on the road above as an entry drive drops past a fountain with pools marking the head of a ravine. The water of the ravine was to be diverted through a series of garden landscapes tracing the pathway to the beach, bringing one first to the graveled auto court before slipping under the house to reemerge by the ramp leading to the sea. After leaving the entry drive, one is drawn downward by steps curving into the great patio. The space here is formed by the arc of a heavy colonnade, a curving wall, and a gently rising ceiling partially reaching over a large boulder surrounded by a pool in the center of the space. The curves of the room lead to an encounter with a grouping of similar large stones that continue outside in a scattered pattern as they fall down the hillside beyond. Invitation to spatial compression is followed by a controlled opening of the distant vista framed by this most unique inside/outside patio room as the eye is pulled toward the flat plane of the bay in the distance, its

Fig. 5. Boulder House, Palm Springs, California. Project, 1951. Site plan. From *L'Architecture d'aujourd'hui* 24, no. 50 (December 1953)

curving edge embraced by gently surrounding mountains echoing the enclosing motion of the house. The design of the house shapes the way the bay itself is seen in relation to its natural geography. Wright's spatial definition uses these natural features as though they are elements of the design, incorporating them into the architectonics of the house.

This kind of abstraction, with its dissolving geometries in dynamic engagement with the spaces of nature, is also key to Wright's design of the first V. C. Morris House (1944–46; plates 11, 12), in San Francisco, perched at the edge of the continent with views across the Golden Gate and out toward the Pacific Ocean. It is one of the most dramatic of his career. The relationships between orthogonal and orbicular frames of reference, the automobile and the natural world, prospect and refuge, are as active here as in anything he designed. This design also began with a site plan roughly sketched in colored pencil directly on the survey blueprint of the promontory, reaching from a curving entry drive outward over a rocky protrusion extending from a dramatically dropping stone cliff to the hovering circular body of the house. The surveyor's reference grid was literally stretched to establish the house, promenade, and terrace edge from which they spring. This practical, conceptual framework was then used in two and three dimensions to control arcs of movement that ritually place the house at the meeting of sea and sky. The rendering from the street dramatizes the curving motion of the automobile converted into that of the promenade reaching outward, over the terrace edge. The spaces fully engage the view of ocean and sky, the circular floor plate of the living room floats over the surface of the ocean as it reaches toward the horizon, while the softened upturned edges of its orthogonal ceiling gently give way to the depth of the sky. The promenade and the terrace from which it springs establish a dissolving Cartesian framework from which to measure our placement in the natural world. We are not just in the world, we are enveloped in our understanding of it as well, and this is what Wright's abstraction seems to engage so powerfully. The one becomes a tool to reach the other. Should we see it as a continually evolving relationship of means to ends, or as a continuous series of metaphorical relationships with one always sliding into another, connecting the ground we stand on with the living symbolism of sea, sky, nature, self? The use of abstraction present in Wright's architecture from the beginning of his practice, the use of linear and planar emphasis on the formal structures of environment and perception, has here reached perhaps its furthest point as it engages this most abstract of possible landscapes. This is what the horizon is after all, the horizontal that becomes vertical as it meets the sky.

Notes

1. Curtis Meyer, letter to Wright, April 17, 1947, G084C01, Frank Lloyd Wright Foundation Archives (The Museum of Modern Art | Avery Architectural & Fine Arts Library, Columbia University, New York). This scheme was eventually rejected, primarily due to concerns about upkeep of the excessive length of gravel roadway during the Michigan winters. The second scheme Wright proposed—twenty-one individual lot possibilities without the explicit choice mechanism—was partially built, although it appears the landscaping he initially designed was never carried out.

2. Frank Lloyd Wright, *An Organic Architecture, The Architecture of Democracy* (London: Lund Humphries, 1939), pp. 16 and 33–34.

3. Wright, quoted in the section "Two Cloverleaf Subdivisions Near Kalamazoo, Michigan," in the second of two special issues designed by Wright and devoted to his work, *Architectural Forum* 88, no. 1 (January 1948): 84.

4. Sara Weisblatt Schastok, "Façade, Landscape, and Worldview—Frank Lloyd Wright and The Acres," *Memar, Iranian Bimonthly on Architecture and Urban Design*, no. 96 (April/May 2016). Weisblatt Schastok grew up in one of Wright's Galesburg houses.

5. Frank Lloyd Wright, *An Autobiography* (New York: Duell, Sloan and Pearce, 1943), pp. 337–38.

6. Wright's aerial rendering of the Boulder House (plate 7) contains a small caricatured representation on the right-hand side of the modernist-style Desert House that Edgar Kaufmann had commissioned Richard Neutra to build a few years earlier.

7. Wright, quoted in the section "Taliesin III" in the first of two special issues designed by Wright and devoted to his work, *Architectural Forum* 68, no. 1 (January 1938): 3.

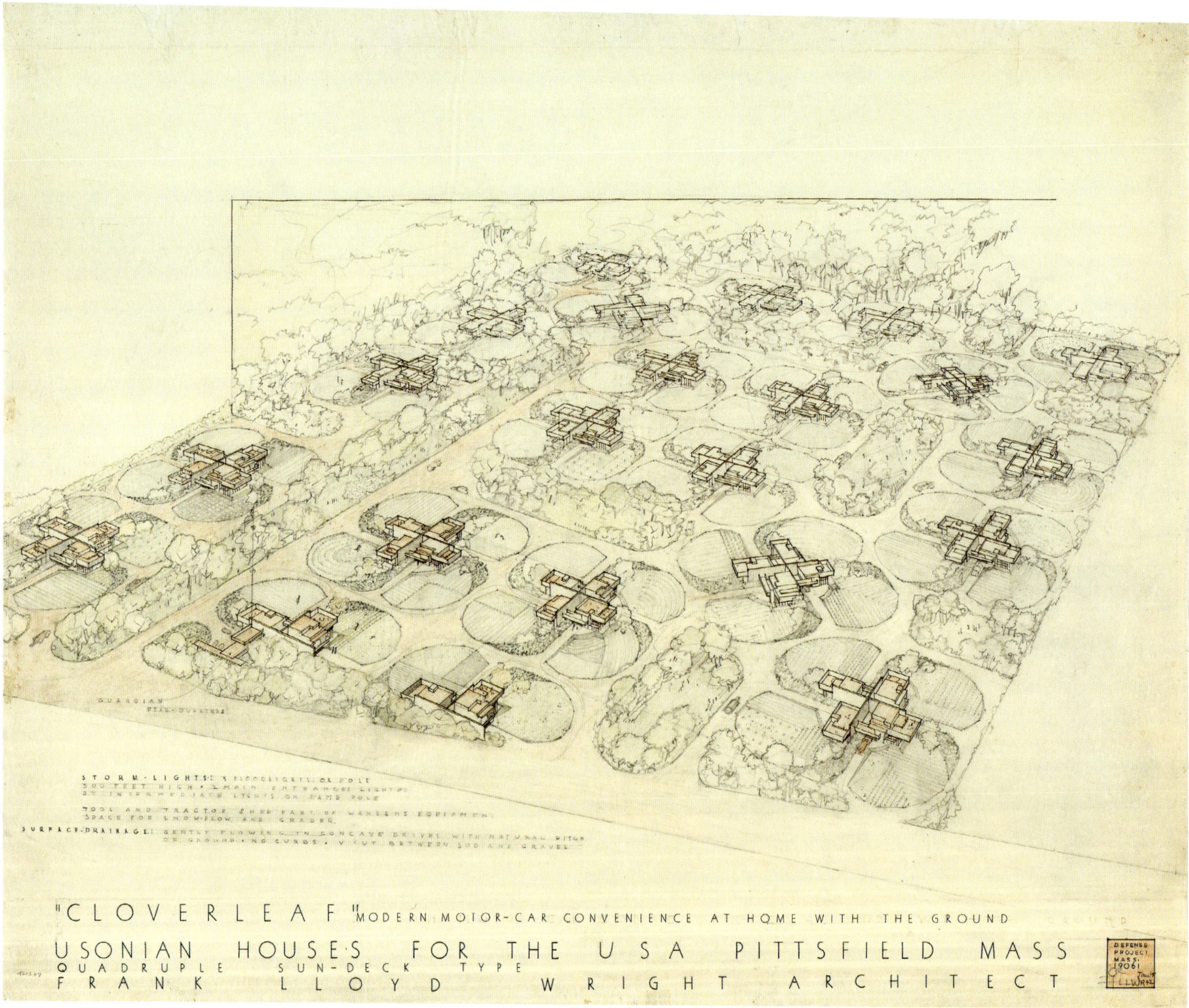

1. Cloverleaf Housing, Pittsfield, Massachusetts. Project, 1941–42. Aerial perspective.
Pencil, colored pencil, and ink on tracing paper, 29 3/8 x 36 in. (74.6 x 91.4 cm)

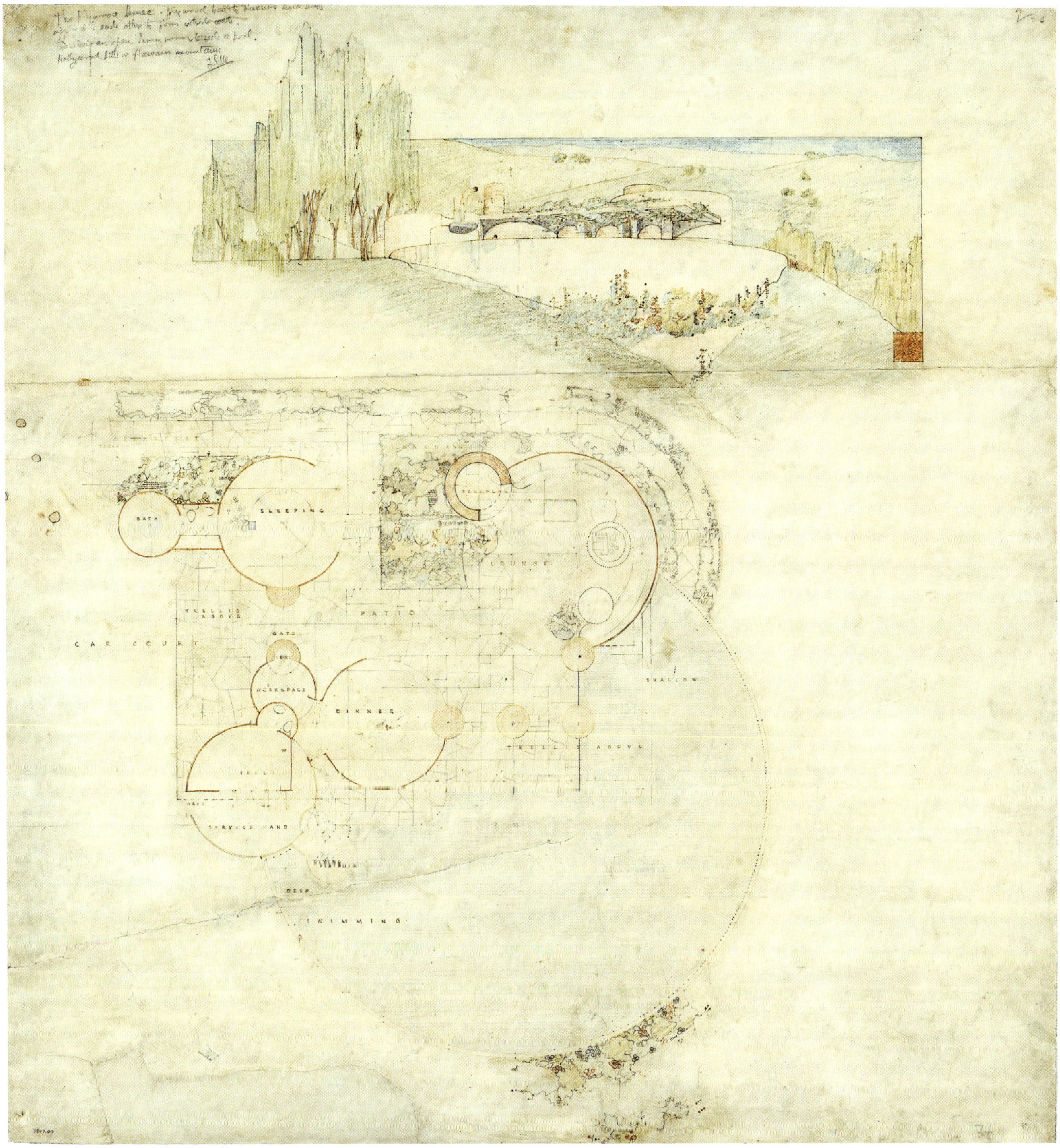

2. Jester House, Palos Verdes, California. Project, 1938–39. Perspective and ground-floor plan.
Ink, pencil, and colored pencil on paper, 34 3/8 x 32 1/4 in. (87.3 x 82 cm)

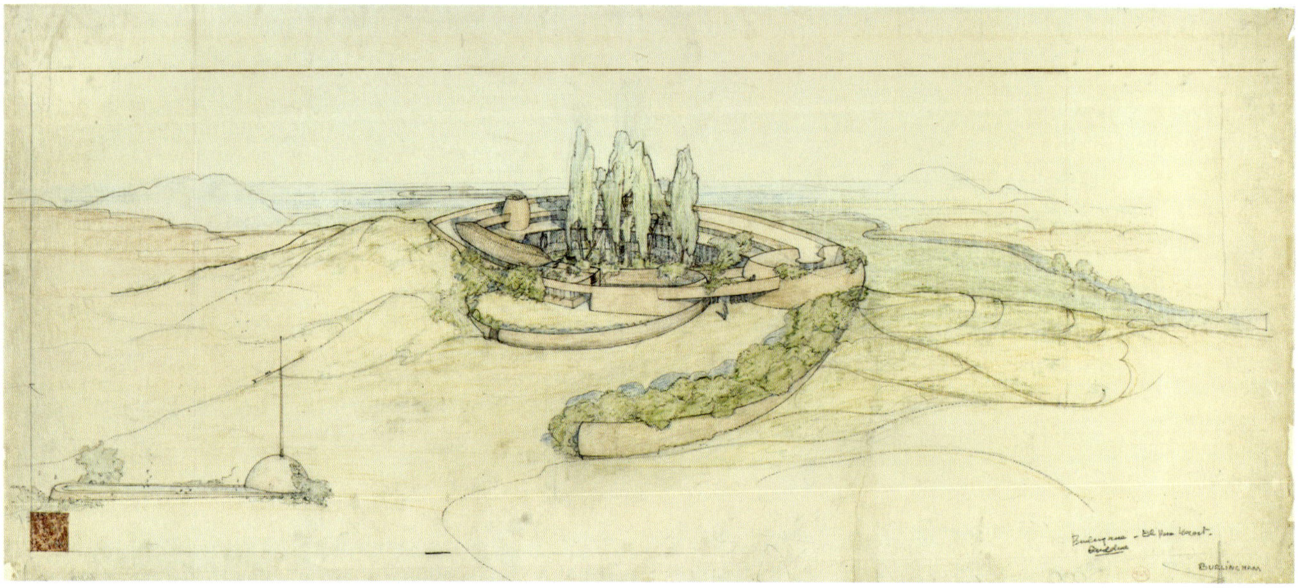

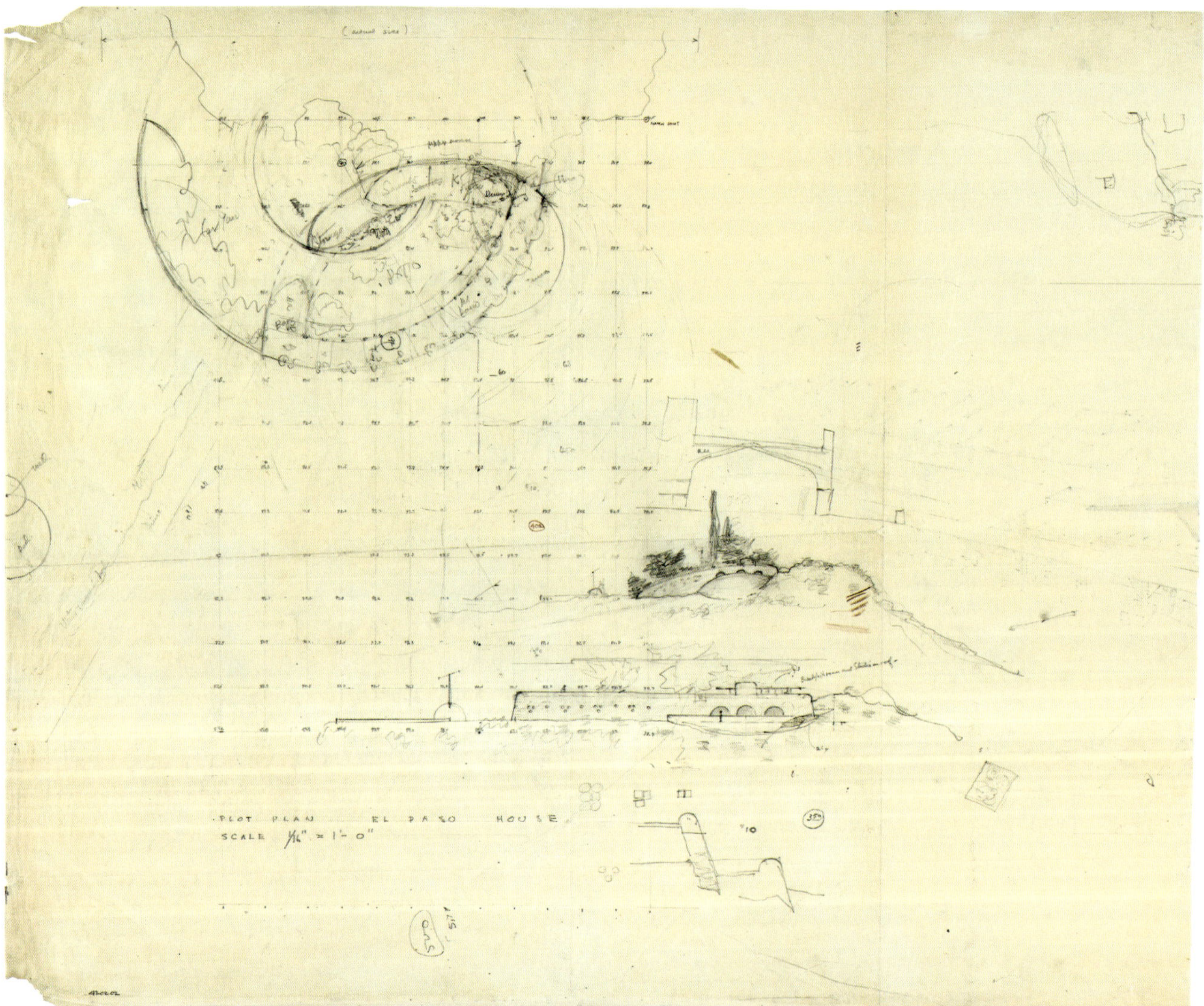

3. Burlingham House, El Paso, Texas. Project, 1940–42. Perspective.
Ink, colored pencil, and pencil on tracing paper, 18 3/8 x 41 3/8 in. (46.7 x 105.1 cm)

4. Burlingham House, El Paso, Texas. Project, 1940–42. Preliminary plot plan with elevation and perspective.
Pencil and colored pencil on tracing paper, 35 5/8 x 43 1/8 in. (90.5 x 109.5 cm)

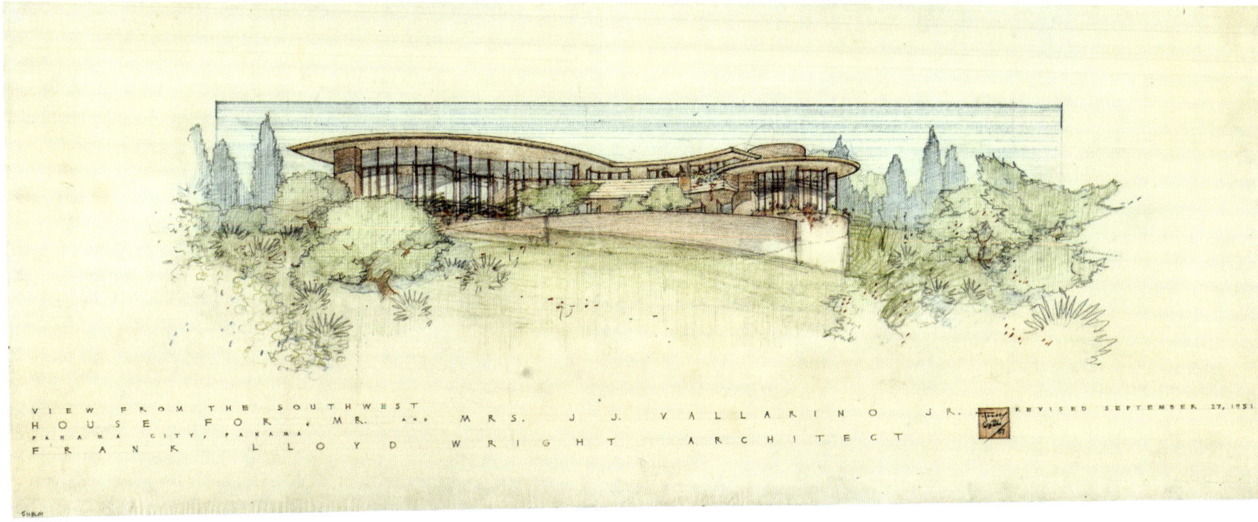

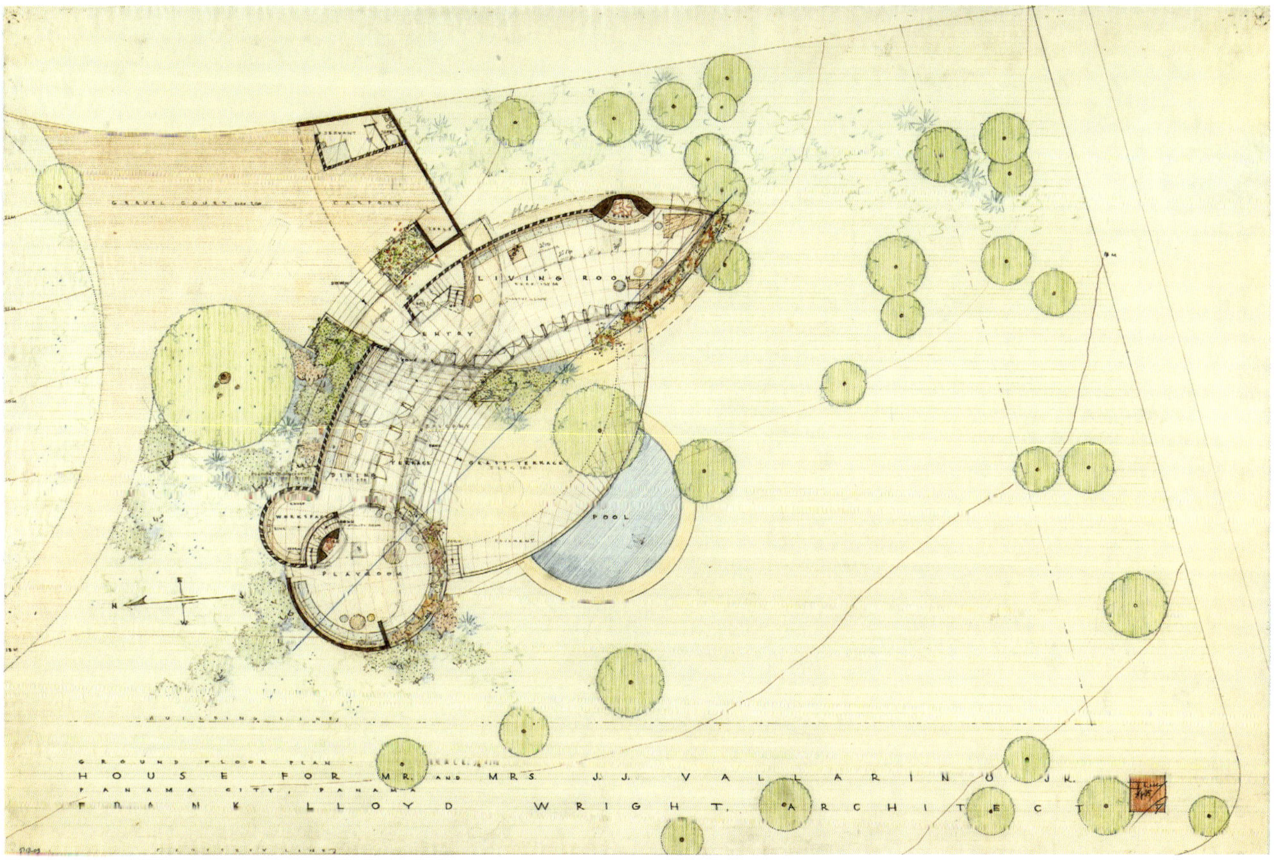

5. Vallarino Jr. House, Panama City. Project, 1951–57. Perspective from the southwest.
Ink, colored pencil, and pencil on tracing paper, 13 ³⁄₄ x 34 ¹⁄₈ in. (34.9 x 86.7 cm)

6. Vallarino Jr. House, Panama City. Project, 1951–57. Ground-floor plan.
Ink, colored pencil, and pencil on tracing paper, 23 ⁵⁄₈ x 35 ³⁄₄ in. (60 x 90.8 cm)

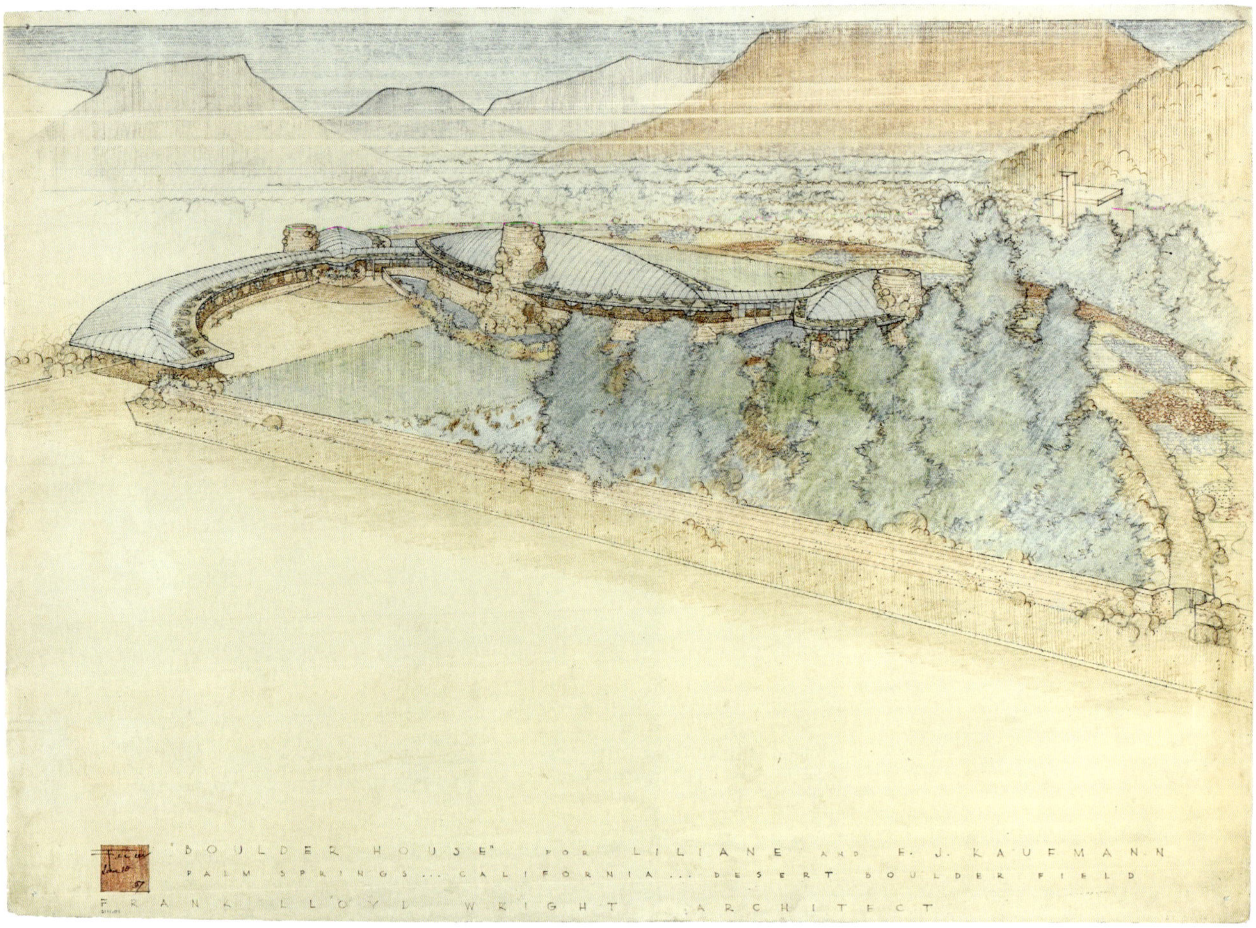

7. Boulder House, Palm Springs, California. Project, 1951. Aerial perspective.
Ink, pencil, and colored pencil on tracing paper, 25 1/4 x 35 3/8 in. (64.1 x 90 cm)

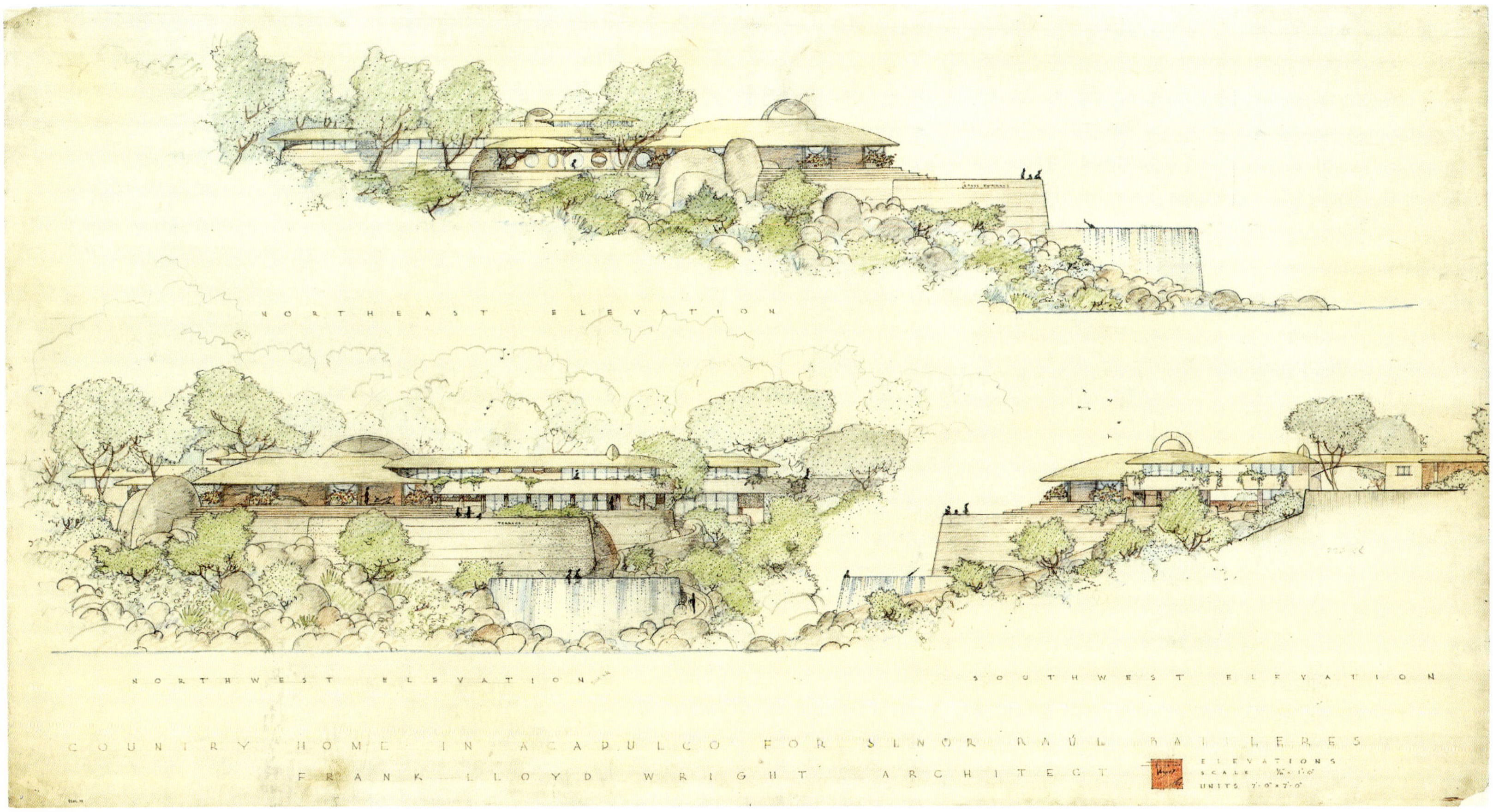

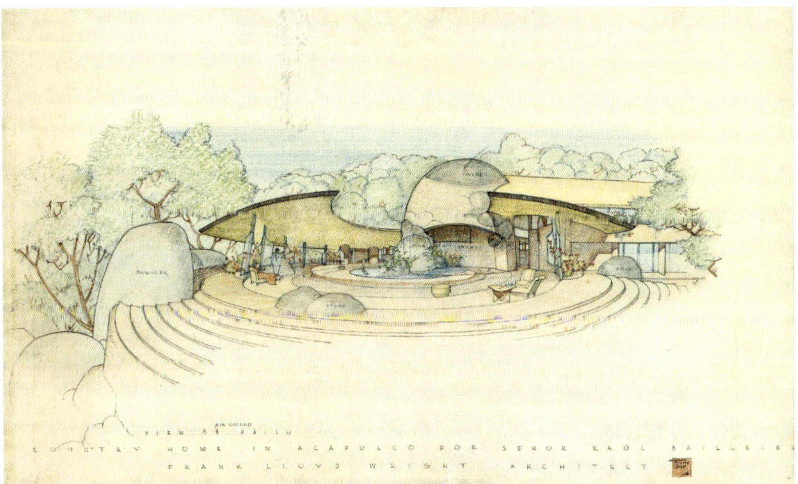

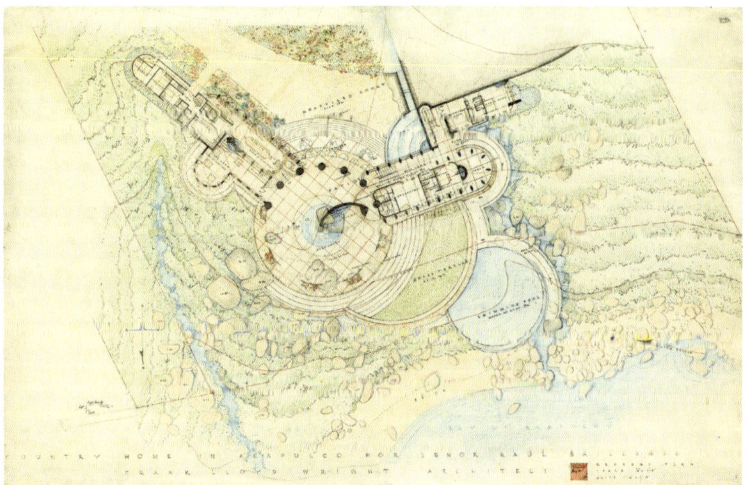

8. Baillères House, Acapulco, Mexico. Project, 1952. Northeast, northwest, and southeast elevations.
Ink, pencil, and colored pencil on tracing paper, 31 1/8 x 58 1/4 in. (79.1 x 148 cm)

9. Baillères House, Acapulco, Mexico. Project, 1952. Cutaway perspective of the patio.
Ink, pencil, and colored pencil on tracing paper, 31 3/4 x 52 7/8 in. (80.6 x 134.3 cm)

10. Baillères House, Acapulco, Mexico. Project, 1952. Site plan.
Ink, pencil, and colored pencil on tracing paper, 35 3/4 x 56 in. (90.8 x 142.2 cm)

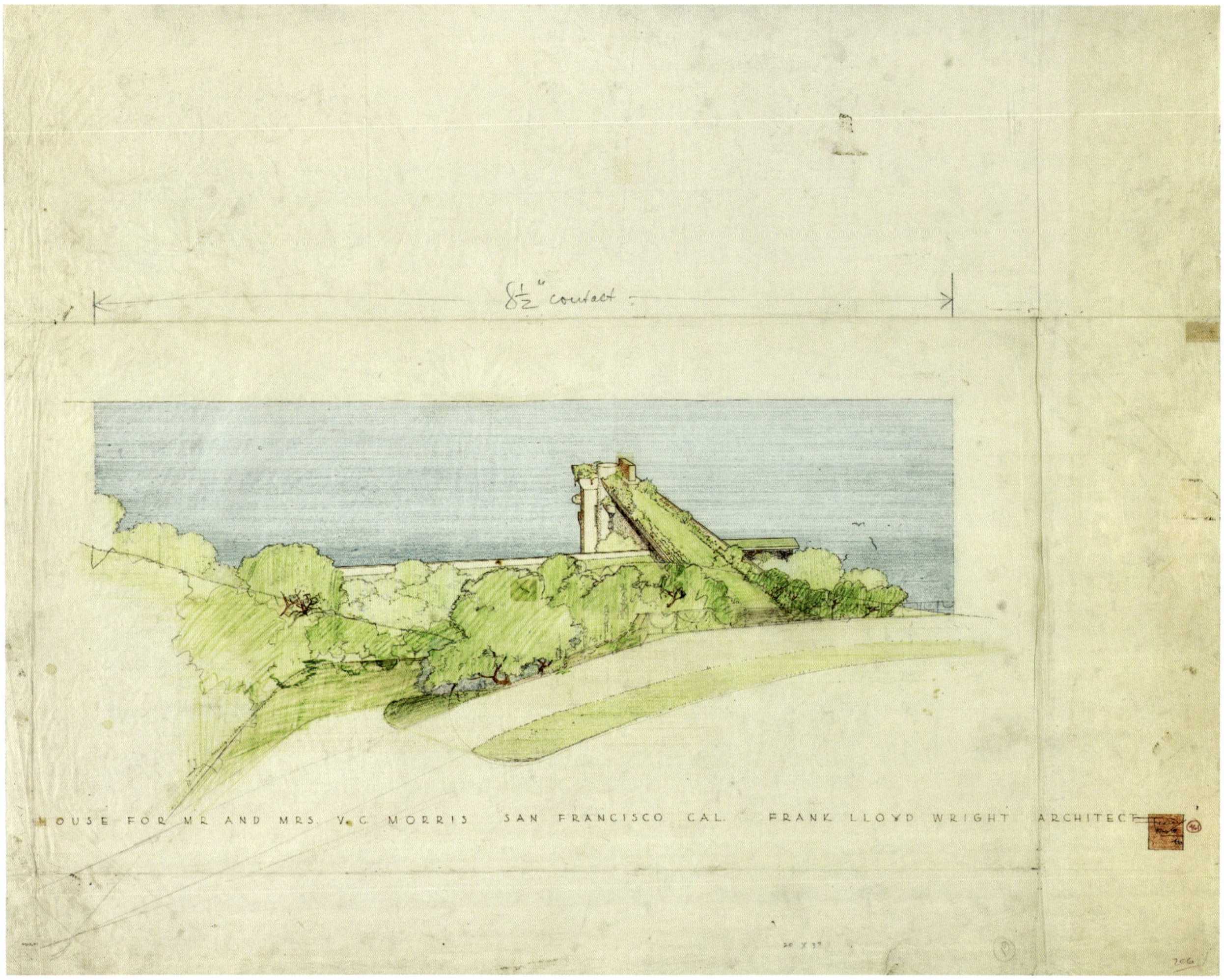

11. V. C. Morris House, San Francisco. Project, 1944–46.
Perspective overlooking the Golden Gate strait.
Ink, pencil, and colored pencil on tracing paper, 35 ⅛ x 44 ¾ in. (89.2 x 113.7 cm)

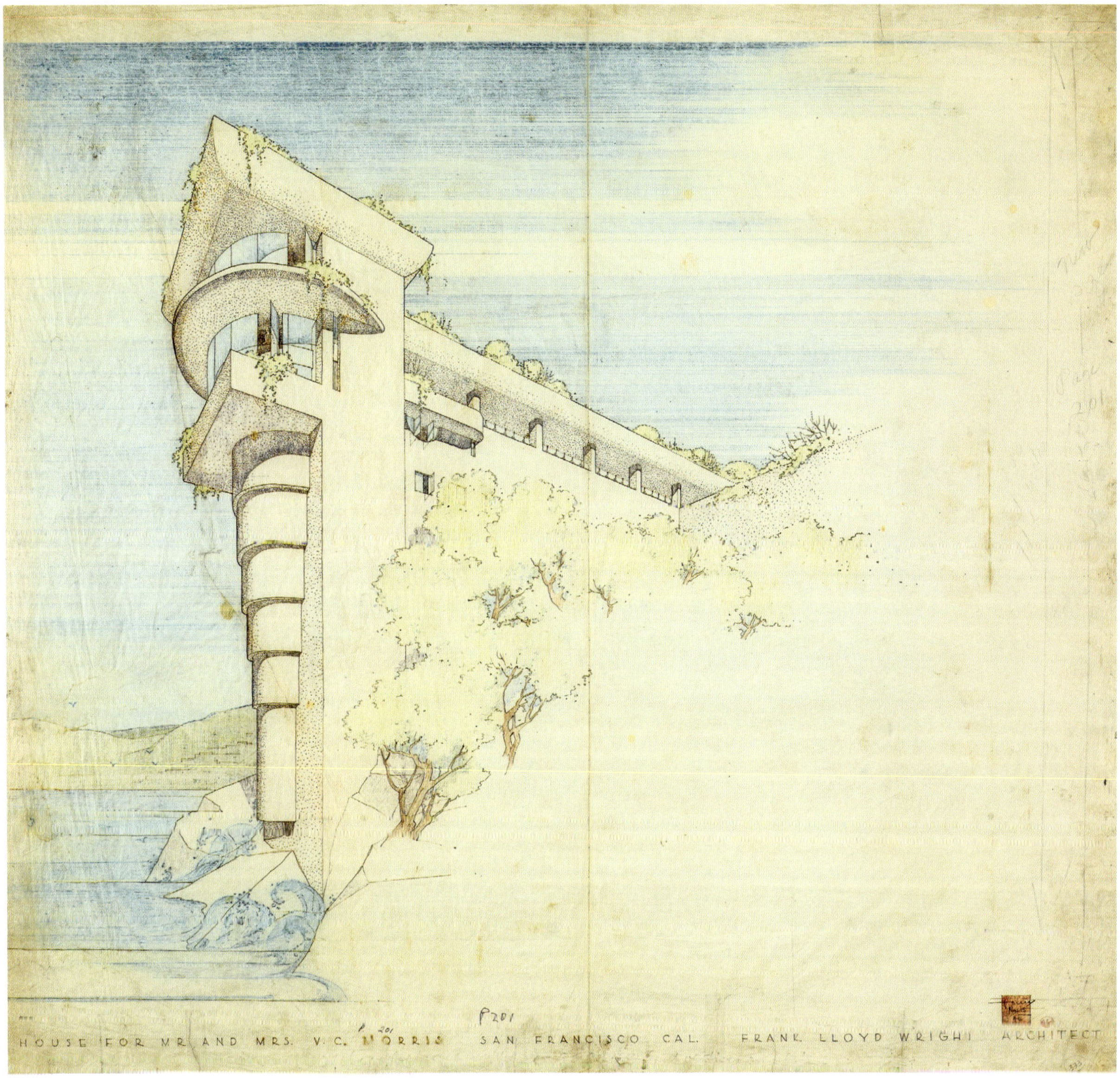

12. V. C. Morris House, San Francisco. Project, 1944–46. Perspective from below.
Ink, pencil, and colored pencil on tracing paper, 40 1/8 × 41 7/8 in. (101.9 × 106.4 cm)

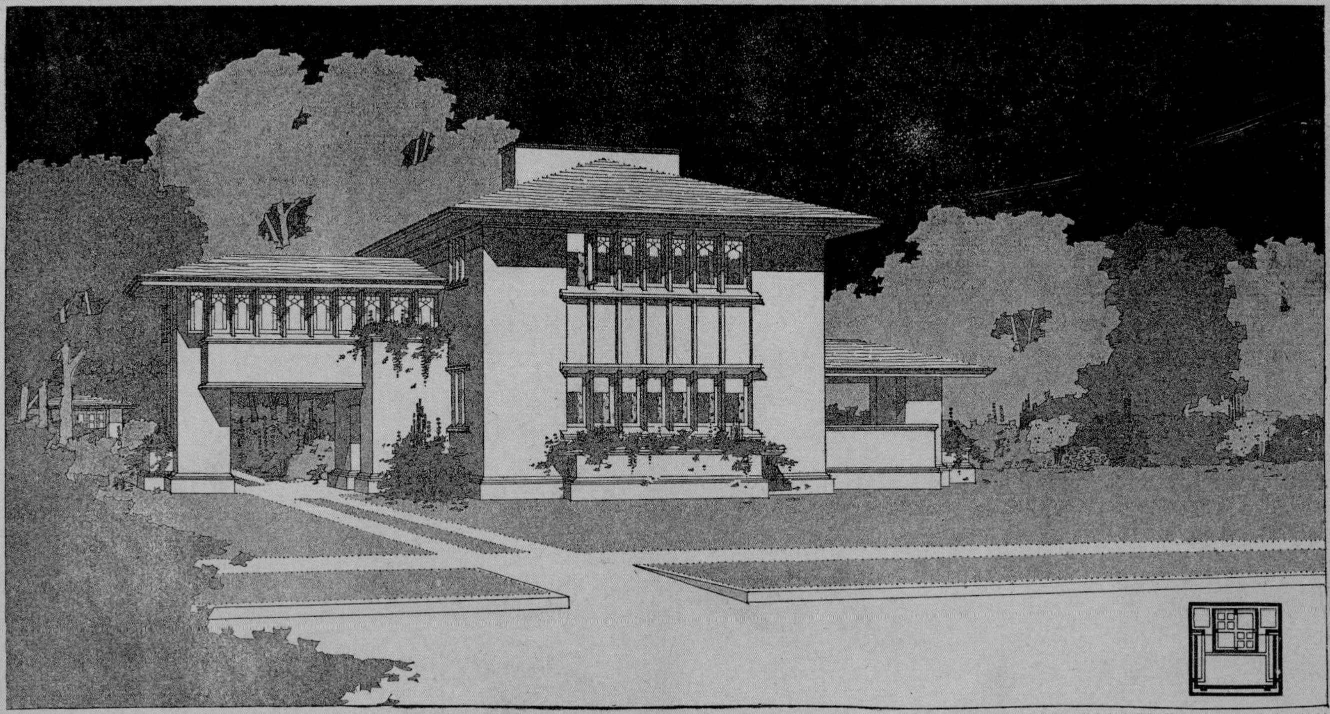

This home is being built by P. D. Diamond & Co. in Ridge Homes, the new restricted residential subdivision being offered by Burhans-Ellinwood & Co. at Tracy, 103d Street and Hoyne Avenue.

YOU CAN OWN AN AMERICAN HOME

BEFORE the summer is over you can be the possessor of an American Home, built for YOU from the plan YOU select. You and your family can be enjoying its unique, beautiful design, its convenient arrangement, its enduring construction.

You can occupy it late this summer or early this coming fall. The price will be guaranteed in advance. The arrangement for payment will meet your convenience.

People in Chicago are just beginning to realize that American Homes are not high priced. Because American Homes look better and have the air of being out of the class of ordinary houses, many home builders have hesitated even to investigate them.

Now that they understand that an American Home costs no more, or even less than others, they are buying rapidly.

We want you, if you are contemplating owning a home now or in the future, to talk to us. All we ask is the opportunity to place before you the facts regarding the moderate prices and our special arrangements which will allow your American Home to be built NOW instead of in the distant future. But first may we remind you of the special advantages of American Homes, which would make you buy even if the price were much higher.

This Is Distinctly American Architecture

American Homes reflect American spirit. They are the most recent triumph of Frank Lloyd Wright, recognized at home and abroad as America's greatest architect. His fame is world-wide, though his most important work has been to teach the American people how they can live in houses that are beautiful, convenient, and enduring.

An American Home is as truly the product of the country and as thoroughly national as a French chateau or an Italian villa.

Homes With Personality and Beauty

American Homes have character. They command recognition. Their dignity, their quiet lines, their strength and their individuality, make them stand forth from the mass of ordinary designs.

These houses are the one, new, stirring note in this oldest and most important of all the arts—the art of home building. As a great writer has said: "They have music and meaning in them."

Convenient, Practical Enduring

When you first see an American Home, either the actual structure or the drawing which we show you, you will be struck by its beauty, its cheery, homelike appearance.

When you enter an American Home you will marvel at the skill which could so perfectly combine charm of outline and effect with absolute convenience and practicability for everyday use.

American Homes are "livable" places for you and your family to spend your lives in. They seem "home" to you from the day you take possession. They make for cheer and comfort and happiness.

Cross-lighting and cross-ventilation make them healthful. Scientific designing gives ample space where it is needed and saves steps. Every woman will be delighted with these plans. They reduce her responsibilities, whether she executes personally or merely supervises household duties. All the little extras and advantages that mean so much in the daily routine of home maintenance are found in American Homes.

The Home You Would Plan

American Homes are the kind you yourself would plan. In fact, you will plan yours, for you will choose, from among the many, exactly the one that suits your every need as to space and the number and arrangement of rooms. All the faults of the ordinary house plan are eliminated. No waste space, no dark corners. Every square foot of an American Home has its use and its value to you.

And you have the choice of so many designs that you are sure to find one that is essentially YOUR home, the home you have sought but never before found.

A Guaranteed Price No "Extras"

If you have ever built for yourself, or if your friends have, you know that the bugbear of home-building is the long list of "extras" that mount up as the construction goes forward.

These "extras" can not worry you when you purchase an American Home. The price is guaranteed. You know in advance exactly what your American Home will cost. And the quality of material and workmanship is guaranteed.

Built by Established Contractors

The American System does not alter present building conditions. American Homes are being erected by established contractors and builders who are enthusiastic over the practical character of the construction, and beauty and permanence of the finished edifice.

Come to Our Office—Learn How YOU Can Own An American Home

To you who live in apartments or in a house not your own, decide now to have a beautiful home of your own. Learn how easily you can become the owner of an American Home—within the next few months. Our arrangement will surprise you. You will find the terms suited to your convenience. Payments can be made monthly. American Homes range in price from $3,000 up.

And see the plans of American Homes. They are different and more complete. Some drawings show not only the walls, doors and windows, but the position of the furniture. It is as if the roof were lifted off. You look into your future home as it will be when you occupy it.

You can study the specifications that protect you at every stage of construction. You will be quoted the guaranteed price—no "extras"—on your completed home ready for occupancy, with quality guaranteed and no building worries.

A visit to our office places you under no obligations whatever. So come at your earliest opportunity. Let us prove every advantage of American Homes. You are to be the judge. We gladly place the facts before you and leave the decision to you. But act at once. For your American Home can be built this summer if you wish, under this broad, generous plan.

Or Write for Suggestions Suiting Your Requirements

If you cannot conveniently meet with us at our office, we will send you a number of beautiful illustrations, together with interesting facts about American Homes.

BUILDERS

- **Elmhurst** GEO. R. CHAPMAN, S. E. Corner Kenilworth Ave. and St. Charles Road, Telephone Elmhurst 34
- **Berwyn** ELLINWOOD & BRAGG, 6808 Windsor Avenue, Phones Berwyn 525, Randolph 3886
- **North Shore, West Side, La Grange to Naperville** AMERICAN HOME BUILDING CO., Room 810, Chicago Savings Bank Building, 7 West Madison Street, Phone Majestic 7859
- **South Side, Riverside, Hollywood** P. D. DIAMOND & CO., 2211 W. 110th Pl. Ph. Beverly 812, Loop Office: Room 808, 7 West Madison St
- **Gary** INGWOLD MOE, Pres. of the Gen'l Construction Co., 501-4 Gary Theatre Bldg. Phone Gary 84 or 58
- **Champaign** J. F. HESSEL
- **Decatur** E. C. RAKOW, 209 Empress Bldg.

TO BUILDERS: These houses are built by builders having exclusive rights in their territories. There are still desirable territories not yet closed, for which we will be glad to hear from strong builders who can appreciate the sales possibilities of this enterprise. This applies not only to the immediate Chicago district, but to the surrounding Middle West which is handled from the Chicago office.
TO SUBDIVIDERS: Nothing could better put the stamp of quality on any subdivision than the building of some of these American Homes, designed by Frank Lloyd Wright. We will be glad to show you how easily this is possible.

LOCAL REPRESENTATIVES OF THE AMERICAN HOME BLDG. COMPANY

- **Waukegan & Lake Forest** Barnum & Wells, Coon Building, Waukegan, Phone Waukegan 1093
- **Highland Park** Henry K. Coale & Son, New Pearl Theatre Bldg. Phone Highland Park 17
- **Ravinia and Glencoe** McGuire & Orr, G. H. Engelhart, Manager, Phone Glencoe 13
- **Hubbard Woods & Winnetka** McGuire & Orr, Winnetka, W. J. Moir, Manager, Phone Winnetka 672
- **Kenilworth and Wilmette** J. A. Shane, 1122 Central Av., Wilmette, Phone Wilmette 1079
- **"L" Terminal, Wilmette** McGuire & Orr, Samuel McCane, Manager, Phone Wilmette 227
- **Central Street, Evanston** Hanney Sons, Inc. End of car line, Phone Evanston 2260
- **Rogers Park** M. J. Roughan, 1535 Jarvis Avenue, Phone Rogers Park 697
- **Oak Park and Austin** Biggs Bros. 5625 South Boulevard, Phone Austin 136
- **River Forest** Thos. E. McBride, Ashland and Lake Streets, Phone River Forest 4830
- **Maywood** Chas. Heller, Madison St. and Fifth Av. Phone Maywood 156
- **Forest Park** Theo. L. Lobstein & Co. 7207 West Twelfth Street, Phone Forest Park 2044
- **Norwood Park** Geo. J. Eckhoff, 6022 Avondale Avenue, Phone Newcastle 984
- **La Grange** Robertson & Robinson, Phone La Grange 688
- **Hinsdale** E. F. Davis, 5 Washington Street, Phone Hinsdale 663
- **Special** M. S. Hubbard, 25 N. Dearborn St., Chicago, Phone Central 1111

Pettit & Rockwell, Chicago Savings Bank Building, 7 West Madison Street—Telephone Central 677

CHICAGO BRANCH OF THE RICHARDS CO., MILWAUKEE, WIS.

American System-Built Houses. Project, 1915–17.
From *Chicago Sunday Tribune*, July 8, 1917

MICHAEL OSMAN

AMERICAN SYSTEM-BUILT HOUSES

AUTHORSHIP AND MASS PRODUCTION

In 1917, the Richards Company, owned by the real estate developer and industrialist Arthur L. Richards of Milwaukee, advertised houses in a few Sunday editions of the *Chicago Daily Tribune*. In the middle of one full-page ad, the Company boldly announced: YOU CAN OWN AN AMERICAN HOME (opposite). These homes, explained the accompanying text, were designed by Frank Lloyd Wright, "America's greatest architect."[1] At the bottom of the ad was a list of builders from around Wisconsin, Illinois, and Indiana who could deliver the product represented in the perspective drawing at the top. Wright's focus in designing his American System-Built Houses was on construction systems—that is, the use of building elements produced in factories that employed machine processes to minimize the need for skilled labor, making a more affordable product. By the late 1930s, still interested in designing middle-class houses for Americans, Wright would turn from designing with mass-produced parts to using standard details for drafting-room production. Rather than modular systems made in factories, he developed a set of guidelines to direct his many apprentices in producing what he called his Usonian houses. Employing these standards for around sixty built houses both cheapened the cost of design, since the apprentices' labor was free, and extended the reach of Wright's signature. Differences between these two approaches—using factory-made building elements versus drafting-room standards—show the types of authorship available to architects during the first decades of the twentieth century. Together they illustrate the flexibility of the interface between Wright's practice and different methods of mass production.

Wright was outspoken about positioning the machine at the center of architectural design as early as 1901. He promoted using factory-made parts and novel materials not only to reduce construction costs and make buildings more accessible, but also to assure that they were culturally vital.[2] His design for a Fireproof House, which was to cost $5,000, had appeared in the *Ladies' Home Journal* in 1907 and incorporated some of these ideas, including the use of concrete. But Wright only fully invested his practice in the development of cost-saving methods for construction as a result of the Richards commission, starting in 1915. For Wright, this was an opportunity to pursue his interest in designs based on machine work, while for Richards the value of Wright's signature offered an esteemed name to help market the houses that would range widely in both size and cost.[3]

To reduce labor costs, Wright worked with factories owned by the Richards Company to limit the amount of carpentry required on the construction site. Shop drawings, like that of a windowsill, make visible the complexity involved in translating skilled carpentry into factory work (plate 1). The house plans were organized around modules, and mass-produced elements such as windows, mullions, doors, sash details, and interior elements—designed to be consistent across all the houses—would brand the American System-Built Houses as products that belonged to Wright's much-coveted "style" (plate 2a–f).

Richards hoped to compete with both professional architects and the Sears, Roebuck and Co.'s mail-order houses that, by the first decade of the twentieth century, were offered through that company's network of factories, warehouses, and distribution facilities, not to mention its staff of accountants for financing and architects who aided clients with design and decor (fig. 1).[4] Some of the methods used to construct the Sears houses overlapped with those proposed for the System-Built Houses. For example, Richards and Wright followed Sears's innovations in "ready-cut" lumber delivery. This meant that there was almost no need for a saw on the job site, reducing the carpenter's labor by as much as half. But unlike the Richards Company's advertisements, the Sears catalogs described the business as "A Big Organization at Your Service," in which every customer could customize their house before its delivery. Thus, although they were machine-made, Sears houses incorporated many slight differences to accommodate a wide range of attitudes toward middle-class comfort.[5]

Wright was less accepting of this open approach to mass-producing houses. In an address to a group of businessmen in Chicago, Wright compared his System-Built Houses to the competition:

I believe that the architecture in America that fails to take into account the machine and modern organization tendencies is going to be of no great benefit to the people . . . [but] . . . I do not want any mistake made about this new "System." These buildings are not in any sense the ready cut buildings we

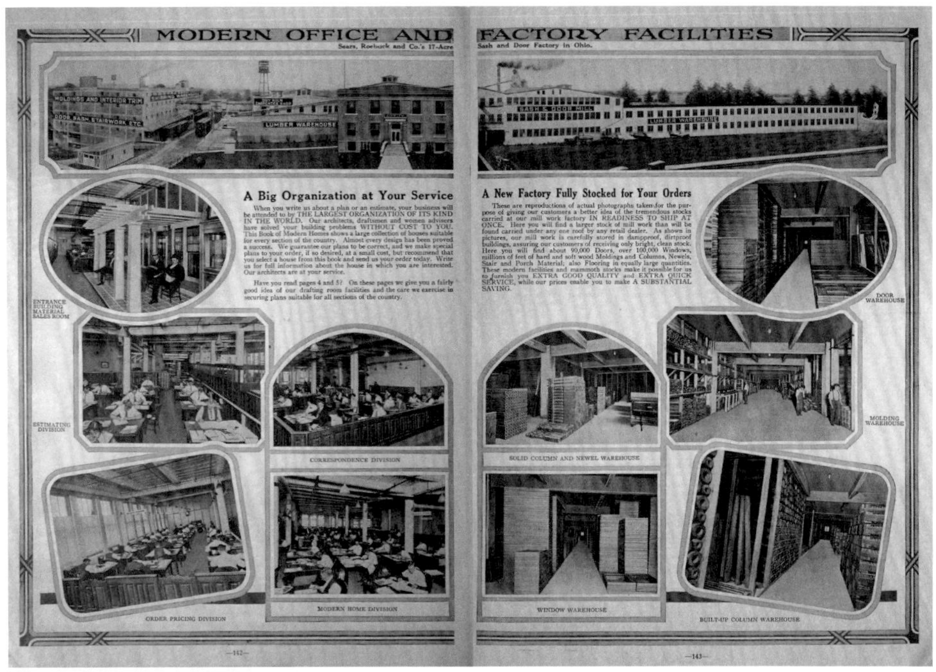

Fig. 1. Pages from Sears, Roebuck and Co. catalog, "Honor Bilt Modern Homes" (Chicago, 1918)

have all heard of where a little package of material is sold to be stuck together in any fashion. The American System-Built House is not a ready cut house, but a house . . . *systematized in such a way that* the result is guaranteed. . . . *I want to deliver beautiful houses to people at a certain price, key in packet.*[6]

Because factory labor reduced direct contact between the architect and all aspects of house-construction, the very reproducibility of the buildings required identifying the architect's authorship as the inventor of the *system* rather than the designer of any one building. Unlike Wright's earlier houses built in Chicago and its suburbs, the System-Built Houses were not works designed around a client's desires; rather, they offered a limited number of options to a potential buyer. Wright acknowledged the transformation in his authorship with a statement in the lower-right-hand corner of every drawing for the project: a declaration that all the components of the system were also elements of a patent application. While there is no evidence that these documents were ever sent to the U.S. Patent Office, the stated intention of assigning intellectual property to the system is still telling.[7] Wright's insistence on beauty, systemization, and predictable results—rather than the flexibility and scale of the operation offered by Sears—illustrates the assertion of his authorship for both the client and the builder as being part of an industrial infrastructure.

Though the Richards Company succeeded in constructing only around two dozen such houses, all in one Milwaukee neighborhood, Wright's practice oversaw the production of one thousand drawings of the system. Indeed, the volume of material related to this project is the largest of any held in the Frank Lloyd Wright Foundation Archives. This was a massive effort: employees produced documents for marketing, contracts for clients, communications with industrial producers, and construction documents for the selected builders.[8] Yet despite his direct involvement in such state of the art infrastructure for mass distribution, Wright claimed to have never applied managerial methods to his own office. In his 1932 autobiography, Wright emphasized his refusal to engage in any form of office management: "There was never organization in the sense that the usual architect's office knows organization. Nor any great need of it so long as I stood at the center of the effort. Where I am, there my office is: my office is me."[9] This statement points to the architect's view of his authorship as the reason for the combined labor of all his employees—and thus an extension of himself.

Given this disavowal of modern managerial culture, it is perhaps surprising that in 1918 an image of the atrium of Wright's Larkin Building (1902–06), in Buffalo, New York, was selected as the frontispiece for *Office Management: Its Principles and Practice*, a book applying Frederick Winslow Taylor's organizational methods to office work.[10] The business press, moreover, viewed Larkin's mail-order processing center as "a model administration building," representing "a magnificent monument to fidelity to a business ideal."[11] A master working drawing for the first-floor plan indicates that important aspects of the company's administrative needs were incorporated into the building's design, including a lighting plan that located all the floor outlets, wall lamps, ceiling lamps, graphophones, and telephones (fig. 2). Perhaps the clearest sign of bureaucracy's integral role in the building design was the central placement of the desks of Darwin Martin and William Heath, the secretary and managers of the company.[12] Thus, Wright was amply aware of the value of management and its infrastructure to white-collar labor; his comments in his autobiography indicate a shift in his attitude toward authorship.

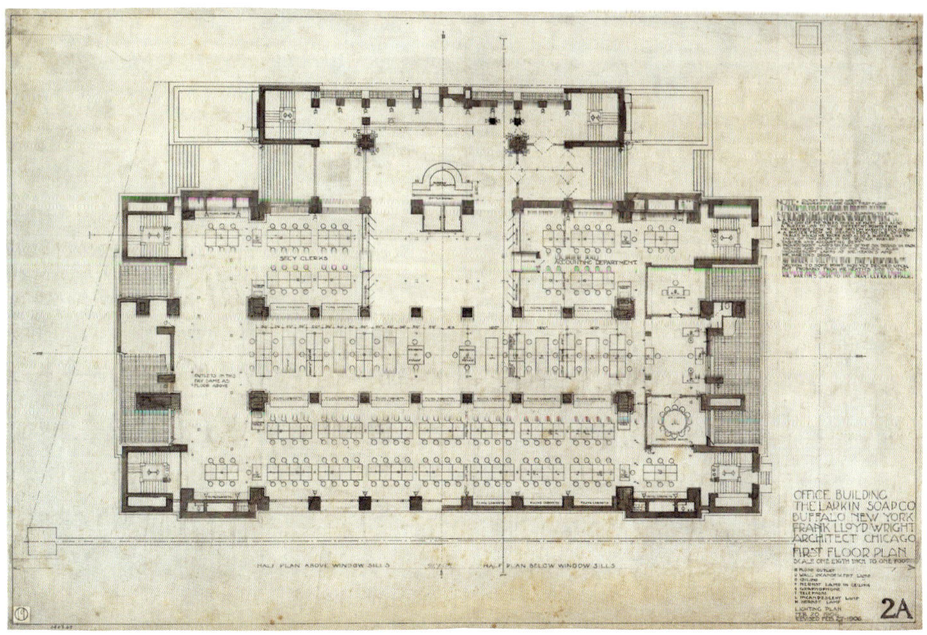

Fig. 2. Larkin Building, Buffalo, New York. 1902–06. First-floor plan. Ink and pencil on drafting cloth, 24 ¼ x 37 in. (61.6 x 94 cm)

In 1932, after a series of personal disasters and little to no work since the stock market crash of 1929, Wright established the Taliesin Fellowship, a school of architecture located on the site of his ancestral home in Spring Green, Wisconsin. Without a baseline income to maintain an office, Wright "employed" would-be architects—that is, apprentices—in the Fellowship, who paid an annual tuition of $650. (The University Pennsylvania, by comparison, charged its undergraduates $400 in that year.) By 1933 tuition at Taliesin had nearly doubled. Fellowship apprentices—initially numbering around twenty—paid this large sum to learn how to produce Wright's designs and, by extension, became the labor force behind the architect's drawings throughout his later years. At Taliesin, Wright's authorship was opened to the apprentices as a result of an educational infrastructure that guided their labor, presenting a sharp contrast to the managerial strategies used in the business world, such as those manifested in the organization of the Larkin Building plan.[13]

To contain this new group of student workers, Wright proposed building a drafting room with connected dormitories as an extension to the remodeled Hillside Home School on the Taliesin property, at some distance from the main house. Under expert supervision, the apprentices quarried nearby stone, produced lime from limestone, milled oak boards from trees felled on neighboring lands, and constructed the building in which they would work and live. Edgar Tafel, one of those early apprentices, recalled that the pedagogical method was fundamentally hands-on: cooking, cleaning, and continuously expanding the complex were essential to the Fellowship. "In the drafting room, as elsewhere at Taliesin," he wrote, "we learned by doing. In the beginning, with senior draftsmen to supervise, Mr. Wright had us copying drawings of his early buildings and working on drawings for the rooms under construction at Hillside."[14] Notice the emphasis on copying: while it was a common practice in other offices at the time, at Taliesin copying was one means to integrate the economy of a school with that of an office, all in the service of reproducing Wright's signature.

The integration of learning and working is clear in the Broadacre City project (1929–35), begun by the first group of Taliesin apprentices to illustrate Wright's views on urbanization in his book *The Disappearing City*, published in 1932.[15] Largely a response to Le Corbusier's proposals to replace urban congestion with high-rise buildings set in a green landscape, this publication solidified Wright's vision for a suburban infrastructure for the continent.[16] The project thus exemplified what Wright called Usonian ideals in a 16-square-mile (41-square-kilometer) swath of land, represented by a model measuring 12 ft. 8 in. (3.9 meters) square (fig. 3). In 1935 the model was displayed at the newly built Rockefeller Center in New York and partly funded by the Pittsburgh department store owner Edgar Kaufmann, who was Wright's most supportive client during the Great Depression, commissioning his famed residence

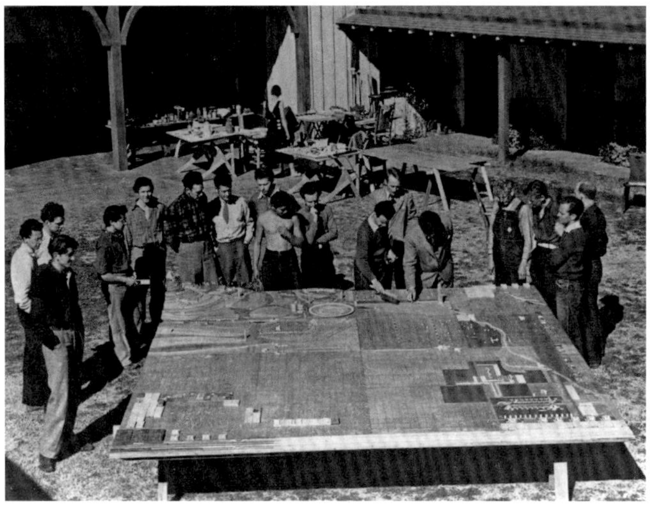

Fig. 3. Broadacre City. Project, 1929–35. Wright and his apprentices working on the model in Arizona. n.d. Photograph by Edgar Tafel. Historic Architecture and Landscape Image Collection, Ryerson and Burnham Archives, The Art Institute of Chicago

Fallingwater (1934–37). But Kaufmann was not the only source of funding for the model; the apprentices also underwrote it with their tuition, and the labor used to construct it was, after all, provided by them. Within a year of the model's display, the Fellowship began designing Usonian houses based on the values it described.

While the System-Built house designs were named "American" and illustrate Wright's views of a nation centered on machines and patents, the name "Usonian" reflected his ideas about the shifting priorities brought about by the Depression. Usonian houses were designed to take advantage of the greater affordability of skilled labor resulting from the era's high unemployment; master craftsmen could be asked to work in a narrow range of materials with refined construction techniques. The resulting level of craft and oversight through the Fellowship guaranteed Wright's signature without the legal structure of intellectual property.[17]

Herbert Jacobs, a client whose house Wright would later name Usonian I, recalled a visit to Taliesin in 1936 in which he and his wife were led by "twenty architectural apprentices . . . through a maze of slat-topped drafting desks to where the architect was sitting."[18] Jacobs was surprised that such a famous architect would entertain as small a commission as a house for $5,000. The final budget, after meeting with Wright, was set at $5,500, including the $450 architectural fee.[19] The intimate yet hierarchical setting at Taliesin offered an infrastructure that made such commissions economically viable at a time that was generally less supportive of experiments in domestic architecture. Indeed, no Usonian houses would be financed by the Federal Housing Administration under the National Housing Act of 1934. One explanation for this is that FHA standards deterred banks from underwriting loans for the houses because of their unconventional building systems, such as the unique wall assembly or Wright's proposed method for delivering radiant heat through a concrete slab. Against the expanding availability of housing debt, these homes could only be realized with the combination of free design labor and freely available client funds.[20]

While the Jacobs House (1936–37; plate 3) was experimental in many ways, there were attempts to make the building prototypical. Consider the plan, where the 2-foot-by-4-foot (0.6-by-1.2-meter) module organized the distribution of walls to minimize material waste (plate 4). This rectangular grid reinforced, at a domestic scale, the one-acre Broadacre module, although the latter was not a perfect two-square. But, in the expansion of Wright's signature, the detail sheets drawn for the project (plate 5) proved to be more significant than the geometry of the plan. These smaller elements became the "grammar" for many of the Usonian houses designed over the next twenty years.[21] Among other things, the details describe the characteristic pine board and batten walls, with a plywood core instead of studs. Thinner than conventional walls, the Jacobs

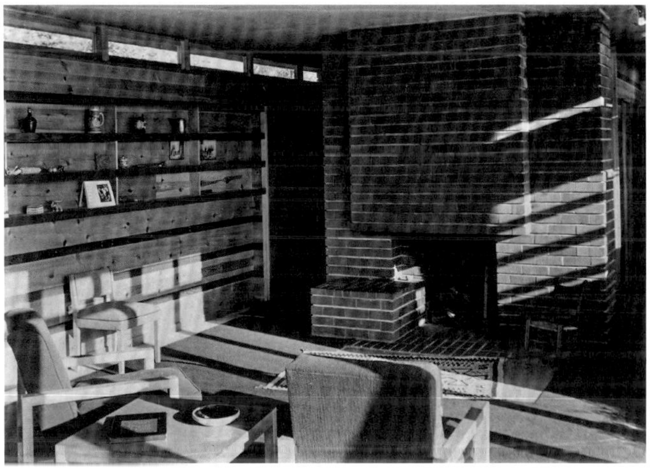

Fig. 4. Jacobs House, Madison, Wisconsin. 1936–37. Living room

House walls attained structural integrity by turning corners and incorporating bookshelves (fig. 4). These were not, however, simple walls to build. While conventional construction hides rough work under layers of sheathing and molding, these walls exposed essential details to showcase the carpenter's craft. For example, the window details of the Usonian houses contained far fewer elements than the windows for the System-Built Houses, yet they required the carpenters to build up the frames from stock lumber, and, without plaster, there was no way to hide errors.

Over the next twenty years, one hundred forty Usonian houses were designed. Many employed the Jacobs details, now summarized in one drawing called the "Standard Detail Sheet." Eight such sheets are preserved in the Archives, the last of which was drawn on May 23, 1940, and revised on September 23, for a demonstration house planned, but never built, for the courtyard of The Museum of Modern Art (plate 6). Rather than copy drawings of old projects, new apprentices were asked to trace these standard details and integrate them into the houses they designed in the Fellowship. In place of adding mass-produced parts to attain the architect's signature, the Standard Detail Sheet became an instrument that allowed the design process itself to be mass-produced and centrally controlled.

Once drawings for a Usonian house were completed at Taliesin, an apprentice often brought the drawings to the site where he would act as the general contractor, overseeing the work of tradesmen from the area. This full-service operation meant detailed dimensions could be excluded to allow for interpretations to be made in situ. The organizing grid and standard details were intended as sufficient guidelines for realizing the houses. Thus, rather than a machine-enabled system made up of normalized parts for construction, standard details for designing in the drafting room made an apprentice's education central to reproducing a style that could always point back to Wright's authorship. The Standard Detail Sheets helped regulate the production of houses under the guiding influence of a set of small-scale decisions. Such "internal standards" were not unique to architectural production—they can be found in numerous industrial practices—but they represent a form of control over design that departs from a modernist historiography that has often focused on industrialized construction in such materials as steel or concrete. The Usonian houses are evidence that architectural authorship could also be expanded in a modern economy with methods that reproduced a signature object with the help of many well-trained hands, including those of skilled craftsmen.

Notes

1. A tear sheet of the advertisement is held in the Frank Lloyd Wright Foundation Archives (The Museum of Modern Art | Avery Architectural & Fine Arts Library, Columbia University, New York), 1506.162. It appeared in the *Chicago Sunday Tribune*, July 8, 1917, p. 9. Others appeared on September 17, 1916, March 4, 1917, and June 3, 1917.

2. See, for example, "The Art and Craft of the Machine" (1901), in *Frank Lloyd Wright: Collected Writings*, vol. 1, *1894–1930* ed. Bruce Brooks Pfeiffer (New York: Rizzoli and Frank Lloyd Wright Foundation, 1992–95), pp. 58–68.

3. One advertisement mentions: "Small homes range in price from $2750 to $3500 larger homes $5000 to $100,000." See "American Homes," *Chicago Sunday Tribune*, March 4, 1917, p. 7. See also Shirley du Fresne McArthur, *Frank Lloyd Wright: American System-Built Homes in Milwaukee* (North Point Historical Society, 1983); and Kenneth Martin Kao, "Frank Lloyd Wright: Experiments in the Art of Building," *Modulus* 22 (1993): 66–93.

4. Arthur L. Richards, letter to Wright, February 6, 1917, R001C06, Wright Foundation Archives (MoMA | Avery).

5. Sears, Roebuck & Co. catalog, "Honor Bilt Modern Homes" (Chicago, 1918).

6. "The American System of House Building," *Western Architect* (September 1916): 120–21. Emphasis added.

7. The contract, sent by the Richards Company to Wright in November 1916, stipulates that Wright would have the plans and specifications "properly patented and copyrighted" in his name. The Richards Company claimed "exclusive right and privilege" to use these patents and copyrights. Richards Company to Wright, W306A01, Wright Foundation Archives (MoMA | Avery).

8. William Allin Storrer, *The Architecture of Frank Lloyd Wright: A Complete Catalog* (Chicago: University of Chicago Press, 2002), pp. 198–210.

9. Frank Lloyd Wright, *An Autobiography* (New York: Longmans Green, 1932), p. 236.

10. Lee Galloway, *Office Management: Its Principles and Practice* (New York: Ronald Press, 1918).

11. George Twitmyer, "A Model Administration Building," *Business Man's Magazine* 19 (April 1907): 43.

12. Both men had commissioned houses from Wright. For a full treatment of the Larkin Building, see Jack Quinan, *Frank Lloyd Wright's Larkin Building: Myth and Fact* (Chicago: University of Chicago Press, 1987, 2006).

13. Edgar Tafel, *Apprentice to Genius: Years with Frank Lloyd Wright* (New York: McGraw-Hill, 1979), pp. 15–16.

14. Ibid., p. 164.

15. Frank Lloyd Wright, *The Disappearing City* (New York: William Farquhar Payson, 1932).

16. Neil Levine, *The Urbanism of Frank Lloyd Wright* (Princeton, N.J.: Princeton University Press, 2016), p. 157.

17. These homes were to belong more strictly to the United States, whose territory Wright called "Usonia." He claimed to have derived the term from Samuel Butler. See John Sergeant, *Frank Lloyd Wright's Usonian Houses: The Case for Organic Architecture* (New York: Whitney Library of Design, Watson-Guptill Publications, 1976).

18. Herbert Jacobs with Katherine Jacobs, *Building with Frank Lloyd Wright: An Illustrated Memoir* (San Francisco: Chronicle Books, 1978), p. 3.

19. Frank Lloyd Wright, "The Usonian House I," in *The Natural House* (New York: Horizon Press, 1954), pp. 81–91; Donald Kalec, "The Jacobs House I," *Frank Lloyd Wright and Madison: Eight Decades of Artistic and Social Interaction*, ed. Paul Sprague (Madison: University of Wisconsin Press, 1992), pp. 91–100.

20. Louis Hyman, *Debtor Nation: The History of America in Red Ink* (Princeton, N. J.: Princeton University Press, 2011).

21. George Chadwick, "The Challenge of Being a Taliesin Fellow" (1940), in *Writings on Wright: Selected Comment on Frank Lloyd Wright*, ed. H. Allen Brooks (Cambridge, Mass.: MIT Press, 1983), p. 60.

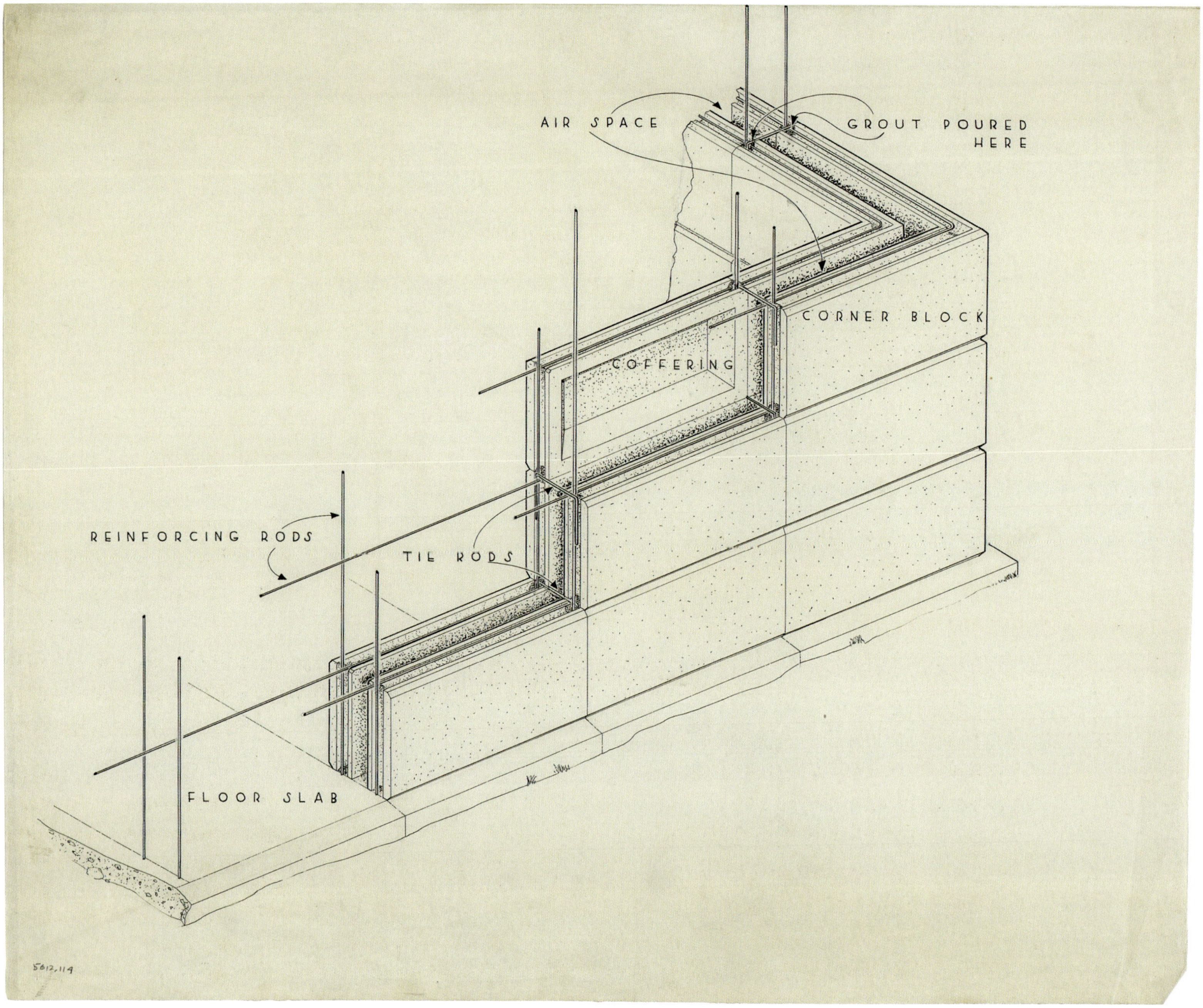

MATTHEW SKJONSBERG

DO IT YOURSELF
USONIAN AUTOMATIC SYSTEM

Usonian Automatic system. Project, early 1950s. Axonometric diagram, 1954.
Ink on tracing paper, 20 ½ x 25 in. (52.1 x 63.5 cm)

Most can raise the flowers now,
For all have got the seed.

—Alfred Tennyson, "The Flower"

With the Usonian Automatic construction system, Frank Lloyd Wright provided citizens of Usonia—Wright's preferred term for a culturally advanced North America—with the means of "doing it themselves," of building their own homes and communities. Though designing ways to provide moderate-cost housing on a large scale had preoccupied Wright for years—and resulted in his invention of numerous construction systems—the Usonian Automatic would be different: almost open source in its sensibility, it was explicitly intended to allow anyone to build their own buildings, of their own earth, on their own ground.

An axonometric drawing, first published in 1954 in *The Natural House*, demonstrates how the Usonian Automatic system worked (opposite).[1] The idea was simple: concrete blocks reinforced with steel rods running through vertical and horizontal joints, not unlike the way a textile is woven on a loom. Its open-ended nature meant that it was also scalable, capable of creating small houses, larger civic centers, as well as infrastructure, such as retaining walls, terraces, and roadways. And most importantly, Wright intended that anyone could use the system, as its basic principle—weaving—required little in the way of skilled labor, expertise, or advanced technology. Moreover, the materials were easy to obtain. Wright intended that users of his system would themselves cast the concrete blocks using soil from their own property as the aggregate. The system was entirely standardized, consisting of just twelve variants of cast-concrete blocks. An individual could use the system at a small scale or cooperate with others to build larger structures. In this way, the Usonian Automatic system approximated democratic relationships between self-reliance and community, between individual initiative and cooperative action.

What does it mean to draw a system rather than a building? A system is open-ended, capable of evolving and changing, whereas a blueprint proscribes a final product. Wright envisioned that the Usonian Automatic system would develop over time, yielding a more democratic civic fabric—both materially and socially. He explained its political potential, describing such an approach to building as "becoming to a free society because, though standardized fully, it yet establishes the democratic ideal of variety—the sovereignty of the individual. A true architecture may evolve."[2] The Usonian Automatic system was to be nothing less than an instrument for social equity.

PRECEDENTS

Wright's first designs for moderate-cost housing appeared in the *Ladies' Home Journal* at the turn of the twentieth century, attempting to democratize access to his house designs using mail-order strategies common at the time. He subsequently experimented with factory-produced housing in his American System-Built designs of 1915–17 (plate 2a–f). This system reduced costs by prefabricating building components in a factory, which were then constructed by licensed contractors to ensure the quality of the results. The American System-Built Houses were an early attempt by Wright to harness the efficiencies of industry and mechanization, while still producing a high-quality and beautiful product.

Wright had, at least theoretically, engaged with industry as an agent of democracy as early as 1901, when he read his seminal essay "The Art and Craft of the Machine" to an audience at Hull House, a multifaceted civic organization in Chicago. In his speech, Wright argued the machine was the "great forerunner of democracy." He cited Victor Hugo's argument in *Notre-Dame de Paris* (1831) that the printing press, by emancipating knowledge in the form of reproducible type, had superseded the symbolic and civic functions previously ascribed to architecture: the book had replaced the building. According to Wright, for architecture to remain relevant it must learn the lesson of the printing press, "the first great machine, after the great city."[3] To this end, Wright sought to instrumentalize architectural production, to use the machine as a labor-saving tool that would bring greater beauty, variety, and dignity to civilization.[4] The *Chicago Tribune* summarized Wright's argument as such: "This idea . . . says that there should be neither slave nor slave-like products. It asserts instead that machine production . . . can be and should be genuinely artistic."[5]

Wright achieved moderate success interfacing architecture and industrial production with the American System-Built Houses, and by the 1920s, while working in California, he began to experiment with another construction system that embraced a new material better suited to the desert climate of his environs: concrete. Residential construction at this time rarely used concrete—"that despised outcast of the building industry,"[6] as Wright described it—but he began to see possibilities in its malleability: "Concrete is a plastic material—susceptible to the impress of imagination. I saw a kind of weaving coming out of it. Why not weave a kind of building? . . . steel for warp and masonry units for woof in the weaving . . . I was getting interested again."[7]

The first projects built with concrete blocks were a series of houses in Los Angeles, where concrete responds better than wood to the incessant sun, and is also fireproof. First at the Millard (La Miniatura) House (1923–24) and then in subsequent designs such as the Ennis House (1924–25), Wright grappled with the tectonic challenges of concrete—namely its amorphous, plastic quality—by casting the concrete into richly patterned blocks made with earth taken from the building site.[8] This process imbued the concrete with the texture and natural color of the surrounding landscape, thus transforming the material into "a thing of beauty—textured like the trees."[9] At the Ennis House, close associates supervised the construction process, which capitalized on the open-ended weaving process and scalability of this system—what Wright came to describe as his textile-block system (plate 7)—to build a rambling complex. The house and retaining walls are nearly indistinguishable, stitched across the hilly site and serving multiple functions, such as roadways for access and water catchment, and terraced gardens for soil conservation and to create a cooling microclimate (plate 8).

The Ennis House, as well as Wright's other concrete-block experiments in Los Angeles during the 1920s, succeeded in transforming a banal, ubiquitous material into a beautiful and scalable system of construction. However, the system had limited applicability with regard to democracy and participatory processes because it still required, at least to some degree, skilled labor. Wright acknowledged this conundrum in the context of his Usonian house projects of the 1930s, another attempt to produce moderate-cost housing that relied on prefabricated "sandwich panels" made by sheathing a core of plywood in board and batten. Sandwich panels lowered the cost of Usonian houses, but their design and construction was complex and precise, requiring apprentices to master the standard details and then travel to supervise construction. As Wright himself later wrote, "a home like this is an architect's creation. It is not a builder's nor an amateur's effort. There is considerable risk in exposing the scheme to imitation or emulation."[10]

The widespread social and economic crises of the 1930s reinvigorated Wright's ambitions for architecture to advance democracy; however, the Great Depression also forced him to reconfigure the relationship between architecture and mechanization. He successfully employed the textile-block system in the construction of the Arizona Biltmore Hotel, in Phoenix, which opened in February 1929, but his most ambitious project employing the system, the San Marcos-in-the-Desert Hotel (1928–29) in nearby Chandler, was derailed by the stock market crash that October. In 1930 Wright gave a series of lectures at Princeton University in which he expressed concern that machine power and the standardization it brings threatened to diminish rather than increase the quality of architecture and human life.[11] His trepidation about mechanization and architecture extended to housing and real estate. Wright later criticized mass housing developments—prefabricated tract housing in the suburbs and high-density, high-rise housing in cities—that were emerging to address widespread housing shortages precipitated by large numbers of veterans returning home after World War II:

Animals are penned or stabled. Humans are "housed!" . . . We Americans planted here on earth a sweeping assertion of man's spirit—the "sovereignty of the individual" . . . it is important now to take the factory to the house . . . the right of every man [is] to be true to his better self as himself, free to dream and build. . . . Recognize the machine as the appropriate magnificent tool of pre-fabrication to be used for man, not on him.[12]

Factory production, it seemed, had resulted in the very "slave-like" conditions and products that Wright had forewarned against in his 1901 speech "The Art and Craft of the Machine," leading him to explore new ways for architecture to realize the lessons of the printing press and, in so doing, advance social democracy. Since his first engagements with mass production in the early twentieth century, Wright had sought to reduce costs while maintaining the highest design standards by outsourcing complex processes to factories or to his own highly trained associates. With the Usonian Automatic system, Wright advanced an alternative to machine production that would "take the factory to the house."

USONIAN AUTOMATIC

In 1938 Wright gave a lecture to the Federal Architects' Association in Washington, D.C., where he boldly claimed, "I don't build a house without predicting the end of the present social order."[13] In just over a decade, Wright invented a new construction system that did not rely on machines or trained craftsmen but instead was simplified, open-ended, and accessible to non-experts: self-build. In 1949 Wright reinvented his textile-block system as the Usonian Automatic, streamlining the system until it consisted of just twelve standard block shapes, from which a wide variety of structures at different scales could be constructed (plate 9a–d). Wright explained that "automatic" meant that now homeowners could build these houses themselves. And they did—at least to some extent.

Some homeowners, such as Elizabeth and William Tracy, of Seattle (1955), and Bette and Theodore Pappas, of St. Louis (1955), cast their own blocks and effectively built their houses. Beverly and Gerald Tonkens, of Cincinnati (1954), engaged Wright's grandson and Taliesin apprentice Eric Lloyd Wright to supervise the construction of their house by a local contractor—still allowing the family and the children to participate, if less strenuously. In each case the houses were built using the twelve standard blocks—including those for walls, roof, and fascia, and the particularly beautiful perforated corner blocks with glass inserts (fig. 1 and plates 10, 11).

The Usonian Automatics harnessed the spirit of the machine, rather than factory modes of production. As a system, it was capable of endless reproduction and accessible to anyone, even if it was perhaps too complex to be considered truly do-it-yourself. This approach had material as well as political advantage over Wright's earlier wood-based construction systems because concrete blocks were scalable as well as relatively sustainable, an important consideration as Wright became worried that "Usonian forests" were being endangered by overuse. "Wood," he acknowledged, "grows more precious as our country grows older."[14] Moreover, the tectonic properties of wood relative to concrete limited the variety and sizes of buildings that could be constructed of it. If, as Wright believed, individual houses were the building blocks of cities, and thus of political and social realities, concrete offered the ability to build at the scale of a community.

Indeed, through all the building materials he worked with, Wright sought a system that would bridge house and community. In the last of his published Princeton lectures, titled "The City," he illustrated the text with an image captioned "Small Town Hall, plastered frame, 1912–1913."[15] The project is, in fact, one of the American System-Built Houses of 1915–17, and not a town hall at all (plate 12).[16] Nevertheless, it is notable that Wright illustrates "The City" with an individual house, and that this house is given a civic function. The date given the project has another interesting civic association, as 1912–13 were

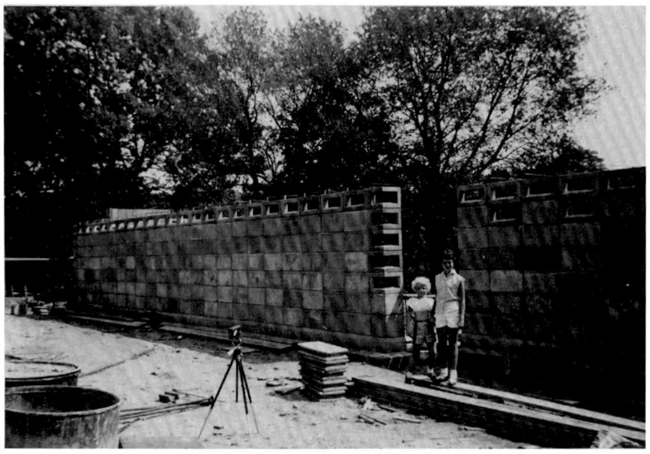

Fig. 1. Tonkens House, Cincinnati. 1954. Wall construction using Usonian Automatic system

the years the City Club of Chicago held an international competition for a neighborhood design, to which Wright submitted a remarkable entry (see p. 179, fig. 4) an early prototype for Broadacre City (1929–35). The proposal was a square field edged with a linear transit spine, commerce bordering its main roads, a latticework interpenetrated by housing, and its civic functions clustered within a linear park system. The city, woven through the existing urban grid as an armature, is revealed as aggregation and composition, nature and culture, bottom up and top down. Wright's nuanced design attributed a civic dimension to housing, balancing individual and communal spheres.

Lecturing on Broadacre City years later, Wright advocated for the construction of such small town halls, calling them "little forums" and praising their ability to gather diverse peoples and viewpoints together in one space:

Why don't you build such little forums? Build one . . . down there in the labor section where the labor fellows could get up and sass away at each other and their bosses sass back as you know they are doing right now in the papers. They could do it better down there in the Forum. . . . We need to educate and stimulate our people to take a big hand in this thing we call Democracy. We must talk it out. *To do it ourselves we must get together to express our own ideas. Isn't that in the very spirit of democracy?*[17]

Little forums created opportunities to practice democracy by providing a physical and social space for communities to reconcile their differences. In 1941 Wright would take this idea a step further by founding *Taliesin Square Paper: A Nonpolitical Voice from Our Democratic Minority*, a series of self-printed pamphlets published by the Taliesin Fellowship that were vehicles for Wright to express and circulate his political views. Wright clearly understood, in ways that seem especially prescient in today's political climate, the complex relationships between physical and social communities and between the media and democracy. He advised the same audience he lectured to about "little forums" also to create "little papers":

Let them "cut loose." Only make sure that they are of A1 liberal democratic quality; that they are really grass roots stuff or better. . . . God knows we are so very tired of being spoon-fed by this great newspaper corporation now so compactly organized for profit that it will never let anything get through that is inimical to its own interests or that has any reflection to cast upon "vested" interests in general. Let's once again hear from the American people![18]

Little papers, of course, had the ability to circulate ideas more broadly than buildings, recalling Hugo's poetic description of the emancipated pages of the printing press blowing in the wind like the birds leaving the cathedral at dawn. Just as the printing press democratized access to knowledge, Wright's self-build system aimed to democratize access to architecture.

Wright's most successful merger of do-it-yourself construction systems and democratic ambitions was arguably in the "little forums" of Taliesin and Taliesin West. Wright envisioned Taliesin as a model democratic community—an enactment of the democratic potential, both social and architectural, a corollary to that which was latent in the Usonian Automatic system. He had earlier tested the limits of self-build concrete blocks at the scale of a small community when he was commissioned to design the campus of Florida Southern College in 1938 (plate 13). There Wright had deployed the textile-block system of the 1920s, sending Taliesin apprentices to instruct the Florida students in building with the system, and in a democratic synthesis of education and participatory labor—at a civic scale the

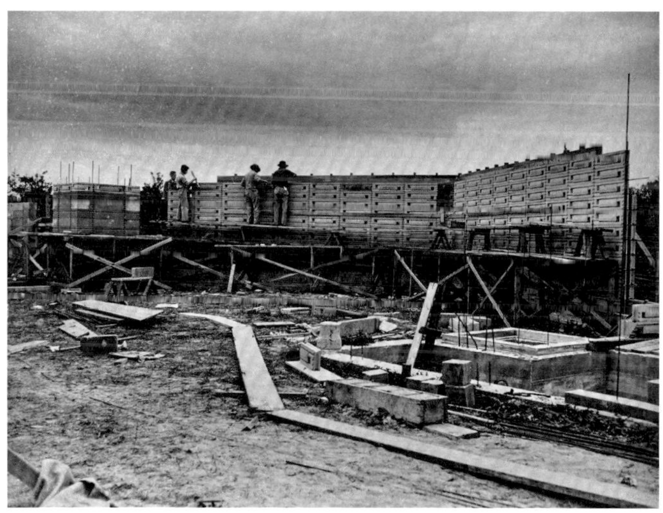

Fig. 2. Florida Southern College, Lakeland. Begun 1938. Wall construction

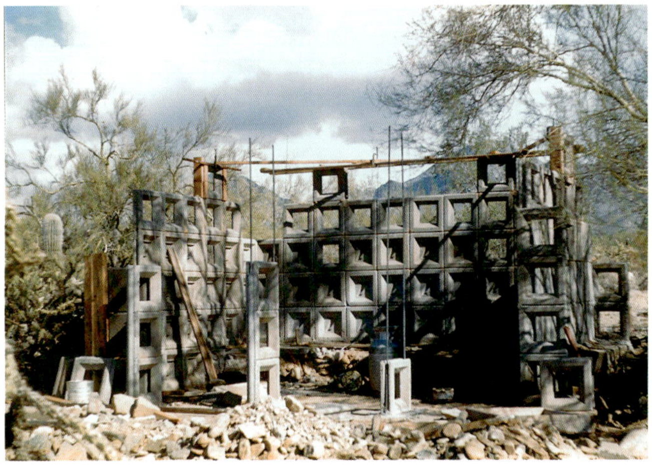

Fig. 3. Taliesin West, Scottsdale, Arizona. Begun 1938. Desert shelter using concrete blocks, 1954. Photograph by Robert Beharka. Collection Jeanine Ferris Beharka

students helped to build their own campus (fig. 2). However participatory the construction process of Florida Southern College, the students still benefited from the considerable oversight and guidance of skilled apprentices and Wright himself. At Taliesin West, Wright was able to further realize his ambitions for do-it-yourself construction to advance democratic social relations.

In 1954—notably the same year that the Usonian Automatic axonometric drawing was published in *The Natural House*—Wright suggested that all the Taliesin apprentices should create designs using the system. These design assignments were submitted collectively in December of that year and can still be found in the Frank Lloyd Wright Foundation Archives. One of the apprentices built a variation of the Usonian Automatic on one of the existing tent sites at the desert campus (fig. 3). In 1955 apprentice David Dodge conducted a survey of all the tent sites, delineating in precise detail the combination of ecological and architectural factors that informed these micro-communities. It is perhaps notable that Dodge drew both the published axonometric drawing and the little-known plan of Fellowship tents, suggesting something of the cumulative, varied, and nonlinear character of the relationships between assertions of individual sovereignty and aspirations for civic design.

Invoking the forest as a metaphor for living communities that balanced the individual with the social whole, Wright described the textile-block house as a "tree itself standing there at home among the other trees."[19] Current research in forest ecology shows that diverse species of trees not only exchange information through their roots, assisted by mycorrhizal networks in the soil, but materials as well—indicating that about half of the carbon in these trees was supplied by other trees in their community.[20] Beyond mere analogy, the emerging discipline of sociobiology suggests that what is true for plant communities is also true for humans—it is by the delicate weaving of roots that resilient communities are established. The Usonian Automatic is thus a call to both individual initiative and to cooperative action, acknowledging that from the tapestry of our lives a civic fabric is also woven—between private and public, garden and park, small scale and large.

Notes

1. Frank Lloyd Wright, *The Natural House* (New York: Horizon Press, 1954).
2. Ibid., p. 205.
3. Frank Lloyd Wright, "The Art and Craft of the Machine" (1901), reprinted in *The Essential Frank Lloyd Wright: Critical Writings on Architecture*, ed. Bruce Brooks Pfeiffer (Princeton, N.J.: Princeton University Press, 2008), p. 24.
4. Ibid., pp. 28–29.
5. "Art and the Machine (March 4, 1901)," accessed January 26, 2016, http://archives.chicagotribune.com/1901/03/04/page/6/article/among-the-new-books.
6. Frank Lloyd Wright, *An Autobiography*, 3rd ed. (New York: Duell, Sloan and Pearce, 1943), p. 241.
7. Ibid., p. 235.
8. Kenneth Frampton, "The Text-Tile Tectonic: The Origin and Evolution of Wright's Woven Architecture," in *On and By Frank Lloyd Wright: A Primer of Architectural Principles*, ed. Robert McCarter (New York: Phaidon 2011), pp. 181–83. Robert Sweeney has argued that Wright's experiments in concrete block construction followed the Bollman House, designed by his son Lloyd Wright in 1922, and that Wright's first concrete-block house, the Millard House, was not, by definition, a textile-block house. See Robert L. Sweeney and David G. DeLong, *Wright in Hollywood: Visions of a New Architecture*, annotated edition (Cambridge, Mass.: MIT Press, 1994), pp. 20, 204–05.
9. Wright, *An Autobiography*, p. 242.
10. Wright, *The Natural House*, p. 89.
11. Frank Lloyd Wright, *Modern Architecture, Being the Kahn Lectures for 1930* (Princeton, N.J.: Princeton University Press, 1931). Reprinted in Pfeiffer, ed., *The Essential Frank Lloyd Wright*, pp. 159–216.
12. Frank Lloyd Wright, "Away with the Realtor," *Esquire*, October 1958.
13. Frank Lloyd Wright, *Washington Post*, sec. 2, October 26, 1938. Quoted in Robert Twombly, *Frank Lloyd Wright: His Life and His Architecture* (New York: John Wiley & Sons, 1979), p. 261.
14. Frank Lloyd Wright, "In the Cause of Architecture: Wood" (1928), in *Frank Lloyd Wright on Architecture: Selected Writings (1894–1940)*, ed. Frederick Gutheim (New York: Grosset & Dunlap, 1941), p. 113.
15. Wright, *Modern Architecture, Being the Kahn Lectures*, pp. 99–100.
16. Neil Levine, *The Urbanism of Frank Lloyd Wright* (Princeton, N.J.: Princeton University Press, 2015), p. 406n51.
17. Frank Lloyd Wright, [Address at Milwaukee Art Institute] Talk No. III (December 5, 1945), manuscript no. 2401.277, p. 15.
18. Ibid., pp. 15–16.
19. Wright, *An Autobiography*, p. 242.
20. Tamir Klein, Rolf Siegwolf, and Christian Körner, "Belowground Carbon Trade among Tall Trees in a Temperate Forest," *Science* 352, no. 6283 (April 15, 2016): 342–44.

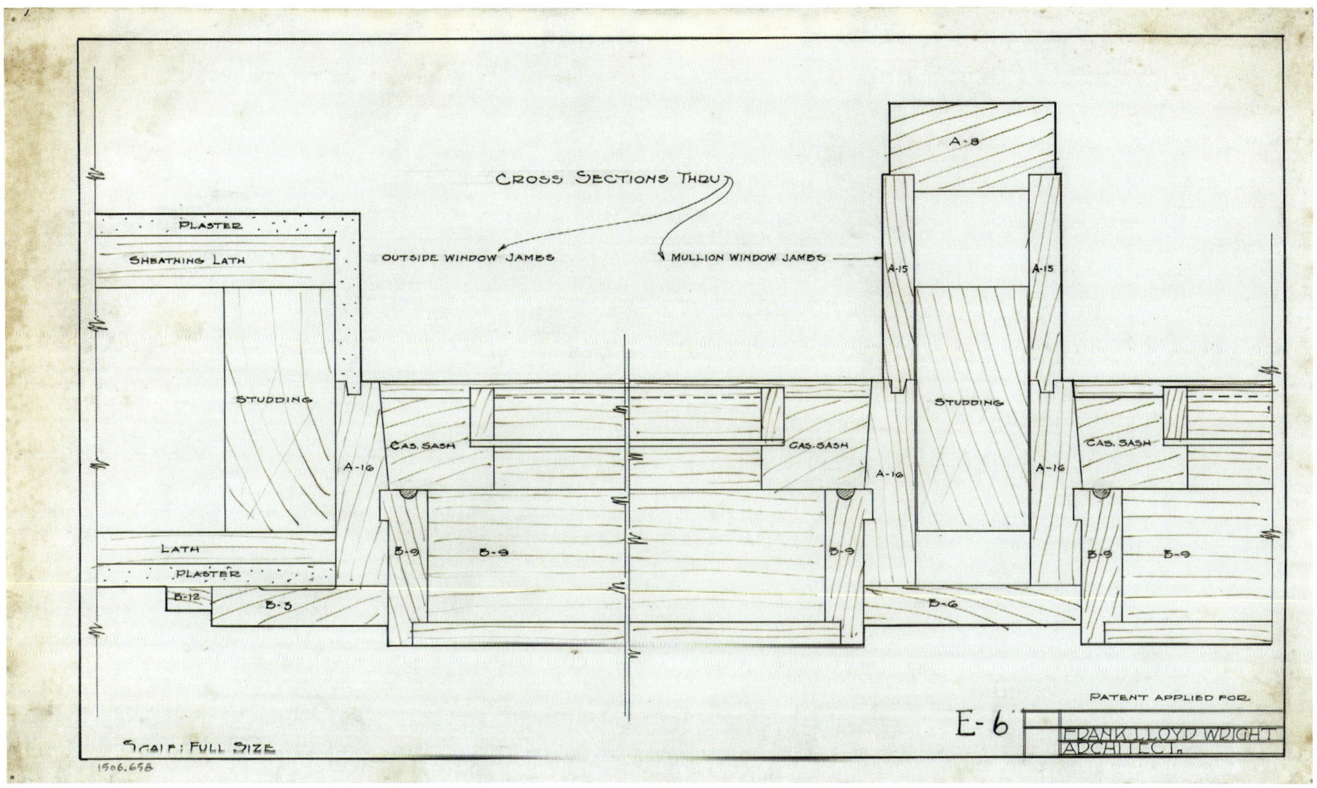

1. American System-Built Houses. Project, 1915–17. Window detail.
Ink on drafting cloth, 12 x 20 ¼ in. (30.5 x 51.4 cm)

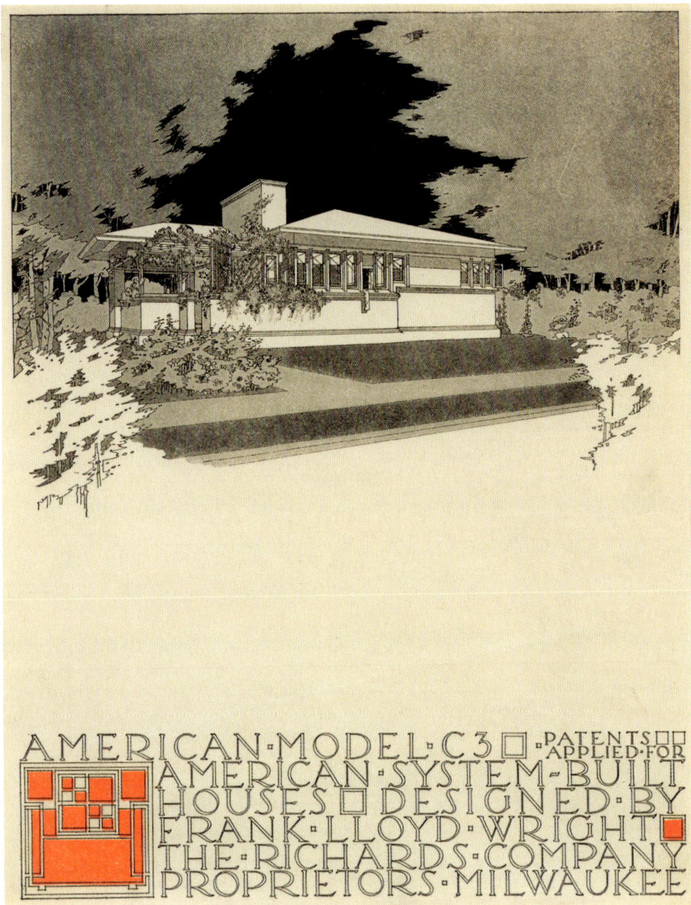

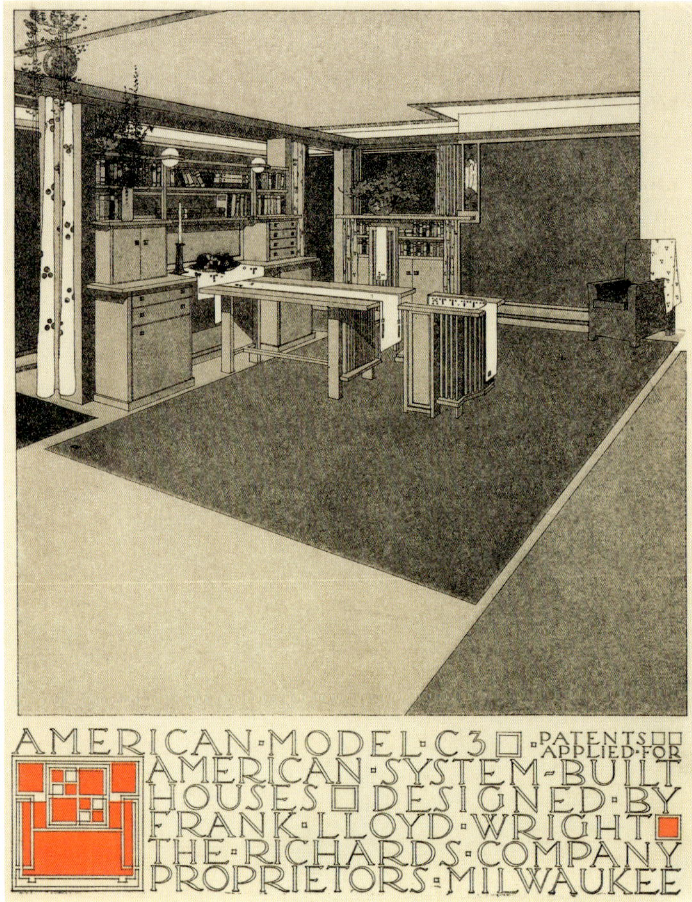

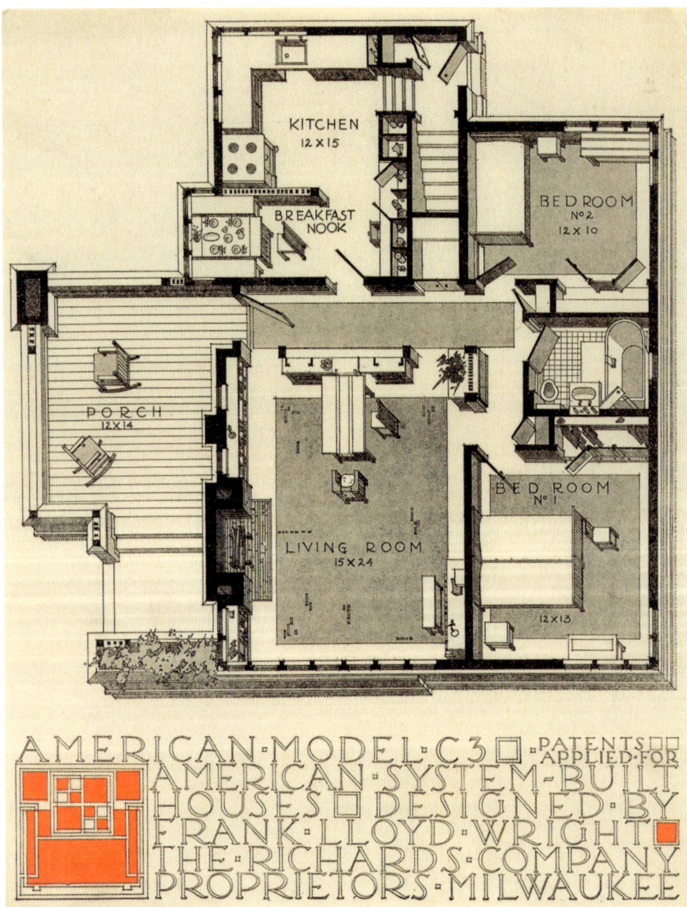

2a–f. American System-Built Houses. Project, 1915–17. Models C3, D101, D1, A101.
Lithographs, each: 11 x 8 ½ in. (27.9 x 21.6 cm).
The Museum of Modern Art, New York. Gifts of David Rockefeller, Jr. Fund, Ira Howard Levy Fund, and Jeffrey P. Klein Purchase Fund

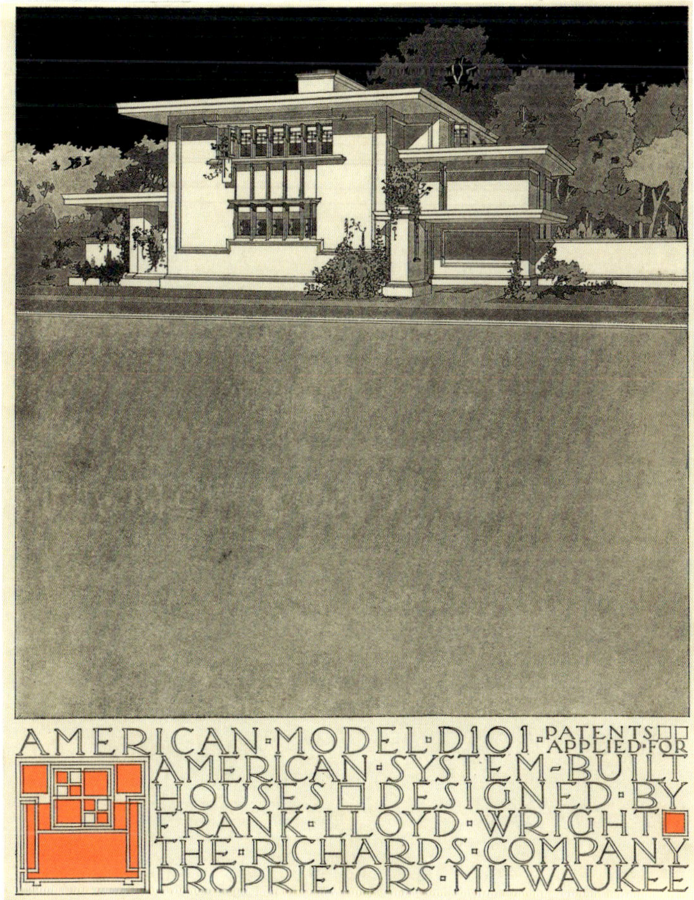
AMERICAN·MODEL·D101·PATENTS APPLIED·FOR
AMERICAN·SYSTEM-BUILT
HOUSES DESIGNED·BY
FRANK·LLOYD·WRIGHT
THE·RICHARDS·COMPANY
PROPRIETORS·MILWAUKEE

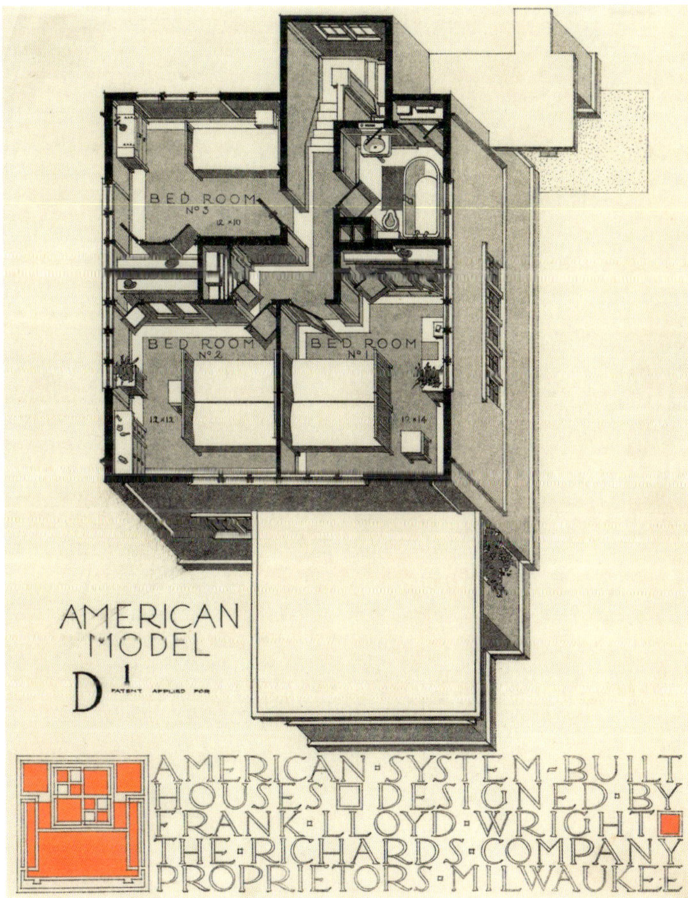
BED ROOM No 3
BED ROOM No 2
BED ROOM No 1
AMERICAN
MODEL
D1
PATENT APPLIED FOR
AMERICAN·SYSTEM-BUILT
HOUSES DESIGNED·BY
FRANK·LLOYD·WRIGHT
THE·RICHARDS·COMPANY
PROPRIETORS·MILWAUKEE

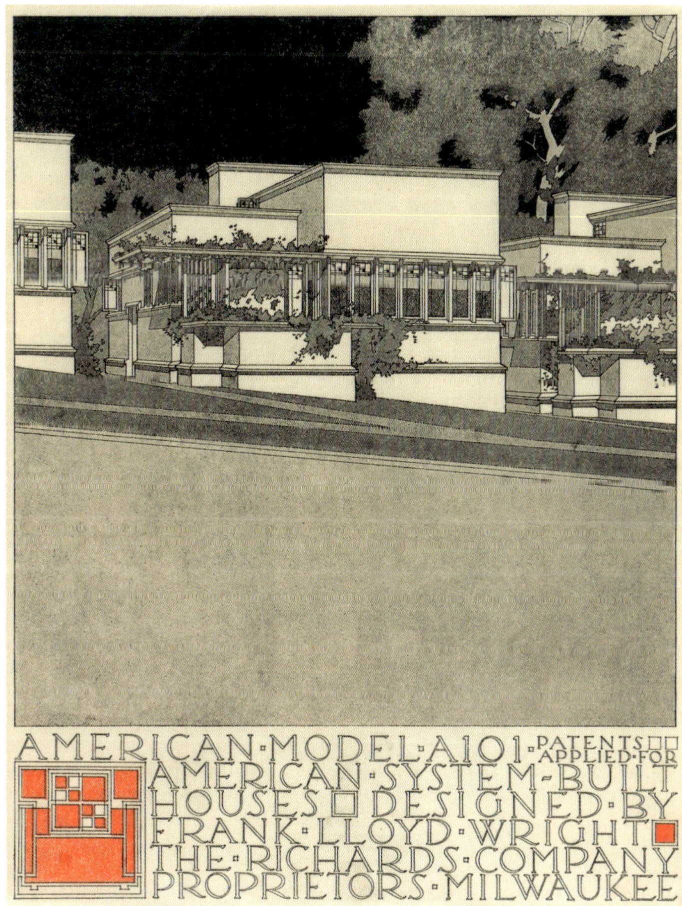
AMERICAN·MODEL·A101·PATENTS APPLIED·FOR
AMERICAN·SYSTEM-BUILT
HOUSES DESIGNED·BY
FRANK·LLOYD·WRIGHT
THE·RICHARDS·COMPANY
PROPRIETORS·MILWAUKEE

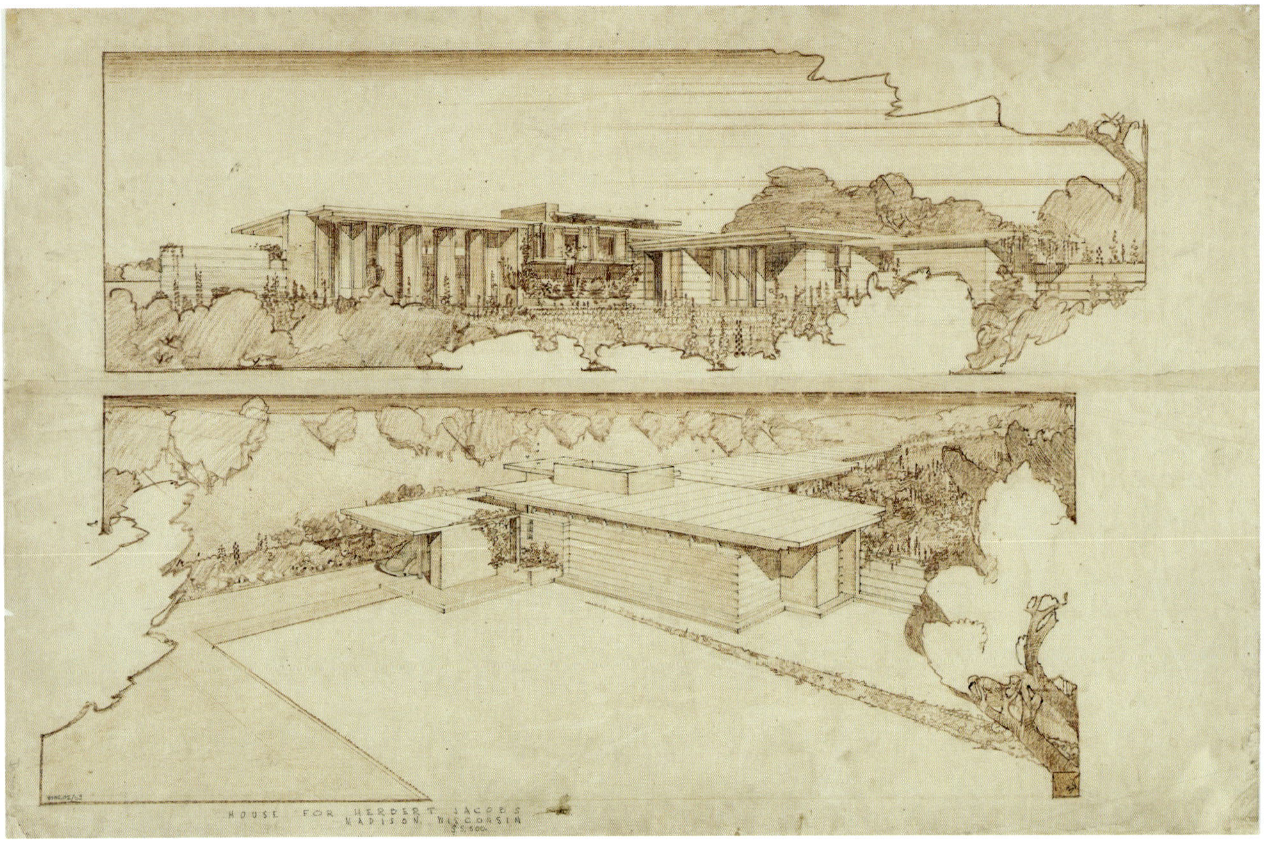

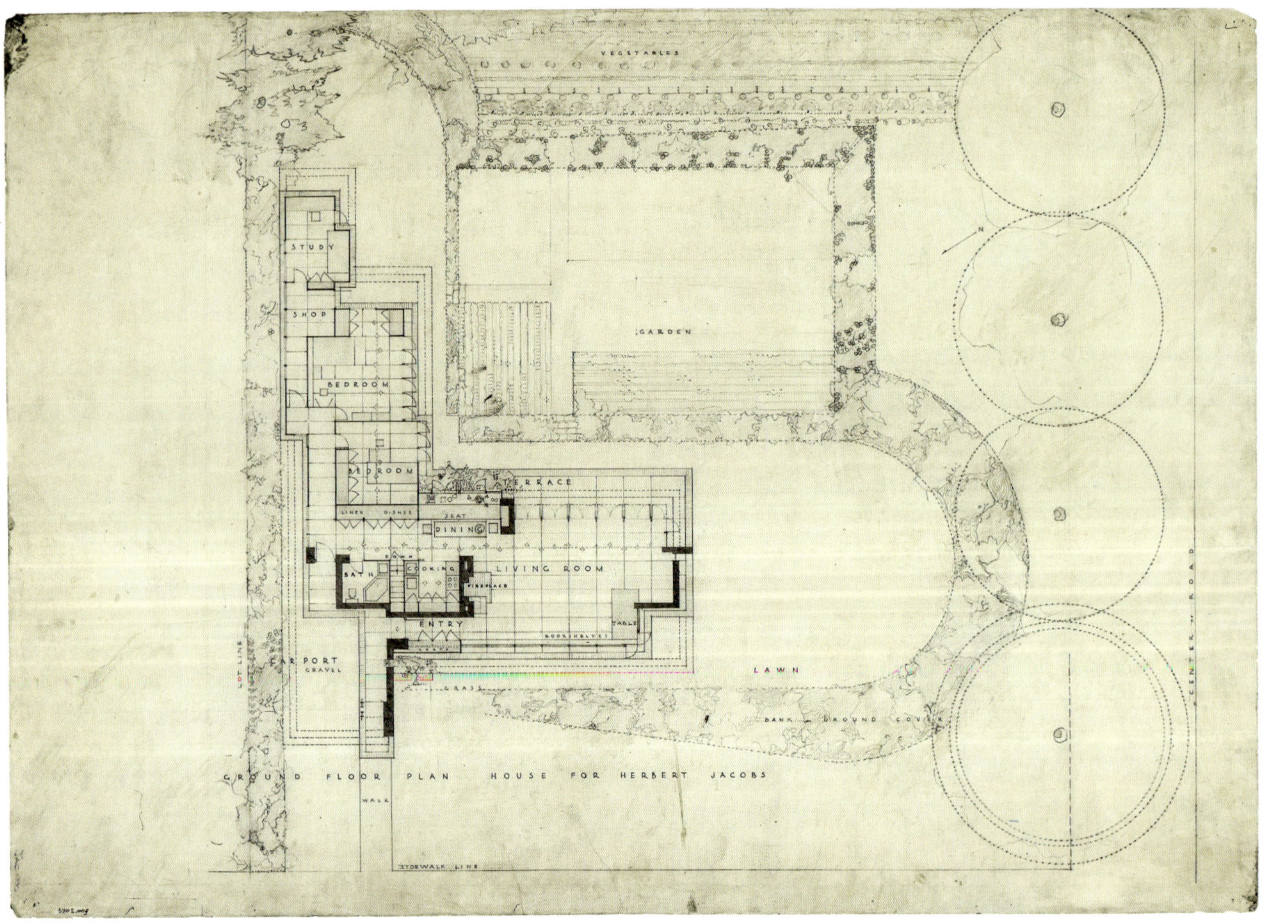

3. Jacobs House, Madison, Wisconsin. 1936–37. Exterior perspectives.
Pencil and colored pencil on paper, 21 ¾ x 32 in. (55.2 x 81.3 cm)

4. Jacobs House, Madison, Wisconsin. 1936–37. Ground-floor plan.
Pencil and ink on tracing paper, 24 ⅛ x 34 in. (61.3 x 86.4 cm)

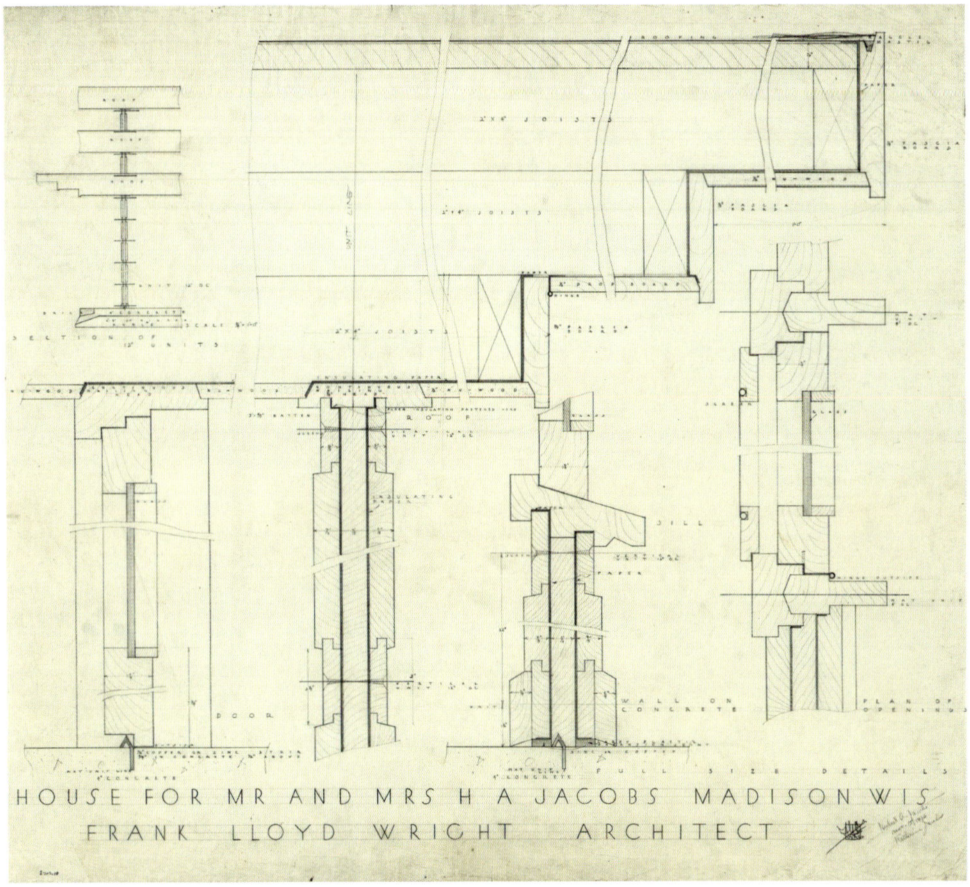

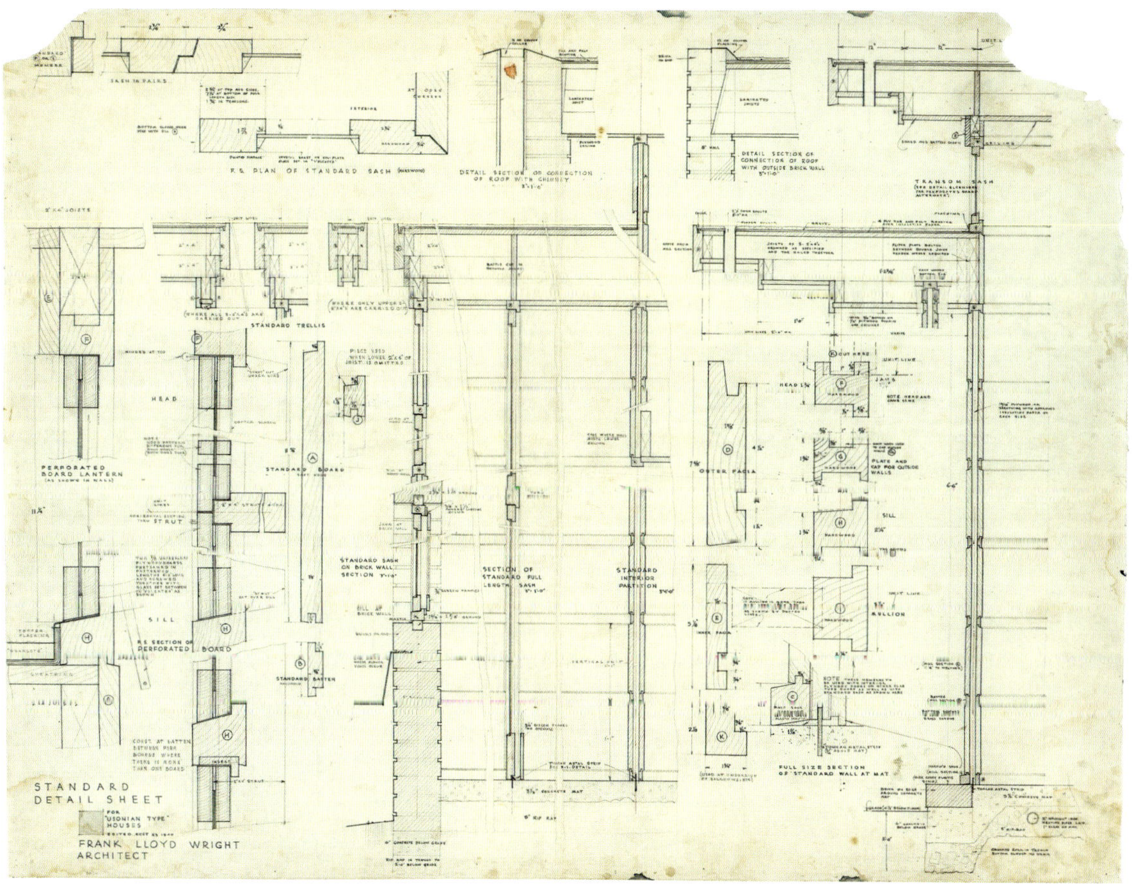

5. Jacobs House, Madison, Wisconsin. 1936–37. Construction details.
Pencil on tracing paper, 30 ¾ x 34 in. (78.1 x 86.4 cm)

6. "Usonian Type Houses." Project, 1940. Standard detail sheet.
Pencil and ink on tracing paper, 36 x 47 in. (91.4 x 119.4 cm)

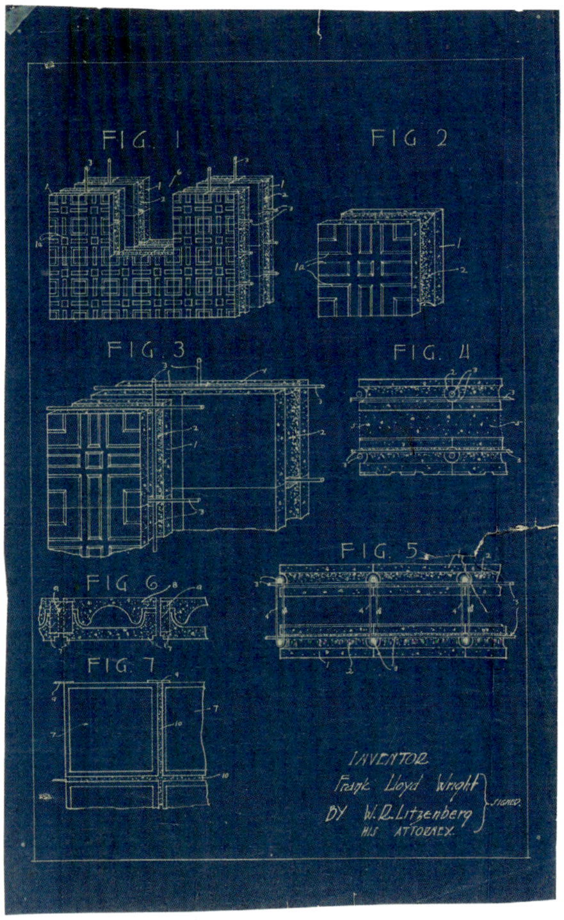

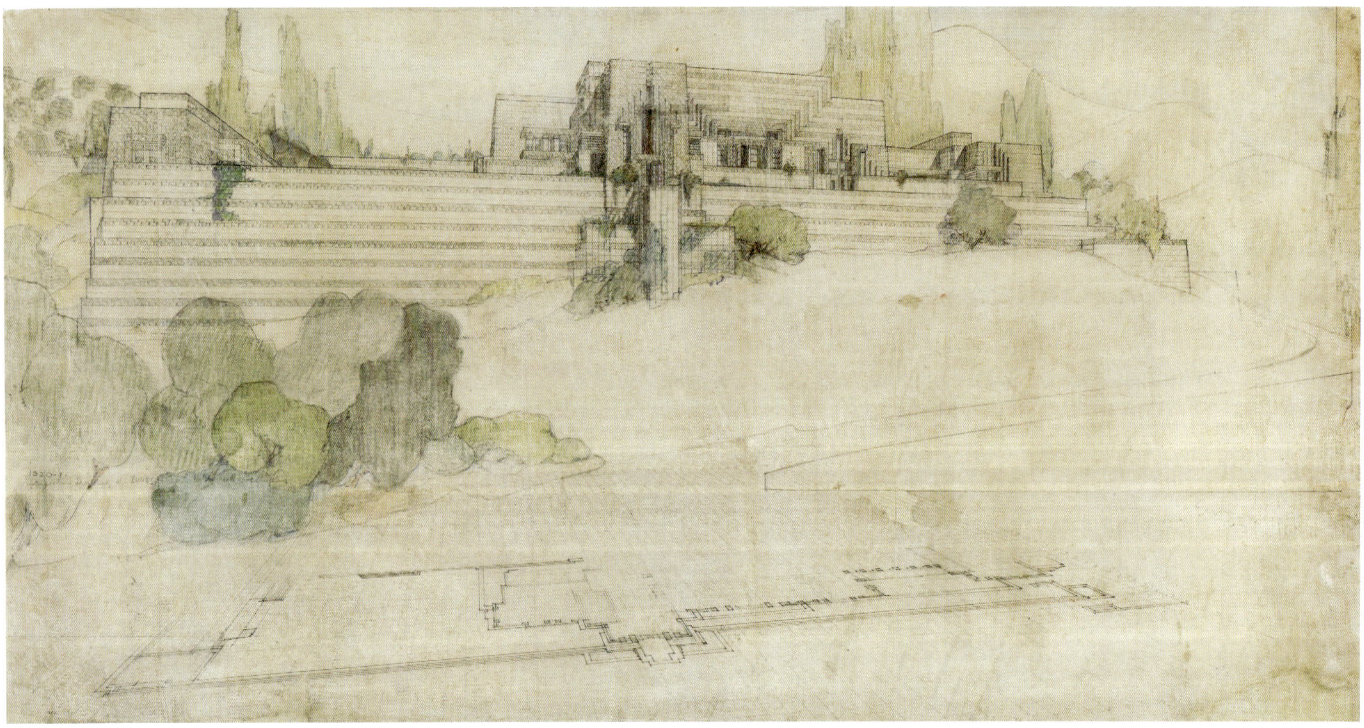

7. Textile-block system. Begun 1923. Details.
Ink on blueprint, 14 ¼ x 8 ⅞ in. (36.2 x 22.5 cm)

8. Ennis House, Los Angeles. 1924–25. Plan and perspective from the southwest.
Pencil, colored pencil, and ink on tracing paper, 20 ⅛ x 39 ⅛ in. (51.1 x 99.4 cm)

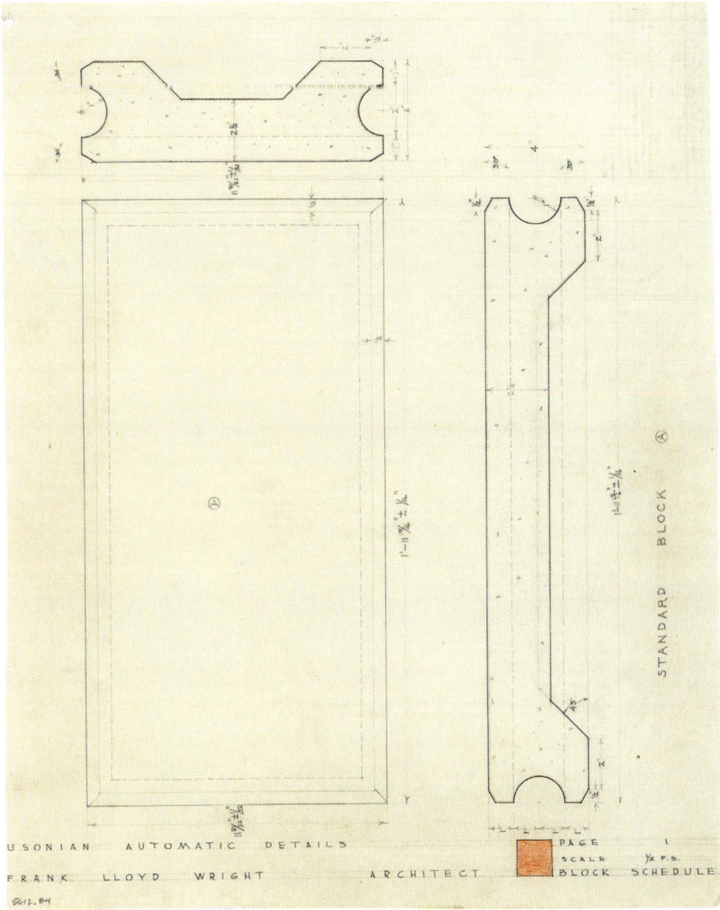

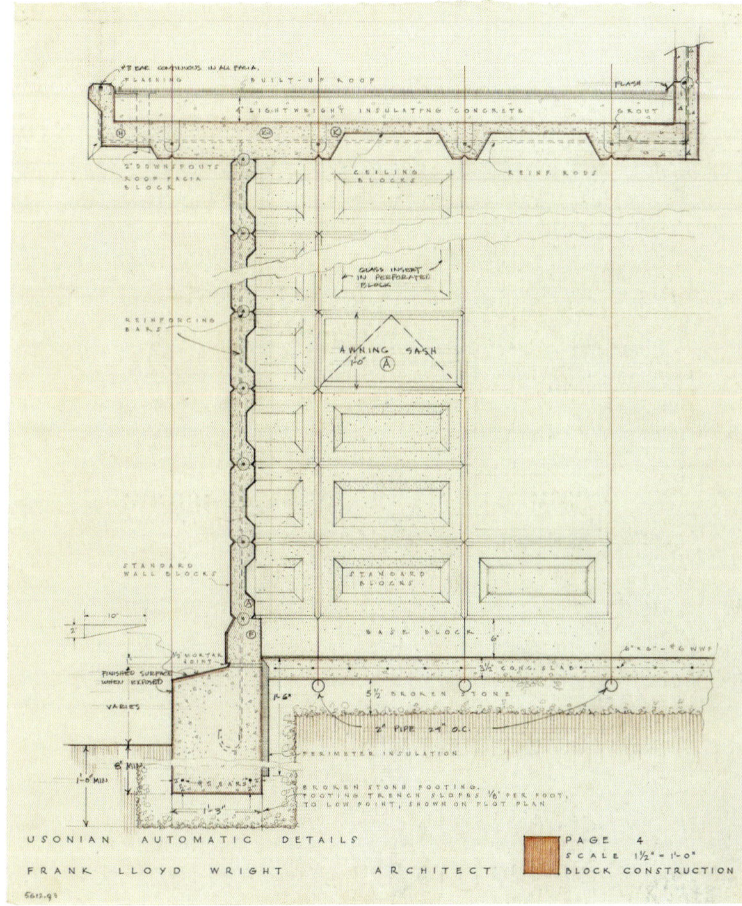

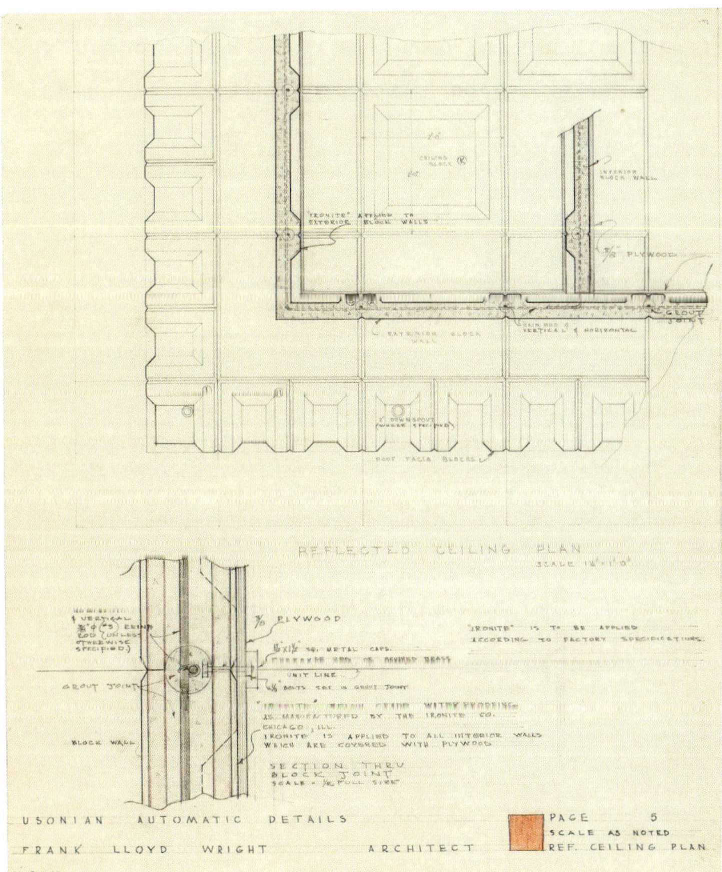

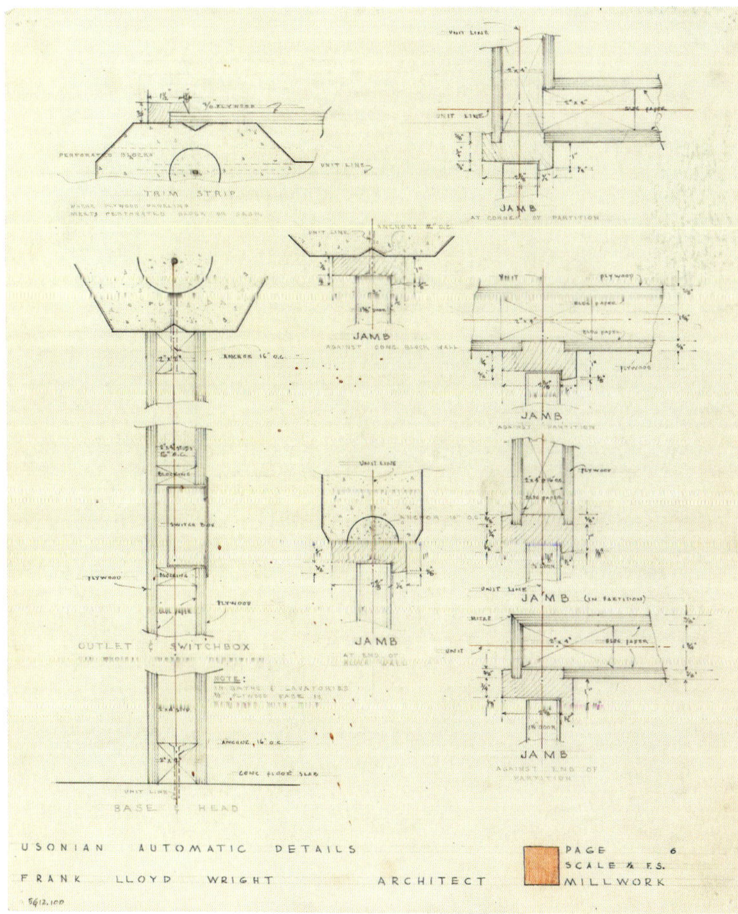

9a–d. Usonian Automatic system. Project, early 1950s. Construction details. Pencil, colored pencil, and ink on tracing paper, each approx. 18 x 15 in. (45.7 x 38.1 cm)

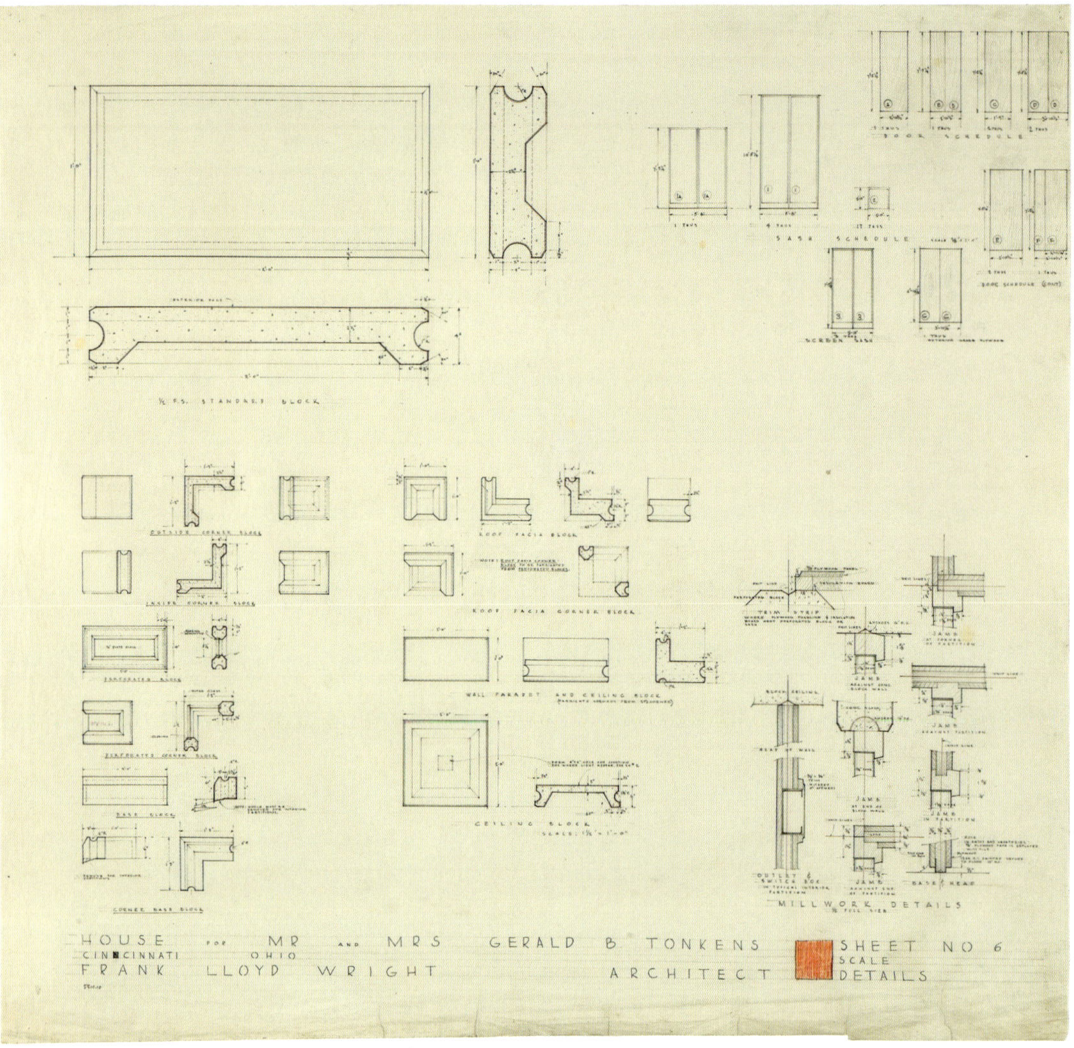

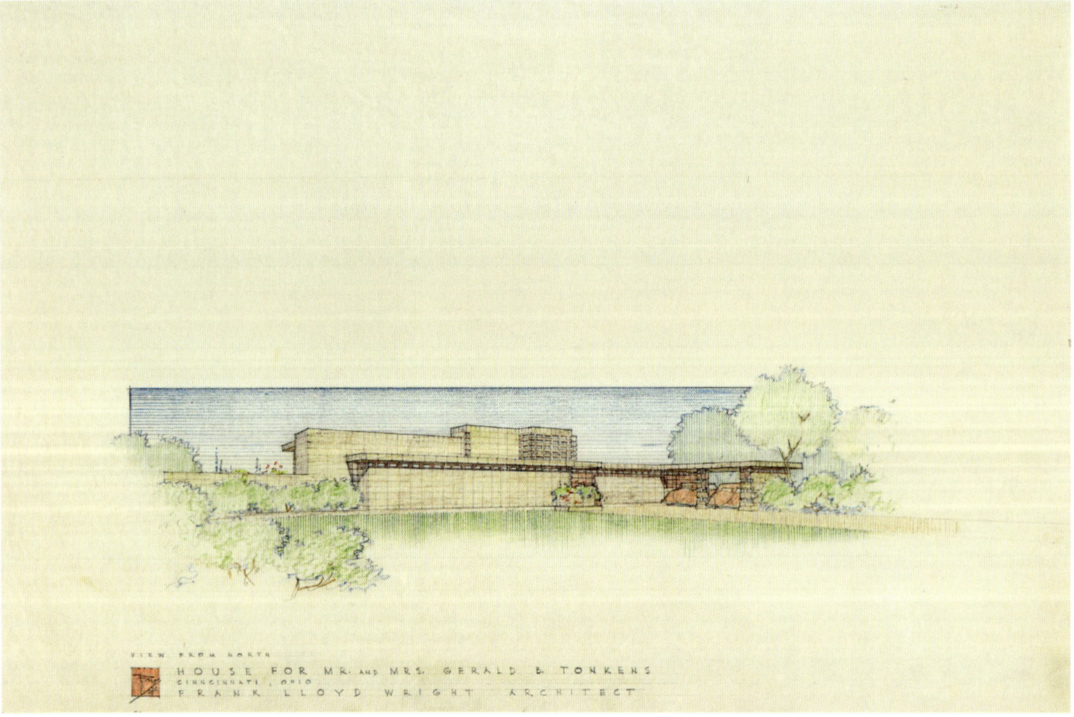

10. Tonkens House, Cincinnati. 1954. Millwork and block details.
Pencil and colored pencil on tracing paper, 36 ¼ x 37 ¾ in. (92.1 x 95.9 cm)

11. Tonkens House, Cincinnati. 1954. Perspective from the north.
Pencil and colored pencil on tracing paper, 23 ⅞ x 33 ¾ in. (60.6 x 85.7 cm)

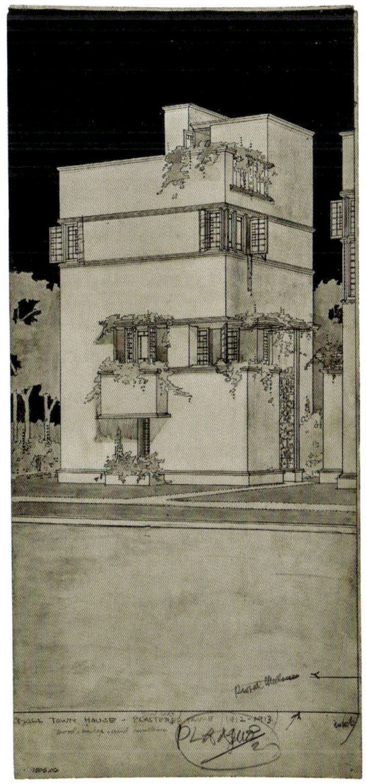

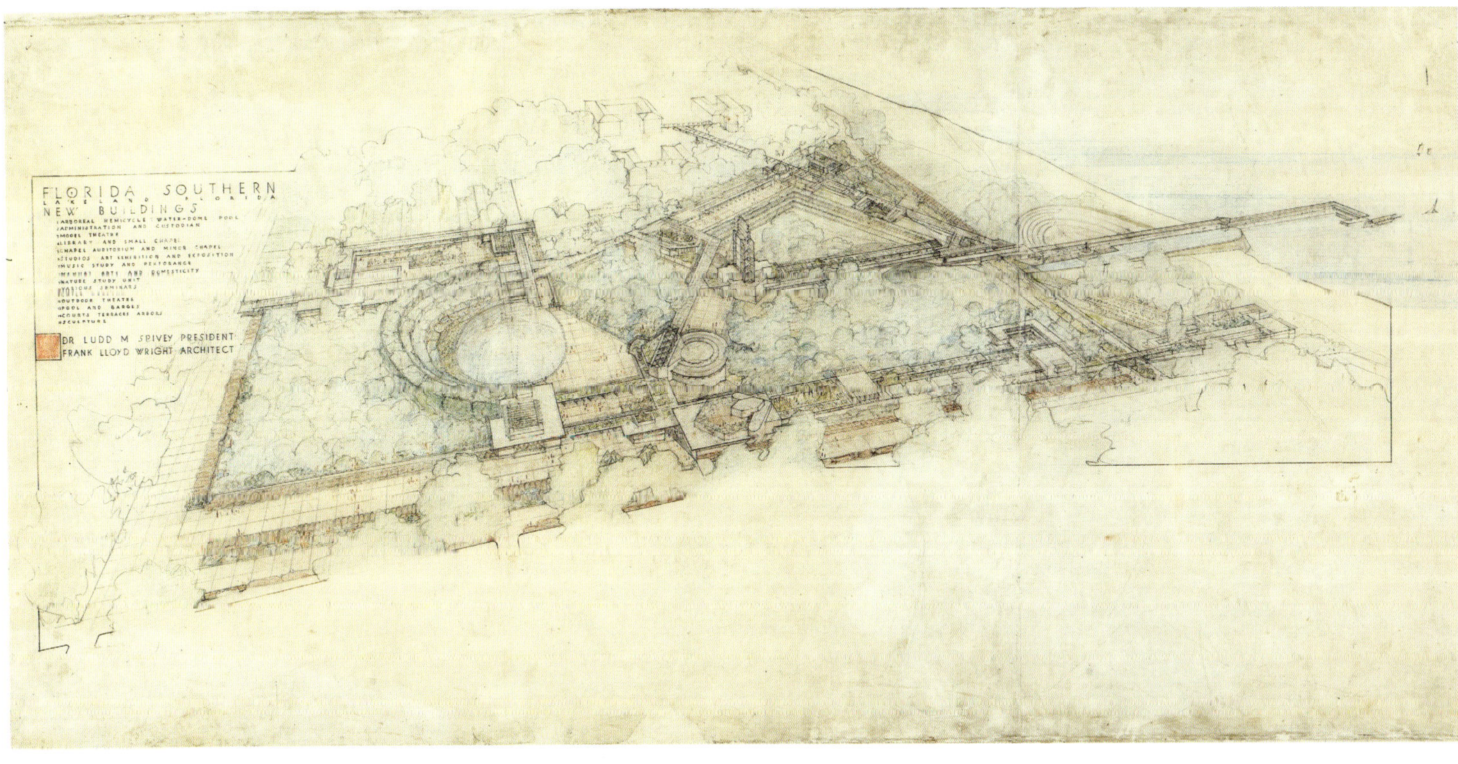

12. American System-Built Houses. Project, 1915–17. Perspective.
Ink and pencil on paper, 16 1/2 x 7 5/8 in. (41.9 x 19.4 cm)

13. Florida Southern College, Lakeland. Begun 1938. Aerial perspective.
Ink, pencil, and colored pencil on tracing paper, 24 x 47 5/8 in. (61 x 121 cm)

NEIL LEVINE

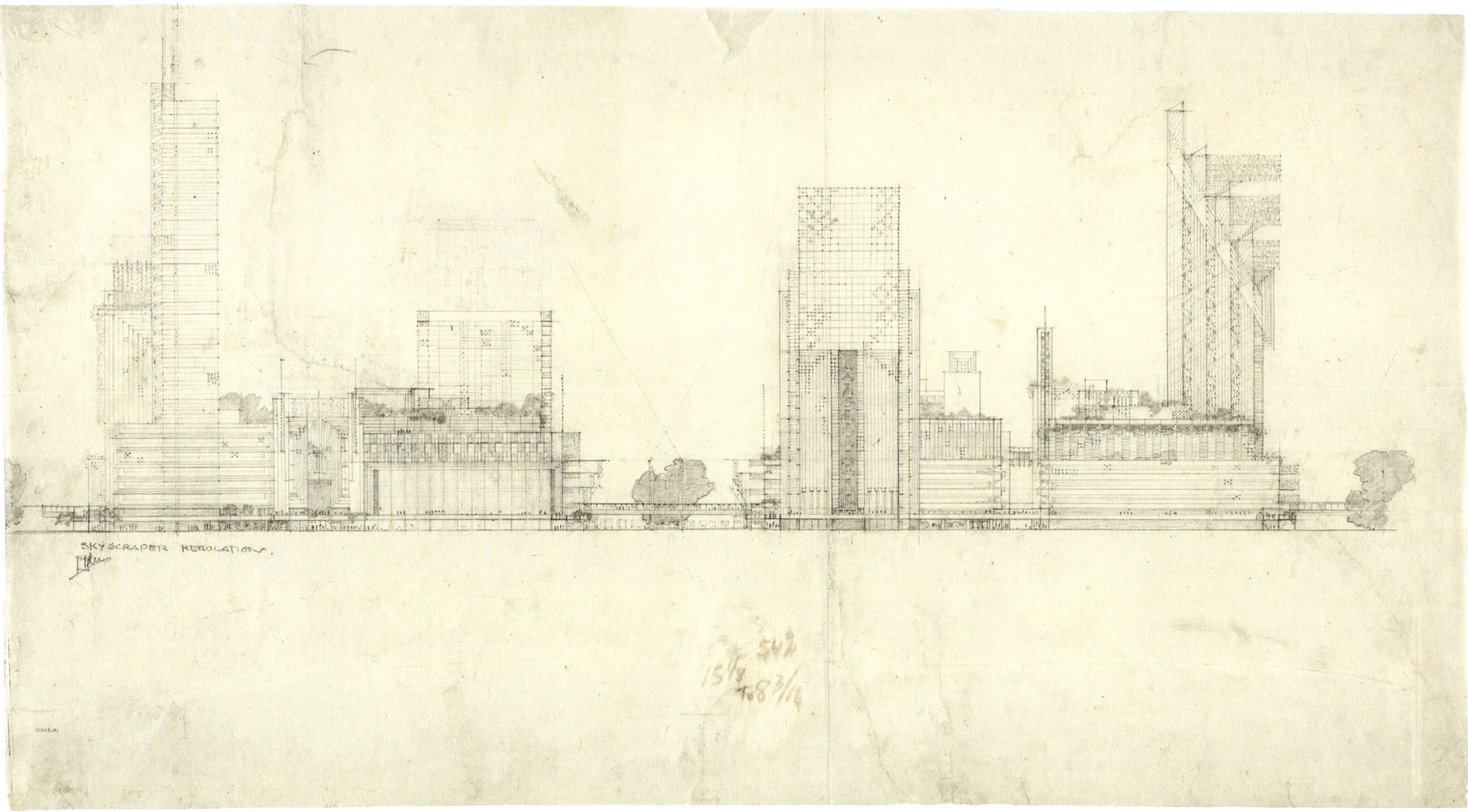

WRIGHT'S URBANISM AND THE SKYSCRAPER REGULATION PROJECT

Skyscraper Regulation, Chicago. Project, 1926. Elevation. Pencil and colored pencil on tracing paper, 20 x 32 7/8 in. (50.8 x 83.5 cm)

Frank Lloyd Wright's numerous designs for reorganizing the urban fabric and revitalizing the core of the city span his seventy-year practice and clarify the development of his work in relation to the evolution of twentieth-century urbanism.[1] The least well-known and least studied of these projects is the one for a nine-block area of the Chicago Loop, the city's downtown commercial district (opposite). Produced in 1926, it came at the midpoint in his thinking about urbanism and marks a transition from designing for the city's surrounding residential neighborhoods to civic, cultural, and mixed-use projects for the city center itself. What Wright called the Skyscraper Regulation project for the "remodeling of the city" was a response to the extraordinary boom in skyscraper construction during the Roaring Twenties accompanied by severe congestion due to the rapid increase in vehicular traffic.[2]

The focus by architectural historians and critics on Wright's utopian Broadacre City (1929–35), a slightly later proposal for decentralization that favored an anti-urban, ruralist alternative, has generally served to marginalize and undermine the importance of the many urban designs that came before and after it. So little known and so profoundly misunderstood is the Skyscraper Regulation project that when it was first published, as late as 1959, it was dated to 1931 and described as a spin-off of the architect's scheme to house the 1933–34 Chicago Century of Progress International Exhibition in a single skyscraper.[3] It was thus seen as essentially a building-type study. In the 1970s, in one of the most widely read books on the history of American urbanism, a highly respected Italian architectural historian characterized the project as "a design of a skyline for Chicago," whatever that might mean.[4] With the advantage of studying the drawings in the Frank Lloyd Wright Foundation Archives, we can now more accurately assess the scope and meaning of the project. Far from being a design for an ideal skyscraper or for the picturesque massing of several, the Skyscraper Regulation project is about nothing less than counteracting the problems of increased building bulk and vehicular congestion in downtown Chicago in response to the city's new zoning ordinance (1923) while providing a novel mixed-use solution of integrated parking, office space, and apartment living.

SKYSCRAPER REGULATION PROJECT DRAWINGS

The six drawings for the project illustrate a system of raised sidewalks and through-traffic streets as an essential component of a nine-block area the architect began working on perhaps by late 1925. The preliminary sketch of an elevation and partial site plan is dated January 1926 (plate 1). This, along with the five other drawings, appears to be either completely or mainly in the architect's hand. The sketch shows two full city blocks, approximately 400 by 370 feet (122 by 113 meters) each, plus two partial blocks and a partial elevation. The sheet is crammed with marginal notes explaining the scheme. In the legend in the lower-right-hand corner, under Wright's signature and date, is the title "Sky-Scraper Regulation. Augmenting the Gridiron. Remodeling of the City." To this is appended the phrase "Beyond these provisions the city should spread out—." The second drawing in the sequence is a larger-scale plan showing the same two full blocks plus partial plans of the seven contiguous ones (plate 2). The main streets, side streets, and alleys are also carefully delineated.

There are two elevations and a section depicting two city blocks. One elevation has a narrow street between the two blocks, while the other shows the blocks separated by a ten-lane street with a median strip (see p. 172). The section also depicts the wider street and has a store sign for the "American Hardware Co." accompanied by the date "March 5 1926" (plate 3). In this drawing, the "alley court" on the left, the "avenue" in the center, and the "alley" on the right are all labeled. The sixth drawing, which includes a plan, section, and elevation, is a detailed study of a corner intersection showing vehicular and pedestrian traffic patterns plus store locations.

While the Archives can tell us much, they do not tell us everything. There is no known client for the project and no evidence of an actual commission. It is very possible that the project was done on a purely theoretical basis. The challenge of the 1923 zoning ordinance, which divided the city into Use and Volume districts and regulated the height, bulk, and lot coverage of individual buildings, clearly intrigued Wright, as can be appreciated in his project for Chicago's National Life Insurance Building (1923–25; see page 220). Its sawtooth, setback design followed quite directly the guidelines laid down in the code as well as the type-solution New York architects developed in response to that city's precedent-setting ordinance of 1916.

The Skyscraper Regulation design expanded the solution to the larger urban context, where many of the other critical issues not directly addressed by the narrow focus of the Chicago ordinance on the individual building could be considered. These included parking, traffic congestion, mixed-use development, and, finally, the adumbration of a superblock concept for rewriting the zoning code at the scale of the city grid itself. The scheme was to represent, as Wright noted on the initial sketch plan, "the Zoning law and setback ordinances carried to a logical conclusion." Among its specific legal impositions were that skyscrapers would be limited to certain corner lots, and that all those designated "skyscraper lots" had to pay a "super tax when [a] tall building is built." In addition, it is noted on the sketch, all "skyscrapers must devote at least two sub-basements to parking."

Wright's point of departure was the typical perimeter-block condition deriving from the city's grid plan. An eight-story street-line height, considerably lower than that allowed by the zoning law, defines each block, except at alternate corners, where towers rise to heights of 350 feet (107 meters) and more. The lower floors, which conform to the street grid, create courtyards of varying dimensions, some filling the entire center of a block where the alley has been vacated. The buildings surrounding the courtyard blocks accommodate shopping, apartment living, entertainment, hotels, and commercial office space. Shops also line the raised sidewalks of most of the street sides of the block, where an "Amsterdam Theater" and a "Hotel Embassy" can likewise be seen.

The courtyards become public gathering places serving various functions. Much larger than earlier atrium courts or arcades, they are open to the sky and predict the mall-like spaces of later superblock designs like New York's Rockefeller Center (initial phase 1929–40). In the Skyscraper Regulation project, the ground plane is raised to the second floor to form a deck over a two-level parking facility, one floor of which is below grade and the other at street level (there is also truck delivery access under the alleys). Both the larger and smaller interior courtyards provide secluded spaces within the tight-knit fabric of downtown streets, where light and air and greenery find their place and where restaurants, cafés, and other facilities permit the apartment dweller, hotel occupant, and office worker to relax and congregate isolated from the surrounding street traffic.

Some of the eight-story perimeter-block buildings are shown as having balconies overhanging the streets below. The buildings themselves have setbacks at the seventh and eighth floors along both streets and alleys, but are flush on the court sides. A much deeper setback, even a double one in some cases, provides accommodation for floor-through penthouse units overlooking both courtyard and street. These manipulations of the zoning rules for height and bulk give the Skyscraper Regulation project a subtlety at the smaller scale of European cities, even as the location, alignment, and variation in height of the corner skyscraper towers manifest most fully Wright's effort to carry the Chicago zoning ordinance "to a logical conclusion."

Wright felt locating the towers exclusively at the corners would have the least environmental impact. Some retain the stepped-back, symmetrical form of the National Life project, while others are composed of more discrete, asymmetrically organized volumetric units, very possibly indebted to some of the proposals for the Chicago Tribune Tower (1922) by European architects, most notably Knud Lönberg-Holm. Wright's towers vary in height from about eighteen to just under forty stories. More important, their lower sections alternate from a north-south to an east-west alignment, and the placement of the skyscrapers themselves is staggered in a pinwheeling fashion to allow for light and air to penetrate the densely built-up city grid.

Going beyond the scope of the 1923 ordinance, the Skyscraper Regulation project developed a spatial network in a three-dimensional, multilevel system. Pedestrian and vehicular circulation occur at five different levels. The levels also serve to segregate one type of movement from another: cars and trucks are at street level and one level below grade; sidewalks for pedestrians are elevated to the second level and connect to bridges crossing streets; finally, pedestrian bridges at the sixth level cross both streets and alleys to link the courtyard blocks to one another. The second-floor store display windows on the raised sidewalks form a continuous arcade-balcony ringing the perimeter-block buildings. Below, where sidewalks would have been, are delivery lanes for trucks, drop-off locations for taxis, and short-term parking spaces. Stairs connect the elevated sidewalks to the street, belowground parking, and subway stations at the corner intersections. These intersections form the critical junctions in the plan, where the bridges one level above the raised sidewalks carry pedestrians from block to block, obviating the need to cross the crowded streets.

MULTILEVEL CITIES OF DISAGGREGATED TOWERS

To understand more fully the Skyscraper Regulation project we must reach outside the archive to see how the design engages its context, both historical and cultural. In addition to the limitation on building size (and consequent overcrowding) called for by the new zoning code, the futuristic, multilevel aspect of Wright's design had much in common with the most popular new recipe of the 1920s for overcoming congestion and reducing traffic accidents. The idea of elevated sidewalks went back to the first decade of the twentieth century. In the United States it made a celebrated appearance as *King's Dream of New York*, the frontispiece of Moses King's 1908 views of the city.[5] This early example attested to the promise the idea held for the modern city and the basic appeal it had to the popular imagination.

These concepts were illustrated on the front page of the January 1910 *New-York Tribune* article about the engineer Henry Harrison Suplee's proposal to rationalize New York's circulation system.[6] The image was republished three years later on the cover of *Scientific American* (fig. 1) announcing the article by Suplee that called for the "absolute segregation of foot travel from any kind of vehicles" as the only means to secure "relief" from congestion and provide "a free and safe path" for the pedestrian.[7] The cutaway perspective shows three subsurface levels, the partially exposed upper one for vehicles, and two levels of pedestrian sidewalks. Tiers of bridges connect the sidewalks and

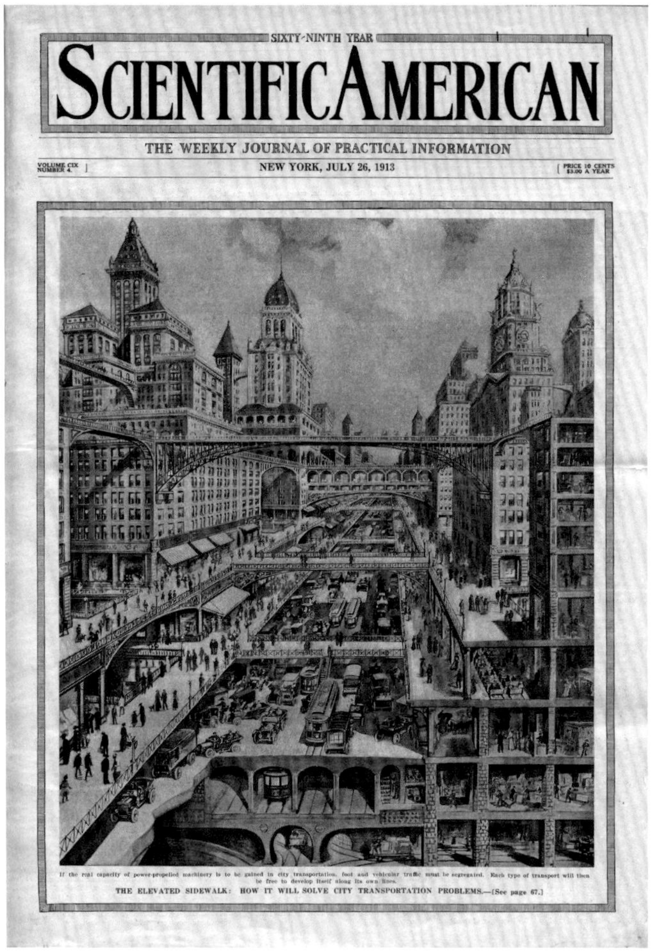

Fig. 1. Cover illustration for Henry Harrison Suplee, "The Elevated Sidewalk," *Scientific American*, July 26, 1913. Originally published in the *New-York Tribune*, January 1910

buildings that line the street, their protruding towers predicting the 1916 New York zoning law. The drawing would become a template for later projects of the sort.

As Jean-Louis Cohen has shown, the *Scientific American* image had a large reach in Europe.[8] In its wake, a number of important architects and planners produced multilevel skyscraper-city projects. Aside from those by Le Corbusier (1922/25), there were ones by Auguste Perret (1922–25), Ludwig Hilberseimer (1924), and Cornelis van Eesteren (1926), among others. Although the New York architect Harvey Wiley Corbett would be a leading champion of the multilevel city and certainly the best-known proponent of the idea among professionals, in Europe as well as America, a most interesting aspect of the concept was that it was embraced by people from all walks of life. It was discussed as often in letters to the editor of daily newspapers as it was in journals of architecture and planning. New York and Chicago both participated in this discourse.

One of the first professional calls for the "construction of elevated streets" came in the form of an editorial in early 1921 from the New York architect and city planner Arnold W. Brunner.[9] It was Corbett, however, who gave prominent visual form to the concept in the mid-1920s (fig. 2). His scheme, developed in collaboration with Hugh Ferriss in 1923 on the Regional Plan of New York and Its Environs, was first published in the Sunday edition of the *New York Times* in February 1924.[10] The three-level design had, like Wright's Skyscraper Regulation project, sidewalks raised to the second-floor level plus cross streets depressed beneath the main north-south avenues. In the following summer came Corbett's important article "Different Levels for Foot, Wheel and Rail," published in *American City*.[11] While reiterating much of his earlier *Times* spread and including the same drawings plus others dramatizing the existing conditions and efficacy of the proposed solution, the later article also contained "an imaginary view of the future city of New York" by Ferriss showing how the multilevel idea might be expanded into a system of superblocks such as Wright was about to propose.[12] A major summation of the scheme, with an expanded description and new illustrations, was published in *Architectural Forum* in early 1927, but by that time Chicago had its own versions of the concept in projects by Edward H. Bennett (Daniel Burnham's former partner), Wright, and others.[13]

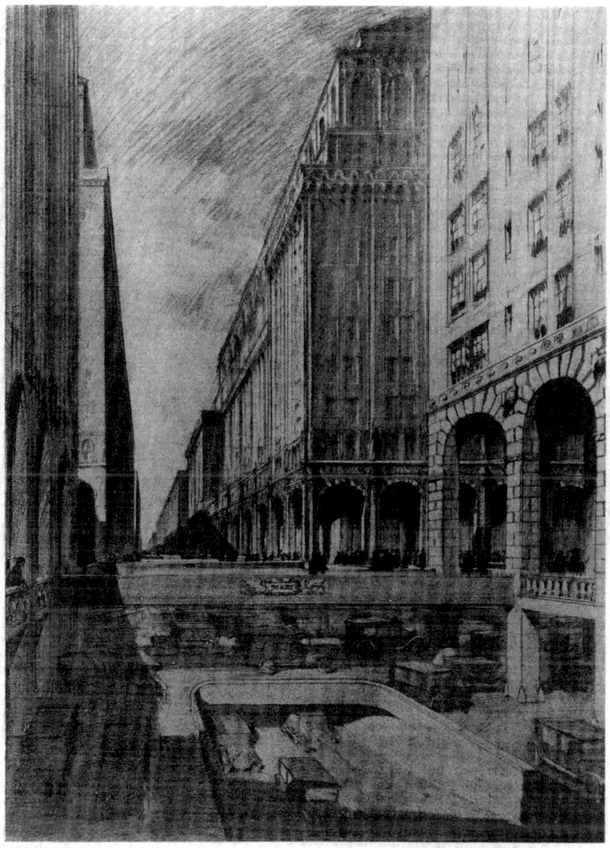

AN AVENUE OF THE FUTURE, SHOWING ELEVATED SIDEWALKS, PASSENGER CAR ROADWAY, AND TUNNEL FOR TRUCKS

Fig. 2. Harvey Wiley Corbett (American, 1873–1954) with Hugh Ferriss (American, 1889–1962). Multilevel street project, New York, 1923–24. Perspective. Reproduced on the cover of *American City*, July 1924. From *Architectural Forum*, March 1927

Chicago witnessed a groundswell of popular interest in the prospect of creating a multilevel street system in the early to mid-1920s due to the worsening traffic conditions in its singularly concentrated central business district and the debate over whether or not to build a subway to ease the burden on Loop streets. An often-cited proof of the city's can-do spirit was the wholesale raising of its street level in the late 1850s and 1860s to accommodate the construction of the nation's first sewage system. Between late 1922 and early 1926, at least six letters to the editor promoting elevated sidewalks and depressed cross streets and/or subways were published by the city's leading newspaper, the *Chicago Daily Tribune*. Two of these were signed by the prominent real estate figure Gordon Strong, an important Wright client at the time.[14]

The *Tribune* was not innocent in printing these pleas. Between 1923 and 1926, the newspaper published more than ten editorials demanding such a program of construction, two of which referred to Corbett. The first, "Unstrangling the Loop," was accompanied by the project the paper itself commissioned for double-decking Madison Street, where its offices were then located.[15] The most well-publicized proposal for establishing a multilevel street system in Chicago closely followed Corbett's, indeed, nearly to the point of imitation (fig. 3). Produced at more or less the same time as Wright's, the one by Bennett, then consulting architect to the Chicago Plan Commission, appeared in two of the city's newspapers—the *Herald and Examiner* and the *Evening Post*—in mid-January 1926 and in brochure form in mid-April. Separating pedestrians from vehicular traffic would, Bennett promised, turn "all streets and every street in the loop into channels of easily flowing wheel and pedestrian movement."[16]

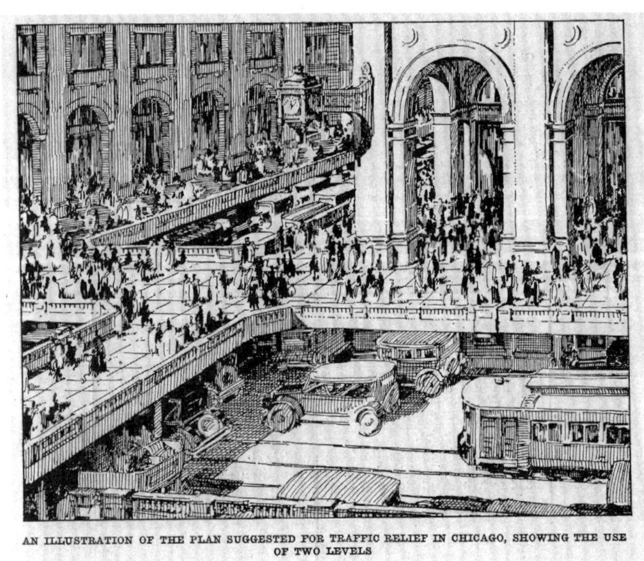

Fig. 3. Edward H. Bennett (American, 1874–1954). Multilevel street project, Chicago. 1926. From *American City*, July 1926

Bennett acknowledged that his idea was proposed "in New York, a year or so ago" and that "it has been definitely suggested . . . for Chicago by others."[17] The reference to New York was clearly to Corbett; but could the one to Chicago have included Wright? We will probably never know. Still, even for the question to arise makes one realize how closely the Skyscraper Regulation project aligned with both traditionalists such as Corbett and Bennett and the more radical Europeans, not to speak of the populist embrace of "sidewalks in the air" by the media.

Rather than substantiating the image of Wright as an arch-individualist, outside the mainstream and bent on flouting the rules, the picture that emerges from the analysis of the Skyscraper Regulation project points to someone very much part of his times, willing to work within regulations and participating in the professional discourse. Moreover, it illustrates a significant engagement with contemporary issues of city planning and thus prompts us to look both backward and forward for further evidence of Wright's abiding interest in urbanism.

FLASHBACK AND FLASH-FORWARD

If the Skyscraper Regulation project illustrates an important continuity in Wright's practice, it also demarcates an abrupt shift in methodology. From this central turning point, we shall see how the ideal, template-like character of the Skyscraper Regulation project grew out of the designs that preceded it, in contrast to those in the final three decades of Wright's career that have a more contingent, interventionist character. The latter also dispense with the underlying grid derived from the eighteenth-century U.S. Rectangular Land Survey that controlled Wright's urban planning through the 1920s.

Although Wright declined Daniel Burnham's offer to work for him at the time Burnham's office was becoming the leading force in American city planning, he early on conceived the residential commissions he received through the lens of urban design. His 1896 project for a twenty-two-house development for an entire block on the outskirts of Chicago transformed the typical subdivision by grouping the individual houses around a central, common garden in a manner soon to be adopted by Garden City advocates (plate 4). Just as telling is the hand-drawn square grid underlying the design. It defines the terrain of the community of houses in terms echoing the larger metropolitan grid on which Chicago's street system was based.

The idealism of the square grid, with its Jeffersonian origins, would determine the critical project of these early years. In response to a request from the *Ladies' Home Journal* in 1900 for the design of a model moderate-cost house, Wright created what he called the Quadruple Block Plan, explaining that any house design had to be understood as part of a general community plan (plate 5). Thus the first so-called Prairie-style house was born out of a development plan for four houses connected to one another in a pinwheeling fashion that gave dynamic form to the 1896 communal garden. The balance between community and privacy was replicated by Wright in several plans for subdivisions in 1903–04, both commissioned and speculative (plates 6, 7). These culminated in the broad application of the Quadruple Block Plan in 1912–13 to a design for a Chicago neighborhood of approximately five thousand people in response to the City Club's competition to improve local living conditions (fig. 4). Including commercial, government, educational, and recreational facilities, Wright's design offered an atypical solution—neither in the City Beautiful nor the Garden City mold—that gave local identity to the neighborhood while ensuring it would be embedded in the larger metropolitan community through an acceptance and fine-grained manipulation of the Chicago grid.

If the Skyscraper Regulation project, as an abstract template for development, was considered a logical outcome of these earlier efforts, Wright's later responses to actual urban problems and conditions resulted in very different formal solutions. This can be most clearly illustrated by the Crystal City project for Washington, D.C. (1940; plate 8), whose program aligned quite closely with that of the Skyscraper Regulation project. For an undeveloped site at the edge of downtown, Wright designed an interconnected group of prismatic towers that rises independently of the surrounding streets in a parklike setting. Housing both apartments and hotel rooms, the megastructure sits atop a multistory base that would have contained the world's largest indoor parking facility while also serving as a shopping center, entertainment facility, and outdoor terrace offering views over the monumental core of the city.

The three other major urban interventions of the period are different in that they were all for civic or cultural centers. The civic center for the shore of Lake Monona in Madison, Wisconsin—designed in 1938 and reworked several times during Wright's lifetime before being built posthumously in much altered form—was consciously meant to relate to an earlier City Beautiful plan for the site, but using modern materials and techniques to create a megastructure partially cantilevered over the lake (plates 9, 10). By placing the main programmatic elements, including automobile access and parking, under a semicircular street-level terrace echoing the auditorium shape within, the civic center became a public forum. With the lake as backdrop and the city as foreground, Wright pictured the theaterlike outdoor space as a place of spectacle (plate 11).

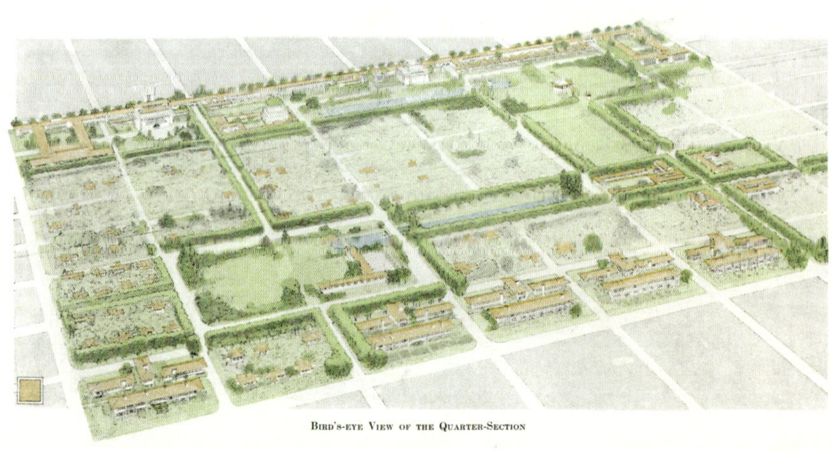

Fig. 4. Scheme of Development for a Quarter-Section. From *City Residential Land Development: Studies in Planning, Competitive Plans for Subdividing a Typical Quarter Section of Land in the Outskirts of Chicago*, ed. Alfred B. Yeomans (Chicago: University of Chicago Press, 1916)

For Pittsburgh, which had suffered terribly from deindustrialization and suburbanization, Wright designed a gigantic spiral-shaped ziggurat for the derelict core of the city, where three rivers meet to form the historic Point (1947; plate 12). The megastucture was intended to house everything from an opera house and rooftop multiuse sports stadium to hamburger stands and gadget shops along a 4-1/2-mile-long (7.25-kilometer-long) ramp that could accommodate the 125,000 cars expected to use the center on a daily basis. The intention was to counteract the process of decentralization by endowing the core with a new community focus and traffic node, making it a link between the suburbs and the downtown.

Wright's final postwar design, for a cultural center for Baghdad (1957), was developed in response to a program by the Iraqi government to hire Western "starchitects" to create signal examples of modern architecture in the city. His multibuilding project was the only one to form the basis of an urban plan (plates 13, 14). Echoing the shape of the original Round City of Baghdad were buildings for an opera house and university within a complex containing museums and other cultural and entertainment facilities. The reclaimed island in the Tigris River was to become a destination point and place for indoor and outdoor public gatherings.

The Baghdad project was the culmination of Wright's vision for making urban space a place of sociability, be it the communal gardens of the earliest residential developments or the public fora of the later interventions. At the center of this effort stands the Skyscraper Regulation project, whose opening up of the downtown commercial blocks to social uses clearly predicted the later Rockefeller Center and the many multibuilding, superblock urban developments that followed in the postwar period.

Notes

1. For a fuller treatment of the subject, see my book *The Urbanism of Frank Lloyd Wright* (Princeton, N.J.: Princeton University Press, 2016).
2. The title and quotations are from the handwritten legend on the preliminary sketch plan (plate 1).
3. Frank Lloyd Wright, *Drawings for a Living Architecture* (New York: Horizon Press, 1959), p. 174.
4. Giorgio Ciucci, "The City in Agrarian Ideology and Frank Lloyd Wright: Origins and Development of Broadacres," in Ciucci et al., *The American City: From the Civil War to the New Deal*, trans. Barbara Luigia La Penta (Cambridge, Mass.: MIT Press, 1979), p. 329.
5. A summary of the early stages in imagining such multilevel street systems is given in Jean-Louis Cohen, *Scenes of the World to Come: European Architecture and the American Challenge, 1893–1960* (Montreal: Canadian Centre for Architecture, 1995), pp. 31–37.
6. "Costly Street Widenings, as Manhattan Crowds Increase, Might Be Obviated by Planning This Kind of Thoroughfare" and "Sees Future New York," *New-York Tribune*, January 16, 1910.
7. Henry Harrison Suplee, "The Elevated Sidewalk," *Scientific American* 109, no. 4 (July 26, 1913): 67. The cover drawing has often been wrongly attributed to Harvey Wiley Corbett.
8. See note 5 above, where the image again is attributed to Corbett.
9. "To Relieve Traffic Congestion in New York," *American Architect* 119 (March 30, 1921): 395.
10. Harvey Wiley Corbett, "Triple-Decked Streets for Traffic Relief," *New York Times*, February 3, 1924, sec. 8. Hilberseimer republished some of the Corbett drawings in his *Groszstadtarchitektur* (1927).
11. Harvey Wiley Corbett, "Different Levels for Foot, Wheel and Rail," *American City* 31 (July 1924): 2–6.
12. The Ferriss drawing was published on the front page of the *New York Times Magazine*, May 25, 1924.
13. Harvey Wiley Corbett, "Problem of Traffic Congestion, and a Solution," *Architectural Forum* 46 (March 1927): 201–08.
14. Gordon Strong, "Skyscraper Streets," *Chicago Daily Tribune*, letter to the editor, September 24, 1924; and "Three-Level Streets," letter to the editor, *Chicago Daily Tribune*, June 15, 1925.
15. "Unstrangling the Loop," *Chicago Daily Tribune*, May 12, 1923.
16. Edward H. Bennett, "Subway Condemned as Loop Congestion Cure," *Chicago Herald and Examiner*, January 15, 1926.
17. Edward H. Bennett, "Chicago's Advance to Bring Traffic Paths High in Air," *Chicago Herald and Examiner*, January 18, 1926.

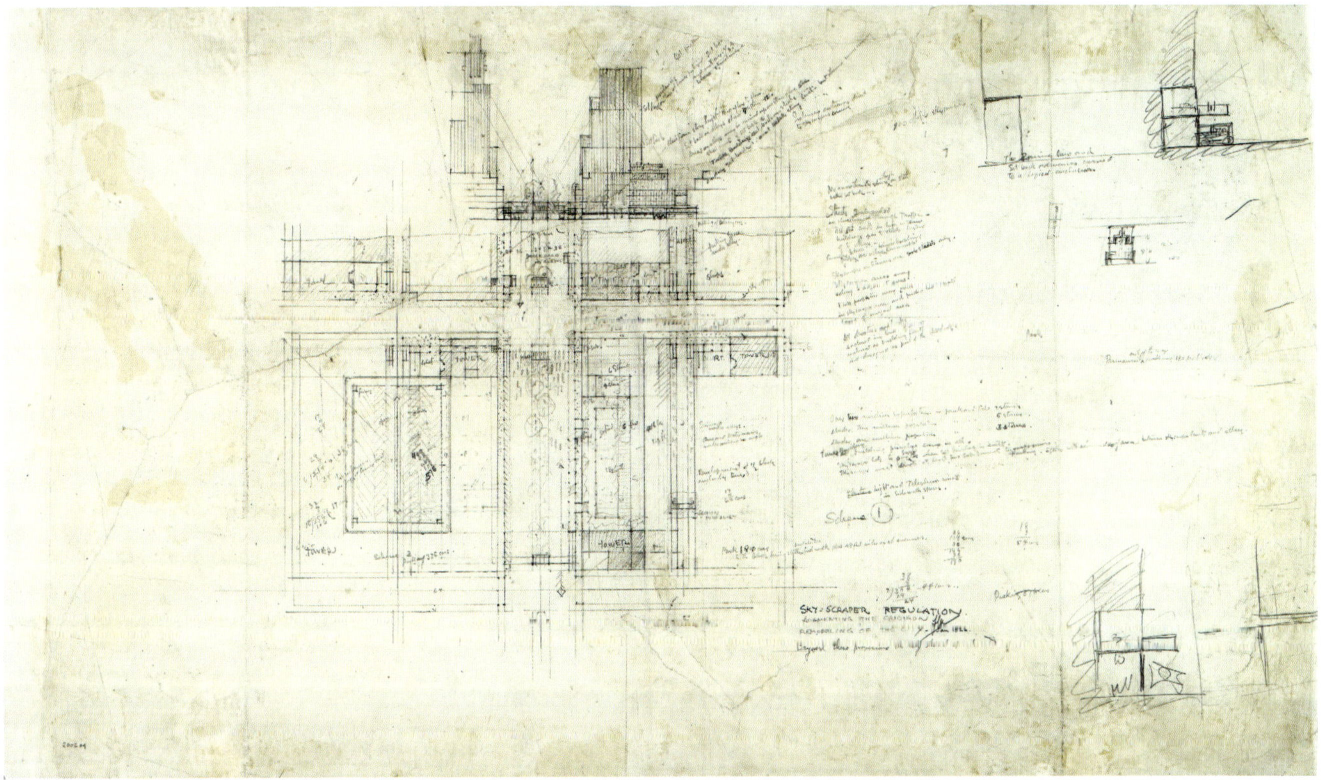

1. Skyscraper Regulation, Chicago. Project, 1926. Preliminary elevation and partial site plan.
Pencil on tracing paper, 20 x 34 1/2 in. (50.8 x 87.6 cm)

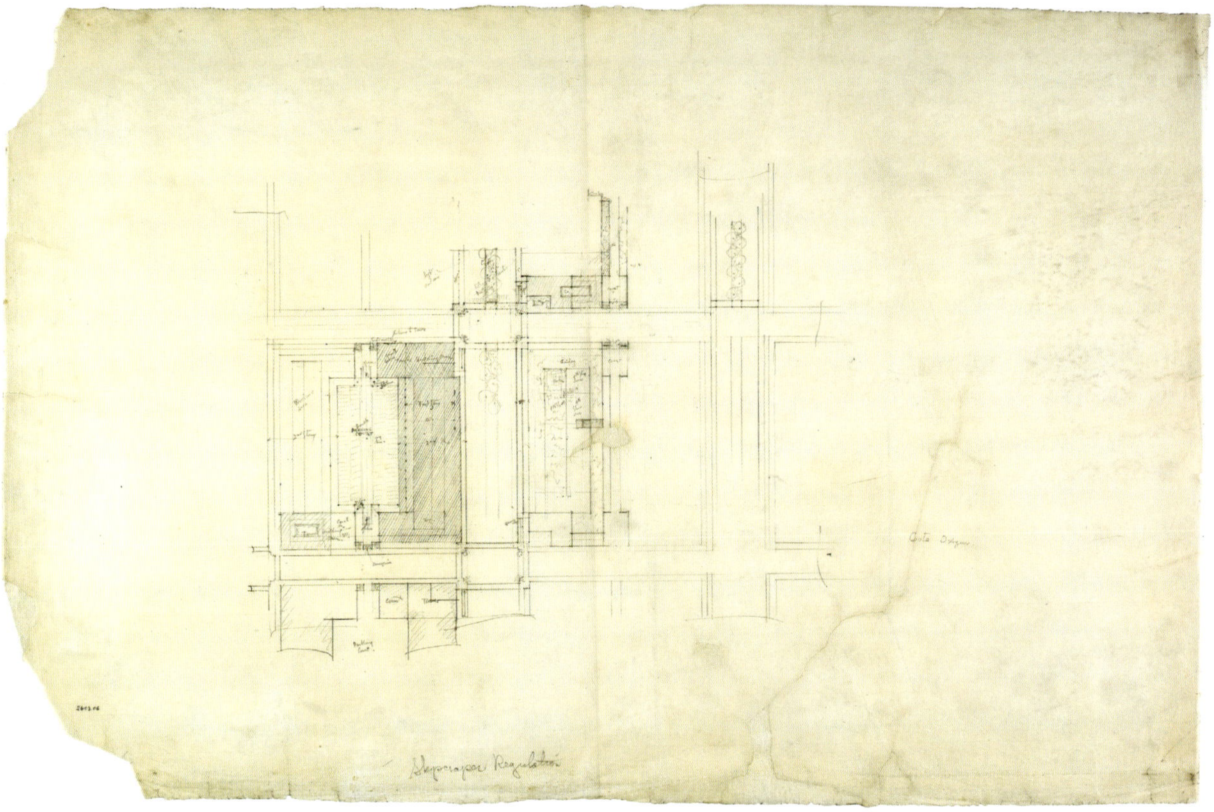

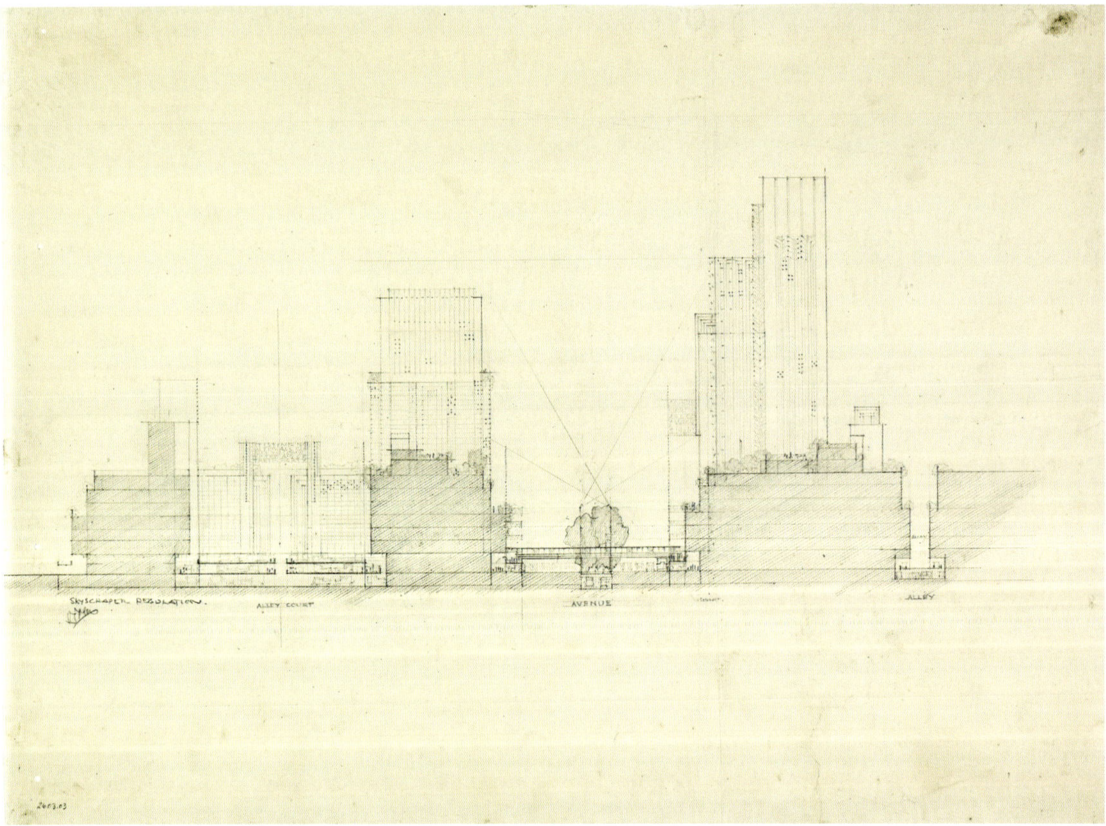

2. Skyscraper Regulation, Chicago. Project, 1926. Plan.
Pencil on tracing paper, 23 3/8 x 36 in. (59.4 x 91.4 cm)

3. Skyscraper Regulation, Chicago. Project, 1926. Section.
Pencil on tracing paper, 20 x 27 3/8 in. (50.8 x 69.5 cm)

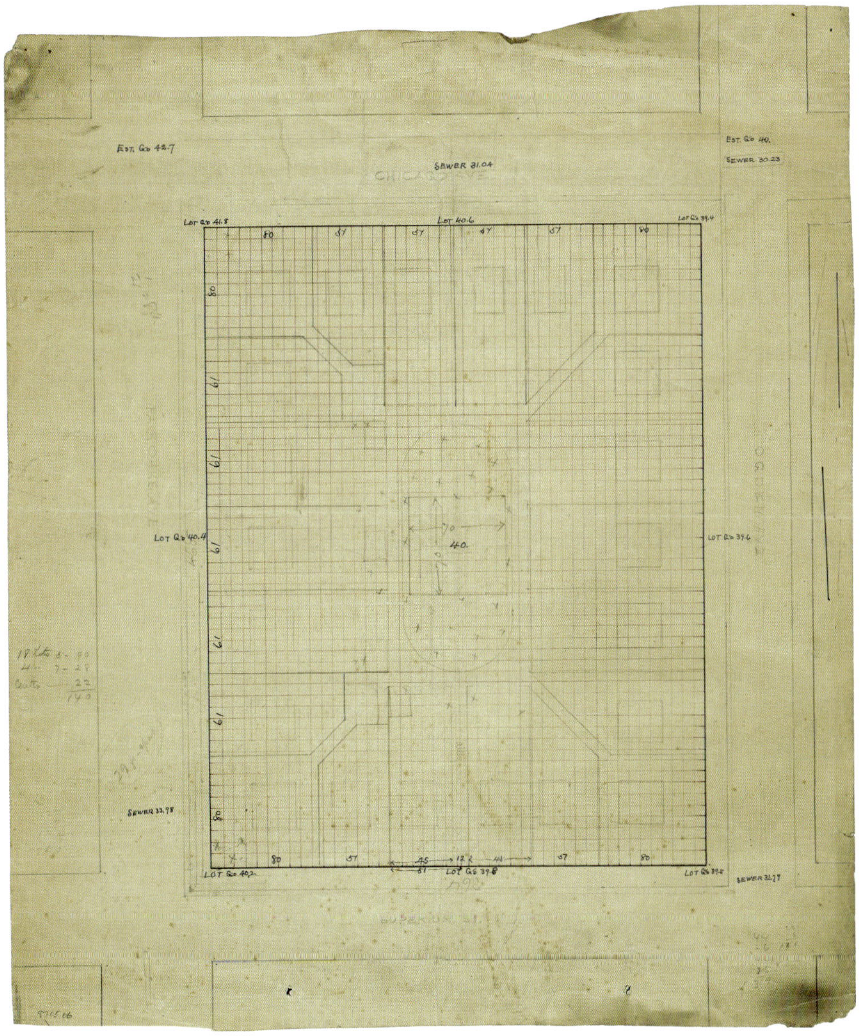

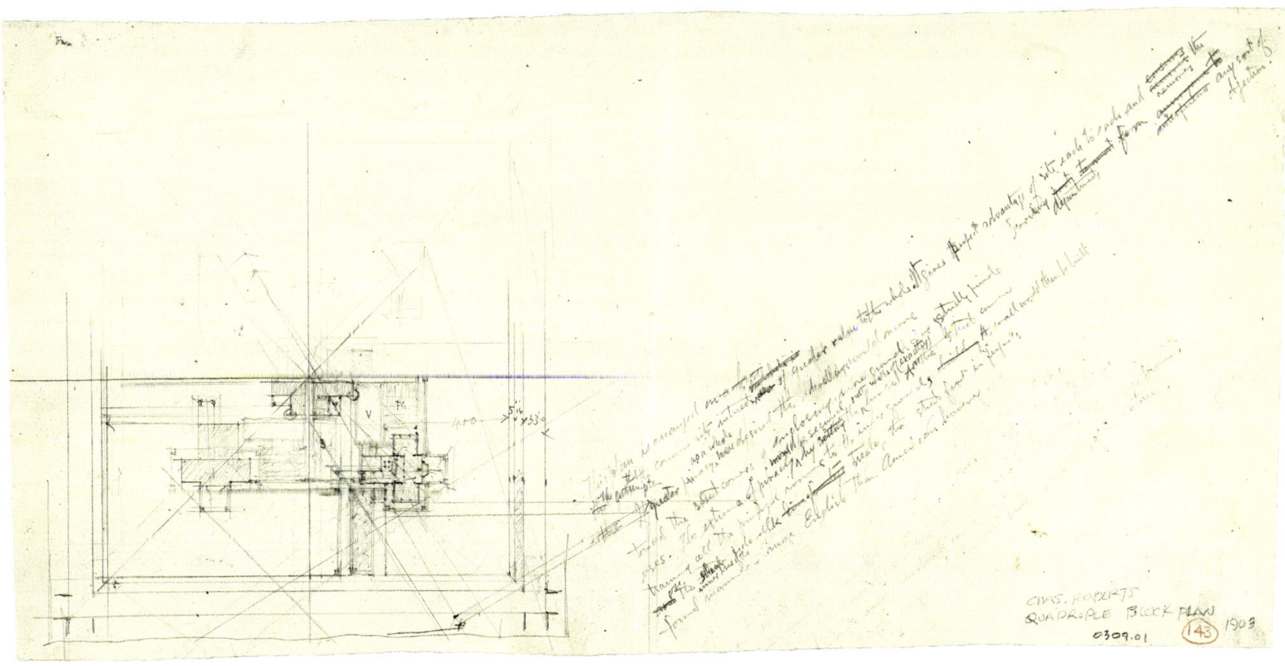

4. Development Plan for Charles E. Roberts, Ridgeland (later Oak Park), Illinois. Project, 1896.
Site plan. Ink and pencil on paper, 22 ⅞ x 19 ⅛ in. (58.1 x 48.6 cm)

5. Quadruple Block Plan for *Ladies' Home Journal*.
Project, 1900–01. Preliminary plan, postdated 1903.
Pencil and colored pencil on paper, 16 ¼ x 11 ¼ in. (41.3 x 28.6 cm)

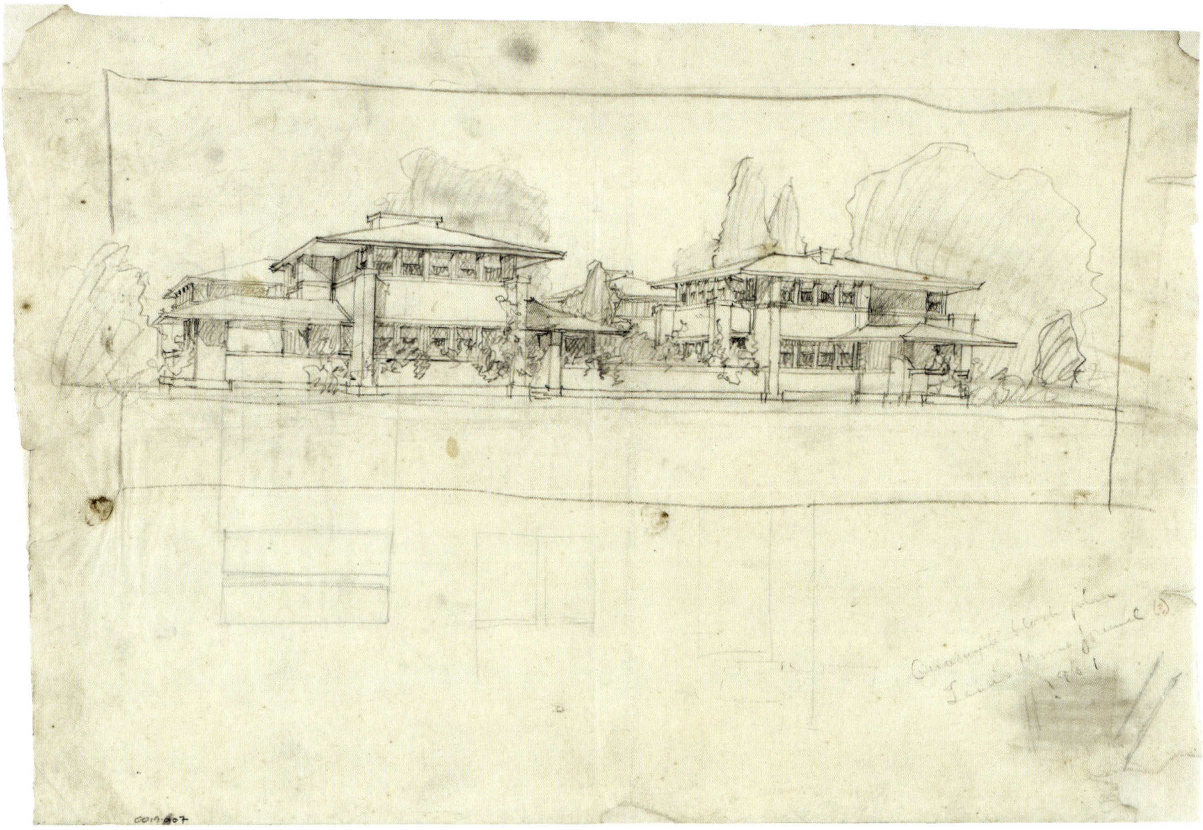

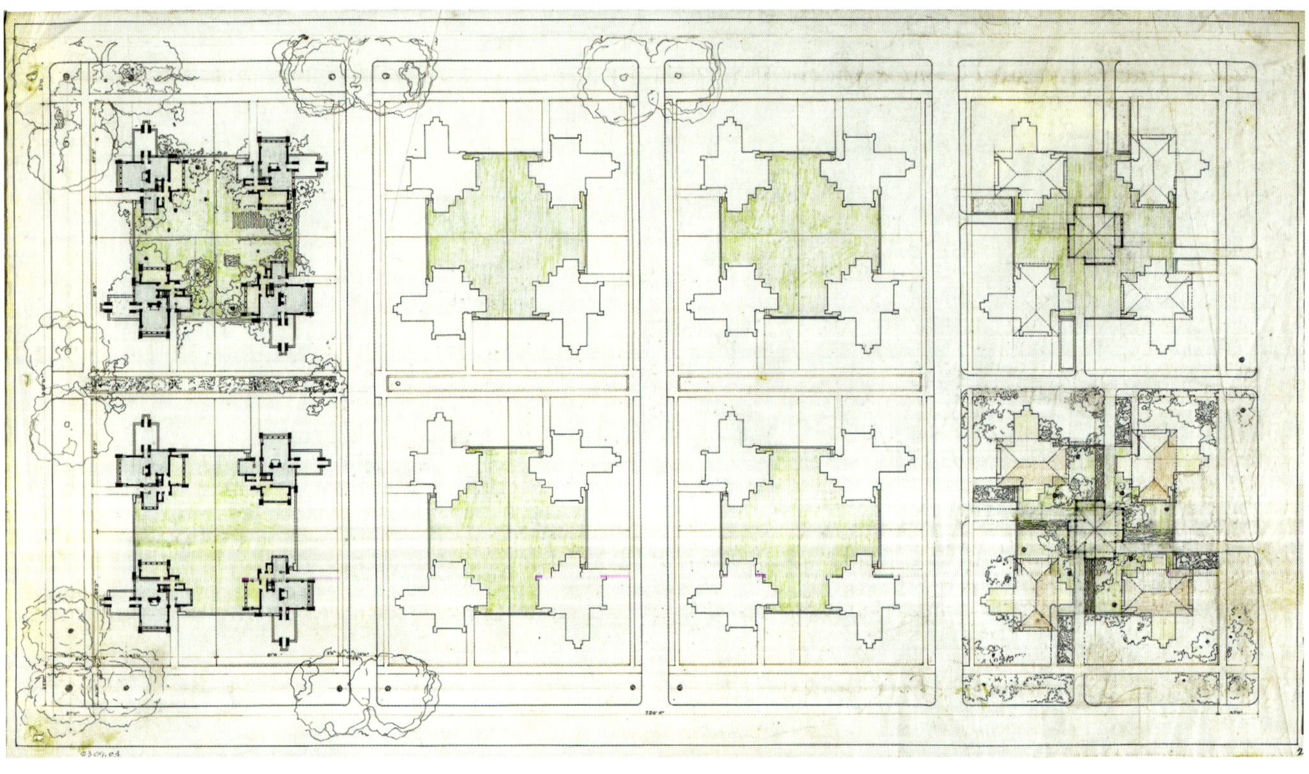

6. Development Plan for Charles E. Roberts, Oak Park, Illinois. Project, 1903–04. Perspective.
Pencil on tracing paper, 14 5/8 x 21 7/8 in. (37.1 x 55.6 cm)

7. Development Plan for Charles E. Roberts. Project, 1903–04. Site plan.
Ink and colored pencil on drafting cloth, 15 3/8 x 27 1/4 in. (39.1 x 69.2 cm)

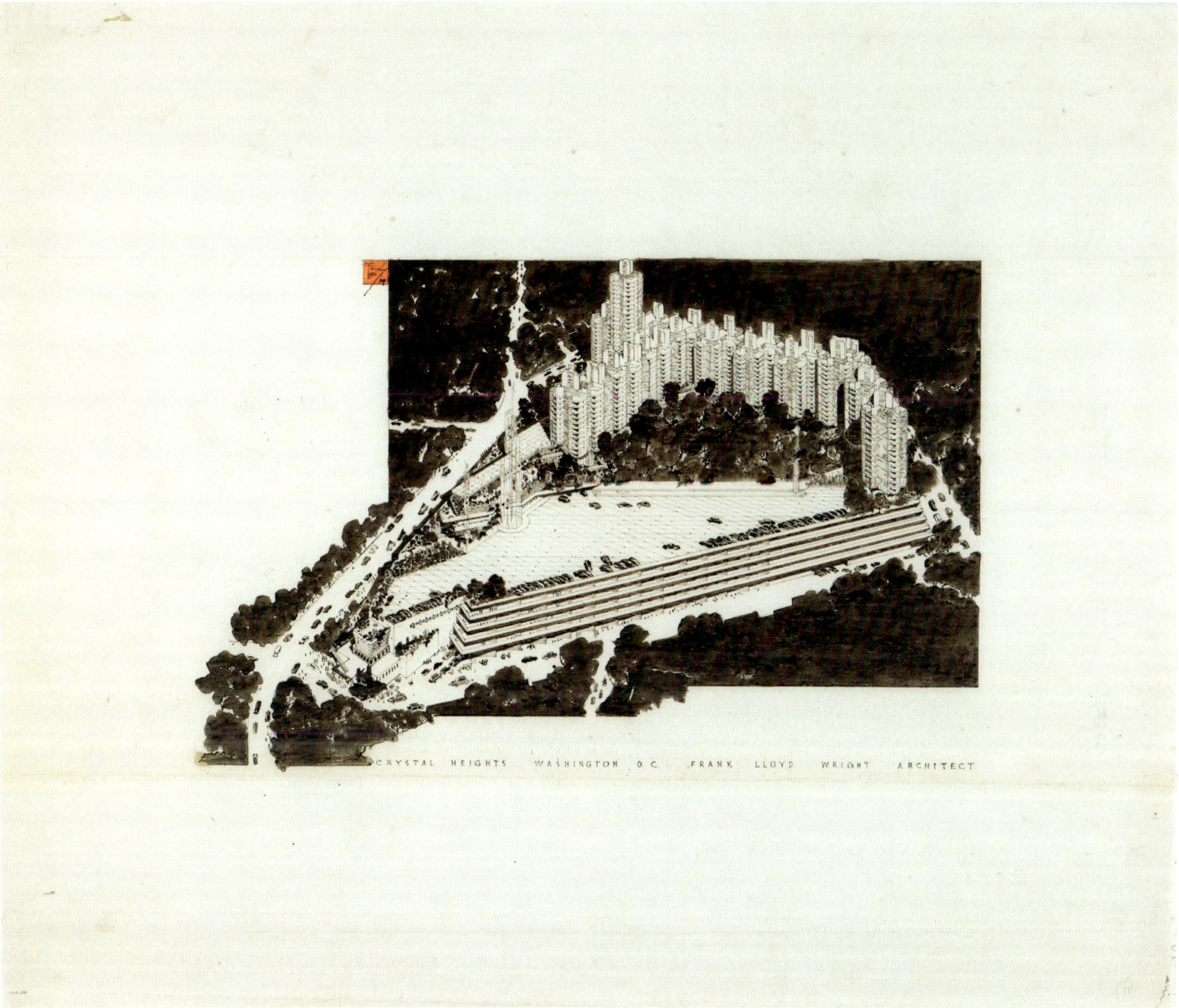

8. Crystal City, Washington, D.C. Project, 1940.
Aerial perspective from the south, antedated 1939.
Ink and ink wash on tracing paper, 20 ½ x 34 ⅛ in. (52.1 x 86.7 cm)

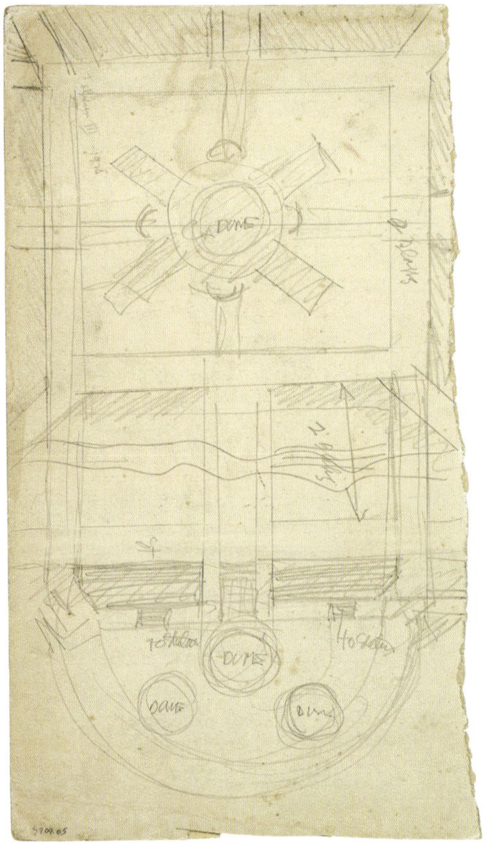

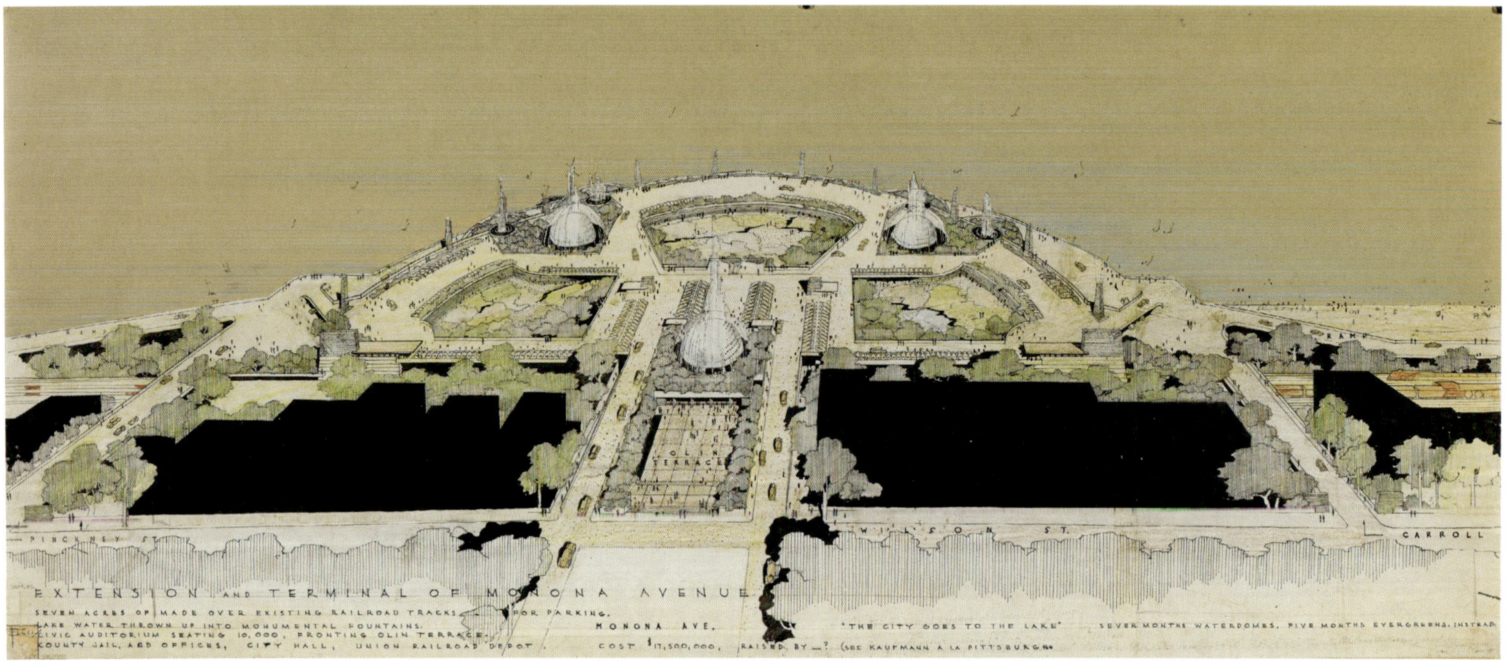

9. Madison Civic Center, Madison, Wisconsin. Project, 1938–59.
Concept study for the site plan, 1938.
Pencil on board, 16 x 9 in. (40.6 x 22.9 cm)

10. Madison Civic Center (Monona Terrace), Madison, Wisconsin. Project, 1938–59.
Aerial perspective from the northwest, 1953.
Ink, colored pencil, and pencil on tracing paper mounted to paper, 18 x 40 in. (45.72 x 101.6 cm)

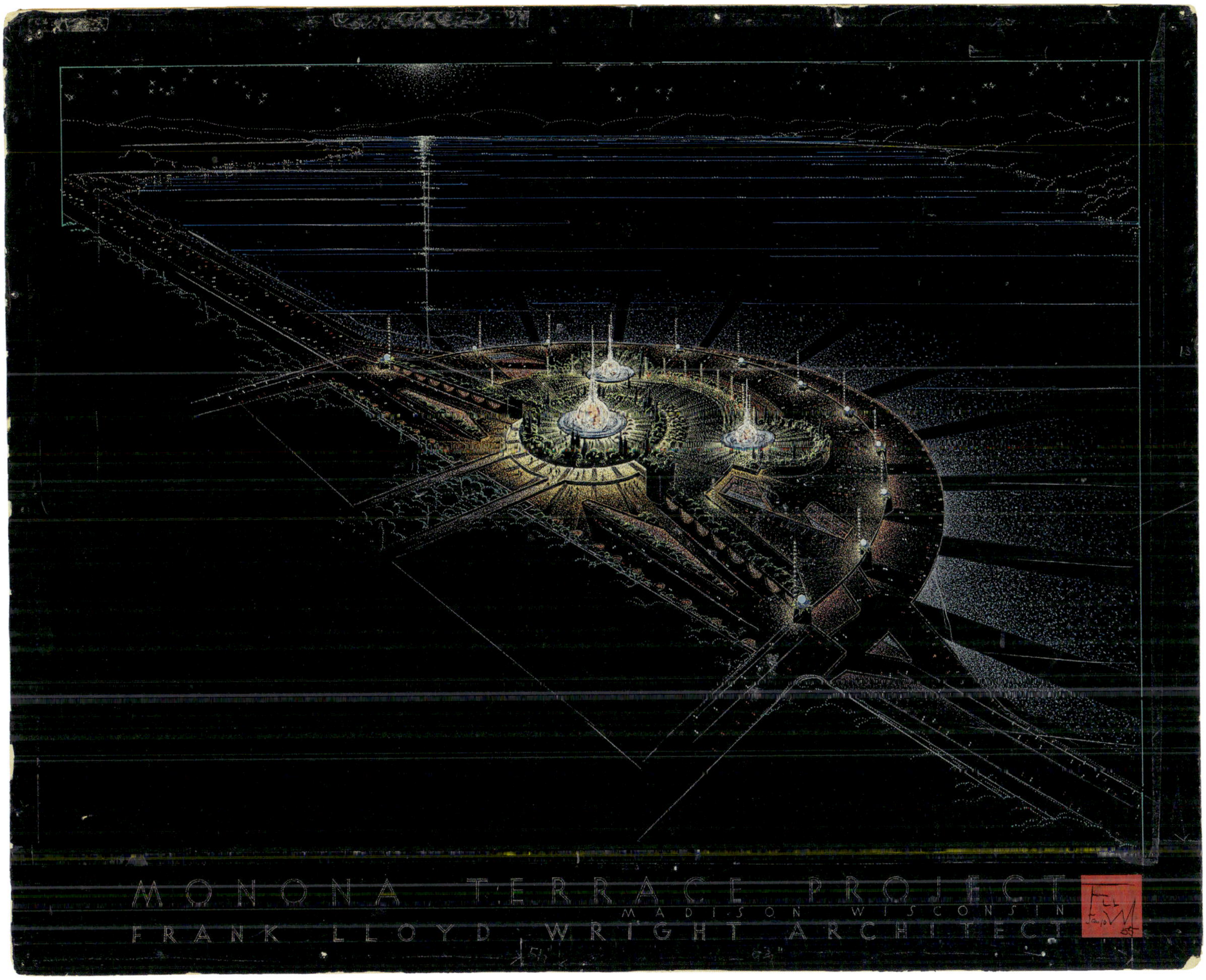

11. Madison Civic Center (Monona Terrace), Madison, Wisconsin. Project, 1938–59.
Night perspective from the west, 1955. Ink and pencil on paper mounted to plywood,
20 x 40 in. (81.3 x 101.6 cm)

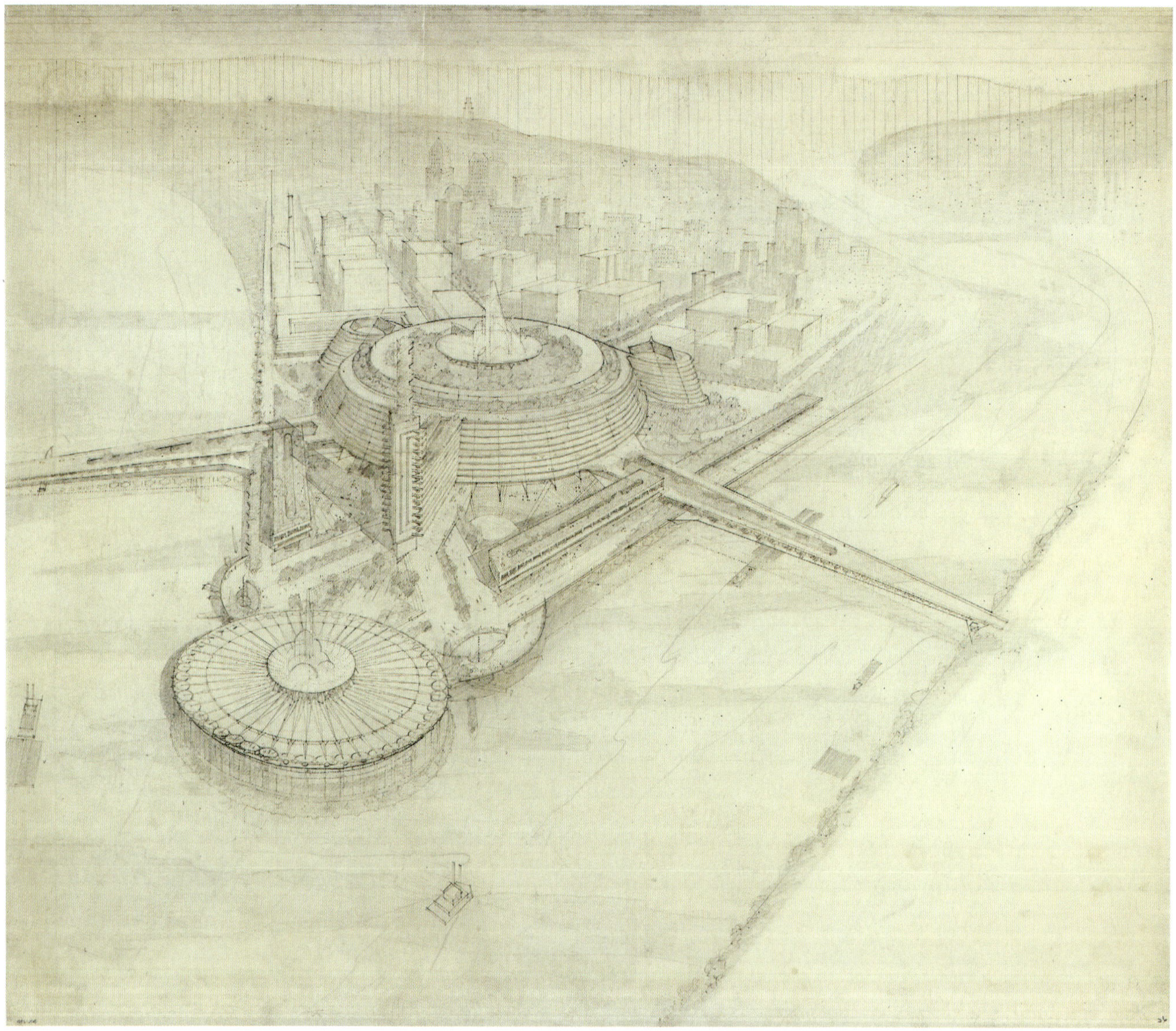

12. Point Park Civic Center, Pittsburgh. Project, 1947. Aerial perspective of the first scheme from Mt. Washington looking east-northeast. Pencil and ink on tracing paper, 31 1/2 x 36 1/2 in. (80 x 92.7 cm)

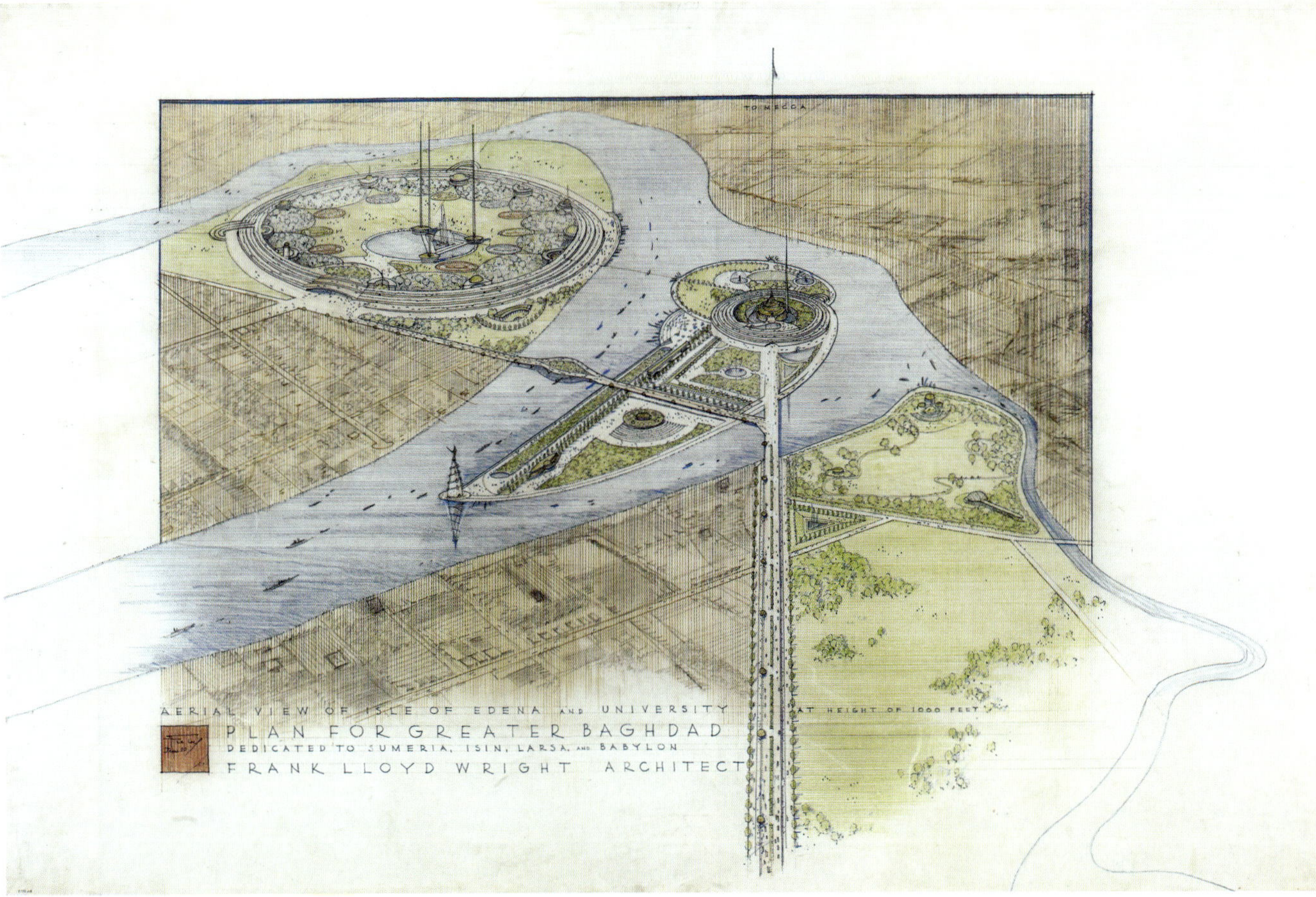

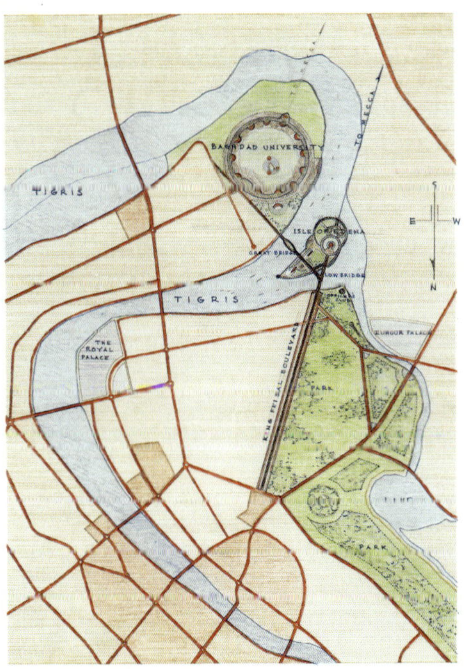

13. Plan for Greater Baghdad. Project, 1957.
Aerial perspective of the cultural center and university from the north.
Ink, pencil, and colored pencil on tracing paper, 34 7/8 x 52 in. (88.6 x 132.1 cm)

14. Plan for Greater Baghdad. Project, 1957. General urban plan.
Ink, pencil, and colored pencil on tracing paper, 20 1/2 x 15 7/8 in. (52.1 x 40.3 cm)

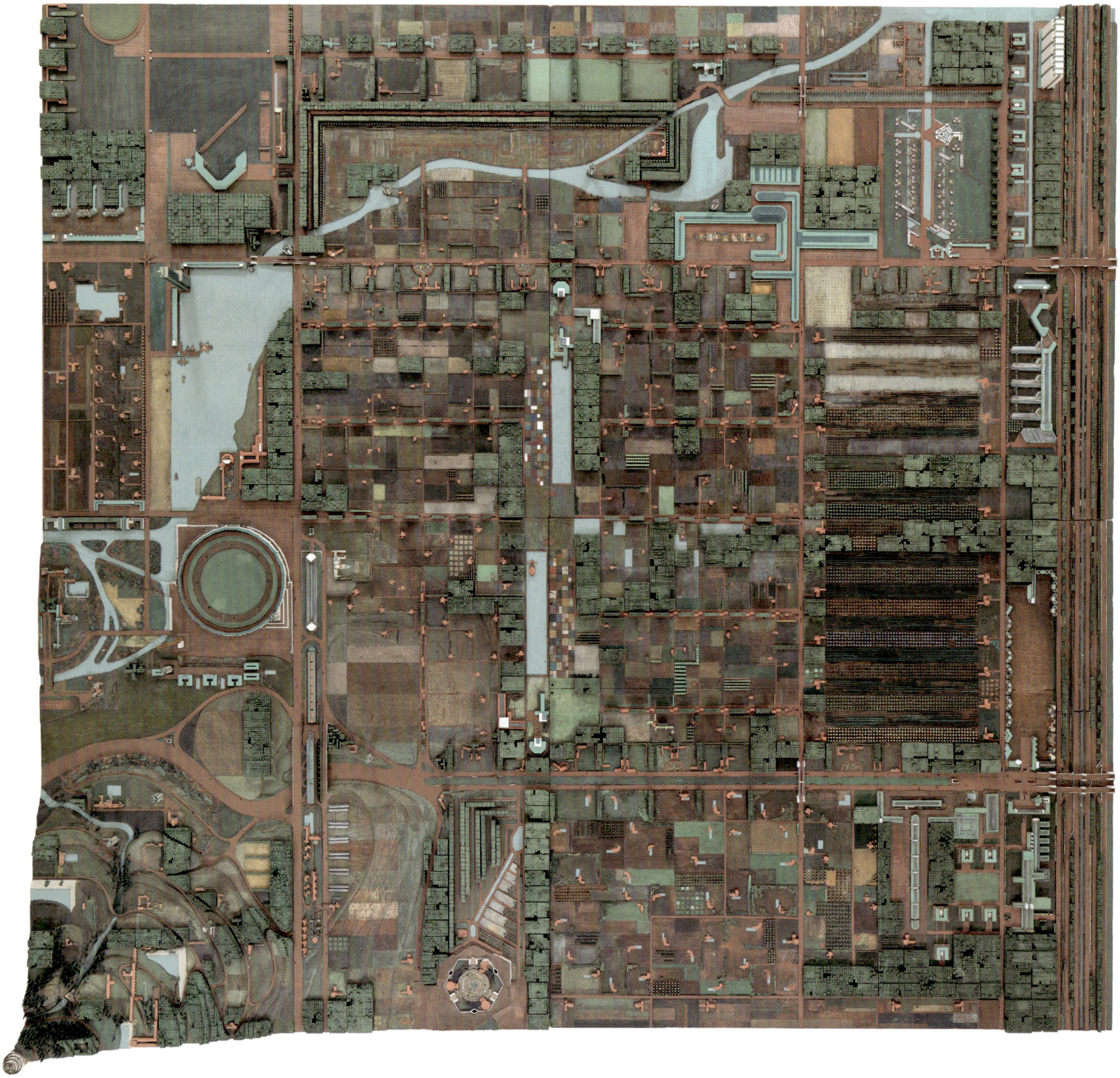

Broadacre City. Project, 1929–35. Model, 1934–35.
Painted wood, cardboard, and paper, 9 in. x 12 ft. 8 in. x 12 ft. 8 in.
(22.9 x 386.1 x 386.1 cm)

DAVID SMILEY

BROAD ACRES
AND NARROW LOTS

The United States is built on fantasies of land, open vistas onto a wondrous future or an idealized past. Yet this land has long been claimed, surveyed and platted, assessed and insured, bought and sold, subdivided, rented, mortgaged, and taxed. From this paradox of imagination and calculation emerged the early-twentieth-century metropolis, with monumental and elegant districts, commercial buildings competing for the sky, smoke-producing factories, and endless blocks of tenements choking on sewage. And while the triumphs of the metropolis were celebrated, many social observers, policy-makers, architects, and planners saw a breakdown of urban functions and civic meaning. Frank Lloyd Wright's proposal for Broadacre City (1929–35) was a remarkable response: an architectural claim that the metropolis was obsolete. In its place, Broadacre was to be a "Usonian" synthesis—an unprecedented landscape unsullied by convention or history, consisting simply of "architecture and acreage" (opposite).[1] With its low-density carpet of small plots, predominantly one- and two-story buildings and seemingly infinite territory, undergirded by well-managed technologies, the ruralized landscape of Broadacre would sustain new levels of individuality and freedom, far more democratic than a traditional metropolis could ever support. Yet the 4-square-mile (10.4-square-kilometer) area of the Broadacre City model would give home to only 1,400 families, which, according to the 1930 Census, would barely satisfy the definition of an "urban place."[2] How, then, can Broadacre be understood? Not simply urban or rural or suburban, but somehow their hybrid, its social life and spatial experience elude clear definition.

■■■■

Challenged by the growing national and international discourse of urban theory and design, Wright emphatically confronted what many observers in the late 1920s called "the problem of the city." After 1930, his lectures and writing assumed an increasingly prophetic tone, demanding a new scale and approach to collective life. The first sketch for Broadacre City, from 1934, demonstrates how new forms of platting and building might shape a new way of life. Wright's marginal notes are explicit, and the sketch shows deliberately zoned land allotments (plate 1): long, tractor-friendly "little farms" line the lower and right perimeter; at upper left, nestled by natural boundaries, a tight grid of "subdivided land"—a "minimum of one acre to the family"; and, at upper right, a dozen "residences of more luxurious class." These groupings—along with factories, warehouses and distribution centers, roadside markets, gas stations, and a landing field—are connected by a network of roads. A theater and "collections clubs" provide for shared cultural life; a park, golf course, and lake offer opportunities for recreation; and all are joined by an overall "natural feeling . . . developed according to its nature." The sketch comes across as neither city nor suburb but as an evenly inhabited swath of subdivided land.

Wright described Broadacre as having "no major or minor axis," nor overt symmetry.[3] He found classical traditions of composition and order deeply problematic, since they embodied centralized power and authoritarian rule, not nature or democracy. Broadacre was a program of "ruralism" in which American equality and self-determination were ensured not by composition or overt order but by the provision of unencumbered *land* to each man and his family.[4]

▪▪▪▪

For more than two tumultuous decades spanning the turn of the century, Wright lived in Chicago and knew firsthand the social costs of urban capital. He shared with many observers the belief that urban greed—the "merciless money increment"—made every man a "soulless unit," and genuine social interaction impossible.[5] For Wright and other Progressives in the early twentieth century, the metropolis had become the central obstacle to human growth; the "big city," he wrote in 1932, "is no longer modern."[6] The metropolitan thicket had become ungovernable, with lots too small and numerous, too many owners, too many tenants, and haphazard regulation. Architects, planners, policy-makers, and urban leaders examined remedies in new forms of land disposition and regional organization. In the hands of city planning departments and banking institutions, "progress" and "community improvement" increasingly demanded large-scale "district replanning."[7] For Wright, change would necessarily be radical while others argued for less dramatic reform, yet both viewpoints shared a strong antipathy to the geographies of laissez-faire capital.

One framework for alternative settlement patterns was offered by the Regional Plan Association of America (RPAA), whose members—including Lewis Mumford—argued for the use of hydroelectric power to disperse cities and towns across the landscape, leaving parks and agricultural land between.[8] The result would be a modern pastoral, joining nature and urbanization, low-density living and the machine, domesticity and collective life, all of which might overcome the destructive arc of the overbuilt, "anxious" metropolis.[9] Wright, too, saw electrification as a means by which the city "spreads out far away and thin," and while he was disdainful of RPAA proposals for Garden City satellites—instead seeking a network of homes—he shared with them an antagonism to the existing metropolis and a great optimism that new technologies, including the airplane, telephone, automobile, and highways, would create a new politics of regionalized settlement.[10]

Clarence Stein and Henry Wright demonstrated RPAA principles with their plan for the town of Radburn, New Jersey (fig. 1), which was recognized as a new land-development system superseding traditional gridiron patterns. It consisted of a series of residential "superblocks," each formed by semi-attached homes and organized around cul-de-sacs for automotive access. Each house backed onto a tiny yard with direct pedestrian access to a community park with school, playground, picturesque paths, and other recreational amenities. Only a few of the superblocks or commercial spaces were built before the Great Depression halted work, yet the Radburn idea was widely praised for its recalibration of private land and housing patterns in support of shared space. While similar principles were studied more than a decade before Radburn—including Wright's own City Club competition project (1912–13) (see p. 179, fig. 4)—the Radburn superblock became the widely circulated prototype demonstrating that new layouts of land, unconstrained by traditional blocks and lots, offered a durable model for community cohesion.[11]

The remapping of cities as a means to create social and economic stability was similarly integral to the Regional Plan of New York and Its Environs (RPNYE). This goal was expressed in that organization's publication of Clarence Perry's chapter "The Neighborhood Unit" in their multivolume report of 1929 (fig. 2). The unit strategy was comprised of a multiblock planning layout based on an easily walked 1/2-mile (0.8-kilometer) diameter and an area of about 160 acres (65 hectares), whose perimeter was established by major automotive arteries. The inward-focused diagram was made by locating shopping and apartment buildings on the site's outer edges, and placing civic functions (schools, public buildings, churches) at its center. Between edge and core were residential blocks grouped around small parks, housing about five thousand people of "similar tastes and similar attitudes."[12] This approach to community design offered an explicit means to rethink the social order of an urban landscape by creating bordered territories intended to inspire in residents a strong sense of local identity. Like the superblock, the neighborhood unit was a key technique used by architects, planners, and policy-makers to rethink land organization and distribution. This rationalization of development profoundly reshaped the older, supposedly "blighted" districts of most cities, linking the displacement of lower-income residents and businesses to large-scale real estate speculation and investment.[13] Such strategies were driven, in part, by the social sciences. Early in the century, sociologists began to study "primary" or kin-like relations as well as spatially contiguous communities as bulwarks against the anomie of the metropolis. In the 1920s the University of Chicago boasted one of the leading departments of sociology, where Robert Park, Ernest Burgess, and others became renowned for their extensive mapping of neighborhoods as distinct socio-spatial units, or what they called "natural areas." In fact, some of the Chicago sociologists joined the planners of the RPNYE at the American Sociology Association conference of 1925, where Perry presented the idea of the neighborhood unit. In effect, sociological study and territorial delineation were connected; urban description became urban prescription.[14]

Rethinking the city now included the design of bordered social territories, an approach that was quickly put to the test. In 1931, the Lower East Side Planning Association, a private umbrella group of New York banks and insurance

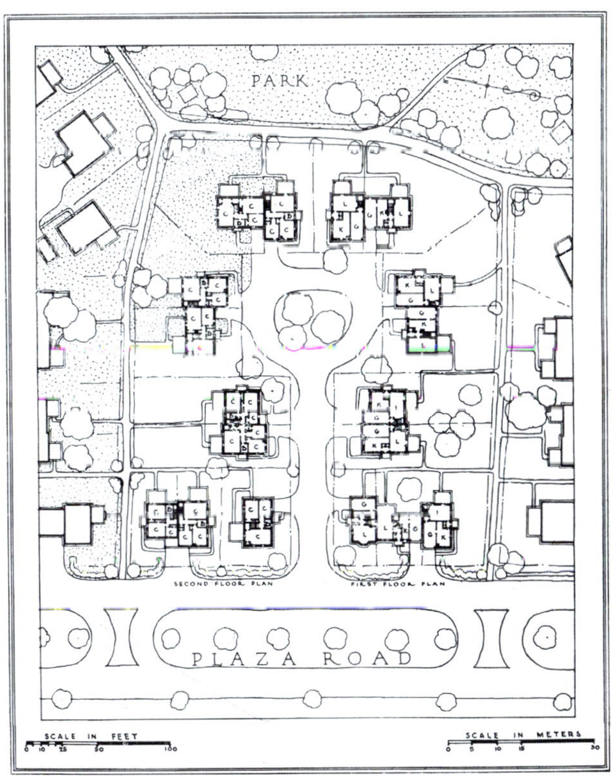

Fig. 1. Radburn, New Jersey, 1927–29. Plan of a superblock. From Clarence Stein, *Toward New Towns for America* (Cambridge, Mass.: MIT Press, 1957)

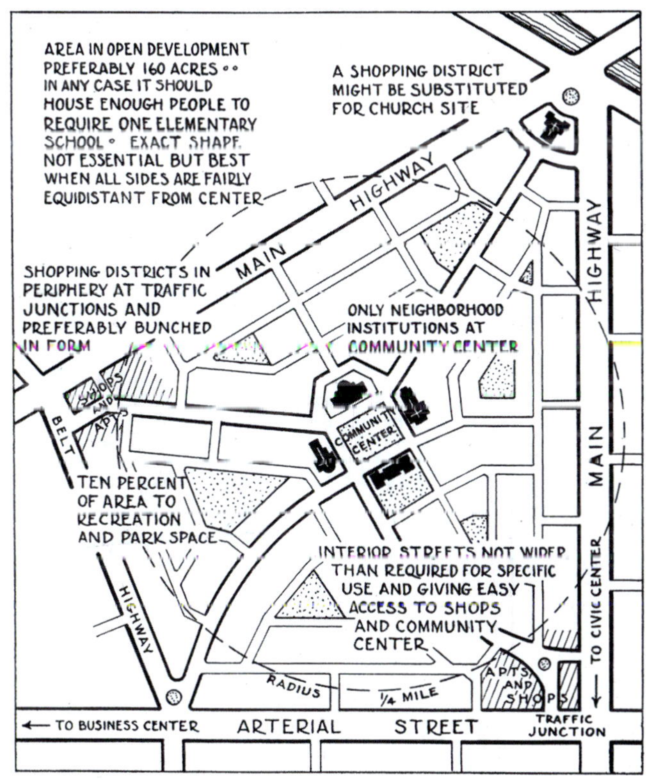

Fig. 2. Clarence A. Perry, "The Neighborhood Unit: A Scheme of Arrangement for the Family-Life Community," in *The Regional Survey of New York and Its Environs*, vol. 7 (New York: Committee on the Regional Plan of New York and Its Environs, 1929)

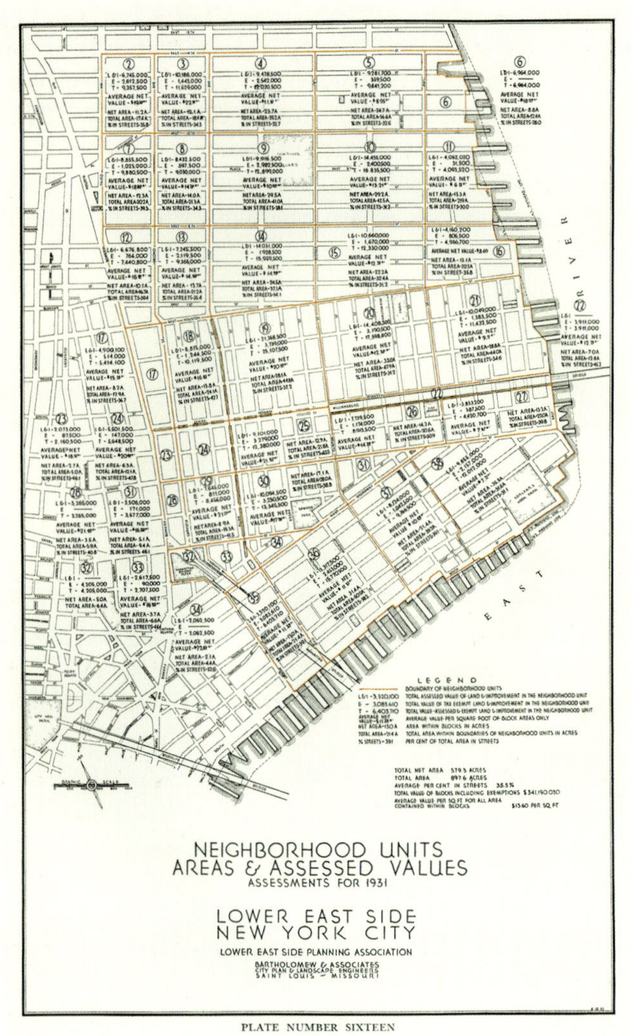

Fig. 3. Harland Bartholomew and Associates, "Neighborhood Units–Areas and Assessed Values," in *Major Traffic Thoroughfares and Transit Plans, Lower East Side, New York City* (New York, 1932)

companies, hired the RPNYE consultant Harland Bartholomew to provide recommendations for "improving"—the term used in professional discourse to describe (or mask) slum clearance, displacement, and new building—the two-hundred-plus-block enclave of the city's immigrant communities. To create a viable scale of intervention, Bartholomew proposed re-platting the area into thirty-eight "self-contained" superblocks—each labeled "Neighborhood Unit"—by closing streets and widening avenues (fig. 3).[15] Such multiblock, slum-clearing projects proliferated during these years and were seen as proof that semi-autonomous neighborhoods could—and should—be created from seemingly undifferentiated urban fabric. In short order, the neighborhood unit and superblock came to dominate the lexicon of land modernization (expressed in modern visual language or not), using precise land techniques to create targeted social spaces, fueling clear development patterns. While these particular methods differed from Wright's view of land organization, Progressive-era thinking about the necessarily changing spatial order of the metropolis threads through all the work.[16]

■■■■

The Broadacre City model was built by Taliesin fellows from late 1934 through early 1935, when it went on display at the Industrial Arts Exposition at Rockefeller Center.[17] It was constructed in four 6-foot-by-6-foot (1.8-meter-by-1.8-meter) sections, each representing 1 square mile (2.6 square kilometers) (plate 2). Wright considered it a demonstration of possibilities, a framework for change rather than a fixed plan. The model shows the transformation of the surveyor's grid into a carpet of planted fields of varied shades and textures, segmented lines of roads, fencing, and trees rolling across the plain and up the hill, and an even scattering of buildings and homes—an "organic modern architecture" that, Wright wrote, will "be seen as landscape."[18] Yet the logic of rationalization remains apparent, quite literally, as the marked ground.

Broadacre's platting of conceptually endless, ostensibly virgin land into townships and freehold lots was largely based on the 6-mile-square (15.5-kilometer-square) *townships*—neither towns or cities, nor units or blocks—of Thomas Jefferson's Land Ordinances.[19] For Wright, this non-hierarchical, egalitarian organization would enable a social life in which individuals could legitimately act out of "intelligent self-interest and honest selfhood," foundational for a revised system of capital joined to a rekindling of democracy.[20] In other words, the grid created equality of opportunity for those willing to take up the challenge of work.

Wright and many observers have emphasized that Broadacre represents only one portion of a potentially limitless fabric. The project has no immediately apprehended, symbolic center, yet the construction of the model in four abutting sections reveals a different logic of centering (compare p. 190 and fig. 4). That Wright worked for many years with intersecting quadrants is well known (see p. 184, plate 7; and p. 134, fig. 2); in all this work, land and property are planimetrically joined but experientially divided by intersecting party walls that extend beyond the structures and along the property line. However, the quadrant projects, unlike those of his houses that pinwheel around their hearths, exert a centrifugal force and direct space outward from the center.[21] In the case of Broadacre, the geometry of planning together with the model's construction reveal a unique tension in the central area, where Wright situated what could be called the homestead zone.

Wright makes room for varied forms of single-family houses at Broadacre City, but the homestead zone specifically consists of "little" homes (and in later versions, "minimum" homes) on a fabric of 1-to-5-acre (0.4-to-2-hectare) parcels. Closer inspection reveals that each lot differs: one includes a large garden or small farm, another evidence of livestock, a workshop, or even a small business. These are neither suburban refuges nor back-to-the-land retreats but productive plots where family, home, garden, workshop, and complementary activities form an organic unit. For Wright, this blending of the home and the homestead is "the only centralization allowable," the lynchpin for the "natural economy" that enables Broadacre to operate.[22]

Wright drew upon a variety of intellectual influences to shape the homestead zone as well as Broadacre's larger social and experiential potential. Accompanying the model were explanatory panels outlining the urban planning principles of Broadacre and the intellectual figures who informed Wright's thinking (plates 3–5). Through the Russian anarchist geographer Pyotr Kropotkin, for instance, Wright expressed his ideal of locally controlled, self-sufficient communities free of centralized regulation, which, at the scale of the worker, would require only "a few hours' devotion to machinery" for daily needs.[23] Wright expanded Kropotkin's autonomous citizenry, seeking a release from wage slavery through individual action unfettered by distant cultures and social conventions.

Wright considered how the homesteader's territory could literally be created in fiscal terms. From economist Henry George, Wright adopted the idea of a single tax, whereby land was unencumbered but taxes would be levied on speculative skyscrapers housing unproductive labor.[24] From the German economist Silvio Gesell, Wright advocated an alternative currency, or scrip, called "free money," which required the purchase of a monthly stamp to maintain face value. This system was designed to discourage the hoarding of cash solely for earning

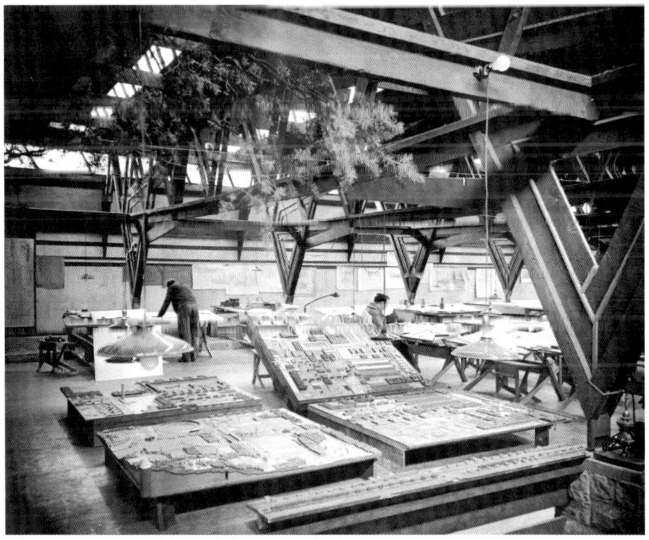

Fig. 4. Broadacre City. Project, 1929–35. Sections of the model at the Taliesin Fellowship Complex, Spring Green, Wisconsin

interest or for use in speculative investments, and to keep money in circulation for productive spending, local consumption, and individual initiative.[25] In a similar vein, Wright's homage to Walt Whitman, Ralph Waldo Emerson, Thorstein Veblen, and Edward Bellamy, among others, was framed around a negotiated balance between self-directed action and those social systems that often hinder that action. The centrality of the homestead zone within the Broadacre model was the fruit of such thinking—a local economy, connected to but not dependent on larger systems; a shift of power from broad political and economic entities to individual and local ones.

Central though it may be, the homestead zone is not hermetic. There are through roads, and it blends with other spaces and functions. Its edge roads have different scales—one is a "main arterial" with a planted median, and others are of varying dimension and vehicular speed. In each direction the zone connects with larger-scaled programs such as roadside markets—places of social exchange and goods distribution (plate 6)—as well as professional blocks and leisure uses, such as a zoo, arboretum, aquarium, lake, and arena. The porosity of the homestead zone implies mobility and spatial continuity, not the border strengthening of neighborhood units and superblocks.

Zooming in, at the heart of the homestead zone—at the center of the center—is perhaps the most vital programmatic area, the education complex. In the model's current state, as well as in most photographs of it, the core of the area is vacant (see p. 190). By contrast, in the initial plans and early model photographs, it is occupied by a high school with a large courtyard, creating a substantial anchor amid the gestural pinwheel (plate 7). As a whole, this complex is an enormous "kindergarten," a symbolic nursery for the cultivation of democratic individuals—balanced, well-read, and creative homesteaders (likely trained with Friedrich Froebel's educational "gifts"). The Broadacre model may show four square miles of a vast regional plan, but Wright focused the view, so to speak, on the educational and enculturation complex at its center.

■■■■

The stability of Broadacre, with its anchoring homestead zone, would not be possible without a complementary mobility. Radburn was called "a town for the motor age," and Clarence Perry's neighborhood unit was part of the "cellular city" made by arterial roads, but mobility in Broadacre is even more deeply woven into the social and built environments.[26] The acre-based allotments of the Broadacre homesteads are also called "one-car house(s)" or "three-car house(s)," etc.[27] One's acre and one's car—rooted identity and free will—are structurally joined, and every facet of daily life, small or large, prosaic to monumental, from the home to the gas station to the stadium is tied to movement. The roadway viaduct is a megastructure, offering mode separation, ten lanes, regional connections, embedded lighting, storage warehouses, and spaces for small industry. Wright's prototype highway interchange enables continuous movement and mitigates the dreaded at-grade crossing about which traffic engineers fretted (plate 8). The mobility *pièce de résistance*, the "automobile objective" (fig. 5), is a cultural center crowning Broadacre's topography, a gathering place for newly mobile individuals.[28] In later years, Wright developed the transportation network in greater, even fantastic detail, taking personal mobility as an expression of liberty and individuality—yet always rendered as part of the weave of landscape infrastructures (plates 9, 10).

Overall, the Broadacre model is a serene, almost timeless landscape, emphasized by the sheer scale and extent of the modulated surface. "The unnatural stricture of verticality," Wright wrote, "can not stand against natural horizontality."[29] This attitude sustained Wright's critique of Le Corbusier's Ville Contemporaine (1922) and the moneyed skyscraper metropolis—yet he included several tall buildings in Broadacre. His design for the residential St. Mark's Tower (1927–29) in New York is re-rendered as a rural building (plate 11), and several dot the model; the county seat, one of the few signs of governance, is also housed in a skyscraper (plate 12), the design reminiscent of Wright's 1926 Chicago Skyscraper Regulation studies. Slender and elegant, the buildings nevertheless carry little civic or rhetorical power in the horizontal expanse of the model; the solid line of the countryside simply dwarfs them.

One outdoor photograph of the model almost merges with the Wisconsin landscape of Taliesin: the one-point perspective of the highway armature points to a distant view of a worked plot of land, several farm buildings, and a tree line (fig. 6). This informal, working landscape is marred only by the power lines, which Wright explicitly forbade: "No poles. No wires in sight." This proscription is but one of several regulations for Broadacre inscribed on the exhibit panel titled A NEW FREEDOM FOR LIVING IN AMERICA (see plate 3). Other rules include the similarly prosaic "No glaring cement roads," but he also made far grander claims, such as "No landlord and tenant" and "No slum. No scum," more than implying a socio economic critique of the metropolitan order. These prohibitions, almost Biblical in tone, attest to Wright's pursuit of a fully planned landscape appropriate to "machine age civilization."[30] Lighting and materials are no less important to Broadacre than its techniques for the construction of a new social order. Most provocatively, the list begins and ends with the very modern conflict between property and freedom: "No private ownership of public needs" complements "No public ownership of private needs." If there is a utopianism in Broadacre, it is here, in a perfectly balanced social order, but for Wright, this was an achievable aesthetic and political undertaking: the whole, he wrote, rests on "general decentralization as an applied principle and architectural reintegration of all units into one fabric."[31] And, finally, this monumental coherence is made possible by the "county architect"—bringing together the Jeffersonian unit of land and civic organization with the uniquely qualified leader; man "must see life as the architect . . . harmonious with nature," Wright wrote.[32]

■■■■

Broadacre embodies a radically individualist thread of Progressivism based on a critique of the metropolis and a new role for land subdivision. Wright called for a "more ordered freedom," claiming land—acres, not blocks and lots—from among the disintegrating physical and intellectual order of metropolitan civilization.[33] The basis of his ordering was a logic of division and delineated territory not unlike the natural area, the neighborhood unit, or the superblock offered by contemporary urbanists, but for Wright, Broadacre's landscape emerged from the individual homestead rather than the urban neighborhood. This was how he joined democracy and capital into a new organic social system, creating a city unencumbered by overarching political or financial institutions. Broadacre entered the historical struggle to manage land under capital based on the capacities of individuals to act and, where needed, to embrace the actions of others.

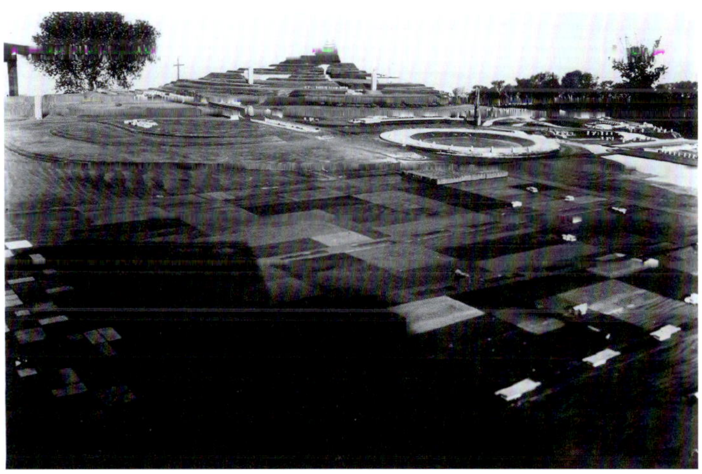
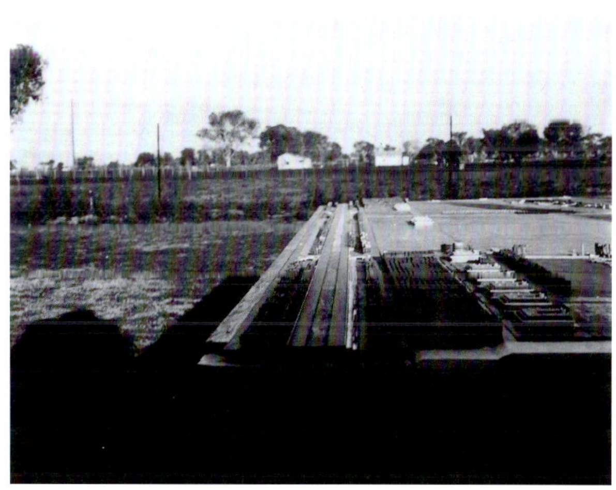

Figs. 5. and 6. Broadacre City. Project. 1929–35. Model under construction showing automobile objective (left) and arterial highway (right). Photographs by Roy E. Peterson

Notes

Many thanks to Lauren Kogod and Alexander Wood.

1. Frank Lloyd Wright, *The Disappearing City* (New York: W. F. Payson, 1932), p. 47.
2. Statistical Abstract of the United States, U.S. Department of Commerce, 1930.
3. This phrase is inscribed on "A New Freedom-for Living in America," panel of Broadacre City model, 1935, Frank Lloyd Wright Foundation Archives (The Museum of Modern Art | Avery Architectural & Fine Arts Library, Columbia University, New York). On symmetry, see Frank Lloyd Wright, "Broadacre City," *Architectural Record* 77 (April, 1935), p. 244.
4. Frank Lloyd Wright, *Modern Architecture: Being the Kahn Lectures for 1930* (Princeton, N.J.: Princeton University Press, 1931), pp. 108–09.
5. Wright, *The Disappearing City*, pp. 4, 63.
6. Ibid., p. 20.
7. John M. Gries and James Ford, eds., *Slums, Large-Scale Housing and Decentralization* (Washington, D.C.: President's Conference on Home Building and Home Ownership, 1932), pp. 4, 66–71.
8. See State of New York, *Report of the Commission of Housing and Regional Planning to Governor Alfred E. Smith* (Albany, N.Y.: J. B. Lyon, 1926) and *Survey Graphic* (May 1925).
9. Wright, *The Disappearing City*, p. 4.
10. Ibid., p. 32
11. See Eugenie Ladner Birch, "Radburn and the American Planning Movement: The Persistence of an Idea," *Journal of the American Planning Association* 46 (October 1980): 424–39.
12. Clarence A. Perry, "The Neighborhood Unit: A Scheme of Arrangement for the Family-Life Community," in *Regional Survey of New York and Its Environs*, vol. 7 (New York: Committee on the Regional Plan of New York and Its Environs, 1929), p. 56; see also the residential diagram by Marcus Whiffen on p. 36.
13. There is a wide literature on the rhetoric and methods of identifying blight. See Wendell E. Pritchett, "The 'Public Menace' of Blight: Urban Renewal and the Private Uses of Eminent Domain," *Yale Law and Policy Review* 21, no. 1 (2003): 13–21.
14. See John D. Fairfield, "Alienation of Social Control: The Chicago Sociologists and the Origins of Urban Planning," *Planning Perspectives* 7 (1992): 418–34; and Sudhir Venkatesh, "Chicago's Pragmatic Planners: American Sociology and the Myth of Community," *Social Science History* 25, no. 2 (Summer 2001): 275–313.
15. Harland Bartholomew, "Toward the Reconstruction of New York's Lower East Side, Part I: An Analysis of the Existing Conditions," *Architectural Forum* 57 (July 1932): 26–32.
16. See Richard Plunz, *A History of Housing in New York City* (New York: Columbia University Press, 1990), pp. 164–246.
17. "Wright's Model of Future City Goes on Display," *New York Herald Tribune*, April 14, 1935, p. 23A.
18. Wright, *The Disappearing City*, p. 96.
19. Neil Levine, "Wright's First Urban Design Initiative: The Development Plan for the Roberts Block, 1896," in Levine, *The Urbanism of Frank Lloyd Wright* (Princeton N.J.: Princeton University Press, 2015), pp. 8–13. Jonathan Hughes, "The Great Land Ordinances," in *Essays on the Economy of the Old Northwest*, ed. David C. Klingman and Richard K. Vedder (Ohio University Press, 1987), pp. 1–15.
20. Frank Lloyd Wright, "An Autobiography, Book Six: Broadacre City (1943)," reprinted in *Frank Lloyd Wright: Collected Writings*, vol. 4, *1939–1949*, ed. Bruce Brooks Pfeiffer (New York: Rizzoli, 1994), p. 252.
21. Donald Leslie Johnson, "Frank Lloyd Wright's Community Planning," *Journal of Planning History* 3, no. 1 (February 2004): 3–28.
22. Wright, *The Disappearing City*, p. 80. Robert Fishman, *Urban Utopias in the Twentieth Century: Ebenezer Howard, Frank Lloyd Wright, and Le Corbusier* (New York: Basic Books, 1977), p. 133.
23. Wright, *The Disappearing City*, p. 46. See Pyotr Kropotkin, *Fields, Factories and Workshops, or Industry Combined with Agriculture and Brain Work with Manual Work* (New York: G. P. Putnam's Sons, 1901), p. 212.
24. Henry George, *Our Land and Land Policy, National and State* (San Francisco, 1871).
25. Silvio Gesell, *The Natural Economic Order*, trans. Philip Pye (San Antonio: Free Economy Publishing, 1934). In 1931 Gesell's American publisher, Hugo Fack, first issued a newsletter called *The Way Out*, issues of which are in the Wright archive.
26. On Radburn as the "town for the motor age," see "These Charming Homes," Advertisement, *New York Times*, May 19, 1929, p. RE9. For the "cellular city," see Perry, "The Neighborhood Unit," p. 31.
27. Frank Lloyd Wright, "Broadacre City," *Architectural Record* 77 (April 1935): 253.
28. Wright, *Modern Architecture: Being the Kahn Lectures*, p. 111.
29. Wright, *The Disappearing City*, p. 24.
30. Ibid., p. 10.
31. Wright, "Broadacre City," p. 253.
32. Wright, *The Disappearing City*, p. 42.
33. Wright, *Modern Architecture*, p. 112.

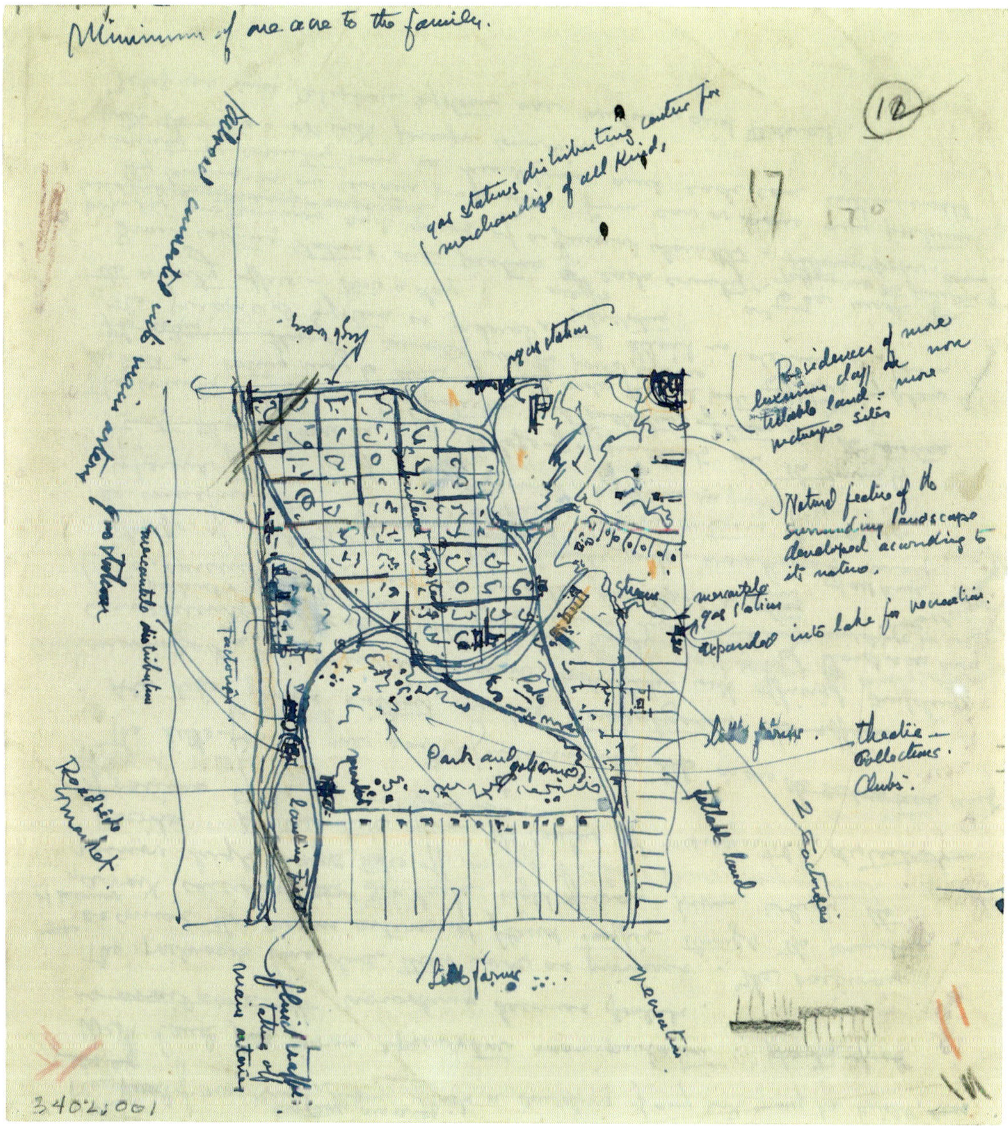

1. Broadacre City. Project, 1929–35. Annotated plan, 1934.
Ink and colored pencil on tracing paper, 9 3/8 x 8 1/2 in. (23.8 x 21.6 cm)

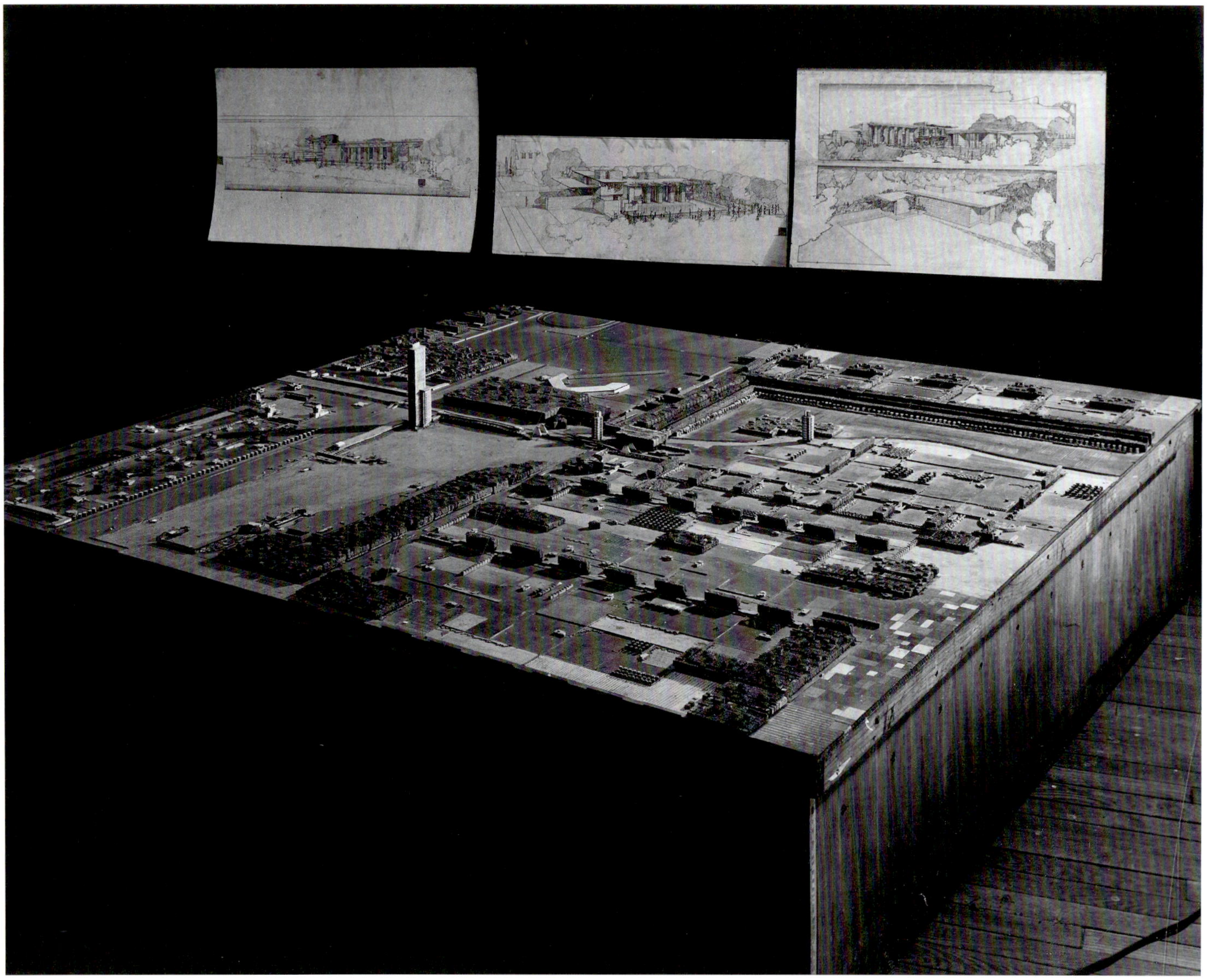

2. Broadacre City. Project, 1929–35. A section of the model installed

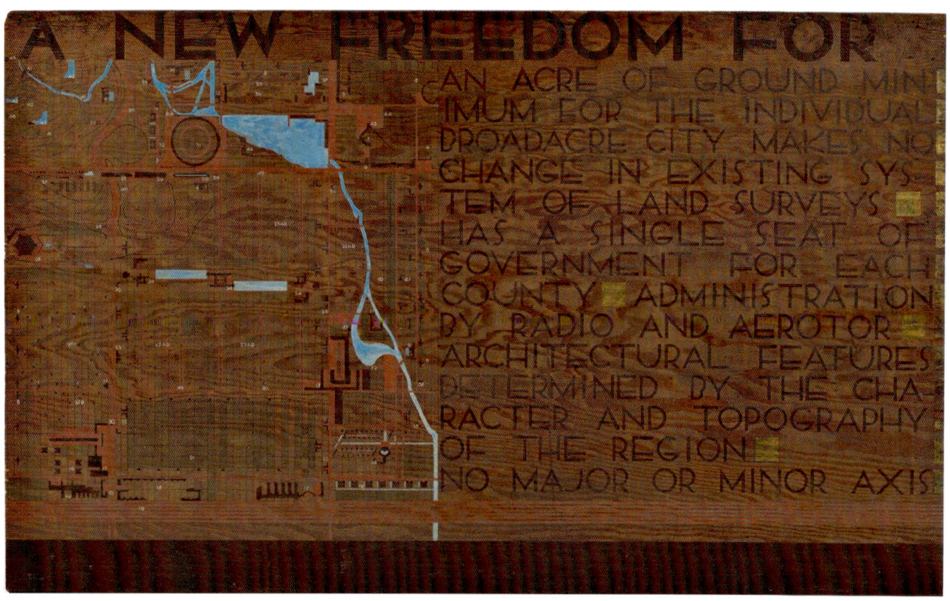

3. Broadacre City. Project, 1929–35. "A New Freedom for Living in America" display panels. Painted plywood, each approx. 48 in. x 6 ft. 7 in. x ⅝ in. (121.9 x 200.7 x 1.6 cm)

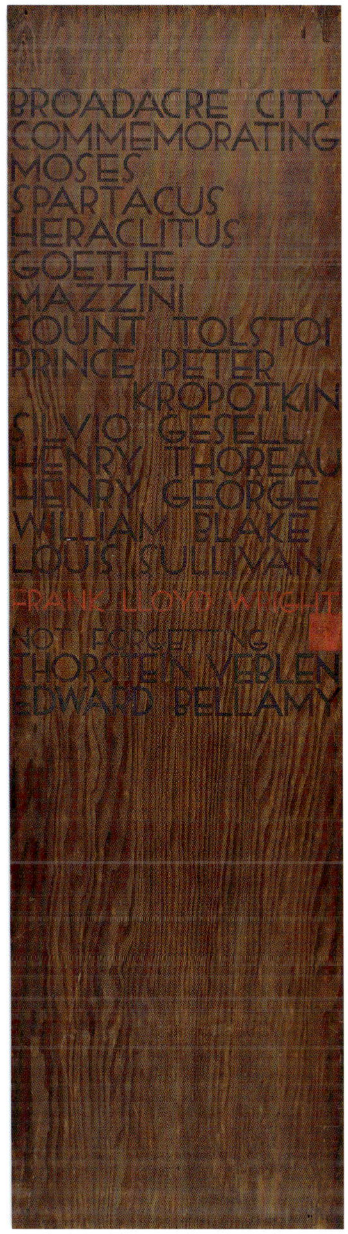

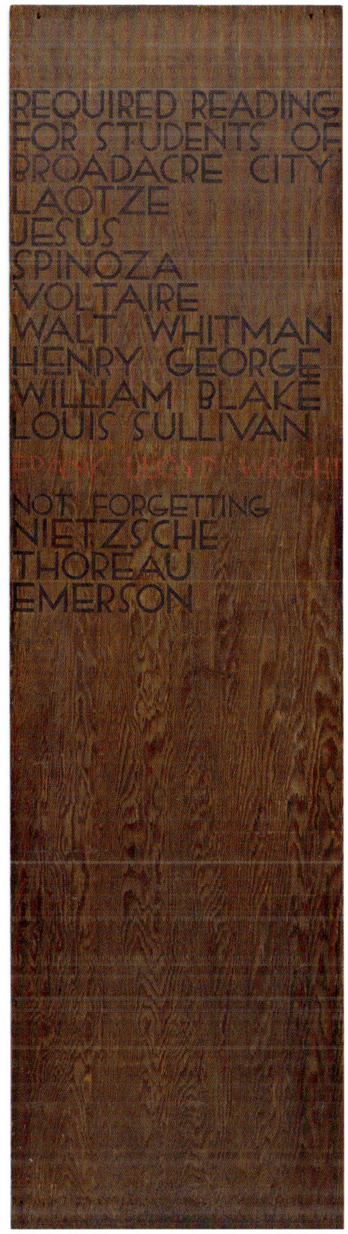

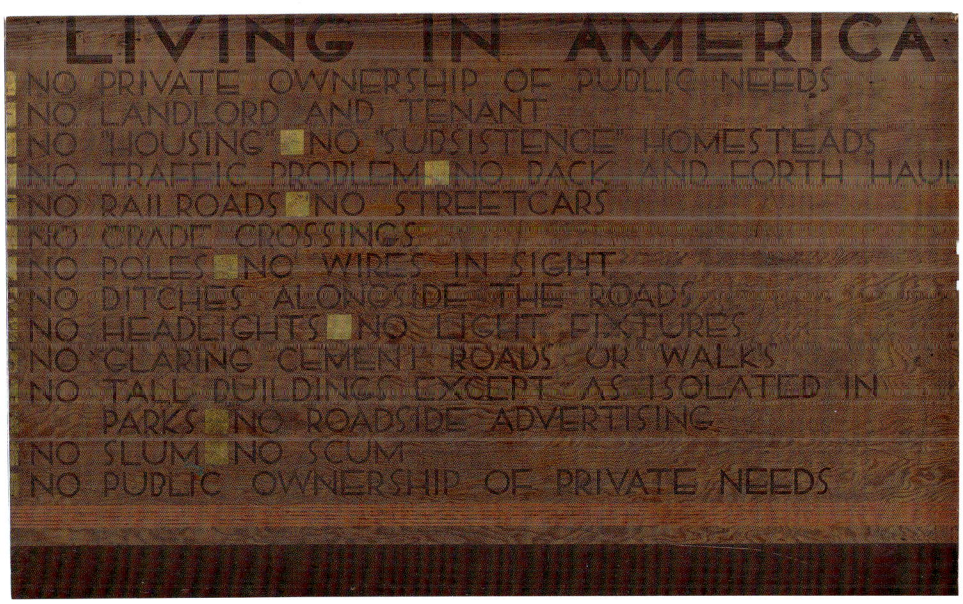

4. Broadacre City. Project, 1929–35. Dedication display panel. Painted plywood, 85 1/2 x 23 7/8 x 5/8 in. (217.2 x 60.6 x 1.6 cm)

5. Broadacre City. Project, 1929–35. "Required Reading" display panel. Painted plywood, 85 1/2 x 23 7/8 x 5/8 in. (217.2 x 60.6 x 1.6 cm)

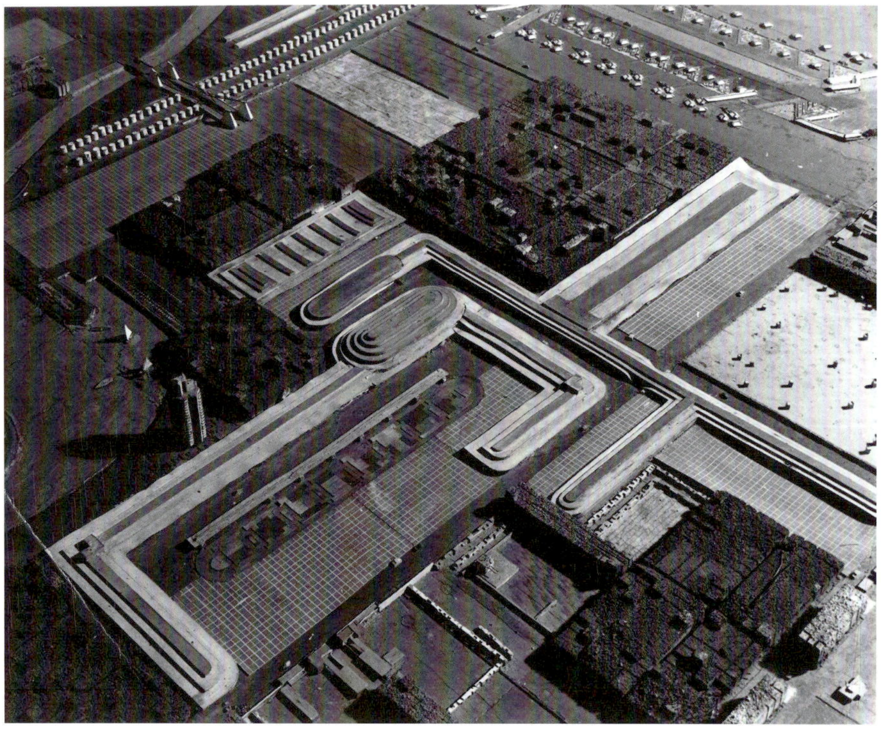

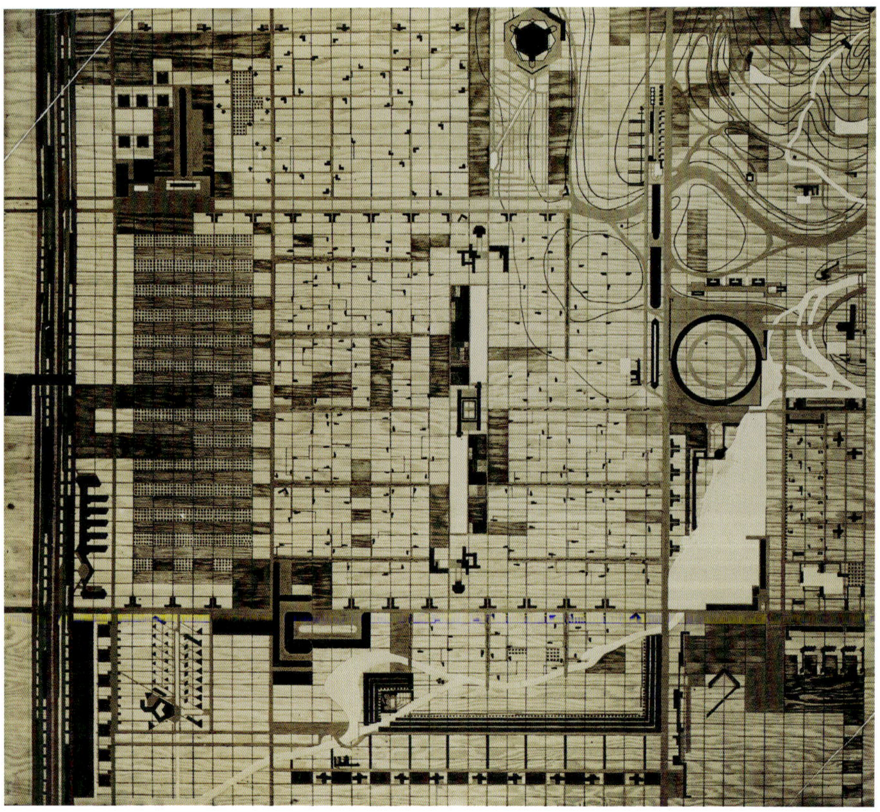

6. Broadacre City. Project, 1929–35. Detail of the model's roadside market

7. "Broadacre City: A New Community Plan." Illustration for *Architectural Record* 77 (April 1935)

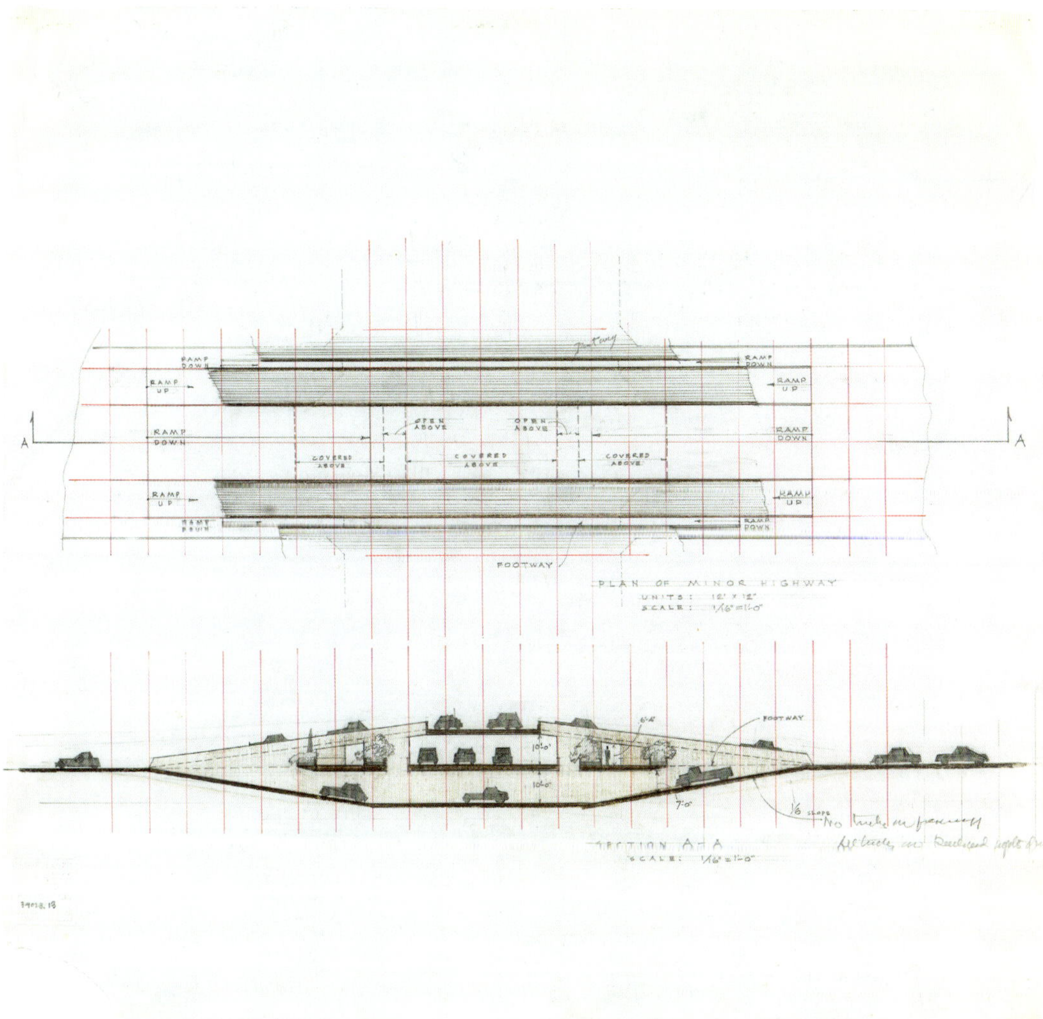

8. Broadacre City. Project, 1929–35. Plan and section of a minor highway.
Ink and marker on tracing paper, 20 ¼ x 21 in. (51.4 x 53.3 cm)

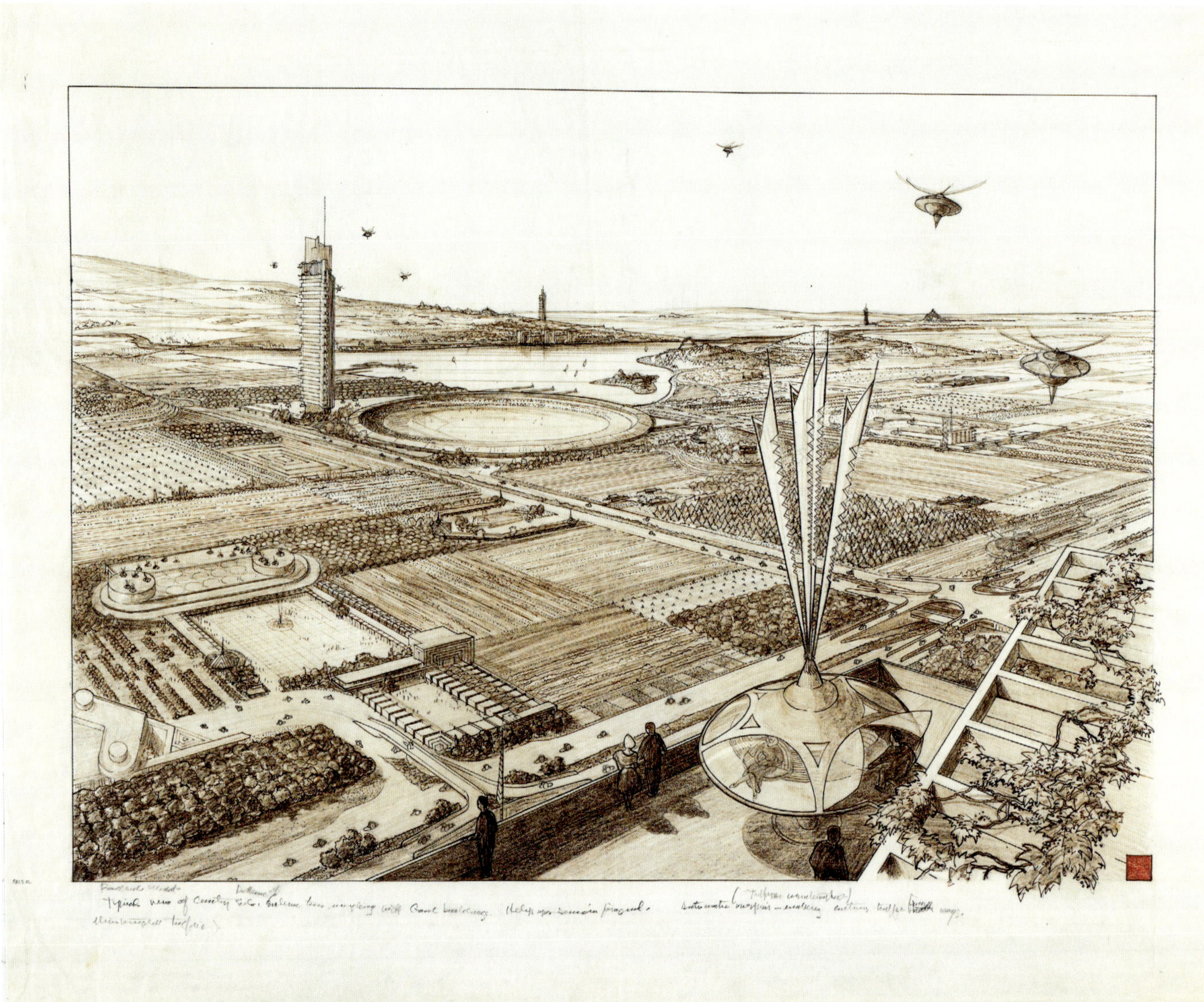

9. The Living City. Project, 1958. Aerial perspective.
Ink, pencil, and colored pencil on tracing paper,
32 1/8 x 38 5/8 in. (81.6 x 98.1 cm)

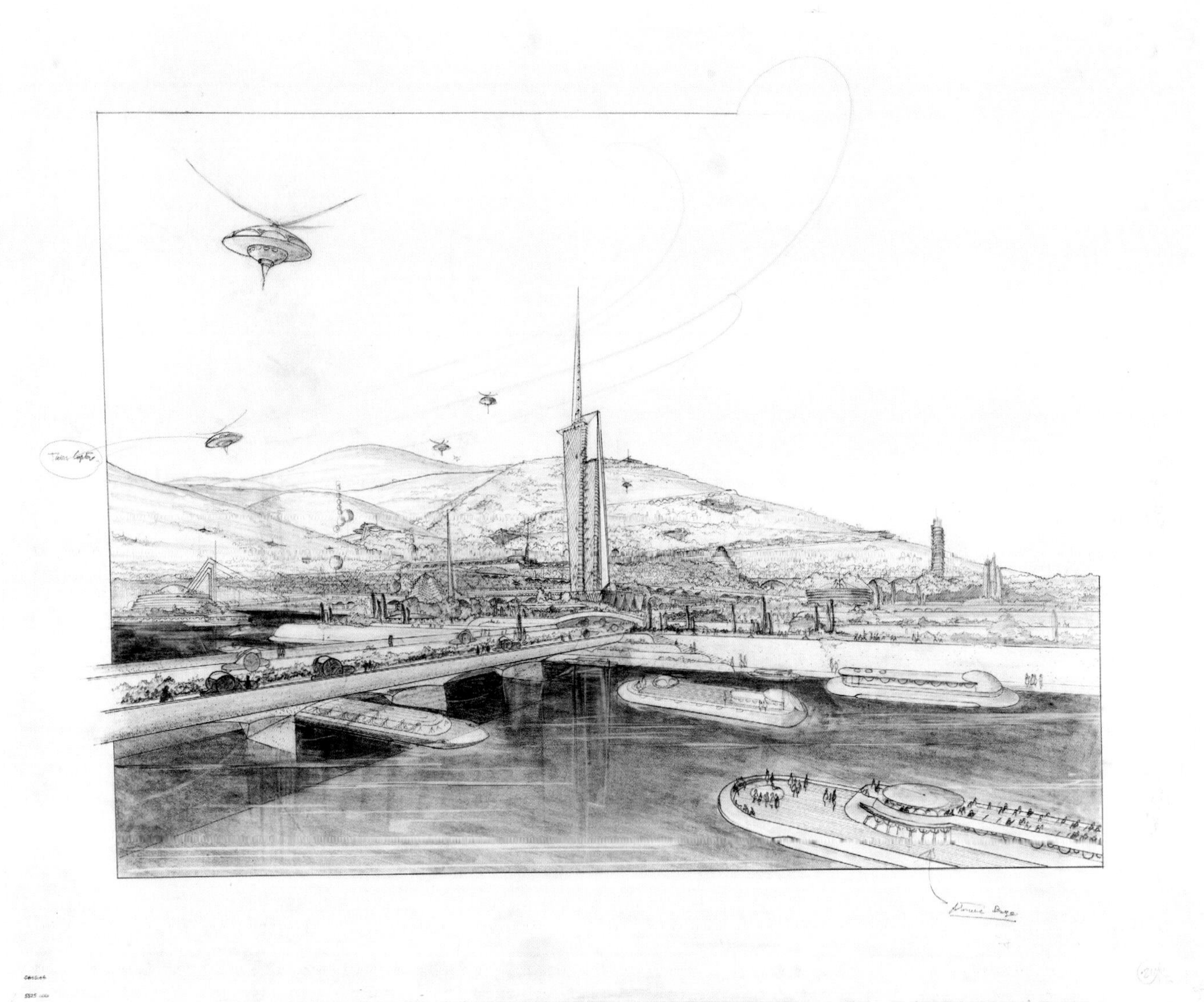

10. The Living City. Project, 1958. Perspective.
Pencil on tracing paper, 32 ¼ x 42 in. (81.9 x 106.7 cm)

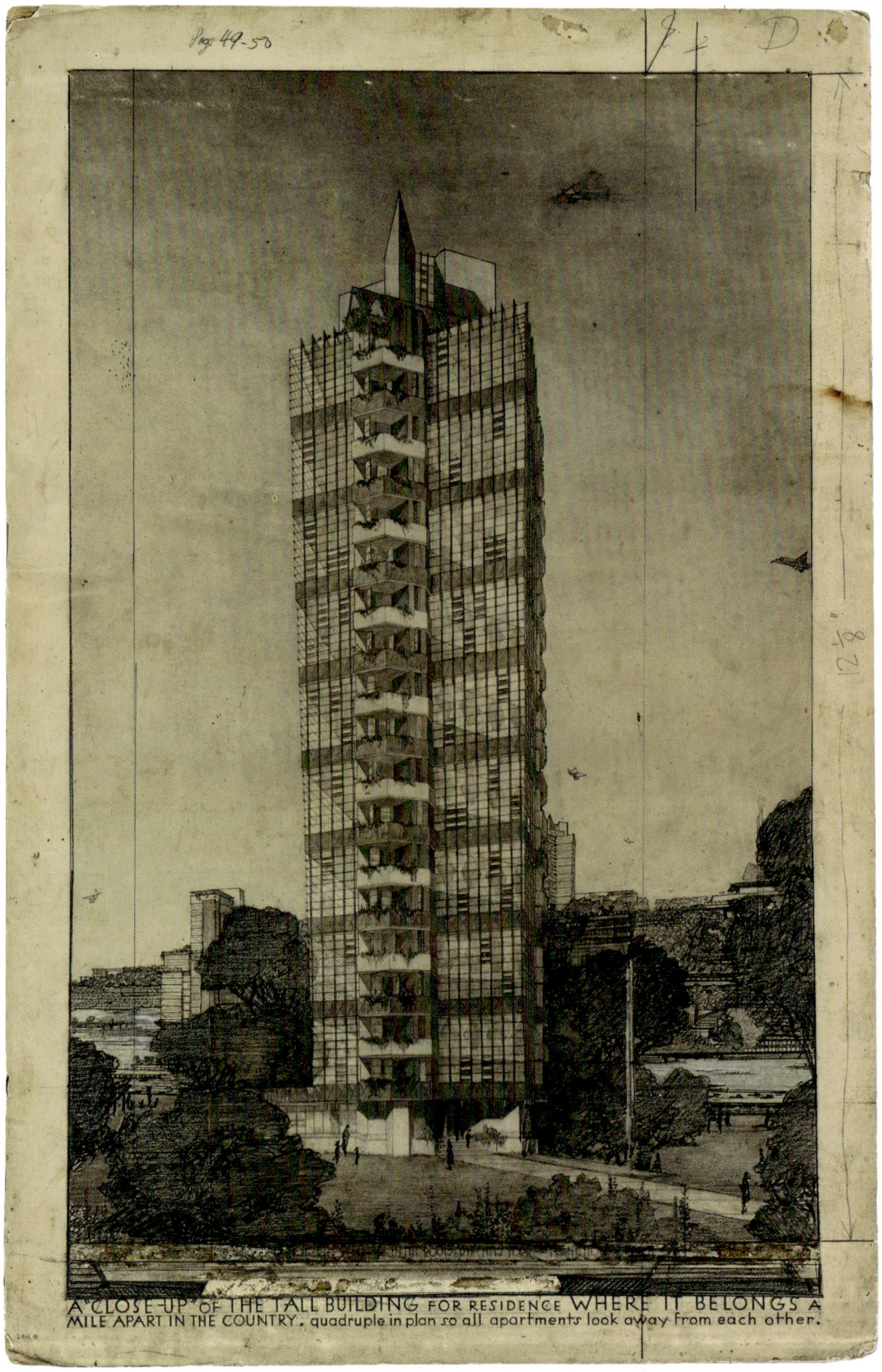

11. St. Mark's Tower, New York. Project, 1927–29. Perspective in the landscape.
Pencil and colored pencil on print mounted to composition board, 33 x 21 7/8 x 3/8 in.
(83.8 x 55.6 x 1 cm)

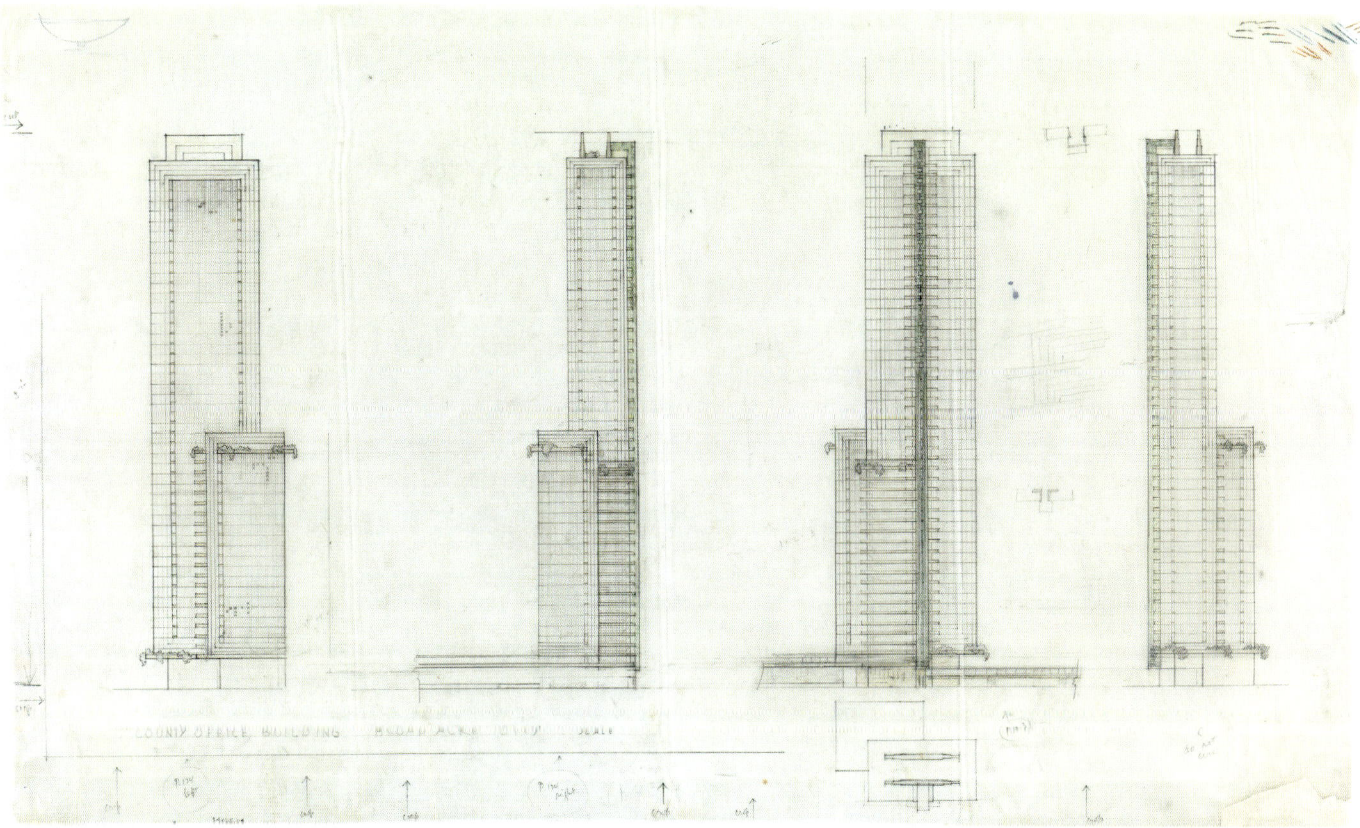

12. Broadacre City. Project, 1929–35. Elevations and schematic plan for the county office building.
Pencil and colored pencil on tracing paper, 20 ½ x 34 ¼ in. (52.1 x 87 cm)

BARRY BERGDOLL

READING "MILE-HIGH"

THE CHICAGO SKYLINE AND THE STAKES OF FAME

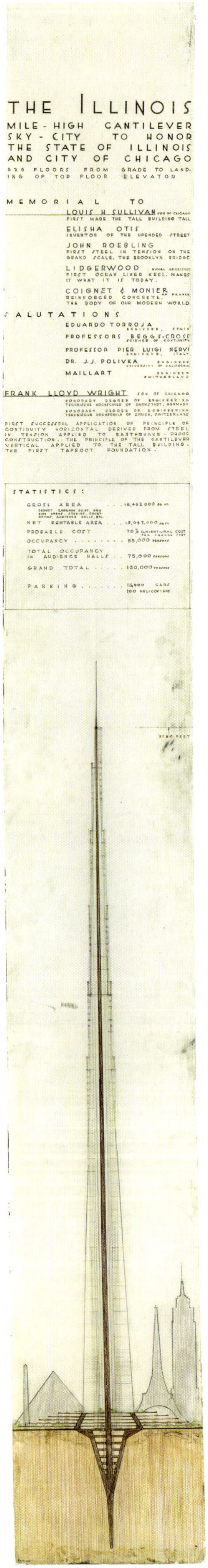

Left: The Mile-High Illinois, Chicago. Project, 1956. Section.
Pencil, colored pencil, and ink on tracing paper, 8 ft. 4 in. x 17 ½ in. (254 x 44.5 cm)

Opposite: Still from the CBS weekly game show *What's My Line?* June 3, 1956

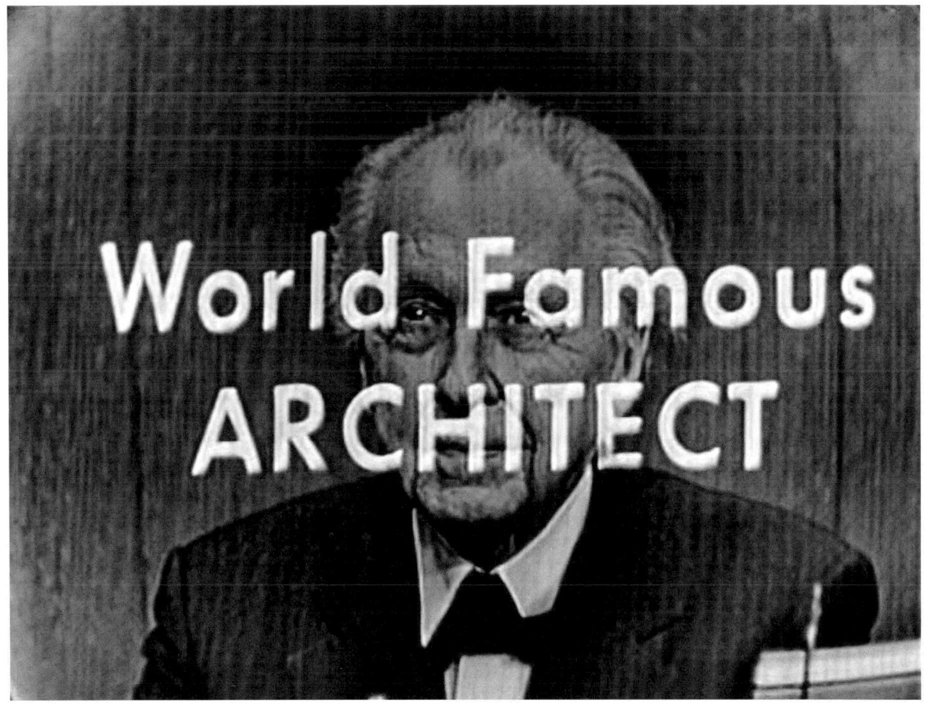

On October 16, 1956, at eighty-nine years of age, Frank Lloyd Wright mounted a press conference to announce a design for an unprecedented mile-high skyscraper—a feat still only halfway reached today in Dubai—for which he had no client, confirmed site, or sign of interest. Television cameras were on hand to record for future broadcast the story, which had been planted and building in the press for months, of Wright's plans for The Mile-High Illinois. Such a bold move was not out of character for an architect who had been preoccupied from almost his first years in practice with crafting his own reputation. Indeed, Wright had long sought to master not only continual architectural innovation but also a rapidly changing media landscape. For decades, his eventful life—divorces, fires, murders, and financial scandals—had captured headlines, as had a number of architectural designs considered so daring they courted structural failure. As early as 1938 Wright appeared on the cover of *Time*, only the second architect to enjoy that honor.[1] And in the final decade of his life he embraced television, appearing already in 1950 on the short-lived *The Faye Emerson Show*, one of the earliest celebrity talk shows.[2] Thus it came as no surprise that Wright had appeared a few months before the 1956 press conference as the mystery guest on the popular television game show *What's My Line?*, where his profession was revealed to the home audience as "World Famous Architect," while blindfolded panelists began to ask probing questions (above). His identity was guessed inadvertently when a panelist asked if he could be in a profession "such as design, or architecture, such as Frank Lloyd Wright." Wright and architecture had, for many Americans, become synonymous.

The key drawing of The Mile-High Illinois project is arguably neither the elevations nor the dramatic colored perspective showing the building in a Chicago stripped of its smaller high-rises to make way for a new prairie surrounding Wright's singular tower. Much can be learned from careful study of a very tall section through the skyscraper (opposite), where the upper third of the drawing, above the thin needle spire of the building, is taken up by a lengthy set of inscriptions, and the lower portion features a a panorama of famous architectural monuments. The inscriptions, which have never been the object of an analysis, reveal Wright's ambitions in this seemingly contradictory gesture of proposing the world's tallest tower even as he continued throughout the 1950s, with his Living City project, to avow a desire to see cities disappear in favor of urban dispersal.[3] This section, on a piece of paper more than 8 feet (2.4 meters) tall, reveals the structural approach that Wright considered one of his most significant inventions—a "taproot" system, analogous to that of a plant's, whereby a central mast is embedded deep in the ground and from which all of a building's floors are cantilevered. It also serves as a kind of graphic manifesto to counter those of European modernists such as Le Corbusier and Ludwig Mies van der Rohe, with whom Wright had been in an understated but intense rivalry since the 1920s. Wright juxtaposes two timescales. One is a pictorial landscape that makes it clear that Mile-High was destined to outpace centuries of striving for height: the Great Pyramid of Giza, the Washington Monument (itself derived from ancient Egyptian obelisks), the Eiffel Tower, and the Empire State Building (plate 2). The other is a set of written inscriptions, an honor roll of great figures past and present that makes it clear that Wright's design is the end result of decades of engineering thinking (plate 1). Rivalry with the Eiffel Tower and the Empire State Building had already been apparent in the marginalia sketches of the towers Wright drew up in proposals for the 1933 Chicago World's Fair, titled "A Century of Progress," for which he first thought of a skyscraper possibly a mile high (fig. 1).

Wright's pictorial timeline relates the history of the relationship of materials to the quest for an efficient monumental height. The Egyptians piled stone upon stone, finding the pyramidal shape most stable, while the Washington Monument, designed by Robert Mills in the 1840s, became the tallest masonry structure in the world at just over 555 feet (170 meters) high. Less than a year after it was finally opened, in 1888, that structure was surpassed by one of a vastly different nature, the great openwork of a tower in iron reaching 986 feet (300 meters). Eiffel's great publicity gesture would remain the world's tallest building until the 1930 completion of Manhattan's Chrysler Building, at 1,046 feet (319 meters), a title lost eleven months later to the Empire State Building, 1,250 feet (381 meters) and 102 stories tall, reaching to 1,454 feet (443 meters) with its antenna. Here the invention of the steel frame, pioneered in the 1880s in Chicago, achieved a height that would not be surpassed for another four decades, a time that would have been shortened had Wright been successful in winning a client for his proposed "cantilevered sky city": 1 mile (1,609 meters) high, with 528 stories to house 130,000 tenants, served by 56 atomic-powered elevators, garages for 15,000 cars, and two helipads for 50 helicopters each.

Was Wright contradicting himself? After all, it seemed when he first unveiled his Broadacre model at Rockefeller Center in 1935—a vision of decentralization—that he was offering an alternative to the high-rise city represented by the new skyscrapers of Manhattan or Chicago, and along with it a critique of capitalist land exploitation. Why an unprecedented piling of usable space on a small footprint, when expansion to the horizon seemed to him at once an American heritage and a future prospect?

Wright's inscriptions on the Mile-High drawing afford clues. He leads off with Louis Sullivan, a "son of Chicago" (although Sullivan was born in Boston), a moniker Wright would use also for himself. Sullivan is the only architect here, praised as the one who "first made the tall building tall." But Wright pursued a different path. As early as his 1913 design for the San Francisco Call Building—which he

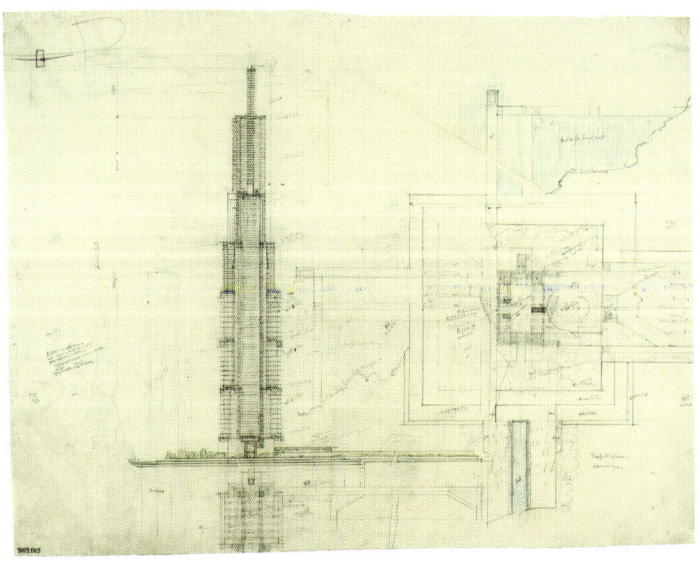

Fig. 1. Skyscraper for A Century of Progress, Chicago World's Fair. Project, 1931. Plans and elevation. Pencil and colored pencil on tracing paper, 27 3/4 x 35 in. (70.5 x 88.9 cm)

memorialized in a large wooden model featured over and over again in his museum exhibitions—he sought to bring architectural form and engineering structure into unity (fig. 2). Adopting a concrete frame designed by the architect rather than dressing a steel frame provided by engineers, as Sullivan had done, Wright announced a unity of expression and of professions: architect and engineer united. Wright pioneered an integrated concrete grid of thin members, resulting in a skeleton and facade that were one. In 1924, the year of Sullivan's death, Wright proposed a different solution for the National Life Insurance Company (plate 3), a self-standing frame draped with a non-structural transparent facade of glass—a curtain wall. Now he entered into competition with younger upstarts, the European avant-garde so notably absent from the Mile-High drawing: Mies van der Rohe, who, in 1921, submitted an entirely glazed triangular tower to the competition for what would have been Berlin's first high-rise (plate 4), and Le Corbusier, with his plan for a modern city made up of glazed towers, exhibited in Paris in 1922.[4] Wright's unrealized design was, in a sense, a belated alternative proposal to the victors in the Chicago Tribune Tower competition of 1922. He countered the masonry-clad frame of the selected design, under construction in 1924, with a luminous design of nearly the same height.

Wright's next tower design, 1927–29, was for a residential high-rise commissioned by the Church of St. Mark's-in-the-Bouwerie, in Manhattan, for which he had originally developed his radical taproot system (see p. 229, fig. 5) that would also figure prominently in the design for Mile-High. Here the central concrete mast that is driven deep in the ground is hollowed in part to accommodate elevator shafts. All floor plates were cantilevered off of this single support, freed of any vertical structure between core and periphery. As the facade was non-load bearing, not all floors needed to extend fully to the building's envelope,

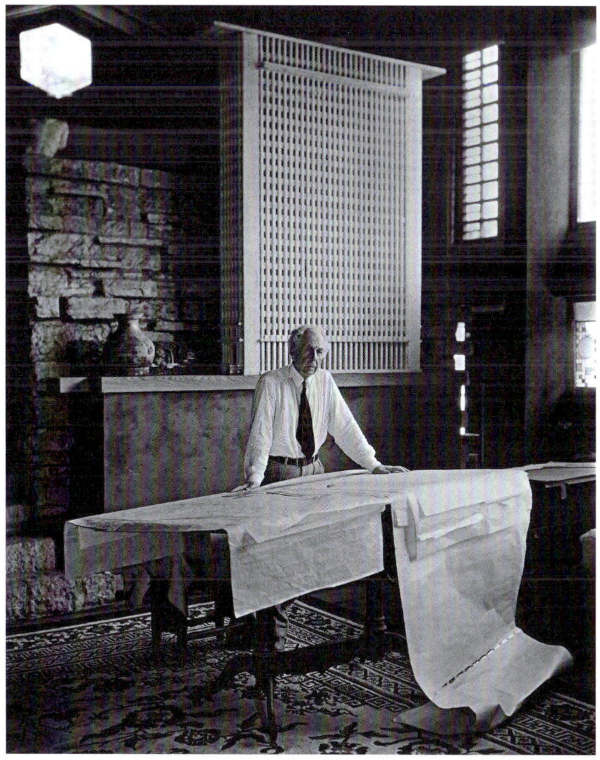

Fig. 2. Wright with a model of the San Francisco Call Building (1913). 1947. Photograph by Pedro E. Guerrero. Pedro E. Guerrero Archives

thereby allowing every other floor to be treated as a mezzanine thus creating double-height duplex apartments.

Although he had realized forms of his taproot structure in two built works by the time he appeared on *What's My Line?*—the Johnson Wax Research Tower of 1943–50 and the H. C. Price Company Tower, begun in 1952 and opened just a few weeks before the broadcast—Wright was frustrated that acclaim for skyscraper innovation seemed to be passing to others. Neither of his towers figured in Carl Condit's seminal 1952 study *The Rise of the Skyscraper: The Genius of Chicago Architecture from the Great Fire to Louis Sullivan*.[5] Even though Condit's account ostensibly stopped with Sullivan, he postulated an emerging "Second Chicago School." Both Sullivan's and Wright's careers had come to premature denouements, Condit maintained. For Wright, "a twenty-year exile in Japan and the Far West erased the memory of him. . . . Moreover his art had had no European counterpart, and Europe after all, was the source of all exciting new ideas."[6] Swiss historian Sigfried Giedion's account of the rise of modernism in *Space, Time, and Architecture* (1941) also claimed that the early innovations of Chicago were taken up most productively by the European avant-garde.[7] Giedion saw Wright's most important work far in the past, and celebrated instead Walter Gropius, by then at Harvard University, as the face of the future. Mies—whom Wright had introduced to the Chicago public in 1938 with a terse "Ladies and Gentleman I give you Mies van der Rohe, but for me there would be no Mies van der Rohe—certainly none here tonight"—was also increasingly in the limelight.[8] For Condit, Mies, by this time at the Illinois Institute of Technology (IIT), in Chicago, was the leader of the Second Chicago School.

If Giedion celebrated the key role of engineers, Wright responded by crafting a heroic lineage of engineering advances waiting to be synthesized by a new genius architect. After Sullivan, the next step was taken by Elisha Otis, inventor, in 1852, of what Wright terms on the drawing "the upended street." In the 1940s the Otis Elevator Company had solved the complex challenge of integrating an elevator into the concrete core of the Johnson Wax tower. And a week before the 1956 press conference in Chicago, Wright thought to consult them on Mile-High. They replied with sangfroid in a detailed four-page letter:

We have checked the sketches you have turned over to us . . . and note the following: 1.) It tapers from a four-sided base, shaped like a kite, starting at the sixth level approximately 370 feet on the long sides up to a triangle approximately 24 feet on a side. 2.) [. . .] We have assumed a straight line decrease in population from approximately 8,000 people on the bottom floor to six people on the 100th floor. 3.) It is noted that the elevators go up in a vertical line, while the building wall recedes, leaving the elevator exposed on the building exterior. With car enclosures of transparent plastic—the occupants can look over the surrounding area. This will, of course, require the cars being completely air-conditioned for both winter and summer. It might work out better to also completely enclose the exposed hoistways with thermal protective glass.[9]

Next comes John Roebling, celebrated as a designer who, with his Brooklyn Bridge, spanned a huge distance by using the tensile strength of steel. He is followed by the little known V. V. Lidgerwood, who perfected a rigid keel system for steel steamships. Le Corbusier had used ships as metaphors of functional design; for Wright they were parallel to his own incorporation of engineering into a daring new structural system that could become, like so many forms of nature, lighter and lighter with evolution. It was left to the next on the list, unrelated French inventors paired here, François Coignet and Joseph Monier, to combine the strength of concrete in compression with that of steel in tension, thereby pioneering reinforced concrete. Coignet had developed a system of reinforced concrete in France in the 1850s, first used in the United States two decades later.[10] Monier was one of the first to realize that in a reinforced concrete slab, forces act differently than in a system of supports and spans. For Wright, this marked the dawn of a new architectural epoch.

The remaining names on the sheet are twentieth-century engineers who were advancing the science of reinforced concrete toward what Wright saw as the ultimate goal: finding form for this "body of our modern world." Wright arranged the figures in the chronological order of their contributions. But it is more revealing to reconstruct the order of Wright's engagement with the Spaniard Eduardo Torroja, the Italian Pier Luigi Nervi, the Czech J. J. Polivka, and the Swiss Robert Maillart, as well as the lesser-known Americans George Erle Beggs and Hardy Cross—whose work he encountered first, in 1930, at the decisive moment when he was invited to Princeton University to deliver the Kahn Lectures, under the title "Modern Architecture."[11] Although the fifth of the lectures addressed what Wright called "the tyranny of the skyscraper," his experience at Princeton helped him advance the quest for efficient height. It was there that he met Beggs, one of the most inventive civil engineers of the period. As early as 1922, Beggs, who was professor of civil engineering at the university from 1914–39, invented a means of predetermining the stress resistance of bridges, dams, and similar structures by modeling complicated engineering structures in paper. On Wright's drawing, Beggs is paired with Cross, professor of structural engineering at the University of Illinois, best known for his work on the moment distribution method and other means of solving dimensions for continuous beams and frames.[12] Both Beggs and Cross perfected the physical science theory behind the realm of continuity in materials and structure that, in Wright's view, would bring structural science into harmony with the underlying laws of natural creation.

Wright remained in touch with Beggs for some years, notably inviting him to visit Taliesin during his planned attendance at an engineering conference in Madison.[13] For detailed calculations he turned to the next figure on the list: J. J. (Jaroslav Josef) Polivka, a Czech émigré engineer, who was to play a decisive role in the last two decades of Wright's quest to advance organic architecture through engineering (fig. 3). Wright was preoccupied with the plasticity of seashells and cocoons as ideal structural examples. Polivka, who would apply the geometry of ruled surfaces to rethinking bridge design, later wrote of a similar fascination with nature in a letter to Wright: "Take for example cobwebs of a spider which definitely should be studied by an engineer whose specialty is to build suspension bridges."[14] Their collaboration began in the most unlikely of ways. In 1946 *Architectural Forum* published an article detailing some of the difficulties Wright had had with engineers over his unconventional structural solutions. The article relates that when steel company engineers determined the daring cantilevers of Fallingwater structurally unsound, Wright sent the client, Edgar Kaufmann, a box to bury in the cornerstone of the house with a letter to posterity, "so that when the house is torn down 2,000 years from now people will know what complete damn fools these engineers are."[15] Polivka, who had never met Wright, dashed off an enthusiastic letter: "I am admiring you as an engineer, although according to a quotation in the last *Forum* issue, these engineers are complete damn fools. . . . You may be right since the Engineers . . . are very seldom guided by the eternal laws of the Nature. . . . [He] knows only beams, girders, columns, and any deviation from his everyday tools is considered as unusual,

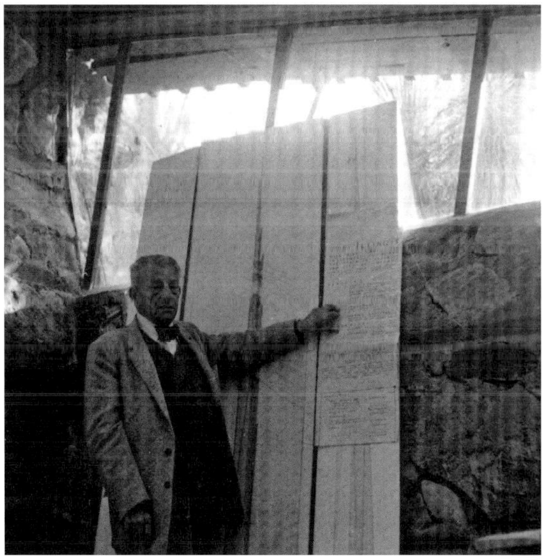

Fig. 3. J. J. Polivka (Czech, 1886–1960) with drawings of The Mile-High Illinois, n.d. University Archives, State University of New York at Buffalo

crazy, or dangerous. Your work confirms and fortifies my ideas and that's why I am so grateful to you."[16] The letter brought in return an immediate invitation (or veritable convocation) to Taliesin West, and began a professional relationship that lasted until Wright's death.

In late April 1946 Polivka made a first visit to Taliesin West and agreed to calculate and verify the experimental structures of a spiral for the Solomon R. Guggenheim Museum (1943–59) in New York. Soon he was an active partner, helping to eliminate visible supports for the coiled ramp, confirming after theoretic reflection and actual modeling that "the tangential curvature of the ramp imparts to the plate the valuable characteristics of a shell, thus reducing the intensities of bending moments and deflections."[17] Here the science of continuity in concrete plates was meeting not only the analogy of the nautilus but also the new science of thin concrete shells, of which the famed engineer Pier Luigi Nervi was a specialist, meriting him too a place on the drawing. Polivka would work closely with Wright as consulting engineer on a number of projects, including the Johnson Wax tower.

In 1947 Polivka, in turn, invited Wright to collaborate on a bid for a new bridge being planned across the San Francisco Bay to relieve traffic on the San Francisco-Oakland Bay Bridge (plates 5, 6). "I feel the new crossing would need your creative genius to become the apotheosis of democratic architecture and engineering," he wrote, demonstrating that he knew how to appeal to Wright's ego.[18] The project extended over years—and many headlines—but even if it was never to be, it arguably linked, in Wright's mind, large-span bridge construction and new challenges for high-rise building. In 1949 Elizabeth Mock, who had been an apprentice at Taliesin as well as a curator and, briefly, director of MoMA's architecture department, published *The Architecture of Bridges*, a history of a progressive struggle for ever lighter structures and ever greater spans. Mock is clearly in tune with Wright and Polivka when she writes, "Most engineers' bridges simply cut through space. Their interest is in flat elevation rather than in the depth plane"; Wright's work, first at Taliesin in a bridge projected over the Wisconsin River (1947) and now in California, "is quite a different matter, for it gave space shape and meaning."[19] According to Mock, Wright had invented what he called a "butterfly bridge," "because its outstretched wings concentrate the load upon a deep central girder." She goes on to explain, "The elegance of the design is best evident in the cross-section. . . . The outer skin is no inert surface, but a 'stressed skin' that works as one with the light stiffening ribs. Structure becomes continuous, flowering out of the plastic nature of the material," consistent with "Wright's conception of architecture as organic."[20] Although Wright had previously designed bridges, Polivka took him to a new development of the idea of continuity in this extraordinary span that crosses the Bay as a huge double helix. Its hollow pier section provides space for the threading through of a new regional railway system, while at mid-crossing it sports a suspended public park (plates 7, 8). Bridges, like so many of Wright's buildings, not only were formed on principles analogous to nature but would themselves flower and leaf in season.[21] Polivka admired the pioneering structural engineer Eduardo Torroja, whose works in Spain from the 1930s were not only striking for their daring sculptural form but also advanced the application of principles of continuity of structure to the use of reinforced concrete. Polivka was keen to introduce Torroja's ideas to America, even serving as the translator of one of his books, *Philosophy of Structures*.[22] Polivka was eager that Wright and Torroja meet, not the least because just as Wright prided himself on his Imperial Hotel (1913–23) in Tokyo having survived the Great Kanto earthquake of 1923, so too had Torroja's hippodrome withstood bombardments in the Spanish Civil War (fig. 4). Polivka offered Wright one of Torroja's books, and in spring 1950 Torroja himself came to visit, an occasion Polivka caught in snapshots, including one of the group visiting Wright's V. C. Morris Gift Shop (1948–49) in San Francisco.[23] Wright and Polivka later took Torroja's work as the starting point for their next collaboration, an unrealized project for a great cantilevered structure at the Belmont Park racetrack in New York, to be financed in large measure by Harry F. Guggenheim, Solomon Guggenheim's nephew.

The last inscription on Wright's monumental drawing—a type of graphic autobiography—is nothing short of his own résumé. It cites his recent honorary degrees, not from architecture schools but from engineering faculties at Darmstadt and Zurich, and proclaims his mile-high design as the FIRST SUCCESSFUL APPLICATION OF PRINCIPLE OF CONTINUITY HORIZONTAL DERIVED FROM STEEL IN TENSION APPLIED TO EARTHQUAKE-PROOF CONSTRUCTION. THE PRINCIPLE OF THE CANTILEVER VERTICAL APPLIED TO THE TALL BUILDING. THE FIRST TAPROOT FOUNDATION. Thus the drawing becomes almost an oversize patent application, as well as a scroll to be unraveled by posterity.

It is, finally, to the immediate political context that we must turn to understand what was at stake. In April 1955 Richard J. Daley was elected Mayor of Chicago, and within days he not only shook up the city's administration but began a building program such as the city had never seen issuing from municipal government. *Fortune* magazine lauded Daley: "What is happening in Chicago amounts, in many ways, to a rebuilding of the city. Chicago has needed the rebuilding in the worst way; it is getting it in a big way. . . . All over the city there is a fury of blasting and leveling."[24] By 1956 the city was entering "the busiest year of building ever in Chicago history, bigger than the years after the Fire. New construction would top a billion dollars."[25] Wright began to plan his own bid, and turned for support to an old hand at skyscraper hype, the *Chicago Sunday Tribune*, which had commissioned its own skyscraper in the 1920s to be "the most beautiful building in the modern world."[26] Is it any mistake that Wright's outsize building with no client should be labeled by its architect as THE ILLINOIS? A reporter was summoned to Taliesin for a scoop a full six weeks before Wright's press conference and the *Tribune*'s front page reported "Wright Plans a Mile-High Building Here":

Full of vigor and plans for the future, as usual, the octogenarian architect whose activities have heightened with advancing years, said he has a mile high building on his drawing boards, conceiving it as a 510 story structure to provide office space for 100,000 employees of the state of Illinois, Cook county, and the city of Chicago. . . . "The Empire State Building would be a mouse by comparison," Wright said. . . . Long noted as a foe of skyscrapers, which he once described as weeds growing one upon another, Wright described his projected Goliath of skyscrapers as the ultimate in centralization. "If we're going to have centralization, why not quit fooling around and have it, because it looks like it will take a century to decentralize as it is."[27]

On September 3 the *Chicago Daily Tribune* proclaimed it "the big plan Chicago has been waiting for—the one plan which will show the world that we really do intend to become the greatest city ever. . . . Chicago will have in its possession the engineering marvel of the world—a tourist attraction drawing more visitors to our city than any world's fair."[28] The same day, reports appeared in the *New York Herald Tribune* and the *Los Angeles Times*. "Is Wright Wrong?" a *Washington Post and Times-Herald* headline asked. "The airplane people don't think too much of the plan. They point out that, descending from a mile up in the air, a man is apt to get an earache, if not a nosebleed. 'It might help if the elevator operators passed

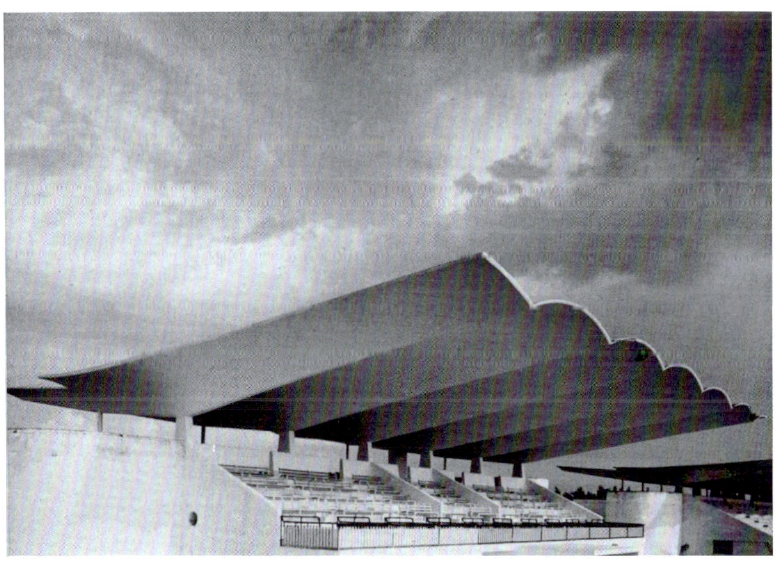

Fig. 4. Eduardo Torroja (Spanish, 1899–1961). Zarzuela Hippodrome, Madrid. 1934–35

out chewing gum on the trip down,' an airline executive said."[29] The following week both *Time* and *Newsweek* joined the growing chorus. "Told that Chicago's Mayor Richard J. Daley had been cautiously noncommittal about the proposition, Wright asked: 'Who's Daley? He couldn't be very bright if he's mayor of Chicago,'" *Time* reported in its "People" gossip section.[30] His assessment, however, would soon change.

By mid-September 1956 the papers reported that Wright would give details of his proposal at a press conference at the Hotel Sherman, the largest hotel west of New York and a center of Chicago society. The genius behind the scenes was Chicago architect Jesse (Cary) Caraway, an early fellow at Taliesin (1935–42), who a year earlier had shown his skills masterminding a fundraiser to help pay off Wright's disputed tax bill.[31] Now even grander publicity was at stake for the future of Taliesin, with Wright seeking to secure an endowment for the Fellowship as well as the property. According to the *Tribune*, a dinner would climax a three-day exhibit of Wright's works.[32] Mayor Daley would also proclaim October 17 as Frank Lloyd Wright Day. Finally, details about a spectacular new mile-high tower began to flow, as the competition intensified with those who were dominating the building boom—including Mies, who was still receiving kudos for his residential towers at 860 and 880 Lake Shore Drive (fig. 5). "I detest seeing the boys fooling around and making their buildings look like boxes," Wright told the press. "Why not design a building that really is tall? . . . Long ago I observed trees after the passing of a cyclone. Those with deep taproots were the ones that survived."[33] He explained his building would go at least 160 feet (48.8 meters) into the earth; indeed, on Wright's sectional rendering the taproot is depicted as almost as deep in the earth as the Empire State Building is tall in the sky. "The external sheathing of the various floors will be suspended on wire. The whole will give the design impression of a great tree, with the floors radiating as limbs, and the sides hanging in suspension like leaves."[34]

The competition between Wright and Mies came to the fore and the designs became more daring. In 1954 Mies had proposed a dazzlingly wide clear-span building to replace the Chicago Convention Center (fig. 6), site of the 1952 Republican National Convention that nominated Dwight D. Eisenhower. Mayor Daley now hoped to rebuild it to host the Democratic National Convention of 1956. At IIT, Mies was forming a school, and "Miesian" was becoming an adjective to describe architecture emanating from Chicago. If Mies was trying to win on the horizontal plane, Wright would now, paradoxically enough, seek to stand out by exceptional height. "I predict that before long, there will be not one, but hundreds of buildings like the 'Illinois' erected everywhere—not necessarily a mile high, but perhaps a quarter or a half-mile high or even less," Wright explained to the *Tribune*.[35] In response to Daley's declaration of Frank Lloyd Wright Day, Wright changed his position, proclaiming, "This is the only Chicago Mayor since 1893 who has boldly enlisted himself on the side of culture."[36]

Every bit as brash as Wright's rhetoric was the 22-foot-high (6.7-meter-high) photographic enlargement of a nearly 9-foot-tall (2.7-meter-tall) perspective drawing Wright had completed days earlier and that now towered over the guests at dinner, as well as over the architect and the mayor at the press conference (plates 9–12).[37] This perspective was perhaps less erudite than the section analyzed here, but it was more startling and photogenic. Local television stations vied to have the prop brought to their studios, and debate about the project continued in the press for days. Images of the rendering began to appear not only in U.S. newspapers and magazines but were solicited abroad, notably by the *Illustrated London News*. It showed not only the "Illinois"—Caraway

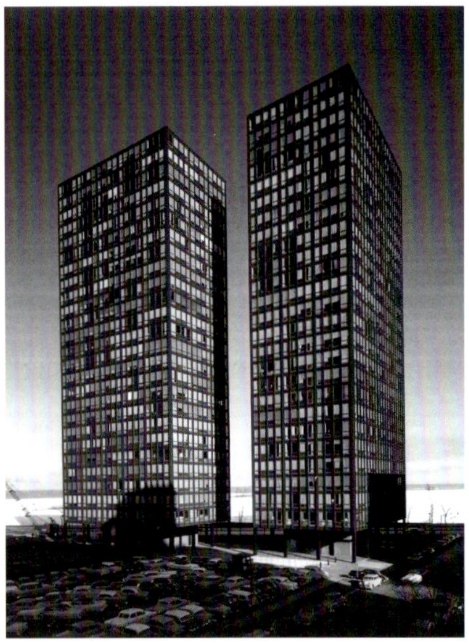

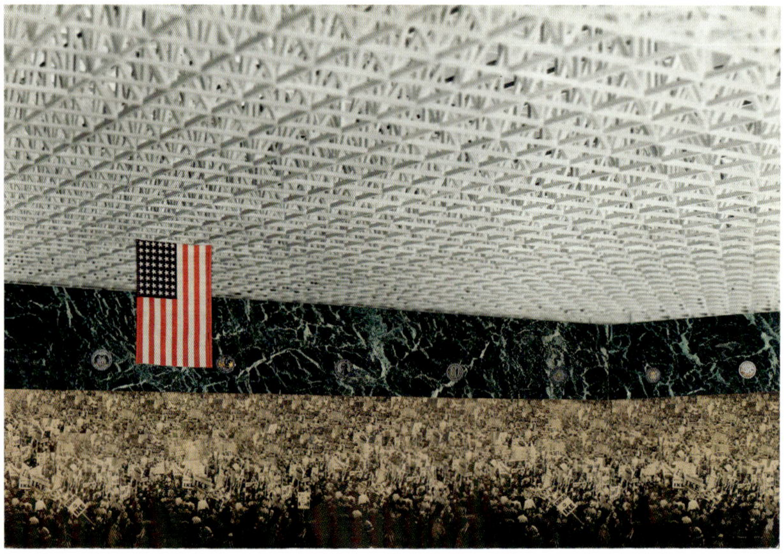

Fig. 5. Ludwig Mies van der Rohe (American, born Germany, 1886–1969).
860/880 Lake Shore Drive Apartment Buildings, Chicago. c. 1948–51. Aerial view.
The Museum of Modern Art, New York. Architecture and Design Study Center

Fig. 6. Ludwig Mies van der Rohe. Convention Hall, Chicago. Project, 1954. Interior perspective.
Cut-and-pasted reproductions, photograph, and paper mounted on composition board, 33 x 48 in. (83.8 x 121.9 cm).
The Museum of Modern Art, New York. Mies van der Rohe Archive. Gift of the architect

called it a "cloudscraper"—but also, in the background, a second tower, a fifty-four-story residential high-rise also designed by Wright, the Golden Beacon, then being contemplated by Chicago financier Charles F. Glore, Jr. "Chicago is a badly overgrown hamlet here on the prairie," Wright announced, and if one looks closely it is clear that he imagined his new towers as catalysts for the city's historic fabric to melt away, the landscape to be returned to prairie, an expansive green landscape dotted with widely spaced towers.[38] This was an idea that he had already explored in the model of Broadacre in the 1930s, where towers approximately a mile apart punctuated the countryside. Perhaps for Wright, the seemingly contradictory gesture of designing the world's tallest skyscraper and advocating for the dissolution of traditional cities went hand in hand. The letters Wright received in response record a mixed reaction. Congratulatory telegrams arrived, notably from Torroja in Madrid. A Chicago high school student effused that Chicago would finally rival New York, with its Empire State Building. However another Chicagoan protested, "For years I have been your staunch defender against all manner of adverse and ignorant criticism against your architecture," but she professed bewilderment: "Where is the preacher of decentralization? . . . This can only be a monument to the ego of Frank Lloyd Wright."[39]

The spire of Mile High was to include a state-of-the-art television studio in its uppermost nine stories, topped by a 300-foot (91.4-meter) television antenna, capable, so the architect claimed, of broadcasting without relay to the whole country. Wright had been interviewed on television—that medium so central to Wright's ambitions of framing his own image—by Hugh Downs in 1953, but the high moment of his increased visibility in the media was his appearance in 1957 on the program *The Mike Wallace Interview*.[40] Wallace focused on recent discussions of Wright's libertarian social and political views and raised questions about his moral standards, while still allowing occasional moments for Wright to work at building his fame as a designer. Wright declared that "an engineer is only a rudimentary architect," and raised the polemical tone beyond Wallace's expectations. Wallace was so satisfied that he invited Wright back for a second segment. Wright in turn began to question his ability to control the new medium, quipping to a reporter in 1958 that "TV is chewing gum for the eyes."[41] Despite his attempts to control history, his account of his work as the culmination of developments in the engineering of reinforced concrete has never emerged as a dominant thread in American modern architecture. But Wright understood the stakes of fame, as his fundraising dinner brought in some $25,000—a huge sum at the time—for Taliesin. Further television invitations flowed in. At the NBC studios in Rockefeller Center, where two decades earlier he had unveiled his model of Broadacre, he insisted on a high stool to increase his physical stature on screen to complement his commanding words. Despite the challenges Wright faced in crafting his own legacy, he remains one of the few nearly everyone can cite when asked to name an architect, even if his Mile-High skyscraper design was swiftly lost to the annals of forgotten dream projects.

Notes

1. Ralph Adams Cram (1863–1942) was the first, on December 13, 1926.
2. Despite courting publicity, in 1957 Wright famously quipped: "I don't mind the fame, but I hate the notoriety." *Look* magazine, Sept. 17, 1957.
3. Frank Lloyd Wright, *The Living City* (New York: Horizon, 1958). On Wright and the skyscraper, see Anthony Alofsin, ed., *Prairie Skyscraper: Frank Lloyd Wright's Price Tower* (New York: Rizzoli, 2005); and Barry Bergdoll, "Frank Lloyd Wright and the City: Density vs. Dispersal," *Frank Lloyd Wright Quarterly* 25, no. 1 (Winter 2014): 23–38.
4. On Mies's skyscraper, see Barry Bergdoll, "Sheer Glass Wrapping for a New Architectural Expression, Mies van der Rohe's Entry *Honeycomb* for the Bahnhof Friedrichstrasse Competition," in *Bauhaus: A Conceptual Model*, ed. Bauhaus-Archiv Berlin, Stiftung Bauhaus Dessau, and Klassik Stiftung Weimar (Ostfildern, Germany: Hatje Cantz, 2009), pp. 115–19.
5. Carl W. Condit, *The Rise of the Skyscraper: The Genius of Chicago Architecture from the Great Fire to Louis Sullivan* (Chicago: University of Chicago Press, 1952). The book was later reissued in a revised form as *The Chicago School of Architecture: A History of Commercial and Public Building in the Chicago Area, 1875–1925* (Chicago: University of Chicago Press, 1964).
6. Ibid., pp. 166–67, 215.
7. Sigfried Giedion, *Space, Time, and Architecture: The Growth of a New Tradition* (Cambridge, Mass.: Harvard University Press, 1941).
8. Wright, quoted in Franz Schulz, *Mies van der Rohe: A Critical Biography* (Chicago: University of Chicago Press, 1995), p. 23.
9. O. J. Doyle, District Manager, Otis Elevator Company, letter to Wright, October 13, 1956, 0050A01-04, Frank Lloyd Wright Foundation Archives (The Museum of Modern Art | Avery Architectural & Fine Arts Library, Columbia University, New York).
10. See LPC report for Landmarks Preservation Commission, June 27, 2006, Designation List 378 LP-2202, New York and Long Island Coignet Stone Company Building, later the Office of the Brooklyn Improvement Company, 360 Third Avenue (aka 370 Third Avenue, 230 Third Street), Brooklyn. Built 1872–73; William Field and Son, architect.
11. Frank Lloyd Wright, *Modern Architecture: Being the Kahn Lectures for 1930* (Princeton, N.J.: Princeton University Press, 1931).
12. Leonard K. Eaton, *Hardy Cross: American Engineer* (Carbondale: University of Illinois Press, 2006).
13. See Beggs, letter to Wright, June 12, 1936, B045A05, Wright Foundation Archives (MoMA | Avery).
14. Polivka, letter to Wright, February 15, 1946, Box 1, Folder 1, J. J. Polivka Papers, 1945–1959, University Archives, The State University of New York at Buffalo.
15. "The Modern Gallery," *Architectural Forum* 84 (January 1946): 82.
16. Polivka, letter to Wright, February 15, 1946.
17. Polivka, letter to Wright, June 17, 1946 (carbon copy), Box 1, Folder 1, J. J. Polivka Papers. See also D. Martín-Saiz, "Jaroslav J. Polivka y el Guggenheim Museum de New York," *Informes de la construccíon* 65, no. 531 (July–September 2013): 261–74.
18. Polivka, letter to Wright, July 21, 1947, Box 1, Folder 4, J. J. Polivka Papers. See also Richard Cleary, "Lessons in Tenuity: Frank Lloyd Wright's Bridges," in *Proceedings of the Second International Congress on Construction History*, ed. Malcolm Dunkeld et al. (Cambridge, UK: Construction History Society, 2006), pp. 741–58.
19. Elizabeth Mock, *The Architecture of Bridges* (New York: The Museum of Modern Art, 1949), p. 120.
20. Ibid.
21. Polivka prepared his own text, "Aesthetics of Bridges"—never to be published—in which it became clear that his quest for patents on new performative roles for ruled surfaces had been expanded to include Wright's cause in architecture: "To maintain and enhance the beauty of the natural environment, we shall have to keep constantly in mind that the buildings and cities to be built are not more constructions of sticks and stones, nor 'machines for living' but are organizations of human perceptions and meanings, and should have character." J. J. Polivka Papers. Clearly now his reading list included Lewis Mumford, the nemesis Le Corbusier, and the hero Frank Lloyd Wright's *An Autobiography* (New York: Duell, Sloan and Pearce, 1943).
22. Eduardo Torroja, *Philosophy of Structures*, trans. J. J. Polivka and Milos Polivka (Berkeley: University of California Press, 1958).
23. J. J. Polivka Papers.
24. Daniel Seligman, "The Battle for Chicago," *Fortune* (June 1955), quoted in Thomas Dyja, *The Third Coast: When Chicago Built the American Dream* (New York: Penguin, 2013), p. 288.
25. Ibid., p. 338.
26. See Katherine Solomonson, *The Chicago Tribune Tower Competition: Skyscraper Design and Cultural Change in the 1920s* (Chicago: University of Chicago Press, 2003), p. 37.
27. *Chicago Sunday Tribune*, "Wright Plans a Mile-High Building Here," August 26, 1956, p. 1.
28. *Chicago Daily Tribune*, "Voice of the People: Wright's Skyscraper," September 3, 1956, p. 18.
29. *Washington Post and Times-Herald*, "Is Wright Wrong? Architect's Mile-High Building Stirs Controversy," September 8, 1956.
30. *Time*, September 10, 1956. Also see the article "Tall Tale," *Newsweek*, September 10, 1956.
31. David V. Mollenhof and Mary Jane Hamilton, *Frank Lloyd Wright's Monona Terrace: The Enduring Power of a Civic Vision* (Madison: University of Wisconsin Press, 1999), p. 140.
32. "Dinner Oct. 17 to Fete Frank Lloyd Wright," *Chicago Daily Tribune*, September 17, 1956.
33. Wright, quoted in Thomas Buck, "Sky City Plan No Idle Dream, Says Wright: Famed Architect Tells How Idea Developed," *Chicago Daily Tribune*, October 17, 1956, p. 48.
34. Ibid. Also quoted in Jane King Hession and Debra Pickrel, *Frank Lloyd Wright in New York: The Plaza Years, 1954–1959* (Layton, Utah: Gibbs Smith, 2007), p. 47. The *Christian Science Monitor* gave more detail: "The entire building is more airplane in character than the usual heavy building construction. For instance the support of the outer walls and of the floors is pendant, and the science of continuity is everywhere else employed from inside outward. All floor slabs are extended across the central core. All loads are thus balanced over central supports except the outer perimeter of slabs and walls, which are suspended. The type of construction is similar to that of the airplane and ocean liner." "Wright Sees Mile-High Buildings of Future: Architect Compares Framework to Tree," *Christian Science Monitor*, November 23, 1956.
35. Ibid.
36. "Wright Limits Kind Words to Two Subjects: Raps All but Daley and Own Building Plans," *Chicago Daily Tribune*, October 18, 1956, p. 12.
37. "Wright Sees Mile-High Buildings of Future: Architect Compares Framework to Tree," *Christian Science Monitor*, November 23, 1956.
38. "Wright Limits Kind Words to Two Subjects."
39. Box 1047, Folder 032 (LOC #1047.032), Wright Foundation Archives (MoMA | Avery).
40. Charter Preston and Edward A. Hamilton, eds., *Mike Wallace Asks: Highlights from 46 Controversial Interviews* (New York: Simon & Schuster, 1958), pp. 122–25.
41. Ed Sullivan, "Little Old New York," *Morning Herald* (Uniontown, Pennsylvania), January 10, 1958, p. 22.

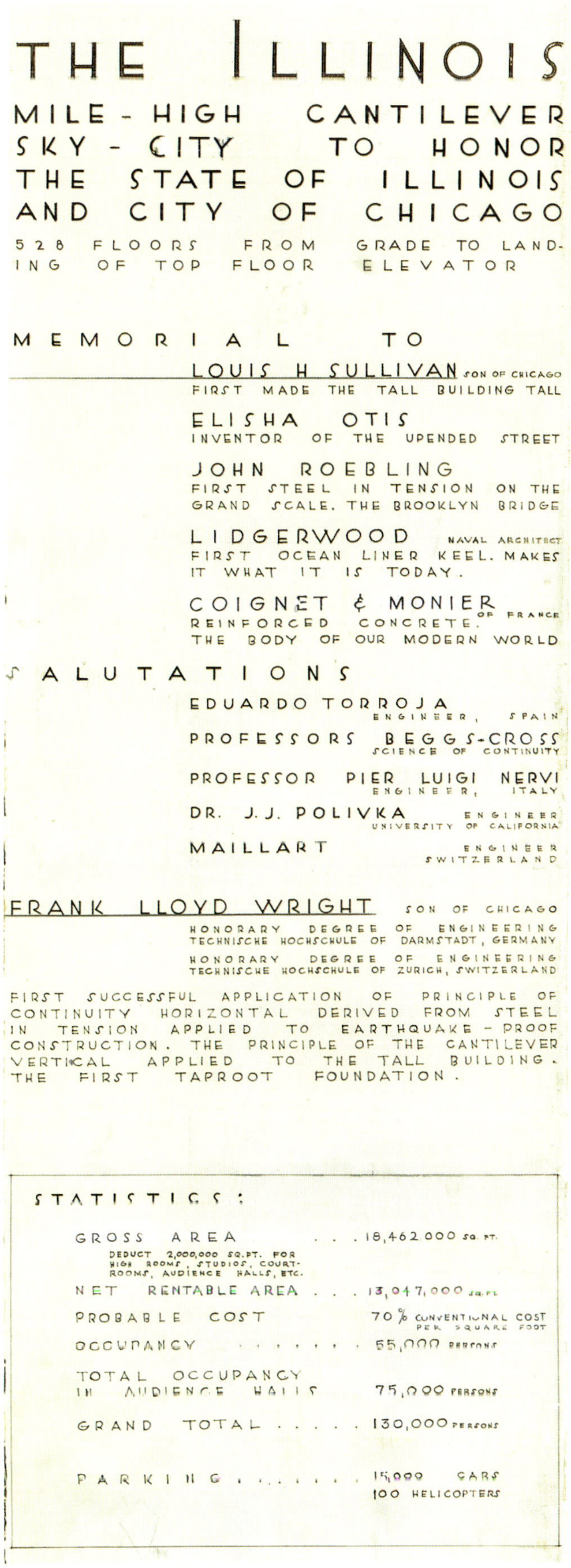

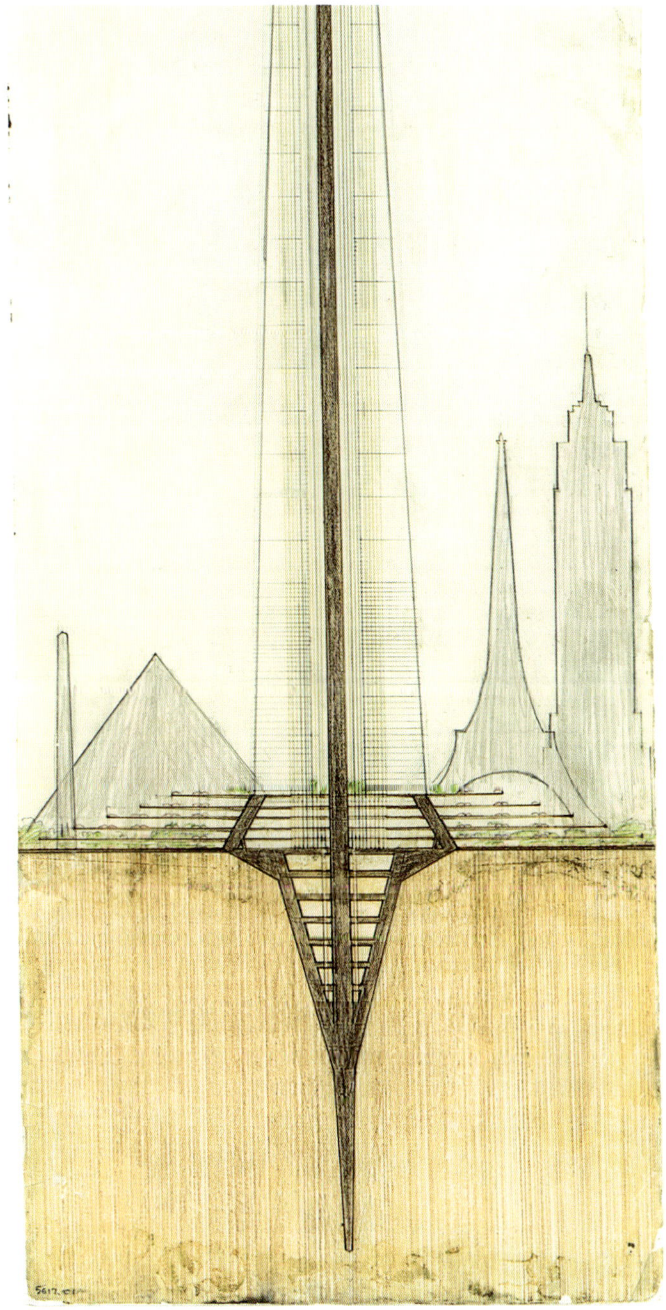

1. and 2. The Mile-High Illinois, Chicago (details). Project, 1956. Dedication to famous architects and engineers (left) and height comparisons to the Washington Monument, Great Pyramid of Giza, Eiffel Tower, and Empire State Building (right). Pencil, colored pencil, and ink on tracing paper, 8 ft. 4 in. x 17 ½ in. (254 x 44.5 cm)

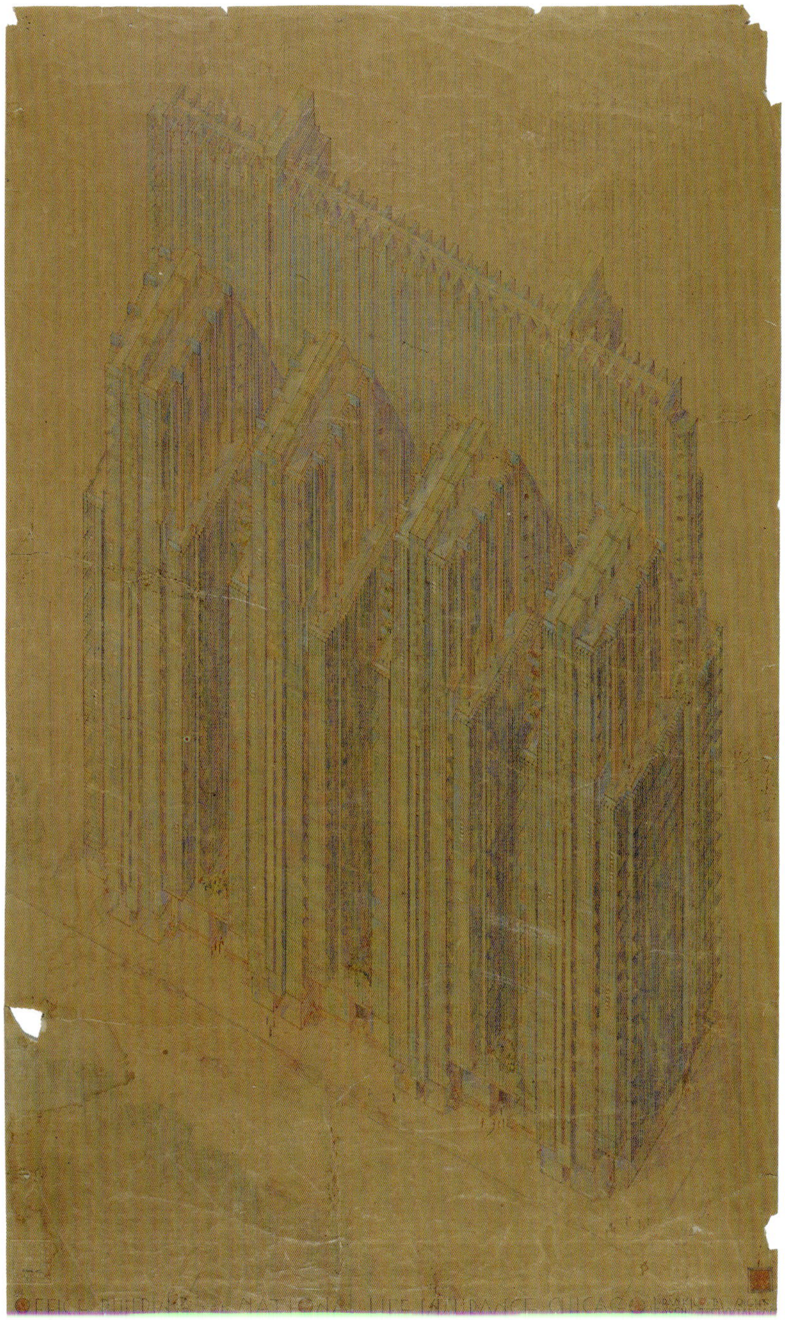

3. National Life Insurance Company Building, Chicago. Project, 1923–25.
Colored pencil on tracing paper, 40 x 24 in. (101.6 x 61 cm)

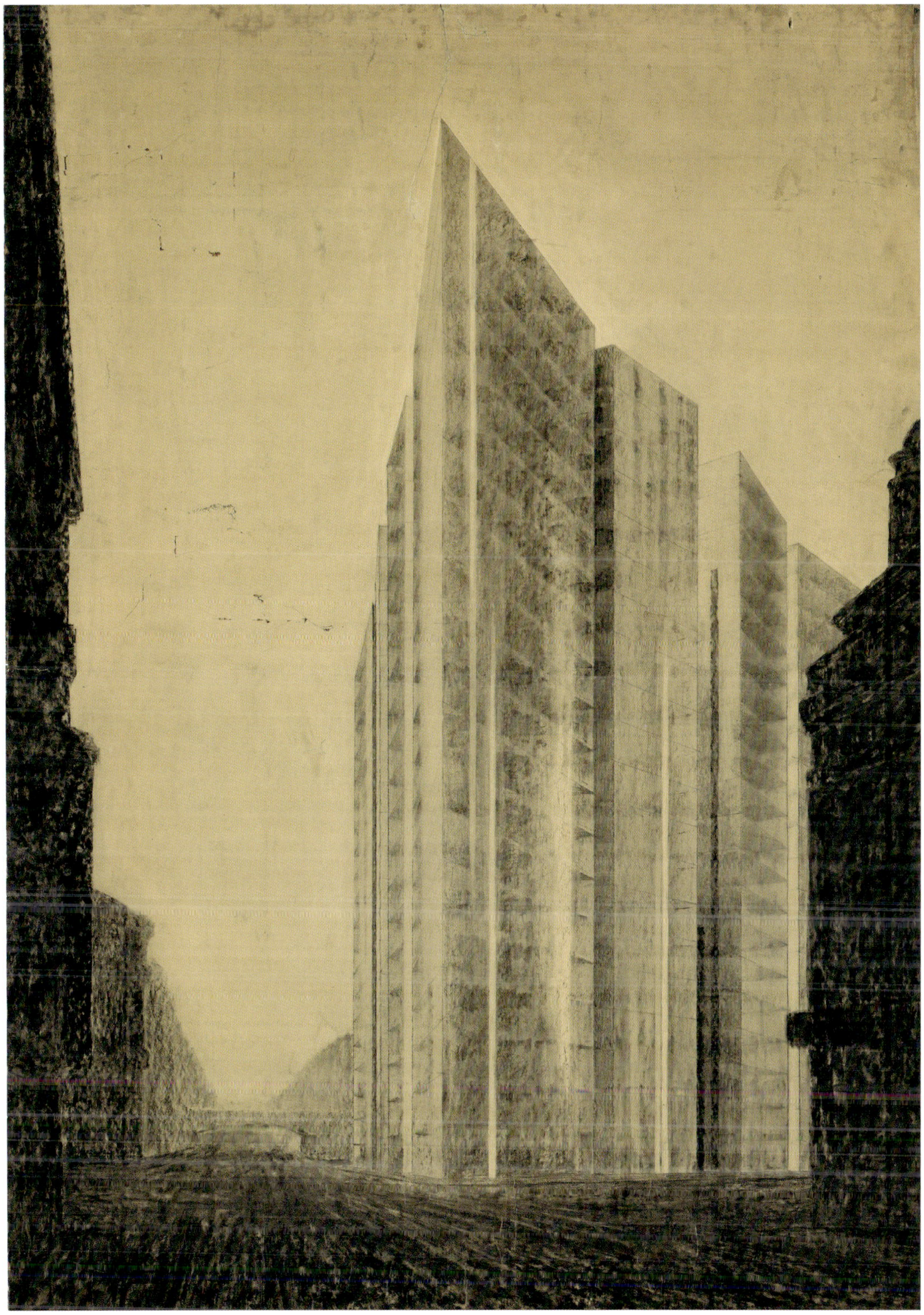

4. Ludwig Mies van der Rohe (American, born Germany. 1886–1969).
Friedrichstrasse Skyscraper, Berlin-Mitte, Germany. Project, 1921. Exterior perspective from the north.
Charcoal and graphite on paper mounted on board, 68 ¼ x 48 in. (173.4 x 121.9 cm).
The Museum of Modern Art, New York. Mies van der Rohe Archive. Gift of the architect

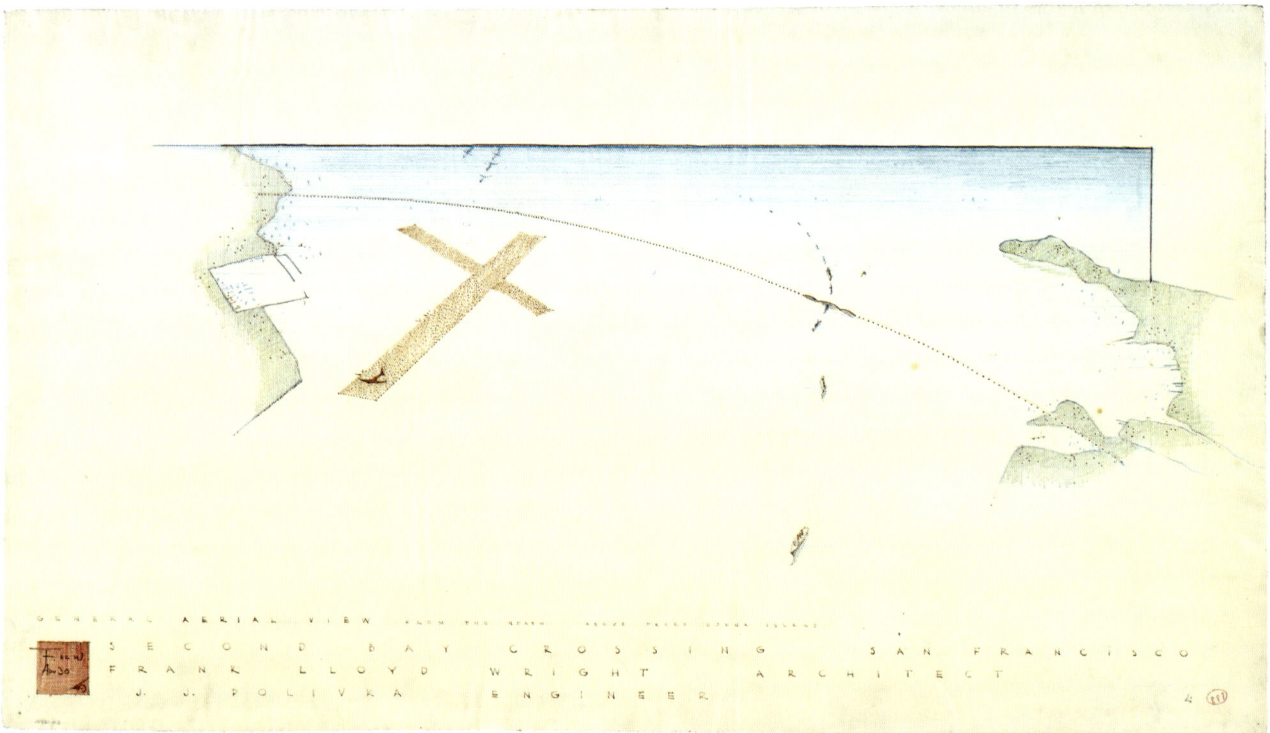

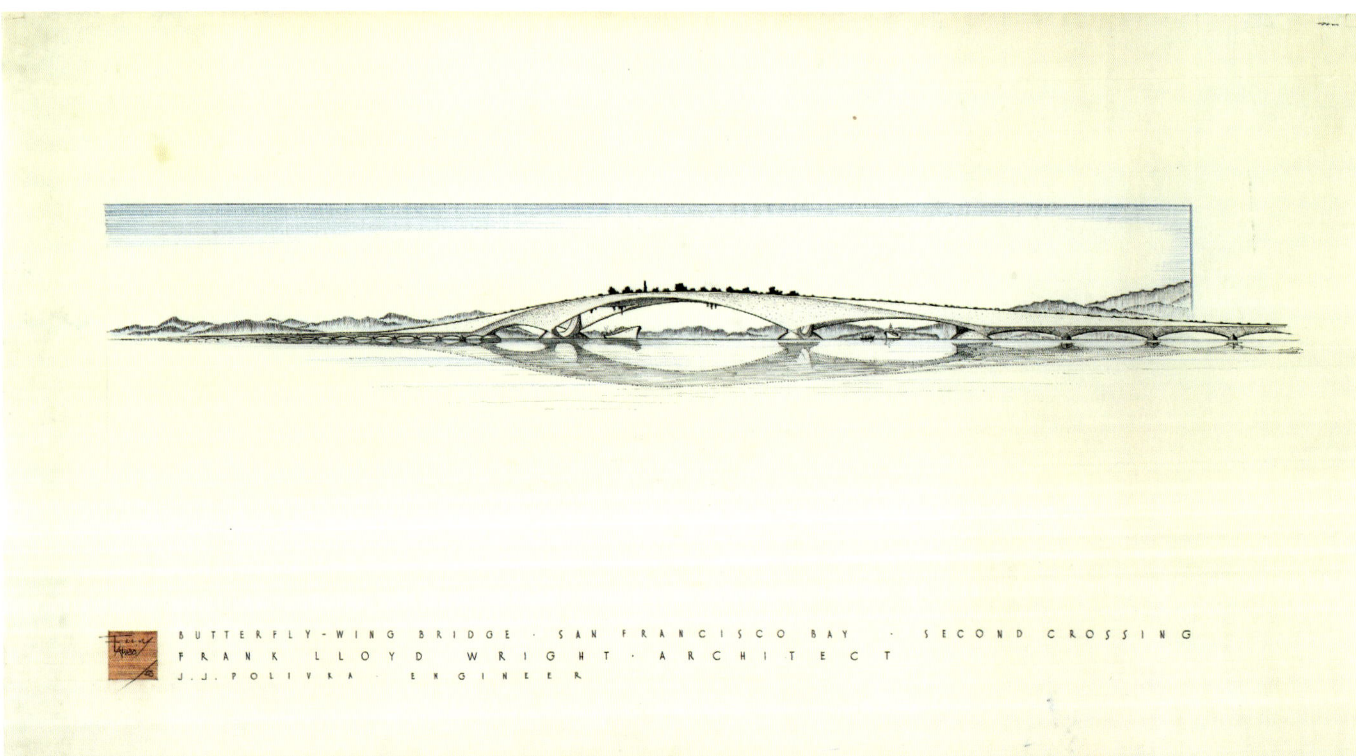

5. Butterfly Wing Bridge, San Francisco. Project, 1949–53. Aerial view from the north.
Ink and colored pencil on tracing paper, 19 3/4 x 35 1/4 in. (50.2 x 89.5 cm)

6. Butterfly Wing Bridge, San Francisco. Project, 1949–53. Perspective.
Ink, pencil, and colored pencil on tracing paper, 23 1/8 x 42 1/8 in. (58.7 x 107 cm)

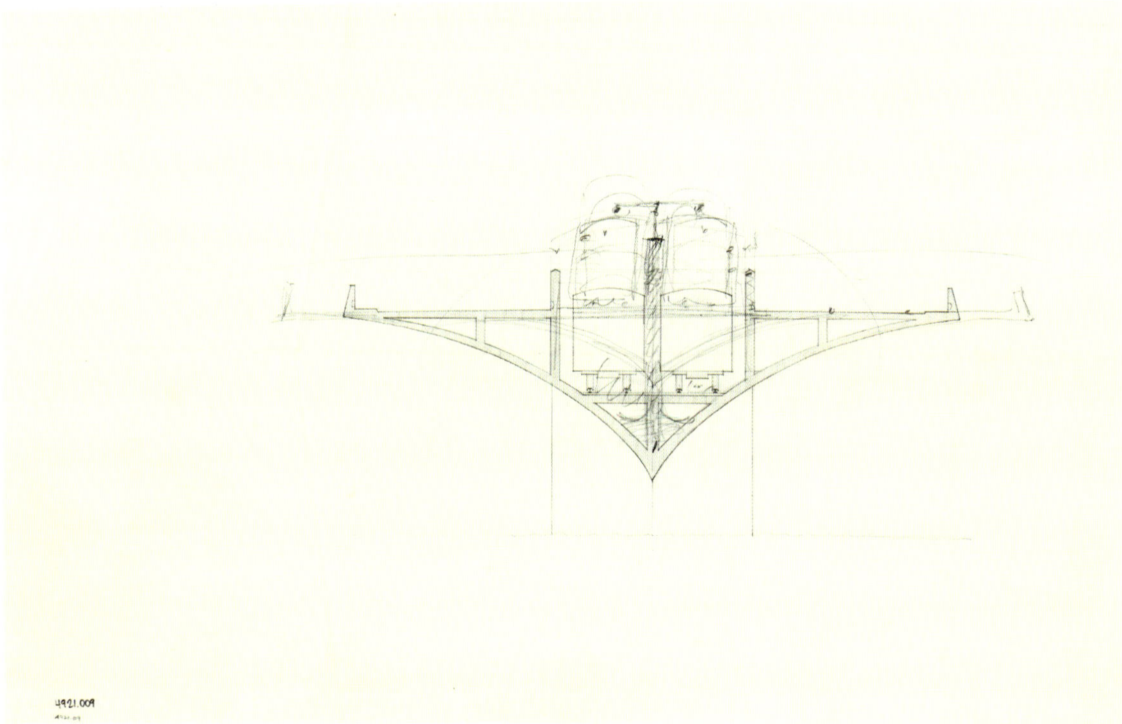

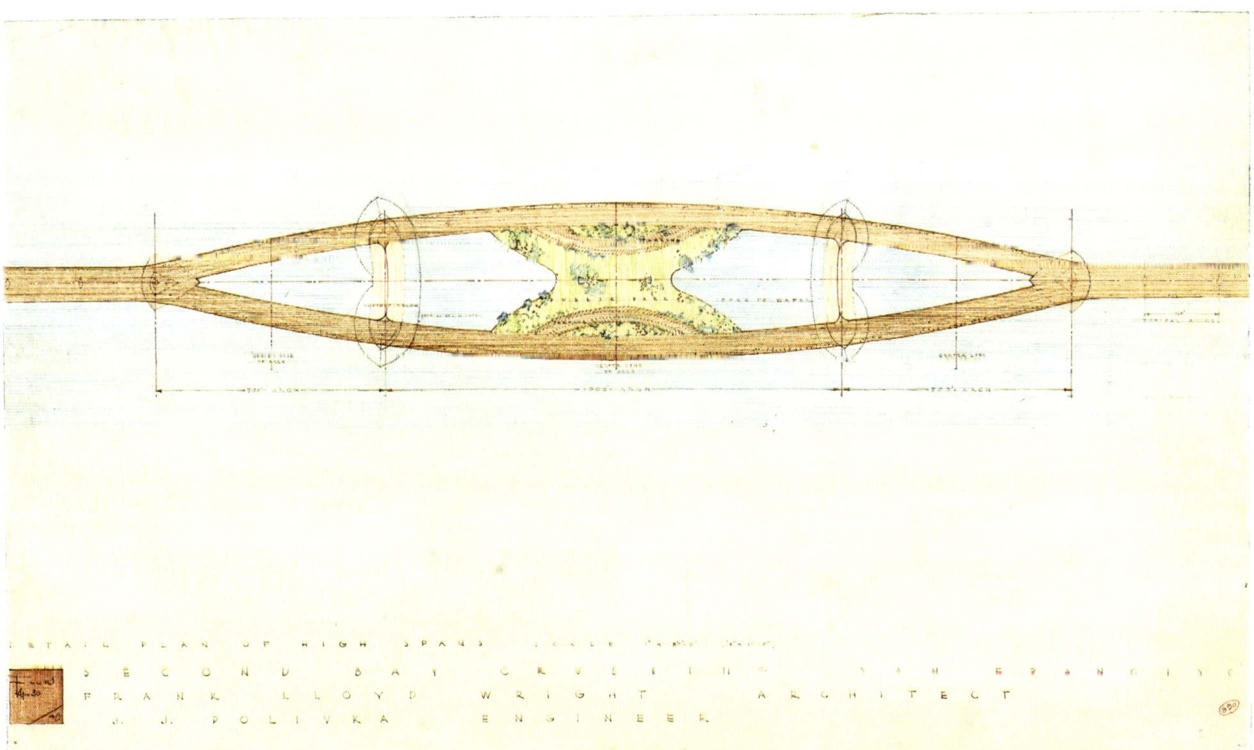

7. Butterfly Wing Bridge, San Francisco. Project, 1949–53. Cross section.
Pencil on tracing paper, 22 3/4 x 36 1/4 in. (57.8 x 92.1 cm)

8. Butterfly Wing Bridge, San Francisco. Project, 1949–53. Detail plan of the upper spans.
Ink and colored pencil on tracing paper, 19 1/2 x 33 1/2 in. (49.5 x 85.1 cm)

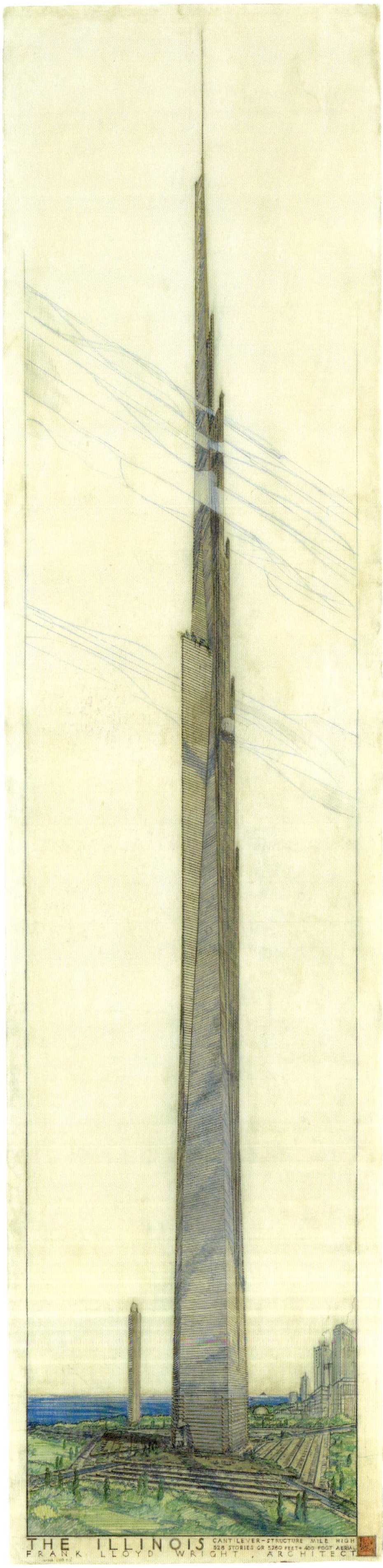

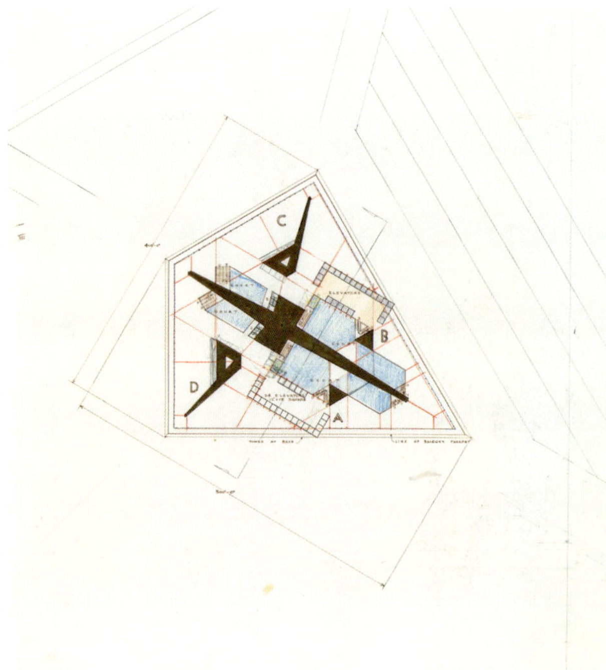

9. The Mile-High Illinois, Chicago. Project, 1956. Perspective with the Golden Beacon Apartment Building project (1956–57). Pencil, colored pencil, and gold ink on tracing paper, 8 ft. 9 in. x 30 in. (266.7 x 76.2 cm)

10. The Mile-High Illinois, Chicago. Project, 1956. Ground-floor plan. Pencil, colored pencil, and gold ink on tracing paper, 27 ¼ x 25 in. (69.2 x 63.5 cm)

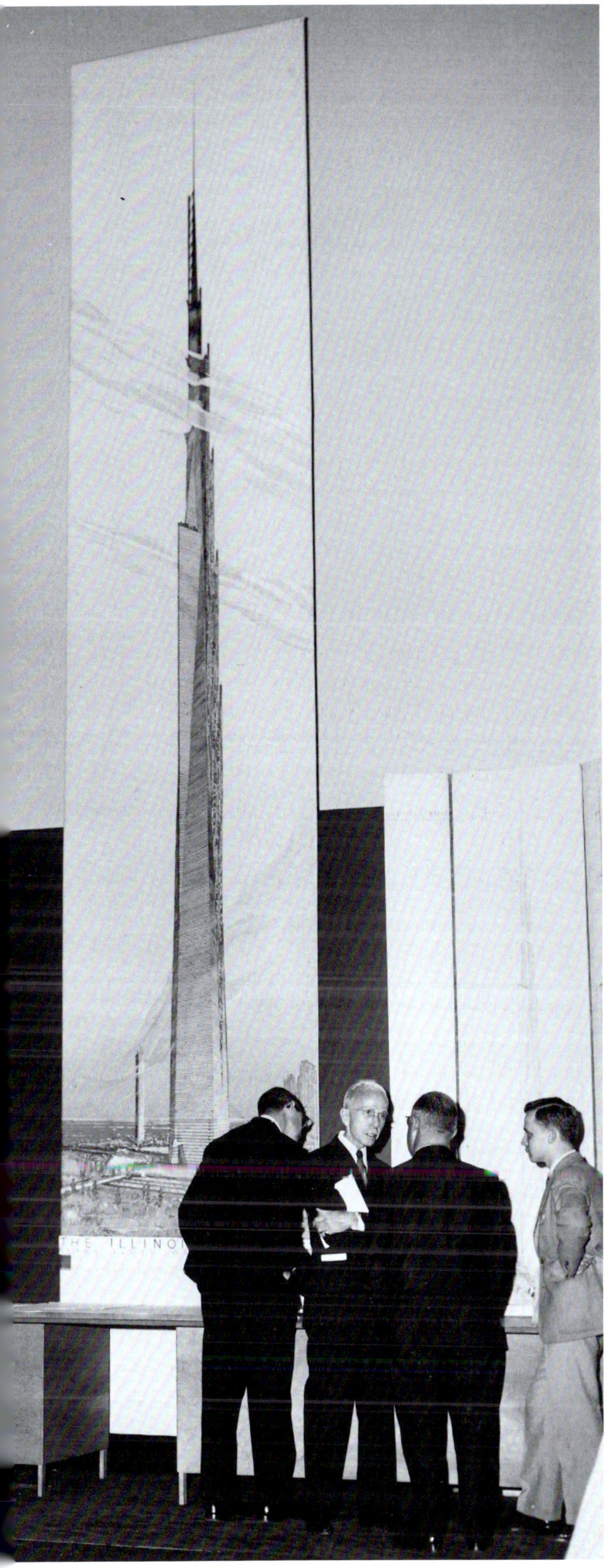

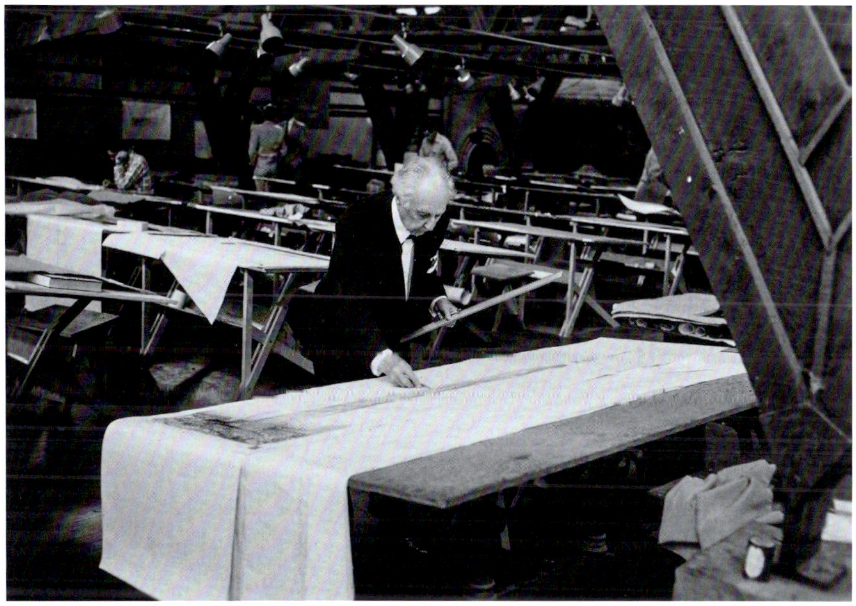

11. Unveiling the 22-foot-high (6.7-meter-high) visualization of The Mile-High Illinois at the October 16, 1956, press conference in Chicago

12. Wright working on a drawing of The Mile-High Illinois. 1956. Photograph by Edgar Obma

CONSERVING AND EXHIBITING THE NEW YORK MODELS

ELLEN MOODY

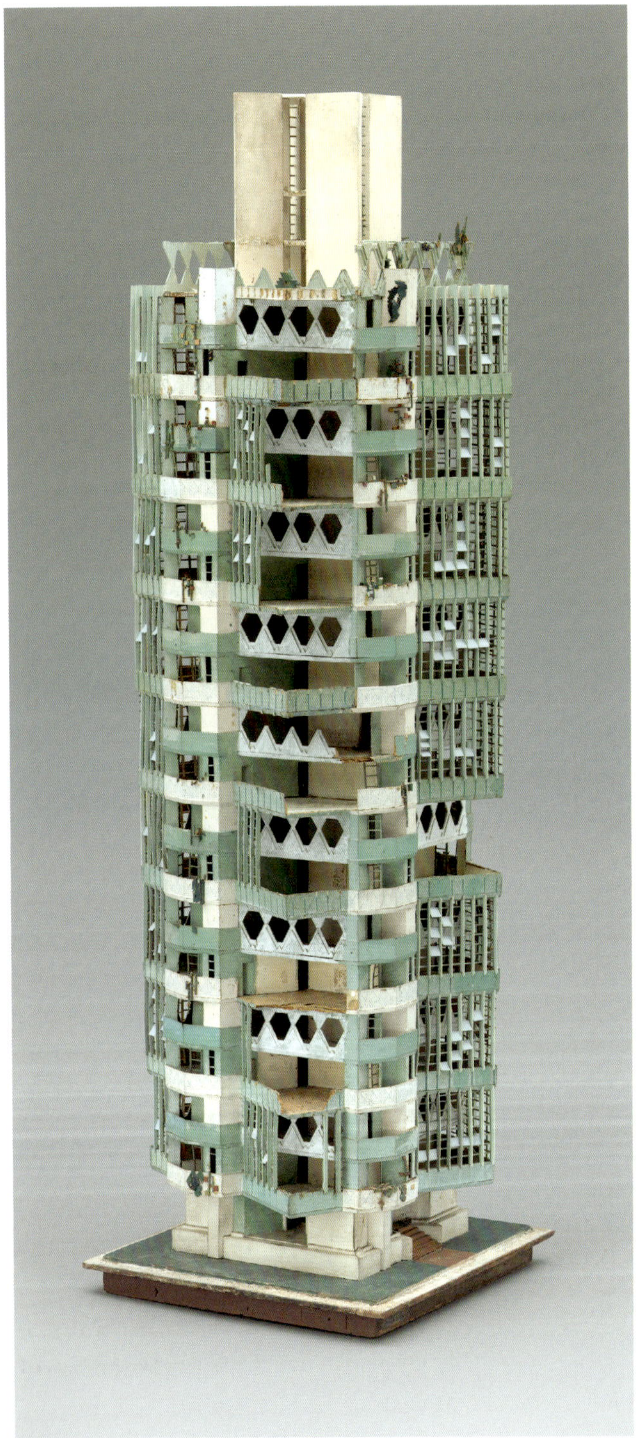

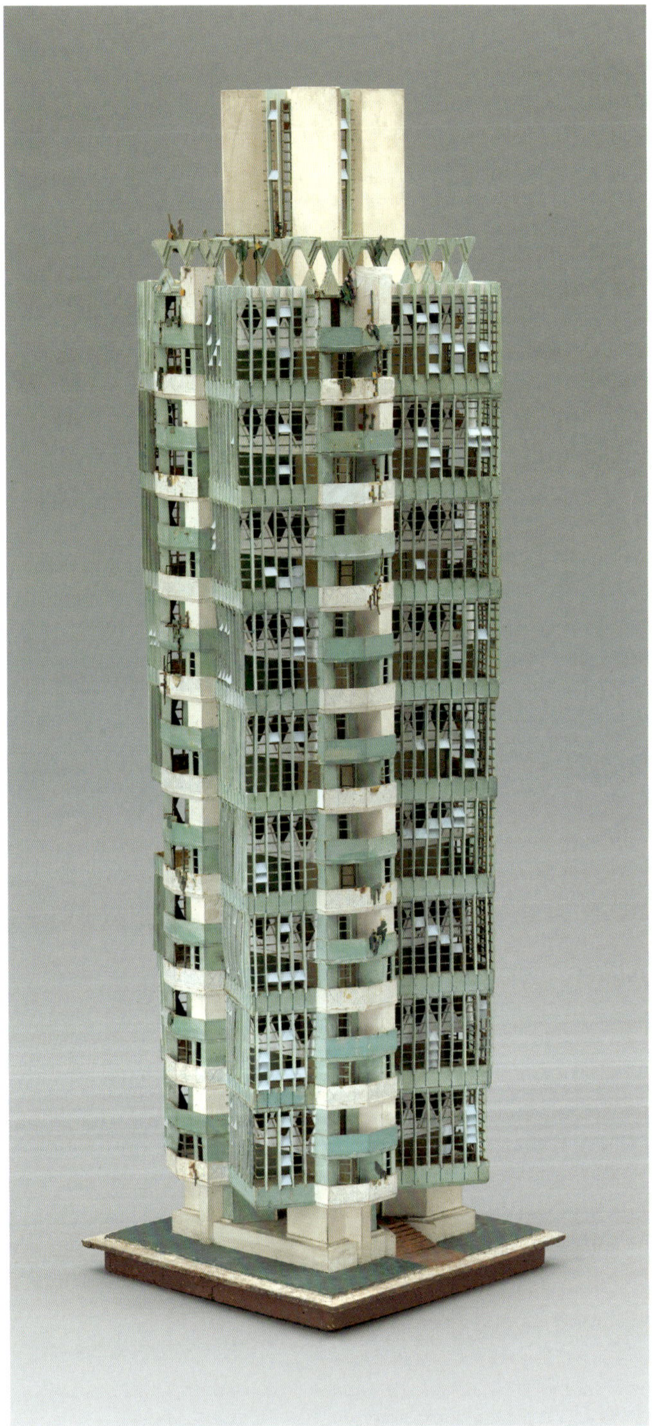

St. Mark's Tower, New York. Project, 1927–29.
Views of unrestored (left) and restored (right) portions of the model.
Painted wood and cardboard, 53 x 16 x 16 in. (134.6 x 40.6 x 40.6 cm)

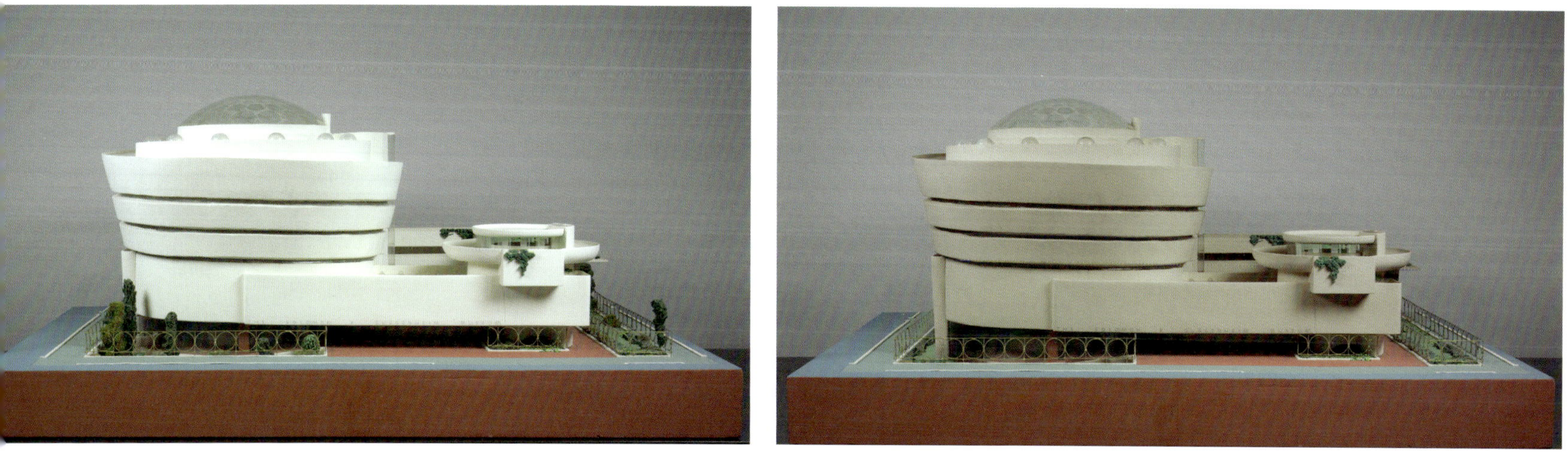

Art conservators find themselves sleuthing at least as often as cleaning or repairing. Any object requiring conservation comes with a history that, once revealed, informs the treatment. The architectural models in The Frank Lloyd Wright Foundation Archives arrived at The Museum of Modern Art with virtually no records, so their histories had to be found elsewhere: in correspondence, drawings, and photographs, as well as in clues provided by the models themselves.[1]

The modern architectural model has received some recent attention in the museum world, perhaps most notably in the 2012 exhibition *The Architectural Model: Tool, Fetish, Small Utopia* at the Deutsches Architekturmuseum in Frankfurt. However, little has been written on the specific role of models in Wright's practice.[2] Often architectural models are a means to an end, a tool for designing. But for Wright, who claimed that an architect should "conceive the building in the imagination, not on paper but in the mind, thoroughly, before touching paper," models had little to do with the actual work of designing.[3] On the contrary, his surviving models are fully realized, meticulously detailed presentation pieces that were used to persuade clients and promote designs, rather than to develop them.

But however detailed, these models were not treated as definitive. This essay takes the examples of two of Wright's designs for New York, St. Mark's Tower (1927–29; opposite) and the Solomon R. Guggenheim Museum (1943–59; above), to demonstrate how his models were reworked and adapted to the architect's shifting goals. These two projects also exemplify extremes in the range of conditions found in the models that survive in the Archives and the divergent approaches to restoration undertaken at MoMA. In this essay I will outline how pertinent details in the models' histories were uncovered, and the decisions my colleagues and I made that led to their different treatments.

ST. MARK'S TOWER

In 1929 Wright switched from the traditional model-making medium of plaster to cardboard, a material touted at the time to be "light and durable," and that could "reproduce in miniature any ideas the Architect may have."[4] His earliest known cardboard model is of his proposed skyscraper residence, St. Mark's Tower (1927–29). Though perhaps preferable to plaster in the short term, anyone's belief in cardboard's durability would be quickly dispelled upon seeing the model on its arrival at MoMA in 2012. It was in a dire state: about fifty percent of the cardboard floors and walls built around the plywood core were missing, and the surviving elements were acidified, discolored, and embrittled, causing warping and separation in the intact pieces (fig. 1).

On close inspection, though, one could find traces of a previous, cohesive structure that made brilliant use of its humble materials. The model's exterior was once made up largely by mullions, painted green to suggest weathered copper, and left empty, inviting the viewer to imagine them filled with transparent panes of glass. An occasional cardboard window pane was present, tilted outward to demonstrate that windows could be individually opened and closed, and painted blue as if reflecting the sky (fig. 2). Exterior walls were decorated with geometric designs for copper reliefs and rectangles representing window boxes that contain small, brightly painted paper and wood squares—abstracted plants that cascade over the balconies. Packed with the model was a bag of detached parts, including a set of scale Wright-designed furniture—an armchair, table, piano, fireplace, and screen (fig. 3). This painstaking detail of a miniature Wright-designed interior would make it all the easier for a viewer to imagine life in one of the tower's deluxe apartment units.

Solomon R. Guggenheim Museum, New York. 1943–59.
Model in its current condition (left) and digital simulation of its restoration (right).
Painted wood, plastic, glass beads, ink, and watercolor on paper, 28 x 62 x 44 in.
(71.1 x 157.5 x 111.8 cm)

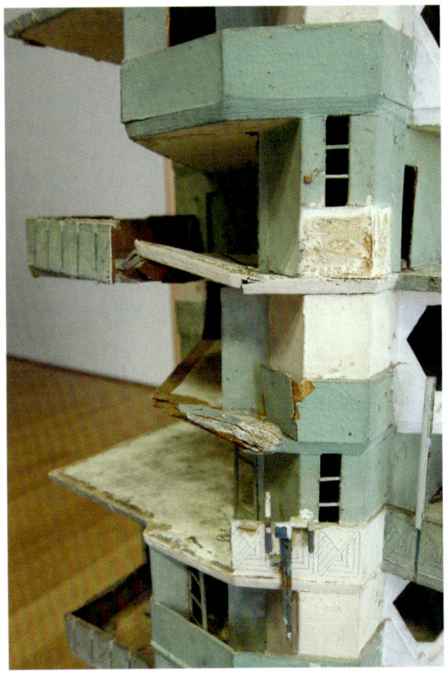

Fig. 1. St. Mark's Tower. Model before restoration

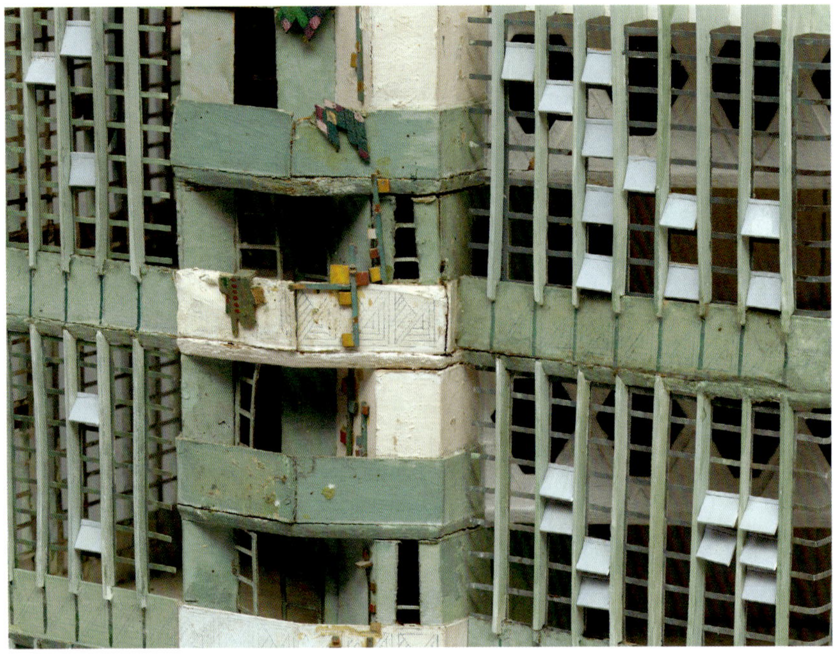

Fig. 2. St. Mark's Tower. Detail of the model's windows

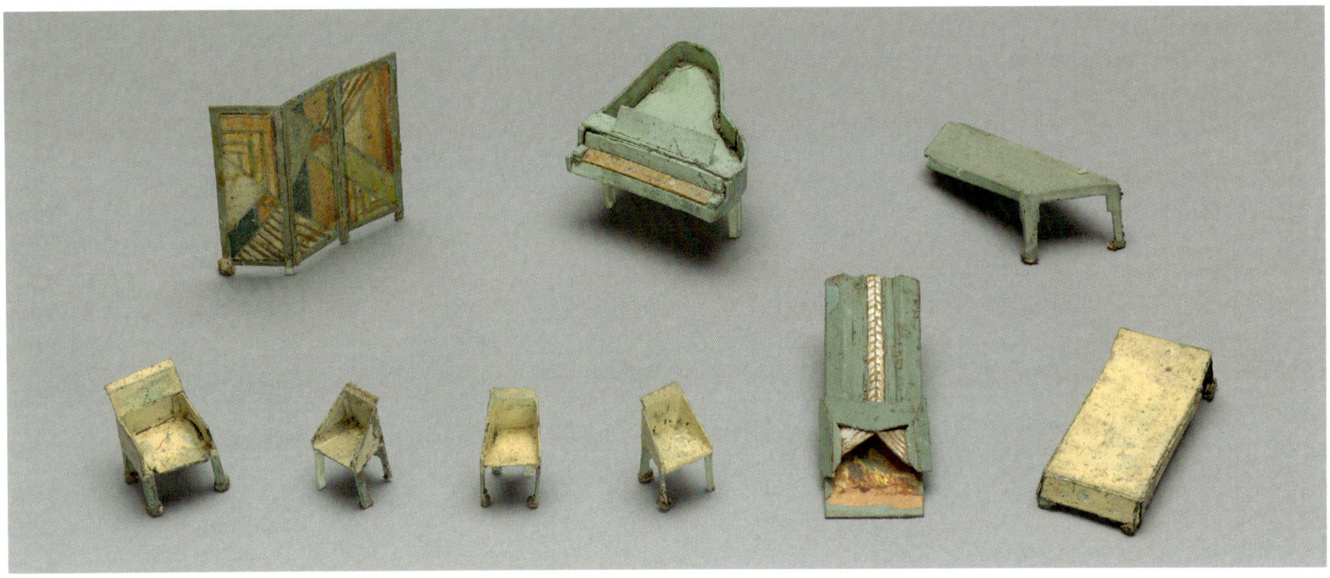

Fig. 3. St. Mark's Tower. Scale furniture designed by Wright

HISTORY

In 1927 Wright received a commission for a residential tower to be erected on the property of the Church of St. Mark's-in-the-Bouwerie (fig. 4). His first project in New York, the building employed Wright's "taproot" structure, which internalized all load-bearing elements to a deep-rooted concrete and steel core, freeing the interior for custom partitioning and making the exterior facade a non-load-bearing curtain wall (fig. 5). Had it been realized, it would have been the first glass skyscraper in New York (this feat only came to pass twenty years later with the United Nations Secretariat Building).

Wright created numerous drawings to illustrate this system to his client, the church's rector, William Norman Guthrie. The model ultimately clarified the design for Guthrie, but also raised for him concerns that a glass exterior on a skyscraper would be psychologically distressing for the building's tenants:

I have been mentally wrestling . . . with insistent doubts of the practicality of your proposal. The model removed my ignorance. I saw that your structure was self-evident, but you did not seem to have reckoned with our persistent human nature and its susceptibility to disastrous contagion. Glass houses—stones, of course, suggested at once! How would anyone feel safe?[5]

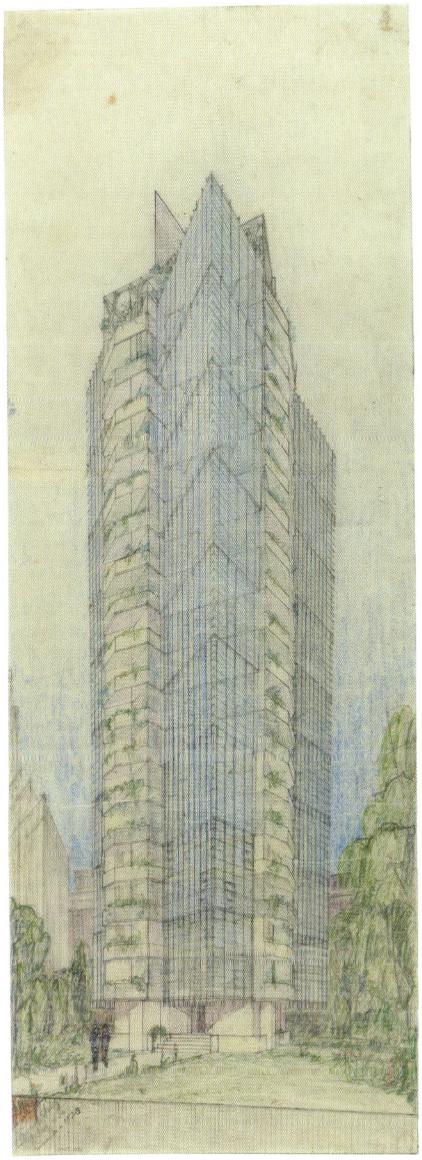

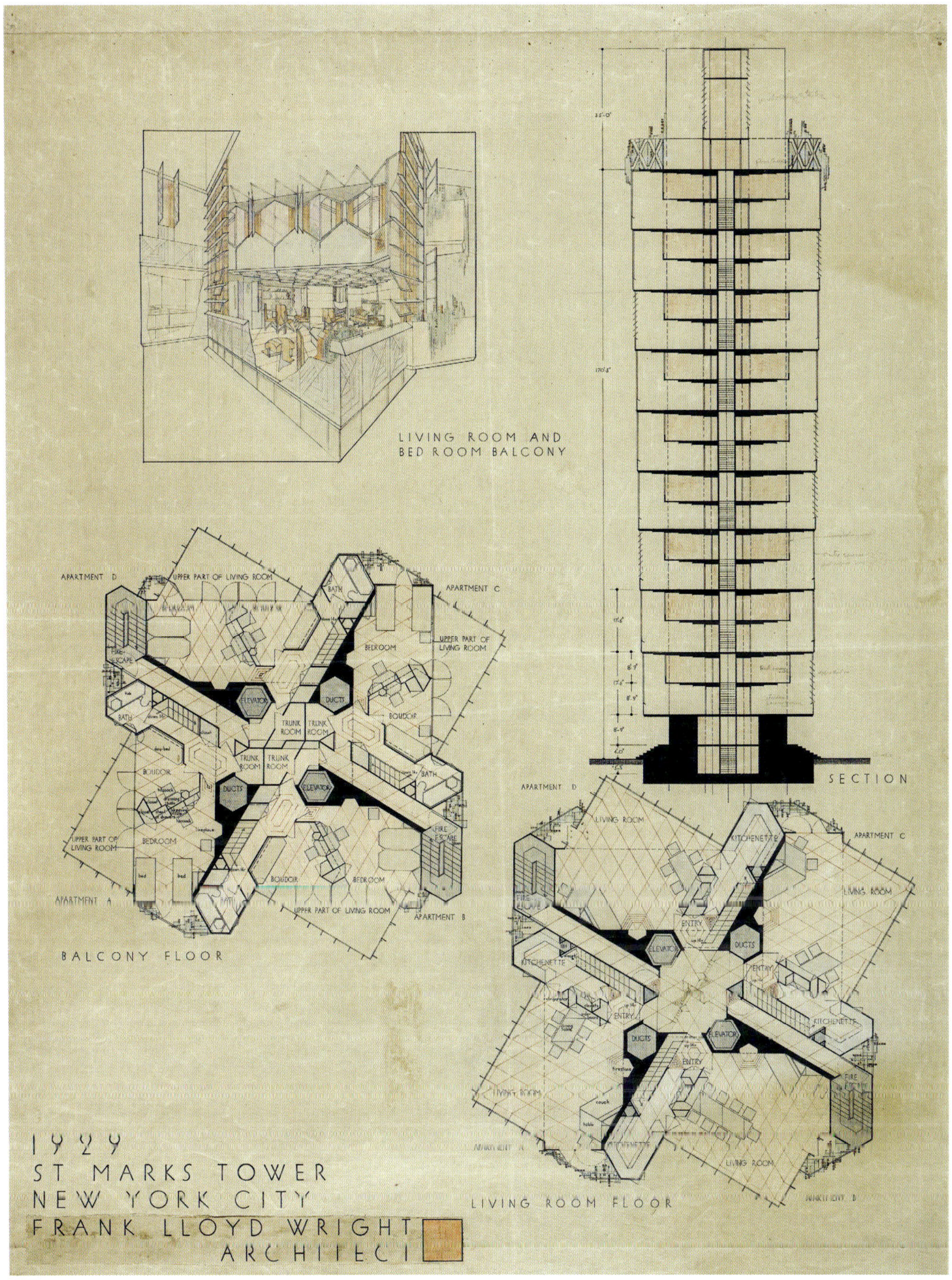

Fig. 4. St. Mark's Tower, New York. Project, 1927–29. Perspective.
Pencil and colored pencil on tracing paper, 28 x 10 1/8 in. (71.1 x 25.7 cm)

Fig. 5. St. Mark's Tower, New York. Project, 1927–29. Plans, section, and cutaway perspective, 1929. Ink, pencil, and colored pencil on cloth, 46 1/2 x 35 1/2 in. (118.1 x 90.2 cm)

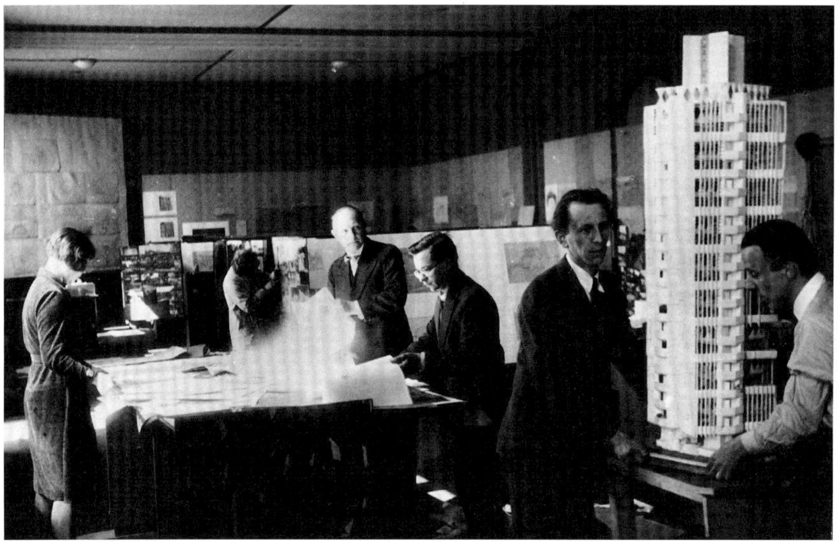

Fig. 6. St. Mark's Tower. Model at the Stedelijk Museum, Amsterdam. 1931

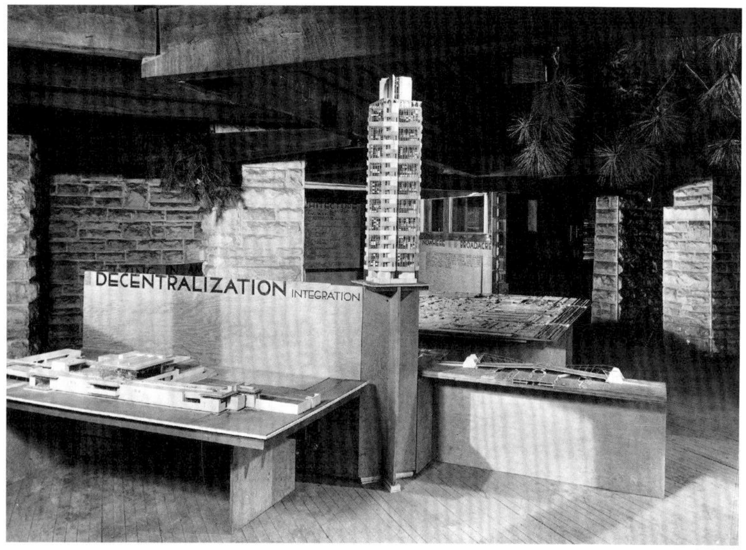

Fig. 7. St. Mark's Tower. Model installed with Broadacre City project at the Taliesin Fellowship Complex, Spring Green, Wisconsin. n.d. Photograph by Roy E. Peterson

The subsequent stock market crash in 1929, in combination with the expense and risks inherent in Wright's novel, untested design, led to the church's abandonment of the scheme. However, the photographs of the model in the Archives reveal an extensive afterlife: rather than retiring the model to storage, the architect enlisted it as a publicity tool. First, it was included in an exhibition of Wright's work that toured America and Europe in 1930–31: *Frank Lloyd Wright, 1893–1930* (fig. 6). Four years later, it traveled with another exhibition, this time centered on Broadacre City (1929–35), Wright's proposal for a decentralized urban plan (fig. 7). In this context, the model illustrated the "city-dweller unit," a series of skyscraper residences that Wright envisioned for his new model of urban dispersal, which would allow those relocating from urban environments to adjust to country living.[6]

Featuring his designs—especially those that had not been realized—in traveling exhibitions was an efficient way for Wright to promote his present practice and future ambitions. Museum visitors across the globe were exposed to his models and drawings, which often found themselves under the same roof as well-known paintings and sculptures. Their standing was further burnished when they were reproduced in the press. The model for St. Mark's Tower, which appeared in many press clippings, was not only photogenic, but with Wright posed alongside it, helped to define the architect as a singular visionary. One such image shows two superimposed St. Mark's Tower models emerging from Wright's head, evoking thought bubbles, or perhaps Zeus's birth of Athena (fig. 8).

Details visible in photographs taken before 1935 diverge somewhat from the surviving model's appearance. In the early images, the vertical mullions on the exterior extend along the length of the building as decorative moldings (fig. 9); today they are truly window mullions, serving only to hold the glass in place and stopping at each unit's exterior wall. The geometric designs on the exterior walls, found on the model today in two forms—one incised with a fine blade and the other rendered more boldly in blue pencil (fig. 10)—are barely visible in these early photographs, suggesting that they were all originally incised. Lastly, several lower-level units are devoid of a windowed exterior, whereas evidence on the model—in the form of paint lacunae and residual adhesive where the missing mullions detached—suggest that in a later version every unit was enclosed by windows.

Photographs from the 1935 Broadacre exhibition and thereafter show a model that more closely resembles the surviving form, indicating that major changes took place in these first years since the model was built (fig. 12). Collectively, these changes convey a shift in Wright's vision for both the building and model. The mullions were likely altered to make the geometric designs on the exterior walls more legible. These designs—most of which were emboldened with the blue pencil for the Broadacre show—are more apparent when uninterrupted.[7]

The appearance of units without a windowed exterior on the earlier iteration is explained by the model furniture whose placement in the model itself is evidenced by losses in paint on two lower-level units, where fireplaces

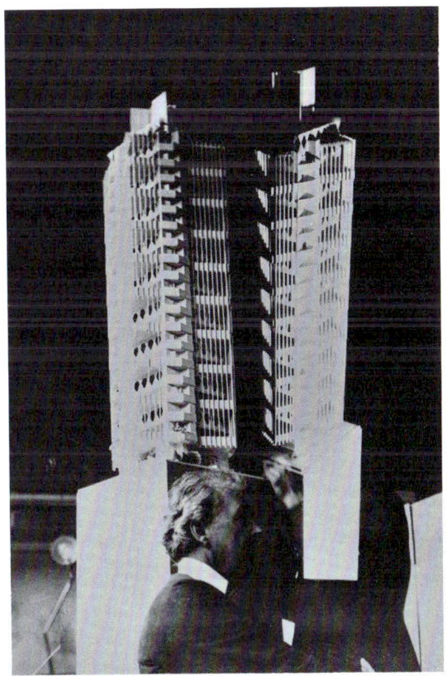

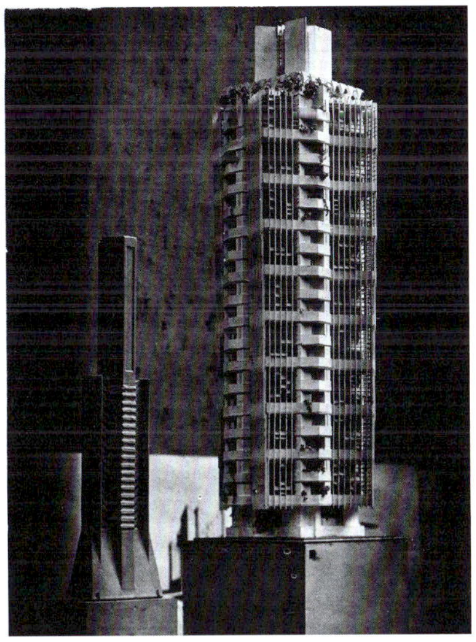

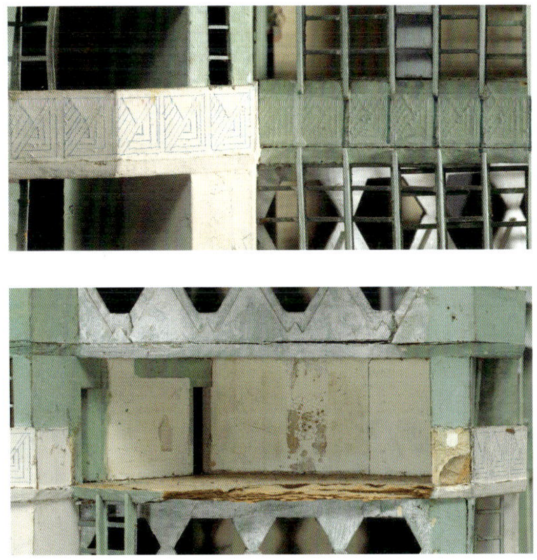

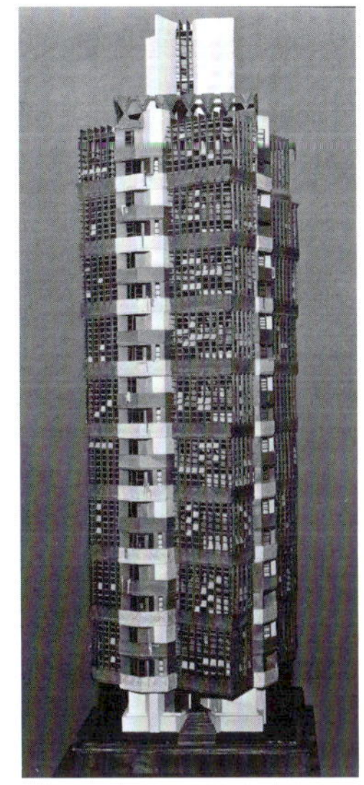

Fig. 8. St. Mark's Tower. Wright with superimposed images of the model

Fig. 9. St. Mark's Tower. Model beside the Skyscraper Vase at the Art Institute of Chicago

Figs. 10. and 11. St. Mark's Tower. Details of the model's rendered and incised molding (top) and former furniture locations (bottom)

Fig. 12. St. Mark's Tower. Model after revisions, 1938. The Museum of Modern Art, New York. Department of Architecture and Design Study Center

and a bookshelf once stood (fig. 11). In order to clearly see the interiors Wright had designed—demonstrating how one would furnish a home with a facade made entirely of glass—the mullions on these units were omitted in the earlier version. For the model's second iteration, when it became a supporting player in the grander concept of Broadacre City, windows were added to the furnished units, obscuring the interiors, but making the model appear more cohesive. By this time the furnishings were less important to Wright as a selling point: the focus was meant to be outward, toward the expansive landscape of a decentralized community, rather than inward, to the reassuring domestic spaces he had designed for New Yorkers six years earlier.

Based on photographs and paint analysis, the model underwent few restorations following the Broadacre show. It was shown at MoMA in 1940 in *Frank Lloyd Wright: American Architect*, then in Philadelphia, Florence, and Paris in 1950–52 for *Sixty Years of Living Architecture*. A photograph from the 1970s shows it at Taliesin, largely intact. The damages occurred between then and 1994, when a condition survey was carried out for a retrospective at MoMA. These damages are the result of a combination of factors: the uncontrolled environment where it was stored and the model's acidic materials.

TREATMENT

When loss to an object is as severe as it was to St. Mark's Tower, the conservator's very practice is brought into question: extensive restoration may mask the original object. As with all restoration treatments, the conservator must find a balance between representing a work's concept, which relays what was in the mind of the creator when he made it, and its original materials, which carry evidence of its history, and the hand, or "aura," of the creator. A treatment of a badly damaged object that privileges its concept can lead to heavy-handed measures that may compromise the object's physical integrity, whereas one that privileges the original material—typically expressed as a lack of action—is apt to fetishize deterioration. Guiding this decision is a "minimalist" approach generally embraced by conservators today: one that prioritizes an object's stability and preservation, and, if deemed desirable, introducing the least amount of compensation needed to reduce the appearance of distracting damages.

Once the St. Mark's model was cleaned and stabilized to prevent further loss, a range of options was considered. One, it could be left in its current, fragmentary state. Damages on utilitarian objects are often left as evidence of the object's purpose—such as wear on props from a performance, or light spots on a lamp shade. The damage the model suffered, however, has little to do with its use. Another option was to restore it entirely, erasing all trace of deterioration so that a viewer could appreciate Wright's design without the distraction of damage. This would mean, though, that more than fifty percent of the model would be comprised of new material, fashioned by a twenty-first-century hand. Ultimately, a compromise was reached: it was decided to restore it partially, leaving a quarter of it in its damaged state, to strike a balance between restoring Wright's vision and respecting the history of the object. From a specific angle, the model would look completely restored, but the unrestored portion would retain its material history (see p. 226).

Since the model underwent several iterations, the question of which version to preserve arose. For the sake of congruency with the remaining material, most of the restoration was carried out in the predominant, later style, with truncated mullions, and blue geometric designs. However one facet of the current restoration recalls the earlier iteration of the model, which exhibited furnished units. Using drawings of the building's interiors in the Archives, the scale furniture that arrived with the model was arranged in one of its living rooms, and the exterior mullions on this unit were left unrestored for easy viewing.

Materials chosen for the restoration were distinct from the originals: new walls, floors, and mullions were fashioned from acid-free paperboard rather than cardboard, painted with acrylic paint rather than oil, and decorated with designs that were laser-printed rather than penciled. Using standard examination tools such as magnification and ultraviolet radiation, future conservators and scholars can easily differentiate the materials introduced in this restoration from the rest of the object. Furthermore, the adhesive used to make these additions is formulated to be reversible in water.[8] These choices are in keeping with today's conservation best practices, which have future generations in mind: if they choose, conservators down the road may revisit, revise, and even undo the additions.

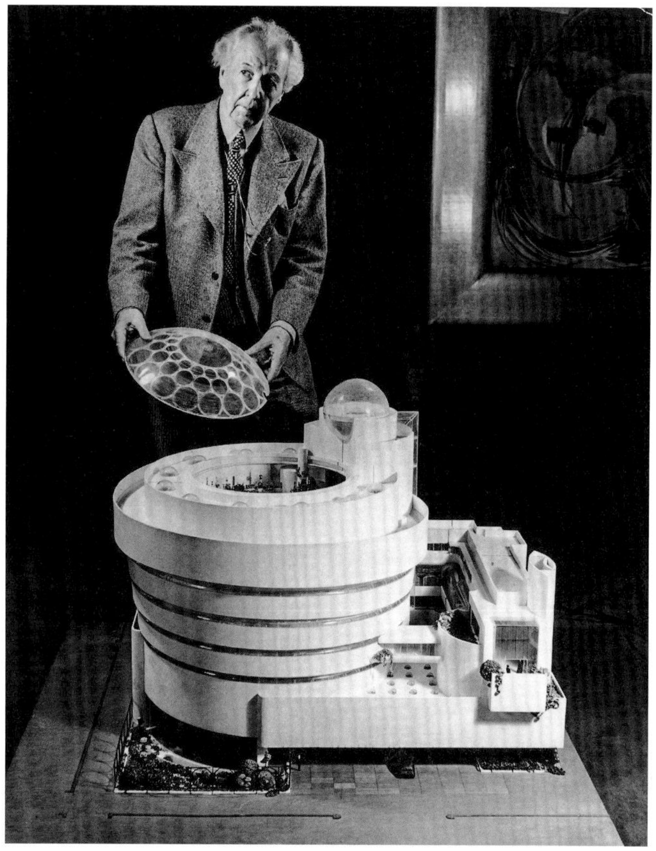

Fig. 13. Solomon R. Guggenheim Museum, New York. 1943–59. Wright posing with the model, 1945. Photograph by Ben Schnall

THE SOLOMON R. GUGGENHEIM MUSEUM

In contrast to St. Mark's Tower, the model for the Solomon R. Guggenheim Museum arrived at MoMA in pristine condition (see p. 227 left). There were no appreciable losses to the substrate or paint layer, which extended continuously over the surface, with no scuffs or cracks. The top half of the spiral detaches from the rest of the model to reveal tiny abstract paintings, executed with pen on paper, adhered to the museum walls. This presentation reflects Wright's insistence that the Guggenheim's collection was best served unframed, mounted directly to the walls, which were sloped ever so slightly backward to catch natural light. Examining these paintings, it became clear that the model's current "pristine" condition was in fact the result of a restoration. First, the paintings exhibited significantly more deterioration than the model: they were torn, dog-eared, and discolored. Second, in some cases, the white paint on the interior walls—which matched that on the exterior—extended over the edges of the paintings. Conversely, portions of the wall directly behind the paintings were gray. All of this suggests that the paintings were originally against a gray background, which was later painted white. As has been demonstrated by the model of St. Mark's Tower, altering a model after its initial "completion" was not unusual in Wright's practice. But the architect's particular distaste for a white interior is well established in his correspondence. Writing to Harry Guggenheim about the museum's director, James Johnson Sweeney, who favored white as a backdrop for the collection, Wright said that to whitewash the interiors would give the museum the effect of "something like you can see in the toilets of the Racquet Club."[9]

HISTORY

This disagreement over the wall colors is one of many clashes between Wright and his clients over the sixteen years it took to complete the museum. In 1943 Wright had been enlisted by Solomon R. Guggenheim and Hilla Rebay, then the director of the Guggenheim Museum of Non-Objective Painting, to create a home for the collection. Sweeney was selected as Rebay's replacement in 1952, and he oversaw the construction of the building, finding himself increasingly at odds with the architect over how the art should be displayed. Early in the planning stages Wright employed a spiral form, representing his idea of how art should be experienced. He had explored this form in the unrealized Gordon Strong Automobile Objective and Planetarium of 1924–25, a building conceived mainly for the purpose of observation, of both the scenic landscape of Maryland as well as the solar system. Wright's early sketches of the Guggenheim included an observatory at the top of the structure, suggesting that he saw in a museum the potential for multiple modes of viewing.

The model, unveiled by Wright at a press preview in New York in 1945, was made of plywood, cardboard, and plastic, the last of which was selected specifically because it could be easily molded to create the shape of the spiral and the impressive domed skylight. The interior was intricately detailed: galleries were fully rendered, with partitions and replicas of Guggenheim's paintings, demonstrating Wright's display concept. Abstract landscaping was intricately carved from wood and embellished with glass beads. Images of the model, in particular those including the architect, attest to its promotional qualities. Mirroring the image in which the St. Mark's Tower model is pictured emerging from Wright's head, in *Time* magazine we see the architect again in the role of Creator, appearing in giant form above the building, about to complete it with its skylight (fig. 13).

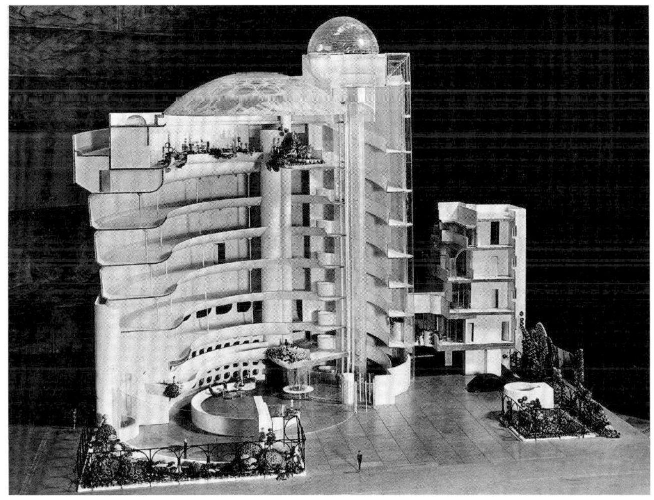

Fig. 14. Solomon R. Guggenheim Museum. Early model, opened to reveal the interior

Earlier images of the Guggenheim model show a significantly different model from the one now at MoMA. Photographs of the model show the observatory, which is now absent; that it had four right-angled spirals instead of three tapered ones; and that it opened to display the interior on a vertical axis rather than a horizontal one (fig. 14). The surviving model is also clearly larger, taking up nearly an entire city block, as the museum does today. The iteration seen in these early photographs was in fact damaged in transit, on its way from New York to Taliesin in 1947.[10] A new model was commissioned, which allowed Wright to incorporate alterations that had been made over the past two years, including the acquisition of the neighboring southern plot of land.

It is widely held that the earlier model was destroyed, implying that the surviving model was a distinct undertaking, made from scratch.[11] Evidence on the model itself suggests otherwise. The acrylic skylight, for one, was evidently reused, as it looks identical to that shown in earlier images. Further, radiographs of the spiral reveal that the original form was used as a "skeleton" for the new: the earlier, vertical profile is present on the interior of the form, with the new, tapered profile pinned to the exterior (fig. 15). This second, larger iteration, completed in 1947, was featured in Wright's touring exhibition *Sixty Years of Living Architecture*, which concluded in a temporary pavilion adjacent to the museum in 1953. Between this date and the museum's construction in 1956, Wright continued to modify his design, as exemplified by photograph of the model in the Archives, with his alterations penciled directly on top (fig. 16).

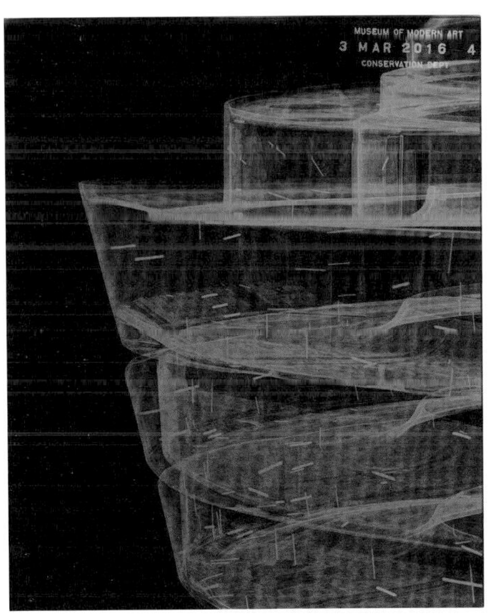

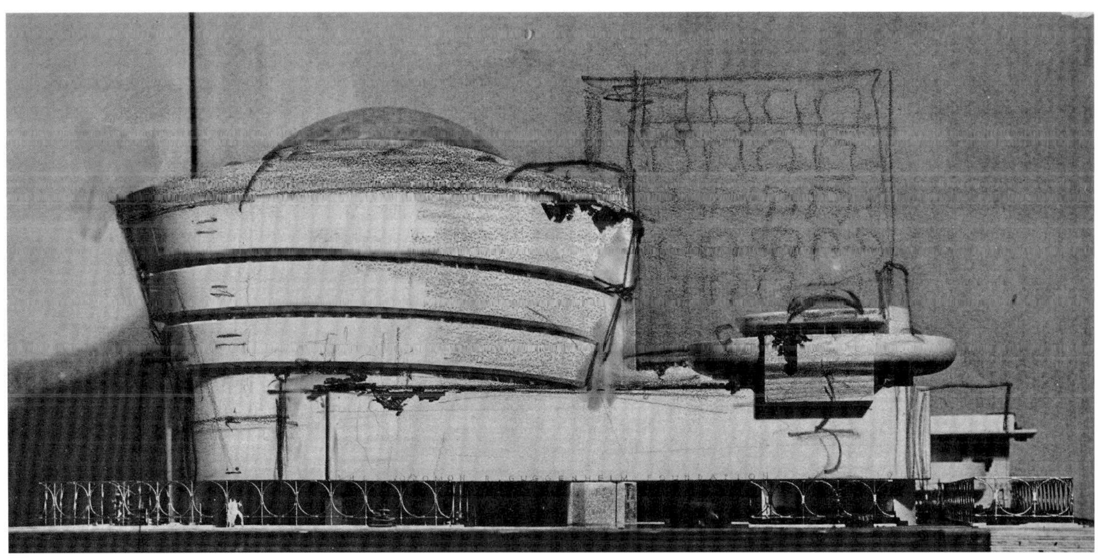

Fig. 15. Solomon R. Guggenheim Museum. Radiograph of the model's spiral ramp, 2016

Fig. 16. Solomon R. Guggenheim Museum. Photograph of model with Wright's modifications. Gelatin silver print with pencil, 5 x 9 3/4 in. (12.7 x 24.8 cm)

The 1947 modification, which may have spruced up the model's appearance at the time, does not account for its white finish today, which seems uncharacteristically pristine for a seventy-year-old paint job, and, more importantly, goes against Wright's well-established preferences.[12] To better understand the history of the paint layers on the model, two types of analysis were performed. First, cross-sectional analysis, wherein a tiny chip of paint, no larger than a pinhead, was removed from the exterior and viewed under magnification on its side to reveal the layers of paint applied beforehand. The cross section (fig. 17) shows that three layers of light, neutral shades sit below the white surface. The lowest layer, presumably the one applied in 1947, is darker and warmer than the upper layers, closer to ocher or beige than white.

The second analysis was employed by MoMA's conservation scientists to characterize the binders of the paints.[13] The bottom layer was found to be an alkyd, a commercial paint prevalent in the 1940s, while the topmost layer was found to be polyvinyl acetate, a paint that gained popularity in the second half of the twentieth century. The color of the model today, then, is likely the result of a treatment that happened after the 1947 modification.

Clues to the model's history can be found in the standing building, which today, like the model, is a cool shade of white. During a restoration campaign over 2005–08, the museum had its own paint history analyzed by architectural conservators, who took cross sections that reinforce the fact that Wright had intended for the building to be a darker, warmer shade than it is today. That is, the cross sections of the building closely resemble those of the model: darker neutral shades below progressively lighter, cooler ones (fig. 18). Additionally, the Guggenheim Archives holds a brochure for exterior paint (fig. 19) that would be used on the building, with Wright's initials approving a beige—decidedly non-white—square. Lastly, color images in the museum archive—and, surely, those who remember the museum in its first twenty years—attest to the building's original beige exterior. As tastes changed over the years, however, and long after Wright's death in 1959, the building became cooler and whiter. Presented with this evidence of an original darker, warmer hue, the New York City Landmarks Commission nevertheless elected to keep the newer color, which they felt better complemented new neighboring buildings, including a 1992 limestone addition to the museum built by Gwathmey Siegel & Associates. In this restoration effort they were not seeking to recover Wright's original vision, but to recognize "the evolution of the Guggenheim" over time.[14] In turn, as it continued to be exhibited after Wright's death, the model was also repeatedly whitewashed; perhaps because the earlier paint layers were grimy or discolored, restorers matched their repainting palette not to the model, but to the building the model represented.

TREATMENT

One may argue that the modifications the Guggenheim model underwent after Wright's death—namely, the replacement of abstract, carved wooden landscaping with the more figurative plant-based trees, in addition to an overall whitening of the surface—form valuable evidence of the model's continued evolution, which echoed that of the museum itself. But the Guggenheim model does not share the functionality or neighborly responsibilities of the actual building. Moreover, it is now housed in MoMA's Department of Architecture and Design, where the intentions of the creator are typically prioritized over modifications by others.

To restore the model to its 1947 incarnation, however, especially given its relatively good condition, would be invasive and risky. Changing its overall color, by either adding a new layer of paint or by removing all but the original layer, would require disassembly, a precarious venture for old cardboard and plastic joined together with pins and aging adhesive. Given that the shape is intact as Wright left it, with color and landscaping as the only evident posthumous departures from his vision, MoMA curators and conservators opted for a virtual approach to restoration. The model was captured in high-resolution images that were then recolored with image-editing software, using the lowest layer of paint as a color guide. The new landscaping was then digitally removed, creating an approximation of how the model would look

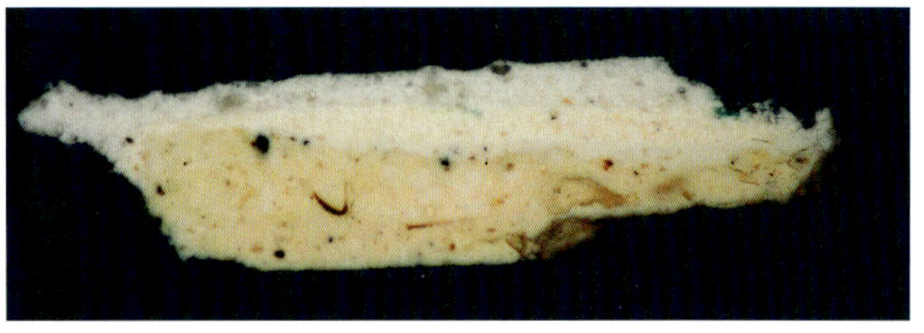

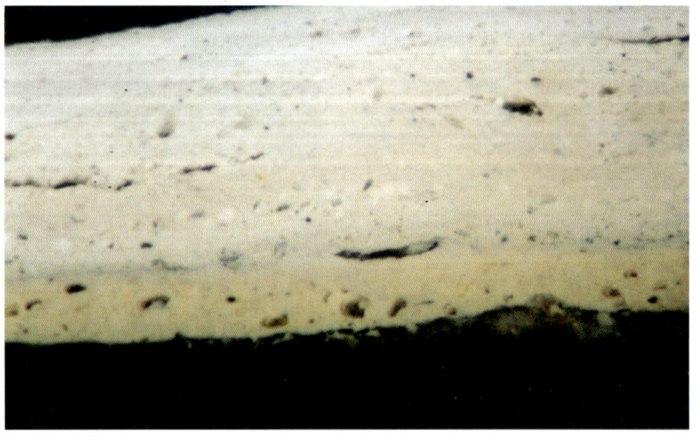

Fig. 17. Solomon R. Guggenheim Museum. Cross section of a paint chip from the model

Fig. 18. Solomon R. Guggenheim Museum. Color stratigraphy of paint layers removed during the museum's 2005–08 restoration. Solomon R. Guggenheim Foundation, New York

had its 1947 form been preserved (see p. 227 right). When the resulting rendering is displayed alongside the physical model, changes made in the later restorations are immediately apparent.

It is perhaps unsurprising that both the St. Mark's Tower and Guggenheim models, which took several forms and had variable uses in Wright's lifetime, have continued to change in appearance and purpose since his death. They are exhibited now as they never have been before: St. Mark's Tower in a hybrid state, combining two past iterations in a partial restoration, and the Guggenheim, shown alongside its virtual, "unrestored" doppelgänger. This presentation is by no means definitive or prescriptive. The curators' and conservators' intention is to provide a fuller account of the models' histories—including their past and present conservation efforts—to ignite discussion about the roles these objects play in our understanding of Wright's practice.

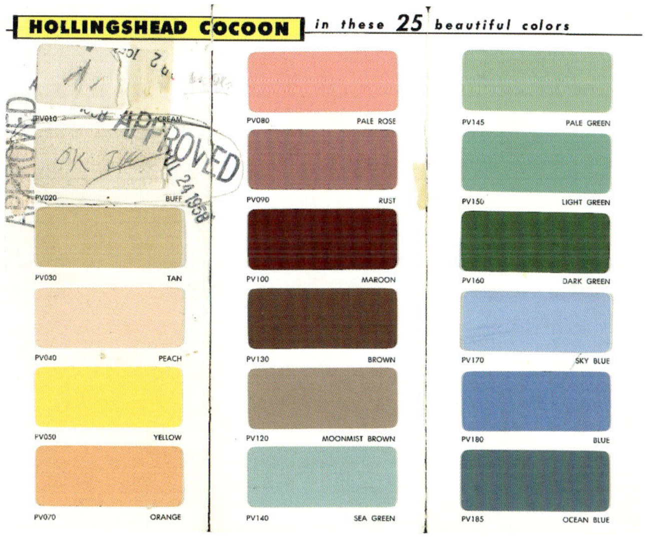

Fig. 19. Hollingshead Cocoon exterior paint brochure, n.d. Solomon R. Guggenheim Museum Archives, New York

Notes

1. This study would not have been possible without the generous support of many. I am especially grateful to the following for their efforts and assistance: Roger Griffith, Jim Coddington, Lauren Klein, Chris McGlinchey, Lynda Zycherman, Megan Randall, Jennifer Gray, Betsy Hawley, Barry Bergdoll, Shelley Hayreh, Nicole Richard, Janet Parks, Paul Galloway, Pamela Popeson, Patricio del Real, Glen Boornazian, Rael Lewis, Neil Levine, Kathryn Smith, and Paul Kruty.

2. While there is discussion of Wright's exhibitions that featured models—for example, Kathryn Smith, "The Show to End All Shows: Frank Lloyd Wright and The Museum of Modern Art, 1940," in *The Show to End All Shows: Frank Lloyd Wright and The Museum of Modern Art, 1940*, ed. Peter Reed and William Kaizen, Studies in Modern Art 8 (New York: The Museum of Modern Art, 2004) and Neil Levine, *The Urbanism of Frank Lloyd Wright* (Princeton N. J.: Princeton University Press, 2016)—their precise utility and history have not been investigated.

3. Wright, "In the Cause of Architecture, I: The Logic of the Plan," *Architectural Record*, January 1928. Reprinted in *Frank Lloyd Wright Collected Writings*, vol. 1, *1894–1930*, ed. Bruce Brooks Pfeiffer (New York: Rizzoli, 1992), p. 249.

4. Architect's Models Co. Philadelphia, letter to Frank Lloyd Wright, December 1, 1910, A001A06, Frank Lloyd Wright Foundation Archives (The Museum of Modern Art | Avery Architectural & Fine Arts Library, Columbia University, New York).

5. Guthrie, letter to Wright, May 20, 1930, G007 E01, Wright Foundation Archives (MoMA | Avery).

6. Frank Lloyd Wright, *The Disappearing City* (New York: William Farquhar Payson; 1932), pp. 70–71.

7. This omission of vertical moldings over the copper reliefs was used in Wright's H. C. Price Company Tower in Bartlesville, Oklahoma (1952–56), the ultimate realization of Wright's taproot design, which exhibits the same principals of St. Mark's Tower.

8. Jade R, a white aqueous adhesive emulsion containing ethylene vinyl acetate (20/80) copolymer that has been modified to be sensitive to water.

9. Wright, letter to Harry Guggenheim, March 17, 1958, G191810, Wright Foundation Archives (MoMA | Avery).

10. A letter confirming damage to the model was sent from Albert E. Thiele to Eugene Masselink, October 29, 1947, Solomon R. Guggenheim Foundation, New York.

11. This is no doubt due to the fact that in his correspondence with his clients, Wright writes of "remaking the model" at "great expense." Wright, letter to Albert E. Thiele, April 17, 1947; and Wright, letter to Solomon Guggenheim, April 23, 1947, Solomon R. Guggenheim Foundation, New York.

12. Gillermo Zuaznabar, "Color Form and Meaning in the Guggenheim Museum," in *The Guggenheim: Frank Lloyd Wright and the Making of the Modern Museum* (New York: Solomon R. Guggenheim Museum, 2009), pp. 101–09.

13. The paint was characterized using Fourier transform infrared spectroscopy.

14. The New York City Landmarks Preservation Commission, Certificate of Appropriateness #08-5025, issued November 20, 2007.

ARCHITECTURAL DRAWING: MATERIALS, PROCESS, PEOPLE

JANET PARKS

Graphic expression was an important component of Frank Lloyd Wright's architectural ideas, an integral part of his lifelong passion for the arts, for Japanese prints, and for printing projects. His drawings are powerful, captivating both the public and the professional audience. They can be compared to works as diverse as the haunting prints of Giovanni Battista Piranesi, the masterful watercolors of the American architect Alexander Jackson Davis, and the nocturnal visions of New York City by Hugh Ferriss. Wright's work also had multiple periods—early, middle, and late—like the career of a painter. Drawings as different as those for Unity Temple (1905–08), Fallingwater (1934–37), and Marin County Civic Center (1957–70) emerged from the same creative spirit.

Wright used the publication and exhibition of drawings to promote his architecture throughout his career. The summa of his early projects is the lithograph portfolio *Ausgeführte Bauten und Entwürfe von Frank Lloyd Wright*, also known as the Wasmuth portfolio, published in 1910 in Berlin. His many texts showcased drawings of his projects in architectural journals, notably the monographic issues of the January 1938 *Architectural Record* and the 1948 *Architectural Forum*. Wright's work was exhibited in nearly every year of his career.[1] Prompted by the 1952 traveling exhibition *Sixty Years of Living Architecture*, Edgar Kaufmann, Jr., an early apprentice of Wright's, published a book of the architect's drawings to "reveal something of the spirit as well as the working ways of one of our century's great men."[2]

Wright's drawings and papers were secured as an archive at Taliesin West, in Arizona, after his death, in 1959. Today, interest in these drawings is high, but, just as H. Allen Brooks observed in 1966, the processes for making them remains little-known.[3] With the Frank Lloyd Wright Foundation Archives open to study, the drawings can be reexamined in the context of correspondence, oral histories by apprentices, photographs, and other documents.

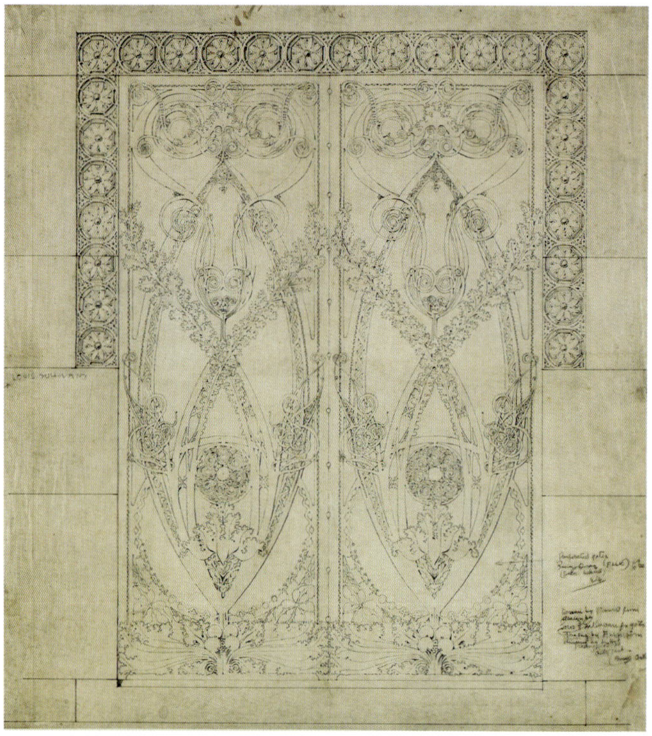

THE STUDIOS

In 1890, when Wright was working in Chicago as head draftsman in the office of Dankmar Adler & Louis Sullivan, few architectural schools existed in the United States (fig. 1). Most architects and their staff began as office boys and low-level draftsmen, if they had any technical training at all.[4] In 1897 the Illinois state legislature enacted a licensing requirement for architects. Practicing architects like Wright were grandfathered in without taking the examination, but many opposed the requirement, equating it to the regulation of street vendors.[5] Even so, Wright often employed licensed or educated architects. Among the drafting staff at the Oak Park studio, Walter Burley Griffin and Marion Mahony, trained at the University of Illinois and Massachusetts Institute of Technology respectively, were the first to take the Illinois licensing exam, scoring high marks.[6] William Drummond passed the exam in 1902. Isabel Roberts, who worked mainly on ornamental glass designs for Wright, had trained at Masqueray-Chambers, a New York architectural atelier for women.[7]

When Wright began his independent practice, in 1893, he hired professional renderers, but by the end of the decade the Oak Park staff was executing the presentation drawings. Wright and many of his contemporaries were active in the Chicago Architectural Club, whose major event was the annual exhibition held at the Art Institute of Chicago beginning in 1894. The catalogues for these displays were heavily illustrated.[8] The 1894 catalogue reproduces as item 381 Wright's black-ink competition drawing for the Milwaukee Public Library and Museum, the preliminary version of which survives in the Archives (fig. 2). The 1900

Fig. 1. Louis Sullivan (American, 1856–1924). Wainwright Tomb, Bellefontaine Cemetery, St. Louis, Missouri. 1892. Ornamental gate rendered by Frank Lloyd Wright. Ink and pencil on drafting cloth, 27 5/8 x 23 3/4 in. (70 x 60.2 cm). Avery Architectural & Fine Arts Library, Columbia University, New York

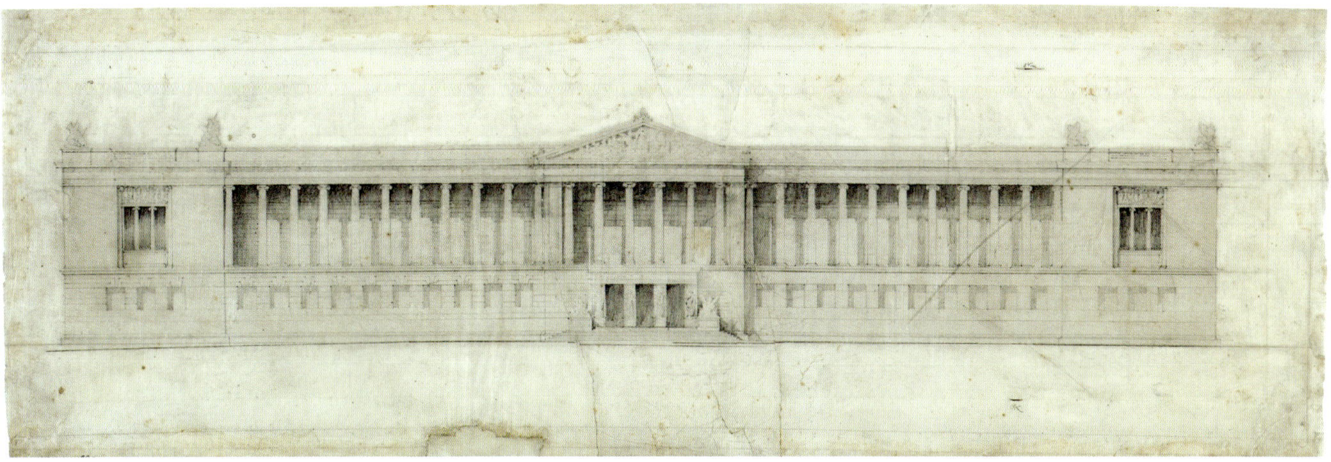

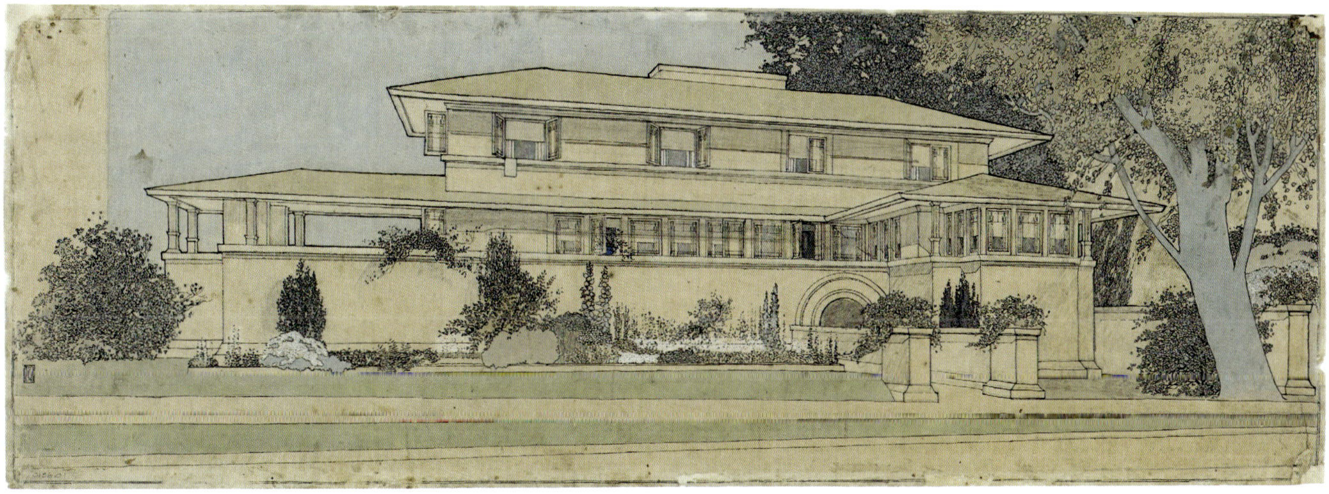

catalogue reproduces several renderings that show a new visual direction, a spare watercolor presentation with no figures and few trees to detract from the architecture.

The most talented graphic hand belonged to Mahony. Firsthand accounts differ about which drawings Mahony drew but none dispute the primacy of her style in the Oak Park studio. Her linear sensibility added an ornamental element to perspective drawings of Wright's work (see p. 35, plate 5).[9] Birch Burdette Long, a professional renderer in the studio, worked in a similar style (fig. 3), but he left Chicago for New York in 1903, leaving Mahony as the dominant force. Other draftsmen began to draw convincingly in this manner as well, so that when Brooks interviewed former draftsmen Barry Byrne, John H. Howe, and John Van Bergen on the authorship of the drawings used as the basis of the Wasmuth plates, they agreed on only four images.[10]

The Wasmuth portfolio gave Wright the opportunity to present his work within a unified aesthetic. The lithographic plates were often copied from existing renderings or from photographs of the built projects themselves, while working drawings were refined into a compatible stylized presentation. The working plans for the Heurtley House (fig. 4), for example, were stripped of their dimensions and technical information and reproduced together with the second-floor plan and perspective on the same vertical sheet in the published portfolio (fig. 5). Wright designed the layout and supervised his son John and Taylor Woolley in the redrawing of each project according to this aesthetic, in which a delicate line quality—almost a silhouette of the building's volume—contrasts with a light wash treatment of surface planes.[11]

Between Wright's return, in 1910, from preparing the Wasmuth portfolio in Europe and his resettlement at Taliesin in Wisconsin in 1928, his firm produced drawings in a variety of styles. The Wasmuth aesthetic persisted in the Bogk House (1916–17) and Goethe Street House drawings (1913). Continuing in this vein was Emil Brodelle, a talented renderer responsible for the Midway Gardens and the Imperial Hotel perspectives, both 1913–14. John Wright and Woolley, both of whom had worked on the Wasmuth, returned to the firm as well. During this period Wright hired a number of European-trained architects. The drawings for the American System-Built Houses (1915–17), also

Fig. 2. Milwaukee Public Library and Museum. Project, 1893. Elevation. Pencil on paper, 9 3/4 x 28 1/8 in. (24.8 x 71.4 cm)

Fig. 3. Thomas House, Oak Park, Illinois. 1901. Perspective. Ink, gouache, and pencil on tracing paper, 7 7/8 x 21 7/8 in. (20 x 55.6 cm)

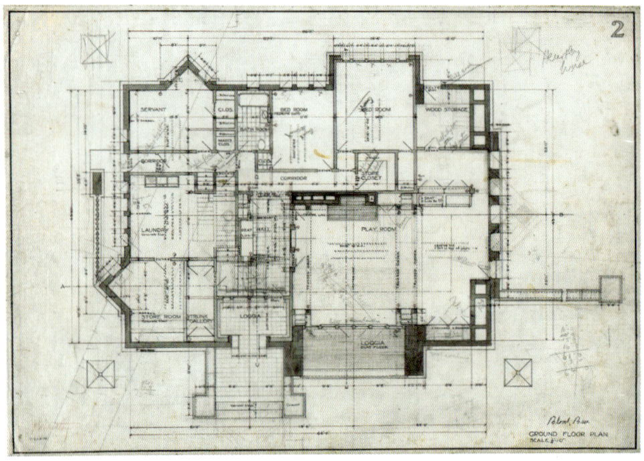

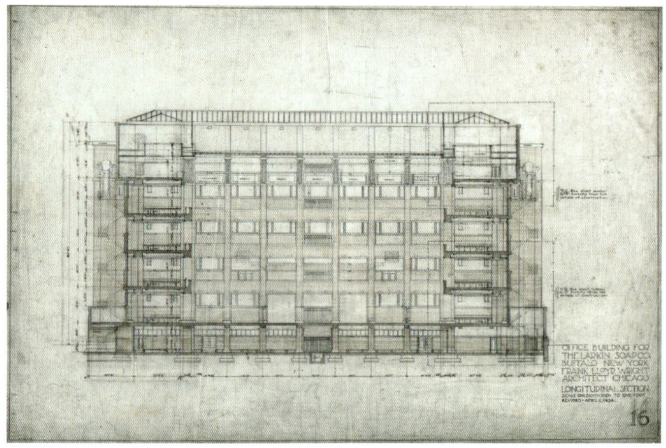

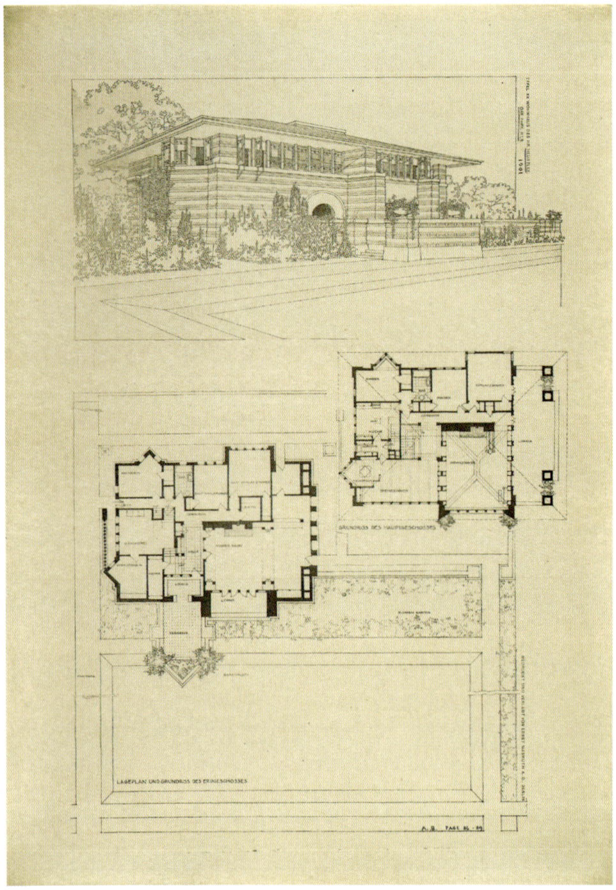

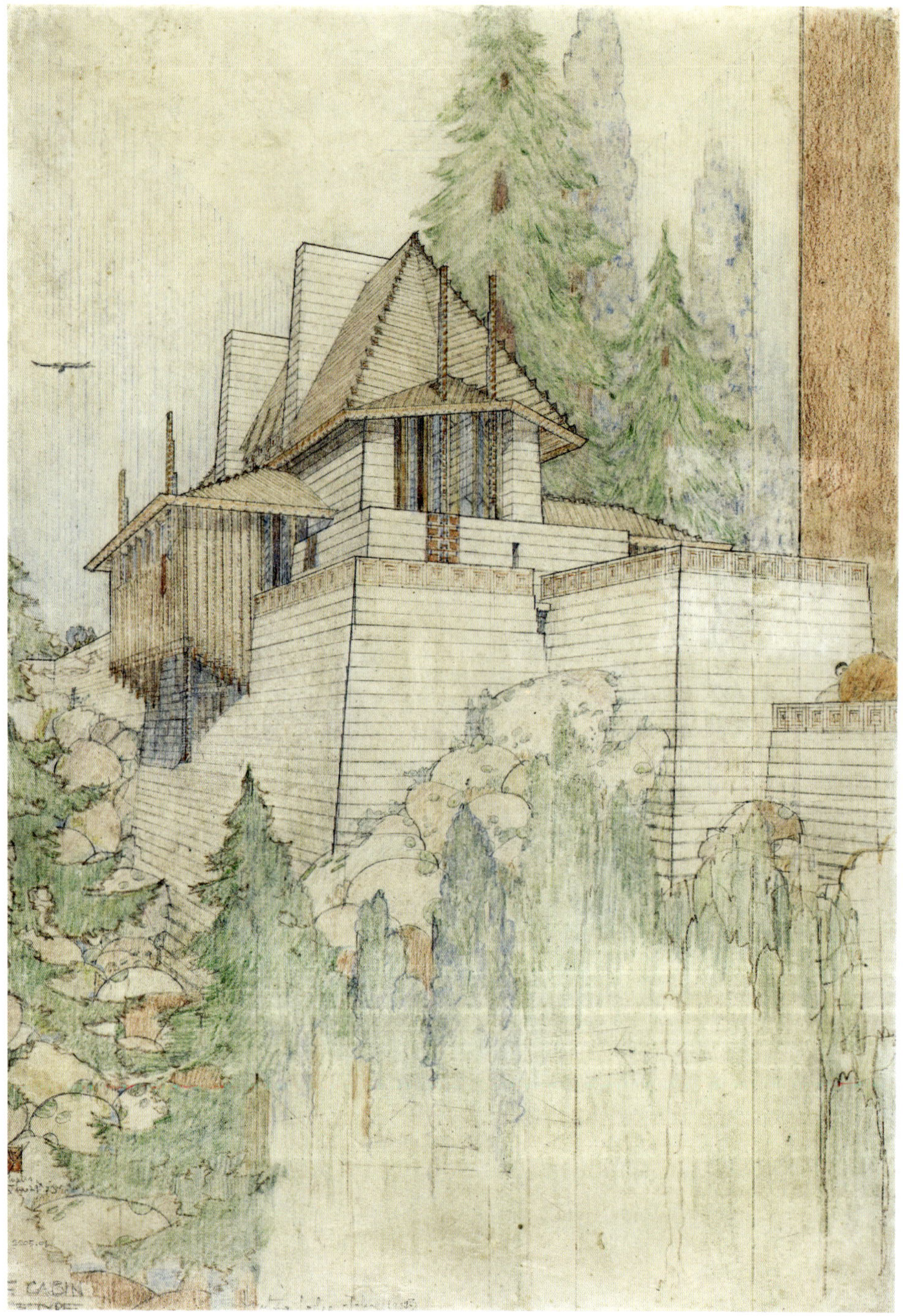

Fig. 4. Heurtley House, Oak Park, Illinois. 1902–03. Ground-floor plan. Ink, pencil, and colored pencil on drafting cloth, 20 5/8 x 29 1/2 in. (52.4 x 74.9 cm)

Fig. 5. Heurtley House, Oak Park. Illinois. 1902–03. Perspective, ground-, and first-floor plans. Plate XX from *Ausgeführte Bauten und Entwürfe von Frank Lloyd Wright* (Berlin: Ernst Wasmuth, 1910). Avery Architectural & Fine Arts Library, Columbia University, New York

Fig. 6. Larkin Building, Buffalo, New York. 1902–06. Longitudinal section. Ink, ink wash, and pencil on drafting cloth, 24 3/8 x 36 3/4 in. (61.9 x 93.3 cm)

Fig. 7. Lake Tahoe Resort, Lake Tahoe, California. Project, 1923–24. Perspective of a cabin. Pencil and colored pencil on tracing paper, 21 3/4 x 15 in. (55.2 x 38.1 cm)

executed in the Wasmuth style, are generally credited to Antonin Raymond, a Czech who arrived in 1916, with contributions by the Austrian Rudolf Schindler, who joined the office in 1918.

For complex projects such as the Larkin Building (fig. 6), and later the Imperial Hotel (1913–23) and the Hollyhock (Barnsdall) House (1918–21), working drawings were developed at a larger scale, detailed extensively, and standardized by sheet size. Schindler signed drawings for the Hollyhock House, among others, while Wright was in Tokyo working on the Imperial Hotel. In the 1920s Wright designed projects, largely unbuilt, for which the drawings were done in soft pencil and colored pencil on tracing paper—conceptual presentation renderings rather than conventional production drawings (fig. 7). Wright's own hand is most evident in these works; others in the studio, including his son Lloyd, followed suit.

During these years the staff included the Swiss architect Werner Moser, the Austrian Richard Neutra, the Japanese architects Kameki and Nobuko Tsuchiura, and the Canadian William Smith. After Wright resettled in Wisconsin, he hired more Europe-trained architects: Vladimir Karfik (present-day Slovenia), Heinrich Klumb (Germany), Michael Kostanecki (Poland), and Rudolf Mock (Switzerland). Takehiko Okami (Japan) and the Americans George Cronin and Donald Walker were also on staff. The studio still produced conceptual drawings in pencil and colored pencil on tracing paper but pencil-and-ink drawings on heavier tracing paper were the media for working drawings. In 1932, a time of few commissions, Wright opened the Taliesin Fellowship, a school for architectural apprentices who would "learn by doing." When the last of the Europeans departed, Moser in 1931 and Klumb in 1933, Wright assumed charge of a community of younger apprentices, many with no practical background at all. The predominant office style remained the same, with working drawings now executed on lighter tracing paper in fine pencil line, a style that prevailed through the 1930s.

Among this group of apprentices, John Howe quickly became head draftsman, having received training from Klumb. Howe's graphic genius matched up well with Wright's; both had an affinity for colored pencil and pencil on lightweight supports, the office style for the remainder of Wright's career. Howe's contribution to this style was his mastery in using ink lines, often in light-brown ink, to underscore the surfaces and volume of the buildings. After Wright's death, in 1959, Howe remained head draftsman with Taliesin Associated Architects until 1964. After his departure, the drafting styles of individual architects emerged.

DRAFTING MATERIALS

Wright once wrote that by nature he tended to the linear and rectangular—the T square and triangle—and away from the curvilinear forms of Louis Sullivan's ornament (see fig. 1).[12] Many photographs of him in the drafting room confirm this practice. His hand is evident in the conceptual drawing for the Oak Park studio (fig. 8), an elevation drawn with straight edges. The borders around the elevation are covered with annotations, calculations, and notes in Wright's small and slightly rounded handwriting.

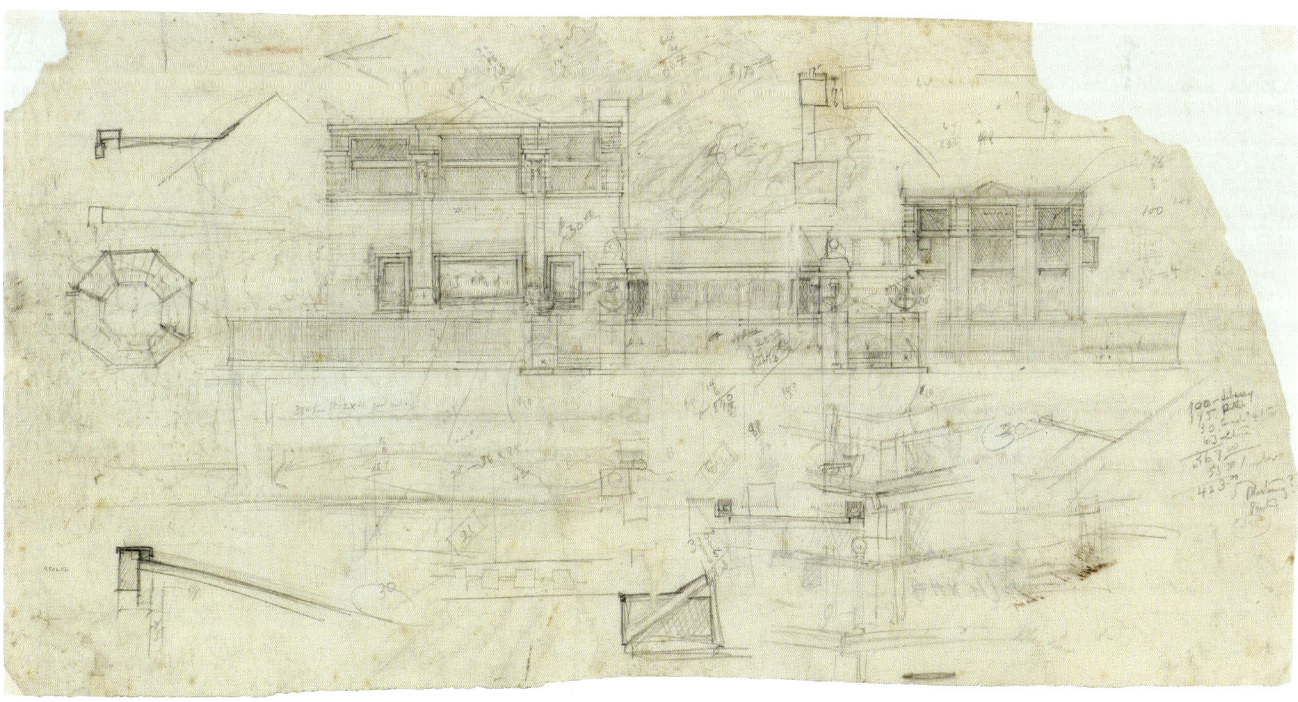

Fig. 8. Wright House and Studio, Oak Park, Illinois. 1895–98. Plan and elevation studies for the studio addition. Pencil on tracing paper, 15 5/8 x 30 in. (39.7 x 76.2 cm)

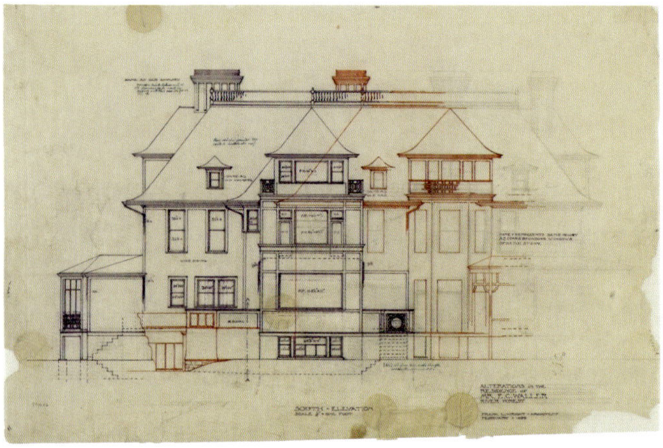

Fig. 9. Waller House, River Forest, Illinois. Alterations, 1899. South elevation. Ink on tracing paper, 19 x 29 in. (48.3 x 73.7 cm)

The Oak Park studio used standard drafting materials. Translucent supports—drafting cloth with black ink and tracing papers with a variety of media—were used for working drawings; multiple prints could be made from them during construction. For Wright's remodeling of John Root's Waller House (fig. 9) the staff redrew Root's drawings on tracing paper, although they could have printed his original cloth drawings, which Wright owned.[13] Red and purple inks, a drawing practice used by many architectural firms in Chicago, respectively indicated the original house and the changes. The purple ink also could be used for aesthetic purposes, as in the drawings for the Moore House (fig. 10). Nearly thirty years later, Wright redesigned the Moore House after a fire and again employed the two-color method in the drawings to differentiate the surviving structure from his reconstruction.

Large projects like the Imperial Hotel and the Hollyhock House needed durable drawings from which many prints could be made. The use of black ink on drafting cloth, a technique taught in architecture schools, suited this purpose, but once Wright's trained American and European architects had left his office he rarely used it. In the Wright Foundation Archives of 55,000 drawings, only about 10 percent are ink on cloth and fewer than 100 were drawn after the Hollyhock House and Imperial Hotel were completed.[14]

The drawings of the 1920s broke from the Wasmuth pattern, showing greater freedom in Wright's own hand and the incorporation of work by his son Lloyd. Tracing papers and colored pencils were often used, for example in Smith's and the Tsuchiuras' drawings for the Ennis, Millard (La Miniatura), Storer, and Freeman textile-block houses. Neutra and Moser worked on the drawings for the National Life Insurance Company Building (1923–25) and the Nakoma Country Club (1923–24). For the Doheny

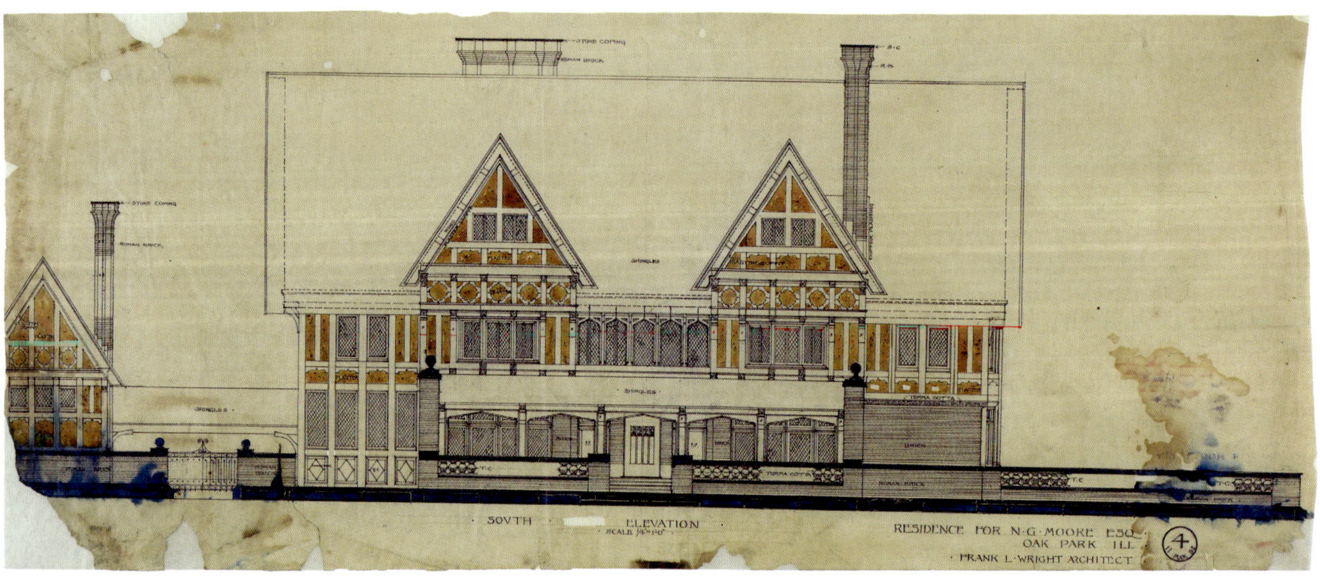

Fig. 10. Moore House, Oak Park, Illinois. 1895. South elevation. Ink on paper, 15 ³/₄ x 37 ¹/₄ in. (40 x 94.6 cm)

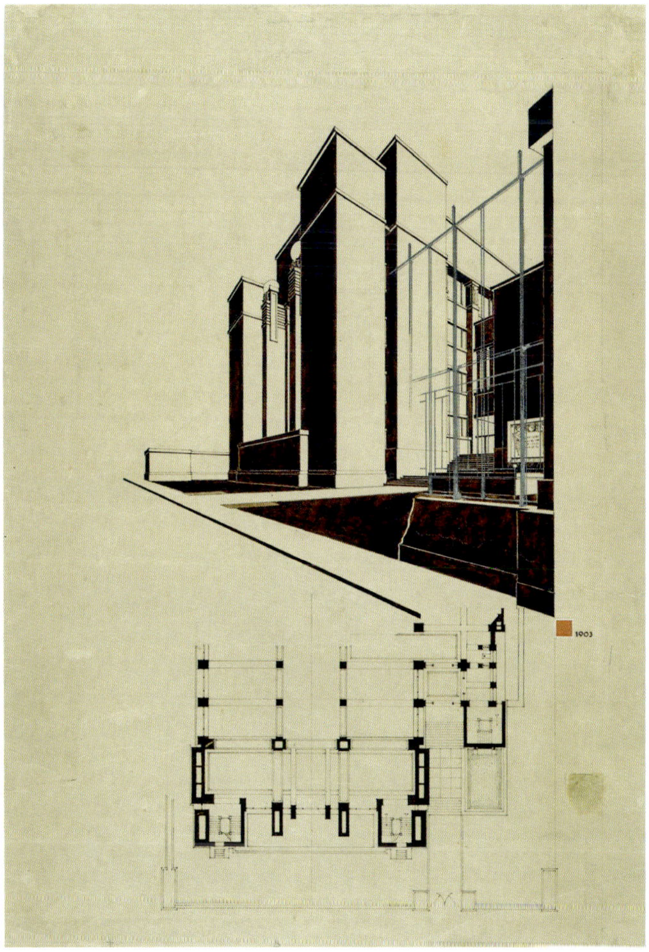

Fig. 11. Larkin Building, Buffalo, New York. 1902–06. Perspective and detail of the plan, c. 1930. Ink and pencil on paper, 34 1/2 x 21 1/8 in. (87.6 x 53.7 cm)

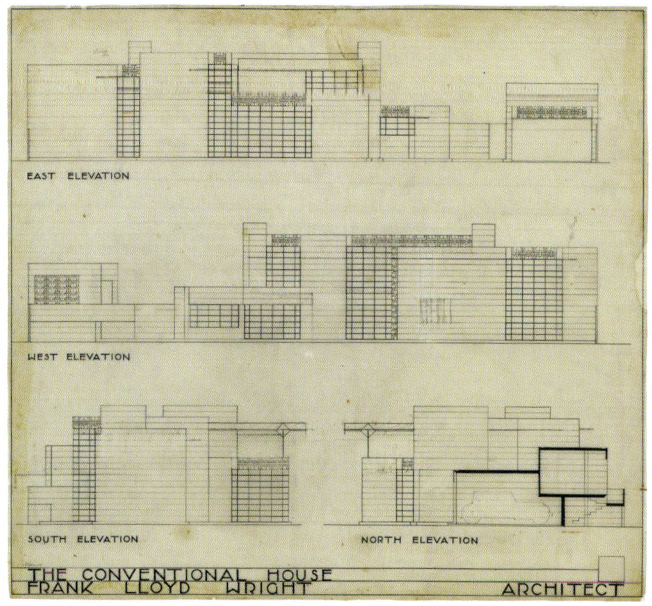

Fig. 12. The Conventional House. Project, 1932. Elevations. Ink on tracing paper, 25 1/2 x 27 7/8 in. (64.8 x 70.8 cm)

Ranch Development and Lake Tahoe Resort projects Wright and his son produced many pencil and colored-pencil drawings on thin sheets of off-white tracing paper. Graph lines, if they appear, were hand drawn in multiple colors—red, yellow, and blue.

In keeping with his passion for Japanese art, Wright often drew on Japanese paper and even printed his photographs on it.[15] Many Imperial Hotel drawings were executed on Japanese rice paper, as were drawings of the Booth House (1911–12) and many drawings from the 1920s. Kameki Tsuchiura mentioned Wright working on a waxed Japanese rice paper, brought back by Wright from Tokyo, that worked well with colored pencil.[16] In a letter of 1938 to Arata Endo, Wright remarked, "I miss the Japanese tracing paper we used to use—the thin silky kind," and he asked Endo to have the paper company Haibara send him twenty-four rolls of tracing paper because there was nothing comparable in the United States and "we use such an awful lot of it."[17] Curtis Besinger, a Taliesin apprentice from 1939 to 1955, also recalled the use of Japanese paper for many drawings.[18]

Wright was also open to unconventional drawing supports. Following European criticism of the architect's work, Klumb, chief draftsman from 1929 to 1933, suggested that they "reduce his renderings to two-dimensional black on white graphic presentations that modern architects are addicted to."[19] These were reproduced on roll-up window shades, according to Klumb, and used for the 1930 Princeton lectures (fig. 11), after which they were included in a 1931 exhibition, organized by H. T. Wijdeveld and Eric Mendelsohn, that toured Europe for ten months. Following in the modern graphic style is the drawing for The Conventional House of 1932 (fig. 12), executed in black ink on heavier, smoother tracing paper. Resin-coated tracing paper, a heavily calendared tracing paper favored by European architects for its smooth surface and translucency, was used for drawings for the Moore House reconstruction in 1923.

STUDIO PROCESS

Memoirs and oral histories from the Taliesin apprentices, particularly those by Howe and his assistant Besinger, are informative about both general studio practice and specific drawings. Howe spent twenty-seven years with Wright, most as head draftsman; Besinger, an architecture graduate of the University of Kansas, arrived in 1939 and stayed until 1955. Their descriptions of the Rogers Lacy Hotel design of 1946–47 are typical of their accounts. Wright's design concept (fig. 13) was fully developed by the time he put pencil to paper and his drawing is laid out on a modular grid, with floor heights, notations, and two variations of the tower design. The paper was extended several times as the building's scale stretched past the original sheet, and a small sketch pasted over a hole cut out of the sheet indicated a change in the design. From this drawing Howe gathered information to create plans, elevations, sections, and perspectives. The rendering (fig. 15) was by Howe alone—Wright's pencil did not touch it.[20] The presentation set of working drawings was executed chiefly by Besinger (fig. 14), who recalled that they were drawn on delicate Japanese paper cut from 30-inch (76-centimeter) rolls. This drawing surface allowed only the slightest touch of the pen, for fear of blotting, and no erasures. Colored pencil was applied for tinting, sometimes on the verso of the sheet.[21]

This process—conceptual designs by Wright, working drawings by the head draftsman—would have been standard procedure in his studios. Stories abound about Wright's ability to lay out the essential elements of a design in a few quickly realized drawings. He liked an audience and knew how to put on a show for his staff to convey his ideas to them. On Christmas Day of 1928, at Taliesin in Wisconsin, Walker observed a four-hour drawing session in which Wright laid out the basic scheme for a tower for the Church of St. Mark's-in-the-Bouwerie, declaring when he had finished, "Don, that is architecture. Make me some working drawings."[22]

The Oak Park studio had been much smaller than the Taliesin offices, but its operation was essentially the same. Byrne relates, "When projects were turned over to me to develop into working drawings, the original Wright-made studies would come into my hands with the plan established and the main theme of the exterior design clearly defined in elevation. The development of all implied but not delineated portions of the project then became the problems of the student draftsman, subject to the master's approval and often to his corrections."[23]

Howe recalled that soon after his arrival at Wright's studio, Klumb gave him details of the Willey House (1932–34) to draw. He learned to do the full range of working drawings on the Hanna House (fig. 16), including a plan with foliage similar to the drawing published in the 1938 issue of *Architectural Record* dedicated to Wright.[24] Among the manuscripts in the Archives is a list of drawings prepared for this issue, crediting them to nine apprentices: Howe, Cornelia Brierly, Benny Dombar, Blaine Drake, Burt Goodrich, Bob Mosher, Wes Peters, Edgar Tafel, and Jim Thomson.[25] Several of the drawings in the issue are part of the Archives, as well as some prepared for it but not published and others preserved in slightly different forms from the published versions.

Both Howe and Besinger describe Wright making corrections directly on drawings, using no overlay, so that to revise the drawings the draftsman had to erase the corrections and then redraw the changes.[26] According to another

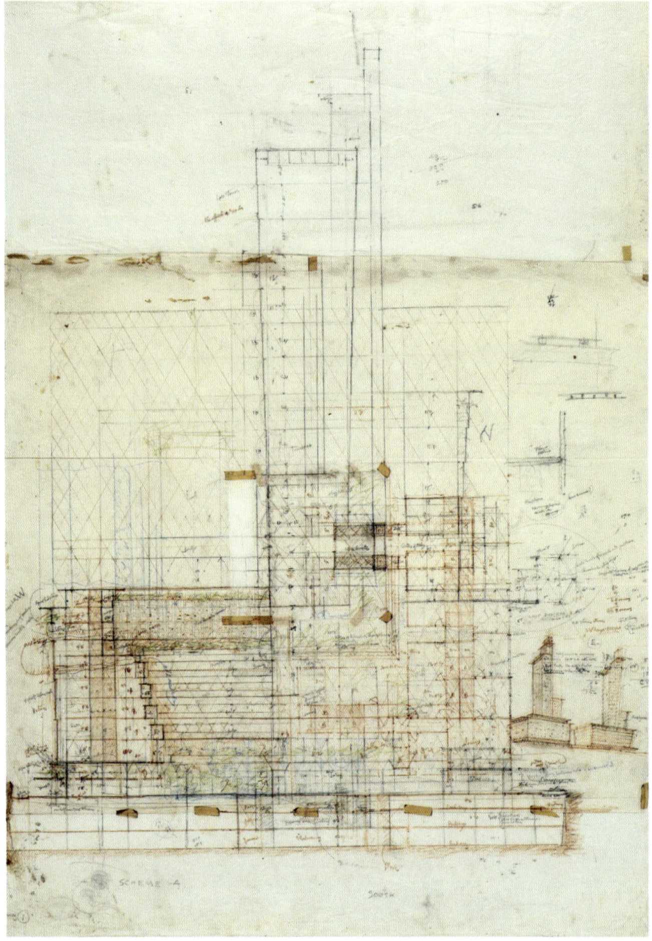

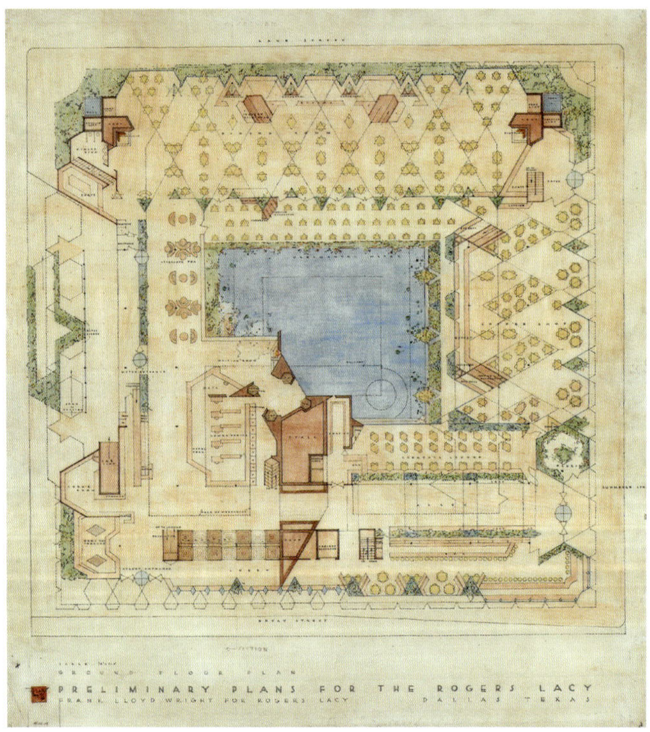

Fig. 13. Rogers Lacy Hotel, Dallas. Project, 1946–47. Section and perspective studies. Pencil and colored pencil on tracing paper, 50 ½ x 35 ½ in. (128.3 x 90.2 cm)

Fig. 14. Rogers Lacy Hotel, Dallas. Project, 1946–47. Ground-floor plan. Ink, pencil, and colored pencil on tracing paper, 33 ¾ x 30 ¼ in. (85.7 x 76.8 cm)

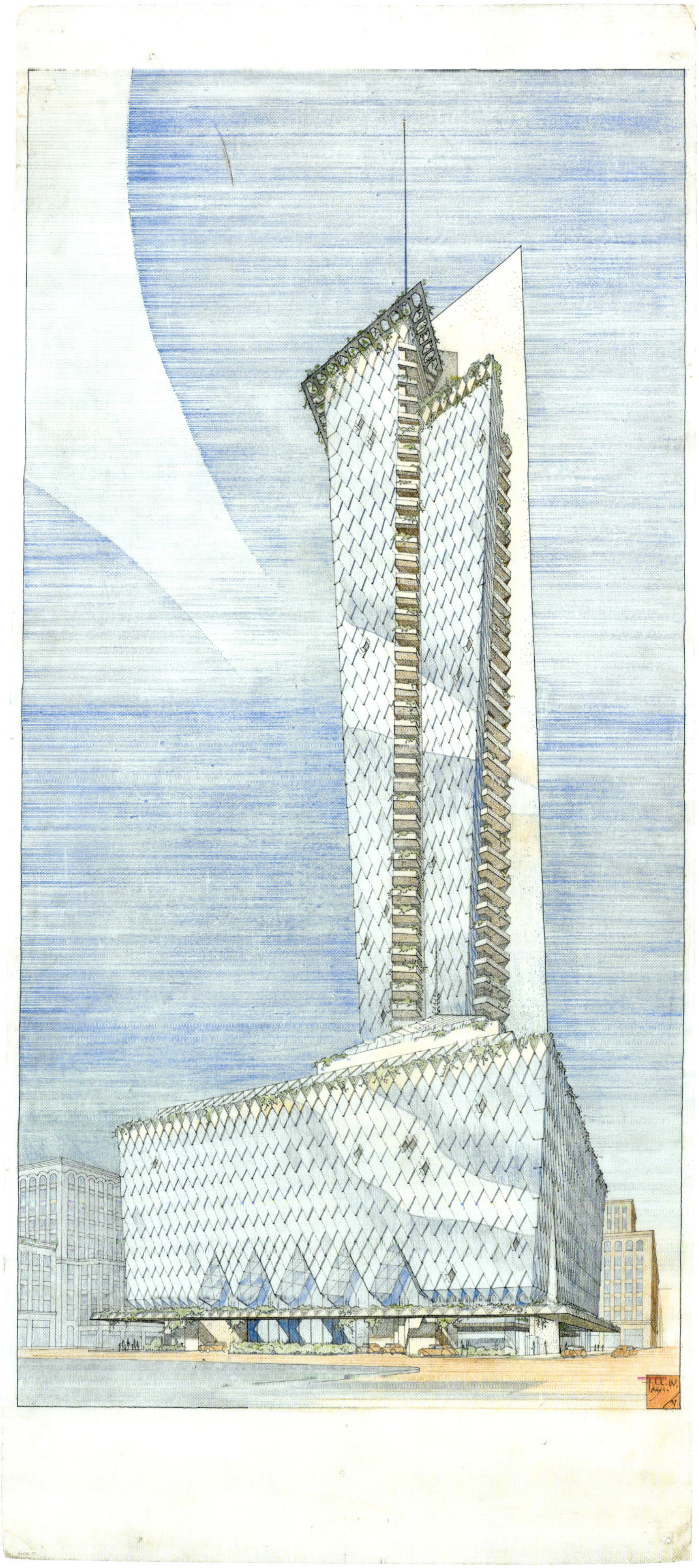

Fig. 15. Rogers Lacy Hotel, Dallas. Project, 1946–47. Perspective.
Colored pencil and ink on tracing paper, 52 ¾ x 29 ¾ in. (134 x 75.6 cm)

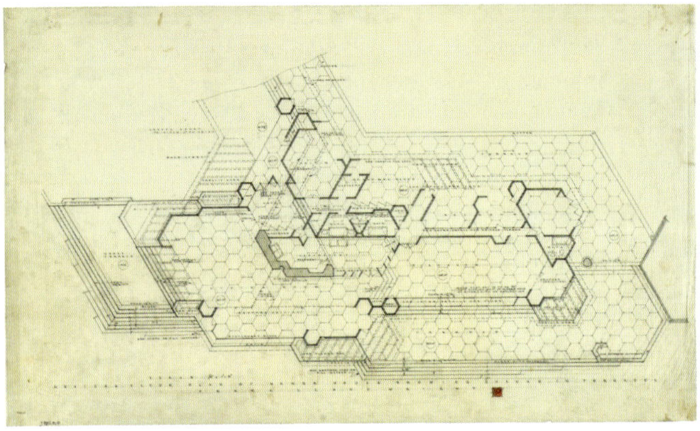

Fig. 16. Hanna House, Palo Alto, California. 1936–37. Ground-floor plan. Pencil on tracing paper, 25 1/4 x 42 1/8 in. (64.1 x 107 cm)

early apprentice, Yen Liang, Wright liked soft pencils and considered the eraser "the most important architectural instrument."[27] This prompted Howe to keep a second set of clean drawings (unknown to Wright, he hoped) that could be updated quickly for prints to be made for the client. Besinger remembered Wright making numerous changes on the drawings for the Usonian house (1953) temporarily constructed on the site of the future Solomon R. Guggenheim Museum:

[We] spent a very intense afternoon erasing and redrawing. . . . Unfortunately, as was true of many such revisions . . . no record of the changes survives. John [Geiger] and I did not make another set of drawings, nor did we make prints before starting work. As we erased and redrew we eliminated any record of the previous house, including Mr. Wright's work on the drawings. What remained was the result of the changes and not a record of the changes themselves.[28]

After Wright simplified the design for the Neils House (1949), whose clients were eager to start construction, Besinger finished the drawings rather than returning them to the original draftsman.[29] In this case there are two plans, one a final version and one showing the traces of reworking.

The Neils House plans also illustrate the predominant use of a module, here a square unit of 4 feet (1.2 meters; conceived in other projects as triangles or hexagons), as the organizational principle for a plan. No dimensions are provided for the rooms or the overall length of the house, although a scale is given. In the Oak Park studio nearly fifty years earlier, Charles E. White had noted Wright's use of modules for elements of the design, like windows, but not the organizational concept of the plan.[30] The Heurtley House plan, for example, has dimensions called out by room and overall areas, and the module of the casement window—of 2 1/2 feet (0.76 meters)—is discreetly included (see p. 238, fig. 4). As Wright's career progressed, though, the module became more prominent. By the time of the Hollyhock House, the plan was placed on a grid of red ink. The system was pervasive during the years of the Taliesin Fellowship, as Besinger writes:

The houses were designed on a grid, generally a rectangular unit system. Dimensions were determined by the location of parts in relation to this grid. One had to have studied the standard detail sheet and to have understood the position of the parts in relation to the grid in order to calculate dimensions. Once a person had done this he found the system of construction logical and simple.[31]

Besinger also noted that this system required fewer drawings per project, and that the absence of "the usual strings of dimensions which located walls, doors, windows, etc." made the design difficult for some builders to bid on. But the system may have been easier for apprentices to learn, enabling the studio to execute a greater number of projects.[32] Howe recounted that a typical drawing took him a day: "One had to move fast to stay ahead of Mr. Wright."[33] Working freehand, Howe drew first in pencil, then in colored pencil, then in brown ink, the last being used to highlight the fascia in the design.[34] Wright often finished off drawings himself by filling in the greenery surrounding the structure.

Besinger summarizes the flow of projects through the studio in three general categories. The first involved a new geometry or concept that captured Wright's attention and resulted in first sketches by Wright in an almost completely realized form. Next were projects in which Wright laid out the general site arrangement and plan, leaving it to the senior apprentices to work out the details before final drawings. And last, to keep up with incoming requests, were projects designed by one of the apprentices and reviewed and revised by Wright before the final set of drawings.[35]

Wright's career lasted seventy-two years and at his death he left a remarkable fifty-one projects on his desk, in various stages of development and realization. Like most architects he maintained staff capable of developing designs in his vocabulary and grammar, as he himself had done for Sullivan. The size and structure of his studios depended on the circumstances of his life, reflecting periods of productivity and turmoil alike. The establishment of the Taliesin Fellowship provided Wright with the energy and skills of the young and devoted apprentices who made possible the third act of his remarkable career, which produced nearly half of his total number of projects. His archival legacy permits the exploration of these relationships and practices, shedding light on the individuals involved and their interactions. Equipped with that knowledge, further examination of the drawings will continue to deepen the understanding of one of history's great creative minds.

Notes

1. See Edgar Kaufmann, Jr., "Frank Lloyd Wright's Architecture Exhibited," *Metropolitan Museum of Art Bulletin* 40, no. 2 (Fall 1982): 5.

2. Kaufmann, in *Taliesin Drawings: Recent Architecture of Frank Lloyd Wright Selected from His Drawings. Comments by Edgar Kaufmann, Jr.*, Problems of Contemporary Art no. 6 (New York: Wittenborn, Schultz, 1952), p. 5.

3. See H. Allen Brooks, "Frank Lloyd Wright and the Wasmuth Drawings," *Art Bulletin* 48, no. 2 (June 1966): 193.

4. On the licensing of architects in Illinois, see Mary N. Woods, *From Craft to Profession: The Practice of Architecture in Nineteenth-Century America* (Berkeley: University of California Press, 1999), p. 44.

5. See Paul Kruty, "A New Look at the Beginnings of the Illinois Architects Licensing Law," *Illinois Historical Journal* 90, no. 3 (Autumn 1997): 154–72.

6. See Myron A. Marty, *Communities of Frank Lloyd Wright: Taliesin and Beyond* (DeKalb: Northern Illinois University Press, 2009).

7. See Nancy K. Morris Smith, ed., "Letters, 1903–1906, by Charles E. White, Jr. from the Studio of Frank Lloyd Wright," *Journal of Architectural Education* 25, no. 4 (Autumn 1971): 105. For the 1900 U.S. census Roberts identified herself as an art student, and from 1910 on as an architect. See John Dalles, "The Pathbreaking Legacy of Ryan and Roberts," in *Reflections from Central Florida: The Quarterly Magazine of the Historical Society of Central Florida* 7, no. 3 (Summer 2009): 8–9. Marion Mahony listed herself as an artist in the 1900 census.

8. PDF's of these catalogues are available on the "Exhibition History" page of the website of the Art Institute of Chicago, at www.artic.edu/research/exhibition-history (accessed November 2016).

9. See White, in Smith, ed., "Letters, 1903–1906, by Charles E. White, Jr.," p. 110; and Barry Byrne, "Review of Arthur Drexler, The Drawings of Frank Lloyd Wright," *Journal of the Society of Architectural Historians* 22, no. 2 (May 1963): 108–9.

10. Brooks, "Frank Lloyd Wright and the Wasmuth Drawings," p. 93.

11. Wright's original designs for the portfolio survive as an album of drawings in the John H. Howe papers, box 2. See http://digital.library.wisc.edu/1711.dl/wiarchives.uw-whs-mss00842 (accessed December 2016). A facsimile of this album was given to Avery Library in June 2016.

12. Wright, *Genius and the Mobocracy* (New York: Duell, Sloan and Pearce, 1949), p. 55.

13. John Root's drawings for the original Waller House are now in the Frank Lloyd Wright Foundation Archives (The Museum of Modern Art | Avery Architectural & Fine Arts Library, Columbia University, New York).

14. New York architects such as Ely Jacques Kahn and Raymond Hood used drafting cloth mainly for large commercial projects. In the mid-1960s, Harrison & Abramovitz produced drawings on drafting cloth for the Metropolitan Opera House at Lincoln Center. See examples in the Avery Architectural & Fine Arts Library, Columbia University.

15. See, e.g., "Shrubs," a photograph in the John Lloyd Wright collection, Avery Architectural & Fine Arts Library.

16. Kameki Tsuchiura, quoted in Edgar Tafel, *About Wright: An Album of Recollections by Those Who Knew Frank Lloyd Wright* (New York: Wiley, 1993), p. 94.

17. Wright, letter to Arata Endo, August 24, 1938. E021A06, Wright Foundation Archives (MoMA | Avery). Haibara had provided mural painters for the Imperial Hotel's Peacock Room and had printed advertisements for the hotel.

18. Curtis Besinger, *Working with Mr. Wright: What It Was Like* (Cambridge: Cambridge University Press, 1995), p. 156.

19. Heinrich Klumb, quoted in Tafel, *About Wright*, p. 100. Klumb was responding to the European criticism of Wright's work in reviews of Heinrich de Fries, *Frank Lloyd Wright. Aus dem Lebenswerke eines Architekten* (Berlin: Verlag Ernst Pollak), 1926.

20. Video interview with Howe, February 14, 1990, transcript, pp. 18–19. Wright Foundation Archives (MoMA | Avery). I thank Jack Quinan for bringing this interview to my attention.

21. See Besinger, *Working with Mr. Wright*, pp. 154–58.

22. Donald Walker, quoted in Tafel, *About Wright*, p. 96.

23. Byrne, "On Frank Lloyd Wright and His Atelier," *Journal of the Association of Collegiate Schools of Architecture* 18, no. 1 (June 1963): 4.

24. Video interview with Howe, transcript, pp. 1 (Willey House), 4 (Hanna House). See also *The Architectural Forum* 68, no. 1 (January 1938).

25. 2401.232, Wright Foundation Archives (MoMA | Avery). Matthew Skjonsberg kindly brought this page to my attention.

26. Besinger, *Working with Mr. Wright*, p. 29; video interview with Howe, transcript, p. 4.

27. Yen Liang, quoted in Tafel, *About Wright*, p. 130.

28. Besinger, *Working with Mr. Wright*, p. 253.

29. Ibid., p. 204.

30. See Smith, ed., "Letters, 1903–1906, by Charles E. White, Jr.," p. 105.

31. Besinger, *Working with Mr. Wright*, p. 32.

32. Taliesin Associated Architects had begun to annotate its drawings with standard strings of dimensions by the 1970s.

33. Video interview with Howe, transcript, p. 9.

34. See Jane King Hession and Tim Quigley, *John H. Howe, Architect: From Taliesin Apprentice to Master of Organic Design* (Minneapolis: University of Minnesota Press, 2015), pp. 45–63.

35. Besinger, *Working with Mr. Wright*, p. 225.

VISUALIZING THE ARCHIVES

CAROLE ANN FABIAN

The Frank Lloyd Wright Foundation Archives comprise the evidence of Wright's monumental corpus of work in myriad formats. The acquisition of this crucial resource by Columbia University's Avery Architectural & Fine Arts Library and The Museum of Modern Art demonstrates the shared commitment of these two institutions to preserve these holdings; to uncover new knowledge about Wright, his work, and its impact; and to provide broad access for scholars, students, stewards of the historic Wright sites, and the interested public alike. At Avery, we are exploring a number of strategies to reveal the contents of this massive archive to all constituencies.

Archival practice operates under two general organizing principles: the aggregation of a body of materials related to one primary creator or entity, and the creation of archival finding aids—an intellectual arrangement of the materials. For the archivist and scholar, the traditional finding aid is a familiar point of entry to a collection. In devising finding aids, an archivist aims to provide structural guidance from an agnostic view of the body of work, and to leave no trace of interpretation. The scholar first encounters the archive through the finding aid, and in that encounter she expects an experience of discovery: a close and deep reading of primary materials resulting in a new insight, argument, or research outcome. But the Wright Foundation Archives also interest a broad public, an audience that compels us to rethink how best to reveal its voluminous holdings in ways that are more transparent, provide an at-a-glance understanding of the Archives as a whole, and offer pathways to deeper discovery of those projects of greater interest. In seeking to balance traditional archival processing practices with alternate methods of representing the Archives, we are exploring data-visualization techniques—the product of aggregation and analysis of archival records as data—to communicate the complexity of information held in ways that are more accessible and appealing. A visual analysis of the correspondence data in the Archives, for example, could graphically represent Wright's circle of correspondents—a social network charting the density of his "conversations" with interlocutors across space, time, and themes. For the projects illustrated here, we visually encoded our holdings of Wright's drawings with the goal of representing the density of the archival evidence for Wright's creative output through locational, temporal, and typological views.

We focused our analysis on the sum of drawn evidence in three sample geographies of varying scales: local (Buffalo, New York); national (Japan); and regional (the Middle East). This information is coded by color to indicate programs. The temporal reading is represented as a smoothed histogram at the bottom of each visualization that represents the span of Wright's career, within which the region's projects are located. The histogram is divided into three bands representing Wright's built, unbuilt, and destroyed work.

While all these analyses share a visual vocabulary, each describes different aspects of Wright's creative output. The Buffalo visualization illustrates an important locus of Wright's early career and documents connections with local clients. Readily apparent is his relationship with Darwin D. Martin, for whom Wright designed ten projects over as many years. The visualization plots records for sixteen projects. Among these, the 179 drawings for the Larkin Building (demolished in 1950) serve as the primary evidence for this Wright masterwork of technical innovation and commercial design.

The visualizations also provide a view of Wright's engagement outside of the United States. Specifically, we see times of tremendous activity in Japan (1913–23) and in the Middle East (1927/1957–59). The graphics quantify a volume of work focused on public spaces and urban design in these regions. Nearly 800 drawings for the Imperial Hotel in Tokyo overwhelm evidence of his other Japan projects, and, like the Larkin Building drawings, document one of Wright's most significant though no longer extant works. The Plan for Greater Baghdad is represented by 105 drawings; these together with his writings about the project represent the body of evidence for this last great—though unbuilt—work.

These early experiments in data visualization hold the promise of a more direct and engaging understanding of the Archives as a whole. Beyond this effort, we hope to link digitized versions of drawings, correspondence, films, and photography to a series of data visualizations. While visualizations can represent our vast collection of material, these holdings are not the full expression of Wright's output. They cannot represent what is missing from the Archives, such as the other side of a correspondence between Wright and a patron, drawings lost to fires at Taliesin, Wright material held in other public or private collections, or elements simply lost over the years. Nonetheless, by leveraging data strategies and digital technologies we aim to represent the most complete and transparent view possible of the whole evidence of the Archives, and thereby enhance understanding of and access to this vast and remarkable body of work.

BUFFALO

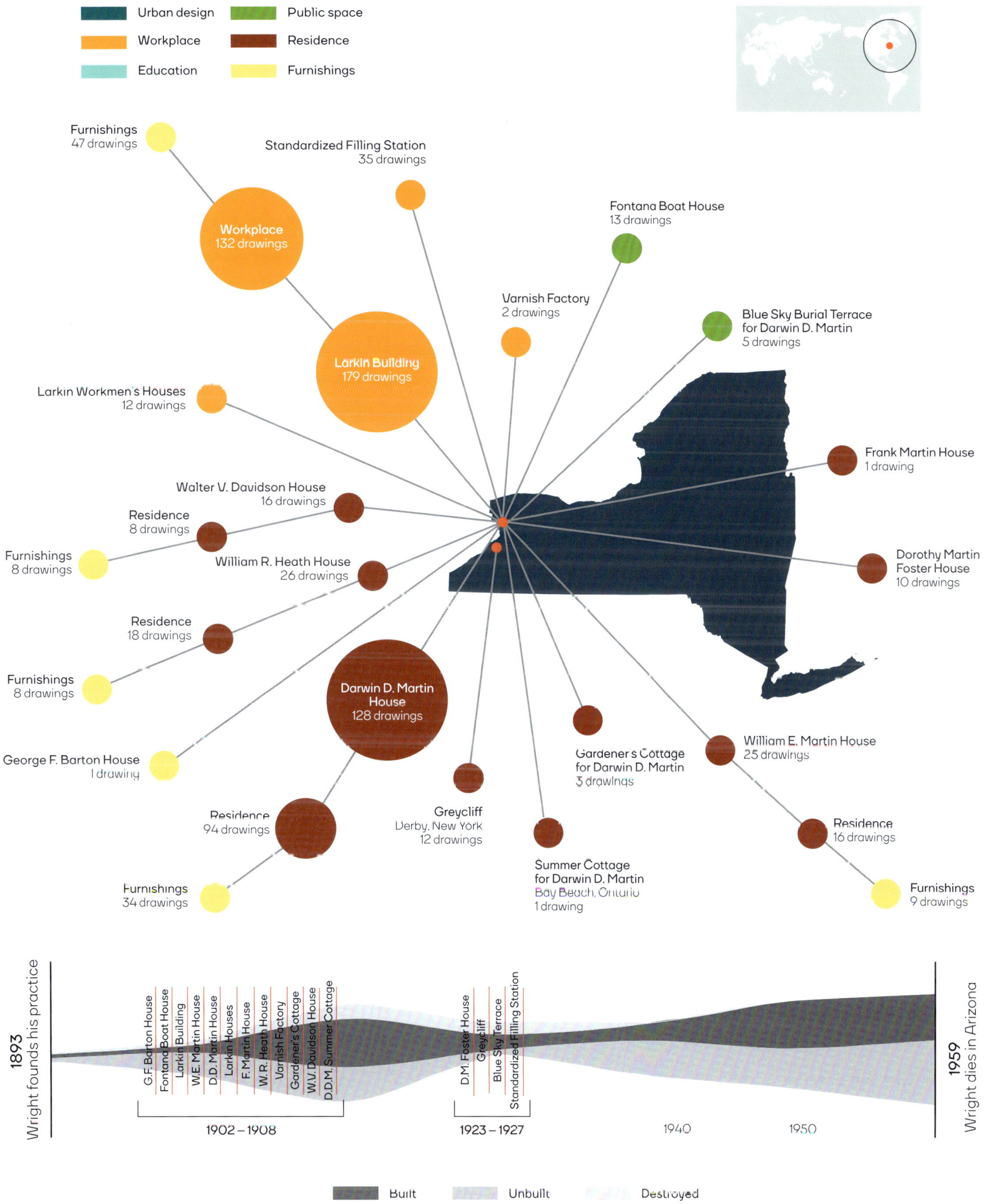

Urban design
Public space
Workplace
Residence
Education
Furnishings
Furnishings
47 drawings
Standardized Filling Station
35 drawings
Workplace
132 drawings
Fontana Boat House
13 drawings
Varnish Factory
2 drawings
Blue Sky Burial Terrace
for Darwin D. Martin
5 drawings
Larkin Building
179 drawings
Larkin Workmen's Houses
12 drawings
Frank Martin House
1 drawing
Walter V. Davidson House
16 drawings
Residence
8 drawings
Furnishings
8 drawings
William R. Heath House
26 drawings
Dorothy Martin
Foster House
10 drawings
Residence
18 drawings
Furnishings
8 drawings
Darwin D. Martin
House
128 drawings
George F. Barton House
1 drawing
Gardener's Cottage
for Darwin D. Martin
3 drawings
William E. Martin House
25 drawings
Residence
94 drawings
Greycliff
Derby, New York
12 drawings
Residence
16 drawings
Summer Cottage
for Darwin D. Martin
Bay Beach, Ontario
1 drawing
Furnishings
34 drawings
Furnishings
9 drawings
1893
Wright founds his practice
G.F. Barton House
Fontana Boat House
Larkin Building
W.E. Martin House
D.D. Martin House
Larkin Houses
F. Martin House
W.R. Heath House
Varnish Factory
Gardener's Cottage
W.V. Davidson House
D.D.M. Summer Cottage
1902 – 1908
D.M. Foster House
Greycliff
Blue Sky Terrace
Standardized Filling Station
1923 – 1927
1940
1950
1959
Wright dies in Arizona
Built
Unbuilt
Destroyed

JAPAN

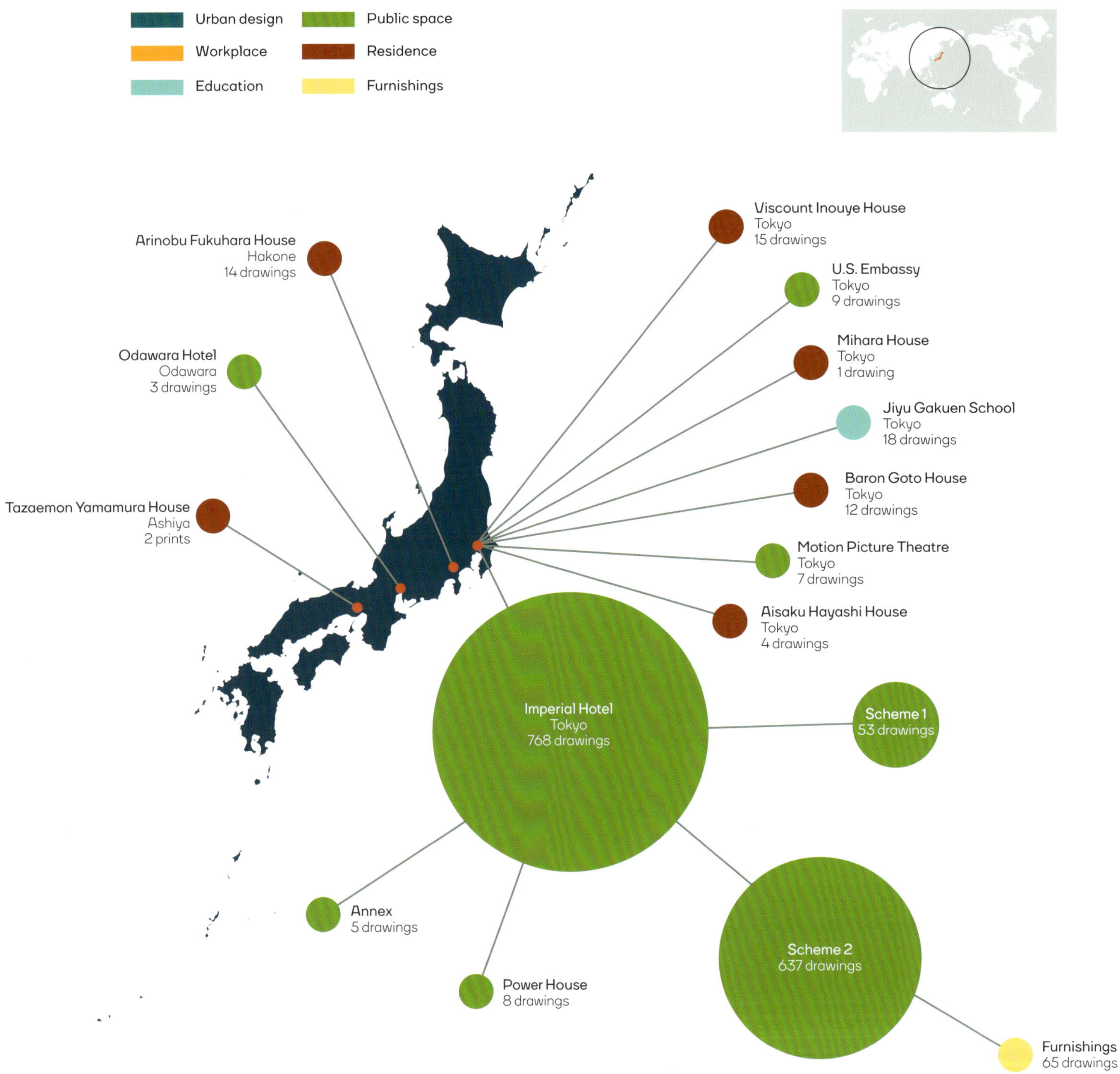
Urban design
Public space
Workplace
Residence
Education
Furnishings
Arinobu Fukuhara House
Hakone
14 drawings
Odawara Hotel
Odawara
3 drawings
Tazaemon Yamamura House
Ashiya
2 prints
Viscount Inouye House
Tokyo
15 drawings
U.S. Embassy
Tokyo
9 drawings
Mihara House
Tokyo
1 drawing
Jiyu Gakuen School
Tokyo
18 drawings
Baron Goto House
Tokyo
12 drawings
Motion Picture Theatre
Tokyo
7 drawings
Aisaku Hayashi House
Tokyo
4 drawings
Imperial Hotel
Tokyo
768 drawings
Scheme 1
53 drawings
Scheme 2
637 drawings
Annex
5 drawings
Power House
8 drawings
Furnishings
65 drawings

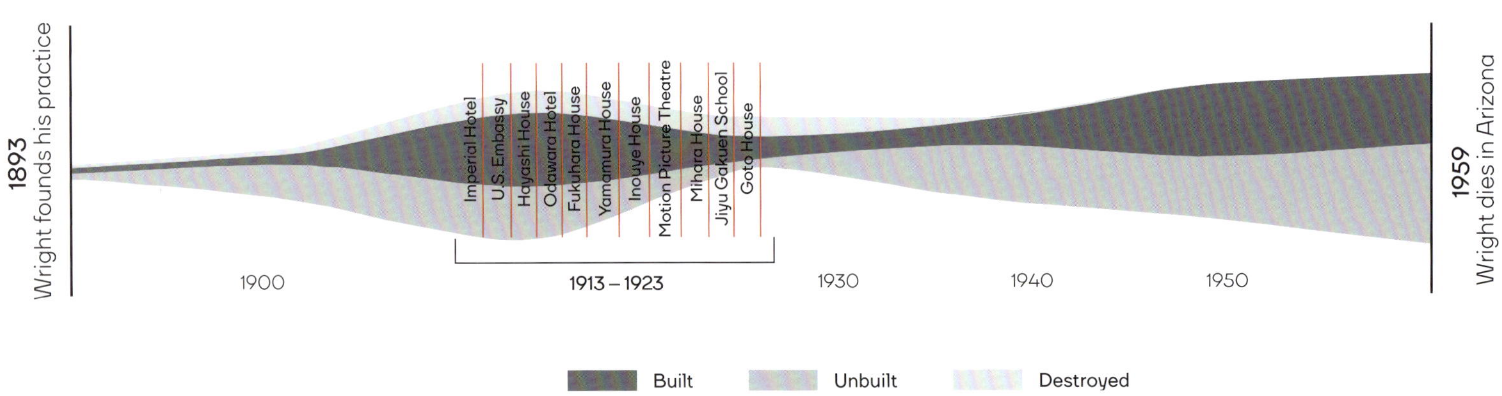
1893
Wright founds his practice
1900
Imperial Hotel
U.S. Embassy
Hayashi House
Odawara Hotel
Fukuhara House
Yamamura House
Inouye House
Motion Picture Theatre
Mihara House
Jiyu Gakuen School
Goto House
1913 – 1923
1930
1940
1950
1959
Wright dies in Arizona
Built
Unbuilt
Destroyed

THE MIDDLE EAST

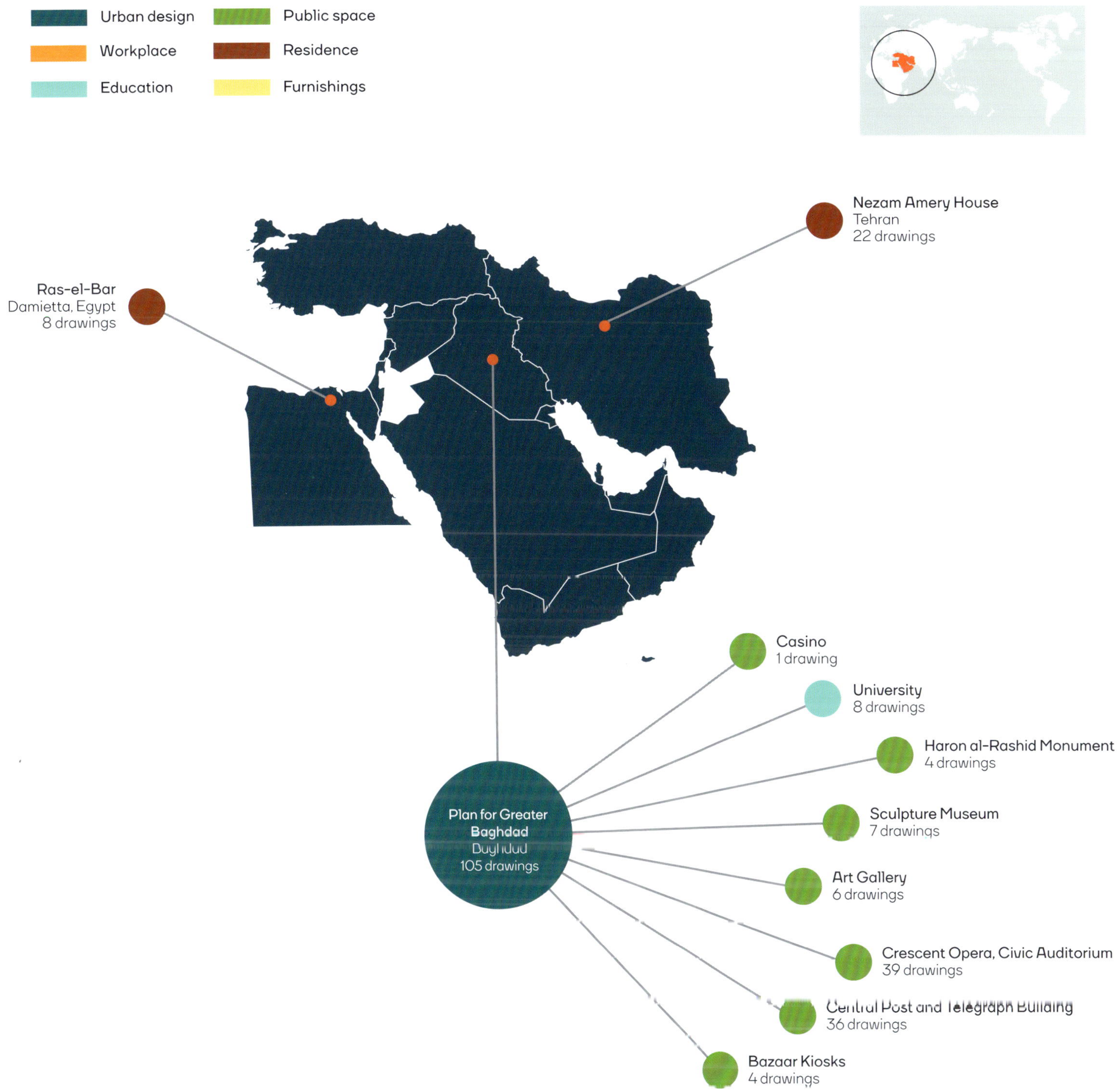

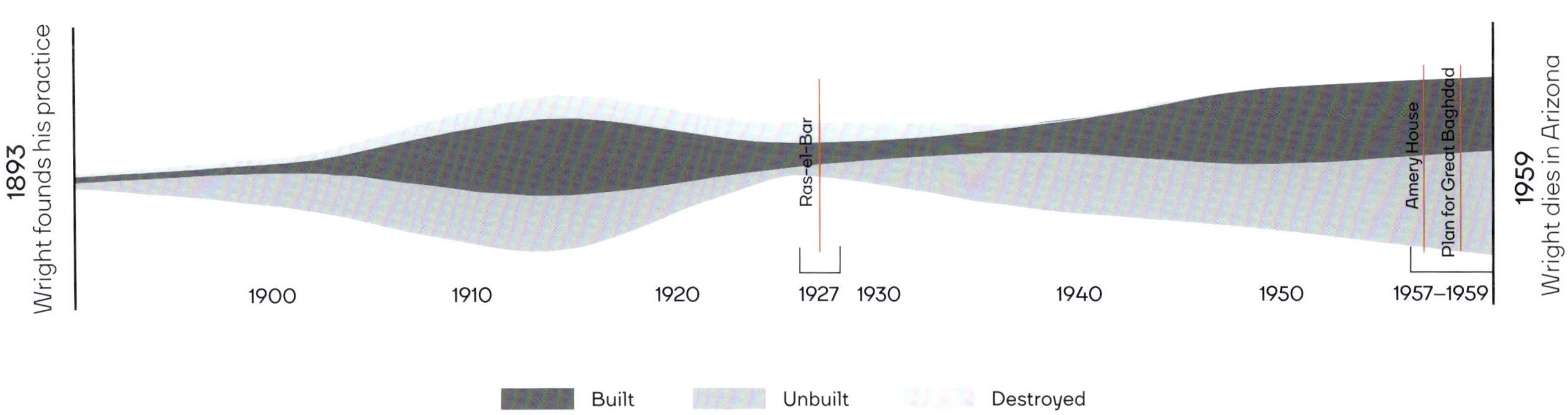

INDEX OF IMAGES

ACKNOWLEDGMENTS

The transfer of the Frank Lloyd Wright Foundation Archives to The Museum of Modern Art and Avery Architectural & Fine Arts Library at Columbia University—begun in 2012 and nearly complete as of this writing—has been a monumental task. It is difficult to draw a sharp boundary between the ongoing commitment and contributions of staff members at both institutions and those who are to be thanked for the work of assembling this catalogue and the accompanying exhibition, *Frank Lloyd Wright at 150: Unpacking the Archive*. First and foremost, special thanks go to Carole Ann Fabian, Director, and Janet Parks, Curator of Drawings & Archives, at Avery Library for their collaboration, from the beginning of discussions with the Frank Lloyd Wright Foundation on moving the archival materials from Scottsdale, Arizona, and Spring Green, Wisconsin. Since the conclusion of the tripartite agreement in 2012, Wright has loomed large at Avery Library in everything from the reorganization of storage and access in the Drawings & Archives collection to matters of cataloguing, data management, and a very significant increase in demands from readers and researchers both on- and off-site. Preparation for exhibitions has added to the volume of work and attention demanded of Avery's modest but dedicated staff, first for the rapid assembly of a 2014 exhibition, *Frank Lloyd Wright and the City: Density vs. Dispersal*, and now with this major undertaking. Most of the library staff has been engaged in one way or another, but most particularly Margaret Smithglass, Registrar and Digital Content Librarian; Shelley Hayreh, Archivist, Drawings & Archives; Pamela Casey, Architecture Archivist; Nicole Richard and Jason Escalante, respectively current and former Drawings Collection Assistant; and Chris Sala, Architecture Bibliographer and Indexer. They have sustained this project on a near daily basis. Additional thanks go to Andrea Merrett, David Colosi, and Paul Guidos for their stamina in helping to physically unpack the archival materials arriving at Avery Library.

None of this would have been possible without the support of the Frank Lloyd Wright Foundation. First and foremost we thank Bruce Brooks Pfeiffer for discussions on the future of the Archives in the new setting of New York. We are grateful to Stuart Graff, President and CEO, for his support, and to Margo Stipe, Curator and Registrar of Collections, as well as Oskar Munoz, Indira Berndtson, and Elizabeth Dawsari, for years of stewardship over the vast array of materials preserved for decades by the Foundation. They have also helped in countless ways with the physical transfer of the collection, and with continued expert intellectual engagement with these materials in their new home. Former President Sean Malone offered years of support, and Nicholas Olsberg, former consultant to the Foundation, played an important role in the initial stages of the transfer of stewardship.

Special thanks also go to the group of scholars, critics, and historians who generously gave of their time and ideas during a workshop held in the early stages of brainstorming the exhibition: Donald Albrecht; Anthony Alofsin; Carole Ann Fabian; Dianne Harris; Neil Levine; Ken Tadashi Oshima; Nicolai Ouroussoff; Spyros Papapetros; Felicity Scott; Joseph Siry; Martino Stierli; and Claire Zimmerman.

We also thank the scholars who helped to "unpack" parts of the archive, both on the exhibition walls and in the essays published in this volume: Michael Desmond, Louisiana State University, Baton Rouge; Carole Ann Fabian, Avery Architectural & Fine Arts Library, Columbia University; Elizabeth S. Hawley, City University of New York; Juliet Kinchin, The Museum of Modern Art; Neil Levine, Harvard University; Ellen Moody, The Museum of Modern Art; Therese O'Malley, National Gallery of Art, Washington, D.C.; Ken Tadashi Oshima, University of Washington, Seattle; Michael Osman, University of California, Los Angeles; Spyros Papapetros, Princeton University; Janet Parks, Avery Architectural & Fine Arts Library, Columbia University; Matthew Skjonsberg, Swiss Federal Institute of Technology, Lausanne; and Mabel O. Wilson, Columbia University. They have been engaged with the project continually over the last two years, from framing the topics it covers to the choice of materials it contains. We are grateful for their continued availability for countless discussions and questions and for their openness to this curatorial experiment. Thank you also to David Smiley, Columbia University, for his essay on Wright's seminal project Broadacre City, an important touchstone in this book.

Above all, the ambitious scope of the project is due to our generous lenders, who have entrusted us with works from their collections and accommodated the long and often unpredictable process of putting together an exhibition. In addition to Avery Architectural & Fine Arts Library, Columbia University, we extend thanks and appreciation to the Wisconsin Historical Society, Madison; University Archives, State University of New York at Buffalo; Library of Congress, Washington, D.C.; John Hope and Aurelia E. Franklin Library, Fisk University, Nashville; University of Chicago Library; Solomon R. Guggenheim Museum, New York; Frank Lloyd Wright Foundation, Scottsdale, Arizona; The Metropolitan Museum of Art, New York; Bentley Historical Library, University of Michigan, Ann Arbor; The Paley Center for Media, New York; Freemantle Media, London; Harry Ransom

Center, University of Texas at Austin; Albert and Shirley Small Special Collections Library, University of Virginia, Charlottesville; Teachers College, Columbia University; State Archives of North Carolina, Raleigh.

We are extremely grateful to our private lenders, Laura Stirton Aust and Tom Aust.

We warmly thank the individuals at each institution who provided essential assistance: Lisa Marine at Wisconsin Historical Society; William Offhaus at SUNY Buffalo; Simonette dela Torre at the Library of Congress; DeLisa A. Minor Harris at Fisk University; Patti Gibbons at University of Chicago Library; Kate Sloss and Tali (Chiyong) Han at the Solomon R. Guggenheim Museum; Margo Stipe at the Frank Lloyd Wright Foundation; Catherine Mackay at The Metropolitan Museum of Art; Malgosia Myc at the University of Michigan; Cristina Meisner and Steve Wilson at The University of Texas at Austin; Heather Moore Riser at the University of Virginia; Jennifer Blomberg at State Archives of North Carolina; Maria Pagano at The Paley Center for Media; and Melanie McClure at Freemantle Media.

At The Museum of Modern Art, exceptional staff from nearly every department has lent support to this project. Our utmost thanks go to Glenn D. Lowry, Director. The leadership and counsel of Ramona Bannayan, Senior Deputy Director for Exhibitions, Collections, and Programs; Todd Bishop, Senior Deputy Director, External Affairs; James Gara, Chief Operating Officer; and Peter Reed, Senior Deputy Director for Curatorial Affairs, have been essential. Trish Jeffers, former Director of Human Resources, and her successor, Odessa Matsubara; Laura Coppelli, Associate Director; and Joyce Wong, Human Resources Manager, have helped us with staffing. The Departments of Painting and Sculpture, Film, Photography, and Drawings and Prints contributed to the exhibition's interdisciplinary aspirations through their generous interdepartmental loans. In the Department of Painting and Sculpture, we warmly thank Ann Temkin, Marie-Josée and Henry Kravis Chief Curator. In the Department of Film, we extend thanks to Rajendra Roy, Chief Curator, and Katie Trainor, Film Collections Manager, who have helped us with viewing and inventorying the films that accompanied the Archives in their transfer to New York. In the Department of Photography, we give many thanks to Quentin Bajac, Joel and Anne Ehrenkranz Chief Curator. In the Department of Drawings and Prints, we thank Christophe Cherix, the Robert Lehman Foundation Chief Curator.

The exhibition would not have been possible without the exceptional generosity of our supporters. Foremost thanks go to the Hyundai Card Company for their major support in funding *Frank Lloyd Wright at 150: Unpacking the Archive*. We express sincere thanks to Sue and Edgar Wachenheim III through the Central National Gottesman Foundation, and also to the Graham Foundation for Advanced Studies in the Fine Arts. Additional support is provided by the Annual Exhibition Fund.

The commitment and savvy of our colleagues in the Department of Development have been integral to the realization of this project. We are grateful to Meagan Johnson, Director of Institutional Giving and Development Operations; Caralynn Sandorf, Director, Major Gifts and Campaign Operations; Lauren Stakias, Director, Exhibition and Program Funding; Sylvia Renner, Senior Development Officer; and Claire Huddleston, Development Officer. For fashioning the exhibition's public presence, we thank the Departments of Marketing and Communications: Kim Mitchell, Chief Communications Officer; Margaret Doyle, Director of Communications; Paul Jackson, former Communications Manager, and Sara Beth Walsh, Senior Publicist; Rebecca Stokes, Director of Digital Initiatives; Carolyn Kelly, Coordinating Editor; Victor Samra, Digital Media Marketing Manager; and Janelle Grace, Publicity Coordinator.

At the heart of the exhibition are the works themselves and the careful choreography of their presentation. The Museum's Department of Conservation has been our guide in the care of works entrusted to us by the exhibition's lenders. We are especially grateful for the help of Roger Griffith, Associate Sculpture Conservator; Erika Mosier, Conservator; and Ellen Moody, Assistant Projects Conservator, who worked expertly over the past few years on Wright materials, most notably the models of St. Mark's Tower and the Solomon R. Guggenheim Museum, which are featured in the exhibition and catalogue. Sincere thanks also to their colleague Jim Coddington, former Chief Conservator, for his sage advice. Additionally, special thanks goes Alexis Hagadorn, Head of Conservation, and Vasare Rastonis, Mellon Conservator for Special Collections, at Columbia University for their work on materials coming from Avery Library. In the Department of Exhibition Design and Production, we extend our deep appreciation to Betty Fisher, Senior Design Manager, for an exhibition design that is as discerning as it is elegant, and to Peter Perez, Foreman, Frame Shop. It has been a privilege to work with colleagues of such deep experience and insight. Chiara Bernasconi, Assistant Director in the Digital Media Department, has been instrumental in the complex project of producing films of the guest scholars, and we thank additionally the Director, Edward Roy, and the j6mediaworks team. In the Department of Graphic Design, Ingrid Chou, Assistant Creative Director; Jocelyn Meinhardt, Associate Writer and Editor; Claire Corey, Production Manager; Damien Saatdjian, Art Director; and Danielle Hall, Senior Graphic Designer, pooled their creative expertise to give resolution to the exhibition's far-ranging geographic and bibliographic content.

For a meticulous attention to detail while always keeping sight of the schedule, we're indebted to our colleagues in the Department of Exhibition Planning and Administration. We express thanks to Jennifer Cohen, Associate Director. Nancy Adelson, Deputy General Counsel, has been our invaluable advisor on all legal matters. In coordinating the exhibition's extensive checklist of works, we are beholden to the skill and resourcefulness of the Department of Collection Management and Exhibition Registration; Stefanii Ruta-Atkins, Head Registrar; Steven Wheeler, Associate Registrar; Victoria Manning, Assistant Registrar; Ian Eckert, Manager, Collection and Exhibition Technologies; and Kat Ryan, Senior Coordinator, Collection and Exhibition Technologies. Our colleagues Tunji Adeniji, Director of Facilities and Safety; Daniel Platt, Director of Security; Rob Jung, Manager; Sarah Wood, Assistant Manager; and Tom Krueger, Assistant Manager, have been indispensable to the management of operations, in-house transportation, installation, and security.

In the Department of Education, we appreciate the support of Wendy Woon, The Edward John Noble Foundation Deputy Director of Education; Pablo Helguera, Director, Adult and Academic Education; Sara Bodinson, Director, Interpretation and Research; Jess Van Nostrand, Assistant Director of Exhibition Programs and Gallery Initiatives; Sarah Kennedy, Associate Educator, Lab Programs; and Leticia Gutierrez, Associate Educator, Education, Gallery, and Learning Programs. Their interpretative ingenuity and knowledge of public programming has made the project accessible to a broad spectrum of people and given it articulation beyond the galleries. The Museum's Library and Archives has been a resource across the development of the project. We thank Milan Hughston, former Chief of Library and Museum Archives; Michelle Elligott, Chief of Archives; Jennifer Tobias, Librarian; and David Senior, Senior Bibliographer. In Imaging Services, we are grateful to Erik Landsberg, former Director; Robert Kastler, Production Manager; Roberto Rivera, Production Assistant; Peter Butler, Collections Photographer; and John Wronn, Collections Photographer. Special thanks goes to Dwight Primiano of Avery Digital Imaging Studio, who produced many of the high-quality photographs indispensable to this book.

The preparation of this book is the collective work of a dedicated team in the Department of Publications. Christopher Hudson, Publisher; Chul R. Kim, Associate Publisher; David Frankel, Editorial Director; Marc Sapir, Production Director; Hannah Kim, Marketing and Book Development Coordinator; and Emily Hall, Editor, have structured our efforts and ensured our success. Our inspired editor, Libby Hruska, took on the daunting task of editing texts from sixteen authors. She has been both thoughtful and steadfast. We are grateful for her editorial acumen, which has enriched the text and made it eminently readable. Amanda Washburn, Senior Designer, created a perceptive design that gracefully weaves the book together as a whole, and makes each page one on which to linger and garner new insights. Additional thanks to Jill Weidman, Isobel Cockerell, and Janet Tam for their assistance with graphics and indexing.

Finally, we are deeply grateful to the members of the Department of Architecture and Design. Encouragement has come from every corner. Our most sincere thanks go to the indefatigable Phoebe Springstubb, Curatorial Assistant, who took on all manner of catalogue production and quite literally made this book a reality. Her knowledge, dedication, and efficiency were invaluable. We also thank Arièle Dionne-Krosnick, Curatorial Assistant; Elizabeth S. Hawley, Museum Research Consortium Fellow; Department Interns Luis Michal and Catherine Acosta; and Martino Stierli, Philip Johnson Chief Curator of Architecture and Design. In the various phases of its development the exhibition has been the work of many hands. Emma Presler, Department Manager; Paul Galloway, Collection Specialist; and Pamela Popeson, Preparator, have answered every question and provided a core of support. Indispensible assistance has come from Sam Fox, former Department Assistant, and from his successor, Nadine Dosa.

Barry Bergdoll
Curator, Department of Architecture and Design,
The Museum of Modern Art

Jennifer Gray
Project Research Assistant,
Department of Architecture and Design,
The Museum of Modern Art

IMAGE CREDITS

Numbers in parentheses refer to accession numbers.

The Frank Lloyd Wright Foundation Archives (The Museum of Modern Art | Avery Architectural & Fine Arts Library, Columbia University, New York). © 2017 Frank Lloyd Wright Foundation, Scottsdale, Ariz. All rights reserved

Photographs by Dwight Primiano, Avery Digital Imaging Studio: **1** (0506.003), **2 top** (8701.001), **2 bottom** (9305.013), **3** (0111.002), **4** (0611.003), **8** (2104.004), **10** (2505.039), **12** (3602.004), **15** (5746.001), **16** (0405.011), **18 right** (0803.0026), **22** (2702.055), **24** (4110.008), **26** (4110.001), **30** (2306.033), **33 top** (0405.028), **33 bottom** (0405.0024), **34 top** (0208.015), **34 bottom** (0803.0011), **35 top** (0602.001), **35 bottom** (9905.033), **36** (1705.026), **37 upper left** (1910.064), **37 upper right** (1910.262), **37 lower left** (1910.201), **37 lower right** (1910.188), **39 top** (1118.001), **39 bottom** (1505.001), **40 bottom** (2704.049), **40 top** (9510.016), **41 bottom** (2704.048), **41 top** (2704.091), **52 bottom** (3205.010), **52 top** (3202.029), **54 bottom** (3205.001), **54 top** (3205.002), **55** (3202.008), **56 and back cover** (3301.001), **57** (3420.009), **58** (3404.006), **59** (3414.001), **60** (1025.088), **62 right** (1113.077), **63** (1902.004), **65** (1915.015), **66 left** (1025.088), **69 right** (n.n.), **69 left** (n.n.), **70 bottom** (1409.053), **70 top** (1409.042), **71 top** (1509.050), **71 bottom** (1509.650), **72** (1025.088), **73** (1509.044), **74** (1509.674), **75** (1509.665), **76** (1509.005), **77 top** (2101.012), **77 bottom** (1706.003), **78** (2405.012), **83 right** (2702.058), **88** (2405.013), **89 top** (2405.008), **89 bottom** (2405.004), **91 right** (9905.009), **92 top left** (0620.001), **92 bottom right** (9506.012), **94** (3301.052), **95 right** (3803.489), **96** (2904.001), **106** (2904.002), **108** (2301.008), **109** (2601.007), **110** (2601.008), **111** (2601.009), **112** (2601.001), **113** (2601.005), **114** (1401.008), **116** (1401.063), **117** (2002.012), **120** (4824.0010), **121** (1910.382–385), **122** (4824.070), **123 top** (1401.007), **124 bottom left** (9905.017), **125 top left** (9806.003), **125 top right** (3003.023), **125 bottom** (2709.001), **126** (5121.002), **127** (2604.003), **128** (5611.001), **129 top** (5611.049), **129 bottom** (1910.726), **130** (4824.008), **131** (4824.010), **132** (4828.001), **134 top** (3703.0229), **134 bottom** (3906.007), **137** (5109.002), **138** (5111.006), **140** (4203.007), **141** (3807.003), **142 top** (4202.001), **142 bottom** (4202.002), **143 bottom** (5113.003), **143 top** (5118.001), **144** (5111.001), **145 bottom left** (5202.013), **145 top** (5202.014), **145 bottom right** (5202.016), **146** (4303.001), **147** (4303.004), **148** (1506.162), **151** (0403.065), **153** (3702.003), **156** (5612.114), **160** (5510.005), **161** (3816.045), **163** (1506.658), **166 top** (3702.002/003), **166 bottom** (3702.005), **167 top** (3702.018), **167 bottom** (3813.011), **168 top** (2111.002), **168 bottom** (2401.003), **169 top left** (5612.084), **169 top right** (5612.093), **169 bottom left** (5612.098), **169 bottom right** (5612.100), **170 top** (5510.010), **170 bottom** (5510.001), **171 top** (1506.006), **171 bottom** (3805.002), **172** (2603.001), **181** (2603.004), **182 top** (2603.006), **182 bottom** (2603.003), **183 top** (9705.006), **183 bottom** (0309.001), **184 top** (0309.022), **184 bottom** (0309.003), **185** (4016.004), **186 bottom** (3909.002), **186 top** (3909.005), **187** (5632.001), **188** (4821.004), **189 top** (5733.008), **189 bottom** (5733.004), **195** (n.n.), **197 right** (3402.043), **197 left** (3402.044), **199** (3402.001), **200 top** (3401.017), **202 top** (3402.024), **202 bottom** (3402.014), **203** (3407.013), **204** (5825.002), **205** (5825.006), **206** (2905.093), **207** (3410.004), **210** (3103.003), **220** (2404.002), **222 bottom** (4921.027), **222 top** (4921.003), **223 bottom** (4921.002), **223 top** (4921.009), **225 left** (5639.001), **225 right** (6007.025), **229 left** (2905.006), **230 left** (3100.015), **230 right** (3402.048), **231 left** (2905.002), **231 second from left** (2905.001), **233 top** (4305.0638), **233 bottom right** (4305.0627), **237 top** (9306.001), **237 bottom** (0106.001), **238 top left** (0204.006), **238 top right** (0403.079), **238 bottom right** (2205.001), **239** (9506.002), **240 top** (9902.002), **240 bottom** (9503.018), **241 left** (0403.002), **241 right** (3201.003), **242 top** (4606.031), **242 bottom** (4606.004), **243** (4606.001), **244** (3701.010)

Department of Imaging and Visual Resources. The Museum of Modern Art, New York: **42** (9000.002), **66 right** (1161.054), **123 bottom** (1161.040), **190** (9000.003), **200 bottom** (9000.003), **201** (9000.003), **208 and 219** (5617.001), **224 left** (5617.002), **224 right** (5617.008), **226** (9000.037), **227** (9000.009), **228** (9000.037), **229 right** (2905.011), **231 second from right** (9000.037)

Historic Architecture and Landscape Image Collection, Ryerson and Burnham Archives, The Art Institute of Chicago: 90 (40497), 152 (M525087)

© 2017 Artists Rights Society (ARS), New York / VG Bild-Kunst, Bonn. Department of Imaging and Visual Resources. The Museum of Modern Art, New York: 49 (right), 216 (right), 221

© 2017 / Artists Rights Society (ARS), New York. Department of Imaging and Visual Resources. The Museum of Modern Art, New York: 49 (left)

The Aust Family Trust: 87

Avery Architectural & Fine Arts Library, Columbia University, New York: 27, 47 (left and right), 82 (right), 91 (left), 124 (top left), 236, 238 (bottom left)

© Estate of Lester Beall/Licensed by VAGA, New York. Department of Imaging and Visual Resources. The Museum of Modern Art, New York: 44 (right)

Courtesy Jeanine Ferris Beharka: 162

Courtesy Sally Guy Browne and Helen Langhorne. Jackson Davis Collection, Albert and Shirley Small Special Collections Library, University of Virginia: 99

© FremantleMedia North America: 209

© 2017 Pedro E. Guerrero Archives: 211

Courtesy Solomon R. Guggenheim Foundation, New York: 234 (bottom)

Courtesy Solomon R. Guggenheim Museum Archives, New York: 235

From *The Imperial: The First 100 Years* (Tokyo: Imperial Hotel, 1990): 64

Jens Jensen Drawings and Papers, Bentley Historical Library, University of Michigan: 38 (HS15326)

Missouri History Museum, St. Louis: 19

The Museum of Modern Art, New York. Department of Architecture and Design Study Center: 231 (right); photograph by Hedrich-Blessing: 216 (left)

The Museum of Modern Art, New York. Department of Conservation: 228 (top left), 233 (bottom left), 234 (top)

Courtesy the State Archives of North Carolina: 100

Jesse Nusbaum Collection, courtesy Palace of the Governors Photo Archives (NMHM/DCA): 84 (060451)

Julius Rosenwald Fund Collection, John Hope and Aurelia E. Franklin Library, Special Collections, Fisk University: 107

© Ben Schnall/The LIFE Images Collection/Getty Images: 232

Courtesy Sears Holdings Archives, Hoffman Estates, Illinois: 150

Courtesy University Archives, State University of New York at Buffalo: 18 (left), 213

From Eduardo Torroja, *The Structures of Eduardo Torroja* (New York: F. W. Dodge Corporation: 1958): 215

Special Collections Research Center, University of Chicago Library: 98

Department of Special Collections and University Archives, W. E. B. Du Bois Library, University of Massachusetts Amherst: 29

Wisconsin Historical Society: 28 (WHS-25570), 46 (WHi-127913), 95 (left) (WHS-26504)

© 2017 Frank Lloyd Wright Foundation / Artists Rights Society (ARS), New York. Department of Imaging and Visual Resources. The Museum of Modern Art, New York: cover, 6, 124 (right), 164–65; Library of Congress Prints and Photographs Division: 53 (LC-USZC4-2193), 86 (LC-USZC4-2206), 93 (LC-DIG-ppmsca-30673), 105 (LC-USZC4-2192)

Published in conjunction with *Frank Lloyd Wright at 150: Unpacking the Archive* at The Museum of Modern Art, New York, June 12–October 1, 2017. Organized by The Museum of Modern Art, New York, and Avery Architectural & Fine Arts Library, Columbia University. Organized by Barry Bergdoll, Curator, Department of Architecture and Design, The Museum of Modern Art, and the Meyer Schapiro Professor of Art History and Archaeology, Columbia University, with Jennifer Gray, Project Research Assistant, Department of Architecture and Design, The Museum of Modern Art.

The exhibition is made possible by Hyundai Card.

Generous funding is provided by Sue and Edgar Wachenheim III and by the Graham Foundation for Advanced Studies in the Fine Arts.

Additional support is provided by the Annual Exhibition Fund.

Major support for this publication is provided by The Dale S. and Norman Mills Leff Publication Fund and by The Museum of Modern Art's Research and Scholarly Publications endowment established through the generosity of The Andrew W. Mellon Foundation, the Edward and John Noble Foundation, Mr. and Mrs. Perry R. Bass, and the National Endowment for the Humanities' Challenge Grant Program.

The Frank Lloyd Wright Foundation Archives (The Museum of Modern Art | Avery Architectural & Fine Arts Library, Columbia University, New York) was acquired through the generosity of MoMA's Committee on Architecture and Design Funds; the Michael H. Dunn Memorial Fund; Avery Library; and the Edgar A. and Frederic Bancroft Fund, Columbia University Libraries.

Produced by the Department of Publications
The Museum of Modern Art, New York
Christopher Hudson, Publisher
Chul R. Kim, Associate Publisher
David Frankel, Editorial Director
Marc Sapir, Production Director

Edited by Libby Hruska with David Frankel
Designed by Amanda Washburn
Production by Hannah Kim
Data visualizations by Janet Tam with Jill Weidman
Color separations by t'ink, Brussels
Printed and bound by Gorenjski Tisk Storitve, Slovenia

This book is typeset in Firs and Cardea.
The paper is 150 gsm Magno Matt.

Published by The Museum of Modern Art, New York
11 West 53 Street, New York, New York 10019-5497

Distributed in the United States and Canada by ARTBOOK|D.A.P.
155 Sixth Avenue, New York, New York, 10013,
www.artbook.com

Distributed outside the United States and Canada by Thames & Hudson Ltd.
181A High Holborn, London, WC1V 7QX,
www.thamesandhudson.com

Library of Congress Control Number: 2017933712
ISBN: 978-1-63345-026-4

Printed in Slovenia

All works reproduced in this volume are from the Frank Lloyd Wright Foundation Archives (The Museum of Modern Art | Avery Architectural & Fine Arts Library, Columbia University, New York) unless otherwise specified.

Front cover: "September Abstractions, The Desert" (detail). c. 1926–27. Cover design for *Liberty* magazine. Colored pencil on paper, 14 ¼ x 24 ⅛ in. (36.2 x 61.2 cm). The Museum of Modern Art, New York. Gift of Jo Carole and Ronald S. Lauder

Back cover: Taliesin Fellowship Complex, Spring Green, Wisconsin. Begun 1932–33. Aerial perspective. Pencil and colored pencil on tracing paper, 17 ⅛ x 20 ⅛ in. (43.5 x 51.1 cm)

p. 1: Hardy House, Racine, Wisconsin. 1905. Perspective. Watercolor, ink, and pencil on paper, 18 ¾ x 5 ⅜ in. (47.6 x 13.7 cm)

p. 2, top: "Drawing shown to lieber Meister when applying for a job." 1887. Pencil and colored pencil on tracing paper, 15 ⅜ x 25 ¼ in. (39.1 x 64.1 cm)

p. 2, bottom: Winslow House, River Forest, Illinois. 1893–94. Perspective. Watercolor and pencil on paper, 12 x 32 ⅝ in. (30.5 x 82.9 cm)

p. 3: Lexington Terraces Apartments, Chicago. Project, 1901 (revised 1909). Aerial perspective. Ink, ink wash, pencil, and cut-and-pasted paper on paper, 16 ½ x 32 ¾ in. (41.9 x 83.2 cm)

p. 4: Unity Temple, Oak Park, Illinois. 1905–08. Perspective. Watercolor and ink on paper, 12 x 25 ⅛ in. (30.5 x 63.8 cm)

p. 6: Millard (La Miniatura) House, Pasadena, California. 1923–24. Perspective from the garden. Pencil and colored pencil on paper, 20 ¾ x 19 ⅝ in. (52.7 x 49.8 cm). The Museum of Modern Art, New York. Gift of Mr. and Mrs. Walter Hochschild

p. 8: Doheny Ranch Development, Los Angeles. Project, 1923. Perspective and plan of House A. Pencil and colored pencil on tracing paper, 16 ⅛ x 20 ½ in. (41 x 52.1 cm)

p. 10: Gordon Strong Automobile Objective and Planetarium, Sugarloaf Mountain, Maryland. Project, 1924–25. Perspective. Pencil and colored pencil on tracing paper, 19 ¾ x 30 ¾ in. (50.2 x 78.1 cm)

p. 12: Fallingwater (Kaufmann House), Mill Run, Pennsylvania. 1934–37. Perspective from the southwest. Pencil and colored pencil on paper, 15 ⅜ x 27 ¼ in. (39.1 x 69.2 cm)

p. 15: Marin County Civic Center and Fairgrounds, San Rafael, California. 1957–70. Aerial perspective looking west. Ink, pencil, and colored pencil on tracing paper, 34 ½ x 6 ft. 2 ⅜ in. (87.6 x 188.9 cm)

TRUSTEES OF THE MUSEUM OF MODERN ART

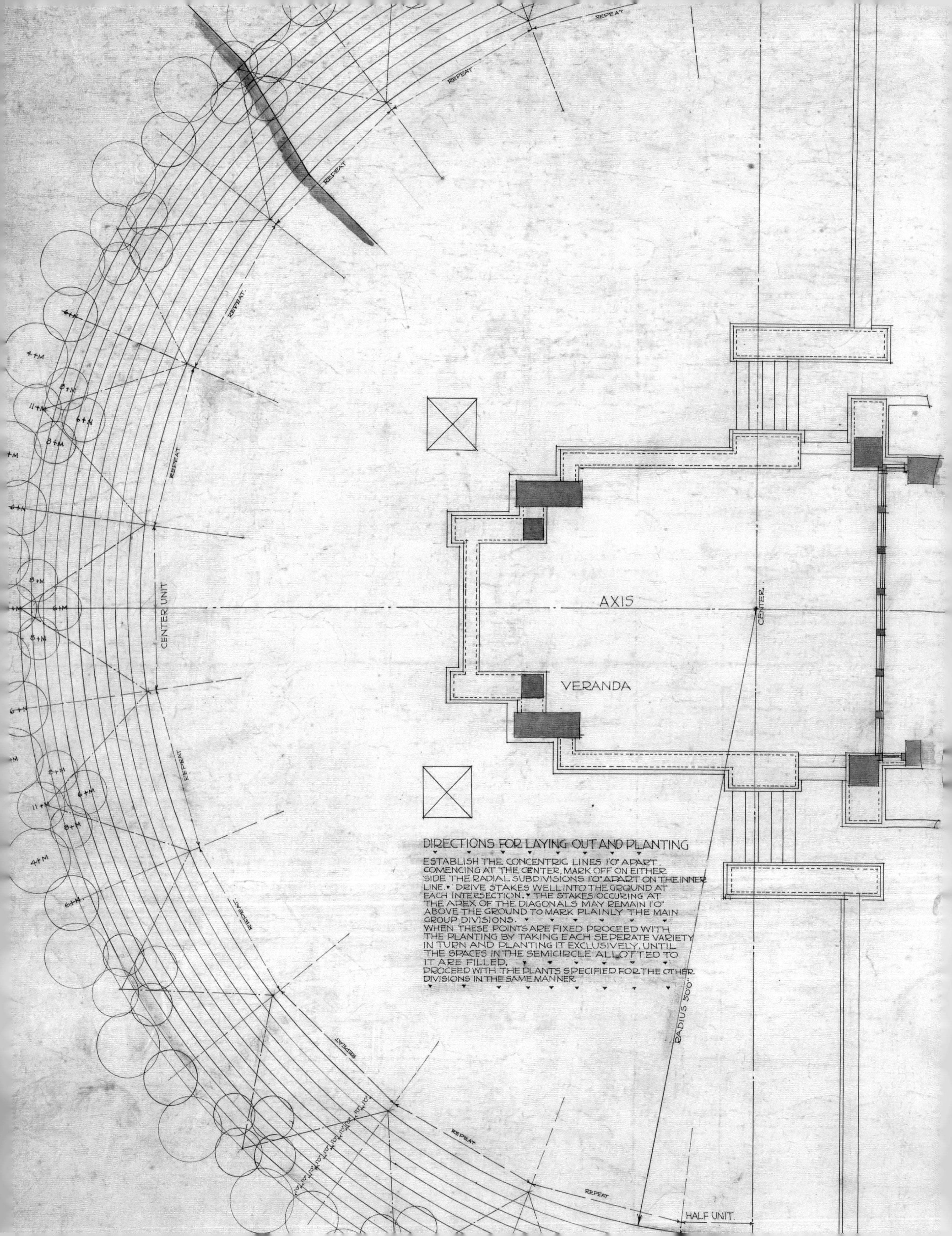
AXIS
CENTER
CENTER UNIT
VERANDA
REPEAT
RADIUS 50'0"
HALF UNIT.
DIRECTIONS FOR LAYING OUT AND PLANTING
ESTABLISH THE CONCENTRIC LINES 1'0" APART.
COMENCING AT THE CENTER, MARK OFF ON EITHER
SIDE THE RADIAL SUBDIVISIONS 1'0" APART ON THE INNER
LINE. DRIVE STAKES WELL INTO THE GROUND AT
EACH INTERSECTION. THE STAKES OCCURING AT
THE APEX OF THE DIAGONALS MAY REMAIN 1'0"
ABOVE THE GROUND TO MARK PLAINLY THE MAIN
GROUP DIVISIONS.
WHEN THESE POINTS ARE FIXED PROCEED WITH
THE PLANTING BY TAKING EACH SEPERATE VARIETY
IN TURN AND PLANTING IT EXCLUSIVELY, UNTIL
THE SPACES IN THE SEMICIRCLE ALLOTTED TO
IT ARE FILLED.
PROCEED WITH THE PLANTS SPECIFIED FOR THE OTHER
DIVISIONS IN THE SAME MANNER